COMPREHENSIVE DICTIONARY
OF PSYCHOANALYSIS

COMPREHENSIVE DICTIONARY
OF PSYCHOANALYSIS

Salman Akhtar M.D.

KARNAC

First published in 2009 by
Karnac Books Ltd
118 Finchley Road, London NW3 5HT

British Library Cataloguing in Publication Data

A C.I.P. for this book is available from the British Library

ISBN-13: 978 1 85575 471 3

Edited, designed and produced by The Studio Publishing Services Ltd,
www.publishingservicesuk.co.uk
e-mail: studio@publishingservicesuk.co.uk

Printed in Great Britain

www.karnacbooks.com

CONTENTS

To

All the individuals whose work is cited in this book, for they are the ones who have collectively constructed the vocabulary of psychoanalysis, *with celebratory gratitude.*

All those contributors to analytic literature whose work I have inadvertently omitted or inoptimally represented, *with sincere apologies.*

All those colleagues who would resist the temptation to point out my errors and omissions, *with brotherly humour.*

My wife, friend, and fellow psychoanalyst, Monisha Nayar, *with profound love.*

Salman Akhtar, MD, was born in India and completed his medical and psychiatric education there. Upon arriving in the United States in 1973, he repeated his psychiatric training at the University of Virginia School of Medicine, and then obtained psychoanalytic training from the Philadelphia Psychoanalytic Institute. Currently, he is Professor of Psychiatry at Jefferson Medical College and a Training and Supervising Analyst at the Psychoanalytic Center of Philadelphia. He has served on the editorial boards of the *International Journal of Psychoanalysis* and the *Journal of the American Psychoanalytic Association*. His more than 300 publications include nine books: *Broken Structures*; *Quest for Answers*; *Inner Torment*; *Immigration and Identity*; *New Clinical Realms*; *Objects of Our Desire*; *Regarding Others*; *Turning Points in Dynamic Psychotherapy*; and *The Damaged Core*, as well as twenty-seven edited or co-edited volumes in psychiatry and psychoanalysis, and six collections of poetry. Dr Akhtar has delivered many prestigious addresses and lectures, including a Plenary Address at the Second International Congress of the International Society for the Study of Personality Disorders in Oslo, Norway (1991), an Invited Plenary Paper at the Second International Margaret S. Mahler Symposium in Cologne, Germany (1993), an Invited Plenary Paper at the Rencontre Franco-Americaine de Psychanalyse meeting in Paris, France (1994), an Invited Keynote Address at the Annual Meetings of Division 39 of the American Psychological Association (1994), the Plenary Address at the Annual Meetings of the Canadian Psychoanalytic Association (2002), and a Keynote Address at the IPA Congress in Rio de Janiero, Brazil (2005). Dr Akhtar is the recipient of the *Journal of the American Psychoanalytic Association*'s Best Paper of the Year Award (1995), the Margaret Mahler Literature Prize (1996), the ASPP's Sigmund Freud Award (2000), the American Psychoanalytic Association's Edith Sabshin Award (2000), Columbia University's Robert Liebert Award for Distinguished Contributions to Applied Psychoanalysis (2004), the APA's Kun Po Soo Award (2004), and the APA's Irma Bland Award for being the Outstanding Teacher of Psychiatric Residents in the country (2005). An internationally-sought speaker and teacher, Dr Akhtar is also a Scholar-in-Residence at the Inter-Act Theatre Company in Philadelphia.

ACKNOWLEDGEMENTS

Dr Michael Vergare, Chairman of the Department of Psychiatry at Jefferson Medical College, helped sustain the academic environment where I could conduct my work in a meaningful fashion. The department's two Vice-Chairs, Drs Mitchell Cohen and Elisabeth Kunkel, as well as its Director of Residency Training, Dr Kenneth Certa, gave me ample opportunities and freedom to continue my scholarship. Dr Robert McFadden and Ms Pamela Kasinetz, my associates in running the department's outpatient clinic, and Dr Jacob Widroff, the clinic's Chief Resident, protected me from administrative chores on numerous occasions. Drs Rajnish Mago, and Stephen Schwartz, fellow faculty members in the department, also helped in subtle and indirect ways. To all these individuals, my sincere thanks indeed.

As can be imagined, work of this magnitude can hardly be done alone. I have been fortunate that, whenever I needed help, I was able to find it. Regardless of whether it involved finding a particular reference, locating an old or out of print book, translating a foreign language phrase or passage, checking the origin of an obscure term, or selecting terms pertaining to specialized areas of applied psychoanalysis, there was someone to whom I could turn for help, someone who was glad to help; none of my frantic phone calls or e-mails remained unanswered. The list of those who helped me and to whom I am utterly grateful is long and includes fellow psychoanalysts from my depth-psychological alma mater, the Psychoanalytic Center of Philadelphia, analytic colleagues from all over this country and abroad, psychiatrists, friends and acquaintances, family members, students, supervisees, and still others who defy categorization. An alphabetical list of those from the mental health field alone includes Drs Jennifer Bonovitz, Ira Brenner, Daniel Freeman, Peter Hoffer, Abigail Kay, Susan Levine Mark Moore, Henri Parens, Andrew Smolar, and David Steinman (all from Philadelphia) as well as Rosemary Balsam (New Haven, CT), Melvin Bornstein (Birmingham, Michigan), Fred Busch (Boston), Diana Constance (Bloomfield Hills, Michigan), Henk-Jan Dalewijk (Amsterdam), James Fosshage (Boston), Axel Hoffer (Boston), Theodore Jacobs (New York), Angelica Kloos (Washington, DC), Eddy de Klerk (Amstelveen, Holland), Saida Koita (Miami), Laurie Kramer (Great Neck, NY), Manasi Kumar (London), Sergio Lewkowicz (Porto Allegre, Brazil), Bert van Luyn (Amsterdam), Paul Mosher (Albany, NY), Edward Nersessian (New York), Monroe Pray (Baltimore), Dwarkanath Rao (Ann Arbor, Michigan) , Joseph Reppen (New York), Irvin Rosen (Topeka, KS), Julian Stern (London), Pratyusha Tummala-Narra (Novi, Michigan), Madhusudana Rao Vallabhneni (Toronto), and Vamik Volkan (Charlottesville, VA).

I wish to thank Mr Cesare Sacerdoti, the former Publications Director of the International Psychoanalytical Association, for putting me in touch with Mr Oliver Rathbone of Karnac

Acknowledgements

Books, the publisher of this book. I am also grateful to Messrs Michael Molnar and Ivan Ward of the Freud Museum in London, who shared valuable details on aspects of Freud's office included in this book.

Three other individuals deserve special mention. Shalini ('Tini') Maitra, the daughter of my good friends, Shantanu and Rachana Maitra, traced the origin of many terms with diligence. My personal friend, Dr James Anderson ('Andy') Thomson, Jr supported me at each step of this sojourn. His kind words of encouragement sustained my effort and his marathon derived quip, made during a conversation near the end of this project, that 'look, you can see the stadium now' rejuvenated my pace just when I had begun to feel exhausted. My secretary, Melissa ('Missy') Nevin, typed and collated this behemoth of a manuscript besides helping in innumerable other ways, which include deciphering my handwriting, conducting library searches, scanning internet sites, finding source materials, making phone calls to find missing pieces of information, and assuring that multiple copies of the manuscript always existed so that a computer glitch would not cause a fiasco of unbearable proportions. She put up with my demands which, not infrequently, had a bit of infantile urgency about them. To Tini, Andy, and Missy, my gratitude is profound. I feel similarly towards my assistant, Jan Wright, as well as to The Studio Publishing Services in the UK, all of whom went through and survived the occasionally tortuous copy-editing process with me and were forever forthcoming and graceful.

Finally, I wish to thank my wife and fellow psychoanalyst, Monisha Nayar. Her love, friendship, patience, sacrifices, editorial comments, and computer skills that far exceed mine were invaluable in the course of my writing this book. If I could say it in Urdu, my mother tongue, I would have said: *Tum na hotey to kuchh nahin hota*.

Salman Akhtar
Philadelphia, June 2009

INTRODUCTION

Like a dream, this book owes its origin to sources from both 'below' and 'above'. An early stimulus for it was provided by Henk-Jan Dalewijk and Bert van Luyn, who suggested that I prepare a handout defining various terms I was using during a teaching workshop at their hospital in Amersfoort, Holland. Some major professional achievements and comparably significant disappointments around the same time led to the confidence and the need, respectively, for my undertaking this gigantic task. And, as might be expected, the influence of childhood experiences also played a role here. Prominent among these were my parent's profound love of language, happy memories of cricket-related records and mnemonics, and the painful episode of a ruined rare stamp collection. The motives for writing this book thus included a didactic imperative for clarity, celebratory muscle-flexing, compensatory self-assertion, extension of family legacy in a new direction, and reparative drive towards some early wounds.

Motives aside, the nature of such praxis itself demands explanation. Many questions arise. What is my purpose in writing this book? How did I select the terms and concepts included here? Did I consult the existing psychoanalytic glossaries? Was the number of entries fixed from the beginning or did it keep increasing as the project unfolded? How often did I revisit a definition I had 'satisfactorily' completed? Did I really do all this work by myself? All alone? How confident was I of my ability to bring it to completion? And, finally, how do I feel about this, the finished product in your hands?

Let me start with the purpose of this book. Well, the fact is that the book has many purposes. To begin with, it is intended to create a civilized order out of a delicious chaos. The vastly improved access to the psychoanalytic literature as a result of computerization has not resulted in synthesizing the scattered material into a harmonious gestalt. This dictionary makes an effort to do that. It recounts the origin of each term, mentions the nuances that were added later on, and brings the term's definition up-to-date with our current psychoanalytic knowledge. Wherever possible, it synthesizes the views of a concept by differing 'schools' of psychoanalysis, and thus strives to create a common vocabulary for a layered and complex conceptualization. It also provides clinically useful hints by commenting on the technical implications of the terms and concepts defined. And, by citing major references in connection with each entry, it acts as a source for furthering one's knowledge in this or that particular area of psychoanalysis. Finally, by including both familiar terms (that are in everyday use) and unfamiliar ones (including those which have become obsolete and those which never caught on in the first place) the *Dictionary* seeks to deepen and expand the scope of psychoanalytic language.

As far as the selection of the terms and concepts is concerned, my method was the following. I first consulted the major psychoanalytic glossaries (Eidelberg, 1968; Rycroft, 1968; Moore and Fine, 1968, 1990; and Laplanche and Pontalis, 1973) and the index to the *Standard Edition* of Sigmund Freud's works to develop a basic list from which I would begin working. Then I went over the index of Otto Fenichel's (1945) compendium of early psychoanalytic literature and Alexander Grinstein's (1966) index to the psychoanalytic writings to add more terms and concepts. Subject indexes of text books and encyclopedias of psychoanalysis (Nersessian & Kopff, 1996; Moore & Fine, 1995; Erwin, 2002; Person, Cooper, and Gabbard, 2005) also came to my rescue. Not fully satisfied with the result, I moved on to Paul Mosher's (1990) *Title Key Word and Author Index to Psychoanalytic Journals: 1920–1990*; its updated electronic version, the so-called PEP disc was my next stop. Finally, I hand-searched the volumes of three major psychoanalytic journals, namely, *The Journal of the American Psychoanalytic Association*, *International Journal of Psychoanalysis*, and *Psychoanalytic Quarterly*, for more terms and concepts.

I wanted to cast my net even more widely and go beyond the clinical realm. It seemed to me that ideas from 'applied 'psychoanalysis also need to be included here. Therefore, I sought the help of my friends and colleagues involved in Holocaust studies, immigration literature, psychoanalytically informed political work and culture-specific psychoanalytic concepts from non-Western societies (e.g., India, Korea, and Japan) and collected more terms. And, as I began doing the required reading and then writing definitions, I repeatedly came across new terms and new concepts that demanded inclusion. For a long time, such lexical encounters were exhilarating and jubilant. Finding yet another member of our rich lexicon would fill my heart up with thrill and joy. Gradually, however, such discoveries became burdensome. The work began to cause me fatigue. Still later, imbued with hostile projections on my part, new words began to appear menacing. The humility I had earlier felt in learning more every day grew into anger at those who invented novel terms. Had they only familiarized themselves with others' writings on the subject, they would not have 'dared' to be inventive. Clearly, I was oscillating between depressive and paranoid positions.

I would write a definition and be satisfied with it only to learn more about the topic later and feel the need to rework the earlier write-up. One moment, epistemic gluttony passed itself off as academic honesty. The next moment, the masquerade was in the opposite direction. Completion, the goal which I desperately desired, seemed elusive. *Caught in the Web of Words* (Murray, 2001), I became both *The Professor and the Madman* (Winchester, 1999). I read at home, in my office, on planes, trains, subways, and I read while crossing streets. I even read while driving and at all these places, jotted down important points in my mind and, sometimes, on paper. I ignored some responsibilities and met others half-heartedly. I could not keep up with electronic and written correspondence. Letters and e-mails went unanswered, papers unread. At times, I thought I was going mad. At other times, I *knew* I was mad. Deeply and privately. I would write one or two definitions, and add two or three more to the list. The more I wrote, the more there was to be written. Like Sisyphus, I was trapped in an unending endeavour.

The wish to give up whispered its poisonous lullaby to me more than once. But all this began only when I was about two-thirds the way through the project. Why did I not give up? I do not know what it was, but some inner discipline, some ancestral calling, some sense of scholarly purpose kept pushing me. Like Korczak Ziolkowski (1908–1982), the Polish-American orphan from Boston who grew up to undertake the carving of the world's largest statue (in honour of the Indian chief, Crazy Horse), I was determined. I kept working. And, surely, a day came when the Snow of Insurmountability melted and the Sun of Happy Endings began to shine. Now I was proud and humming with joy.

The task I had undertaken was not only formidable in its magnitude, it was also exceedingly complex. Part history, part literature, part psychoanalysis, and part sheer detective work, it required diverse skills and significant containing capacities. It involved paying close attention to one topic at a time and then, with an equal degree of resolve, to give it up and move on to the next one needing attention. The work also demanded good manners. This applied to both my own contributions and to those of others. About including my work, I had to walk on the tightrope between the sin of self-promotion and the travesty of masochistic self-effacement. Regarding the work of others, too, there were dilemmas to be negotiated. To begin with, some analysts came across as temperamentally more inventive than others; they liked to make up new terms all the time. These had to be included but this created the unintended illusion that others—equally talented but less given to lexical innovations—had not contributed to psychoanalysis in significant ways. Another major challenge was posed by the issue of precedence: who had used a certain term first? This became more difficult when a particular term (e.g., 'malignant narcissism', 'self-object') had been widely associated with a renowned individual's name but turned out to have been coined by someone else. At times, the same term (e.g. 'phallus', 'oral triad') had entirely different meanings in different hands. At other times, the same concept had been described under different names (e.g., 'golden fantasy' and 'Nobel Prize complex'). Complications, complications. And then there were terms and expressions whose origin could not be traced to a paper, book chapter, or a monograph; they originated in the course of administrative meetings of this or that psychoanalytic society (e.g., 'analysability'), or popped up during informal conversations over drinks (e.g., 'neuropsychoanalysis'). How did I find this out?

Others entered the stage at this point in the play. Wife, friends, colleagues, familiar and unfamiliar members of 'The American', secretary, supervisees, students, some young kids from my neighbourhood, close and remote family members, all offered me assistance in finding this or that fact, telling me such and such interesting anecdote, and, above all, to 'hold' me in their forebearance and grace as I plodded along towards the finish line and, one fine afternoon in June 2008, crossed it.

Now, the final question: how satisfied am I with the end product? No answer to this question can bypass Sigmund Freud's (1937c) celebrated 'terminable and interminable' phrase. The writing of a dictionary is hardly something that can be regarded as complete. If writing dictionaries were a profession, Freud would have surely included it among the ones he called 'impossible'. A dictionary does not come to an end. The author only approximates an illusory closure, reaches a compromise between scholarly failure and literary satiety. I am no exception. I know that what I have been able to accomplish is wide-ranging, informative, and theoretically well-grounded. But I also realize that what I have placed in your hands is ultimately an incomplete and flawed product. It perhaps omits, or inoptimally represents, the work of some analysts and overemphasizes that of others. Though I am loath to admit this, it is certainly possible that, due to the limits of my scholarly reach, some misattributions have occurred and a few important concepts are not included here.

My hope is that, despite its weaknesses, this compendium of psychoanalytic terminology will become a useful source of knowledge for psychoanalytic students worldwide, an impetus to think and rethink the ideas we take for granted in our discourse, and a tool for teaching and research both within and outside the field of psychoanalysis. Above all, though, I want my reader to join me in the spirit in which this work was undertaken. This spirit is one of adventure, play, dreaming big dreams, and then having the determination and perseverance to turn them into reality.

'I do not overlook the fact that the path from the letter A to the end of the alphabet is a very long one, and that to follow it would mean an enormous burden of work for you. So do not do it unless you feel an internal obligation—only obey a compulsion of that kind and certainly not any external pressure'

(Sigmund Freud in a letter to Richard Sterba, 3 July 1932, when the latter had begun work on a psychoanalytic glossary. Sterba's *Handworterbuch der Psychoanalyse* (1936–1937) was published in an incomplete form with entries only from the letters A to G. It never reached the end of the alphabet.)

A

Abreaction: concept introduced by Sigmund Freud in 1893 to denote the fact that pent-up emotions associated with a trauma can be discharged by talking about it. The release of affect occurred by bringing 'a particular moment or problem into focus' (Freud, 1914g, p. 147) and as such formed the cornerstone of Freud's early cathartic method of treating hysterical conversion symptoms. Over the later course of evolution of psychoanalysis, however, the concept of abreaction lost its centrality to the treatment method. It came to be recognized as secondary to insight derived from interpretation. None the less, Edward Bibring (1954), in his widely-read paper 'Psychoanalysis and the dynamic psychotherapies', included abreaction among the five therapeutic tools of psychoanalysis (the other four being 'suggestion', 'manipulation', 'clarification', and 'interpretation?'; separate entries on each of them are to be found in this dictionary). Bibring regarded abreaction, or 'emotional reliving', as offering evidence and establishing credibility of the actuality of repressed material to the patient. Vamik Volkan (1976) agreed with this, but added that abreaction in the 'classical' sense also occurs in treatment. He noted that abreaction differs from 'emotional flooding' (see separate entry) in so far as some secondary process functioning and observing ego is retained in the former. As a result, during an abreaction, the patient can make connections between his emotional and ideational fields of experience while he cannot do so during emotional flooding.

Abstinence: it was in the course of elucidating 'transference love' and what might be appropriate therapeutic stance in regard to such 'love' that Sigmund Freud (1915a) sternly declared that 'the treatment must be carried out in abstinence' (p. 165). By this, he meant that the analyst must not gratify the patient's demands for overt or covert erotic indulgences. To do so would appease the neurotic suffering by substitute pleasures and thwart its deeper resolution by the means of interpretation. While initially restricted to libidinal pressures in transference, the 'rule of abstinence' applies to negative transferences also. The analyst must not be tempted to disprove that he or she is not as 'bad' as the patient thinks. All in all, the principle of abstinence requires that we neither attempt to modify the transference by indulging the patient nor by changing our behaviour or by insisting upon our own view of who we actually are. Four more things need to be emphasized regarding the 'rule of abstinence': (1) abstinence must not be equated with remaining silent in response to the patient's overtures; Herbert Schlesinger (2003, pp. 152–154) has cogently advocated this point, noting that the analyst's silence can, at time, be felt as an action—even a hostile action—by the patient; (2) abstinence affects both the analysand and the analyst; the former has to tolerate the deprivation and the latter has to sit on his or her impulses to gratify the patient; (3) abstinence can co-exist with occasional and gentle encouraging remarks that support the patient's analytic ego; and (4) abstinence, in its remote derivatives triggered by events in the intersubjective matrix of analysis, might also involve not eating, drinking, or smoking (cigars!) during the sessions by both parties.

Accident proneness: the failure in the function of self-preservation leading to frequent accidents generally results from a complex interplay of factors. These include: (1) expressing mental conflicts in bodily terms; (2) counterphobic adventures to deny castration anxiety; (3) turning aggression against the self; (4) dramatizing sexual fantasies, especially during adolescence. Liselotte Frankl (1963), who identified these factors, distinguished age-specific accidents from those accidents that reflect a more permanent character disturbance. She suggested that early treatment of children and adolescents and freeing some of the aggression which had been turned against the self can diminish the frequency of accidents and also lessen the incidence of later neurotic developments. See also Theodore Dorpat's (1978) paper, which concludes that 'psychic factors play a part in some, but not all, accidents' (p. 282).

Accidental encounter with patients: see 'Extra-analytic contacts'.

Accordion phenomenon: this phenomenon is observed during psychoanalytically oriented unofficial diplomacy and was first described by Vamik Volkan (1987). As the dialogue takes place between 'enemy' groups with the help of psychoanalytically oriented facilitators, the participants suddenly experience a rapprochement. This closeness is followed by a withdrawal from one another and then by closeness all over again. Volkan likens this to the playing of an accordion—squeezing together and then pulling apart. Derivatives of aggression within the participants, even when they are hidden, and attempts to protect large-group identities are the underlying basis for this behaviour. Volkan (2006) believes that effective discussion of real-world issues cannot take place unless one allows such 'accordion playing' to continue for a while so that the pendulum-like swing in sentiments can be replaced by more secure feelings about participants' large-group identities.

Acculturation: the gradual process of adaptation to post-migration changes in the topographical, political, historical, and socio-economic aspects of one's life. The immigrant becomes more familiar with the conventional ways of behaviour in his new homeland. Altered socio-economic status necessitates psychological shifts and emotional adjustment. Facility with the new language improves and identity undergoes transformation (Akhtar, 1995) to include new avenues of self-expression and altered superego dictates.

Acculturation gap: Sudha Prathikanti's (1997) term for the difference between older and younger members of an immigrant family in their familiarity and comfort with the culture of the country of adoption. This difference can make communications between the two generations difficult and lead to chronic misunderstandings and conflict between them. A clinical counterpart of this gap becomes evident when an immigrant analyst undertakes the treatment of a fellow immigrant from his or her country of origin. While the two seem to have similar cultural backgrounds, the degree to which the values of their new culture have been assimilated by them might vary, leading to difficulties in communication (Akhtar, 2006).

Act of faith: Wilfred Bion's (1970) term for the analyst's intervention that has arisen from a sudden intuition and has, for one shining moment, left all prior experience and knowledge behind. The 'act of faith', or 'F', does not represent the system 'K' (see 'L, H, and K') or the register of knowledge. It represents the absolute truth, or what Bion calls the 'O' (see separate entry). Bion regards the 'act of faith' as representing a scientific state of mind only when it is not filled with supernatural fantasy and is devoid of memory and desire.

Acting in: the term 'acting in' was coined by Meyer Zeligs (1957) to distinguish 'acting out' within the analytic hours from 'acting out' outside the analysis. 'Acting in' may be restricted to bodily movements and postural changes on the couch through which unconscious conflicts are manifested, or it may involve more elaborate behaviours which express repressed memories. It might manifest genetic or extra transferential fantasies as well as unconscious transference-based desires (Paniagua, 1998). In either case, something is put into action instead of words. Repeating has replaced remembering in these instances. Viewed this way, 'acting in' is a form of resistance. However, when the conflictual material pertains to the preverbal periods of childhood and has not had adequate psychic representation and 'mentalization' (Fonagy & Target, 1997), then such behavioural communication might be the only way through which it can find its way to the clinical surface. Here, discerning the communicative value of 'acting in' takes technical precedence over its resistance potential. In this context, it is interesting to note that, in a later publication, Zeligs (1960) himself regarded 'acting in' as a mid-point between 'acting out' and free-association.

Acting out: this English language psychoanalytic term has been derived from the German *agieren*, 'to act') which Sigmund Freud (1905e) used in describing certain aspects of the case of Dora. Freud said that 'she acted out an essential part of her recollections and fantasies instead of producing it in the treatment' (p. 119). Acting out was thus seen as a resistance to remembering and free association. In the later published and now celebrated paper, 'Remembering, repeating, and working through' (1914g), Freud extended the meaning of the term by including the possibility that besides serving as a resistance, acting out could also be a way of remembering. Either way, acting out referred to the behavioural discharge rather than verbal recall of repressed mental contents mobilized during the course of analytic treatment. Departures from Freud's restricted use of the term began to occur fairly soon. These extended the concept of 'acting out' to habitual impulsivity emanating from personality pathology and, in fact, all sorts of socially or morally unacceptable behaviour. Thus, sexual deviations, drug addictions, alcoholism, and antisocial behaviour came to be subsumed under 'acting out' (Abt & Weissman, 1965). Helene Deutsch (1966) went even further, and declared that 'we are all actors-out because nobody is free of regressive trends' (p. 131); even creativity was a form of acting out for her. Lamenting such overextension and in an uncannily prescient statement, Joseph Sandler, Christopher Dare, and Alex Holder (1973) stated that 'it is perhaps unfortunate that some such term as "enactment" was not used in the literature to distinguish the general tendency to impulsive or irrational action from acting out linked with the treatment' (p. 100). They could not have guessed that, some twenty years later, their term 'enactment' would gain immense popularity in psychoanalytic literature, especially in North America.

Action language: developed as an alternative to the conventional psychoanalytic vocabulary of forces, mechanisms, and structures, Roy Schafer's (1976) 'action language' describes all psychological goings-on in terms of dynamic processes. This entails that one give up nouns (e.g., libido) and adjectives (e.g., strong ego) in referring to psychological phenomena. Instead, one would speak in terms of verb–adverb formulations (e.g., 'he carries out his cruel acts towards others without consciously registering them'). In relation to psychological activity also, Schafer's 'language' dictates that we speak of someone not as having 'become friendly' but as 'behaving in a more friendly manner than before'. Such conceptual bedrock would eliminate the distinction between motivational forces and resulting actions, since all would be action; preparatory, preliminary, constitutive, and final steps would all be regarded as a part of an action sequence. Although Schafer's proposal did not gain wide acceptance and, in fact, was rather harshly criticized (Barratt, 1978), it can be seen as an early nudge towards renouncing 'one person' psychology in favour of the contemporary relational and intersubjective perspectives.

Active defensive primal repression: see 'Primal repression'.

Active technique: term associated with certain interventions introduced into psychoanalytic technique by Sandor Ferenczi (1919a, 1921). In the beginning, there were two such measures: (1) *injunctions*: interventions aimed at converting repressed impulses into manifest actions, and (2) *prohibitions*: once repressed impulses have been transformed into actions, telling the patient to stop those very actions. The thinking behind these measures was that a certain amount of acting out facilitates the recall of repressed material. In a later work, co-authored with Otto Rank (1924), Ferenczi introduced a third component of the active technique: (3) *setting a deadline for*

termination: the purpose of this is to facilitate the mourning of unachievable instinctual goals. While Ferenczi (1925a) later abandoned the 'active technique', echoes of his technical voice continued to reverberate in the clinical chambers of psychoanalysis. Sigmund Freud's injunction for phobics to face their feared objects (quoted in Alexander & French, 1946) is but one example of this. Many decades later, Harold Kolansky and Henry Eisner (1974) spoke of 'spoiling' of pre-oedipal developmental arrest in impulse disorders and addictions in order to stir up more analysable intrapsychic conflicts. A similar notion is discernible in the technical stance for the treatment of sexual perversions by Charles Socarides (1988), of intensely pleasurable hatred by Otto Kernberg (1992), and of pathological optimism by Jacqueline Amati-Mehler and Simona Argentieri (1989), and Salman Akhtar (1996). For the Freud–Ferenczi controversy around the latter's 'active technique' and other therapeutic experimentations, see the contributions of Andre Haynal (1988, 2005), Axel Hoffer (1991, 2006; Hoffer & Hoffer,1999), and Peter Hoffer (2003, 2008)

Activity: according to Robert Emde (1988), 'activity' is the most important among the 'basic motives of infancy' (see separate entry) for behaviour and development during infancy. The tendency for 'activity' is in-built and brings with it 'increasing organization and understanding of the world, independent of learning or reinforcement' (p. 28). The infant's activity is matched by parenting behaviours which tend to maximize efforts at tasks of increasing complexity. Emde includes three other dimensions of 'basic motives of infancy': (1) 'social fittedness', (2) 'affective monitoring', and (3) 'self regulation' (see separate entries on each).

Activity and passivity: words in daily use that are employed in psychoanalysis for three specific purposes: (1) to characterize the aim of an instinctual drive; (2) to characterize the ego's attitude towards id, superego, and external reality; and (3) to characterize the overall level of arousal and functioning of the mind at any given time. In the *first* sense, activity and passivity, respectively, refer to the instinctual drive seeking an object for its gratification or rendering the self as an object for gratifying someone else's corresponding drive. Thus, sadism is active and masochism passive in terms of instinctual aims, and the same is true of voyeurism and exhibitionism, respectively (Freud, 1915c). This motif of activity and passivity is to be found outside of the Freudian id psychology as well. Wilfred Bion's (1967) motivational vectors of 'L, H, and K' (see separate entry) all come in active and passive forms (i.e., the wish to love and be loved, to hate and be hated, and to know and be known). This touches upon the *second* usage outlined above. In this view, the ego can adopt an active stance towards id (e.g., by expressing instinctual desires in a controlled manner) or superego (e.g., by defying the dictates of one's conscience). Or, it can adopt a passive attitude towards the other psychic agencies (e.g., by being overwhelmed by instinctual impulses and mindlessly carrying them out, or surrendering to the hard rebukes of the superego by becoming depressed or suicidal). Similarly, the ego can take an active or passive stance towards the demands of external reality. The *third* usage of active–passive is in terms of the overall level of mental activity. Combination of high ('active') and low ('passive') levels of mental activities characterizes a balanced life. Too much passivity can lead to inertia, lack of productivity, and psychic death. Too much activity might reflect a manic defence (see separate entry) and be equally unproductive. Quiet states of mature solitude, introspection, and even simply 'lying fallow' (see separate entry) help regenerate psychic coherence and authenticity. Robust activity then gives them an expression. Glorification of one or the other pole (active/passive) of mental life is unwarranted and might reflect cultural prejudice. Another instance of bias was the equation of activity with masculinity and passivity with femininity. This obviously incorrect assumption was the result of the phallocentric bias of the early psychoanalytic theory.

Actual neurosis: although the notion of 'actual neurosis' was present in Sigmund Freud's writing as early as 1894, the term itself was not introduced by him until 1898; Freud distinguished 'actual neurosis' from 'psychoneurosis' on *two grounds*: (1) the former resulted from disturbance in contemporary sexual life while the latter was caused by psychological trauma in childhood; and (2) the symptoms of 'actual neurosis' were due to the physiological reactions and therefore lacked the psychodynamic depth of the problems associated with psychoneurosis. Freud went on to divide 'actual neurosis' into two types: 'neuraesthenia' (which resulted from sexual excess, especially frequent masturbation), and 'anxiety neurosis' (which resulted from diminished frequency or poor quality of sexual discharge). These conditions were not deemed amenable to psychoanalytic treatment by Freud. A corollary of his early toxicologic (as opposed to purely psychological) theory of anxiety, Freud's concept of 'actual

neurosis' is now regarded as obsolete. Any symptoms that might result from excess or lack of sexual activity would now be regarded as secondary consequences of the psychological disturbance leading to the disturbed erotic life in the first place (Fink, 1970).

Actualization: an expression that is used in three different ways in psychoanalysis. (1) *The first use* pertains to the situations when a growing child's fantasies are suddenly given credence by an event in the external reality. For instance, if an oedipal phase boy meets with an accident and fractures his leg, the castration anxiety he had been struggling with becomes 'actualized'. Such 'actualization' contributes to the propensity for 'fixation' (see separate entry). (2) *The second use* of the term 'actualization' is in the context of an individual transforming his wishes and day-dreams into a concrete product (e.g., a statue, a building, a mechanical invention, a painting, or a book) in external reality. (3) *Finally*, within the clinical situation, 'actualization' finds its counterpart in the 'role-responsiveness' (Sandler, 1976) of the analyst, whereby the letter momentarily lives out the transference attributes assigned to him or her.

Adaptation: Heinz Hartmann's (1958) term for the capacity to cope appropriately and advantageously with one's environment. When the individual alters the environment to meet his needs, the resulting adaptation is called 'alloplastic'. When, however, the individual modifies himself in response to the environment, the adaptation is called 'autoplastic'. Extremes of autoplastic adaptation are seen in severely inhibited behaviours as well as chameleon-like adjustment to the demands of external reality. Extremes of alloplastic adaptation are evident in the act of migration, divorce, and, curiously, also in the capacity to invent new things. Mostly, however, the two forms of adaptation exist and are not seen in such extreme forms. This is clearly seen in marriage, an institution that demands both alloplastic and autoplastic adaptations.

Adaptive perspective: see 'Metapsychology'.

Addiction: while Sandor Rado (1933) hinted that addiction might, to a certain extent, be the cause of psychopathology rather than its result, and Norman Zinberg (1975) asserted that the psychic attributes of addicts are often the result of a chronic social alienation and restricted ego autonomy, most analysts view addiction as a primary psychopathology. Indeed, there is a fair amount of agreement in the psychoanalytic literature on addiction. (1) *From the drive theory perspective*, addiction is correlated with oral dependency and regression from genital to masturbatory pleasure (Abraham, 1908; Fenichel, 1945; Freud, 1897, 1905a); (2) *from the ego psychology perspective*, affect primitivization, the ego's vulnerability to regressive solutions, use of denial, lack of self-governance, and predominance of primitive defences are implicated (Abraham, 1908; Krystal & Raskin, 1970; Mack, 1981; Rado, 1926); (3) *from the object relations viewpoint*, a borderline character organization (Kernberg, 1967; Waska, 2006) and loss of transitional relatedness are seen as major features; (4) *from the self psychology perspective*, addiction is seen as a failure of self-regulation (Levin, 1987). While not ignoring the role of oedipal factors, almost all authors conclude that the 'fundamental wound of the addict's ego' (Simmel, 1948, p. 27) is caused by early, preoedipal damage to the personality. At the same time, they acknowledge the role of social variables and constitutional vulnerabilities, which perhaps explains the fact that not all individuals with preoedipal ego damage develop addiction.

Addiction to near-death: described by Betty Joseph (1982), this is a malignant form of self-destructiveness which manifests as 'over-working, almost no sleep, avoiding eating properly or secretly overeating if the need is to lose weight, drinking more and more, and perhaps cutting off from relationships' (p. 449). Within the clinical situation, such individuals express themselves in a masochistically animated manner and tend to develop marked 'negative therapeutic reactions' (see separate entry). They also display an intense pull towards suffering and 'seduce' the analyst to become harsh and critical towards them. There seems to be a kind of 'mental or physical brinksmanship' (*ibid.*, p. 450), in which seeing oneself suffer and remaining unhelpable plays a secretly exciting role (at the same time, the pull towards sanity and life is deposited, via projective identification, in the analyst). It is extremely difficult for such patients to give up their masochistic gratification and to replace it with pleasurable object relations.

Adhesive equation: Frances Tustin's (1993) concept for the behaviour and psychology of autistic children who are chronically stuck to their mothers in such a manner that there can be no space between them and hence no true object relationship can develop. She distinguished this concept from adhesive identification (see separate entry). 'In *adhesive equation*, the subject feels the *same* as the object with no space between them, while in *adhesive identification* the subject feels *similar* to the object and there is space between them' (Tustin, 1992, quoted in Mitrani, 2001, p. 32).

Adhesive identification: concept originated by Esther Bick (1964, 1968) to denote an archaic form of object-relating which premiums proximity with the object for the purpose of self-coherence. This type of relatedness precedes the desire to get inside the object by projective identification. Most marked during early infancy, such object-relation places the object in the position of a 'psychic skin' (see separate entry) that can contain the infant's emotional experiences, since these are inchoate and as yet incompletely differentiated from its bodily sensations. Bick's ideas have been further elaborated upon by Donald Meltzer (1975).

Adhesive identity: see 'Adhesive equation'.

Adhesive libido: a concept introduced by Sigmund Freud in 1905a. Employing terms such as *Haftbarkeit* (adhesiveness) and *Klebrigkeit* (viscosity), Freud said that, in certain instances, a libidinal fixation shows greater tenacity than usual. Individuals with this propensity 'cannot make up their minds to detach libidinal cathexes from one object and displace them on to another, although we can discover no special reason for this cathectic loyalty' (1937c, p. 241). Freud held 'adhesive libido' to be largely constitutional in origin, and felt its intensity to increase with age. To be sure, a proposition of this sort had prognostically nihilistic implications and might have permitted many early analysts to explain away their negative countertransference reactions and therapeutic failures. A dramatic example of this is the following recollection of Margaret Mahler about her failed analysis with Helene Deutsch. 'In the course of the first session, Mrs. Deutsch proceeded to tell me, summarily, that I had a "sticky libido"' (Stepansky, 1988, p. 60). This notwithstanding, there is a statement of Freud's (1918b) which offers a more psychodynamic (as opposed to constitutional) and, hence, potentially more hopeful view of the situation. Talking of Wolf Man, Freud states that 'Any position of the libido which he had once taken up was obstinately defended by him from fear of what he would lose by giving it up and from distrust of the probability of a complete substitute being afforded by the new position that was in view' (1918b, p. 115). Here 'adhesiveness' is a product not of somatic constitution, but of fear, which, in turn, might emanate from mixed elements of fantasy and reality and hence be amenable to further exploration.

Adhesive pseudo-object relations: described by Judith Mitrani (1994), this is an aberration of development rooted in traumatic experiences of marked privation during intrauterine and neonatal life. Gradual dawning of objectivity, and even the congealing of true subjectivity, are compromised. Their place is taken by premature and false relating in which objects are experienced as inanimate things 'to be absorbed, exploited, manipulated, or avoided by the subject in a desperate attempt to gain a sensation of existence, safety, and impermeability' (Mitrani, 2001, p. 38). Separation from them causes a catastrophic collapse of the self.

Adolescence: while it might be more or less pronounced in different cultural settings, the psychosocial transition that begins with puberty and ends with the consolidation of young adulthood does seems to bring forth highly specific developmental tasks to be mastered. Collectively, these challenges and their solutions are grouped under the rubric of 'adolescence'. Consolidation of identity is at the centre of this turmoil (Erikson, 1956). While psychological separateness in childhood depends upon a secure internalization of parental homeostatic functions, the process is now reversed. In this *second individuation process of adolescence* (Blos, 1967), disengagement from early objects becomes necessary. This, coupled with an upsurge of sexual drive at this stage, results in ego instability. Living in close proximity with parents while arriving at the threshold of genital primacy (Freud, 1905a), and the sexual fantasies it propels, causes anxiety. Defensive withdrawal and fighting then ensues. These measures also allow dependent longings (which are mobilized due to the ego's facing so many internal and external challenges) to be kept in check. Progressive and regressive trends alternate, at times with disturbing rapidity. The former herald new self-configurations and non-incestuous, extra-familial object relations. The latter lead to magical thinking, intense idealizations, and a return to anal-phase struggles around control issues. 'The adolescent mind is essentially a mind of the moratorium, a psychosocial stage between childhood and adulthood, and between the morality learned by the child, and the ethics to be developed by the adult' (Erikson, 1950, pp. 262–263). Devaluation of parents and idealization of peers gradually gives way to a mid-way ego position with realistic appraisals of both. In the process, some *depersonification of superego* (Jacobson, 1964), i.e., mellowing of the literal parental dictates around issues of morality, takes place. Gender differences in identity development also become evident (Fischer &

Fischer, 1991). For the boy, the door to regressive closeness with mother is barred because it threatens his gender identity. For the girl, regression to a close tie with the mother, with its push–pull tensions, is more evident. Both boys and girls struggle with renouncing sexual aims towards primary objects. Peter Blos, Senior (1967, 1984) suggests that it is only during adolescence that negative oedipal strivings are truly given up. This contributes to the psychic image of the kind of person one aspires to become. Indeed, Blos declares that 'the adult ego ideal is the heir of the negative oedipus complex' (1984, p. 319). This development, coupled with broadened ego-autonomy and softened superego, results in a deeper individuation and a unique formulation of personal identity.

Adolescent detachment: elaborating upon Freud's (1905a) observation that a certain 'detachment from parental authority' (p. 227) is essential for the growth of the new generation, Roy Schafer (1973a) introduced the term 'adolescent detachment'. This referred to the adolescent's vehement effort to 'stamp out' the parental influence upon his mind and, in a misguided effort to do so, his avoiding them, acting aloof, and becoming disdainful towards them. Not having fully resolved the ties to his parents of childhood, the adolescent revolts against his actual contemporary parents.

Adolescent identity crisis: see 'Identity crisis'.

Adoption trauma: Luis Feder's (1974) concept pertaining to the psychological trauma that results from being adopted. In his view, most such children were conceived under problematic circumstances, have been subject to the adoption agency's 'family romance fantasies' (see separate entry), and to a pre-adoptive idealization by their adoptive parents that gradually lifts to reveal ambivalence, if not unmitigated hostility. While adoptive children do tend to face some extra difficulties in growing up, 'adoption trauma', as described here, is far from ubiquitous. The complex emotional struggles of adopted children and their parents have been elucidated by Elaine Frank and Denise Roe, Katherine Reed, Carlotta Miles, Martin Silverman, and Marshall Schechter in a volume enticingly titled *Thicker than Blood* (Akhtar & Kramer, 2000).

Adult development: see 'Developmental tasks of adult life'.

Advice: see 'Psychoanalytically informed advice'.

Affect: term customarily used in psychoanalysis for 'emotion' or 'feeling'. According to Leo Rangell (1995), 'differentiation between these terms has been attempted from time to time but has not led to any satisfactory or generally accepted formulation' (p. 381). Psychoanalytic perspective on affect has evolved in tandem with the overall progress of psychoanalytic theory. Early on, David Rapaport (1953a) delineated three phases of this evolution: (1) *from 1890 to 1900*, during which 'affect' was equated with energy and 'strangulation' of affect was seen as the cause of symptoms; (2) *from 1900 to 1923*, when affects were seen as physiological discharges into the interior leading to both the expression and experience of emotions; and (3) *from 1923 to 1926*, when affects were seen from multiple vantage points and their development and refinement came to be associated with increasing ego dominance. To this list of historical phases, one can add later developments, when affects came to be regarded as primary communicative pathways for the relationship between self and its objects (Emde, 1983; Mahler, Pine, & Bergman, 1975; Spitz, 1965; Stern, 1985), as well as the building blocks of self and object representations (Kernberg, 1975a; Klein, 1940) and even the organizers of drives themselves (Kernberg, 1992, 1995). Besides these metapsychological issues, there are *seven phenomenological binaries* to consider regarding affects. These include: (1) primitive *vs.* advanced affects; (2) single *vs.* mixed affects (Glover, 1939); (3) fixed *vs.* labile affects; (4) affects built up due to instinctual tension *vs.* affects resulting from instinctual release; (5) drive related affects (e.g., love, hate) *vs.* ego related affects (e.g., pleasure and mastery); (6) affects as motives for defence *vs.* affects as expressions as defence (Brenner, 1975; Rangell, 1978); and (7) conscious and unconscious affects. Regarding the last mentioned matter, Freud seems to have been 'inconsistent' (Rangell, 1995, p. 382), mostly saying that affects have to be conscious but occasionally implying otherwise. More recently, Sydney Pulver (1971, 1974) has suggested that affects can exist in the unconscious as fully formed repressed contents, or as predispositions to congeal into a particular emotional manner of responding. See also the work of Ranier Krause and Jorg Merten (1999), which elucidates the affective distinctions between neuroses and severe psychopathology. In the former, there is an excess of conflictual affects, while in the latter there is restriction of affect with one negative 'lead affect' taking over the mind.

Affect intolerance: phrase originated by Stanley Coen (1997, 2002) to denote the difficulty some patients (and analysts) have in bearing the emergence of intense emotions associated with love, dependent longing, erotic desire, and hatred during the analytic sessions. Coen emphasizes the necessity to explore the patient's fearful fantasies about why they regard such feelings to be intolerable. He connects such 'affect intolerance' with 'fears of relinquishing a pathological object relationship, within which certain key feelings had seemed unbearable to both child/patient and parent' (2002, p. xxiii). The analyst who seeks to help his patient master such anxieties must be prepared to feel the dreaded affects on the patients' behalf for a long time before attempting interpretation and reconstruction.

Affectionate and sensual currents: even before he turned his attention specifically to the topic of romantic love, Sigmund Freud (1905a) had noted that the human process of the choice of love object is diphasic. The first move towards the object begins between the ages of two and five and is characterized by infantile sexual aims. However, repression renders such longings as merely an 'affectionate current' which, in turn, has to be synthesized by the 'sensual current' appearing during puberty. Seven years later, Freud developed his understanding of love in a seminal statement that still remains the cornerstone of the psychoanalytic understanding of love. He noted 'two currents whose union is necessary to ensure a completely normal attitude in love . . . These two may be distinguished as the *affectionate* and the *sensual* currents' (1912a, p. 180, original italics). The affectionate current was ontogenetically earlier and arose in connection with the early psychosomatic care by the primary objects, especially the mother. The sensual current was more specifically sexual and arrived on the scene with puberty. When the two currents could not be synthesized, the sphere of love bifurcated into tenderness and passion. Individuals thus afflicted 'love (whom) they do not desire and where they desire they can not love' (*ibid.*, p. 183). The components of the two currents were further elucidated by psychoanalysts following Freud. The affectionate current consists of concern, empathy, tenderness, optimal distance, and mutual playfulness (Akhtar, 2009a) and the sensual current consisted of the elements described by Otto Kernberg (1991) under the rubric of 'erotic desire' (see separate entry).

Affectionate transference: Stefano Bolognini's (1994) designation for a kind of transference feeling that usually emerges towards the later phase of analysis. The affectionate transference results from 'the transposition in the analysis of an ameliorated internal object relationship involving sexual specificity, gratitude, and quite free appreciation of the object and of the subject's own relational potential, while at the same time respecting reality and the relevant limits' (p. 83). Such transference differs from 'erotic', 'erotized', and 'loving transferences' (see separate entries).

Affective core: Robert Emde's (1999) term for 'an early appearing and organized set of consistent parameters for an individual's emotional experience and expression' (p. 325). Although the infant's 'temperament' (see separate entry) does contribute to it, the 'affective core' reflects a more sustained emotional tone which is present on an everyday basis and which continuously influences the behaviour. Such ongoing emotional background is evolved from experiences with early caretakers and, in a dialectical fashion, has an impact upon the latter. The 'affective core' is anchored in the memory system; current emotional experiences evoke the past ones and past experiences have an impact upon the perception and processing of the present ones.

Affective monitoring: according to Robert Emde (1981, 1988), 'affective monitoring' is one of the four 'basic motives of infancy'; the other three are 'activity', 'self regulation', and 'social fittedness' (see separate entries on each). 'Affective monitoring' refers to the infant's proclivity to check experience according to what is pleasurable and unpleasurable. Such monitoring helps the infant regulate his own behaviour while guiding the mother's care giving activities.

Affective organ language: see 'Primal psychophysiological self'.

Affectualization: term coined by Grete Bibring and colleagues (Bibring, Dwyer, Huntington, & Valenstein, 1961) who denote a characterological tendency to overemphasize the emotional aspects of an issue in order to avoid a deeper, rational understanding of it. 'Feeling is unconsciously intensified for the purposes of defense' (p. 64). Such deployment of 'emotionality as a defense' (Siegman, 1954) becomes incorporated as a character trait in some individuals, especially those with a hysterical personality (Valenstein, 1962). Affectualization is the exact opposite of intellectualization, which channels instinctual energy into intellectual debates and ruminations. It resembles manic defence in its precluding a deeper and duller contact with psychic reality. It differs from 'manic defence' in so far as it lacks the mental cluttering and denial typical of the latter.

Affirmative interventions: term introduced into the psychoanalytic literature by Bjorn Killingmo in 1989. Such interventions are distinct from interpretive interventions, with the latter being aimed at deciphering and unmasking hidden meanings. Affirmative interventions, in contrast, are aimed at establishing plausibility that the patient's experience is indeed valid and meaningful. They comprise (1) an *objectifying element* that conveys the sense to the patient that the therapist can feel what it is to be in the patient's shoes (e.g., 'Your tense silence, distraught appearance, and avoidance of me all tell me that you are profoundly upset and find the situation unbearably painful'). This renders the affective experience of the patient less private; (2) a *justifying element* that introduces a cause-and-effect relation, thus placing the patient's feeling state in the context of a reasonable sequence of events (e.g., 'No wonder you feel so upset at my announcing my vacation, since you feel desperately lost without me and, on top of that, feel so helplessly excluded from my decisions in this regard'); and (3) an *accepting element* that imparts a historical context to the current distress by including the mention of similar experiences from the patient's past (e.g., 'I know that my leaving hurts you deeply because it reminds you of the time when you were 4 or 5 years old and your parents would go away for weeks at a time, leaving you pining for them'). Affirmative interventions strengthen the therapeutic alliance and enhance the recognition of the emotional turmoil as a transference reaction.

Agency: beginning with David Rapaport's (1953b) metapsychological essay on ego activity through Roy Schafer's (1976) 'action language' (see separate entry) and George Klein's (1976) delineation of ego pleasures, to Ethel Person's (2001) emphasis upon personal power in the conduct of life, the concept of 'agency' has pervaded contemporary psychoanalytic discourse. Essentially, it can be thought of as 'the person's capacity to live by the term "I want", or "I shall seek" or "I shall not", that is awareness of and behavioral implementation of personal aims' (Pine, 2005, p. 16). 'Agency' refers to an inner state of awareness and choice of action. While unconscious factors might contribute to it, the experience of agency itself is conscious, active, and self-owned in its nature. It is not felt as reactive, and thus contains a psychostructural shadow of Donald Winnicott's (1960) concept of 'true self' (see separate entry).

Aggression: a broad and inherently multi-disciplinary topic, 'aggression' defies a brief summary.

Even within psychoanalysis, a uniformly agreed upon definition is difficult to find. Many reasons account for this: (1) too many words ('aggression', 'aggressivity', aggressiveness', 'aggressive behaviour', 'aggressive drive', 'aggressive instinct', and so on) are used interchangeably in this realm; (2) the word 'aggression' itself has come to denote many phenomena, ranging from drive to behaviour, (3) the tension between an active–assertive and hostile–destructive view of aggression also compounds issues under consideration, and (4) a tendency towards circular reasoning abounds here, as when assertive and non-destructive behaviour is called 'aggressive' and then advanced as proof that not all aggression is destructive in aim. Broadly speaking, however, one can divide the psychoanalytic perspective on 'aggression' into four categories: (1) *Sigmund Freud's views:* these show an important shift from regarding aggression and especially sadism, as a runaway 'component of the sexual instinct which has become independent and exaggerated and, by displacement, has usurped the leading position' (1905a, p. 158) to the elevation of aggression as an independent instinctual drive (Freud, 1920g). After maintaining that aggression is a component of sexual instinct for over a decade, Freud made the 'startling' (Jones, 1957, p. 266) declaration that aggression or 'aggressive drive' is a drive of the 'death instinct' (see separate entry), which, together with life instinct, constitutes the two main forces in the struggle of life. In polar opposition to his 1905 view that destructive aggression resulted from the thwarting of the instinct for mastery, Freud (1930a) now suggested that 'the instinct of destruction, moderated and tamed, and, as it were, inhibited in its aim, must, when it is directed to objects, provide the ego with the satisfaction of its vital needs and with control over nature' (p. 121); (2) *Melanie Klein–Heinz Hartmann divergence:* the conceptutal chasm between Freud's two views on aggression gave rise to the bifurcation of psychoanalytic theory. Klein became the most 'uncompromising' (Gay, 1988, p. 402) exponent of death instinct and Hartmann dismissed it as a fanciful 'biological speculation' (1939, p. 11). Hartmann did not, however, discard the notion of primary aggressive propensity in man; this led the 'death instinct' to be conceptually transformed, as it were, into 'aggressive instinct', something most classical analysts felt comfortable with; (3) *theoretical dissent by the British Middle School and North American Self Psychology:* theorists in these camps (e.g., Michael Balint, Roanld Fairbairn, Donald Winnicott, and Heinz Kohut) either down-played or rejected the instinctual underpinnings of aggression and located its origin in actual frustration at the hands of early caretakers. Aggression was seen by them as a reactive, not primary, phenomenon which contained an element of hope; and (4) *The contemporary reformuations:* these include Otto Kernberg's (1991, 1992) view that aggressive drive evolves from the integration of aversive affects; Henri Parens' (1989) delineation of three trends in aggression: non-destructive aggression, non-affective destructiveness and hostile destructiveness which was the end result of chronic frustration, and Gerald Stechler's (1987) proposal that if a child's 'assertion' (see separate entry) meets a punitive response from parents, the child reacts with negative affects, which cause contamination of assertion with aggression. When this is extensive, to all appearances an 'aggressive drive' has been set in motion. Clearly, the theory of aggression has travelled a long distance from its origins in the instinctual model, through affect-based hypotheses to relational paradigms. To be sure, these perspectives interact with each other and lead in complex ways to the end product of 'aggression'.

Aggression-reassignment surgery: since the male transsexual's fervent wish to be surgically transformed into a woman (an idealized and envied object that he seeks to merge with) is largely a matter of repudiating his phallic aggression and denying his unconscious hatred of women, James Kavanaugh and Vamik Volkan (1980) wryly suggested that the popular phrase 'sex-reassignment surgery' might be replaced by the psychodynamically accurate 'aggression-reassignment surgery'!

Aggressive drive: see 'Aggression'.

Aggressive energy: see 'Psychic energy'.

Aggressive instinct: see 'Aggression'.

Agoraphilia: Peter Glauber's (1955) term for the inordinate fascination for the outdoors, viewing ruins, climbing mountains, and hiking through wilderness. 'Agoraphilia' is not a reaction to agoraphobia. It is a derivative of necrophilia (see separate entry) in which 'the love of the dead mother and the need to master the fears of her, have become the love and mastery of, or triumph over, the petrified aspects of Mother Nature' (p. 703). A fantasy of rebirth is frequently associated with 'agoraphilia'.

Agoraphobia: a morbid psychological state characterized by fear of open and public spaces and a strong aversion to leaving familiar surroundings unless accompanied by a reassuring companion.

While such fear is often the end product of a repressed prostitution fantasy identified long ago by Sigmund Freud (1897, p. 253), this conceptualization now seems a bit dated. What is perhaps away from familiar surroundings (and their implicit ego supports and superego admonishments) can release instinctual impulses which, in turn, can be frightening to an otherwise inhibited individual. Other factors also play a role. In an early paper on 'locomotor anxiety', Karl Abraham (1913b) noted that neurotic inhibitions of mobility emanate not only from defences against constitutionally strong pleasure in movement and unconscious sexual fantasies, but also from difficulty in separating from love objects. Some years later, Helene Deutsch (1929) declared the involvement of a partner to be the crucial determinant of the agoraphobic's malady. However, she felt that hostile and controlling fantasies were frequently hidden underneath the apparent need for libidinal supplies. Heinz Kohut (1980), more recently, concluded that agoraphobic's consciously felt need for a friendly companion is the key to what lies in his psychic depths, namely, the continued search for a maternal object. Clearly, the symptom of agoraphobia seems to have many determinants, including constitutional hesitancy, powerful attachment needs, sexualization of locomotion and freedom, hostile fantasies towards caretakers, and a regressive diminution of separateness and ego autonomy.

Aim of the instinct: see 'Instinct'.

Aim-inhibition: in order to understand this concept, one has to recall that an instinct, according to Sigmund Freud (1915b) is 'the measure of the demand upon the mind in consequence of its connection with the body' (p. 122) and it has four aspects: source, impetus, aim, and object. The 'aim' of an instinct is the specific action which discharges excitement and brings about satisfaction. 'Aim-inhibition' refers to an intrapsychic situation whereby an instinct, rather than finding total discharge, seems content with 'certain approximations to satisfaction' (Freud, 1923a, p. 258). Examples of this are one's relations with adult children and with friends, i.e., situations where sexual elements of desire are subject to repression and ego restraint. Responding with sarcasm, rather than violence, to a provocation constitutes another example.

Ajase complex: described by Heisaku Kosawa (1931), this psychological constellation is named after a character from an old mythological fable from India. In this tale, Prince Ajase imprisons his father, King Bimbsara, on the political instigation of a senior member of their court. Then he learns that his mother, Queen Vaidehi, is secretly sending the King food and other supplies. He attacks his mother with a sword and nearly kills her. Later in his life, however, he begins to feel a strong sense of remorse which leads him to break out in pustulent sores all over his body. Kosawa contrasted the tale of Oedipus with that of Ajase. Oedipus killed his father in order to posses his mother, but Ajase tried to kill his mother because he felt that he was losing possession of her. Kosawa stated that both types of murderous impulses (i.e., parricidal and matricidal) result in guilt and remorse, but such feelings are stronger when the hostility is primarily directed at the mother.

Alexithymia: originated by Peter Sifneos in 1967 (cited in Nemiah & Sifneos, 1970), this term denotes a cognitive style that is peculiarly uninformed by affects. The emotions themselves remain undifferentiated and poorly verbalized. The individual appears rational and his discourse is true to factual details. However, there is a striking lack of imaginativeness, empathy, spontaneity, and playfulness. Found mostly in patients with psychosomatic and addictive disorders, 'alexithymia' renders the patient unsuited for psychoanalytic therapy. This conclusion is strengthened if one regards the condition to be essentially neurophysiological. Viewing it as a characterologic defence or even a developmental deficit (caused in part by being raised by parents who were disinterested in the patient's mind during his or her childhood) can mobilize a ray of therapeutic hope, however (Sifneos, 1975).

Alien self: term coined by Peter Fonagy, Gyorgy Gergely, Elliot Jurist, and Mary Target (2002) for those self-states which have emerged as a result of inappropriate and inadequate mirroring by childhood caregivers. Lacking well-attuned mirroring, the child internalizes a mismatched mental state as a part of the self. This causes internal disorganization and presses for projection outwards. Fonagy and co-authors refer to such split-off and projected parts as the 'alien self'.

Alienation: a sense of estrangement from the emotional connections and values of one's family and society. To a certain extent, this is expected during adolescence. However, more marked feelings of this type suggest psychopathology. 'Alienation' is also evident during the early phases of immigration from one country to another. In distinction of this relatively phenomenological level, the term 'alienation' has been given a deeper metapsychological slant by Jacques Lacan (1955). He proposed that 'alienation' is the inevitable consequence of the subject's identification with its specular image during the 'mirror stage'. As a result, the ego is essentially based upon fantasy and therefore the subject is inherently and inescapably split within himself. Masud Khan (1979) carried this idea further into his study of sexual perversions, stating that perverse fantasies, gadgets, and pornography 'alienate the pervert from himself, as, alas, from the object of his desire' (p. 9).

Allergic object relationship: a particular type of object relationship described by Pierre Marty (1958) in connection with patients with chronic allergic reactions. This object relationship is characterized by 'the subject's incessant endeavor to come as near as possible to the object until he merges with it, as it were in an indistinct mass' (p. 98). The gobbling up of the object is immediate, complete, arachaic, and violent. It results in a deep and boundless identification of the subject with the object confusion.

Alloerotism: Sigmund Freud's (1899a) counterpart of his own concept of 'autoerotism' (see separate entry), referring to the libidinal investment in an object other than oneself. Freud divided 'alloerotism' into two subtypes: (1) homoerotism or the libidinal cathexis of an object of the same sex; and (2) hetroerotism or the libindinal cathexis of an object of the opposite sex. Both types of libidinal investments served to deflect cathexis from the self on to an external object.

Alloplastic adaptation: see 'Adaptation'.

Alpha-elements: Wilfred Bion's (1962a,b) designation for those mental registrations that are made directly from sense impressions and emotional experiences. These, in turn, are used in the formation of conscious and unconscious thinking during wakefulness, dream thoughts, and as triggers for further knowledge. 'Alpha-elements' are building blocks of language as well. The word 'dog', for instance, is an 'alpha-element' which propels thinking and adds to knowledge. Bion (1963) clarifies this in the following manner: 'Having found the name and thereby bound the phenomena, the remainder of history, if so wished, can be devoted to determining what it means—what a *dog* is; the name is an invention to make it possible to think and talk about something before it is know what that something is' (pp. 87–88).

Alpha function: Wilfred Bion's (1962a,b) designation for the mental activity essential for the reception, elaboration, and communication of experiences. Bion kept the term itself devoid of meaning, thus providing psychoanalytic theory 'an equivalent to the concept of a variable in mathematics' (Bleandonu, 1994, p. 150). 'Alpha-function' operates on sense impressions and felt emotions, transforming them into thinkable thoughts or 'alpha-elements' (see separate entry). It is, therefore, the cornerstone of knowledge acquisition. Bion emphasized that, under normal circumstances, this function is operative during both wakefulness and sleep; it is thus responsible for the generation of waking thoughts as well as the thoughts that lie behind a dream. When 'alpha-function' fails to operate, sense impressions and subjective feelings remain in their precognate state.

Alter: see 'Dissociative self'.

Alter-ego personalities: see 'Narcissistic personality types'.

Alter-ego transference: a concept from 'self psychology' (see separate entry) which suggests that some analysands need to experience an essential likeness with their analysts in order to strengthen their selves. Such 'transference' is based upon the insufficiency of narcissistically stabilizing childhood experiences of similarity and affinity with parents. 'Faced with growing up in a world experienced as alien, the child sometimes manifests the intensity of this need in the creation of imaginary playmates' (Wolf, 1994, p. 73). 'Alter-ego transference' similarly creates a partner in the clinical situation who is seen to suffer from the same tragedies and share same values as that of the patient. Fittingly, another name for this type of transference is 'twinship transference' (Kohut, 1971).

Alterity: see 'Autochthony, cosmogony, and alterity'.

Altruism: striving to broaden the understanding of altruism and to undo its customary linkage with masochism, Beth Seelig and Lisa Rosof (2001) wrote a remarkable essay under the title of 'Normal and pathological altruism'. They delineated five types of altruism: (1) *Proto altruism*, which is largely biological and instinctive; it is 'hard-wired' in the human brain and contributes to the ordinary maternal protectiveness towards her infant, though, clearly, such an attitude has other determinants as well; (2) *Generative altruism*, which reflects the non-conflictual pleasure in fostering the achievements and success of others; (3) *Conflicted altruism*, which subsumes Anna Freud's concept of 'altruistic surrender' (see separate entry) as well as generative altruism that has been drawn into emotional conflict; (4) *Pseudo altruism*, which comprises pleasureless compulsive generosity serving as a defensive cloak for unconscious sadomasochism, and (5) *Psychotic altruism*, where delusionally driven self-sacrifice for others' welfare and messianic acts of saving the world dominate the clinical picture.

Altruistic surrender: concept outlined by Anna Freud (1946) in describing the tendency of some individuals to be surprisingly tolerant, and even encouraging, of the instinctual gratifications they would never permit themselves. A strict superego made them renounce their wishes, but a 'clever' ego arranged a situation where they obtained vicarious gratification of these wishes by projecting them upon carefully selected proxy individuals who had little compunction in living out such desires. Melanie Klein's (1946) concept of projective identification, especially when it involves the psychically endangered 'good' aspects of the self (Hamilton, 1986), comes very close to Anna Freud's 'altruistic surrender'. Also pertinent is the behaviour of the 'shy narcissist' (see separate entry) who 'lives out his own ambition vicariously by playing "second fiddle" to someone whose success he has himself silently engineered' (Akhtar, 2000, p. 54).

Amae: a Japanese term which denotes an intermittent, recurring, culturally patterned interaction in which the ordinary rules of propriety and formality are suspended, allowing people to receive and give affectionate ego support to each other (Doi, 1962, 1989; Taketomo, 1986). Daniel Freeman, a North American psychoanalyst with extensive knowledge and experience of Japanese culture, regards amae to be an 'interactive mutual regression in the service of ego, which gratifies and serves the progressive intrapsychic growth and development of both the participants' (1998, p. 47). While echoes of early maternal refuelling of a growing child's ego can be discerned in it, the interaction typical of amae extends beyond childhood to spread over the entire life span of the individual (Freeman, 1998). The adult engaging in amae is not regressed or fixated, but capable of a healthy access to interpersonal sources of ego-strengthening.

Ambitendency: a term coined by Margaret Mahler, Fred Pine, and Anni Bergman (1975) to denote the simultaneous display of two contrasting behaviourally manifest attitudes by a child in the rapprochement subphase (from 14–15 months to about 24 months or so). For instance, the child might cry and smile virtually at the same time, kiss mother and then suddenly bite her, and approach mother and, at the last moment, dart away from her. Such behaviour is suggestive of internal ambivalence towards closeness and distance from the mother. The former is sought for soothing purposes, but brings along the fear of regression and merger. The latter is sought for the pleasure of freedom, but carries with it the risk of separation and aloneness.

Ambition: expressing the hard-wired infantile potential for exploratory activities and exercising autonomous ego functions, the psychological attitude called 'ambition' (the wish to achieve, succeed, master, and advance) has origins in gratifying as well as in conflictual aspects of childhood experience. The 'healthy' factors contributing to ambition include the confidence that results from being 'the mother's undisputed darling' (Freud, 1917b, p. 156), identification with industrious and success-orientated parents, validation of one's talents and efforts, pleasurable 'experiences of efficacy' (Wolf, 1994) during latency and adolescence, and secondary rewards (e.g., fame, money) in external reality. The painful experiences contributing to ambition are childhood feelings of inferiority and shame; these might result from being orphaned as a child or from having bodily defects that lead one to be ridiculed by others. In such cases, a powerful wish to rectify the narcissistic imbalance can, at times, lead to great creative and social achievements. Clinically more relevant are cases of the opposite type, i.e., those with too little ambition. Here, the differential diagnosis of a defective ego *vs.* guilt-based inhibition becomes important, since it can guide therapeutic strategy. Finally, there is the issue of gender difference in the context of ambition. Adrienne Applegarth (1997) has highlighted the impact of parental channelling of the girl's ambition in the direction of marriage and motherhood; this can lead to heightened conflict between femininity and work-related success in women.

Ambivalence: term originated in 1910 by the renowned Swiss psychiatrist Eugen Bleuler to denote the existence of contradictions in the realms of: (1) *volition:* the desire to do something and not do that very thing, (2) *intellect:* simultaneously believing in two contradictory ideas, and (3) *emotion:* feeling love and hate for the same person. Bleuler regarded 'ambivalence' as one of the four cardinal signs of schizophrenia (the other three being autism, looseness of associations, and affective disturbances) but acknowledged that, to a lesser extent, it could exist in normal people too. Sigmund Freud (1911e) borrowed Bleuler's concept to explain the simultaneous occurrence of positive and negative transference in individuals undergoing psychoanalysis. He was selective in incorporating Bleuler's ideas and used the term 'ambivalence' for emotional matters alone. His most significant clinical application of the concept is in his paper 'Mourning and melancholia' (1917e), where the occurrence of depression following object loss is explained by the ambivalence directed at the lost object being redirected at the self. Freud's phenomenological and dynamic use of the term 'ambivalence' was later extended to the developmental realm by Karl Abraham (1924a). According to Abraham, a growing child passes from pre-ambivalent (oral–sucking) stage through an ambivalent (oral–biting) stage to a post-ambivalent (genital) stage of development. These ideas found more powerful elaboration in the writings of Melanie Klein (1935, 1940). One thing, however, must always be kept in mind, and it is that ambivalence is not the same thing as having mixed feelings towards someone. Charles Rycroft (1968) has most clearly made this point. He says that ambivalence 'refers to an underlying emotional attitude in which the contradictory attitudes derive from a common source and are interdependent, whereas mixed feelings may be based upon a realistic assessment of the imperfect nature of the object' (p. 6).

Anaclitic depression: term coined by Rene Spitz (1946) for a syndrome that develops in infants who are separated from their mothers at a very early age. The symptoms begin with weeping and clinging, but soon move on to wailing and losing weight. This is followed by withdrawal, facial rigidity, and motor retardation. If the mother returns, or a devoted substitute is found before four or five months pass, the syndrome can be reversed. Spitz emphasized that anaclitic depression is a direct result of ruptured care and differs from adult depression, where the internalization of ambivalence towards an object forms the key dynamic.

Anaclitic object choice: Sigmund Freud (1914c) distinguished two types of object choices made by human beings: (1) narcissistic object choice, and (2) anaclitic object choice. In the former, the individual chooses someone who has some real or imagined similarity with him. In the latter, the individual chooses someone who satisfies dependent longings, and thus represents a parent of

childhood. The word 'anaclitic' is, after all, derived from the Greek *anaclisis*, meaning 'to lean upon'. Given this perspective, homosexuality was seen as narcissistic and heterosexuality as anaclitic. The idea was that, pursuing an anaclitic object choice, a man will find a woman who feeds him and a woman will find a man who protects her. The anaclitic object choice was seen to emanate from the self-preservatory instinct and its purpose was to provide psychic sustenance. The loss of such a relationship could precipitate a mournful reaction of considerable proportions (see 'Anaclitic depression').

Anaclitic regression: term introduced by Masud Khan (1960) for 'a gradual and controlled regression to what the patient described as "a state of being nothing" and the emergence from it' (p. 149). During this period, this particular patient gave up looking after himself and had to rely on friends' support for daily existence. He also showed a 'near-absolute' dependence on his analyst, who, too, had to help the patient with some real life activities. However, by being held in alert and vital holding attention, the patient gradually emerged from this state and resumed the analytic work in the usual fashion. See also the related entry on 'new beginning' and the recent thought provoking paper on the concept of 'therapeutic regression' by Laurence Spurling (2008).

Anagogic interpretation: term originated by Herbert Silberer (1914) for a mode of decoding symbolism in dreams and myths that brings out its universal, transcendent, and ethical dimension. Unlike the usual psychoanalytic tendency to decipher symbols along personal and sexual lines, *anagogic* (Greek for 'to bear upwards') interpretations elevate the concrete into the spiritual. For instance, from a traditional analytic stance, a dream of buying a big house might be related to a competitive wish, a desire to expand one's family, or a soothing defence against feelings of inferiority in other realms of life, and so on. From an 'anagogic' perspective, however, the same dream can be seen as expressing a desire to expand one's mind so that one can include concerns and problems faced by others; the dream will be viewed as a statement of blossoming civic-mindedness.

Anal character: Sigmund Freud's (1908b) paper 'Character and anal erotism' and Ernest Jones' (1918) paper 'Anal erotic character traits' contain elucidations of personality attributes derived from anal fixation that remain unsurpassed today. Typical of anally-fixated individuals was the triad of orderliness, parsimony, and obstinacy. 'Orderly covers the notion of bodily cleanliness, as well as conscientiousness in carrying out small duties and trustworthiness. Parsimony may appear in the exaggerated form of avarice; and obstinacy can go over into defiance' (Freud, 1908b, p. 169). While acknowledging the role of upbringing, especially the struggles around toilet-training, Freud emphasized that 'such people are born with a sexual constitution in which the erotogenicity of the anal zone is exceptionally strong' (p. 170). Today, 'anal' character traits are viewed as deriving from a mixture of constitution, fixation, defensive flight from conflicts over dependency, and regression from oedipal phase conflicts. The tight connection between anality and miserliness has also been relaxed to include oral determinants of impaired capacity for giving to others.

Anal eroticism: see 'Anal phase'.

Anal narcissism: Leonard Shengold's (1985) term for a regressive return to being dominated by the anal–sadistic organization (Abraham, 1924b) and the associated reduction of ego to body ego. As this happens 'relationships become self-centered and hollow; people are reduced to things; values to stuff' (p. 59). Charles Hanly's (1982) and Janine Chasseguet-Smirgel's (1984) formulations of regressive and sadistic narcissism are also along the same lines.

Anal phase: refers to the developmental period between ages 18 months and 36 months as viewed from the perspective of psychoanalytic instinct theory. Posited first by Sigmund Freud (1908b), this phase is marked by the shift of the child's instinctual interest from the mouth to the anus. Pleasure now is derived from the stimulation of the anal mucous membrane by the passage of faeces. Anus, anal sphincter, act of defecation, and faeces preoccupy the child. They offer the opportunity for gratifying libindal impulses (withholding faeces in the hope of greater stimulation of the anal mucous membrane) as well as aggressive impulses (forcefully expelling the faeces). At first, the object of such 'anal eroticism' and 'anal sadism' is faeces itself. However, with increasing socialization of impulses via toilet training, the retentive and expulsive anal pleasures come to involve parental objects, especially the mother. Anal auto-eroticism changes into anal object relations. Relinquishing faeces becomes a gift to the mother and a sign of affection (Freud, 1917b, p. 130) and withholding it a hostile act and a sign of rebellion. That the child frequently oscillates between these extremes in a state of 'anal ambivalence' was further elucidated by Karl Abraham (1921). Three other aspects of the anal phase warrant mention: (1) the faecal stick can become a psychic 'forerunner' (Freud, 1918b, pp. 4, 84) of the penis and this can conflate giving up of stools with castration; (2) an unconscious equation of stool–penis–baby can get established and contribute to fantasies of anal birth and to sexual desires for anal penetration; and (3) the difficulty in renouncing faeces, which after all, is a part of oneself, automatically leads to a tendency to somehow get it back; the impulse to 'coprophagia' and 'cutaneous reintrojection' via smearing are manifestations of this tendency. Needless to add, the vicissitudes of these complex sensations, fantasies, and conflicts have a far-reaching impact upon character formation (Freud, 1908b, 1909d; Jones, 1918; Abraham, 1921). Object relations, especially as they involve matters of control *vs.* compliance and retentiveness *vs.* giving, are especially affected by the outcome of anal phase conflicts. It is therefore surprising, if not disturbing, to note the inoptimal attention of contemporary analysis to the anal phase. This could be in part due to the overall shift of theory from a drive-based, body-orientated model to an object-relations model, and in part due to the tracing of struggles of ambivalence further back to the earliest mother–infant relations. Cultural abhorrence of anal matters perhaps also adds to the 'heuristic repression' of the anal phase. Prominent exceptions to this tendency are to be found in the writings of Bela Grunberger (1989), Janine Chasseguet-Smirgel (1984), and Leonard Shengold (1988).

Anal sadism: see 'Anal phase'.

Anal universe: Janine Chasseguet-Smirgel's (1984) euphemistic designation of the dominance and idealization of anality over genitality in the setting of a 'perverse character' (see separate entry). Such 'universe' comprises denial of differences between sexes and generations. Male and female, old and young, parents and children, are all viewed as alike and indistinct from each other. The distinction between a faecal stick penis and the fertile, life-giving penis of the father is minimized. 'Infantile sexuality' (see separate entry) is glorified and placed on an equal, if not higher, footing with adult, genital sexuality. All things pertaining to the anal phase are idealized, and a false emphasis upon beauty and aesthetics is then employed as a defence to hide the inner hollowness.

Analysability: while Sigmund Freud (1905) had declared that one who is likely to tolerate the rigours of psychoanalytic treatment and benefit from it should possess 'a reasonable degree of education and a fairly reliable character' (p. 263), the term 'analysability' did not appear in the literature until much later. The first mention of it is to be found in the bulletin of the 1948 American Psychoanalytic Association Meetings. It is not certain, but it seems that Robert Knight was the person who coined the term (Paul Mosher, personal communication, January 3, 2007). A period of great enthusiasm followed, whereby repeated attempts were made to distil the personality characteristics that might predict suitability for analytic treatment. Henry Bachrach and Louis Leaff (1978), in their review of sixteen clinical and eight quantitative-predictive studies of analysability, concluded that individuals most suitable for psychoanalysis are those who have 'good ego strength, effective reality testing and sublimatory channels, and are able to cope flexibly, communicate verbally, think in secondary process terms, and regress in the service of ego' (p. 885). Such persons are usually young, do not display serious narcissistic or superego pathology, and possess psychological mindedness. Bachrach and Leaff's (1978) conclusions were upheld by later studies (Erle, 1979; Erle & Goldberg, 1984; Rothstein, 1982; Zimmerman, 1982). However, the enthusiasm for finding the ideal personality make-up for analysis gradually waned. Many reasons account for this: (1) the restricted age range recommended by these studies came under serious question; (2) as psychoanalytic conceptualizations moved towards two-person psychology and intersubjectivity, the issue of a proper 'fit' between the patient and the analyst acquired a prognostic status comparable to analysability, and (3) finally, the tight and somewhat idealized portrayal of the analysable individual was a counterpart to a similarly tight and idealized view of psychoanalysis. With the greater assimilation of Kleinian and British independent traditions, and with the advent of self-psychology and attachment theory based models, the view of analytic treatment shifted and the notion of analysability lost its appeal. To be sure, not all people benefit from psychoanalysis (Varvin, 2003b); psychotic, antisocial, and seriously perverse and addicted individuals are certainly not suitable for analysis. One does look for ego-resilience, honesty, perseverance, and psychological mindedness in a potential candidate in analysis, and there has been some effort (Peebles-Kleiger, Horwitz, Kleiger, & Waugaman, 2006) to rejuvenate the concept of 'analysability'. However, it turns out to be less a matter of 'who is analysable?' and more of 'who is analysable *vis-à-vis* what conflicts, at what era

of their lives, by what sort of analyst, and under what circumstances'.

Analysand: refers to an individual undergoing psychoanalysis. With delicious wit, Charles Rycroft (1968) has said that 'the word owes what little currency it has to the fact to the fact that it makes it possible to avoid calling students patients' (p. 7).

Analysing instrument: term introduced by Otto Isakower (1963) for the joint construction of a functional entity by the analyst and the analysand that helps create, sustain, and advance the analytic process. Both parties contribute to its emergence and functioning. The analysand does so by abiding by the rule of free-association and the analyst by maintaining a free-floating attention—and, as Joseph Sandler and Ann-Marie Sandler (1998) would add years later, 'free-floating responsiveness'—towards the analysand's material. Both parties have to experience some regression for such mutuality to emerge and for unconscious material to surface, be verbalized, and deciphered. If the 'analysing instrument' is functioning properly, the analyst's interventions remain authentic, well-timed, and tactful, the analysand, in turn, responds with bringing forth more material that confirms and/or advances the emergent line of understanding. Isakower's ideas regarding 'analysing instrument' were given further precision by Leon Balter, Zvi Lothane, and James Spencer Jr (1980) and have been, more recently, meaningfully evoked by Theodore Jacobs (2007).

Analyst induced termination: this phrase can encompass three different situations in which ending of an analysis is undertaken at the analyst's behest. This might be due to the analyst's (1) serious illness, (2) relocation to another city, or (3) growing awareness that continuing the analysis would be a perverse capitulation to the analysand's unconscious coercive wish to stay forever in treatment. While the first two situations are important in their own right (see 'analyst's illness' and 'analyst's relocation'), and while the originator of the term 'forced termination', Paul Dewald (1966), had used it in the context of his relocation (see also Glick, 1987; Schwarz, 1980), it seems preferable to use 'analyst induced termination' or 'forced termination' only for the third contingency described above. Such usage keeps it in the realm of chosen technique rather than a technical accommodation of the exigencies of the analyst's life. This said, one can revisit the history of such a drastic technical intervention, which goes back to Sigmund Freud's (1918b) injunction to the

Wolf Man and to Sandor Ferenczi and Otto Rank's (1924) 'active technique' (see separate entry). The purpose of 'analyst induced termination' in these and other instances is to confront the patient with the reality that some instinctual aims shall never find gratification. The idea is to force the mourning of this 'loss' to begin. Doing this becomes necessary in analyses where clinical work has become subjugated to the patient's 'pathological hope' (Amati-Mehler & Argentieri, 1989), tenacious 'someday fantasies' (Akhtar, 1996), 'malignant erotic transference' (Akhtar, 1994), replacing life by analysis, and developing an 'insight addiction' (George Awad, personal communication, January 2001). Needless to add, the analyst's bringing up the issue of termination and forcing the end, as it were, are fraught with technical and ethical difficulties. Peer consultation, return to supervision, and even to some personal treatment, reading the existing literature, working through the countertransference, and, perhaps, a legal consultation, might all be needed to take this step in meaningful way.

Analyst's authority: in a concluding overview of the various contributions (by the likes of Christopher Bollas, Charles Brenner, Charles Hanly, Irwin Hoffman, Otto Kernberg, and Roy Schafer, to name a few) to the 1996 *Psychoanalytic Quarterly's* special issue on the 'analyst's authority', Lawrence Friedman (1996) distils the following important points (1) Sigmund Freud (1916–1917) held that the psychoanalyst has authority of a beloved parent; (2) such 'relationship authority' is distinct from authority derived from possession of knowledge (Brenner, 1996); (3) as analysis advanced, the analyst also came to be a 'moral authority'; his superego was taken as a model by the patient (Strachey, 1934) even though he avoided being directive about the patient's life decisions; (4) however, despite the analyst's getting off such a pedestal, the patient often hears his words as having moral authority; (5) analyst's authoritative manner can cause false compliance on the patient's part but, as Otto Kernberg (1996) points out in this special issue, it can also be reassuring to the patient that the analyst is indestructible; (6) analyst's authority can also be seen as a role which includes maternal, paternal, and oedipal modes of cognition (Bollas, 1996); these can be discerned in both male and female analysts (Hanly, 1996); (7) most contributors to this special volume located 'analyst's authority' in their procedure rather than in their knowledge; this is 'procedural authority'; (8) with the shift of analysis away from a deterministic outlook towards relationism and unpredictability, the place of 'knowledge authority' has diminished (see also Rubin, 1996). Charles Hanly (1996), however, emphasizes that the 'analyst's authority' is tightly linked with the search for objective truth. Friedman concludes by noting that 'modern analysts are realistically (and uncomfortably) aware that they transmit a host of subtle unintended, and ultimately unforeseeable messages, and they even acknowledge that some larger configuration of the treatment relationships always hovers just outside their vision' (p. 263). At the same time, it remains true that 'functional authority', of a sort, is unavoidable on the analyst's part; 'authorship of treatment implies authority about mental processes and illness' (*ibid.*, p. 264). There is also the ever present risk of authority turning into authoritarianism, which is, regrettably, not an infrequent occurence in the practice and profession of psychoanalysis (Levine, 2003; Ross, 1999).

Analyst's death: the personal reflections of Thomas Wolman (1990) upon the death of his training analyst six months after termination, the follow-up interviews with the analysands of recently deceased analysts, or reflections upon their self-reports by Abraham Freedman (1990) and Tove Traesdal (2005), and the report by Stephen Firestein (1990) on the experiences of thirteen patients whose analysts had died while their treatments were in progress, constitute almost all of the literature that exists on this topic. It appears that the analysts facing a fatal illness are vulnerable to denial, and patients are not infrequently given too little or too much information, leaving them traumatized. The fact is that 'once the patient has inferred that the analyst is seriously ill or if the news has been directly confirmed, the treatment has ended. Even if the analyst and the analysand continue to meet, the treatment of the patient has concluded. This is true because the roles are instantly reversed; the patient feels that he or she must in many ways serve as therapist for the analyst. The setting for the work has lost its usefulness for the patient' (Firestein, 1990, p. 334). The following guidelines, drawn from the work of the authors mentioned above, can mitigate the situation deteriorating further and becoming seriously traumatic for the patient: (1) the analyst must inform the patient of his illness; (2) he must deal with the patient's response in realistic as well as interpretive–reconstructive ways, but not use such an approach to delay ending their work; (3) the analyst must offer to help with referrals for the subsequent care of the patient; (4) the analyst must seek analytic consultation himself in order to work through his vulnerability to denial and to offset the vastly increased risk of countertransference based errors of clinical judgment; (5) the analyst must maintain a professional will, which assigns a family member or a colleague (with their informed consent) as the person who will inform his patients of his death (whose contact information should be listed clearly in this will) and which includes an ethical and legally appropriate way of handling the clinical records of his patients; and (6) finally, it should be remembered that the management of the patient's crisis after the analyst's death is of crucial importance and is markedly affected by how the seriously ill and dying analyst had handled himself *vis-à-vis* the patient. Firestein suggests that all analysts should develop an understanding with two trusted friends that they will intervene if the analyst '(1) shows signs of I in his work life; (2) experiences sudden total incapacitation or dies' (p. 338).

Analyst's fears: Warren Poland (cited in Mathias, 2008), has described four different ways in which fears arise within the analyst: (1) elicited by the patient, (2) originating within the analyst himself, (3) pertaining to the analytic process, and (4) from the realities of the human condition. Poland emphasized that the analyst cares, and is therefore vulnerable to fears of attachment and loss. Besides, he also has to tackle the fears of resistance and unfamiliar realms that open up in the course of his work both within the patient and himself. 'Fear is a feeling and, as with all feelings, the analyst must sort out its roots and then figure out how to turn his or her fear to the service of his work' (Mathias, 2008, p. 9).

Analyst's greed: extrapolating the ideas of Melanie Klein (1931, 1937) on the phenomenon of 'greed' (see separate entry), Amnon Issacharoff (1979) has commented upon the 'analyst's unconscious greed', or simply 'analyst's greed'. He notes that such greed is especially aroused by a patient who comes across as withholding. If the analyst suppresses his greed, it becomes difficult to maintain an empathic link with the patient. If, on the other hand, the analyst gives in to his greed, he becomes restless and intrusive. Moreover, 'the eager analyst pursues things wonderful, instead of things true, and his fervent desire colors them with ambivalent light' (p. 40). A reversal of the analyst's greed can give rise to excessive 'generosity' of attention and what Lawrence Epstein (1979) has called the 'compulsion to interpret'; unconscious impulses to attack and punish the patient can also contribute to such compulsion.

Analyst's illness: Paul Dewald (1982a), Sander Abend (1982), and Harvey Schwartz (1987) are among the few analysts who have addressed the impact of physical illness of the analyst upon the analytic process. Their papers, along with later contributions by other analysts, including Abraham Freedman, Susan Lazar, and Normund Wong, have been put together in a comprehensive volume on the topic edited by Harvey Schwartz and Ann-Louise Silver (1990). A somber chorus of sublimated anguish, the book describes how the 'analyst's illness' can pose a threat to his or her analysing capacity, get denied by both parties in the clinical dyad, stir up transference and countertransference chaos, create dilemmas around the issue of self-disclosure, and so on. The last mentioned point especially commands attention. There seems to be some disagreement between various analysts when it comes to divulging information about their illness; Abend takes a more cautious stance than Dewald, for instance. The argument for non-disclosure is that giving information burdens the patient and precludes an important avenue for the exploration of transference fantasies. The argument for disclosure is that having some reality information satisfies the patient's ordinary need for causality and diminishes the tax on his credulousness. Schwartz sides with Abend, and declares that 'the therapeutic power of one's painstakingly developed analytic neutrality is never more revealed to be an exquisite instrument for evocation of patient's deepest and most feared fantasies as when the frame is momentarily ruptured' (p. 691). To be sure, the matter of 'analyst's illness' is complex and goes beyond the arresting question of telling and not telling the patient about it, or, to put it in more 'liberal' terms, of telling how much and to whom and for what purposes. There are many other aspects to the situation, including the long-term consequences for transference and countertransference, alterations in the analyst' working capacity, impact on the analyst's views on life and death, the analyst's position *vis-à-vis* his peers and his analytic society, and so on. This list can be extended to include organizational policies regarding the physically ill and impaired analyst, ethical guidelines, and legal matters involving this realm.

Analyst's intuition: according to Ronald Britton and John Steiner (1994), the analyst, in a state of free-floating attention, suddenly becomes cognizant of one particular facet of the patient's material (e.g., a fact, a pun, a pause, a nuance of affect) which, in turn, gives rise to an interpretation. However, such intuition and the resulting creative use of this 'selected fact' (see separate entry) must be distinguished from the crystallization of an overvalued idea in the analyst's mind. Sigmund Freud's (1937c) stern reminder that an interpretation is nothing more than 'a conjecture which awaits examination, confirmation, or rejection' (p. 265) is important to note.

Analyst's irreducible subjectivity: going a step further than Evelyne Schwaber (1992), who emphasizes listening from the patient's perspective but acknowledges analysts' frequent failure to do so, Owen Renik (1993) declared that 'instead of saying that it is *difficult* for an analyst to *maintain* a position in which his or her analytic activity objectively focuses on a patient's inner reality, I would say that it is *impossible* for an analyst to be in that position *even for an instant*' (p. 559, original italics). Renik stressed that, while an analyst can acknowledge his 'irreducible subjectivity', he cannot eliminate it. Technical implications of this include (1) a more relaxed attitude regarding the inevitability of 'countertransference enactments' (see separate entry), (2) the acceptance of the idea that '*unconscious* personal motivations expressed in action by the analyst are not only unavoidable but *necessary to the analytic process*' (p. 563, original italics), and (3) the realization that the analyst's explicitly communicating his or her own construction of reality, especially when it differs from that of the patient, is central to analytic technique.

Analyst's masochism: Heinrich Racker's (1958) observation that analysts with prominent masochistic traits are vulnerable to putting their sadistic internal objects into the patient. The 'analyst's masochism' is aimed at making the analysis fail or, at least, be riddled with difficulties. According to Racker, such masochism may also represent 'an unconscious tendency to repeat or invert a certain infantile relationship with his parents in which he sacrifices himself or them. The analyst may seek to suffer now, through his analytic "children", what he had made his own parents suffer, either in fantasy or reality' (p. 559).

Analyst's office: literature on this topic is meagre. This is surprising, since most analysts recognize that their patients are fascinated by things in their offices. Indeed, analysands might develop transferences both because of and to various artefacts, especially the analytic couch. This concern leads some analysts to have rather spartan décor; however, this too can evoke transferences. Pertinent in this context is Stephen Kurtz's (1989) observation that Sigmund Freud had filled up every conceivable space in his office with things of beauty and

value to compensate for the loneliness he felt in sitting behind the patient. The profusion of books, paintings, and sculptures in analysts' offices seems attributable to the following four factors: (1) most analysts are cultured individuals, knowledgeable in humanities and aesthetically inclined; the cultural artefacts represent their authentic existence; (2) their identification with Freud and his office; (3) spending long hours with conflict and pain necessitates (both as healthy adaptation and manic defence) surrounding oneself with *objects d'art*; and (4) analyst's unconscious reliance upon the evocative and containing power of physical objects. In this way, things in the office come to acquire totemic (Freud, 1912–1913), and shamanic (Kakar, 1991) attributes. The technical handling of changes in the office is also an issue. Some patients, especially those lacking object constancy, find such alterations quite destabilizing. While interpretive handling is ideal, in some instances it is not altogether a bad idea to inform the patient of an anticipated change in the office décor (Akhtar, 2009c).

Analyst's persona: term introduced by Susan Levine (2007) to denote 'the self we step out of at the close of each session and the self we step into as the patient enters the room' (p. 81). In other words, the 'analyst's persona' is that face of the analyst's self which is available to be perceived by the patient. While largely predictable and constant, this persona does show subtle variation of tone and content with each individual patient. Self-disclosures and self-revelations that occur within the range of the 'analyst's persona' or outside of it feel different to both parties in the clinical dyad. All in all, Levine's concept underscores the tension between authenticity and restraint in the clinical setting on the analyst's part.

Analyst's pregnancy: like any other special event affecting the analyst (e.g., illness, bereavement), her becoming pregnant has an impact upon the clinical work. It intensifies transference, challenges technical neutrality, stirs up sibling and oedipal rivalries, and mobilizes primal scene memories (Etchegoyen, 1993; Fenster, Phillips, & Rapoport, 1986; Mariotti, 1993; Penn, 1986). This, however, does not have to disrupt the analytic process; indeed, analysis may at times deepen as a result of such external stimulus.

Analyst's relocation: many technical challenges are posed by the 'analyst's relocation' to another city, state, or country. Such dilemmas have been a part of the profession's history (given that many analytic pioneers had to leave their lands of origin in the wake of Hitler's onslaught). However, they did not write about their dislocation due to a multitude of reasons (Akhtar, 1999b); the pain was rather too great. The literature on 'analyst's relocation' is therefore sparse and relatively new. The first paper on the topic is by Paul Dewald (1966); this was followed by other contributions (Weiss, 1972; Aarons, 1975; Martinez, 1989). From these papers, five variables emerge as being important in working through this affectively charged transition: (1) the extent of information regarding relocation that needs to be shared; (2) the necessity, desire, risks, and inevitability of some personal disclosure beyond the strict issue of relocation; (3) the time period allowed for this reality based interruption of analytic work ;(4) the continuing analysis of transference while making arrangements and referrals for the patient's ongoing care ; and (5) the manifold increase in vulnerability to countertransference errors. To this list, Monisha Nayar , in a paper presented at the 2008 Fall Meeting of the American Psychoanalytic Association, added three more variables: (1) the consideration of 'post-termination contacts' (see separate entry), or, to use her more accurate expression, 'post-interruption contacts'; (2) the impact upon the analyst's professional identity, especially in light of the fact that his relocation also involves the loss the 'holding ' function provided by his local analytic community; and (3) the differential impact of the 'analyst's relocation' on child and adult patients. The issue of the 'analyst's relocation', therefore, appears far from simple, and a psychoanalyst contemplating a geographical move would benefit from collegial input and by familiarizing himself or herself with the literature cited above.

Analyst's reverie: drawing his ideas from Wilfred Bion's (1962a,b) concepts of 'container' (see separate entry) functions of the mother, including 'maternal reverie' (see separate entry), Thomas Ogden (1994) describes 'analyst's reverie' as a relaxed, subdued, and floating mentation that captures the analysand's unspoken and unspeakable thoughts via highly personal and even idiosyncratic bits of analyst's mental activity. This is far from a sign of inattentiveness or resistance on the analyst's part. Instead, it 'represents symbolic and protosymbolic (sensation-based) forms given to unarticulated (and often not yet felt) experience of the analysand as they are taken place in the intersubjectivity of the analytic pair (i.e. in the analytic third)' (p. 83).

Analyst's wish to regress: Stanley Coen's (2000, 2002) phrase to denote the temptation felt by the analyst to join his patient in a state of mutual regression. Such regression obliterates the capacity to examine one's countertransference affects and pushes one towards a less differentiated relatedness to the patient. Essentially, it constitutes 'an abdication of the analyzing function in favor of a more infantile relatedness with the patient and with the therapist's internal objects' (2002, p. 139). Coen distinguishes such regression from the analyst's fluid reverie, which retains the capacity to examine one's countertransference pulls for the sake of the patient's treatment.

Analyst's work ego: first described by Robert Fliess (1942), this concept refers to the functions of the analyst that are integral to his conducting analysis. These comprise receiving the patient's strivings, making a 'trial identification' (i.e., transiently putting himself in the patient's shoes), and, through both these manoeuvres, grasping the patient's psychic reality. The analyst maintains a 'free-floating attention' (see separate entry) and enters into a 'conditioned day-dreaming' (i.e., reverie stimulated by the patient's associations) on behalf of the patient. To accomplish all this, the analyst has to acquire a 'work ego' (p. 221) with special perceptual capacities and unique relationships with the id and superego. By tolerating instinctual deprivation during the clinical hour, such ego induces the superego to lend its powers for the ego's free use. 'The superego's judicial function becomes thereby what might be called the analyst's "therapeutic conscience"' (p. 222) and its 'function of critical self-observation is utilized for the recognition of instinctual material which has transiently been acquired by identification with the patient' (p. 226). These ideas of Fliess were elaborated upon by Stanley Olinick (Olinick, 1976; Olinick, Poland, Grigg, & Granatir, 1973) who underscored that the 'analyst's work ego' (1) is relatively autonomous from drives and conflicts, (2) is capable of self-observation, (3) draws upon the full range of his emotional and intellectual capacities, (4) is open to regressive processes within its own self in order to learn about the inner world of the patient, and (5) is motivated by altruism. Victor Calef and Edward Weinshel's (1980) paper titled 'The analyst as the conscience of analysis' also touches upon these areas, and the interested reader would benefit by looking it up.

Analytic candidate: an individual who is undergoing training to become a practising psychoanalyst. Most such individuals have a background in medicine, clinical psychology, and social work, though occasionally those individuals with degrees in humanities, nursing, education, and divinity also seek analytic training. In order to be qualified as an analyst, the individual has to undergo a personal analysis, attend didactic seminars in analytic theory and technique, and analyse three or four patients under the close supervision of senior analysts.

Analytic couch: see 'Couch'

Analytic education: see 'Analytic training'.

Analytic introject: term introduced into psychoanalytic literature by Peter Giovacchini (1972) to denote the internalization of an analyst (more accurately, his or her analytic attitude) by the analysand. The formation of such an internal structure is not deliberately engineered, either by the analyst or the analysand; it is not a matter of mimicry or behavioural emulation. Instead, it refers to the painstaking and gradual evolution of impulse control, self-reflection, enhanced curiosity and concern about oneself, and a capacity to derive ego pleasure from truthful knowledge and mastery of one's inner world. The analyst's unwavering dedication to analytic attitude and refraining from offering his or her own self as a model of real-life identification is precisely what helps the formation of an analytic introject. The optimal functioning of such a new structural element in the analysand's psyche deepens 'therapeutic alliance' (see separate entry) and is most clearly evident as the termination phase come closer.

Analytic listening: any consideration of 'analytic listening' must begin with the injunctions made by Sigmund Freud that the analyst should maintain an attitude of 'not directing one's notice to anything in particular' (1912–1913, p. 111) and 'adjust himself to the patient as a telephone receiver is adjusted to the transmitting microphone' (*ibid.*, p. 116). Together these statements advocate the attitude of 'evenly suspended attention' (see separate entry) in listening to the patient's material. Of note in the second statement is that Freud says one ought to adjust oneself to the 'patient' rather than to the patient's utterances. Such relaxed and lambent cognition helps the analyst capture important links between disparate elements of the patient's material as well as seemingly unintended upwards cues from the latter's unconscious. While these ideas of Freud remain the cornerstone of 'analytic listening', contemporary psychoanalysts have added significant insights to this realm. These include (1) Charles Brenner's (2000) proposal that a selective and shifting focus of attention is more useful than 'evenly suspended attention' in listening to analy-

tic material; (2) Evelyne Schwaber's (1983, 1995, 1996, 2005, 2007) emphasis upon listening from the patient's perspective and its contrast with Jacob Arlow's (1995) attunement to discerning unconscious fantasies; (3) the distinction in types of listening, dictated by what Carlo Strenger (1989) has termed 'classic' and 'romantic' visions of psychoanalysis. The former prompts listening geared to deciphering ways in which the patient's wishes and fantasies colour his perception of past and present realities while the latter mobilizes listening geared to healthy strivings for wholeness and authenticity; (4) Bjorn Killingmo's (1989) reminder of the necessity for the analyst to oscillate between sceptical listening and credulous listening in accordance with shifts in the patient's level of psychostructural organization; (5) George Makari and Theodore Shapiro's (1993) reminder that 'analytic listening' attends to non-linguistic communications and to the linguistic categories pertaining to narrativity, symbolic reference, form, and interactive conventions; (6) Henry Smith's (2000) emphasis that analytic listening is an 'ongoing conflictual process, containing all the components of conflict and shaped in every moment by both the patient's and the analyst's conflicts' (p. 95); (7) the role of the analyst's reverie and meandering subjectivity (Benjamin, 1995, 2004; Jacobs, 2007; Ogden, 1994) in listening to the patient, either because the material is co-created or because the patient's disowned affects and unthinkable thoughts have been deposited in the analyst by 'projective identification' (see separate entry); (8) the trend of 'close process attention' (see separate entry) which advocates focus on the minutest shifts in the flow of the patient's free associations; and (9) Salman Akhtar's (2007d) observations on the potential instinctualization of analytic listening and the technical strategies consequent upon such occurence.

Analytic management: Donald Winnicott's (1963) term for the psychoanalytically orientated care of rather severely ill (e.g., psychotic, antisocial) patients, especially those who were hospitalized. He believed that such patients could not use interpretations meaningfully, and mostly needed 'holding' and 'ego coverage', protecting them from 'psychotic anxiety' (see separate entry). Winnicott also used the concept of management in the relation to the treatment of children and adolescents, and even of adults undergoing psychoanalysis. There, he felt, the degree of 'management' (i.e., adaptation of the analytic environment to suit the needs of a particular patient) required depended upon the extent of regression.

Analytic posturology: Felix Deutsch's (1952) designation for the psychoanalytic study of bodily postures and their oddities. Derived from Wilhem Reich's (1933) regard for the physical dimension of character armour (e.g., stiffness of the paranoid, lyrical grace of the hysteric, statuesque aloofness of the phallic-narcissist), such speculations gradually lost their novelty. Some contemporary authors did continue to speak of the peculiar 'temperature and boundary sensitivity' (Bach, 1985, p. 21) of some individuals, and that 'furtive pain around the mouth' (Wheelis, 1966, p. 148) discernible in the prosperous crowd at a wine tasting or a private art exhibit. The most prominent contributor to contemporary analytic posturology has been James McLaughlin (1987, 1992), who has written extensively on the significance of non-verbal behaviours (e.g., hand movements, crossing legs) of the patients on the couch.

Analytic screen: Lilla Veszy-Wagner's (1961) term for a phenomenon in the subjectivity of the analyst, which consists of the analyst as observer, the patient as a whole self, and all those objects of the patient's love and hate that contribute to the patient's problems. The 'analytic screen' differs from countertransference, since it is not a reponse to a specific person, but to a constellation existing within the analytic situation. The structure of the 'analytic screen' is triangular and accessible through direct and indirect observation. Such a screen, at its base, emanates from the analyst's own primal scene fantasy. 'All elements of later sublimated primal screen are to found in the analytic screen, and nowhere else could curiosity and restitution blend into one harmonious attitude as they can in a psychoanalytical observer' (*ibid.*, p. 41).

Analytic supervision: this constitutes one of the three components of training to become a psychoanalyst; the other two are personal psychoanalysis and a didactic curriculum of analytic concepts. Analytic supervision consists of the trainee having to meet, on a regular basis, with a senior analyst in order to present the patient he is treating and to learn the nuances of clinical technique. The frequency of these meetings is usually once a week, though a lesser frequency is at times acceptable for more advanced trainees. Typically, the trainee presents clinical material, either verbatim or via recollection, that includes both the patient's associations and his or her interventions. The supervisor carefully listens, raises questions, explores the thinking behind the candidate's interventions, suggests additional ways of listening and speaking, points out pertinent literature for reading, and judiciously helps unmask countertransference difficulties. The supervisor is not the analyst of the supervisee's character, only of the supervisee's analytic ego as it is engaged in the clinical situation under scrutiny (Haesler, 1993). When things go well, and if both parties in the supervisory dyad are so inclined, the supervisor can also become a professional mentor of the supervisee. However, this is not the main aim of supervision. Help with professional and academic matters can, at times, be defensively used against anxiety and ineptitude of conducting supervision. This is contrary to the aim of the process, which is primarily intended for imparting knowledge and the skills of clinical analytic work.

Analytic surface: the term was implicitly introduced by Sigmund Freud (1905e) when he declared that 'I start out from whatever surface (the patient's) unconscious happens to be presenting to his notice at the moment' (p. 12). This indicated that some elements in the patient's material constituted the starting point of the interpretive process; the dictum of interpreting from surface to depth (Fenichel, 1941; Loewenstein, 1951) arose from this notion. However, the concept of analytic 'surface' itself remains ill-defined. Cecilio Paniagua (1985) attempted to fill this lacuna by noting that 'surface' is constituted by readily observable phenomena, such as pauses, shifts of affect, striking omissions, etc. A comprehensive elucidation of the concept was provided by Steven Levy and Lawrence Inderbitzin (1990), who noted that 'disturbances, discontinuity, and disequibria' (p. 374) in the analytic relationship constitute components of the 'analytic surface' just as much as aspects of the patient's verbal and non-verbal behaviour. Levy and Inderbitzin note that four authors stand out as having elucidated the 'surface' concept in ways that have great technical significance: (1) *Merton Gill* (1979, 1982) who argues forcefully for the analysis of transference in the here-and-now; 'the analytic surface for Gill consists of instances in which some aspect of the material emerging in the analytic situation can be identified as a transference distortion or displacement connected with some (often minor) detail or event actually occurring during the session' (Levy & Inderbitzin, 1990, pp. 378–379); (2) *Paul Gray* (1973, 1982, 1986), for whom the surface consists of the way identifiable defensive ways alter the course of patient's associations; the focus is on the analysand's thinking processes and the aim is to unmask intrapsychic conflict; (3) *Anton Kris* (1982) for whom 'analytic surface' is tightly connected with continuities and discontinuities in the patient's free association and whose goal is to expand the analysand's freedom in this regard; and (4) *Evelyne Schwaber* (1983, 1986), who emphasizes listening from the patient's perspective and for whom the 'surface' consists of attunement to divergences between the patient's and the analyst's perspective. Levy and Inderbitzin note that it is likely that 'different analysts and analysands have varying proclivities for recognizing different surfaces' (p. 387). None the less, the concept of 'analytic surface' remains important for technical and didactic purposes. The interested reader would benefit by looking up the report of a panel discussion on the topic (Seelig, 1993), in which Dale Boesky, Marianne Goldberger, Warren Poland, and Henry Smith participated. Also worth noting is the observation by Donald Spence, Linda Mayes, and Hartvig Dahl (1994) that clustering of shared pronouns (e.g., you/me) constitutes an aspect of 'analytic surface' to which the analyst frequently responds by making an intervention.

Analytic tact: see 'Tact'.

Analytic third: coined by Thomas Ogden (1994), this term refers to the intersubjective experience which is a product of a unique dialectic generated between the individual subjectivities of the analyst and analysand within the clinical setting. 'The analytic third is a creation of the analyst and analysand, and at the same time the analyst and analysand (qua analyst and analysand) are created by the analytic third' (p. 93).

Analytic training: it is in accordance with Max Eitingon's (1925) proposal that a 'tripartite model', consisting of personal analysis, didactic courses, and supervised clinical work, was universally adapted as the standard format for training to become a psychoanalyst. Eitingon, a loyal lieutenant of Sigmund Freud, himself helped set up such training centres in Berlin, Moscow, Paris, Calcutta, and Jerusalem. While his model became the norm, 'reforms' to it have been suggested from the early days of psychoanalysis (e.g., Balint, 1948) up to today (e.g., Wallerstein, 1993; Kernberg, 2000, 2006, 2007; Tuckett, 2005). Essentially, these 'reforms' are aimed at (1) diminishing conceptual and technical orthodoxy, (2) reducing or eliminating rigid administrative hierarchies, (3) diminishing conflict of interest among various participants in the educational process, (4) making the didactic curriculum broader, culturally sensitive, and internationally representative, and (5) creating an open-minded atmosphere that relies on an exchange of ideas rather than authoritarianisms and indoctrination.

Annihilation anxiety: it is readily conceivable, if not conceptually necessary, to add the fear of annihilation to the fears (e.g., fear of loss of love object, fear of loss of object's love, fear of castration) included under the rubric of classical 'danger situations' (see separate entry). Indeed, this was implicit in Sigmund Freud's comparison of the experience of anxiety with the effects of 'mortal danger' (1916–1917, p. 396) and explicit in his declaration that what the ego fears most from the external and internal overstimulation is 'being overwhelmed or annihilated' (1923b, p. 57). Other metaphorical ways to capture this dread include referring to fears of falling apart, or going crazy, or of being fragmented, imploded, and psychically destroyed. Such expressions are found in the works of analysts who elaborated on this aspect of Freud's views on anxiety. Prominent among these are Melanie Klein (1932, 1948a), and Donald Winnicott (1962), who spoke of 'psychotic anxieties' and 'unthinkable anxieties', respectively (see separate entries). In a comprehensive, if somewhat overinclusive, review of literature, Marvin Hurvich (2003; see also Hurvich, 1989) underscores the following points: (1) 'annihilation anxiety' originates in early infancy; (2) it can, however, be reactivated by later phase-specific anxieties; (3) a combination of excessive constitutional aggression and servere traumatic experiences leads to ego weakness which, in turn, increases the vulnerability to 'annihilation anxiety'; (4) such anxiety may exist in pre-verbal forms or may acquire retrospective fantasy content from later development phases; (5) it is generally associated with propensity towards psychosis but might also underlie non-psychotic conditions especially those of addictive, psychosomatic, and perverse varieties; and (6) 'annihilation anxiety' mobilizes defences that are particularly recalcitrant. Despite its considerable heuristic and clinical significance, the concept of 'annihilation anxiety' did not gain as wide acceptance in North America as it did in Europe and Latin America. This seems partly related to psychoanalytic politics, since the early North American analysts were devotees of the Anna Freud–Heinz Hartmann axis and eschewed ideas they regarded to be 'too Kleinian'. Going a step further, Robert Langs (1981) stated the following: 'Another constellation of motivations which, in general has eluded classical analysts . . . is comprised of the distinctly primitive anxieties, including the dread of annihilation . . . It seems likely that classical psychoanalytic theory and technique has been designed to some extent as a defense against such primitive anxieties' (p. 545).

Anniversary reactions: a term originally coined by Josphine Hilgard (1953) for the outbreak of psychological symptoms in a parent when his or her child reaches the age at which the parent had experienced a childhood trauma. In a later paper (Hilgard & Newman, 1959), this definition was extended to include symptomatology appearing in an adult patient at an age which coincides with the age of the parent who died during the patient's childhood. Fascinatingly, for women, loss of father did not tend to cause symptoms on the anniversary reflecting father's death, but when they reached the age that corresponded to how old the mother was at the time of father's death. 'Anniversary reactions' may not be always related to precise dates, but to times of the year, festivals, seasons, holidays, and other periodicities. George Pollack (1970, 1971) has comprehensively reviewed the literature on this topic and added many illustrations from the artistic and literary world. George Engel (1975), in a poignant paper, has described his own anniversary reactions following the death of his twin brother, Frank Engel; the two were Chairmen of Psychiatry and Pathology departments of a medical school, respectively, and gave one lecture annually to each other's class, pretending to be the other twin!

Anonymity: in his paper titled 'Recommendations to physicians practising psycho-analysis', Sigmund Freud (1912e) instructed that 'the doctor should be opaque to his patients and, like a mirror, should show them nothing but what is shown to him' (p. 118). He suggested that the analyst not reveal personal facts of his or her life to the patient, since doing so interferes with the proper development (and, hence, resolution) of transference. Thus, along with 'abstinence' and 'neutrality', 'anonymity' became a central element of the analytic posture. Contemporary views (Gill, 1994; Hoffman, 1983) hold that while a 'mirror', or as it came to be known, 'blank screen', model is neither desirable nor possible (after all, patients know their analyst's name, office address, and often religious affiliation, while also noticing his aesthetic preferences via his office décor), the analyst ought to avoid confirming or denying the patient's speculations about him or her in order to remain a viable object for projection of transference fantasies.

Anomie: a term coined by the renowned French sociologist Emile Durkheim (1858–1917) to describe the personal unrest and alienation that result from a major alteration or breakdown of social values and standards. While this is not a psychoanalytic concept *per se*, it is of use when one considers the psychological situation of individuals living under great social turmoil.

Anorexia nervosa: see 'Eating disorders'.

Antilibidinal ego: see 'Fairbairn's description of endopsychic structure'.

Antisocial behaviour: not restricted to 'antisocial personality disorder' (see separate entry), behaviour that goes against the societal norms and tends towards criminality is seen in association with a number of psychiatric conditions and psychostructural organizations. Otto Kernberg (1989) has listed a hierarchical differential diagnosis of 'antisocial behaviour' that, from the most severe to the least severe, includes the following *seven categories*: (1) antisocial behaviour disorder, (2) the syndrome of malignant narcissism, (3) narcissistic personality disorder with antisocial behaviour, (4) other severe personality disorders (e.g., paranoid, infantile) with antisocial features, (5) neurotic conditions with antisocial features, (6) antisocial behaviour as part of a symptomatic neurosis, and (7) dyssocial reaction which was a normal or neurotic adjustment to a highly abnormal social environment.

Antisocial personality disorder: while Sigmund Freud did not use the term 'antisocial personality disorder', he made the observation that 'the man who, in consequence of his unyielding constitution, cannot fall in with the suppression of instinct, becomes a "criminal", an "outlaw" in the face of society' (1908b, p. 187). He thus hinted at (1) a constitutional factor in the etiology, (2) weakness of repression, and (3) non-renunciation of omnipotence, as important aspects of the disorder. In 1914c, he stated that criminals fascinate us because they maintain 'an unassailable libidinal position we ourselves have since abandoned' (p. 89). However, it was left to August Aichhorn (1925) to offer the first detailed psychoanalytic explanation of the antisocial character. In his view, a failure to move from the pleasure principle to the reality principle and a malformation of superego lurks in the background of such pathology. Both extreme indulgence and excessive severity towards the child impede the renunciation of pleasure principle. Otto Fenichel (1945) emphasized the instability and lovelessness of such individuals' childhoods, noting that, under such circumstances, capacity for reciprocal object relations suffered and Oedipus complex and its solutions were disorganized, weak, and inconsistent. Most prominent among the latter contributors to the psychoanalytic understanding of antisocial personality are Kurt Eissler (1949, 1950), who offered a detailed clinical picture of the syndrome, Adelaide Johnson and Martin Szurek (1952), who described the concept of 'superego lacunae' (see separate entry) and Otto Kernberg (1984), who provided a through differential diagnosis of 'antisocial behaviour' (see separate entry). In Eissler's view, antisocial personality consists of a predominately narcissistic orientation in which even the seemingly 'islands of true devotion' (1949, p. 12) hide selfish motives. There is an addiction to novelty, commitment to a paranoid world view, and spells of infantile helplessness alternating with self-inflating omnipotence. Salman Akhtar (1992b), in a comprehensive review of psychoanalytic literature on the topic, concluded that 'antisocial personality disorder' consists of overt and covert manifestations in six areas of psychosocial functioning: (1) self-concept, (2) interpersonal relations, (3) social adaptation, (4) love and sexuality, (5) ethics, standards, and ideals, and (6) cognitive style. The individual with antisocial personality disorder is overtly grandiose, charming, affable, earnest, seductive, strikingly unburdened by social mores, and impressively knowledgeable and articulate. However, covertly he is inferiority-laden and confused about himself, scornful of others, incapable of love and loyalty, profoundly lacking in the capacity for remorse and guilt, unable to sustain any vocational interest, and possessing only exhibitionistic titbits of knowledge. Active or passive criminal tendencies often accompany the condition, but, since criminality is not a psychological concept, these should not form the basis for the diagnosis.

Antisocial tendency: Donald Winnicott's (1956a) term for those attitudes and actions of an individual that compel the environment to be important. It is as if, by behaving in a certain manner, the individual is forcing the environment to attend to him. The 'antisocial tendency' invariably comprises stealing and destructiveness. Stealing is not meant to obtain a specific thing but to find a person over whom one can have unlimited rights. Similarly, destructiveness is aimed at hurting someone with an underlying hope of being accepted by that person. This 'nuisance value' (p. 311) is an essential aspect of the antisocial tendency whose manifestations include imperiousness, greediness, messiness, stealing, lying, outrageousness, and destructiveness. Winnicott traced the origin of the antisocial tendency to a traumatic experience of deprivation in childhood. There has been 'a loss of something good that has been positive in the child's experience up to a

certain date, and that had been withdrawn; the withdrawal has extended over a period of time longer than that over which the child can keep the memory of the experience alive' (p. 309). It is this rupture of homeostasis that the individual is seeking to repair. Winnicott explicitly stated that the treatment of the antisocial tendency is not psychoanalysis but 'management, tolerance, and understanding . . . a going to meet and match the moment of hope' (p. 309). The therapist must offer a new opportunity for ego relatedness, since it was an environmental failure in ego support that originally led to the antisocial tendency.

Anxiety: refers to an unpleasant and dysphoric sense that something bad and potentially disastrous is about to happen. Anticipation of danger mobilizes defensive operations and binds the tension. What could not be 'bound' by such ego manoeuvres is left over as the consciously experienced 'anxiety'. This is accompanied by myriad physiological manifestations including palpitation, sweating, difficulty in breathing, frequency of urination, etc. While these symptoms can also accompany fear, 'anxiety' and fear differ in their nature and origins. 'Anxiety' is a response to an internal and unconscious danger, and fear is a reaction to a readily regognizable threat from external reality. Within psychoanalysis, 'anxiety' plays a crucial role, since symptoms of psychopathology are viewed as attempts to avoid this experience. As far as the causation of anxiety is concerned, Sigmund Freud had two theories. His first theory (Freud, 1895d) held that anxiety is caused by libido that is not adequately discharged; the concept of 'actual neurosis' (see separate entry) was a corollary to this perspective. His second theory (Freud, 1926d) viewed anxiety as a response to a threat to the individual; this threat emanated from a sense that he or she was about to face a re-creation of the 'danger situations' (see separate entry) typical of childhood. Freud also distinguished between 'automatic anxiety' and 'signal anxiety' (see separate entries); the former resulted from being overwhelmed by danger and the latter by anticipating danger.

Anxiety hysteria: Wilhelm Stekel's (1908) term for what would today be called phobic neurosis or, simply, phobia. In 'anxiety hysteria', the libido, which is separated from the original pathogenic idea by repression, is not converted into a somatic symptom, but set free in the shape of anxiety (Freud, 1909). This anxiety is subsequently bound to a specific object, creating a morbid fear of it.

Anxiety neurosis: originally described by Sigmund Freud (1895d), this syndrome comprises general irritability, chronic feeling of dread and its physiological concomitants, such as dizziness, insomnia, excessive sweating, and palpitations. A sub-variety of 'actual neurosis' (see separate entry), this syndrome resulted from the accumulation of sexual tension (e.g., due to sexual abstinence or frequent coitus interruptus) and insufficient psychological working-over of somatic excitation. This view of 'anxiety neurosis' is now outdated; free-floating anxiety is now deemed secondary to the threatened break-through of dangerous or immoral impulses. The fear of break-through is either because of the (constant or reactive) strength of the repressed impulses, or due to ego weakness.

Aphanisis: term introduced by Ernest Jones (1927) to denote a fear that sexual desire might disappear. Deriving from the Greek word, *aphanes* (meaning invisible), Jones' term was intended to emphasize that loss of sexual desire constituted a much greater and developmentally earlier dread than the loss of a specific sexual object necessitated by castration anxiety of the oedipal phase. The fear of 'aphanisis' was associated with the fear of separation from love objects, and caused severe anxiety.

Apparent therapeutic disability: phrase coined by Stanley Coen (2002) for some patients' stance that they simply cannot tolerate and process conflict and, as a result, avoid responsibility for what is wrong inside them. They are given to endless repetitions of essentially the same traumatizing scenarios. In such patients, there seems to be a 'covert angry wish to transform the therapeutic relationship into a version of an unsatisfactory mother–child relationship' (p. 36). The analyst treating them begins to feel hopeless and defeated, in an unconscious collusion with what these patients are trying to create. Coen suggests that, instead of sorting out whether such a proclivity is defect-based and 'unanalysable,' or defensive and analysable into component wishes and fears, a more 'fluid, dynamic, and shifting perspective of therapeutic engagement' (p. 37) should be taken, whereby empathically attuned holding, waiting, and affirming oscillates with confrontation, interpretation, and reconstruction.

Applied analysis: see 'Applied psychoanalysis'.

Applied psychoanalysis: refers to the employment of basic psychoanalytic principles (e.g., psy-chic determinism, overdetermination, dynamic unconscious, transference) in order to explicate and understand cultural phenomena at large. Set in motion by Sigmund Freud himself, who made astute observations on biography (1911c), fiction (1907a), and sculpture (1914b), the field of 'applied psychoanalysis' has grown in leaps and bounds since the early days of psychoanalysis. There are journals specifically devoted to this aspect of psychoanalysis (e.g., *Imago, Psychoanalysis and Contemporary Thought, International Journal of Applied Psychoanalytic Studies*) and national and international associations of professionals interested in the discipline. The encounter between psychoanalysis and social anthropology, history, and politics is in part necessitated by the profound changes occurring in the Western culture at large. Prominent among these are information explosion, narcissism of the 'me-generation', the impact of visual media, and a fearful clinging to conventionality (Eizirik, 1997). The fact that massive immigrations across continents has resulted in a changed demography of nations in general and of psychoanalytic patients and practitioners has also pushed the balance in the direction of a renewed 'culturalization' of psychoanalysis. The diverse realms addressed by it include art (Gedo, 1983; Kris, 1952; Nagera, 1967; Rose, 1996; Spitz, 1985), cinema (Gabbard, 1999; Gabbard & Gabbard, 1999; Sabbadini, 2007); literature (Hamilton, 1969, 1976; 1979; Fitzpatrick-Hanly, 1986, 1993, 2003, 2005; Levine, 1995), music (Nagel, 2008; Nagel & Nagel, 2005), opera (Tarnopolsky, 2000), Hindu mythology and philosophy (Doniger, 1976; 1981; Courtright, 1985; Rao, 2005; Reddy, 2005: Vallabhaneni, 2005), Islam (Akhtar, 2008), migration (Grinberg & Grinberg, 1989; Akhtar, 1999b), school bullying (Sacco & Twemlow, 1997; Twemlow, 2000), ethnic conflict (Volkan, 1997, 2004, 2006), prejudice (Parens, Twemlow, Mahfouz, & Scharff, 2007), terrorism (Akhtar, 1997; Varvin & Volkan, 2005), law (Lifson & Simon, 1998), monetary investments and business (Lifson & Geist, 1999; Tuckett & Taffler, 2008), and, quite recently, architecture (Hendrix, 2006; Winer, 2005; Winer, Anderson, & Danze, 2005). However, it is psychoanalytically informed biographies that draw most attention from the lay public; prominent among these are the biographies of Gandhi (Erikson, 1969), Lawrence of Arabia (Mack, 1976), Joseph Conrad (Meyer, 1970), Kemal Atatürk (Volkan & Itzkowitz, 1984), Houdini (Meyer, 1976), Nixon (Volkan, Itzkowitz, & Dodd, 1999), George Bush (Frank, 2004), and Osama bin Laden (Olsson, 2007). While the field of 'applied psychoanalysis' can shed meaningful light on sociocultural phenomena and, at times, yield useful insights for the clinical enterprise of psychoanalysis, it also carries some inherent risks and pitfalls. These include (1) the tendency towards psychoanalytic colonialism, whereby principles and nuances of the field under study (e.g., music, art) are usurped lock, stock, and barrel in favour of those derived from psychoanalysis; (2) the potential for 'wild analysis' (see separate entry), whereby the lack of a live respondent to one's ideas permits heavy-handed speculation and conjecture without corrective input from the protagonist under study; and (3) the vulnerabilty to cross-cultural biases and blindspots, whereby 'in-culture' perspectives are ignored and omitted from the field of study and even devalued. While more recent efforts in 'applied psychoanalysis' are taking these hazards into account, more soul-searching, greater efforts at operationalizing methodolgy, and further cross-disciplinary dialogue is certainly needed here. See Charles Hanly's (1992) monograph *The Problem of Truth in Applied Psychoanalysis* for an elucidation of the difficulties in enterprise of 'applied psychoanalysis', Richard Cornfield's (1999) report of a panel discussion on the historical and conceptual vicissitudes of 'applied psychoanalysis', Eric Nuetzel's (2003) application of idiodynamics to 'applied psychoanalysis' and the Spring 2008 issue of the *Psychoanalytic Quarterly*, which is devoted to this topic.

Apprentice complex: phrase originated by Otto Fenichel (1945) to denote a certain kind of love derived from the boy's negative oedipal strivings. Here the son enters into 'a temporary feminine submission to the father in order to prepare himself for a later masculine competition with him' (p. 85). Such 'psychology of the pupil' (p. 277) is riddled with ambivalence, since the ultimate goal here is to replace the master. The relationship between the negative oedipus complex and aggression in the male has been elucidated by many subsequent authors, especially Daniel Jaffe (1983) and John Munder Ross (1999).

Area of creation: Michael Balint's (1968) term for an experiential realm of the mind where there is no external or internal object present. 'The subject is on his own and his main concern is to produce something out of himself; this something to be produced may be an object but not necessarily so' (p. 24). Besides artistic creation, mathematics, and philosophy, this mental area includes 'understanding something or somebody, and last but not least, two highly important phenomena: the early phases of becoming—bodily or mentally—"ill" and spontaneous recovery from an "illness"'

(p. 24). Balint went on to state that, even when the subject is without an object, he is not entirely alone. He is most probably with 'pre-objects' i.e., dim fragments of non-self representations that congeal into objects only after the work of creation has been done. The 'area of creation' appears in the clinical situation, according to Balint, when we encounter a silent patient. While, most of the time, such a patient is running away from something, at other times, he might be running towards something, i.e., a state in which he can do something about his problem himself. The latter type of silence need not be interpreted; the analyst must wait till the patient 'returns' from his reverie with a 'solution' to his malady of the movement.

Archaic ego states: the persistence into adult life of ego experiences that seem to represent very early, infantile forms of perceiving the inner and outer reality. Sigmund Freud (1919h, 1930a) used this expression in connection with mystical experiences of merger with the universe at large, and also with regard to uncanny experiences of *déjà vu* and encountering ghosts, animals that speak in human tongues, and personal doubles. Mystical experiences represented the early undifferentiated state of ego, and the uncanny experiences revived the infantile animistic beliefs. Ernst Kris's (1956) later introduction of the concept 'regression in the service of ego' (see separate entry), however, opened up the possibility that emergence of such 'archaic ego states' might not necessarily be pathological and could fuel creativity. Testimony to this is provided by the credulity-stretching paintings of Heironymous Bosch and Salvador Dali, the devilish etchings of M.C. Escher, and the magical surrealism in the novels of Gabriel Garcia Márquez and Salman Rushdie.

Arrogance, curiosity, and pseudo-stupidity: three features of a hateful syndrome outlined by Wilfred Bion (1967). (1). *Arrogance* results from narrow-mindedness in the realm of feeling and perception. This, in turn, is caused by the hostile obliteration of the concept of 'whole objects' (see separate entry) and their replacement by dehumanized figures toward whom malice can be directed without empathy and remorse. The hateful devaluation of the object is accompanied by a heightening of secondary narcissism, and this also contributes to arrogance. (2). A peculiarly naïve *curiosity* about others paradoxically accompanies such dehumanization. However, this curiosity does not express a genuine wish to understand others. Rather, it reflects puzzlement about their motivations on the part of an individual who has little knowledge of his own intrapsychic life. (3). *Pseudo-stupidity* is a consequence of the massive tendency toward projection and the resulting inability to internalize new knowledge. An individual with pseudo-stupidity feels immensely surprised when his hostile acts are found as such by others. He is also unable to alter his paranoid views in the light of new knowledge. Together, 'arrogance, curiosity, and pseudo-stupidity' give rise to a clinical picture of a mindless certainty, omnipotence, and intellectual smugness.

As-if personality: term introduced by Helene Deutsch in 1942 to describe a character disorder that 'forces on the observer the inescapable impression that the individual's whole relationship to life has something about it which is lacking in genuineness and yet outwardly runs along "as-if" it were complete' (p. 302). However, these individuals themselves do not seem aware of their defect in feeling. They seem superficially well adjusted and might even display appropriate emotional responsiveness. Yet something subtle and intangible is missing, leading their friends and acquaintances to wonder what is wrong with them. They do, however, show attunement to others' expectations, which helps them to adapt to their environment. They lack authenticity and display a tendency toward rapid narcissistic identifications with others. These identifications are not assimilated into the self-system, but are acted out in a superficial manner. This tendency to mimic others helps buttress their weak inner self. It also serves to deny any difference and disagreement with others and thus assures their continued support. Aggressive tendencies are split off, lending such individuals an air of 'negative goodness' and of mild amiability. All this contributes to a corruptible value system and striking defects of morality. 'As-if' personalities invariably give a history of maternal deprivation and unstable, shifting, and multiple caretakers during the first few years of childhood. Their failure to find sustained objects for emotional investment has prevented the process of identification from progressing beyond imitativeness. Their inner psychic structure is weak, and the superego (the proper development of which requires a meaningful oedipal experience) is grossly deficient. Resembling the patients described by Deutsch, but different in being inappropriately effusive, rather than cold, are patients described by Priscilla Roth (1994). They display a 'saccharine overcompliance and little believable warmth' (p. 393), and seem to be parodying what is actually most valuable in human emotions. Their inauthenticity has, however, resulted from a close tie to a 'false object' (see separate entry).

Asceticism–greed dilemma: according to Salman Akhtar (2003a), this conflict is among those characteristically experienced during midlife. It is stirred up by the subjective awareness that life is short and time is running out. Based upon such awareness, the individual finds himself at the crossroads of asceticism and greed. The former pushes him towards renunciation, futility, and anhedonia. The latter pushes him towards manic denial, renewed acquisitiveness and pseudo-youthfulness. Although different cultures tilt towards one or the other pole of the solutions for this conflict, the most acceptable outcome in all cultures results from a synthesis of the two extreme possibilities. This leads to the individual developing an enhanced capacity for experiencing pleasure in sensual and material realms, and yet being less dependent upon them.

Assertion: according to Gerald Stechler (1987) 'assertion' emanates from a universal exploratory tendency and 'aggression' (see separate entry) from a universal self-protective system. The former is spontaneous, the latter a reaction to external events. The former is in the service of mastery and is usually associated with joyful affects. The latter reacts strongly and with dysphoric affect to threats from outside. If a child's 'assertion' meets a punitive response from parents, the child reacts with negative affects which cause contamination of 'assertion' with 'aggression'. Joseph Lichtenberg (1989) includes the need for exploration and 'assertion' in his list of motivational systems. Henri Parens' (1989) concept of 'non-destructive aggression' also subsumes a similar concept. What all these investigators seem to be proposing is that 'assertion' involves active engagement with, and manipulation and control of, the external reality in the service of exploration and mastery. Motor aspects of such ego activity are generally underscored, though 'assertion' also involves intellectual forthrightness. While originally ego-syntonic and reflective of what, in early psychoanalytic theory, were called 'ego instincts' (see separate entry), 'assertion' can certainly get caught up in conflict; symptomatic pictures of counterphobic bravado and tongue-tied social awkwardness might develop as a consequence.

Association: while the notion that seemingly disparate psychic elements might be linked and form an 'association' that can be observed and examined existed in the psychoanalytic doctrines of nineteenth century Germany, Sigmund Freud (1895d, 1900a, 1912e) gave it a significant twist. He proposed that (1) ideas are linked with each other not in a passive way, but via dynamically meaningful connections, (2) such 'associations' correspond to organized clusters of the individual's memory, and (3) the flow and flux between a set of associations and between different sets of association might remain unconscious or become conscious, depending upon the acceptable or conflictual nature of the issue involved in them. Such conceptualizations propelled Freud to renounce hypnosis and 'pressure technique' (see separate entry) and move on to employing 'free-association' (see separate entry) on the patient's part as the cornerstone of his treatment method.

Asymmetric logic: see 'Bi-logic'.

Asymmetry gradient: while psychoanalysis does involve a profoundly significant emotional relationship between two individuals, a certain asymmetry must exist within the dyad. One party (the patient) reveals the deepest aspects of his or her mind and the other remains relatively anonymous and abstinent from the indulgence of self-disclosure. Relational warmth and personal anonymity on the part of the analyst are important because the patient must experience both affinity and distance within the dyad. The former facilitates trust and self-revelation. The latter helps in learning about oneself and assimilation of new insights. In Leo Stone's (1984) words, the former meets the condition of 'resemblance' necessary for the development of transference and the latter places the analyst in the position to interpret the transference. The analyst must be on the 'same page', but not on the same footing as the patient. However, the gradient of the asymmetry must be carefully titrated (Thoma & Kachele, 1994) lest it add to the patient's feeling inferior and alienated. Fred Pine's (1997) reminder that the usually helpful aspects of psychoanalytic frame (e.g. couch, time limits, not revealing where one is going for vacation) can be traumatic to some individuals is in this very spirit. Asymmetry with the clinical dyad, caused by these measures and the analyst's anonymity and neutrality, must not exceed what the analysand's ego can bear without undue suffering.

At-one-ment: expression used by Wilfred Bion (1970) to describe a mental state that intuitively grasps 'the absolute truth in and of any object' (p. 30). This implies the transformation of 'O' (see separate entry) or absolute truth into 'K' (see separate entry), or knowledge. Such transformation can happen in two ways. The first involves the help of memory and desire to create a new formulation. The second is unstained by memory or desire; it involves a direct and intuitive under-

standing. This is called 'at-one-ment'. Memory and desire might be evoked by 'at-one-ment', but do not precede it.

Atonement: see 'Atonement–forgiveness dyad'.

Atonement-forgiveness dyad: Irwin Rosen's (2009) phrase for what he regards as the ever-present link between the phenomena of 'atonement' and 'forgiveness' (see separate entry). By 'atonement', Rosen means an act of reparation that is preceded by, and is accomplished through, an 'identification with the aggressed' or an unconscious joining with the victim in his suffering. It is through such empathic and pained 'at-one-ment' that the damaged object is repaired and forgiveness elicited from it.

Attachment theory and psychoanalysis: originated by John Bowlby (1940, 1944, 1958, 1960, 1963, 1980), 'attachment theory' is an empirically derived set of hyposthese that have the infant's need for a secure bond with the mother at its core. Departing from 'classical' psychoanalytic theory, which gave premium to instincts as the basis of human motivation, 'attachment theory' stressed that the emotional tie with the primary caregiver (mostly the mother) was a primary drive and the main factor in psychic structualization. Bowlby studied maternally-deprived children and proposed that they have an excessive need for love; this turns into demand and protest before retreating into listless withdrawal. Bowlby's ideas were based upon behavioural observations and it borrowed terms and concepts from ethology. Early psychoanalysts, including Anna Freud (1960) and Rene Spitz (1960), regarded them as mechanistic and lacking the rich nuances of a psychology dealing with unconscious processes; Bowlby's inattention to the Oedipus complex also troubled them. Such critical outlook on 'attachment theory' persisted well into the 1970s (Engel, 1971; Hanly, 1978; Roiphe, 1976). During the 1980s and 1990s, however, attempts at rapprochement between 'attachment theory' and psychoanalysis began (Bretherton, 1987; McDevitt, 1983; Emde, 1983; Nachman, 1991; Holmes, 1993). The organizing role of the early infant–mother relationship became well-established and so did the idea that insecure attachment patterns contribute to later psychopathology. Bridges began to be constructed between the developmental models of Anna Freud, Donald Winnicott, and Maragaret Mahler on the one hand, and Bowlby and later attachment with Ainsworth, Blehar, Waters, and Wall (1978) and Main, Kaplan, and Cassidy (1985), on the other. Peter Fonagy (2001) has noted that attachment difficulties might underlie some aspects of 'borderline personality disorder' (see separate entry). He (2001) also provides the most lucid step-by-step review of this history as well as that of how attachment theory relates to ego psychology, the work of the British independent school, and the contemporary relational approaches. He also describes the work of 'psychoanalytic attachment theorists', among whom he includes Karlen Lyons-Ruth, Morris Eagle, Jeremy Holmes, Arietta Slade, and Alicia Lieberman. Fonagy notes that both attachment theory and psychoanalysis hold that personality development is best studied in relation to the child's social environment. Though 'attachment theory' takes the cognitive underpinnings of emotional development more into account, psychoanalysis is also beginning to pay attention to this variable. Finally, both theoretical models emphasize and accept the crucial significance of feelings of security and safety in childhood. See also the thoughtful paper on the potential overlaps and differences between 'attachment theory and psychoanalysis' by Siegfried Zepf (2006). An eminently readable synopsis of the basic proposals of 'attachment theory' has recently been provided by Sonia Austrian and Toni Mandelbaum (2008).

Attacks on linking: Wilfred Bion's (1958) designation of mental operations aimed at destroying connections between (1) the patient and analyst, (2) different parts of the patient's own self, (3) internal and external reality, and (4) between these two realities and the psychic apparatus that perceives and registers them. The origin of the proclivity for 'attacks on linking' goes back to phantasied, primitive violence against the bond with the maternal breast and that between the genitals of the two parents. When libido dominates over aggression, the anxiety consequent upon knowing these links can be tolerated. When aggression dominates over libido, these links cannot be accepted and are attacked. In borderline and psychotic conditions, 'attacks on linking' are marked; as a consequence the personality is left with coldly rational and 'almost mathematical relationships' (Grinberg, Sor, & Bianchedi, 1972, p. 37) with little or no emotional meaningfulness.

Autistic character disorder: basing his conceptualizations on Margaret Mahler's (1965) scheme of the separation-individuation process, Alexis Burland (1986) suggested that an early, severe, and sustained deprivation of maternal care results in an incomplete psychological 'hatching' of the infant. A gratifying symbiotic phase does not follow, as the child fails to establish a robust tie with the mother. This multi-faceted developmental arrest, termed 'autistic character disorder' by Burland, manifests in interpersonal unrelatedness, cognitive lag, pathological narcissism, and much destructive aggression. Although Burland described the syndrome mainly in maternally deprived ghetto children, he did suggest that it was recognizable in adults by their affectionlessness, fragmented identity, cognitive impotence, and mindless hedonism.

Autistic–contiguous anxiety: see 'Autistic–contiguous position'.

Autistic–contiguous position: a developmental organization described by Thomas Ogden (1989) as being antecedent to the paranoid–schizoid and depressive positions (Klein, 1946, 1957) and yet as co-existing in a dialectical relationship with the latter two. Common manifestations of 'autistic–contiguous anxiety' include fears that one is rotting, that one's bodily contents are leaking out, and that one is endlessly falling. Defences against these fears centre upon a 're-establishment of continuity of the bounded sensory surface and ordered rythmicity upon which the early integrity of the self rests' (p. 134). Thus, various ways of self-soothing (including compulsive masturbation), and all sorts of repetitive actions are deployed to keep a falling-apart self intact. Tormenting procrastination also sometimes helps generate 'a palpable sensory edge against which the patient attempts to define himself' (p. 135). Besides such intense expressions seen in autistic and schizoid individuals, the 'autistic–contiguous position' is, in general, responsible for contributing a sense of bounded sensory experience which serves to generate the 'sensory floor' (Grotstein, 1987, cited in Ogden, 1989, p. 134) of all experience, just as the paranoid position creates the bedrock of all certainty and the depressive position of all tenderness in human subjectivity.

Autistic objects: introduced by Frances Tustin (1980), the concept refers to psychotic children's use of physical objects in sensation-dominated ways. These objects are usually small and hard (e.g., keys, little metallic cars). They are not used for their intended purpose. Instead, they are deployed as scaffolds to stabilize the mind. According to Tustin, such objects 'have a bizarre and ritualistic quality and the child has a rigidly intense preoccupation with them . . . They may have no fantasy whatsoever associated with them, or they may be associated with extremely crude fantasies which are very close to bodily sensations' (p. 27). A strange promiscuity in their use coexists with intense attachment to them. Their loss is felt as a loss of a body part, and therefore they are immediately replaced.

Autistic phase: originally proposed by Margaret Mahler (1958) as the period extending from birth until about three months of age, during which the infant largely lives in a world of inner stimuli and shows 'hardly any signs of perceiving anything beyond his body' (p. 170). However, Mahler's followers questioned the validity of this observation. They asserted that the infant was object-related from the very beginning of life. Marjorie Harley and Annemarie Weil, for instance, used the term 'quasi-autistic phase' (1979, p. xiii) while referring to what Mahler had called 'autistic phase'. Significantly, they used this term in their introduction to Mahler's selected papers, which were published while she was alive. Certainly they must have had a 'green light' from the old lady for doing so!

Autistic shapes: term used by Frances Tustin (1980) to describe idiosyncratic swirls and figures of sensation produced upon the surface of the skin with the aid of bodily substances or by physical objects pressed upon the skin. Essentially, these shapes are sensation-dominated ways to create an illusion of safety, strength, and integrity.

Autistic regression: a tendency on the part of the infant to lose connectedness with the external world from time to time, largely owing to the immature neuropsychological apparatuses for sustained attachment. In infants who face intense environmentally induced frustrations from the very start of life and/or have constitutionally weak attachment capacities (or both), the tendency towards loss of object cathexis under stress becomes a fixed pattern, however. This subsequently gives rise to vulnerability to mental absences, blank states of mind, psychotic compensations, non-human experiences, and chronic dread and hatred of reality.

Autochthony: see 'Autochthony, cosmogony, and alterity'.

Autochthony, cosmogony, and alterity: terms employed by James Grotstein (1997) in order to elucidate the different ways the formation and activity of the 'self' (see separate entry) are conceptualized. 'Autochthony' refers to the perspective that the self is defined by its self-creation and its creation of external objects. 'Cosmogony' is a twin of 'autochthony' and refers to the technique of narratology, whereby the use of primary

process and projective identification leads an external event to become personalized. As a concept, 'cosmogony' is quite close to Donald Winnicott's (1969) notion of the creation of a 'subjective object' before the Otherness of the object or the objective object can be comprehended. This brings up Grotstein's third notion, namely 'alterity'. This refers to the fantasy and eventual recognition of the creation and defining of the self by external objects. Grotstein emphasizes that 'autochthony' and 'alterity' exist in a dialectical relationship. Moreover, 'autochthony' and 'cosmogony', by owning one's psychic determinism, paradoxically render it a bit relative; this does not happen in the psychotic, who is 'owned' by his determinism. Together, 'autochthony' and 'cosmogony' constitute forerunners of thinking and thus an internal prophylactic against the impact of psychically external trauma. 'Alterity', in contrast, presupposes the achievement of 'object constancy' via 'separation–individuation' (see separate entries) and forms the foundation of differentiated self-object relations. 'Autochthony' and 'cosmogony' together come under 'psychic creationism', and are essentially reflective of one-person psychology. 'Alterity' is at the heart of 'intersubjectivity' (see separate entry), and thus reflects two person psychology.

Autoerotism: a term used in three different contexts: (1) *descriptive context*: this is the way Havelock Ellis (1894), who coined the term, used it. Here, 'autoerotism' means deriving sexual satisfaction solely from one's own body; genital masturbation is the example *par excellence* of this; (2) *dynamic context*: this is the way Sigmund Freud (1905a) first used the term. Taking the action of sucking as the prototype of 'autoeroticism', he proposed that, in the beginning, the oral sexual instinct is attached to hunger (a manifestation of self-preservatory instinct) and finds satisfaction by feeding at the mother's breast. Later, the oral sexual instinct become detached from hunger; at this point it loses its object and becomes 'autoerotic'. In a sophisticated elucidation of this dynamic, Laplanche and Pontalis (1973) state, 'The "origin" of auto-eroticism is thus considered to be that moment—recurring constantly rather than fixed at a certain point in development—when sexuality draws away from its natural object, finds itself delivered over to phantasy, and in this very process is constituted qua sexuality' (p. 46); and (3) *developmental context*: the notion of an autoerotic stage of development preceding object-relatedness—implicit in Freud's early work (1905a)—was given emphatic credence by Karl Abraham (1924b), who conflated autoerotic stage and early 'oral phase' (see separate entry). Later psychoanalysts, most significantly Ronald Fairbairn (1952) contested this view of an infant, declaring that the child is object-related from the very beginning of life.

Autohypnosis: a set of defensive operations which lead to alteration of consciousness and a 'strange state of mind in which one knows and does not know of a thing at the same time' (Freud, 1894a, p. 117). Described by Leonard Shengold (1989) in detail, 'autohypnosis' comprises three subsidiary mechanisms: (1) *hypnotic evasion*, involving the use of altered consciousness as a defence against libidinal and aggressive drives (Dickes, 1965; Fliess, 1935) and against the emergence of traumatic memories; (2) *hypnotic facillitation*, involving the use of altered consciousness to sanction the discharge of otherwise repudiated impulses; and (3) *autohypnotic vigilance*, involving hypercathexis of certain perceptual functions existing side by side with defensive obliviousness of other environmental cues; an invidividual using such 'autohypnotic vigilance' could come across as 'an expert witness, even a sensitive detective preternaturally alert to clues, and a completely unreliable observer' (Shengold, 1989, p. 142). All three mechanisms are regularly employed by the victims of 'soul murder' (see separate entry).

Autohypnotic vigilance: see 'Autohypnosis'.

Automatic anxiety: Sigmund Freud's (1926d) label for the spontaneous reaction of helpless dread in the face of a traumatic situation. 'Automatic anxiety' is to different from 'signal anxiety' (see separate entry). The former results from encountering a traumatic situation and the latter from anticipating it. 'Automatic anxiety' is more evident during infancy, since the ego capacities at that time are rudimentary. However, at an instinctive and experientially raw level, the concept of such anxiety is also valid for adult life.

Autonomous ego functions: Heinz Hartmann (1958) declared that certain ego functions are not 'derived from the ego's relationships to instinctual drives as love objects, but are rather prerequisite of our conception of these' (p. 15). These functions include intelligence, thinking, perception, learning, motility, and speech. Their origin is to be found in constitutional givens. They have 'primary autonomy', i.e., they develop independent of the sexual and aggressive instincts. However, they can get caught up in instinctual conflicts and lose their autonomy. Under such circumstances, instinctual forces (and their relational scenarios) can enhance or impede the unfolding and growth of autonomous ego functions.

Autonomy *vs.* shame and doubt: this is the second of the eight stages of psychosocial development described by Erik Erikson (1950). It typifies the consolidation (or otherwise) of a sense of self-coherence and agency. Like the other stages (see 'Eriksonian stages of psychosocial development'), this stage too is conceived in terms of two potential outcomes that are polar opposites of each other. The fortunate outcome is that the child becomes capable of self-expression as well as self-control. It is from an optimal balance between these two tendencies that a lasting sense of pride emerges. Lack of self-control and over-control by the parents lead to a lasting propensity for shame; this affect emerges from feeling exposed and conscious of being looked at. 'Doubt is the brother of shame' (p. 253), and has to do with continuing uncertainty about who (the parent or the child) is in charge of the child's sphincteric control.

Autotomy: the impulse to get rid of an organ that creates disturbing sensations. According to Sandor Rado (1942), the notion of castration might be based upon the archaic retaliatory idea of talion as well as upon traces of the ancient biological reflex of autotomy. Otto Fenichel (1945) states that 'an evaluation of the concept of autotomy shows the relativity of the contrast between the satisfaction of an instinct and defence against an instinct' (p. 56). In the contemporary context, 'autotomy' is perhaps most evident in self-caused amputations by psychotic and malignantly self-destructive patients (see Ira Brenner's 2004 text on severe psychological trauma for clinical illustrations). In a symbolic way, even dissociation and fainting can be seen as 'cerebral autotomy', whereby ego-synthesis, temporal continuity, and perceptual linkages are destroyed for defensive purposes.

Autosymbolic experiences: described by Herbert Silberer (1909a), these experiences occur when the individual is drowsy and yet making an effort to think. The struggle between the two pulls elicits the 'autosymbolic experience'. This emerges in a hypnagogic state and consists of a hallucination which puts forth, automatically, as it were, a serviceable symbol for what was being thought or felt at that moment. See Austin Silber's (1970) paper 'Functional phenomenon, contemporary defense' for a thorough elucidation of this concept. Also worth considering is the role of 'autosymbolic experiences' in the genesis of phenomena associated with 'dissociative identity disorder' (see separate entry).

Average expectable environment: Heinz Hartmann's (1939) designation of the necessity of some basic environmental provisions (e.g., nurturance, safety, protection from physical danger, psychological dignity) for the psychic structure to develop in an optimal fashion. The concept includes both ecological and emotional components, and its profound relevance is demonstrated by what human beings are capable of becoming and doing when raised in environments that fall drastically short of such a requirement. The dehumanization of oneself and others seen in feral children, serial killers, and terrorists, though aetiologically different in many regards, demonstrates the effects of a missing average expectable environment (Akhtar, 2003).

Awe: an emotion with mixed elements of fear and reverence that is generally evoked by being in the presence of supreme authority, moral greatness, or mysterious sacredness. A sense of great wonder, a feeling of being a part of a larger universe, and a subjective experience of humility also accompany awe. Using the expression *penis awe*, Phyllis Greenacre (1953, 1956) traced the origin of awe to the momentarily overwhelmed state of the child upon seeing the father's erect penis. Two decades later, Irving Harrison (1975) added that the recognition of the attributes of the mother's body, especially her breasts and nipples, lay down the groundwork for a sense of wonder that is later elaborated into awe. The insistently anatomical moorings of these hypotheses reflect a particular phase of psychoanalytic theory. Christopher Bollas' (1979) description of reverence evoked by maternal transformative functions speaks more pointedly to the matter at hand. Mortimer Ostow's (2001) detailed treatment of the subject of awe also cannot be overlooked. In his view, the capacity to experience awe is hardwired in the temporal region of the brain but is experientially evoked by the encounter between the infant's supine eye and the seemingly large parents with upright locomotion. The 'major discrepancies of scale . . . the large sizes, loud sounds, and bright lights the infant encounters at the hands of his parents and the world in which they live' (Ostow, 2001, p. 206) contribute to the experience of mystified humility and wonder that lie at the core of awe. Later, life exposure to structures whose size is incommensurate with human dimensions (e.g., great mountains, oceans, large cathedrals) and their human counterparts (i.e., 'great people') reawakens this early feeling.

B

Background of safety: Joseph Sandler's (1960) concept that replaced the organizational principle of the ego from avoidance of anxiety to seeking and maintaining a sense of safety. 'Safety feelings' are distinct from those of pleasure. The former is an ego asset while the latter is a consequence of the discharge of id impulses. Under fortunate circumstances, the generation and sustenance of this asset is taken for granted and gives rise to a 'background of safety'. This concept provides 'a motivational framework far better articulated with the interpersonal object relations tradition than a simple drive theory model' (Fonagy & Cooper, 1999, p. 7).

Background of uncanniness: Yolanda Gampel's (1999) phrase for the 'dialectic between reminiscence and forgetting' (p. 61) that becomes an organized psychic structure when people are constantly surrounded by social violence, political instability, and war. Proposed as an opposite construct of Joseph Sandler's (1960) 'background of safety' (see separate entry), the 'background of uncanniness' denotes a state of subliminal disorganization that becomes an integral part of the person growing in socially unstable and dangerous environments.

Bad-enough object: this expression refers to the masochistic individual's persistent tie to a beloved sadistic parent and its repeated re-creation in adult relationships, including the transference to one's analyst. The 'bad-enough' object seems needed for structural and dynamic stability of these individuals. Irwin Rosen, who coined the phrase in 1993, but published it only in 2009, responded to an inquiry about the conceptual ancestry of this idea in the following words: 'While the phrase itself was not used, the inherent idea of the "bad-enough object" (the attraction to an abusive other) was in ample evidence. One need only think of "A child is being beaten" or Berliner's 1947 *Quarterly* paper in which he describes the tie to the beloved–sadistic parent. And, of course the Robert Glick–Donald Meyers (1988) volume on masochism includes papers by Arnold Cooper and Stuart Asch which allude to the same idea without identifying it by name. Additionally, there is an absolute gem of a paper (God rest her soul) by Erna Furman on externalization in latency age children in which she describes the phenomena of seeking or creating the sought-after punisher' (personal communication, December 4, 2006).

Basic assumption group: see 'Basic assumption group and work group'.

Basic assumption group and work group: term used by Wilfred Bion (1961) for a group whose members share 'basic assumptions' (see separate entry). This type of group does not recognize the passage of time. Bion contrasted 'basic assumption group' with 'work group', which is task oriented and aware of the dimension of time and need for change. Later in his career, however, he became convinced that both types of mental activity ('basic assumptions' and 'work group' related) operate in all groups, though in various permutations and combinations.

Basic assumptions: term used by Wilfred Bion (1961) for the common, agreed upon, and anonymous obedience prevalent in a group at a given time. 'Basic assumptions' arise out of intense and primitive emotions; they affect the group's culture and functioning in important ways. Bion described three 'basic assumptions': (1) basic assumption of dependence, which implies a collective belief in a protective diety, leader, or organization that will always provide security for the group; (2) basic assumption of fight/flight, which implies the existence of an external enemy whom one must vanquish or avoid; and (3) basic assumption of pairing, which betrays a messianic hope that someone from the future generations will solve the problems of the group.

Basic core: term proposed by Annemarie Weil (1970) to denote the most fundamental, largely pre-verbal substrate of the psychic structure formed by selective maternal evocations of certain specific aspects of child's inherent cognitive and affective propensities. This core might 'range from great harmony and potential for ego structuring and ego strength to considerable imbalance and vulnerability' (p. 457). Its characteristics persist as a fundamental layer to which later imprints of how the separation–individuation and oedipal conflicts are resolved are added. The 'basic core' 'will partially determine individual nuances of the character of healthier persons or the symptomatology of our patients' (p. 458).

Basic fault: Michael Balint (1968) proposed that there are three areas of the mind: the area of creation (see separate entry), the area of 'basic fault', and the area of Oedipus complex. The area of 'basic fault' is characterized by: (1) a subjective sense on the patient's part that there is a 'fault', not a complex or conflict, deep inside of him, and that this fault must be put right, (2) a feeling that the cause of this fault is that someone has failed to provide, at a crucial point in development, what the patient needed, and (3) a desperate longing for the analyst to make things right in this regard or to, at least, not repeat the trauma. Balint added that five developments indicate that this level has been reached or activated during the clinical work: (1) consensually agreed-upon words lose their meanings and potency; the analyst's interpretations are felt to be attacks and the patient's associations circle endlessly around one theme and do not become any deeper, (2) the patient tends to get under the analyst's skin, uncannily reading his emotions and motivations, (3) if the analyst fails to respond in a manner expected by the patient, an atmosphere of resignation and futility begins to take over, (4) the analyst feels countertransference pressure to indulge in the patient, pacify him, console him; or, the analyst becomes defensively and rigidly entrenched in his usual technique, and (5) the patient feels no gratitude for the analyst's efforts to understand and help him; he feels that it is his due to receive what he is expecting. Balint proposed that such pathology can be traced back to 'a considerable discrepancy in the early formative phases of the individual between his biopsychological need and the material and psychological care, attention, and affection available during the relevant times' (p. 22).

Basic fear: Gert Heilbrunn's (1955) concept that suggests that all human anxiety ultimately comes from the dread of annihilation and this, in turn, is related to the phylogenetically derived fear of being eaten. Summarizing a wide range of observations of the animal kingdom as well as well as those of cannibalistic practices of man, Heilbrunn proposed that vigilance against oral attack in human beings mostly remains dormant, but can readily be activated by external threats. Even the developmentally 'appropriate' separation and castration anxieties are, at their base, linked with the 'basic fear' of being cannibalized. Indeed, Fenichel (1928) had earlier suggested that 'the dread of being eaten is in practice indissolubly connected with the idea of being castrated' (p. 159).

Basic motives for infancy: according to Robert Emde (1988), there are four 'basic motives' for behaviour and development during infancy. These include: (1) activity; (2) self-regulation; (3) social fittedness; and (4) affective monitoring. These are pre-programmed in the human infant and separate entries exist on each of them in this glossary.

Basic needs: based upon a comprehensive review and synthesis of pertinent literature, Salman Akhtar (1999a) has identified six basic psychological needs, which seem to be ubiquitous, though the degree to which they are overt and the ways in which they are met vary across cultures. Their gratification seems necessary for healthy psychic development to occur, for relationships to survive, and for psychoanalytic work to take hold and to continue optimally. These needs are (1) the need for one's physical needs to be deemed legitimate; (2) the need for identity, recognition, and affirmation; (3) the need for interpersonal and intrapsychic boundaries; (4) the need for understanding the causes of events; (5) the need for optimal emotional availability of a love object; and (6) the need for a flexible responsiveness by one's love objects under special circumstances. Ordinarily, these needs are met during the course of treatment with no deliberate effort by the analyst. In the treatment of some patients, however, they require more direct attention. Akhtar's review of literature suggests that terms such as 'ego needs' (Winnicott, 1960) and 'growth needs' (Casement, 1991) are subsumed under these 'basic needs'.

Basic rule: see 'Fundamental rule'.

Basic trust: term coined by Erik Erikson (1950) to denote the sustained inner feeling of optimism regarding oneself and the world-at-large. It develops out of frequent experiences of one's childhood needs being met with satisfaction. Therese Benedek's (1938) concept of 'confident expectation' constitutes an earlier formulation of a roughly similar idea.

Basic trust *vs.* basic mistrust: this is the first among the eight stages of psychosocial development described by Erik Erikson (1950). It subsumes the experience of infancy and very early childhood. Like the other stages (see 'Eriksonian stages of psychosocial development'), this stage, too, conceived in terms of two potential outcomes that are polar opposites of each other. On the fortunate side is the development of 'basic trust' (see separate entry) which manifests, at first, in the child's willingness to let the mother out of sight without undue anger or anxiety. Such sense of trust implies 'not only that one has learned to rely on the sameness and continuity of the outer providers, but also that one may trust one's self and the capacity for one's own organs to cope with urges' (p. 248). On the unfortunate side, which results from unreliable and mostly frustrating maternal care, is the development of 'basic mistrust'. This leads to a life-long tendency towards pessimism, withdrawal, lack of faith, and a paranoid view of life.

Basic unity: Margaret Little's (1960) term for the primordial state of oneness between the foetus and mother which, later on, provides the neonate with the psychic stability needed at the outset of life. For this to occur, a psychological environment approximating the harmony of the intra-uterine state must be provided to the infant. This environmental provision, along with a rudimentary 'memory' of intra-uterine oneness, is internalized and psychically elaborated. When such 'basic unity' has not been established, 'annihilation anxiety' (see separate entry) persists and leads to a life-long search for such unity; this could be in the form of desperate longing for ideologies, religion, and symbiotic relationships.

Beast-baby fantasy: originally described by Rosemary Balsam (1999), 'the beast-baby fantasy' refers to a split view of men often found in women. The fantasy implies significant fear and denigration of the male sex. The 'beast' aspect of this fantasy emanates from the looking girl's fear and excitement about the sexual father. In this role, he violates women, but also craves sexual favours from them. The 'baby' aspect involves a view of men as weak, needy, and stupid. Balsam states that this latter view evokes 'some maternal tenderness that is laced also with hatred' (p. 98).

Beating fantasy: refers to a fantasy of being beaten (and, less frequently, of beating someone). Such a fantasy is usually associated with sexual excitement. It can become a condition for orgasm during masturbation or sexual intercourse. It may remain at a purely ideational level or may be behaviourally enacted by being spanked, and, in its derivative forms, by being blindfolded, handcuffed, and otherwise controlled during sexual intercourse. At their base, such fantasies (and their behavioural manifestations) reflect unconscious guilt over incestuous longings towards the father (Freud, 1919h). In girls, the masochistic attitude is related to positive oedipal strivings and hostility towards the mother. In boys, it reflects a negative oedipal orientation the and feminine strivings that result from it.

Beginning phase: Sigmund Freud (1913c) divided the course of analysis into the beginning, middle, and end stages, noting that, like chess, 'only the openings and end-games admit of an exhaustive systematic presentation' (p. 133). The 'beginning' or 'opening phase' extends from the first analytic session (making the pratical arrangements of schedule, money, etc. take place before the beginning proper) to the time when the 'therapuetic alliance' (see separate entry) is reasonably well-established and fleeting and 'floating transference' (see separate entry) reactions have congealed into a coherent 'transference neurosis' (see separate entry). Usually, this takes two to three months, but in sicker patients this period can take longer. The 'beginning phase' consists of a focus upon (1) helping the patient adjust to the unfamiliar situation of being in analysis, (2) establishing a rapport with the patient and to 'attach him to analysis and to the person of the analyst' (Freud, 1913c, p. 139), (3) judiciously answering a 'naïve question' (Etchegoyen, 2005, p. 611) or two to facilitate the patient's relaxation and collaboration with the analytic work, and (4) demystifying what is taking place in the analytic setting without a compromise of the necessary anonymity and neutrality (Thoma & Kachele, 1994).

Behaviour: term referring to an individual's overt and observable action or a set of actions. Generally speaking, 'behaviour' is deemed a surface phenomenon that is the end product of a complex interplay of drive–defence, impulse–prohibition, feeling–thought, and fantasy–reality constellations. In the clinical setting, an analysand's behaviour is addressed only if it is (1) outlandish and bizarre, (2) disruptive of the therapeutic frame, (3) associated with mutism, and (4) readily 'linkable' to the patient's verbal associations of the moment. An illustration of this last indication is letting a patient know that one has noted his difficulty in leaving the office when the patient is talking about his pain at separations.

Benevolent neutrality: see 'Neutrality'.

Benign and malignant narcissism: see 'Malignant narcissism'.

Benign and malignant regression: terms used by Michael Balint (1968) to designate two types of 'regression' (see separate entry) during the analytic process. Both types need the presence and participation of the analyst. However, they differ in important ways. In 'malignant regression', the patient expects or demands gratification of his needs from the analyst. In 'benign regression', the patient's premium is not upon the expected change in the external world, but upon a tacit consent to use the external world in a way that would allow him to get on with his problems; 'the event that matters is in the patient himself' (p. 142). Malignant regression ends up in a vicious spiral whereby, as soon as some of the patient's needs are satisfied, new cravings crop up. Benign regression, in contrast, leads to the patient's finding altered ways of relating to himself and the world, ways that constitute a 'new beginning' (see separate entry). See also Harold Stewart (1993) on further clinical aspects of 'malignant regression'.

Benign and malignant prejudice: terms introduced into psychoanalytic literature by Henri Parens (2007a) in order to distinguish between the mild discomfort with ethnically or racially different others (which arises from ordinary stranger anxiety) and active hatred of them (which arises from the externalization of hostile destructiveness). The distinction seems logical, nosologically tidy, and suitable for research purposes. However, it leaves unaddressed all gradations of prejudice that might lie between the two extremes. More importantly, the terms 'benign' and 'malignant' are a bit risky to use in this context. One's 'malignant' prejudice, for instance, may appear 'benign' to oneself and others 'benign' attitudes experienced as 'malignant'. This element of subjectivity in these terms casts doubt on their usefulness, though the distinction remains an important one.

Benign circle: Donald Winnicott's (1954) term for the oscillations of the child's efforts to distinguish between his two perceptions of the mother: 'environment mother *vs.* object mother' (see separate entry). There is, at first, the recognition of instinctual experience and its depleting impact upon the mother. This is followed by the inner sorting out of good and bad, and is accompanied by feelings of guilt. The next step is reparation, which, in turn, restores the integrity of the 'environment mother' until the instinctual pressure in the child rises again. The establishment of confidence in this 'benign circle' is the basis for the 'capacity for concern' (see separate entry).

Benign prejudice: see 'Benign and malignant prejudice'.

Benign regression: see 'Benign and malignant regression'.

Bereavement: see 'Grief'.

Bestiality: a broad term referring to sexual contact with animals. This usually occurs in association with predisposing cultural factors, lower levels of education, and schizoid tendencies. Richard von Krafft-Ebing (1892), the pioneer of descriptive classification of sexual perversions, described two syndromes of erotic interest in animals: *zoerastia* (also known as zoerasty) and *zoophilia*. The former involves sexual acts with animals in lieu of a human partner. The latter involves contact with animals (via petting and stroking) to enhance sexual desire for a human partner. Psychoanalytic literature generally does not make this distinction, and employs 'bestiality'—or, to use Daniel Traub-Warner's (1986) more recent term 'bestophilia'—as an overreaching concept. Salman Akhtar and Jodi Brown (2005), who have summarized this literature, conclude that sexual perversions involving animals display withdrawal from intimacy with human beings, reliance on a silent and undemanding partner, symbolic enactment of wide-ranging unconscious fantasies (e.g., those pertaining to sadomasochism, homosexuality, castration), and the use of both a 'transitional object' (see separate entry) and a fetish.

Bestophilia: see 'Bestiality'.

Beta-elements: Wilfred Bion's (1962a,b) designation of those sense impressions and feeling states that have not been transformed into thinkable thoughts, or 'alpha-elements' (see separate entry), by the intervention of 'alpha-function' (see separate entry). 'Beta-elements' are experienced as 'things in themselves'. They are 'not so much memories as undigested facts, whereas alpha-elements have been digested by the alpha-function and are thus "food for thought"' (Bleandonu, 1994, p. 152). Highly vulnerable to projective identification, beta-elements require a reliable 'container' (see separate entry) in order to be metabolized and return in the palatable form of alpha-elements. Only then can they be psychically useful.

Bibring's five therapeutic principles: in a paper that was widely read until the 1980s, Edward Bibring (1954) delineated five therapeutic principles typical of psychoanalysis and dynamic psychotherapies. These included 'suggestion', 'abreaction', 'manipulation', 'clarification', and 'interpretation' (see separate entries). Bibring distinguished between the 'technical' and 'curative' applications of these principles. The former application referred to the use of an intervention for the purposes of safeguarding the continuity of the treatment. The latter application refered to the use of the same intervention for the purposes of ameliorating the patient's psychopathology.

Bicultural identity: term used in two different senses in psychoanalytically orientated immigration studies: (1) to denote the hybrid self that emerges in a person who has long lived in an alien culture and has undergone what Salman Akhtar (1995) has called a 'third individuation'; and (2) to denote the sense of belonging to two cultures in the offspring of immigrant parents. Some authors (e.g., Meaders, 1997) call the former 'transcultural identity' and reserve the term 'bicultural identity' for the latter group.

Bicultural self: see 'Bicultural identity'.

Bi-logic: Ignacio Matte-Blanco's (1975) term for the joint operation of 'asymmetrical' and 'symmetrical' logic in the human mind. The former focuses upon one thing and, of necessity, separates it from the next thing. The latter identifies the individual thing by its class. Consciousness is dominated by 'asymmetrical' and the 'unconscious' by 'symmetrical' logic. Consciousness deals with individual items (beings, things, emotions, or ideas) and unconscious with sets or classes; the latter does not distinguish between part and whole, between self and other, and between opposites of any kind. Matte-Blanco's ideas provide an inductive system to help organize the data of analysis and human mental functioning at large. For intricate connections between 'bi-logic' and the classical concepts of 'primary and seconday processes' (see separate entry) and for the potential links between Matte-Blanco's 'bi-logic' and Gregory Bateson's (1972; see also Bateson, Jackson, Haley, & Weakland, 1956) ideas on various patterns of communication; see the contributions of Eric Rayner and Gerald Wooster (1990), and Horacio Etchegoyen and Jorge Ahumada (1990), respectively. The report of a panel held in honour of Matte-Blanco's contributions by Warren Procci (2000) is also quite instructive. Procci draws three technical conclusions 'the *first* task might be described as working with the patient to an understanding, respect and lessening of fear of the manifestation of symmetrical thinking that operate most clearly in areas such as despair, destructive omnipotence, body's own confusion, areas of emptiness, non-differentiation and confusion. The *second* task has to do with encouraging those vital discriminations that allow for more separate functioning and autonomy. The *third* task is to build on the first two and therefore

to allow a reordering and communication between each person's symmetrical and asymmetrical functions' (p. 572).

Bipersonal field: originated by Madeline Baranger and Willy Baranger (1966) and elaborated upon and popularized by Robert Langs (1976, 1979), this concept refers to the temporospatial space within which the analytic interaction takes place. The field contains both participants, and embodies interactional as well as intrapsychic mechanisms. Every event within the field receives contributions from both participants. The ground rules of psychoanalysis 'not only delimit the field, but also, in a major way, contribute to the communicative properties of the field and to the analyst's hold of the patient and containment of his projective identification' (Langs, 1979, p. 72). Langs has identified three forms of this 'interactional field': (1) Type A, where symbolic communication occurs and the field itself becomes the realm of illusion, (2) Type B, where action is central and projective identification predominates, and (3) Type C, where all communication is destroyed and the field is emptied of meaning.

Bipolar affective disorder: previously known as 'manic depressive illness', this condition is characterized by recurrent episodes of pronounced mood disturbance of elated and depressed types. The former manifests with marked euphoria, grandiosity, pressured thinking, inability to sleep, distractability, and impulsivity; this can progress to irritability, anger, and delusional thinking (primarily of grandiose, and secondarily of paranoid, kind). The latter manifests with dysphoria, lowered self-esteem, psychomotor retardation, anorexia and insomnia, hopelesssness, and suicidal ideation; this can progress to profound despair, withdrawal and mutism, nihilistic and hypochondriacal delusions, and suicidal attempts and even completed suicide. Periods of lucidity can be observed between the episodes, though nearly a quarter of individuals suffering from the disorder continue to show some mood instability even during these intervals (*DSM-IV-TR*, American Psychiatric Association, 2005, (p. 286). The condition has a strong hereditary and constitutional component. This does not mean that psychological factors do not play a role in precipitating these episodes or in giving content to either the depressive or manic symptomatology (Cohen, Baker, Cohen, Fromm-Reichmann, & Weigert, 1954). See also the related entries on 'cyclothymia', 'depression' and 'mania'.

Bipolar self: term coined by Heinz Kohut (1977) to describe the core psychic structure, which consists of 'nuclear ambitions' of early childhood on the one hand, and 'nuclear goals' of later childhood on the other. The former are predominantly derived from the child's relationship with the maternal 'selfobject' (see separate entry) and the latter from parental figures of either sex. There is an 'abiding flow of actual psychological activity that establishes itself between the two poles of the self, i.e. a person's basic pursuits towards which he is "driven" by his ambitions and "led" by his ideals' (p. 180).

Birth fantasies: according to Gilbert Rose (1969), some analysands tend to report fantasies suffused with birth symbolism during the first year of analysis. These fantasies are overdetermined and reflect themes as diverse as defences against death wishes and a sense of entering an altogether new era of life. Such fantasies are also frequent towards the end of an analysis , especially if it has given the patient the feeling of a true 'new beginning' (see separate entry).

Birth trauma: the notion that being born is psychologically traumatic was first proposed by Otto Rank (1924). He then extended this view to suggest that all developmental crises were, in part, a replication of such 'birth trauma' (*ibid.*). While not accompanying Rank to this extreme, Sigmund Freud (1915c) was persuaded that the overwhelmed and defenceless psychic state of the newborn (upon transition from the well-protected ambience of the womb to the highly stimulating external world) might indeed form a developmental prototype of human anxiety.

Bisexuality: a concept that came into the psychoanalytic corpus from two sources: the studies of sexual behaviour by Krafft-Ebing (1892) and Havelock Ellis (1894, 1903, 1905), and the correspondence between Sigmund Freud and his esteemed friend, Wilhelm Fliess (Masson, 1985). The first source emphasized the behavioural aspect of bisexuality, describing in detail the various combinations of heterosexual and homosexual practices in people's lives. The second source emphasized biological basis (e.g., embryonic, anatomic, physiological) for bisexuality, and extending to matters psychological. As a result, three levels of the term 'bisexuality' seem to exist: (1) behavioural, (2) constitutional, and (3) psychological. Bisexual behaviour, emanating from failure of identity synthesis, is always related to 'psychic bisexuality' but the latter does not always lead to bisexual behaviour. And this should not be surprising if one follows how personality development usually unfolds under

normal circumstances. Parents of both sexes form not only objects of identification, but also objects of desire for children of both sexes. As a result, feminine and masculine attitudes (see entries on 'femininity' and 'masculinity') come to reside in all individuals, and so do heterosexual and homosexual erotic inclinations. However, with the predominance of identifications with the same-sex parent and sociocultural faciliatation of the consequent gender role, the 'attitude proper to the opposite sex succumbs to repression' (Freud, 1937c, p. 231). This is not to say that aim-inhibited and/or sublimated forms of bisexuality do not find their way to consciousness. Otto Kermberg's (1991) delineation of the components of 'erotic desire' (see separate entry) includes the sublime emergence of bisexual trends during foreplay and sexual intercourse, and David Guttman's (1980) elucidation of mid-life changes addresses the same issue from the vantage point of ego identity. More recently, Henry Smith (2002a) has pointed out the four different implications of the term 'bisexuality': (1) the ubiquitous presence of maternal and paternal identifications, (2) the fact that every sexual object choice is essentially bisexual, (3) the existence of mixed masculine and feminine traits in all individuals, and (4) actual bisexual practice.

Bizarre objects: Wilfred Bion's (1967) term for the uncanny object perceptions across sensory modalities that are created by the projection of violently destroyed mental links and the accompanying fragmentation of the ego into the external world. In simple words, certain objects in external reality begin to appear frightening and strange, not only because of aggression attributed to them, but because they seem to give their scary messages in a sensory modality not originally intended for them. For instance, the radio smells awful, the chair smiles wickedly, and the shoe starts to sing ballads.

Black hole: Wilfred Bion's (1970) extrapolation of the astronomical term for the description of the subjective experience of collapse into nothingness and meaninglessness. It was in connection with his description of the 'infantile catastrophe' (see separate entry) that Bion used the term 'black hole'; it was intended to metaphorically capture the infantile, traumatic bodily separateness from the mother with its disturbing mental consequences. The term was later developed and applied by Frances Tustin (1988, 1993) to the study of autistic spectrum disorders, and by James Grotstein (1986, 1989, 1990) to the study of schizophrenia. Grotstein (1990) emphasized that this is felt 'not just as a static emptiness but as an implosive, centripetal pull into the void' (p. 257). A thorough review and update of the literature on this topic is provided by Ofra Eshel (1998). Invoking André Green's (1986) concept of the 'dead mother' (see separate entry), Eshel proposes that encounter with it 'constitutes a "black hole" experience in the interpersonal, intersubjective space of her child because of the intense grip and compelling pull of her world of inner deadness. Individuals under her influence are either trapped in her deadening world or, if they succeed in detaching themselves from it, are petrified in their interpersonal space because of the imminent threat of being drawn back in again' (p. 79).

Blanket interpretations: Sandor Feldman's term (1958) for interpretations given on the basis of the analyst's knowledge of theory or experience with other patients, and not on the basis of the analysand's own associations. Such interpretations, even if correct in respect of content, lead to foreclosure of the material and add to the patient's resistance. Martin Stein's (1958) description of a patient's use of analytic clichés constitutes a counterpart of the analyst's use of 'blanket interpretation'.

Body ego: though not included in many psychoanalytic glossaries and encyclopaedias (Eidelberg, 1968; Erwin, 2002; Laplanche & Pontalis, 1973), the term 'body ego' is of considerable significance in so far as it sheds light not only upon the early origins and functioning of the ego but also upon the somatocentric nature of early psychoanalytic theory Freud's (1923b, p. 26) celebrated phrase 'the ego is first and foremost a bodily ego' succinctly conveys both these issues. Regarding the bodily origins of the ego, Freud emphasized that the ego is ultimately derived from bodily sensations and later Willie Hoffer (1949, 1950) noted that the infant's attention is mostly focused upon nursing and avoidance of hunger. As a result, the mouth becomes the first important area of self expression and contact with external reality. Hands, that grasp the mother's breast, and eyes, that look at mother's face during nursing, become the next cathected islands of the self. The knowledge of the ego or the self (used interchangeably at the time of Freud's and Hoffer's theorizing) then spreads to a comprehensive view of one's bodily and mental self. This is the 'hand–mouth–ego integration' sequence. Besides such 'structural' implications of the term 'body ego', there is also a 'dynamic' aspect since, in early psychoanalytic theory, ego functioning was seen as modelled upon body functioning. Thus, introjection

was regarded as representing eating or swallowing, projection as equivalent of splitting, denial as a psychic form of closing one's eyes, negation as turning the head away from an undesirable food item; and so on. Such premium on the body and the associated tendency to regard bodily tensions as the primary motivators of human behaviour gave rise to physicalistic interpretations of a large number of psychoanalytic concepts, the most prominent among them being 'penis envy' (see separate entry), and 'castration anxiety' (see separate entry). In contemporary psychoanalysis, these concepts are reformulated in the light of object-related fantasies.

Body image: refers to the mental representation the individual has of his or her own body. The 'differentiation' subphase of 'separation–individuation' (see separate entry) sets the psychic discovery of one's body—an initial step in creating its mental representation—into motion. Gradually, the earlier unmentalized cathexis of mouth, hands, and eyes get integrated into a primitive 'body schema' that, in turn, is underscored by perceptually locating the musculoskeletal pleasure of crawling and upright locomotion. Discovery of the anatomical differences between the sexes (Freud, 1925j) refines such early body image. This schema gets elaborated during the latency phase, when psychomotor activity and playful mastery of external reality occupy the centre stage, and adolescence, when sexual maturation reshapes the views of one's own body; genital and non-genital masturbation also plays an important role here. By the end of adolescence, a truly composite view of one's body is established in the mind. Later events (e.g., pregnancy, ageing, physical illness) subtly cause additions and deletions to this baseline. Fixation on body image of one particular era of life can lead to difficulty in assimilating changes in later life. Also, fantasy-based and/or environmentally indoctrinated distortions (e.g., one is fat, short, ugly) of body image can contribute to life-long emotional suffering; these often underlie 'eating disorders' (see separate entry) and are subsumed under the psychiatric entity of 'body dysmorphic disorder'.

Body schema: see 'Body image'.

Borderline personality disorder: the prefix 'borderline' was for a long time used in diverse psychiatric contexts and was given a formal status by Adolph Stern (1938) in connection with patients who responded adversely to classical psychoanalysis. His list of ten criteria remains an outstanding description up to today. These included:

(1) narcissism, (2) psychic bleeding, (3) hypersensitivity, (4) rigidity, (5) negativism, (6) feelings of inferiority, (7) masochism, (8) constitutional incapacity to tolerate stress, (9) preponderance of projective mechanisms, and (10) difficulties in reality testing. However, it was not until the empirical study by Roy Grinker, Sr. and his colleagues (1968) and, even more so, the seminal review article by John Gunderson and Margaret Singer (1975) that the specific term 'borderline personality disorder' came into nosological limelight. Its inclusion in the *Diagnostic and Statistical Manual of Mental Disorders III* (APA, 1980) gave the entity an 'official' imprimatur. Borderline personality disorder is seen as consisting of (1) unstable sense of self or identity disturbances, (2) disturbed interpersonal life characterized by vacillating but intense relationships, (3) a superficial neurotic-like picture associated with a tendency towards occasional 'micropsychotic' breaks, (4) contradictory presence of intense affects with a dreadful sense of inner emptiness, (5) impulsivity, (6) chronic rage at others coupled with self-destructiveness, (7) intolerance of being alone, (8) chaotic sexual life, and (9) inordinate sensitivity to rejection by others. Together, these nine features betray the existence of major contradictions in the realms of self-image, affect regulation, and object relations.

Borderline personality organization: introduced by Otto Kernberg in 1967, this term refers to a character structure with (1) identity diffusion, (2) predominance of splitting over repression, (3) lack of self- and object constancy, and (4) marked preoedipal colouration to the Oedipus complex. Oscillations between extremely favourable or unfavourable estimations of the self are frequent. The capacity for comprehending objects in their totality is impaired. Affects pertaining to ambivalence, mourning, and sadness are deficient. Superego integration is minimal and superego forerunners of a sadistic kind are easily projected, creating frightening external persecutors. Such personality organization is not a discrete nosological entity, but the substrate of all severe personality disorders and certain cases of alcoholism, drug abuse, and sexual perversions. The concepts of borderline personality disorder and borderline personality organization are on different levels of abstraction, although they do overlap in some ways. A 'borderline personality organization' underlies all cases of 'borderline personality disorder' (see separate entry). However, not all cases of 'borderline personality organization' present as 'borderline personality disorder'.

Border symbolism: it is widely accepted that the human mind imbues its physical surround with symbolic meanings. Various natural features of the Earth (e.g., rivers, mountains) and man-made structures (e.g., bridges) all come to signify elements of deep unconscious fantasies. In a unique contribution to this area of investigation, Avner Falk (1974) proposed the concept of 'boder symbolism'. According to him, borders between two countries or regions often unconsciously symbolize early parental figures. 'Thus crossing an international border for a man may mean crossing the incest barrier into the mother. It may also mean a search for a bounteous early mother who will unconditionally accept and embrace the child' (pp. 653–654). Falk added that borders not only symbolize such interpersonal barriers, but can also stand for intrapsychic boundaries.

Boredom: a psychological state characterized by a blocked sense of longing for something, an inability to know what is longed for, a feeling of time having slowed down, an impediment to generating wishful fantasies, and an attitude of passive expectation that the external world might offer some satisfaction and yet ending up inconsolable and frustrated. Ralph Greenson (1953) is one of few analysts who have addressed this topic. A less metapsychological grappling with the issue is also to be found in the essay titled 'The league of death' (1966) by San Francisco analyst Allen Wheelis. Together, these authors underscore that a sense of longing coupled with an absence of fantasies of what would quench that longing are the central characteristics of boredom. Underlying the affect is oral hunger and a near-total ego identification with that hunger: the bored person is full of emptiness. In addition, there is repression of hostile fantasies aroused by feeling frustrated and deprived. Such regression, in turn, weakens the ego, which then fails to generate 'entertaining' fantasies. A vicious circle between id-deprivation and ego-weakness is thus set up. Hunger increases in proportion to the repressive diminution of fantasy scenarios. The resulting affect is experienced as boredom.

Borromean knot: A figure consisting of three circles interlinked in a way that, if any one of them is cut, all three become separated. Known as such because it is found on the coat of arms of the Borromeo family, the knot was invoked by Jacques Lacan (1974) to illustrate the interdependence of the three psychic registers of the 'real', 'symbolic' and 'imaginary' (see separate entries on each). The total unravelling of the knot resulted in the three registers of the mind becoming de-linked from each other; psychosis represents such a state of affairs.

Borrowed sense of guilt: the phenonmenon of a 'borrowed unconscious sense of guilt' was first described by Friedrich Eickhoff (1989) in connection with children of Nazis whose parents had used massive denial to ward off any feelings of guilt for their actions; the parental guilt had been deposited in the offspring. In a comprehensive review of literature on this and related affects, Joseph Fernando (2000) categorized 'borrowed sense of guilt' into two types that result from feeling the guilt that: (1) the parent feels but denies, and (2) the parent should feel but does not. The first is a narrow use of the term 'borrowed sense of guilt'. The second refers to the fact that the child himself becomes a target of accusations that he internally levels against the parent. While Fernando does not mention it in his paper, William Ronald Fairbairn's (1940) concept of 'moral defence' (see separate entry) is highly pertinent in this context.

Borrowed unconscious sense of guilt: see 'Borrowed sense of guilt'.

Bound energy: see 'Psychic energy'.

Boundaries: an ill-defined term that seems to subsume eight overlapping concepts: (1) *ego-boundaries* (Freud, 1911b; Federn, 1952), which, on the inside, separate the ego from the fantasy world, and, on the outside, from reality, (2) *boundaries between self and object-representations* (Jacobson, 1964), which help retain the intrapsychic difference in the experience of the self and its internal objects, (3) *interpersonal boundaries* (Akhtar, 2006; Mahler, Pine, & Bergman, 1975) which develop in early childhood and regulate the extent of intimacy possible without the dread of fusion and separateness needed, without the despair of loneliness, (4) *skin envelope* (Anzieu, 1992), which metaphorically contains psychic experience and precludes massive projections and suggestibility, (5) *temporal boundaries* (Erikson, 1950; Kogan, 2006), which help distinguish subjective experience of past from those in the present, (6) *cultural boundaries* (Akhtar, 1999b), which regulate the sense of similarity and difference in a dialogue between people from distinct cultural traditions, (7) *intrapsychic boundaries* (Freud, 1900a, 1921c, 1923b; Hartmann, 1939), which keep major psychic structures at optimal distance from each other (e.g., ego from id, ego-ideal from ego) in order to permit rational ways for the ego to operate, and (8) *ethical boundaries in the clinical situation* (Celenza, 2007; Gabbard & Lester, 1995) which prevent harmful countertransference transgressions of the analytic frame.

Boundaries of the self: this refers to the limiting membrane that develops around the self by the 18th to 20th month of life. While rudimentary at this time, this allows for keeping intrapsychic material and the external reality separate. Gradually, it becomes firmer. The capacity for reality testing and for distinguishing between conception and perception, and between fantasy and reality, depends upon this boundary. Some permeability always remains, however; the extent of this varies from culture to culture. Empathic immersion in the subjective experience of someone else and projective identifications are healthy and not-so-healthy examples, respectively, of such permeability.

Boundary constancy: see 'Spatial representations'.

Boundary crossings: according to Glen Gabbard and Eva Lester (1995), these refer to somewhat benign countertransference enactments that are quickly recognized by the analyst as something to stop and reflect upon. 'Boundary crossings', are likely to occur in isolation, may be inevitable in certain provocative patients, and might even extend the analytic work in a positive direction.

Boundary violations: according to Glen Gabbard and Eva Lester (1995), these refer to egregious countertransference enactments that are chronic, repetitive, and harmful to the patient. Such behaviours on the analyst's part destroy the analytic frame and put the feasibility of analytic treatment into question. Examples of such 'boundary violations' include sexual relations with a patient, or entering into grossly unethical financial dealings with them. Diana Siskind (1997), Howard Levine (2005), Salman Akhtar (2006), and Stephen Sonnenberg and William Myerson (2007) have added the concepts of 'referral boundary violations', 'narcissistic boundary violations', 'cultural boundary violations', and 'educational boundary violations' (see separate entries), respectively, to this list.

Boundary violating therapists: according to Glen Gabbard and Eva Lester (1995), there are four types of 'boundary violating therapists': (1) those suffering from psychoses, (2) predatory psychopaths, (3) therapists who develop serious erotic countertransferences ('love sickness'), and (4) those who masochistically surrender to the patient's unrealistic demands for the gratification of instinctual desires. In a remarkable contribution, Andrea Celenza (2007) has offered further details on the personality characteristics and situational variables associated with therapists, educators, and clergy violating sexual boundaries. Combining psychoanalytic perspective with questionnaire-based empirical research, Celenza elucidates the damage such actions cause and also discusses the rehabilitation measures for the transgressors.

Boy's dis-identification with the mother: according to Ralph Greenson (1968), a growing boy must dis-identify from mother and identify with a male figure in order to develop a solidly masculine gender identity. In the process, the boy must give up the security and pleasure that comes from closeness and identification with the mother. The mother, too, must be willing to let go of him a bit and allow him to identify with the father figure. And, from his side, the father must make such a move desirable for the boy.

Breast envy: term originated by Felix Boehm (1930) for the covetous attitude towards the adult female (i.e., maternal) breast displayed by both boys and girls. In the boy, this can be seen as a counterpart to penis envy, in so far as the breast might have become a penis equivalent by the unconscious mechanism of upward displacement. In the girl, similar envy might represent a desire to possess mother's adult (and oedipal) prerogatives. In both sexes, breast envy receives impetus from preoedipal longing for the mother's capacity to soothe and provide nourishment. This particular dynamic found greater explication later in the work of Melanie Klein (1935, 1940, 1946).

Bridging interventions: term introduced by Otto Kernberg (1975) to denote those remarks of the analyst which emanate from his or her capacity to retain a borderline patient's split and contradictory self and object-representations in mind (since the patient has a tendency to 'forget' affectively one or the other extreme of his experience). The aim of such interventions is to undo the psychic compartmentalization caused by splitting. In elaborating Otto Kernberg's views, Salman Akhtar (1995, 1998) notes that 'bridging interventions' involve the analyst's display—by gentle verbal reminders or a subtle shift in the tone of voice— that he at least has not 'forgotten' the transference

configuration that is opposite to the one currently active. Thus, the analyst might make a mild, *en passant* remark during the course of a lengthier intervention about the patient's hostility when the latter is being too idealizing, and love when the patient is being too demeaning.

Bulimia: see 'Eating disorders'.

Burdens of sanity: Sigmund Freud is known to have said that all psychoanalytic treatment can do is to transform 'hysterical misery into common unhappiness' (1895d, p. 305). However, the constituents of this irreducible 'misery' were left to the imagination. Moreover, Freud was hardly alone in coming to the conclusion that a certain amount of conflict and emotional pain is inevitable in the course of life. Buddha's first Noble Truth comprised this very realization, and Henry David Thoreau (1854) grimly declared that most men live of a life of 'quiet desperation'. Extending these ideas on operational and descriptive levels, Salman Akhtar (2005) came up with a list of six factors that he collectively termed as the 'burdens of sanity'. In his view, a mentally healthy person—or, to be more accurate, the mentally healthy sector of the mind—has to bear the weight of the following six realizations: (1) *factual uncertainty*: life is unpredictable and we have little control over random events that have an impact upon us; (2) *conceptual complexity*: matters of life are far from simple, as there are always multiple perspectives with which any event, thing, or person can be viewed; (3) *moral ambiguity*: what is 'good' and 'bad' is hardly absolute; such decisions are dependent upon context, culture, ear, viewpoints and contingencies; (4) *cultural impurity*: the world has become (actually, has pretty much always been) a hybrid place with contributions of various people, religions, nationalities, and cultures being inextricably linked in the daily fabric of our lives; the search for 'purity' is a regressive delusion; (5) *personal responsibility*: we have to take responsibility for our lived life in its aggression, sexual, and non-instinctual realms, as well as its conscious and unconscious aspects; we have the power of life's agency; and (6) *total mortality*: death is final with no heaven and hell, no reincarnation, no return or resumption whatsoever. To be sure, this last burden is the hardest to bear, and various religious belief systems readily provide a haven from the heavy weight of this realization.

C

Candidate in training: see 'Analytic candidate'.

Capacity for concern: Donald Winnicott (1962) proposed that in the period around 5–12 months, the infant begins to renounce his 'ruthlessness' and show concern for the mother. To be sure, the 'capacity for concern' is rudimentary at this stage, and is further elaborated and consolidated over the course of time. However, this early 'stage of concern' (Winnicott, 1954) is a turning point in development. Unlike Melanie Klein (1940) who had proposed that the child moves into a 'depressive position' (see separate entry) as a result of *his* growing awareness of his attacks against his good mother, Winnicott emphasized that the movement is because of the *mother's* surviving the child's ruthlessness.

Capacity to be alone: according to Donald Winnicott (1958), the 'capacity to be alone' emantes from the repeated and peaceful experience of 'being alone, as an infant and small child, in the presence of mother. Thus the basis of the capacity to be alone is a paradox: it is the experience of being alone while someone else is present' (p. 30). Such aloneness is distinct from withdrawal and loneliness; the latter states actually betray incapacity to be alone and are pathological. The mature capacity for aloneness, in contrast, is ego-replensishing, since it replicates an early state of being psychologically held by a devoted, non-intrusive mother.

Care: according to Erik Erikson (1982), the capacity to genuinely care for people, things, and ideas around oneself is a hallmark of adulthood. In an interesting revelation on his thinking on this subject, Erikson recounted the following episode. 'For my talk on the generational cycle, in fact, I asked Sudhir Kakar for the Hindu term corresponding to Care. He answered that there did not seem to be one word for it, but that the adult is said to fulfill his tasks by practicing *Dáma* (Restraint), *Dána* (Charity), and *Daya* (Compassion). These three words, I could only reply, are well translated into every day English with "to be care-ful", "to take care of", and "to care for"' (pp. 58–59).

Carry-over transference : see 'Reanalysis'.

Castration anxiety: refers to the fear of loss of, or injury to, the genitals, especially the penis. The concept of such anxiety and the fantasies and developmental consequences associated with it (collectively termed 'castration complex') were originally described by Sigmund Freud. Beginning with his observations *vis-à-vis* Little Hans (1909b), the five-year-old boy who had a fear of horses, and culminating in his seminal paper 'Some psychical consequences of the anatomical distinction between the sexes' (1925j), Freud elaborated the following notions: (1) upon noticing the differences in their genitals, both boys and girls react with distress; (2) the boy feels that the girl has been castrated and fears that a similar fate can befall him; (3) the masturbatory pleasure and the exhibitionistic delight in his penis, as well as the later emerging oedipal wishes for his mother, render such 'castration anxiety', in his mind, a punishment coming from the father; (4) this leads the boy to suppress, repress, and renounce his oedipal longing for his mother and internalize the father's authority as his superego; (5) in the girl, the same discovery leads to feeling castrated and inferior, experiencing 'penis envy' (i.e., coveting the 'superior organ', to use Freud's words), and a wish to obtain the penis (or, as a substitute, children) from the father; (6) since the girl does not feel 'castration anxiety' *per se*, the internalization of punishing authority is less crucial, leading to a weaker superego; and (7) while pregenital factors (especially oral and anal separation experience) can contribute to 'castration complex', its essence lies in the excitations, anxieties, and psychical consequences associated with the loss of the penis. After a fairly long reign of complete acceptance, Freud's ideas began to be questioned. The following objections to them are especially worth noting: (1) the use of the term 'castration anxiety' for females has been derided as representing the phallocentrism of early psychoanalytic theory, and alternative terms such as 'female genital anxiety' (Bernstein, 1990) have been offered as better descriptors of the phenomena involved; (2) the proposal regarding the weakness of female superego and its purported reasons has come under harsh criticism, though without altogether dismissing gender-based differences in the superego (Bernstein, 1983; Gilligan, 1982); (3) the anatomical foundations and universality of 'penis envy' has largely been replaced by its object-related substrate and experience-based relativism of the intensity of such scenarios; (4) the girl's wish for a baby is seen to pre-date her so-called 'castration fantasies' (Parens, Pollock, Stern, & Kramer, 1976); (5) in boys, the fear of the loss of, and injury to, testicles has been added to similar concerns regarding the penis (Bell, 1961); and (6) the universality of 'castration anxiety' has been questioned. Eddy de Klerk (2003, 2004), for instance, has suggested that the centrality of this phenomena in Freud's theory might be related to his experience of circumcision as an infant, which left subtle but indelible somatic memories that were activated with the entry into the phallic phase; de Klerk wonders if the concept of 'castration anxiety', developed in a small enclave of neonatally circumcised men, is a universally applicable concept or one with a relatively limited significance. With all these conflicting claims, the theory of 'castration anxiety' and 'castration complex' has lost the place of pride it earlier occupied. As it is, in adults one comes across such phenomena mostly via concerns displaced on to other regions of the body, or on to intellectual and social prowess. Counterphobic denial, leading to unnecessary bravado, and splitting of the ego, leading to 'fetishism' (see separate entry), are other indicators of subterranean 'castration anxiety'. However, in all these situations, an admixture of conflicts from multiple levels of development is unmistakably evident.

Castration complex: see ' Castration anxiety'.

Castrophilia: John Lindon's (1958) term for a relentless pattern of seeking social and professional defeats and disasters. These are unconscious equivalents of castration and gratify masochistic needs emanating from unresolved oedipal wishes. One does wonder whether the term 'castrophilia' might have an entirely different connotation in Havana!

Catastrophic aloneness: in a compelling ethnographic portrayal of serial killers, Sue Grand (2002) described the humiliation, abuse, and outright violence that such individuals have suffered during their childhood. One aspect of such psychic suffocation is 'catastrophic aloneness', i.e., a sense of isolation that is beyond the limits of human tolerance. This devastating and despairing isolation makes one feel sub-human or non-human. Inducing this painful feeling into someone else constitutes one among the many (e.g., sadism, narcissistic reversal of humiliation) motives for serial killing.

Cathartic method: therapeutic technique, evolved by Joseph Breuer and Sigmund Freud (1895d) at the turn of the nineteenth century, which emanated from a theory of undischarged and 'strangulated' (*eigeklemmt*) emotions being the cause of hysterical conversion symptoms. It was argued that liberating such emotions, by bringing to consciousness those traumatic experiences that had given rise to them, would lead to their proper discharge. Such 'abreaction' (see separate entry) would eliminate the energic substrate of the symptom, which will then disappear. With the abandonment of hypnotic and suggestive elements of technique, and with the gradual discovery of the structural and dynamic complexities of the mind, the 'cathartic method' gave way to a more sophisticated method of conducting analytic treatment that relied upon free-association, resistance analysis, and transference interpretation. Emotional release, or 'catharsis', became a subsidiary, even if integral, dimension of analytic therapy.

Cathexis: a neologism invented by the 'informal glossary committee' (Ornston, 1985, p. 391) made up of Ernest Jones, Alix and James Strachey, and Joan Riviere; this group quietly strove to create a psychoanalytic language during the course of translating Sigmund Freud's work into English. The word 'cathexis' was created to replace the German word *Besetzung*, which described the investment of psychic energy in an object or the self; this invention, in James Strachey's own words, 'later became a smash-hit'. One began talking of 'self-cathexis' or 'narcissistic cathexis' on the one hand, and of 'object cathexis' on the other. Issues of intensity and shifting interest also came to play a role in this linguistic context. Note the expression 'hypercathexis' (*uberbesetzung*), or powerful interest, and 'decathexis', or withdrawal of interest. Conflicting interests of id, ego, and superego were highlighted through the phrases 'anticathexis', or the more familiar 'counter-cathexis'. All in all, the term 'cathexis' and its various adjectival and verb forms are accompaniments of the economic perspective of 'metapsychology' (see separate entry). A hydraulic model of the mind and a quantitative dimension is clearly implied in these concepts. While Freud's translators can be 'blamed' for such overly scientific rendition, the variable of intensity (e.g., 'over-reaction', 'downplaying an emotion', 'understatement') is difficult, if not impossible, to avoid in any consideration of mental phenomena. See also Peter Hoffer's (2005) paper elucidating the difficulties in finding an adequate English substitute for the German word *Besetzung* and its various forms.

Censorship: idea proposed by Sigmund Freud (1900a) in the course of explaining the mechanism of dream formation; it was 'censorship' that resulted in the transformation of latent dream thoughts into their disguised representation via the 'manifest dream' (see separate entry). Freud's (1900a, 1915d, 1917b, 1923b) evolving view of 'censorship' includes the following five observations: (1) it is an ongoing activity, (2) it exists between the systems Conscious and Preconscious and between systems Preconscious and Unconscious, (3) it is not only responsible for the disguised material in dreams but also for the resistance to dream recall and interpretation, (4) its placement between systems Conscious and Preconscious is more permeable than its placement between the systems Preconscious and Unconscious, and (5) it is the function of superego; however, Freud (1923b) later attributed 'censorship' to the ego. His ideas were extended by other analysts, especially Joseph Sandler and Anne-Marie Sandler (1983) who, in describing their 'three box model of the mind' (see separate entry), delineated two subtypes of 'censorship'.

Central ego: see 'Fairbairn's description of endopsychic structure'.

Central phobic position: term originated by André Green (2000) to highlight that, in certain patients, there is a peculiar and frequent loss of the capacity for free association and psychological mindedness due to profound inner anxiety. These patients show vagueness of communication and blurring of discourse. They frequently put free association aside and resort to literalness and even somatization. Green postulates that this disturbance is based upon a 'central phobic position' characterized by (1) communicative failures in the form of inability to listen to oneself and the analyst, and difficulty in connecting the dots together even in the material that has been verbalized, (2) the keeping apart of various traumatic constellations by the means of associative avoidance, (3) arousal of profound anxiety at the prospect of bringing these 'encysted' (p. 436) traumatic memories and related associations into contact with each other, (4) a dimly experienced catastrophic threat from the superego's attack and from the fear of ego's disorganization, and (5) the countertransference experience that the analysand is confused and the analyst himself is becoming confused. The 'central phobic position' is most evident in clinical work in patients who are generally more troubled and might be considered 'borderline'.

Change of function: term originated by Heinz Hartmann (1939) for the fact that often a behaviour starts for one purpose and in a given context, but subsequently acquires a different purpose and context. What once was a means to realize an object-related fantasy might turn into a goal itself. The habit of smoking cigarettes is an example *par excellence*. Not infrequently acquired as a sign of adolescent rebellion, phallic exhibitionism, or identification with a public figure or parent who smokes, the habit gradually loses connection with its origins and becomes an automatism that is largely driven by the craving for nicotine.

Character: the reasonably and enduring predictable pattern of an individual's psychosocial functioning. Understood psychodynamically, character is the person's usual mode of reconciling intrapsychic wishes, developmental needs, moral prohibitions, and demands of external reality. Character traits, like neurotic symptoms, are compromised formations between these forces. But character traits are more stable than symptoms and are experienced more as part of one's self. How a person's developing character is affected by his or her parents depends upon the stage of development at which crucial situations involving trauma and conflict arise. It also depends upon whether the child adopts the parents' affirming or prohibiting attitudes and whether he or she seeks to disidentify with them. Inborn affectomotor potentialities ('temperament') also help determine whether conflicts are solved by reality-adjusted, well-integrated and flexible behaviour, or by pathological and inflexible means. Francis Baudry (1995) has provided the most comprehensive synthesis, so far, of the psychoanalytic literature on the topic of character and the reader will benefit from a perusal of it (see also Baudry, 1989).

Character armour: term introduced by Wilhelm Reich (1933) to underscore that rigid character traits often manifest through bodily stance and thus create a defensive wall, as it were, around the deeper psychic structure. Such 'character armour' includes the way people breathe, stand, walk, and move, with all such musculo-skeletal attributes serving the purpose of instinctual discharge and ego defence.

Character integrity: Mardi Horowitz's (2002) term for the 'intrapsychic pattern of organizing, harmonizing, and using beliefs, motives, and values that concern self and others' (p. 554). 'Character integrity' effects how the individual responds to instinctual urges, reality dictates, and internalized moral pressures. As a structure, it is both enduring and subject to slowly accruing change.

Horowitz classifies 'character integrity' in three levels: (1) *high-level* implies complex and relatively harmonious schematizations of self and others. Projective mechanisms are minimal, and discordant affects and moral dilemmas are tolerated and seen as emanating from within oneself; (2) *middle-level* shows lesser capacity for integration of contradictory self and object representations. Instinctual urges and moral dictates against them are constantly at war and decision-making capacity is compromised; (3) *low-level* is characterized by impulsivity, dramatically shifting self assessment, and intensification of affects. The sense of identity is incoherent and unstable. According to Horowitz, this typology is useful in guiding empathic attunement and the level of therapeutic interventions. While he offers more details, the most cogent point he makes in this regard is that 'lower-level patients, and higher-level patients with stress-induced regressions, are more likely to benefit from a slower technique, one that uses small packets of information, explicit repetition of seemingly obvious facts, and help in establishing lucid sequencing through a conflicted train of thought' (p. 569).

Character neurosis: a neurotic constellation in which the ego and superego are altered in order to conform to the dictates of the id. The resulting disorder is ego-syntonic and relies heavily upon 'externalization' and 'rationalization' (see separate entries). An appearance of normality is achieved at the cost of considerable counter-cathexis and behavioural rigidity. In today's terms, 'character neuroses' are roughly equivalent to 'personality disorders' (see separate entry).

Character pathology: see 'Personality disorders'.

Character perversion: term coined by Jacob Arlow (1971) for a particular type of personality constellation in which defences typical of perverse activities appear as character traits. There is no overt sexual perversion, however. Individuals with 'character perversion' ignore the demands of reality and/or seize on peripheral matters to focus upon. Arlow likened this attitude to 'voyeurism' and 'fetishism' (see separate entries), in which the sight of a female genital stirs up intense castration anxiety and leads to repudiation of its reality. Thirteen years later, Janine Chasseguet-Smirgel (1984) independently described the similar appearing 'perverse character' (see separate entry) founded upon the denial of sexual and generational differences. Her explanation, however, rested less on castration anxiety hypothesis and more on seduction by the mother

which made the boy feel that he was already a man. significantly, both Arlow and Chasseguet-Smirgel focused upon male patients when it came to outlining this syndrome. In contrast, Lee Grossman (1992) reported a female case of 'character perversion'. He underscored how 'looking away, looking without seeing, looking without experiencing as real, looking only at parts, looking without focusing, or focusing elsewhere' (p. 587) helped his patient repudiate disturbing aspects of reality.

Character resistance: term introduced by Wilhelm Reich (1933) to underscore that certain behavioural tendencies can serve as a resistance during analysis and that these remain stereotypically the same no matter what the material is against which they are directed. Such rigidity of habitual defensive manoeuvres (e.g., talkativeness, haughtiness, politeness) evolved in order to keep the advancing intrapsychic conflicts in abeyance. In contrast to resistances burn-out of transference, 'character resistance' is more diffuse and less connected to specific fantasies involving the analyst.

Character traits: see 'Classification of character traits'.

Child analysis: although Sigmund Freud's (1909b) treatment of Little Hans, a five-year-old boy with a fear of horses, set the foundations for child analysis, the fact is that this work was accomplished largely by communicating with the boy's father; Freud himself saw the boy only once. None the less, the groundwork was laid and Hermine Hug-Hellmuth became the first clinician to practice psychoanalysis with children. Melanie Klein and Anna Freud soon followed. Since children were neither able to free associate nor abide by the formal structure (e.g., lying on the couch) of analysis, other ways had to be found to decipher and interpret their unconscious dynamics. From such dilemmas arose the awareness that talk and action cannot be separated from each other in their case, and their play activities provided a pathway *par excellence* to the depths of their minds. To what degree the play itself could be equated with free association, how rapidly and directly its symbolic nature could be interpreted, and to what extent a child who was still dependent upon the parents could develop a full-blown transference, soon became matters of controversy between Melanie Klein and Anna Freud and their respective followers. The necessity of a preparatory phase before interpretation, the sessile *vs.* mobile position of the analyst, the impact of ongoing development on psychopathology and technique, and the degree to which the child's parents could or should be involved in the treatment, became other topics of debate and, to a certain extent, remain contested even today.

Childhood amnesia: see 'Infantile amnesia'.

Choice conflict: see 'Decision making function of the ego'.

Choice of neurosis: an expression used by Sigmund Freud (1896, 1913c) to denote the process by which a particular neurotic symptomatology as opposed to another one develops in an individual. The process is highly complex and not entirely fathomable. A large number of variables contribute to such 'choice'. These include constitutional endowment, nature of traumatic events, age and the degree of ego maturity at the time of trauma, subsequent events of both ameliorative and fixating types, vulnerability to regression, and so on. One thing, however, is clear: the term 'choice' here does not refer to the intellectual selection of one among many possible options. As a result, it is safe to say that, in the setting of psychic determinism, the usage of a word like 'choice' bears Freud's characteristic wry stamp.

Chosen glories: Vamik Volkan (1988, 2004, 2006) coined this term to denote the idealization of an ethnic or national group's past triumphs and successes. Recollection of such events is often surrounded by rituals and the events themselves are heavily mythologized over time. 'Chosen glories' are passed on to successive generations through parent/teacher–child interactions and through participation in ritualistic ceremonies recalling past successful events. The mental representations of such glories are saturated with derivatives of the libidinal drive; it is pleasurable to share them with younger generations. The shared importance of such events, whether recent or ancient, real or mythologized, helps to bind the individuals in a large group together. In stressful situations or times of war, leaders reactivate the mental representation of 'chosen glories' (and heroes associated with them) to bolster their large-group identity. A leader's reference to chosen glories excites his followers simply by stimulating an already existing shared large-group marker.

Chosen traumas: according to Vamik Volkan (1987, 2004, 2006), a 'chosen trauma' is the shared mental representation of an event in a large group's history in which the group suffered a catastrophic loss, humiliation, and helplessness at the hands of its enemies. When members of a victim group are unable to mourn such losses and reverse their humiliation and helplessness, they pass on to their offspring the images of their injured selves and psychological tasks that need to be completed. As time passes, the mental representation of the traumatic event becomes a link between the members of that particular group. Indeed, it can become a significant large-group identity marker. A chosen trauma reflects the 'infection' of a large-group's mourning process, and its reactivation serves to link the members of a large group. Such reactivation can be used by the political leadership to promote new societal movements, some of them deadly and malignant.

Christmas neurosis: Bryce Boyer's (1955) label for depression occurring around Christmas as a result of the activation of unresolved sibling rivalries. The celebration of the birth of Christ, a fantasied rival with whom one is unable to compete, re-awaken memories of unsuccessful rivalry with siblings. This stimulates oral conflicts and helpless rage.

Chronic misfits: see 'Misfits'.

Civilizational anxiety: Jonathan Lear's (2007) phrase for the widespread contemporary dread that civilization, as each individual large group knows it, is vulnerable. He notes the emergence of deep divisions between Europe and America, between West and East, between secular and religious peoples, and between various stripes of religious folks. Calling the fear of extinction that each feels 'civilizational anxiety', Lear states that 'there is anxiety about globalization overwhelming traditional cultures, about secularization undermining religious values, about Islam over running Europe, (and) about Western culture overrunning Islam' (p. 294).

Civilizing influence of the daughter: According to Salman Akhtar (quoted in Kieffer, 2008, p. 80) the presence of a daughter in a family exerts a 'civilizing influence' upon the father. Five factors account for this. (i) First of all is the delicateness with which the father handles his female baby; cultural expectations, injunctions from the baby's mother, and his own psychobiological intuition impel a greater amount of aim-inhibition of aggression in the father. In learning to be gentler with his girl than he is with his boy, the father altruistically gives up the satisfaction of his assertive–aggressive impulses. (ii) A second factor is comprised by the greater distance the father takes from his daughter's naked body from early on; in this process, there is suppression, repression, and actual renunciation, via mourning, of dormant voyeuristic impulses (that were, at least in part, a reactivation of his boyhood curiosities about his mother's body). (iii) A third factor is comprised by the daughter being a female who (like mother and, to a lesser extent, sister) is a combination of an object and a selfobject; this increases cross-gender knowledge and empathy. (iv) Teaching ego skills to a girl imparts a sense to the father that execution of tasks is not a so-called phallic prerogative. This diminishes his masculine narcissism and makes him humbler. (v) Finally, having to renounce sexual gratification, while retaining a modicum of the erotic resonance, in response to the girl's oedipal overtures (both during her childhood and later when she is blossoming into a young woman), strengthens the incest barrier in the father's mind. Together, these five factors lead to a measure of restraint, humility, and cross-gender tenderness. The fact that much more poetry has been written by male poets about their daughters than about their sons gives testimony to the irreducible, subterranean discontent with such civility as well as to the sublimated pleasures of restraint.

Clarification: a term coined by Carl Rogers (1942) to denote a therapeutic intervention that helps the patient to 'see much more clearly' (p. 41) and achieve clearer differentiation of the meanings of things to him. 'Clarification' consists of restating the feelings which accompany the main train of thought, or of rearranging seemingly unrelated clusters of thought in a meaningful manner. Such restating does not transcend the phenomenological level and is based entirely upon explicit statements made by the patient. Otto Kernberg (1984) regards 'clarification' to be 'the first cognitive step in which what the patient says is discussed in a non-questioning way in order to bring out all its implications and to discover the extent of his understanding or confusion regarding what remains unclear' (p. 8). Unlike 'interpretation' (see separate entry), clarification does not refer to unconscious material. Consequently it 'does not encounter resistance, at least not in the proper sense as originating from unconscious defenses against the material being made conscious, as it appears in reaction to interpretation' (Bibring, 1954, p. 756). As a rule, patients react to clarification with surprise, intellectual pleasure, and enhancement of self-observing functions.

Classic and romantic visions of psychoanalysis: in a scholarly paper of great clinical relevance, Carlo Strenger (1989) noted that two divergent visions of the human condition underlie a chronic and fundamental rift in the field of psychoanalysis. Strenger named these as the 'classic' and 'romantic' visions. The former holds striving towards autonomy and the reign of reason to be the essence of being human. The latter values authenticity and spontaneity over logic and consensus. Each vision exerts a powerful influence upon psychoanalytic theory. 'The *classic view* sees man as governed by the pleasure principle and the development towards maturity is that towards the predominance of the reality principle. The analyst's attitude towards the patient is a combination of respect and suspicion and the analyst takes the side of the reality principle. The ethic is stoic: maturity and mental health depend on the extent to which a person can acknowledge reality as it is and be rational and wise. The romantic view sees man as striving towards becoming a cohesive self. Development aims at a self which consists of a continuous flow from ambitions to ideals, from a sense of vitality towards goals which are experienced as intrinsically valuable. Mental suffering is the result of the failure of the environment to fulfill the self-object function and the patient's symptoms are the desperate attempt to fill the vacuum in his depleted self. The analyst's attitude towards the patient is one of trust in his humanity and the analyst takes the side of joy and vitality. The ethic is romantic: maturity and mental health consist in the ability to sustain enthusiasm and a sense of meaning' (Strenger, 1989, p. 601). All this has technical consequences. The classic attitude prompts scepticism and a listening geared to deciphering the ways in which the patient's internal reality colours his perception of reality; the romantic vision mobilizes credulousness and a listening geared to discerning the healthy striving for wholeness and vitality in the patient's communications. Not surprisingly, the former attitude yields interventions that address resistance and facilitate uncovering, while the latter yields interventions that support and enhance the validity of patient's experience. Other aspects of technique, not spelled out by Strenger, are also affected by these two visions (Akhtar, 2000). These include (1) *view of transference*: the first approach views transference as a re-creation of early object relations, the second approach regards transference to be a search for new objects; (2) *view of resistance*: the classic approach values verbalization and therefore views the patient's silences as resistance to the process; the romantic approach emphasizes that the patient is always communicating something important to the analyst, and his or her silence is one way of doing so; (3) *recognition of the* *therapist's role*: in the classic approach, the therapist's role is technical and interpretive, while in the romantic approach it is mutative via empathic relatedness and development facilitation; (4) the classic approach regards *the therapist's personality* as significant only in so far as it is a constituent of technique, while the romantic approach regards the warmth and authenticity of the therapist to be of central importance; (5) the classic approach deems *deep regression during the treatment* undesirable, since it threatens therapeutic alliance, while the romantic approach regards it as essential for a new beginning to become possible; (6) while both views acknowledge *acting out* to be inevitable, the classic view considers it an undesirable spilling over into life of material that should be brought to conscious awareness in treatment, and the romantic approach views it as a desperate manifestation of hope that the environment (now embodied by the therapist) will reverse the damage it has done; (7) the main *countertransference* risk of the classic approach is that the analyst might become judgemental while the main risk of the romantic approach is that the analyst might become overindulgent. These distinctions highlight the fact that an exclusive adherence to either of these approaches entails technical tradeoffs. A dedicatedly 'romantic' approach can preclude uncovering, interpretive work, whereas a strictly 'classic' approach can overlook the importance of empathic, stabilizing measures. Most practising analysts, therefore, intuitively strike their own variety of balance between the two positions.

Classification of character traits: Otto Fenichel (1945) categorized 'character traits' into two types: (1) *sublimation type*, whereby a successful aim-inhibition of problematic drives is achieved and 'the ego forms a channel and not a dam for the instinctual stance' (pp. 470–471); and (2) *reactive type*, which are either rigid avoidances (phobic attitudes) or strong oppositions (reaction formations) to instinctual aims. Fenichel added that these two types of traits often co-exist and a characterological diagnosis should be based upon the predominance, and not the exclusive occurrence, of one over the other.

Cloacal anxiety: Karen Gilmore's (1998) term for the 'typically female fear that the genital is dirty, messy, and disgusting, and the feeling that sexual impulses are repellant, explosive, and out of control' (p. 447). Such anxiety is often associated with a feeling of shame. Its origins go back to the first three years of a girl's life, during which the emergent sense of gender identity is impacted upon by anal phase conflicts of aggression and separa-

tion–individuation. Such early 'cloacal anxiety' is reorganized under the influence of oedipal phase issues and elaborated with further development. In Gilmore's view, this anxiety is a typically feminine manifestation of a tension that is ubiquitous in human experience, namely the fear of intensity of drives.

Cloacal theory: designation given by Sigmund Freud (1908c) to children's idea, based upon the ignorance of vagina, that the anus is the orifice used for coitus and for babies to come out of the mother's 'tummy'. The fantasy gains strength from the psychic vicissitudes of the 'anal phase' (see separate entry) as well.

Close process analysis: see 'Close process monitoring'.

Close process attention: see 'Close process monitoring'.

Close process monitoring: a particular type of 'analytic listening' (see separate entry) associated with the technical approach of Paul Gray (1982, 1994). Such listening homes in on the moment-to-moment shifts of emphasis and nuance in the stream of the patient's associations. It pays sharp attention to a pause, an abrupt change of topic, the emergence of an incongruent affect, and an unexplained avoidance of the logically expectable. Observing such occurrences and bringing them to the anaysand's awareness makes resistance analysis possible. Frequently, it also unmasks hidden transference proclivities. Moreover, helping the patient see that thoughts following each other are causally connected strengthens the alliance to carry on analytic work. Gray's ideas have been further elaborated upon by Walter Davison, Monroe Pray, and Curtis Bristol (1990) and Fred Busch (2004). These contributors acknowledge that some patients, especially those in the throes of a regressive transference, might not be able to participate in the 'close process monitoring' driven work. They point out that 'close process monitoring' puts the ego in the centre of analytic technique, that interventions thus derived focus on process more than upon content, and that interventions work best when they underscore 'the shortest possible time interval of process in which the analysand can experience a shift in feeling' (Davison, Pray, & Bristol, 1990, p. 613). While this approach has gained wide respect, an interesting footnote to this matter is that Paul Gray dropped the word 'monitoring', since it gave the impression of the analyst watching something from high above and began calling his approach 'close process attention', a phrase that gradually gave way to the more *au courant* 'close process analysis' (Monroe Pray, personal communication, 7 April 2008).

Co-conscious mentation: term evolved by Charles Oberndorf (1941) from Morton Prince's (1929) description of 'co-consciousness' in the setting of multiple personality disorder. While Prince had used the term for the pre-conscious, or, at times, even unconscious, knowledge of one set of ideas by the other, Oberndorf focused upon the *conscious* awareness of simultaneous thoughts that were unrelated to each other. According to Oberndorf, 'co-conscious mentation' consists of two streams of thought, 'not necessarily flowing in the same direction, but aware of each other through tangential impulses from one current to the other in their flow' (p. 45). The phenomenon of listening to a lecture while planning a response and also noticing the reactions of the audience constitutes an example of 'co-conscious mentation' in day-to-day life. Oberndorf outlined three forms of 'co-conscious mentation': (1) the concomitant passive registration of irrelevant content while paying attention to something else; (2) an ongoing criticism of the content of intentional thought; and (3) thinking about topics unrelated to primary thought. Pathological forms are evident in obsessional ruminations about oneself, and in feelings of 'derealization' and 'depersonalization' (see separate entries on both). More recently, Ira Brenner (2001) has used the term 'co-consciousness' to denote the stage when a strengthened observing ego makes a centrally held awareness of hitherto dissociated selves possible. 'Co-consciousness' is therefore a welcome development in the treatment of 'multiple personality' or 'dissociative identity disorder' (see 'Dissociative character').

Co-consciousness: see 'Co-conscious mentation'.

Cocoon phase: described by Arnold Modell (1975a), this refers to the early phase of the analytic treatment of narcissistic personalities when the patient is heavily defended against affects and attachment to the analyst. The patient acts as if the analyst is not there; he retains an illusory self-sufficiency in the clinical setting. It is as if he were encased in a plastic bubble or cocoon. However, 'a cocoon, no matter how well insulated, needs to be attached to something, and these people who may deny their dependent needs usually crave admiration' (p. 276).

Co-foreconscious mentation: see 'Co-conscious mentation'.

Collated internal object: Masud Khan's (1979) term for the amalgamated introject evolved out of split and discordant objects of the future pervert's childhood. Parallel to the development of such 'collated internal object' is that of an ego 'collage'. It is through the highly sexualized interplay between these structures that the pervert can experience a sense of vitality. The fact that the pervert's internal structure is not integrated leads to his continous proclivity to act out.

Collective unconscious: see 'Primal phantasies'.

Colonial countertransference: see 'Colonialism and psychoanalysis'.

Colonial transference: see 'Colonialism and psychoanalysis'.

Colonialism and psychoanalysis: the penetrating deconstructions of the Western gaze at the colonized people of Africa and Asia by Edward Said (1979) and Frantz Fanon (1952, 1959) constitute the starting points for a consideration of 'colonialism and psychoanalysis'. Also contributing to this stream of thought are Jacques Derrida's (1998) sociopolitical critique of organized psychoanalysis, Christopher Lane's (1998) discourse on psychoanalysis and race, Ranjana Khanna's (2004) book on colonialism and depth-psychology, and Maria Teresa Hooke and Salman Akhtar's (2007) volume about the transgenerational consequences of history in lands whose original inhabitants were brutally decimated by colonial settlers. The recently emerging application of psychoanalytic ideas to understanding and treating 'oriental' folk and 'people of colour' (Akhtar; 1999b; Bonovitz, 1998; Holmes, 1992; Kakar, 1985; Leary, 1995, 1997; Perez-Foster, Moskowitz, & Javier, 1996; Ng, 1985; Smolar, 1999, etc.) adds to the clinical dimension of this realm. The collective conclusion of these diverse tracts is that psychoanalysis, evolved in the West and, in many ways, reflective of White Euro-American norms, has regarded people of former colonies (to varying degrees, now under the influence of neo-colonialism) with an uninformed and biased perspective. And, those viewed through this provincial prism have paid back in the usual currency of the devalued, that is, by idealizing the West, until they are awakened from this collusive dream. Three psychoanalytic realms in which all this is evident include (1) *organizational*, whereby the administration of the International Psychoanalytic Association is divided into three regions, namely Europe, North America, and Latin America. This leaves the entire continents of Africa and Asia unrepresented or, at least, un-named; note, in this connection, that India and Israel, which do have psychoanalytic organizations, are included in Europe and, even more curiously, so is Australia; (2) *academic*, whereby early British analysts like Owen Berkely-Hill (1921) and Claude Dangar-Daly (1930) felt free to write condescendingly of the Hindu character, for instance. The tone of pleasant surprise in the 1970s North American reports on 'inter-racial psychoanalysis' (see separate entry) paradoxically betrayed the prevalence of a mind-set to the contrary. In addition, discussions of 'psychoanalysis and culture', until today, have been frequently limited to Western culture with little mention of Asian and African cultures; the January 2007 issue of *Psychoanalytic Quarterly* is a shining exception to this trend; (3) *clinical*, whereby the impact of the national and cultural difference between White (especially European) analysts and their analysands from erstwhile colonized countries goes relatively unmentioned. That such analyses might be riddled with 'colonial transference' (e.g., idealization, fear, mistrust) and 'colonial countertransference' (e.g., contempt, fear, mistrust) does not receive the attention it might deserve. Masud Khan's analyses (with Ella Freeman Sharpe, John Rickman, and Donald Winnicott) in England, when India had barely become independent from the British rule, most likely also contained such dynamics (Akhtar, 2007a). Even outside of such larger than life drama, attitudes coloured by a colonial mentality are occasionally discernible in the treatment and supervision of analytic candidates from the 'third world' nations (Sripada, 1999).

Colour in dreams: in his seminal work on dreams, Sigmund Freud (1900a) mentioned the appearance of colour in dreams three times. Each time he delared that this represented a visual stimulus. In other words, the wish underlying the dream had been mobilized by something one had actually seen. Subsequent analysts added that (1) dreaming in colour is perhaps more common than reporting of 'colour in dreams' (Miller, 1964); (2) that particular colours may express specific affects and even certain drive organizations; 'through synaesthesia color may simulate other sensory modalities such as sound or movement sensation and vice versa' (Blum, 1964, p. 529); (3) appearance of colour in dreams happens with greater frequency in interracial analyses (Myers, 1977) and (4) in partially colour-blind patients serves as a denial of their handicap (Yazmajian, 1983).

Combined parent figure: Melanie Klein's (1929) term for an imago formed in the child's mind through his or her attacks on the mother's body, especially as it is envisioned in intercourse with the father. The 'combined parent figure' consists of a hostile mother containing a hostile penis and is a source of deep anxiety for the child. The child views the mother's insides as dangerous and finds it to have become more frightening by the entry of his 'bad' father's penis into it. To the little child, 'these united parents are extremely cruel and much dreaded assailants' (p. 213). In addition to its original Kleinian meaning, 'combined parent figure' can also stand for the internal representation evolved by children who are inoptimally exposed to healthy and rational disagreements between parents. Raised in a formalized and rigid manner, where the two parents *always* support each other, even when one of them is being harsh and oppressive towards the child, such children do not have sufficient differentiation between the images of mother and father.

Combined treatment: see 'Medication and psychoanalysis'.

Common mirror dreams: see 'Mirror dreams'.

Compassionate neutrality: see 'Neutrality'.

Compensatory structures: see 'Defensive and compensatory structures'.

Complemental series: Sigmund Freud's (1916–1917) term for the fact that causation of neurotic disorders is dependent upon the interplay between endogenous and exogenous factors. Thus 'fixation' (see separate entry) and 'psychic trauma' (see separate entry) both play a role here. If the fixation is tenacious, even a minor trauma can precipitate symptoms. If the fixation is mild, however, greater trauma is needed to cause illness. And, fixation itself can result from hereditary predisposition or from childhood experience. Such dialectical forces constitute what Freud called 'complemental series'.

Complementary countertransference: see 'Countertransference'.

Complex self: see 'Simple and complex selves'.

Compliance with the introject: described by Phyllis and Robert Tyson (1984), this concept refers to a step in the development of superego. Its achievement is evident when the child shows obedience to the mother's rules and regulations even in her absence. 'Compliance with introject' further consolidates self and object constancy as it ensures the cathexis of the internal mother representation.

Compliance with the object: described by Phyllis and Robert Tyson (1984), this is a step in the development of superego. It preceedes 'compliance with the introject' (see separate entry) and consists of a toddler's obeying his parents' (especially his mother's) dictates and controlling his impulses in order to gain a sense of safety and self-esteem via parental approval. In the specific contexts of excretory functions, Sandor Ferenczi (1925b) termed such compliance as 'sphincter morality' (see separate entry).

Component instincts: Sigmund Freud's (1905a) term for a central feature of 'infantile sexuality' (see separate entry). Sexual gratification through orgasmic discharge via genitals does not characterize 'infantile sexuality'. Instead it is driven by 'component' or 'partial instincts'; the prefix 'component' underscores that these instincts are constituents of the full adult sexuality and not complete in and of themselves. According to Freud, 'component instincts' (1) arise from the evolving erogenous zones (e.g., mouth, anus) of childhood, (2) are independent of each other, (3) can become intermingled, (4) are governed by 'pleasure–unpleasure principle' (see separate entry), (5) have active and passive aims, (6) provide only forepleasure, and (7) fuse with each other over the course of development and come to serve the aims of 'genital primacy' (see separate entry). The last mentioned point has a differential diagnostic significance. In normalcy, 'component instincts' find expression only during foreplay and, through the process of sublimation, in creativity. In neuroses, 'component instincts' remain strong, necessitate powerful defences, and 'return' by attaching themselves to aspects of reality that then become disgust or fear provoking. In sexual perversions, 'component instincts' create a psychic fiefdom of their own, co-opt the part of the ego to live them out, and become capable of yielding and pleasure.

Compromise formation: Sigmund Freud (1896b) talked of the formation of 'a compromise between the repressed ideas and the repressing ones' (p. 170) in his earliest consideration of how obsessional ideas are formed. Gradually, however, this notion spread over a wide array of phenomena and Freud (1900a, 1916–1917) began to view dreams, symptoms, and parapraxes all as resulting from intrapsychic 'compromise formations'. Robert Waelder (1936), in his oft-cited paper 'The principle of multiple function', gave a thorough

metapsychological grounding to this idea; in his view, all feelings, thoughts, and behaviours represent the ego's attempt at a 'compromise formation' between the demands of id, superego, and reality. This perspective became a darling of North American psychoanalysis (e.g., Arlow & Brenner, 1964; Brenner, 1982), which, until recently, was dominated by 'ego psychology' (see separate entry). A nuanced view of psychopathology, character traits, dreams, and events of the clinical hour was the yield of such enthusiasm. At the same time, the drive to see everything as a 'compromise formation' contributed to a stilted view of borderline and psychotic conditions, where the role of defects and deficits of ego functions takes precedence over dynamic compromise formations. Finally, mention must be made of Bradley Peterson's (2002) sophisticated discussion of how 'compromise formations' make ample and free use of the 'indeterminacy' of meanings to satisfy simultaneously the multiple competing of mental existence.

Compromise of integrity: syndrome described by Leo Rangell (1974) where the intrapsychic struggle between the ego and superego leads to splits in the self and the tendency towards dishonesty and deceit. The impetus for compromise of integrity is unbridled narcissism. Comparing 'compromise integrity' to other forms of psychopathology, Rangell noted that 'in the neuroses, the id is sacrificed; in psychosis, reality; in compromise of integrity, the superego' (p. 8). Since the 'fluidity of the superego enables it to serve as a bridge between the individual and the group' (p. 8), the manifestations of 'compromise of integrity' are found in the unethical and complicit behaviour of both individuals and groups.

Compulsive character: see 'Obsessional character'.

Compulsive passion for work: see 'Work compulsion'.

Concentrated analysis: refers to a format for clinical psychoanalysis where more than one session is held in a day, though the treatment is limited to two consecutive days or a weekend. Junquiera Mattos (1996) has reported extensively on this practice and Burton Hutto (1998), a North Carolina based analyst, has written about his own 'concentrated analysis', which took place before it was converted into a conventional treatment. From these reports, it seems evident that the treatment can work this way, and the advantage is that psychoanalysis becomes available to those who live quite far from their analyst. This has clear implications for the spread of psychoanalysis in those areas of the world with few psychoanalysts. Hutto adds that proclivity to acting out and history of early loss might be relative contraindications to 'concentrated analysis'. He also notes that analysis of dreams generally suffers in this type of work.

Concordant countertransference: see 'Countertransference'.

Concretism: term coined by Ilse Grubrich-Simitis (1984) to denote a type of mentality seen in the early stages of the psychoanalytic treatment of the offspring of Holocaust survivors. 'Concretism' is characterized by the loss of 'ego function of metaphorization'; this function is effective in regulating drives by linking reality (inner and outer) with representation, and by creating and sustaining the world of imagination. Individuals with 'concretism' 'regard what they have to say as thing-like. They appear not to regard it as something imagined or remembered, or something having a sign character. The open-ended quality of fantasy life is missing. Instead the expressions have a peculiarly fixed and unalterable quality, which may at first sight strike one as psychotic' (p. 302). However, these patients are not psychotic. They are the children of Holocaust survivors who were subject to dehumanizing cruelties, including meaningless labour, incarceration, and physical torture. They suffered a violent attack not only on their bodies, but also upon their identities and their secondary process thinking. This undermined their capacity for metaphorical use of speech. The transgenerational transmission of such ego impairment resulted in the 'concretism' manifested by the second generation.

Concretization: process by which abstract thinking is given up in favour of literalness and physicalistic causality. 'Concretization' can be due to severe ego regression, as seen in schizophrenia (Arieti, 1974), defensive retreat from fantasy life during adolescence (Blos, 1967), or inhibition of intellect by guilt (Blackman, 2004). With variable intensity and scope, the cognitive direction under these circumstances is towards loss of metaphor, decline in wit, search for external explanations of behaviour, swings into literalness, and compromised capacity for dialogue.

Condensation: a mental mechanism first described by Sigmund Freud (1900a) as being central to the formation of the manifest dream. This mechanism achieves brevity and overlap that are typical of dreams. It operates in many ways. Most commonly, it fuses disparate elements possessing one common denominator into a composite whole. At other times, persons from one era of life or one particular place are shown in the context of an entirely different era or place. Yet another manner in which condensation operates is by omitting portions of latent dream content and letting only unimportant elements appear in the manifest dream. While condensation is most often thought of in connection with dreams, the fact is that many parapraxes (especially, slips of the tongue) are the result of this mechanism as well. Neologisms are also formed by condensation, and so are certain jokes (Freud, 1905c). In all these circumstances, condensation seems to strike a compromise between mental censorship on the one hand, and free expression of feelings and fantasies on the other.

Conditioned daydreaming: see 'Analyst's work ego'.

Confident expectation: see 'Basic trust'.

Conflict: Heinz Hartmann (1939) stated that 'conflicts are part of the human condition' (p. 12) and Ernst Kris (1947) declared that the subject matter of psychoanalysis is nothing but 'human behavior viewed as conflict' (p. 6). Charles Brenner (1976, 1982) provided a wide-ranging explication of this theme and there remains a broad consensus among analysts that the concept of conflict is basic to the understanding of human mental functioning, both in health and illness. However, the word 'conflict' encompasses a large number of phenomena. These can be organized around the following five binaries: (1) *external* vs. *internal conflicts:* the former refer to those between an individual and his environment, while the latter refer to those within his own psyche; (2) *externalized* vs. *internalized conflicts:* the former pertain to internal conflicts that have been transposed upon external reality, and the latter to the psychic problems caused by the incorporation of environmental dictates opposing one's drives; (3) *developmental conflicts* vs. *anachronistic conflicts:* the former refer to conflicts caused by parental challenges to the child's wishes or by contradictory wishes of the child himself (Nagera, 1966), and the latter to conflicts that are not age-specific and underlie psychopathology during adulthood, (4) *inter-systemic* vs. *intra-systemic conflicts:* the former refers to the tension between id and ego or between ego and superego, the latter (A. Freud, 1965) to that between different instinctual tendencies (e.g., homosexual and heterosexual), or different ego attributes (e.g., activity and passivity), or different superego dictates (e.g., modesty and success); (5) *structural conflict* vs. *object relations conflict*: the former refers to a stressful divergence of agenda between the three major psychic structures, namely id, ego, and superego, and the latter refers to a conflict in a psychic structure that is antecedent to such structural differentiation (see entry on 'object-relation conflicts'); and (6) *opposition type conflict* vs. *dilemma of choice type conflict* (Rangell, 1963a), or its partial reincarnation as *convergent* vs. *divergent conflicts* (Kris, 1984, 1985): the former refers to conflicts between intrapsychic forces which can be brought together by a compromise formation, the latter to those conflicts where such negotiation is unlikely and choosing one side of the pull (hence, mourning over renouncing the alternative course) is imperative. These are also called 'either/or conflicts'. In the end, it should also be noted that the centrality accorded to the concept of 'conflict' might reflect the North American ego psychological bent of theorizing. Reviewing the status of this concept in the broader context of psychoanalysis at large, Jorge Canestri (2005) has noted that, in Europe, greater attention has been given to preconflictual states than to 'conflict' *per se*, though the latter is always lurking in the background.

Conflicts of self-protection: Axel Hoffer's (1985) designation of intrapsychic conflicts that develop around efforts to hide 'ego deficits' and the fierce neediness that often accompanies them. 'Feelings of shame and self-contempt are associated not only with the perceived "deficit" itself, but also with the desperate, often vengeful efforts to obtain compensation for it' (p. 773).

Confrontation: not listed in the index of the *Standard Edition* of Sigmund Freud's complete works, and not mentioned in prominent books on psychotherapy (Menninger & Holzman, 1973; Ursano, Sonnenberg, & Lazar, 1998), the term 'confrontation' seems to have made its appearance in the early 1950s. George Devereux (1951) wrote the first paper with the word 'confrontation' in its title. He proposed that 'confrontation' is 'an analytic device only insofar as it leads to the production of some new material, which is eventually interpreted in terms of the logic of the unconscious' (p. 21). Ira Miller (1963) defined 'confrontation' as 'that aspect of what is said to a patient which is aimed at pointing out distortion of reality' (pp. 66–67). In the treatment of relatively ego-syntonic disorders, consistent 'confrontation' serves to institute a conflict within the ego, causing the symptoms to become somewhat

ego-dystonic. In contemporary approaches to borderline patients (Kernberg, Selzer, Koenigsberg, Carr, & Applebaum, 1989; Yeomans, Selzer, & Clarkin, 1992), the technique of 'confrontation' is used less for reality testing purposes and more for helping the patient reflect upon major contradictions within himself.

Confusion of tongues: in a paper that contained this phrase in its title, Sandor Ferenczi (1933) stated that neurosis was the result of sexual abuse by parents and their obfuscation of the child's perception of this trauma. He declared that 'sexual trauma as the pathogenic factor cannot be valued highly enough' (p. 161) and psychoanalytic treatment should give greater importance to empathy, validation, active interventions, and countertransference. The reaction to Ferenczi's paper was, however, quite negative; Sigmund Freud was outraged. He saw it not only as repeating his early 'seduction hypothesis' (see separate entry), but as an attack against his notions about the fantasy life of children and especially his postulate of the 'Oedipus complex' (see separate entry). Subsequent authors have portrayed the battle that then ensued between Freud and Ferenczi as one of the 'saddest, most tragic' (Aron & Harris, 1993, p. 2) and 'darkest moments in the history of psychoanalysis' (Rachman, 1993, p. 89).

Conscience anxiety: see 'Moral masochism'.

Conscious: one among the three psychic systems identified by Sigmund Freud (1900a, 1915a, 1915c) in his 'topographic theory' (see separate entry). The system 'conscious' was closest to the surface and received information from the external as well as the internal (psychic and somatic) worlds. It worked through verbal representations and operated on the basis of 'secondary process' thinking (see 'primary and secondary processes'). Unlike its counterparts in the topographic model ('preconscious' and 'unconscious'), the system 'conscious' did not contain persistent mnemic traces. A barrier separated 'conscious' from 'preconscious'; this barrier was more permeable than the 'censorship' (see separate entry) between 'preconscious' and 'unconscious'. With the replacement of the 'topographical theory' by 'structural theory' (see separate entry), a tendency grew to equate 'conscious' with the ego. However, this is only partly true, since parts of the ego (e.g., those involved in defensive functions) are not conscious at all.

Consciousness: following the 'topographic theory' of the mind, it is tempting to equate 'consciousness' with the activity of the system 'Conscious' (see separate entries). As a consequence, 'consciousness' would appear to be characterized by secondary process thinking and verbal representations; it would be devoid of persistent mnemic traces. However, such a picture is incomplete, since primary process material can certainly enter into 'consciousness' (e.g., during the moments of creative imagination), and word presentations can regress into visual images and other types of 'thing' presentation. Sigmund Freud's (1918a) statement that 'mental processes are in themselves unconscious and only reach the ego and come under its control through incomplete and untrustworthy perceptions' (p. 143) helps explain the situation. Mark Solms (1997), in sophisticated elucidation of the 'consciousness', concludes that it consists of a dual awareness: 'First, we are aware of the natural processes occurring in the external world, which are represented to us in the form of our external perceptual modalities of sight, sound, touch, taste, and smell, etc. Second, we are aware of the natural processes occurring within ourselves, which are represented to us in the form of our subjective consciousness. We are aware of nothing else. These are the only constituents of the envelope of conscious experience' (p. 685). Solms adds that both pereceptions (of the outside and the inside worlds) may affect each other and both are real; one is no more subjective or objective than the other. Moreover, brain processes are no more causally responsible for 'consciousness' than they are for 'uncosciousness' of mental phenomena, so to speak. The particular issue of the *Journal of American Psychoanalytic Association* that carried Solms' article also included incisive commentaries on it by Bernard Baars, Linda Brakel, Marcia Cavell, Nicholas Humphrey, Fred Levin, David Olds, David Rosenthal, Howard Shervin, Jerome Singer, and Max Velmans. These commentaries raised many important questions about 'consciousness' and the reader will benefit by looking them up. The matters touched upon by these discussants included the role of affect in the perception of subjectivity, the limited capacity of conscious experience as compared to the unconscious reservoirs of interactional scenarios, the distinction between reflective consciousness and primary consciousness, the relationship of 'consciousness' to first-person thinking, and so on. See also the interesting paper by Barry Opatow (1997), which proposes that 'consciousness' is itself multilayered and, in the end, inseparable from the activity of desire.

Conservative object: Christopher Bollas' (1987) term for 'a being state preserved intact within a person's internal world: it is not intended to change, and acts as a mnemic container of a particular self state conserved because it is linked to the child self's continuing negotiation with some aspect of the early parental environment' (p. 110). The notion of 'conservative object' seems to have intricate connections with the phenomenon of 'low-keyedness' (see separate entry) described by Margaret Mahler, Fred Pine, and Anni Bergman (1975).

Constancy principle: extrapolating experimental psychologist Gustav Fechner's (1873) 'principle of stability' to an energic model of depth psychology, Sigmund Freud (1895d) proposed the concept of 'constancy principle'. Boiled down to its essence, this notion implies that psychic apparatus seeks to keep all excitations at a fixed level. When environmental cues upset mental harmony, 'constancy principle' mobilizes avoidance mechanisms. When intrapsychic tensions arise, it mobilizes defence mechanisms or permits tension discharge via action. Either way, it strives to keep the level of excitation constant. Three ambiguities are important to sort out in this context: (1) while, in general, increase in tension causes unpleasure and reduction of tension pleasure, this is not always the case; sometimes increase in tension (e.g., during foreplay) is associated with pleasure. As a result, 'constancy principle' cannot be equated with 'pleasure principle' (see separate entry); (2) while 'constancy principle' implies maintaining intrapsychic energy at a fixed level, and 'Nirvana principle' (see separate entry) reducing this energy level to zero, Freud sometimes used the terms interchangeably. At other times, he implied that the latter was more fundamental; (3) one way of solving this contradiction is to view 'Nirvana principle' as the economic basis of 'death instinct' (see separate entry) and 'constancy principle', which safeguards a fixed level of energy (that results from maintaining fused drives and unified structure), as the economic basis of 'life instinct'.

Constitution: a term used somewhat loosely in psychoanalysis to denote the inherent and more or less unalterable genetic endowment in human beings. The term includes hereditary as well as evolutionary dimensions, and refers to both physical and psychological vulnerabilities and assets of the individual. At the same time, it is hardly seen to operate in isolation from the interpersonal influences of one's life, especially those of infancy and childhood. Sigmund Freud emphatically maintained such a synthetic view of character formation. Note the following statement made by him in 1912: 'Psychoanalysis has warned us that we must give up the unfruitful contrast between experience and constitution, and has taught us that we shall invariably find the cause of the onset of neurotic illness in a particular psychically situation which can be brought about in a variety of ways' (1912e, p. 238). Thus, not only ordinary personality formation, but the origin of pychopathological symptoms is to be viewed as emanating from both psychological experience and 'hardwired', bodily strengths and vulnerabilities. Linda Mayes and Donald Cohen (1995), in their comprehensive review of the topic, note that Freud especially noted the role of endowment in five areas: (1) the 'choice' of neurosis, (2) the tendency towards sexual perversions, (3) psychological differences between men and women, (4) the degree of anxiety tolerance, and (5) the response to psychoanalytic treatment. Among possible additions to this list are (i) the existence and subsequent enhancement or atrophy of talents (ii) propensity towards psychosomatic disorders, especially of the auto-immune type, and (iii) resilience in the face of disappointment and trauma. Indeed, in 1937, Freud declared that 'the stronger the constitutional factor, the more readily will a trauma lead to a fixation and leave behind a developmental disturbance' (1937c, p. 220).

Construction: term originated by Sigmund Freud in 1937 for the analyst's formulatation of an account of the patient's forgotten early experience. The analyst draws his inference in this regard from the patient's free associations, transference propensities, non-verbal cues, dreams, and, of course, from the resonance of all these in the countertransference experience. What the analyst offers for the patient to consider is, however, not an exact replication of childhood events. It is a conjecture and, hence, a 'construction' rather than 'reconstruction'. The two words are used interchangeably (Eidelberg, 1968) though, for unclear reasons, the Europeans (Laplanche & Pontalis, 1973; Rycroft, 1968) prefer 'construction' and the Americans (Blum, 1980a; Jacobs, 1986a; Moore & Fine, 1968, 1990) 'reconstruction'. In any case, an intervention of this sort by the analyst furthers recall of childhood memories, often bringing out fresh material for consideration. Even when this does not happen, a credible construction seems to 'achieve the same therapeutic result as a recaptured memory' (Freud, 1937d, p. 266). The patient's finding confirmation of the construction by extra-analytic means (e.g., by talking to relatives, looking up family documents and old photo albums) not only brings him a great conviction about the veracity of the analytic method, it also helps put psychoanalysis on solid scientific grounds.

Contact-shunning personalities: see 'Narcissistic personality types'.

Container: term coined by Wilfred Bion (1962) for the maternal mind which receives the projections of the child and, by that very act, makes it possible for the latter to discover its needs. Bion proposed that the infant is not aware of its need for the 'good breast'; he is aware of an unsatisfied need (the 'bad breast'), which he tries to get rid of. If the mother provides the 'good breast', the infant gets rid of the 'bad breast', depositing it into the mother. Thus, the mother becomes not only the provider of literal and emotional nourishment, but of the metabolism of the child's unpleasant feelings. Bion regards this process as the original prototype for the capacity to think. Thoughts arise in the child's mind as sense perceptions and subjective experiences, but are not processed until the mother empathically deciphers them and returns them to the child as thinkable entities. Of course, the child has to be able to tolerate some frustrations before receiving this feedback, and the mother has to be receptive to the child's perceptions. Bion refers to such maternal attitude as 'container' in structural, and 'reverie' in functional, terms. Gradually the child internalizes her attitude and develops the capacity to think about her own thoughts. Such mother–child interactions are reflected in the analyst–analysand exchanges during the clinical hour. The analyst receives the projections of what the analysand is unable or unwilling to think about. Becoming a 'container' and using his 'reverie' (to decipher, titrate, and arrange the received content), the analyst returns the projected material via his interpretive remarks.

Control case: refers to a patient who is undergoing psychoanalysis by an analytic candidate. Such treatment is conducted under close supervision by a fully qualified, experienced, senior analyst. The frequency with which the analytic candidate meets with his or her supervisor varies from once a week to once a month, depending upon the level of training and clinical experience of the candidate.

Controversial discussions: refers to a series of meetings held over eighteen months between 1943 and 1944 at the British Psychoanalytic Society. During these meetings, four papers (on phantasy by Susan Isaacs, on projection and introjection by Paula Heimann, on regression by Susan Isaacs and Paula Heimann, and on depressive position by Melanie Klein) were presented to explicate and 'defend' the Kleinian viewpoint against the sceptical stance of the 'classical' analysts (i.e., the followers of Anna Freud). Each paper was discussed over a course of many sessions, and much heat was generated. Though tension between the two factions had existed for a long time, the arrival of the Freuds in London in 1938 had made matters worse. It was hoped that the intellectual exchange at these meetings (which only later came to be called the 'Controversial Discussions') might yield a threortical rapprochement. That did not happen. Instead, a bureaucratic solution was found by which the two groups could share 'a minimum code of reciprocal tolerance' (Steiner, 1985, p. 65) and participate in various committees and training activities. 'The final agreement has been known as the "Gentleman's Agreement", though it was entered into by three women: Melanie Klein, Anna Freud, and the President of the British Society, Sylvia Payne' (Hinshelwood, 1991, p. 54). Pearl King and Riccardo Steiner (1991) have painstakingly elucidated the Melanie Klein–Anna Freud schism, including in their text a thorough account of the controversial discussions.

Convergent and divergent conflicts: although Leo Rangell (1963a) had described approximately similar ideas under the title of 'opposition-of-forces type' and 'decision type' of conflicts, the terms 'convergent' and 'divergent' conflicts were coined by Anton Kris (1988). These conflicts differ in four ways: (1) the form of opposition, (2) the resistances they pose, (3) the patterns in which they are resolved, and (4) the kind of insight that evolves from working these conflicts through. The *convergent conflict* consists of two forces (e.g., wish and prohibition) opposing each other head on. Resistance to its proper elucidation is mostly in the form of repression. The pattern of resolution requires the facilitation of free association. And, the insight that comes with the resolution of a 'convergent conflict' often occurs suddenly in the form of recalling a hitherto repressed and 'forgotten' memory, dream, or transference wish. The *divergent conflict* involves two forces (e.g., the contradictory wishes of staying married or getting divorced) pulling in opposite directions and creating an 'either-or dilemma' (Kris, 1977). Resistance to its proper elucidation centres around the dread of loss. The pattern of its resolution requires fuller expression of the two sides of the dilemma. And, the insight that comes with its resolution evolves painfully and gradually; it pertains to the inevitability of mourning in the process of growth and in life in general.

Conversion: term introduced by Sigmund Freud in 1894a to denote the process by which the libido attached to a repressed, conflicted idea is 'transformed into something somatic' (p. 49). This accounted for the seemingly unexplained physical symptoms (e.g., paralysis, gait disturbances, blindness) associated with hysteria. Freud's notion was essentially an economic one. In other words, it pertained to the alterations of psychic energy from one form to another. The notion of conversion also had a symbolic dimension, since the somatic symptom invariably expressed the hidden, repressed idea—usually pertaining to oedipal fantasies—in one way or the other. It is as if the body, rather than the mind, was telling the story of what was troubling the individual. Freud also noted conditions that favoured the occurrence of conversion. These included a constitutional factor that predisposed a particular organ to be suitable for the purpose of signifying an underlying conflict (see 'Somatic compliance'). Later authors, especially Otto Fenichel (1945), Leo Rangell (1959), and Wilfred Abse (1966) advocated an expansion of the term 'conversion' to include psychologically caused physical symptoms in not only hysteria, but a variety of psychiatric syndromes, and arising from developmental levels other than that of the Oedipus complex.

Conversion hysteria: see 'Hysteria'.

Converting psychoanalysis into psychotherapy: while there is a reasonable amount of literature on 'converting psychotherapy into psychoanalysis' (see separate entry) and many psychoanalytic institutes conduct didactic courses on that topic, little attention has been paid to 'converting psychoanalysis into psychotherapy'. Since it is almost certain that instances do occur when analysis does not seem to be working and/or is no longer feasible after having been set into motion, the profession's silence on this topic is curious. Some tentative considerations about this intervention might include: (1) *indications*: the development of psychosis during analysis, serious risk of suicide and homicide, a major life change which makes the patient unable to sustain an analysis, and any other reason for a sincere and well-thought out conclusion that the patient who appeared analysable is not really so: (2) *guidelines*: since issues of countertransference can play havoc here, a decision of this sort should only be made after peer-consultation or, in the case of trainees, with the help of a supervisor. Its timing should be watched and inwardly explored by the analyst. Countertransference should be laid bare in the supervisory or consultatative process for a proper inspection and deeper understanding of the situation. Even when a decision is made to go ahead, effort should be made to include the patient in it. Moreover, it must remain clear to both the patient and the analyst that only a technical procedure, and not the care of the patient in general, is being given up. Whether the change to psychotherapy would be permanent or transient depends upon the resilience shown by the patient and the confidence one can have in his or her ability to once again tolerate the regression and rigour of psychoanalysis. Some of these conundrums were avoided in the past by recommending a period of 'trial analysis' (see separate entry) that would permit a thorough asessment of the patient's capacity to participate in the work of psychoanalysis, which can, for some, prove quite destabilizing. Another important point to note here is, while most analysts (e.g., Bernstein, 1983; Horwitz, 1990; Levine, 1985) tend to go from psychotherapy to psychoanalysis, thinking that the reverse step would injure the patient's narcissism too much, Otto Kernberg (1984) holds that it is easier to move from analysis to psychotherapy than the other way round. Finally, the effects of such intervention should be explored and handled in a manner that is considerate to the patient and close to analytic principles, even if, for the time being, the clinical approach comes to include more than ordinary supportive measures.

Converting psychotherapy into psychoanalysis: while passing mention of some patients' need of ego-strengthening psychotherapy before starting psychoanalysis proper was made earlier (Stone, 1961; Blanck & Blanck, 1974), the credit of bringing focused attention on 'converting psychotherapy to psychoanalysis' goes to Stephen Bernstein (1983) and Howard Levine (1985). Locating their ideas in scattered bits and pieces of patient literature and breaking new ground on their own, these authors described patients who required once a week psychotherapy lasting for almost a year before feeling motivated to invest the time and money required for psychoanalysis. The patients reported upon were 'analysable' but either neurotically feared analysis or lacked sufficient understanding of what it could offer. With the publication of Bernstein's and Levine's papers, ground was set for deeper scrutiny of this realm. A panel discussion on the topic was held at the American Psychoanalytic Association with Merton Gill, Leonard Horwitz, Otto Kernberg, and Ernest Ticho as panelists (Fisher, 1987) and the *Psychoanalytic Inquiry* devoted a special issue to it in 1990. The following ten points can be deduced from these discussions: (1) it is possible to convert psychotherapy into psychoanalysis; (2) this is easier if the psychotherapy has been along psychoanalytic

lines and major breeches of 'anonymity', 'neutrality', and 'abstinence' (see separate entries) have not occurred; (4) it is with three types of patients that the issue of 'converting psychotherapy into psychoanalysis' arises (Horwitz, 1990). These include patients who were initially deemed too ill for analysis, patients for whom external realities and major life crises precluded analysis, and patients who were neurotically afraid or psychologically unsophisticated *vis-à-vis* psychoanalysis; (5) while some analysts (e.g. Kernberg, 1984) believe that 'converting psychoanalysis into psychotherapy' (see separate entry) is easier, most others (Bernstein, 1983; Levine, 1985; Schlessinger, 1990) hold the opposite view, stating that it causes less narcissistic injury and involves fewer adjustments of the therapeutic frame; (6) the 'introductory psychotherapy phase' (Levine, 1985, p. 296) provides an opportunity for clarifying diagnosis, assessing 'analysability' (see separate entry), and strengthening the patient's ego; (7) the impact of this phase upon the opening phase of analysis, and indeed the entire course of analysis, has to be assessed and analysed; (8) in a related vein, the deeper meaning of transition to analysis, including the potential roles of compliance and masochistic surrender, need explanation as well; (9) countertransference reactions (e.g., triumph, excitement, anxiety) stirred up by the patient's shifting to psychoanalysis warrant attention, and (10) finally, the theoretical underpinnings of the transition need to be taken into account. Joseph Lichtenberg and David Levi (1990) astutely note that 'analysts who assume that the central feature of the treatment lies in the analysis of free-associations minimally influenced by internal cues, for example, will be exquisitely sensitive to possible compromises of, neutrality, abstinence, and revelation of knowledge of the analyst . . . in contrast, analysts who assume the central feature of the treatment lies in the exploration of object-related transferences will regard the psychotherapy as an opportunity to form and observe transference phenomena. Cautions that might interest the first group of analysts will seem to the second analytic group less significant' (p. 18).

Coprophagia: subsumed under this term are a group of phenomena involving ingesting body secretions and eating or smelling or playing with faeces, nasal secretions, and other bodily discharges. A number of early analysts, including Karl Abraham, Sandor Ferenczi, Rene Spitz, and Bertram Lewin, have commented on these symptoms, a literature that has been well summarized by Sidney Tarachow (1966). Essentially, 'coprophagia' serves as an attempt to reestablish a threatened narcissistic equilibrium, usually caused by early object loss. The resulting childhood loneliness is compensated by narcissistic over-valuation of body products and by the symbolic reintrojection of what has been lost.

Core conflictual relationship theme: term coined by Lester Luborsky (1976) to denote the central configuration of the relationship a patient develops in regard to his therapist, and how that pattern reflects the core unresolved conflicts at the ontogenetic centre of the psyche. Aspects of the patient's narrative that run across his relationship with the therapist and his relationship with others in his current life are especially helpful in deducing what is the 'core conflictual relationship theme' of that patient. While practising analysts employ such observational methods regularly, Luborsky's approach gave a certain exactitude to such data. Its advantage resides in giving psychoanalytic researchers a new tool to examine and assess the concept of 'transference' (see separate entry), both cross-sectionally as well as over the course of treatment. In subsequent contributions, Luborsky and his colleagues (Luborsky, 1977; Luborsky & Crits-Christopher, 1989, 1990; Luborsky & Luborsky, 1993) sharpened the conceptual underpinnings and empirical applications of these ideas.

Core self and core relatedness: see 'Sense of a core self'.

Corrective emotional experience: phrase originated by Franz Alexander (1948) for an analysand's refreshing discovery that his analyst's attitude differs remarkably from that of his parents. This relaxes the patient and permits him to express himself more freely. In Alexander's own words, 'corrective emotional experience is a consciously planned regulation of the therapist's own emotional responses to the patient's material in such a way as to counteract the harmful affects of the parental attitudes' (p. 287). If the parents were harsh, the analyst deliberately adapts a more tolerant and sympathetic attitude. If the parents were overindulgent, the analyst leans towards firm limit setting. And so on. Alexander's ideas in this regard were received hesitantly, if not with rejection and scorn. The more 'classical' and abstinent analytic practitioners especially questioned the elements of manipulation and gratification in Alexander's technique. The less rigid analysts feared that such indulgences on the analyst's part might render the analysis of transference (especially in its negative aspects) difficult. Nowadays 'corrective emotional experience' is regarded to be

a result not of analyst's accommodations to transference pressures, but of interpretive resolution of that very transference; this can be called the 'corrective analytic experience'. The patient's developmentally driven search for new objects would also be seen to facilitate his or her need and capacity to have a 'corrective emotional experience'. In a contemporary assessment of Alexander's concept, Theodore Jacobs (1990) states that 'we intuitively make adjustments in our approach to patients with the aim of effective contact with them. In so doing, we modulate the tone, pitch, and inflection of our voices, express or inhibit certain bodily movements, and in other ways seek to attune ourselves to the psychological state of another individual. ... The difference in our approach today as compared with Alexander's is that it is only under special circumstances and for particular reasons that the modern analyst makes a conscious effort to behave in ways that contrast with the behavior of parents or other important figures of childhood. Rather, for the most part our attunements are subtle, intuitive, and unplanned' (p. 444).

Corrective empathic experience: phrase coined by Robert Emde (1990) to denote the essential thrust of Heinz Kohut's (1971, 1977) technical stance. This stance regards the provision of empathic listening and affirmation as the central ameliorative factor for those psychologically damaged by the lack of empathy by primary caregivers during childhood.

Cosmogony: see 'Autochthony, cosmogony, and alterity'.

Cosmogonic principle: term used by James Grotstein (1997) to denote the function of the need to bring order to chaos. According to him, the 'cosmogonic principle' involves the use of both 'primary and secondary processes' (see separate entry) to codify the chaotic data of emotional experience to create two tiers of meaning out of them: 'the first is a phantasmal or mythic account, and the second is "realistic". The cosmogonic principle operates in an attempt to create, first, a personal (autochthonous) cosmology, and second, an objective one' (p. 409). See also the related entry on 'autochthony, cosmogony, and alterity'.

Couch: a centrepiece of numerous *New Yorker* cartoons, the 'analytic couch' or, simply, the 'couch', has an intriguing place in psychoanalytic history (Stern, 1978). According to an April 1938 note (Ivan Ward, personal communication, 25 March 2008) by Marie Bonaparte, Martha Freud told her that the 'couch' used by Sigmund Freud was given to him as a gift by a patient named Madame Benevenisti in 1890. Peter Gay (1988) has noted this in his biography of Freud though he says that the Bonaparte note was 'undated' (p. 103). The 'couch' was covered by rugs made in Smyrna (currently, Izmir, Turkey) which Freud had received from Martha Freud's brother as a gift (Michael Molnar, personal communication, 25 March 2008). Freud's use of the 'couch' for seeing patients was perhaps a leftover trait from his days as a hypnotist. However, the rationale he gave (Freud, 1913c) was that he did not like being stared at by patients for hours on end. Gradually, more was added to the rationale for using the 'couch'. Prominent among these were (1) 'couch' precludes visual contact between the patient and analyst and also the former's ability to see the analyst's face (and posture) and thus regulate and tailor his associations; (2) 'couch' creates immobility and blocks discharge of impulses through action; like the sleep–dream situation, this pushes impulses to find discharge via fantasies which, in turn, enrich free association (Khan, 1962; Macalpine, 1950); (3) lying down on the 'couch' reduces overall stimulation from outside; this diminution of external distractions facilitates looking at mental activity. These ideas, and the use of 'couch', became so deeply entrenched that little theorizing was done about all this. The fact that, over years of clinical practice, many experienced analysts (e.g., Harry Stack Sullivan, William Ronald Fairbairn) renounced the use of 'couch' did little to challenge the practice or to encourage critical thinking *vis-à-vis* this issue. Recently, however, some serious attention has been paid to it. Merton Gill (1994) wondered whether the 'rationales' for using the couch were actually 'rationalizations'. He noted that while 'couch' can have usefulness, it can also create problems. The fact that it is seen by some patients and therapists as a 'status symbol' lends it to narcissistic abuse. Moreover, the 'couch' can be used for defensive purposes (e.g., distancing, keeping things a bit unreal) by both parties in the clinical dyad. More impressive, however, is the sophisticated and insightful article on the use of 'couch' by the Boston based analyst, Andrea Celenza (2005). She notes that both lying down on the 'couch' and sitting up on the chair have their own pros and cons. Each can be used defensively. Each can facilitate dialogue and even self-revelation, though perhaps in different ways. Celenza emphasizes that placing the analyst outside the analysand's vision allows, rather like the Rorschach test, for 'wider range of interpretability' (p. 1656) by the patient and might indeed foster self-reflection. It also allows for greater privacy for both parties and thus enhances their capacity for reverie. However, it can also cause distancing. Celenza concludes that, while it is preferable to begin all analyses with the patient on the 'couch', 'perhaps every analysis should, at some point, include both modalities for some period of time, since it is often difficult to know what anxieties lurk where until they are enacted' (p. 1656).

Countercathexis: see 'Cathexis'.

Counterenactments: term employed by Gail Reed (1994) for the analyst's actions that occur in response to the patient's 'enactment' (see separate entry). Using the terms 'reciprocal countertransference enactments' and 'responsive counterenactments' almost synonymously, Reed describes the myriad ways in which such phenomena become manifest. At times, the behaviours involving them are dramatic. At other times, 'counterenactments' 'manifest themselves by silence or over-talkativeness or maladroit wording, or extra-analytically in an action that nevertheless bears the unconscious stamp of the analyst's reaction to the patient's material' (p. 195).

Counterphobia: an unconscious attitude of the ego which propels the individual to undertake, and even enjoy, the very activities that arouse anxiety and fear in him. Dare-devil types of social and motor acts performed by adolescents exemplify such an attitude. A strikingly rapid assimilation into the host culture on the part of an immigrant is another illustration of counterphobia. The pleasure derived from counterphobic activities, however, is not identical with instinctual pleasure; it lacks the simplicity and flesh-bound 'innocence' of the latter. There is a quality of desperation about the 'enjoyment' provided by counterphobic actions. It is as if the individual is not really convinced of his mastery of the underlying anxiety. In fact, a certain leakage of anxiety is not infrequently seen in association with a counterphobic attitude.

Counterphobic assimilation: a term coined by Jagdish Teja and Salman Akhtar (1981) for an immigrant's tendency to rapidly renounce his original culture and adopt the characteristics of the new culture in order to avoid feeling different and therefore sad ,hurt, and angry. Betraying an 'as if' (Deutsch, 1942) quality, such immigrants often change their names or give them a local sounding twist, stop associating with the homoethnic group, and develop 'borrowed prejudices' to buttress their affliation with their host group.

Counter reactions: Charles Chediak's (1979) term for the following four aspects of the analyst's experience with a patient. (1) his overall affective response, (2) his transference to the patient, (3) his empathic identification with the patient, and (4) his emotional reaction to the role being assigned to him by the patient. Chediak regards only the last one to constitute true 'countertransference' (see separate entry). Current custom, however, is to use the term countertransference in a much broader manner.

Countertransference: term coined by Sigmund Freud (1910d) to describe the feelings generated in the analyst 'as a result of the patient's influence on his unconscious' (p. 144). From this pioneering observation, through subsequent eludications by Freud himself and others, to the contemporary views, the saga of 'countertransference' has had many twists and turns (Sandler, Dare, and Holder, 1973; King, 1978; Epstein & Feiner, 1979; Blum, 1987a; Slakter, 1987; De Leon de Bernardi, 2000). *Six major shifts* are discernible in the view of countertransference over time: (1) the 'classical' view held that countertransference was a hindrance to treatment but increasing number of analysts (Winnicott, 1947; Heimann, 1950; Little, 1951; Fromm-Reichman, 1950; Racker, 1953) began to observe that the data of 'countertransference' provides useful information regarding the patient and what is going in the analytic process. This does not mean that 'countertransference' blind spots, collusions, and undue indulgences or deprivations can not be harmful to a patient; (2) the early stance that 'countertransference' could be avoided if the analyst had been well-analysed has given way to agreement that it constitutes an inevitable and integral part of the treatment process; (3) while initially 'countertransference' was restricted to undue and unwanted reactions of the analyst, Paula Heimann (1950), in her seminal contribution 'On countertransference', extended the concept to include all the feelings that the analyst experiences during the analytic session. She liberated the concept of 'countertransference' from its negative connotations, placing it in the centre of psychoanalytic technique; (4) Heinrich Racker (1953, 1957, 1958) broke the monolithic notion of this concept by classifying countertransference phenomena into 'direct' and 'indirect' types. 'Direct countertransference' referred to the analyst's emotional respone to the patient. 'Indirect countertransference' referred to the analyst's emotional response to someone important to the patient (see also Bernstein & Glen, 1978; Jacobs, 1983; Searles, 1979 in this regard). 'Direct countertransference' had two subcategories called 'concordant' and 'complimentary' countertransferences. The former included the analyst's empathic resonance with the patient's felt conflicts; this was, of course, more marked if the analyst also had similar conflicts himself. The latter referred to the analyst's unconscious identification with some unfelt and projected part of the patient's psychic structure; the analyst's emotional experience in this case was 'opposed' to that of the patients. Joseph Sandler, Christopher Dare, and Alex Holder's (1973) reminder that the prefix 'counter' is used in two different ways in the English language, namely to parallel (e.g., counterpart) or oppose (e.g., counter attack) something, is patent in this context. Other considerations in regard to the phenomenology of countertransference include its intensity (from mild to severe), duration (acute or chronic), and clinical visibility (gross or subtle; the latter was termed 'mini-countertransference' by Ernest Wolf in 1979); (5) the early 'classical' position that 'countertransference' was a manifestation of the analyst's unresolved conflicts soon gave way to the Kleinian position that it was 'the patient's creation' (Heimann, 1950, p. 83). This position became quite popular, especially among the analysts working with severely regressed, borderline, and near-psychotic individuals (e.g., Kernberg, 1975, 1984, 1992; Searles, 1960). The rise of relational and intersubjective perspectives (Mitchell, 1988, 1993; Ogden, 1986, 1994) has, however, shifted the pendulum to the midpoint of its arc by emphasizing that both 'transference' (see separate entry) and 'countertransference' are essentially co-created phenomena; and (6) there also has been a shift in the degree to which 'countertransference enactment' (see separate entry) is deemed inevitable. Ideally, the analyst should be able to monitor his affective responses to the patient, dip into them, and, from this, learn about the patient, himself, their interaction, and the analytic process. More often, the analyst shows a certain 'role responsiveness' (see separate entry) to the patient's externalization and grasps the meaning of it analytically only on a *post-hoc* basis. A converse problem is the analyst's resistance to feeling strong affects in the clinical situation (Coen, 2002) and thus becoming unable to analyse the patient's material in its verity and depth. Teaching the matters regarding 'countertransference' to psychoanalytic candidates is therefore of great importance, even though tricky as Alex Tarnopolsky's (1995) paper clearly shows. The involvement of real life issues with 'countertransference' (Slakter, 1987) and of cultural differences (Akhtar, 1999b) are also significant areas of concern here. What remains of utmost importance is the analyst's ability to feel a wide range of affects and fantasies in the clinical situation and to apply his analytic thinking to these psychic productions of his own. Martin Silverman's (1985, p. 176) recollection that Jacob Arlow once said to him that 'a psychoanalyst needs to be soft-hearted as well as hard-headed' says it all.

Countertransference dreams: while Sigmund Freud's (1900a) celebrated dream about Irma's injection was a 'countertransference dream' *par excellence*, subsequent psychoanalysts have refrained from reporting such dreams. Literature on this topic is therefore meager. Donald Winnicott (1947) mentioned a dream about his patient in the 'Hate in the countertransference' paper. Roy Whitman, Milton Kramer, and Brian Baldridge (1969) reported a sleep laboratory study of therapists in training and their dreams the night before they were to make a case presentation; they found that six per cent of the therapist's dreams have patients in their manifest content and an additional thirty-four per cent in the latent content as well. Leon Altman (1980) emphasized the importance of analysing one's countertransference dreams and the role this can play in deepening the understanding of the analytic process. The most comprehensive and thoughtful paper on the topic, however, is by Robert Zwiebel (1985) who concluded that 'countertransference dreams' (1) occur rarely, (2) occur more often during the treatment of individuals with severe personality disorders, (3) occur after analysis has been going on for a long while, (4) occur during problematic phases of the work, (5) contain reactions to certain statements or behaviours of the patient, (6) reflect the analytic process as it is unfolding, and (7) should spur the analyst towards deeper self-analysis; if this does take place, 'countertransference dreams' propel the analysis forward. This last point has been noted by Eva Lester, Rose-Marie Jodoin and Brian Robertson (1989) as well, and has recently been developed further by Susann Heenen-Wolff (2005). See also the paper by Brian Robertson and Mary-Eleanor Yack (1993) for the handling and educative value of such dreams in the course of analytic supervision.

Countertransference enactment: in a paper with this very title, Theodore Jacobs (1986b) reviewed the existing literature on the tendency for countertransference to spill into action. With the help of detailed clinical material, Jacobs noted that subtle 'countertransference enactments' are to be discerned in the way the ground rules of clinical work are managed. He asserted that often it is not 'overt actions, including even troublesome lapses of control, that are the source of analyst's greatest countertransference problems, but the covert, scarcely visisble, yet persistent reactions that pervade his listening and responding' (p. 168). Since Jacobs' important contribution, clinical theory has advanced and a certain spillage of countertransference into action is now generally considered inevitable, especially during the treatment of sicker, and more regression-prone, individuals. What is required from the analyst, however, is vigilance, ongoing self-observation, and a capacity to step back and learn from what has been put into action.

Countertransference hatred: this consists of strong and sustained feelings of aversion and malice felt by the analyst towards the patient; it is a frequent development during the treatment of borderline and severely masochistic patients. The analyst's aversion leads to a wish to withdraw from the patient and his malice leads to cruel impulses towards the patient (Maltsberger & Buie, 1974). Viewing themselves as compassionate individuals, most analysts are vulnerable to mobilizing unconscious 'defences against countertransference hatred' (see separate entry); these invariably cause problems. It is better that the analyst does not bury his feelings deep in his heart. This permits him to work his way through this difficult experience. At worst, the analyst continues to oscillate between emotionally giving up on the patient and attempting to resolve the patient's hatred analytically (Kernberg, 1992). The analyst's felt torment gets gradually translated into a fuller understanding of the patient's inner world. Harold Searles (1986) states that he 'cannot over emphasize the enormously treatment-facilitating value, as well as the comforting and liberating value for the therapist personally, of his locating where this or that tormenting or otherwise upsetting countertransference reaction links up with the patient's heretofore unconscious and unclarified transference reactions to him' (p. 214). Finally, there is the question of whether sharing countertransference hatred with the analysand is ever helpful. Donald Winnicott (1947) noted that this is 'obviously a matter fraught with danger, and it needs the most careful timing. But I believe an analysis is incomplete if even towards the end it has not been possible for the analyst to tell the patient what he, the analyst, did unbeknown for the patient while he was ill, in the early stages. Until this interpretation is made the patient is kept to some extent in the position of infant—one who cannot understand what he owes to his mother' (p. 202).

Creative drive: see 'Primary psychic creativity'.

Creative pause: Lajos Szekely's (1967) term for the time interval between the moment a thinker interrupts his conscious preoccupation with an unsolved problem and the moment when the solution of that problem or a new insight about it suddenly presents itself to him. During the 'creative pause', a controlled regression of thought occurs in the service of the ego, which permits access to possibilities less 'rationally' connected with the problem at hand. This, in turn, facilitates thinking of new solutions.

Creative reparation: see ' Reparation'

Criminal from a sense of guilt: term coined by Sigmund Freud (1916d) to describe a paradoxical situation where a 'misdeed arose from the sense of guilt' (p. 332) and not vice versa. Astutely observing that the morally unacceptable, illegal, or even criminal behaviour of some individuals was a manoeuvre to allay a nagging sense of inner guilt which arose from persistent unconscious wishes to commit the two 'great human crimes' (p. 333) i.e., incest with the mother and parricide. The 'bad' behaviour the individual was thus a sort of plea-bargaining; he seemed to be saying 'punish me for this, not for that', with the latter referring to the unconscious wish for oedipal transgressions. Freud acknowledged that most individuals commit crimes because they lack appropriate morality, but insisted that some do because they have too much morality. The latter do misdeeds to rationalize the pre-existing feelings of guilt within them. While Freud's formulation is striking, his great human crimes— 'Parricide and incest with the mother' (p. 333)— leave something to be desired, for such a restricted definition would lead to the conclusion that women cannot be 'criminals from a sense of guilt'. Moreover, such phallocentric wording (and theorizing that lies behind it) can suggest to the cynic that 'matricide and incest with the father' is somehow not a great human crime. And, what about filicide and infanticide, in this regard? All in all, it seems that the two great human crimes should be re-worded as simply incest and murder. Such reformulation would deepen and expand Freud's aetiologic hypotheses in regard to the 'criminal from a sense of guilt' without robbing his description of its phenomenological elegance.

Cross-gender tranferences: the belief in the power and 'irrationality' of the unconscious led early psychoanalysts (Fenichel, 1945; Glover, 1955) to the opinion that the actual attributes of the analyst's person, including his gender, had little impact upon the development of transference. This was despite the fact that the founder of psychoanalysis himself had suspected that his being a male evoked greater hostile competitivess from male patients (Freud, 1916–1917) and pre-oedipal maternal transferences evolved with greater frequency in analysis conducted by female analysts (Freud, 1931b). Freud's concession that the sex of the analyst can affect the development of transference has been 'confirmed' by more contemporary analysts in several ways. Harold Blum (1971) concluded that the order in which various transferences emerge can be affected by the analyst's gender. Some female analysts (e.g., Karme, 1979) noted that their male analysands do not develop paternal transferences to them, and utilize external figures to express such issues; others (e.g., Goldberger & Evans, 1985), however, offered data to the contrary. And, a survey of experienced psychoanalysts (Mogul, 1982) revealed that oedipal issues were often misunderstood when the transference was automatically assumed to be constant with the analyst's gender. In a thorough discourse on the topic, David Raphling and Judith Chused (1988) emphasized the following six points: (1) 'the sex of the analyst contributes enormously to the transference experience' (p. 102); (2) when the analytic process centred upon dyadic issues, the sex of the analyst is less important, but when the material moves to oedipal issues, the sex of the analyst becomes crucial for unfolding transferences; (3) patients who are tolerant of their own bisexual identifications are more capable of 'cross-gender transferences'; (4) in a same-sex clinical dyad, a heterosexual erotic transference can be mistaken for homosexual desire, leading to anxiety and resistance; (5) children are less inhibited by the analyst's actual gender in developing oedipal longings (Tyson, 1980; Chused, 1982); and (6) 'the analyst's empathic responsiveness may become faulty when he needs to make a transient identification with sexual attributes of an opposite sex transference image' (p. 101). See also the recent contribution on this topic by Shahrzad Siassi (2000).

Crucifixion fantasies: these refer to conscious or unconscious preoccupation with scenes that are disguised versions of the figure of Christ nailed to the cross. Such 'crucifixion fantasies' (Edelheit, 1974) represent the combined image of the parents in the primal scene and, at the same time, by way of the double identification with parents, they also represent the helpless, observing child.

Crying at happy occasions: frequently encountered at weddings and award ceremonies, this phenomenon is determined by a number of psychodynamic factors: (1) guilt at success, which is unconsciously equated with oedipal transgression and incestuous crime (Freud, 1916d), (2) emergence of pre-existing sadness that had been kept in abeyance and is now that happiness is undoubtedly assured, is 'permitted' to enter conscious awareness; crying results from a decrease in the intensity of 'manic defence' (Klein, 1940) under happy circumstances, (3) a paradoxical diminution of omnipotence at the time of major achievements (i.e., 'that is it, no more'!) can also induce pain and crying (Dorn, 1967), (4) a sense of having become separated from some love objects (e.g., at weddings, from parents and siblings, and friends) and thus experiencing a sudden loss of 'optimal distance' from hitherto banked-upon sources of emotional refuelling (Gruenert, 1979), and (5) emergence of remorse over having competed with others and, in imagination, wished them harm; this dynamic is especially operative at award ceremonies, where one nominee among four or five others receives the honour while others applaud with feigned (pained?) grace.

Cultural boundary violations: Salman Akhtar's (2006) term for situations where the analyst imposes his or her values and notions regarding a wide range of social and cultural matters (e.g., how often should an adult offspring call his out of town mother on the phone, should pre-marital sex be a necessary step before the decision to marry) upon the analysand, causing the latter to suffer narcissistic confusion and iatrogenic conflict. More common are 'cultural boundary violations' caused by the analyst's ignoring that such boundaries even exist. This happens when immigrant and racially different patients are analysed with no attention at all to their cultural backgrounds. Such illusory clinical oneness can harm the analysand and, in the long run, do disservice to the profession of psychoanalysis.

Cultural countertransference: see 'Cultural transference and cultural countertransference'.

Cultural holding environment: Henri Parens' (1998) extension of Donald Winnicott's (1960) concept of the 'holding environment', to include the silent but important role of social customs and rituals in ego development. Both 'structures' (e.g. places of worship, ethnic museaums, and monuments) and 'dynamic processes' (e.g. regularly occurring festivals, birth and death anniversaries of heroes) play a role in creation such a 'holding environment'.

Cultural identity: Salman Akhtar's (1999b) term for the aspect of the core self-representation that is aligned and affiliated with the norms, attitudes, values, and communicative idioms of a group of people; while cultural identity is partly determined by ethnicity and religion, regional and linguistic variables perhaps play a larger role in its genesis. For instance, a Muslim from Bangladesh has a Bengali identity, while a Muslim from Iraq has an Arab identity.

Cultural neutrality: Salman Akhtar's (1999b) term for the analyst's capacity to remain equidistant from the values, ideals, and mores of the patient's culture and those of his own. The need for maintaining 'cultural neutrality' is especially important while treating immigrant patients. The development and maintenance of cultural neutrality is facilitated by (1) personal treatment to mitigate paranoid defences, (2) study of the interface of social anthropology with clinical work, (3) treating patients of many cultures, (4) avoiding the pitfall of excessive culturalization of the analytic ego, and (5) leading an open and cosmopolitan life.

Cultural transference and cultural countertransference: terms coined by John Spiegel (1976) to denote, respectively, the feelings, fantasies, and attitudes a patient might have towards the analyst's ethno-racial group or an analyst might have towards the patient's ethno-racial group. The pheomena associated with 'cultural transference' and 'cultural transference' are mutiply-determined, with their roots going down to actual childhood experiences of the two parties in the dyad and transgenerationally transmitted tales of the historical relationship between the ethno-racial groups of the analysand and analyst. Of note here is that such affects and fantasies are bi-directional and can contain both positive and negative feelings. Technically speaking, mild sentiments of this sort subside pretty much on their own as a 'therapeutic alliance' (see separate entry) gets established and the treatment moves forward. More sticky and 'noisy' transferences with a cultural theme should raise the suspicion of either a more aggressive psychoapthology on the patient's part than was suspected (see the related entry on the 'law of suspicious cultural intensity'), or the undetected activity of a gross 'cultural countertransference', or some combination of both. Peer consultation and supervision might help undo knots of this sort. One aspect that still seems to be a bit of a taboo is constituted by difference in political views of the two parties. While, generally speaking, it is all 'grist for the mill', occasions where the feasibility of undertaking, or advisability of continuing, an analysis might come into question are certainly conceivable.

Culture shock: a term commonly used to describe the ego disturbance caused by a sudden and drastic change in the 'average expectable environment' (Hartmann, 1939); it puts the newcomer's personality to the test and challenges the stability of his psychic organization. Cesar Garza-Guerreo (1974) has contributed a most significant paper on this topic.

Cumulative trauma: this term was introduced into psychoanalytic literature by Masud Khan in 1963a. While Ernst Kris (1956) had earlier mentioned a similar concept under the rubric of 'strain trauma', it was Khan who became the leading exponent of this idea. According to him, 'cumulative trauma is the result of the breaches in the mother's role as a protective shield over the whole course of the child's development, from infancy to adolescence—that is to say, in all those areas of experience where the child continues to need the mother as an auxiliary ego to support his immature and unstable ego functions' (1963a, p. 46). These breaches in the mother's role as a protective shield are not singly traumatic. However, their effect accumulates silently and becomes traumatic in retrospect.

Cyclical living: Jerome Kavka's (cited in Pollack 1970, p. 353) designation for the life of those individuals who expect certain catastrophic events to keep occurring in a cyclical fashion throughout their age span. Kavka noted a twelve-year cycle in the life of Ezra Pound, who lost his beloved grandmother at age twelve, and thereafter made significant changes in his life at every twelve-year interval.

Cyclothymia: condition characterized by frequent swings of mood between elation and depression. Severe forms of 'cyclothymia' are associated with 'manic depressive illness', which is currently called 'bipolar affective disorder' (see separate entry); this condition is mostly constitutional and biological in origin though psychodynamic factors can play a role in giving the content to what the individual says he is happy or sad about. Milder forms of 'cyclothymia' are mostly psychogenic in origin and reflect disregulation of self-esteem under environmental cues in narcissistic personalities (Akhtar & Thomson, 1982). See also the related entries on 'depression' and 'mania'.

D

Daedalus experience: Marian Tolpin's (1974) designation of a favourable developmental vicissitude of the infantile grandiose fantasy of being able to fly is transformed into the 'feeling of being uplifted' (p. 216) through creativity and enjoyable self-expression. Tolpin suggests that Winston Churchill's 'elevated and elevating' (p. 227) prose is one such sublimated heir to archaic grandiosity.

Damming up of libido: concept first used by Sigmund Freud in his 1898 description of 'actual neuroses' (see separate entry); these resulted from lack of sexual discharge leading to accumulation of tension within the body-mind. In psychoneuroses, which was caused by intrapsychic conflict related to childhood wishes, 'damming up of libido' was a secondary occurrence. In 1912, Freud added that 'damming up of libido' was not pathogenic in itself. It could lead to actual neurosis or to sublimations. Still later, he (Freud, 1914c) extended the notion of damming up to psychosis, which resulted from the excess of undischarged narcissistic libido. This, in part, explained the 'hypochondriasis' (see separate entry) that is usually seen in the prodromal phase of schizophrenia.

Danger situations: in his elucidation of the origins of anxiety, Sigmund Freud (1926d) spoke of some ubiquitous 'danger situations'. These comprise a real or imagined threat of (1) loss of a love object, (2) loss of the love object's love, (3) castration, and (4) moral condemnation from within oneself. 'Each situation of danger corresponds to a particular period of life or a particular developmental phase of the mental apparatus and appears to be justifiable to it' (p. 146). Some 'danger situations' lose their significance as the individual matures, while others survive by acquiring more up-to-date forms. Still others (e.g., fear of superego's attack) accompany people throughout their lives. 'Danger situations' mobilize anxiety and set ego defences into motion.

Day dreams: occupying a mid-way place between dreams that occur during sleep and fleeting fantasies of waking life, 'day dreams' are multi-factorial derivatives of unconscious fantasies. Not surprisingly then, there exist gender differences in the nature of day dreams which are especially marked during latency and adolescence (Peller, 1958); there is greater amount of aggression and work-related ambition in the boy's day dreams and greater erotic and anticipatory maternal element in the girl's day dreams. In general, day dreams permit the emergence into consciousness of complex wish-defence constellations relating to infantile sexual and narcissistic aims in relatively palatable forms. In talented hands, 'day dreams' serve as a preamble for creative writing (Freud, 1908e). The dilution and aesthetic reworking of instinctual material makes it possible for the readers to connect their own similar fantasies to those of the writer and draw vicarious gratification from the creative product. Thus, the writer becomes the 'community's day dreamer' (Arlow, 1986, p. 58). In contrast to such positive use, there is the tendency to use 'day dreams' as 'psychic retreats' (see separate entry); the pathological nature of this type of day dreaming is evident through their intensity, pervasiveness, and ego-depleting impact.

Day precipitate: while the observation that the manifest content of a dream often provides a blueprint for action was made in passing by Richard Sterba (1946), it was Harvey Kelman (1975) who coined the phrase 'day precipitate' of dreams. He said that the idea arose in the discussions of a study group led by Gary Morris of the Washington Psychoanalytic Institute. Referring to the notion as the 'Morris hypothesis', Kelman stated that the dream is anchored in reality at both ends. The 'day residue' (see separate entry) provides visual images for the manifest content of a dream. The 'day precipitate' of dreams is the acting out of this manifest content in the subsequent session or in the day following the dream.

Day's residue: term coined by Sigmund Freud (1900a) for the triggering function of the preceding day's events in the formation of that night's dream. Actual occurrences, visual impressions, waking thoughts, and unfinished tasks can all become the 'day's residue'. Each is capable of stirring up preconscious ideas to which repressed instinctual wishes can get attached; the latter are then transformed by 'dream work' (see separate entry) to produce the 'manifest dream; (see separate entry). While the 'day's residues' are selected for inclusion in dreams because 'they are congruent with or reminiscent of certain important fantasies or memory schemata' (Arlow, 1969, p. 41), owing to their distance from the current wishes, they help deceive the censorship that is active against unconscious wishes. Exploring the connection between the manifest content of a dream and the events of the previous day can yield useful information in two ways: (1) it can bring to mind more associations and memories related to the day's event itself, and (2) it can lead to the wishes that were mobilized by those events, wishes that underlie the dreams.

Dead father: although this expression appears to be a counterpart to André Green's (1980) 'dead mother' (see separate entry), the fact is that Joyce McDougall (1989b), who introduced it into psychoanalytic literature, used it in a somewhat different manner. It was in the course of reporting the case of an author with a 'writer's block' (see separate entry) and troubled homosexual relations that McDougall suggested that 'the roots of both sexual deviance and creativity may often be traced to early psychic trauma' (p. 218); both are ways to overcome the damage done to the mind. In the particular case reported by McDougall, it was the death of her father when she was fifteen months old (and the subsequent depressive turning away of her mother) that was the central trauma, hence, McDougall titled her paper 'The dead father'. Many years later, though, the more expected metaphorical usage which links the phrase 'dead father' with 'dead mother' was put into practice by Lila Kalinich and Stuart Taylor (2005). Used this way, the phrase refers to a father who lacks paternal functions or has abdicated them, much to the detriment of his offspring.

Dead mother: André Green's (1980) phrase for the internal lack of altruism, concern, and generosity that results from having been raised by a mother whose maternal functions (e.g., devotion, selflessness, forgiveness, survival, soothing, nourishment) were grossly deficient or altogether absent; this was a woman who as a person was alive, but as a mother was dead. She was most likely absorbed in her own inner world of bereavement, anhedonia, and deadness.

Deaggressivization: term proposed by Sigmund Freud (1923b) to denote the process by which the psychic energy of the 'death instinct' (see separate entry) is denuded of its aggressive charge. This might happen by its being bound by libido, or the psychic energy of the life instinct, or by countercathexis, that suppress only the quality of energic charge without affecting its quantity. 'Deaggressivization' contributes to 'sublimation' (see separate entry) and can also underlie neurotic inhibitions of the ego in the realm of aggression.

Deanimation syndrome: described by Janos Schossberger (1963), this consists of a disturbing experience in which people seem to have become puppet-like and their movements appear devoid of spontaneity. Individuals experiencing such phenomena feel detached from the world, anxious, and 'isolated in a world of unintelligible, threatening robots' (p. 480). According to Schossberger, all this usually occurs in pre-psychotic, catatonic, and paranoid conditions, but may also be found in the setting of neurotic organizations and even during the course of free association. 'The psychodynamic balance in deanimation consists either in increased repressive attempts or in an ebbing of libidinal flow. The syndrome appears, therefore, occasionally as a sign of exhaustion of somatic origin, such as strain and over work in adolescents' (p. 528).

Death anxiety: see 'Fear of death'.

Death instinct: based upon observations regarding children's turning traumatic experiences into play, certain analysands' returning over and over again to painful past experiences, the behaviour of those who must go repeatedly through similar calamities, and the dreadful preoccupations of war veterans, Sigmund Freud suggested that there might be a self-destructive 'daemonic force' (1920g, p. 35) at work in them. This force worked in opposition to the pleasure principle and was aligned with a fundamental attribute of mind that searched for reduction of all excitation to quiescence. At its deepest, this search for quiescence—the 'Nirvana principle' (see separate entry)—was aimed at returning the living organism to its previous, inorganic state. He concluded that 'the aim of all life is death' (1920g, p. 38), and thus gave voice to his celebrated concept of the 'death instinct'. A threat to the self at birth, this force is deflected outward by the influence of libido and ego using the agency of somatic musculature. Freud termed this outwardly deflected part of the death instinct the 'aggressive instinct'. In *The Ego and the Id* (1923b), Freud added that the death instinct operates silently. In *Civilization and Its Discontents*, he emphasized that 'aggressive instinct is the derivative and the main representative of the death instinct' (1930a, p. 122). In 'Analysis terminable and interminable' (1937c), Freud again referred to the death instinct and related masochism, negative therapeutic reaction, and unconscious guilt to its derivative, the aggressive drive. And, finally, in the *Outline*, he reiterated his formulation of 'two basic instincts' (1940a [1938], p. 148), one to establish unities and the other to undermine connections and destroy things. Freud emphasized that the 'concurrent and mutually opposing action of the two basic instincts gives rise to the whole variegation of the phenomena of life' (*ibid.*, p. 149). He acknowledged borrowing the expression 'Nirvana principle' from Barbara Low, a Sanskrit expert. The notion of 'death instinct' thus, from the beginning, had an Eastern touch. Gustav Fechner, the renowned physicist whose 'constancy principle' (see separate entry) led Freud to the 'Nirvana principle' was himself involved in Buddhism (Jones, 1957). And Romain Rolland, from whom Freud (1930a) obtained the related concept of 'oceanic feeling' (see separate entry), was an avid reader and biographer of the nineteeth-century Indian mystics, Sri Rama-krishna Paramahansa and Swami Vivekananda. The Indian mystic tradition was thus a back-ground conceptual source for Freud's death instinct. This may have been part of why the con-cept appeared alien to Western minds. With the exception of Melanie Klein (1933, 1935, 1952), her followers, and Kurt Eissler (1971), most subse-quent analysts laid the postulate of death instinct to rest. In the Kleinian tradition, however, the concept remains, and is utilized largely to explain mental operations that seek to destroy sublime and well-synthesized ego attributes and the capa-city for in-depth object relations.

Death instinct reformulated: While, with the exception of Melanie Klein (1933, 1935, 1952) and her followers, most psychoanalysts renounced the concept of 'death instinct', a close examination of psychoanalytic literature shows a recurring notion that there is, in humans, a vague, drive-like, inter-nal pull toward the loss of the boundaries, if not the existence, of the psychic self. Concepts that allude to this internal pull include (1) a deep-seated longing to return to the preoedipal fusion with the maternal breast (Lacan, 1938); (2) the merger fantasies, often associated with feeding and with sleep (Lewin, 1950); (3) the deep-seated wish for loss of human identity by 'metamorpho-sis' (Lichtenstein, 1963); (4) the everlasting wish for 'the lost, original union with the mother' (Jacobson, 1964, p. 39); (5) in the context of neo-natal life, 'the drive to return to an earlier state where all was gratified automatically' (Stone, 1971, p. 236); (6) man's eternal yearning to recap-ture the 'coenesthetically remembered harmony of dual-unity stage' (Mahler, 1971, p. 186); (7) the 'search for oneness' (Kaplan, 1978); (8) neonates' 'inborn and immediate wish to return to the intrauterine state' (Chasseguet-Smirgel, quoted in Akhtar, 1991b, p. 751) and man's 'nostalgia for primary narcissism' (Chasseguet-Smirgel, 1984, p. 29); (9) the 'someday' and 'if only' fantasies

(Akhtar, 1991a); and (10) an attempted reconcilia-tion of 'everything' and 'nothing' fantasies, which occurs 'transiently in dreamless sleep and in the ecstasy of orgasm—but the promise of perma-nence can be realized only after our individual lives are over' (Shengold, 1991, p.7). To be sure, these concepts have diverse theoretical founda-tions, involve fantasy content not attributable to insitinctual primitivity, and contain an unmistak-able libindinal admixture with aggression. Yet, collectively, these notions do demand a contempo-rary reconceptualization of the 'death instinct' (see separate entry) concept. Such examination might confirm the ubiquitous existence in humans of a deep-seated wish for the loss of self-boundaries, perhaps an echo of an early desire for (and mem-ory of) fusion with the mother. It might be that this preverbal pull subsequently accures fantasies from various levels of psychosexual development. Death, too, may enter this scenario, though much after infancy and childhood, perhaps truly not even until middle age. From then onward, the deep-seated desire for fusion with mother might become intermingled with a longing for peace via death; a 'death instinct' has thus been set into motion. On the other hand, individuals who are traumatized by early losses through death, or themselves have faced early life-threatening cri-ses, might incorporate the notion of death into this substrate of fusion/oblivion seeking much earlier. They might give evidence of possessing a 'death instinct' even before middle age. Such a formula-tion of 'death instinct' is clearly different from the original one by Sigmund Freud (1920g). In this reconceptualization, both *death* and *instinct* are words that seem misplaced. Clearly, further think-ing and newer terminology are needed here. The recent paper by Cordelia Schmidt-Hellerau (2006a) is one such attempt to reformulate the death drive in object relations terms.

Death narcissism: see 'Life and death narcissism'.

Death of the breast: Donald Meltzer's (1967, 1979) concept dealing with a development in the clinical situation whereby the patient becomes intensely attentive to the analyst's physical and mental state, highly sentitive to external intru-sions into the analytic process, and desperately desirous of distinguishing the actual person of the analyst from the transference figures projected on to him. The analysand also shows an increased preoccupation with the reproductive aspects of the parental sexuality and struggles with posses-sive jealousy in this area. Meltzer (1979) proposed that underlying this depressive situation is a 'struggle to integrate the split-off parts of the infantile structure, especially the more destructive parts' (p. 141)

Decathexis: term employed for the withdrawal of psychic energy from an idea or an object. The defence mechanisms of repression and isolation (see separate entries) exemplify this process as does secondary narcissism that results from the investment of libido withdrawn from frustrating objects back into the self.

Deceiving superego: Angel Garma's (1968) term for the role of superego in the manic state. Contrary to the 'classical' formulation (Freud, 1921c) that ego and superego fuse during mania, Garma suggested that the superego tricks the ego to renounce genuine libidinal gratification and 'jump from object to object as though one was walking over hot coals' (p. 78). The manic's ego is masochistic and his self-esteem derives from his total submission to the superego. Like a child who is proud of obeying his parents, he can appear happy, but in fact he is satisfying self destructive tendencies unleashed upon him by a cruel superego.

Decision-making function of the ego: described by Leo Rangell (1969), this ego function is directed towards resolving an intrapsychic 'choice conflict' (p. 600). The various steps involved in this process are (1) first the ego permits a small, trial instinctual discharge (mostly in fantasy), (2) then it experiences a reaction response from the superego and from its own reality-assessing aspects, (3) on the basis of this response, the ego feels either a sense of safety or a signal of anxiety, (4) now the ego is confronted with a choice and competition between optional paths of action, i.e., 'what to do next, whether to permit further discharge, or how not to, or how to affect a compromise' (p. 600), and (5) then, based upon an internal scanning process which helps it cross-check the current situation against past ones as well as sort out the conscious and unconscious elements at hand, the ego selects one pathway of action. Rangell goes on to add that while problems of decision-making are involved in many different types of psychopathology, in some patients they form the main symptom. Four types of problems might result: (1) inability to make decisions, (2) reckless decisiveness (Akhtar & Byrne, 1983), (3) vacillation between choices, and (4) inability to reverse a decision after having made one. For psychoanalytic views on political decision-making, see Volkan et al. (1998).

Deep interpretation: term originated by Melanie Klein (1932) in the context of child analysis. She stated that the analyst should not shy away from making a 'deep interpretation' (p. 24) even at the start of the analysis. Disputing Anna Freud's (1927) recommendation of a prepatory phase before interpretive work could be done with children, Mrs Klein emphasized that 'we have to trace not only the representational content but also the anxiety and sense of guilt associated with it right down to that layer of the mind which is being activated. But if we take the principles of adult analysis as a model and proceed first of all to get into contact with the superficial strata of the mind— those who are nearest to the ego and to reality—we shall fail with children in our object of establishing the analytical situation and reducing their anxiety' (p. 25). The interpretation must not only be timely but also 'deep-going' (p. 25). While advocated in working with children, such technical style became the hallmark of the Kleinian approach to the adult patients as well. This elicited criticisms of undue certainty, disregard of resistance, and theoretical dogmatism from a variety of analysts (e.g., Balint, 1968). Recently Fred Busch (2000) has elucidated the arguments on the side opposed to the use of 'deep interpretations'. He distinguishes depth of understanding from the depth of interpretation and advocates careful 'resistance analysis' (see separate entry) before interpretation is proper. In essence, the Melanie Klein–Anna Freud schism continues unabated to date!

Deep self: see 'Designed self *vs.* deep self'.

Defence: see 'Defence mechanisms'.

Defence analysis: term originated by Anna Freud (1936) and popularized by Otto Fenichel (1941). It was an inevitable outcome of the discovery of the ego's role in warding off anxiety and creating symptoms as compromise formations. 'Defence analysis' required that interpretations be directed not only at instinctual fixations, but also at the means used to defend against anxieties caused by resurgent infantile wishes. Without this, analysis was only id analysis. A dictum arose in this context: defences should be analysed before addressing the drives they hide or oppose. However, following it literally (if that was even possible) led to caricatured and incomplete interventions. Charles Brenner (1976) highlighted this in his lucid text on technique. He declared that 'defense analysis is not done and can not be done in isolation, separately and apart from the other dynamic and genetic aspects of conflict' (p. 78). One almost always includes hints of the instinctual derivative being warded off while interpretating a defensive operation. See also John Munder Ross's (2003) recent paper on the topic.

Defence hysteria: see 'Hysteria'.

Defence mechanisms: the terms 'defence', 'mechanisms of defence', and 'defence mechanisms' made their earliest appearance in Sigmund Freud's (1895d) book *Studies on Hysteria*, his paper (1915e) 'The unconscious', and Anna Freud's (1936) monograph *The Ego and the Mechanisms of Defence*, respectively. Freud initially used the expression 'defence' synoynomously with 'repression' but later began to distinguish different types of defences in hysteria, phobia, and obsessional neurosis. It was, however, Anna Freud (1936) who offered the first well-organized and clinically illustrated list of defences. She listed nine mechanisms including 'regression', 'repression', 'reaction formation', 'isolation', 'undoing', 'projection', 'introjection', 'turning against the self' and 'reversal into the opposite'. A tenth mechanism called 'sublimation' was added by her, but it was supposed to be less of a defence than a 'normal' mechanism. Fascinatingly though, decades later in an interview with Joseph Sandler (Sandler & Freud, 1983), Miss Freud said that one does not really count such things! In between these two statements, she (1946) also described the mechanisms of 'denial', 'altrusitic surrender', and 'identification with the aggressor'. Separate entries on all these mechanisms exist in this glossary, and the reader might gather specific details about each mechanism by looking these up. And the list of 'defence mechanisms' has expanded from Miss Freud's original nine through Franz Alexander's (1948) eleven to Jerome Blackman's (2004) one hundred and one. Otto Fenichel's (1945) classification of defences into 'successful' (which bring about a cessation of what is warded off) and 'unsucessful' (where the warded-off material remains in suspension and threatens to break through) is also to be noted. Ten other points need emphasis: (1) all defences aim to reduce anxiety; (2) all defences operate unconsciously; (3) all defences have their roots in childhood; (4) some defences arise in association with specific developmental phases (e.g., reaction formation in anal phase); (5) some defences seem specific to certain psychopathologic syndromes (e.g., conversion to hysteria, undoing to obsessional neurosis); (6) some defences have more 'ego' in them (e.g., undoing) while others more 'id' (e.g., 'turning against the self'); (7) some defences (e.g., 'repression' and 'reaction formation') are permanent, others (e.g., 'undoing') employed when needed, and still others (e.g., displacement) occupy an intermediate place in this continuum; (8) 'defences' are not only defences; they also play a role in normal psychic structure formation (e.g., introjec-tion leading to enrichment of ego and especially superego); (9) while identifiable 'mechanisms of defence' (regardless of their number) do exist, it is also true that any activity can be used for defensive purposes. Anna Freud underscored this by saying that 'falling asleep is certainly not a defense mechanism but it can be used to defend against aggression' (Sandler & Freud, 1983, p. 43); and (10) there is some recognition that 'mature ego defences' can be distinguished from 'primitive ego defences' (see separate entries on all the terms rendered here within quotation marks).

Defence neuropsychosis: label assigned by Sigmund Freud (1894a) to a group of mental conditions in order to distinguish them from disorders caused by constitutional defects or by disturbances in the contemporary sexual life; the last mentioned were termed 'actual neurosis' (see separate entry). 'Defence neuropsychosis', also refered to as the 'neuropsychosis of defence' resulted from the deployment of defences against unpleasant ideas and memories arising out of childhood trauma. In a later paper, Freud (1896) described how the defence operated in specific conditions: in hysteria, the traumatic memory was *converted* into a somatic symptom; in phobia, the anxiety generated by the memory was *displaced* on to an external object; in obsession, the link between the disturbing idea and its accompanying affect was severed and the emotion was *isolated*; in certain hallucinatory psychoses, the recognition that a traumatic event had taken place was *repudiated*, and in paranoia, the origin of psychic disturbance was *projected* on to an outside or person. The concept of 'neuropsychosis of defence', however, was set aside when the role of actual sexual trauma during childhood was eclipsed by the discovery of the child's active fantasy life and especially of the Oedipus complex.

Defences against countertransference hatred: John Maltsberger and Dan Buie (1974) have outlined five such manoeuvres: (1) *repression* (resulting in boredom, excessive day dreaming, and frequent looking at the clock during the sessions, and altogether forgetting the patient's appointments); (2) *turning against the self* (with the analyst becoming doubtful about his skills and masochistically submissive to the patient); (3) *reaction formation* (resulting in excessive helpfulness and omnipotent rescue fantasies on the analytst's part); (4) *projection* (with the analyst beginning to dread that the patient will either attack him or commit suicide); (5) *distortion of reality* (resulting in the analyst's ignoring important information and altering clinical facts, and thus messing up the patient's treatment).

Defences against envy: according to Melanie Klein (1957), the main defences against envy are (i) contempt and devaluation, (ii) omnipotent control, and (iii) narcissistic withdrawal. By *contempt and devaluation*, the subject seeks to diminish his estimation of the object. By exerting *omnipotent control*, the subject forcibly takes over the envy producing qualities of the object. By *narcissistic withdrawal*, the subject shuns envy arousing objects and thus reduces his suffering. Though evident in individuals with all severe personality disorders, the use of these mechanisms is most marked in narcissistic personalities.

Defences against goodness: drawing upon the Kleinian ideas of 'goodness' being an attribute of the 'depressive position' (see separate entry) whereby omnipotence, greed, and envy are set aside in favour of concern, gratitude, and reparation, Roy Schafer (2002) introduced the idea that such 'goodness' is not easy to bear and is, at times, warded-off by characteristic mental mechanisms. Melanie Klein's (1946) idea that endangered good aspects of the self can be deposited into others for safekeeping readily comes to mind in this context, and so does Gregory Hamilton's (1986) elaboration of this Kleinian notion under the title of 'positive projective identification'. These contributions are not mentioned by Schafer in his paper. What Schafer does, however, is to emphasize that in approaching 'depressive position', one can develop 'massive reactions against feeling, believing in, and avowing openly personal goodness, and the goodness of (one's) primary objects' (p. 6). One tends then to hide what is good in oneself and attribute it to others. One also curtails attitudes that would elicit goodness from others towards oneself. All this is done to ward off the anxiety consequent upon renouncing narcissistic and sadomasochistic 'pleasures' and bearing the sweet burden of gratitide and of making reparation to others.

Defences against mental pain: in a comprehensive paper on 'mental pain' (see separate entry), Salman Akhtar (2000) has noted that many defences can be used against this disturbing experience. Each of these can have a pathological or healthy outcome, depending upon the intrapsychic and social context, and upon whether they ultimately permit mourning to take place or not. Essentially, these defences include the following: (1) *psychic retreat and self-holding*: if this is accompanied by a sense of futility and generalized inhibition of drive and ego functions, then the outcome is pathological. However, if the retreat is transient, focal, and is accompanied by an effort to sort out the ego weakening that has resulted from pain, then the outcome is not so bad after all. (2) *Denial and manic defence*: if this leads to 'psychic numbing' (Kogan, 1990), substance abuse, and promiscuity, then the knowledge of what is going on in the internal reality is diminished and the outcome is pathological. However, if the 'manic defence' (see separate entry) involves only the unaffected sector of the personality, then it can serve as an umbrella under which the pain-ridden part can carry out mourning in a piecemeal fashion. (3) *Extrusion of pain and its induction into others*: to a limited extent, self-protective indignation, and even rage, in the face of mental pain can serve adaptive purposes. (4) *Changing the form or function of pain*: such alterations can yield both pathological and healthy outcomes. Among the former are 'concretization' (Bergmann, 1982) through acting out; 'physicalization', that is, turning the mental pain into physical pain; and 'libidinization' (Fenichel, 1934). At the same time, some 'change of function' (see separate entry) *vis-à-vis* mental pain might prepare the ground for its creative sublimation.

Defensive and compensatory structures: terms used by Heinz Kohut (1977) to describe psychological structures built in early childhood to deal with a primary defect in the self. In Kohut's own words: 'I call a structure defensive when its sole or predominate function is the covering over of the primary defect in the self. I call a structure compensatory when, rather than merely covering a defect in the self, it compensates for that defect' (p. 5). Illustrating the latter by evoking his concept of 'bipolar self' (see separate entry) Kohut said that weakness of one pole of self (i.e., exhibitionism) is made up by the strengthening of the other pole (i.e., pursuit of ideals).

Defensive structures: see 'Defensive and compensatory structures'.

Deferred action: outlined by Sigmund Freud, this concept refers to the fact that experience not properly understood at one time can forcefully grab one's attention later and even become traumatic. Freud's (1918b) description of the Wolf Man contains the most lucid illustration of 'deferred action': the witnessing of the primal scene at one and half years of age became comprehensible and traumatic when a dream revived its memory at age four. The fact that the second occurence endowed the first with pathogenic force is the essence of 'deferred action' or, as Ludwig Eidelberg (1968) calls it, 'deferred reaction'.

Deferred obedience: term used by Sigmund Freud (1923b) for the observation that an unheeded parental threat or command may gain potency later on. Freud illustrated this idea by pointing to the seventeeth century painter, Christopher Heizman, who had ignored his father's opposition to his artistic career but succumbed to the filial prohibition upon the old man's death.

Deferred reaction: see 'Deferred action'.

Deferred revision: designation given by Jean Laplanche and Jean-Bernard Pontalis (1973) to Sigmund Freud's (1896) observation that memory traces are frequently subjected to rearrangement in accordance with fresh circumstances. They note that 'deferred revision is occasioned by events and situations, or by an organic maturation, which allowed the subject to gain access to a new level of meaning and to rework his earlier experiences' (p. 112).

Defilement complex: term coined by William Needles (1966) for the psychological consequences that, in his view, result from the proximity between vaginal, urinary, and rectal orifices and functions in the female. To function receptively in a zone otherwise reserved for eliminative procedures might give rise to a sense of 'defilement'. This, in turn, can lead to contempt for her own body that is repeatedly sullied, as well as hostility towards, and desire for revenge on, the defiler. The 'defilement complex' also draws its intensity from the fact that the vagina is often symbolically equated with the mouth. When marked, such a complex might lead to an aversion to accepting a feminine role in the sexual act and, therefore, to vaginismus and dyspareunia.

Defusion of instincts: see 'Fusion and defusion of instincts'.

Deglutitive stage of development: see 'Prenatal stage of development'.

Dehumanization: being human in a psychological sense, involves sharing a ubiquitous motivational substrate with fellow human beings as well as possessing certain psychosocial features that are common to the human experience. These include the capacity for thought and thinking, the acquisition of language, barriers against incest and murder, group affiliation, and the elaboration of myths and rituals. These shared structural and dynamic characteristics are at the heart of feeling and being human. When these characteristics are seriously impaired or totally lost, the psychologi-cal state is best referred to as 'dehumanization'. According to Salman Akhtar (2003), this state is characterized by 'a variable combination of callous disregard for one's body, focal or pervasive mindlessness, inability to contain affects and fantasies by symbolization, a horrifying disaffiliation from others and a profound lack of empathy with them, grotesque reduction or exaggeration of basic psychological needs, non-renunciation of infantile omnipotence, thanatophilia, poverty of language as a dominant mode of communication, and the collapse of barriers erected by civilization against incest and murder' (p. 132). Five, somewhat overlapping, aetiological types of dehumanization are (1) *deficiency-based* dehumanization, seen in feral children; (2) *defect-based* dehumanization, seen in infantile autism and severe cases of Asperger's Syndrome, (3) *regression-based* dehumanization, seen in schizophrenia, lycanthropy, and other psychotic states; (4) *identification-based* dehumanization, manifested by serial killers, and (5) *strategy-based* dehumanization, seen in association with terrorism and suicide bombing (for details, see Akhtar, 2003).

Deinstinctualization: the process by which an activity, fantasy, or affect becomes de-linked from its instinctual substrate. Its occurrence is evident in diminished pressure and urgency of that psychic phenomenon and by the greater dominance of ego over it. Removals or minimization of libidinal and aggressive charges are, respectively, termed 'desexualization' and 'deaggressivization' (see separate entries).

Delusion of clarity of insight: originally described by Donald Meltzer (1976), this phenomenon seems to result from the 'unconscious infantile phantasy of projective identification with the internal object, especially the mother's breast and head, experienced as the font of knowledge and wisdom' (p. 146). A characteristic aggressivization of the 'epistemophilic instinct' (see separate entry) and intellectual functions is evident under such circumstances. Patients who have the 'delusion of clarity of insight' develop cognitive grasp of a situation rapidly and then rigidly cling to it. However, their imagination is impoverished and their understanding is shallow. Other phenomena associated with 'delusion of clarity of insight' are 'sitting in judgement', aloofness, smugness, and superciliousness.

Demand: term used by Jacques Lacan (1958) to denote the infant's vocalization of his needs so that the mother can satisfy them. However, since the gratification depends upon the will of the

Other, therefore 'demand' comes to have two connotations: (1) anticulation of a need, and (2) appeal for the object's love. Similarly, in the clinical situation, the analysand's speech serves the dual function of (1) seeking a reply from the analyst, and (2) seeking the analyst's love or the encouragement and permission to identify with him.

Demaracation of the introject: see 'Re-grief therapy'.

Demarcation exercises: see 'Re-grief therapy'.

Denial: an unconsciously operative ego defence by which an individual reduces psychic distress by repudiating the awareness of a painful, external reality (A. Freud, 1946). Denial can be mild or severe, focal or generalized, and transient or persistent. It can be consonant with healthy mental functioning (e.g., affluent people in India remaining unperturbed when faced with beggars, psychoanalysts in terrorism-afflicted Israel debating clinical nuances), or it can betray psychopathology (e.g., a bereaved person believing that his or her dead relative is actually alive). Some degree of transient denial is common in the early stages of loss and trauma but its persistence and tenacity after some time begins to be worrisome. In medical settings, patients often deny the full impact of knowing their clinical condition. This can often be left unchallenged especially if the patient is largely able and willing to follow the physician's recommendation. For instance, an individual who refuses to acknowledge that he has cancer but is willing to try radiation therapy does not need an unmasking of his defensive posture. (While the foregoing carries the usual emphasis upon repudiation of external reality in denial, it should be noted that, in Melanie Klein's (1935) work, the defence is also seen directed at internal reality. This matter is covered in more detail under 'manic defence').

Denial by exaggeration: see 'Exaggeration as a defence'.

Dependence: since the human infant is unable to survive on its own, reliance on others is its inherent neccessity. At the dawn of life, such 'dependence' is total and, in its neediness, indifferent to the caregiver's (mostly mother's) inclinations and desires. Mother's own joyous ego regression helps sustain this early infantile 'dependence', in so far as the two partners in the dyad form a 'dual unity' (see separate entry). Described from different vantage points as 'mother–infant symbiosis' (Mahler, Pine, & Bergman, 1975), 'absolute dependence' (Fairbairn, 1952), and the state of 'illusion' and 'omnipotence' (Winnicott, 1960), this state of affairs is short-lived. With burgeoning ego maturity, increasing capacity for self-object differentiation, and enhanced reality testing, 'absolute dependence' gives way to 'relative dependence'. The establishment of 'object constancy' (see separate entry) especially diminishes reliance on external objects. This is, however, not a once and for all achievement. Continued availability of love objects and optimal gratification of drives and ego needs strengthens the psychic structure in this regard. Adolescence ushers in a need for disengagement from early objects; caricatured states of independence are frequent at this time. Finally, the young adult arrives at 'mature dependence', which is characterized by mutuality, reciprocity, and acceptance of limits of what others can provide. Anna Freud (1963) has delineated this 'developmental line' (see separate entry) in detail, and Henri Parens and Leon Saul (1971) have elucidated the gradual emergence of 'inner sustainment' (see separate entry) in a growing child. Pathological developments in this realm include both excessive and inadequate dependence on others. The former is manifested via clinging behaviours, vulnerability to 'anaclitic depression' (see separate entry), and addictions. The latter is evident in the autistic spectrum disorders ranging from early infantile autism through Asperger's Syndrome to the more commonly encountered schizoid personality.

Depersonalization: psychiatric term for a subjective experience that one's self is somehow unreal. The subjective experience splits into two: detached observer self and a devitalized experiencing self. 'A feeling of conviction about personal identity is retained, but the sense is stronger than that with the participating self' (Moore & Fine, 1990, p. 52). 'Depersonalization' may occur alone or in combination with 'derealization' (see separate entry). Though earlier explanations emphasized economic shifts in the distribution of libido, current views (e.g., Arlow, 1966) regard 'depersonalization' as the consequence of defences against exhibitionistic and hostile impulses. Paul Bradlow (1973) goes one step further and regards 'depersonalization' to be a result of ego splitting. The underlying fantasy can be expressed as: 'this is not really being experienced (felt) by me, but by someone else. That other person is not human. I am. Therefore I have nothing to be anxious about' (p. 491).

Depersonification of superego: Edith Jacobson's (1964) phrase for the softening of archaic morality emanating from a literal internalization of early parental dictates. Typically, such mellowing occurs during adolescence, when greater ego-autonomy and trial identifications with peers and extra-familial figures yield other ways of negotiating drive pressures. Concrete details of what one learned as being 'good' or 'bad' conduct is replaced by a more abstract morality that is contextually anchored and shows greater loyalty to the spirit of ethical standards than to the letter of the law. While Jacobson described this process as occurring during adolescence, the fact is that refinement of superego functions continues throughout adult life.

Depletion anxiety: term coined by Stanley Cath (1965) to denote the growing awareness among the elderly that their psychosocial reserves are both diminished and vulnerable. Reliance upon one's body becomes shaky. Monetary status dips down and friends begin to die. A fear that no one will be there when help is needed crops up. If the individual's early world has been plagued by persecutory anxieties and feelings of emptiness, the age-specific onset of depletion anxiety 'confirms' infantile fears of retribution and despair.

Deployment: observing that an unmistakable element of power lurked in the background of the defensive structures used by certain narcissistic–masochistic patients, Rena Moses-Hrushovski (1994) introduced the concept of 'deployment'. In her view, such patients showed a stubborn determination to hold on to their misery. They displayed a strong wish for the acknowledgement of their suffering and for a reversal of the injustices inflicted upon them. The force and rigidity with which they carried on their repetitions reminded one of the ways a general 'deploys' his armies, with overt and covert power struggles and an insistent wielding of power at the core of the configuration. The pathological element here is the investment of excessive energy in rigid ways of perceiving, feeling, and acting. Most such patients have been raised by narcissistic parents, exploited, and severely shamed during their childhood.

Deposited representations: see 'Replacement child'.

Depression: a clinical syndrome characterized by sad mood, psychomotor retardation, anhedonia, and the 'vegetative signs' of insomnia, anorexia, weight loss, and diminished sexual desire. Feelings of worthlessness, hopelessness, and guilt are frequent accompaniments and contribute to suicidal tendencies and sometimes to actual 'suicide'

(see separate entry). While attention is increasingly being directed to hereditary predisposition and a neurochemical substrate of 'depression', there is little denying that psychodynamic factors play an important role in most, if not all, clinical cases. Treatment is, therefore, more effective when psychotherapy is combined with medication. As far as the psychological aetiology (or, at least, psychological contributions to aetiology) is concerned, many models have been proposed; those listed below constitute only the most prominent ones: (1) *Karl Abraham* (1911) emphasized the role of intense ambivalence that paralysed the individual's capacity to love; the hatred underlying this incapacity is repressed and then projected on to the world. As a result, the individual feels unloved, hated, and depressed. Abraham traced the depressive's eating difficulties to oral-sadistic conflicts; (2) *Sigmund Freud* (1917e), in his seminal paper 'Mourning and melancholia' distinguished grief from depression on the grounds of the occurrence of guilty self-reproaches in the latter. He proposed that this is due to the substitution of identification for object love; the hostile component of object-investment is redirected at the ego which has become identified with the lost object. In a striking statement, Freud compared the suicidal tendency of the melancholic to the state of falling in love; in suicide, the ego surrenders itself to a 'bad' object, while in love it submits to a 'good' object; (3) *Sandor Rado* (1928) highlighted the narcissistic intolerance of the depressive. He felt that the depressive angrily rebels upon the loss of a narcissistically adoring object, and only when such rebellion fails does he emit a 'great despairing cry for love' (p. 425) in the form of remorse and depression; (4) *Melanie Klein* (1934) distinguished between the unmetablolized and externalized rage of the 'paranoid position' from the genuine, remorseful, and concerned sadness of the 'depressive position' (see separate entries). Her observations were elaborated upon and applied to the distinction between the depression seen in the setting of borderline conditions from that seen in better organized, higher level neurotics (Kernberg, 1970); (5) *John Bowlby* (1961, 1963) suggested that the sequence of protest, despair, and detachment displayed by children separated from their mothers captures the essence of 'despair'. The melancholic pathology lies not in his age at abandonment, but in the misdirection of the resulting anger to himself. The five models mentioned here do not exhaust the list. Major contributions to the psychoanalytic understanding of depression have been made by other psychoanalysts as well, including Edward Bibring (1953) and Edith Jacobson (1946, 1953, 1971). For interesting clinical material, see Harvey Rich (1985) and Vamik Volkan (1985) and for a comprehensive review of these models, see the impressive monograph by Myer Mendelson (1974).

Depressive character: though descriptions of a personality type associated with vulnerability to depression had existed for a long time within both descriptive psychiatry (Kraepelin, 1921; Bleuler, 1911; Kretschmer, 1925) and psychoanalysis (Abraham, 1924b; Glover, 1925; Reich, 1933), the term 'depressive character' itself made its appearance only in the 1950s. Frieda Goldman-Eisler (1953) desribed the 'depressive character ' as having a profoundly pessimistic outlook on life, a passive–receptive attitude, intense feelings of insecurity coupled with a need for the assurance of getting a guaranteed livelihood, and a tendency towards periods of depression and withdrawal. Some years later, Bernhard Berliner (1966) published what is arguably the first paper with the term 'depressive character' in its title; Eli Marcovitz (1966) wrote an accompanying discussion in the same issue of the journal. Together, they portrayed individuals with such character as having unhappy childhoods infiltrated with 'moral masochism' (see separate entry). Often their parents were depressed themselves. The child 'absorbed' suffering and sadness and found such adaptation as the only way to survive. His pain became libidinized and took the place of absent or inadequate nursing and cuddling. A constitutionally stronger than usual oral and skin eroticism, which had characterized such a child to begin with, became intensified owing to early deprivations of loving care. Hurt at the hands of parents gave rise to rage, which contributed to the ferocity of the superego formed under such circumstances.

Depressive position: Melanie Klein's (1940) term for the psychic stance in which all aggression is not projected outwards. This development occurs around 4–6 months of age, and is a consequence of the infant's integrating his or her fragmented perceptions of the mother and bringing together the 'good' and 'bad' mother representations. This gives rise to the replacement of 'part objects' by a 'whole object' (see separate entries). The 'all good' internal object is lost forever, and this gives rise to painful phantasies and exquisite sorrow. The child begins to see that he also has been destructive and that others have not always been 'bad'. He begins to recognize having received goodness and having caused hurt to others. Capacity for concern now arises, and so does the tendency towards reparation and genuine love. Clearly, such capacities are achieved only gradually by the

child. Humility and gratitude are the major attitudinal consequences of the 'depressive position'. The achievement of this position is not a once-and-for-all event, and bearing the emotions associated with it is hardly easy. The temptation to drop them in favour of 'manic defence' (see separate entry) is great. Vulnerability to regression into 'paranoid position' (see separate entry) also remains throughout life. Therefore, the mental functioning at the level of 'depressive position' needs vigilance and safeguarding. Hanna Segal (1956) added that, in some extremely ill individuals, the rudiments of 'depressive position' are experienced only by the therapist in whom they have been deposited by the use of 'projective identification' (see separate entry). The reader would benefit by looking up Robert Hinshelwood's (1989) thorough exposition of 'depressive position'.

Depth-psychology: designation ostensibly originated by Eugene Bleuler (Moore & Fine, 1990) to distinguish psychoanalysis from other psychological approaches to the study of the human mind. The expression 'depth-psychology' became over-extended to include a diverse set of theories about the complexity of human mental functioning and thus lost its value. However, Stanley Greenspan and Stuart Shanker (2005) have recently resurrected this term, offering a straightforward definition for it: 'Depth psychology concerns itself with levels of the mind that influence mental health and mental illness but are often not manifested directly in surface behaviors and in non-clinical settings' (p. 335). Their explication of the term leaves no doubt that they are employing the term synonymously with psychoanalysis. Bleuler would have been delighted!

Depth-rendering interventions: Salman Akhtar's (1998) designation for analytic interventions that impart the knowledge to the patient that multiple meanings co-exist in his or her communication, though at differing levels of abstraction, awareness, and importance. By doing so, 'depth-rendering interventions' give the various aspects of the patient's material a figure–ground relationship with each other. To use a phrase of Julia Kristeva's (1987), such interventions aim at 'layering of significance' (p. 6).

Derealization: psychiatric term for the subjective experience that the outer world is somehow unreal. The experience, occurring alone or in combination with 'depersonalization' (see separate entry), reflects a defensive denial of external reality (Arlow, 1966). It is frequently seen in early stages of schizophrenia, where it forms a component of 'world-destruction fantasies' (see separate entry). However, it can also occur in less drastic circumstances involving difficult reality situations.

Derivative of the unconscious: see 'Derivatives'.

Derivatives: the repressed psychic contents exert 'a continuous upward pressure in the direction of consciousness' (Freud, 1915e, p. 151) and, by pushing towards awareness and motility, become attached to associatively connected ideas that are unobjectionable to the conscious ego. These conscious links to the 'dynamic unconscious' (see separate entry) are called 'derivatives'. It is by facilitating their recognition that the repressed material is inferred and made available for interpretation during the clinical work of psychoanalysis.

Descriptive unconscious: see 'Unconscious'.

Desexualization: term proposed by Sigmund Freud (1923b) to denote the process by which the sexual energy, or 'libido' (see separate entry), was denuded of its charge and turned into neutral energy. By itself 'desexualization' is neither normal nor abnormal; it is integral to the process of 'sublimation' (see separate entry), but can also be seen in inhibited or automatized sexuality.

Designed self: see 'Designed self *vs.* deep self'.

Designed self *vs.* deep self: Carlo Strenger's (1998, 2004) phrase for the dialectical tension between the fragmented, pluralistic, ahistorical, and manufactured persona ('designed self'), that has become increasingly the modal psychic structure these days, and inner, ontogenetically anchored, authentic core ('deep self') that none the less survives the sociocultural and narcissistic assault upon it. Strenger explicates how the conflict between self-creation and the inevitable legacy of one's past impacts upon clinical phenomenology and technique.

Desire: term used by Jacques Lacan (1977) to denote the left-over quantum of 'demand' (see separate entry) after its gratification in reality. Lacan's view of 'desire' emphasizes the following four characteristics: (1) its being unconscious, (2) its being sexual in nature, (3) its uncompatibility with speech, and (4) its distinction from 'demand' and 'need'. 'Need' is biological and is verbalized in the form of 'demand'. In contrast, 'desire is neither the appetite for satisfaction, nor the demand

for love, but the difference that results from the subtraction of the first from the second' (p. 287).

Desomatization: see 'Somatization'.

Destiny neurosis: term used by Heinz Lichtenstein (1963) to denote the driven and unwavering attitude with which certain individuals follow a particular path in life. Lichtenstein traced such compulsion to a mother's strong imprinting of a particular psychic agenda on her newborn child. Such rigid and specific, even though silent, injunction for the child to become this or that is distinct from the normal situation whereby 'the mother imprints upon the infant not an identity but an identity theme' (p. 208) which is capable of variations. Lichtenstein's concept of 'destiny neurosis' has some overlap with Sigmund Freud's (1920) notion of 'fate compulsion' or 'fate neurosis' (see separate entry) although it lacks the masochistic element typical of the latter.

Destructive instinct: see 'Aggressive instinct'.

Destrudo: a term coined by Wihelm Stekel in the early 1920s (Gay, 1988) to denote the psychic energy of the death instinct. Intended to be analogous to 'libido' (the psychic energy of the life instinct), the term never gained Sigmund Freud's favour. As a result, it soon vanished from psychoanalytic literature.

Desymbolization: a term coined by Harold Searles (1962) for a process whereby once-attained metaphorical meanings revert to their earlier, concrete status. The individual reacts to them as being literal and is puzzled by them. While Searles developed this notion in connection with his work with schizophrenic patients, the tendency towards 'desymbolization' can also be seen in other conditions, including organic brain syndromes.

Desymbolizing effect: Ilse Grubrich-Simitis's (1984) concept pertaining to the impairment in the capacity to use and understand metaphors and higher connotative levels of language as a result of the distorted reality in political imprisonment and concentration camps.

Determining power of names: in a paper with this very title, Karl Abraham (1911) highlighted the fact that the name a child is given can impact upon his 'destiny' (i.e., psychologically determined path of life) in a profound way. To be sure, it is not merely the name itself, but the parental fantasies and emotions encrypted and deposited in the child via a particular name that have the 'determining power' here. And, needless to say, all this unfolds in the context of child–parent relationship as well as the vicissitudes of the child's fantasy life, drive economy, and ego development. In later phases of life also, one's name can acquire great emotional significance. The adoption of Anglo-Saxon sounding names by the Jewish analysts fleeing Europe during the Second World War (e.g., Mihaly Bergsmann taking on the name Michael Balint) is a case in point here. The founder of psychoanalysis had himself shortened his first name, Sigismund, to Sigmund!

Deutro-phallic phase: see 'Proto-phallic and deutro-phallic phase'.

Development: psychoanalysis views development as an 'on-going process, in which the psychic structures and functions determining the human personality gradually evolve from the personal experiences of a biologically maturing individual in interaction with important people in his or her environment' (Tyson & Tyson, 1995, p. 395). While many expository and conceptual models exist in the study of this realm (see Tyson & Tyson, 1990) and not all apply with comparable relevance to various periods in the human life span, consensus more or less exists about the following points: (1) hereditary proclivities dialectically interact with personal experience (and fantasies) to create psychic structures; (2) early caretakers, especially the mother, play a profoundly important role in facilitating attachment, evoking inherent potentials, and providing a resilient scaffold for the growth of personality; (3) early environmental influences can influence neural patterning which, in turn, affects the processes of abstraction, self-reflection, and internalization; (4) conflicts between the child's drives and their regulation by the external environment are gradually internalized, giving rise to the capacity to experience intrapsychic conflict; (5) over time, the working of psychic systems tends to accommodate concerns of reality, besides those of instinctual discharge and pleasure; (6) encounter with the triangular family constellation (i.e., child, mother, father) imparts to the personality the capacity to accept generational differences, incest barrier, and respect for the dimension of time; (7) after a period of lull in instinctual activit,y during which task-orientated ego functions flourish, adolescence provides a turmoil-ridden second opportunity to work through the psychic lessons of childhood; (8) forward and backward movements, rather than a linear pathway, characterize 'development' throughout the life span, and (9) 'development' does not stop with entry into adulthood; it is a life-long process and extends through midlife (when a final mourning of unexpressed self-representations and a reworking of reversed oedipal configurations involving one's children takes place) and old age (when a deep and post-ambivalent view of the world one has lived in and is about to leave needs to be evolved) through death. While it is not possible to list all those who have made significant contributions to the psychoanalytic understanding of 'development', to omit the following would amount to a heuristic and historical sin: Sigmund Freud, Melanie Klein, Anna Freud, Rene Spitz, Donald Winnicott, Erik Erikson, Margaret Mahler, Selma Fraiberg, Phyllis Greenacre, John Bowlby, Humberto Nagera, Albert Solnit, Sally Provence, Eleanor Galenson, Peter Blos, Sr., Calvin Settlage, Henri Parens, Louis Sander, Daniel Stern, Phyllis Tyson, Robert Tyson, Robert Emde, Jack Novick, Kerry Kelly Novick, Peter Neubauer, Peter Fonagy, Calvin Colarusso, George Vaillant, and Annemarie Weil. Mention of the numerous contributions made by these outstanding individuals is scattered throughout this glossary.

Developmental arrest: see 'Fixation'.

Developmental conflict: Humberto Nagera's (1966) term for the dilemmas experienced by the child 'either when certain specific environmental demands are made at the appropriate developmental phases, or when the child reaches a certain developmental and maturational level at which specific conflicts are created' (p. 41). Toilet training illustrates the first type of trigger, and maturational arrival at the oedipal phase the second type of trigger for a 'developmental conflict'. Nagera notes that 'developmental conflict' differs from 'developmental interference' (see separate entry) in being a phase-specific, normal, and expectable occurrence. Moreover, while a 'developmental interference' is invariably of external origin, a 'developmental conflict' can become an 'internalized conflict' (A. Freud, 1962) once the environmental demands are instituted within the child's own psychic structure; this is also referred to as an 'internal developmental conflict' (Nagera, 1966, p. 43). Finally, it should be noted that a 'developmental conflict' is usually transitory and disappears more or less completely once the specific developmental phase is over. When this does not happen and the 'developmental conflict' persists, a move towards the formation of a neurotic conflict is evident. Before one can make the diagnosis of the latter with certainty, however, a period of ambiguity is encountered during which the conflicts are better termed 'transitory developmental neurotic conflicts'.

Developmental disharmony: Anna Freud's (1965) term for the 'uneven progression rate in drive and ego development' (p. 218) which contributes to the intensification of an ordinarily evolving 'developmental conflict' (see separate entry). Under normal circumstances, such 'disharmonies' are dealt with by confident support and love from the parents. When this is missing, or when the disharmony is pronounced, serious conflicts arise. Sylvan Keiser's (1969) concept of a greater vulnerability to neurosis in gifted children is a case in point here; the perceptual and cognitive egos of such children are capable of knowing more about their parents weaknesses and instinctual life than their defensive capacities allowed them to metabolize.

Developmental distance: Albert Solnit's (1983) phrase for the gap between two siblings in terms of their inner fantasy life as well as the ego capacities for regulation, anticipation, and adaptation to reality. A finer measure than mere chronological difference, 'developmental distance' helps to ascertain what kind of relationship the two siblings might have with each other. When 'separated by more developmental space, they may be living in widely separated developmental epochs (e.g. a two year old and a his nine year-old sibling) . . . .their ease in communicating, empathizing, and identifying with each other is not nearly as great as in siblings who are developmentally close to each other' (p. 284).

Developmental interference: Humberto Nagera's (1966) term for the derailments of personality developments due to 'happenings, situations, conditions, or events' (p. 17) that significantly depart from the 'average expectable environment' (see separate entry). Circumstances that place unjustified demands upon a growing child (e.g., long separation from mother, premature toilet training, surgery, death of a sibling) alter the normal unfolding of development and lead to psychopathology. The impact of a 'developmental interference' varies with the age of the child, the level of ego and drive maturation at the time of interference, and the prescence or absence of ameliorating factors.

Developmental intervention: Samuel Abrams' (1978) concept of 'developmental intervention' refers to the analyst's supportively underscoring the progressive trend when hitherto unexpressed health capacity emerges as a result of interpretive work. In other words, rather than interpretively deconstruct, the analyst simply acknowledges and upholds the patient's newly acquired ability. The following remarks illustrate the use of this tool. 'It is significant that you were able to experience yourself in a mixed light, not as the usual all-good or all-bad'. Or, 'we can observe that you are now able to see things from someone else's point of view also'. Such interventions provide the patient access to the silent progressive trends activated by the treatment. Abrams states that 'aiding in the distinction between the progressive and regressive may result in a further sharpening of the expressions of the transference neurosis; and, by rendering a progressive potential into consciousness, one might facilitate the emergence of experiential building-blocks necessary for development' (p. 397).

Developmental lines: Anna Freud's (1981a) term for the step-by-step delineation of the evolution of psychic functions from their earliest origins through their intermediate forms to their mature, adult versions. Viewing the gradual development toward adult sexual and love life as the earliest 'developmental line' traced by psychoanalysis, she noted that mature functioning depends on the interaction and integration of drives, ego functions, superego actions, and environmental influence. Miss Freud extended such conceptualization and elucidated three other 'developmental lines', namely, those pertaining to (1) ability to work, (2) peer relationships, and (3) possession of one's own body. She stated that 'disharmonies, arrests, and deviations on developmental lines are responsible for many of the oddities, infantilisms, and borderline features of problem children' (p. 135). Such pathology needs to be distinguished from that consequent upon neurotic conflict, even though the two can mutually reinforce each other. To confuse them with each other 'constitutes a diagnositic error [and] is also a grave disservice to task of matching the child's disorder with the treatment most appropriate for it' (p. 136). The concept of 'developmental lines' was later applied to acquisition of language (Edgcumbe, 1981), relationship with the inanimate surroundings (Akhtar, 2003), and the defence of negation (Litowitz, 1998).

Developmental psychopathology: refers to a diverse group of symptomatology that includes 'developmental arrest', impact of 'developmental disharmony', the perpetuation of 'developmental conflict', and the long-term effects of 'developmental interference' (see separate entries). Contributions of Anna Freud (1962, 1963, 1965), Rene Spitz (1959, 1965), Donald Winnicott (1953, 1960,

1971), Humberto Nagera (1963, 1964, 1966), Albert Solnit (1970, 1982), Sam Abrams (1978, 1983, 1986, 1990), Robert Emde (1980), and Henri Parens (1989) are of seminal importance in this realm.

Developmental tasks of adult life: contrary to the early psychoanalytic assumption that an individual's personality is given its more or less final shape by childhood experiences, contemporary observers hold that development is a life-long process. Not only does 'adolescence' (see separate entry) offer the possibility of reworking early internalizations, adulthood itself engenders potentials for further growth. Indeed each subsequent phase (young adulthood, full adulthood, middle life, and old age) presents new challenges for internal drive economy and external adaptation and, thus, opens up avenues for ego growth. In Erik Erikson's (1950) terms, adulthood includes the mastery of three polarities: 'intimacy *vs.* isolation,' 'generativity *vs.* stagnation', and 'integrity *vs.* despair' (see separate entries on each). In his own words, 'a widening commitment to take care of the persons, the products, and the ideas one has learned to care for' (Erikson, 1982, p. 67) characterizes adulthood. This means leaving behind the uncertainties of the erstwhile psychic life. With the onset of young adulthood (from 22–28), for instance, the emotional volatility, indifference to the world at large, and smug self-acceptance of adolescence are put aside. Four important tasks facing the young adult are (1) forming a 'dream' and giving it a place in the life narrative, (2) finding a 'mentor' (see separate entry), (3) making a decisive vocational choice, and (4) establishing mature love relationships (Levinson, Darrow, Klein, Levinson, & McKee, 1978). The 'dream' may be actively pursued and lived up to, or modified, rebelled against, and even totally dropped. It is, however, an important developmental step to consolidating young adulthood. The same is true of the 'mentor', who is helpful as a guide and facilitator of psychosocial growth but is usually left behind after a few years. Even the vocational and romantic choices of this phase have a bit of trial-and-error quality. By the age of 30, full adulthood is on the scene. The 'dream,' by now modified and de-instinctualized enough to be realistic and broken down into its step-by-step components, is translated into gradual action. Vocational choice becomes firm. Mentors begin to turn into colleagues and the 'ideal spouse representation' (see separate entry) is renounced in favour of a realistic romantic object choice. Marriage and parenthood further strengthen a sense of personal integrity. Raising children can put one's own inner 'object constancy' (see separate entry) to the

test. Being the recipient of a child's rapprochement subphase turbulence, the adult parent has to modulate her or his own reciprocal drives and contradictory representations of the offspring. Subsequently, the capacity to tolerate the child's oedipal intrusiveness and hostility tests the parental capacity to retain 'optimal distance' (see separate entry). Children's passage through adolescence similarly puts a burden upon the parent's ego. Then, middle age comes and brings new challenges (Erikson, 1950; Kernberg, 1980; Levinson, Darrow, Klein, Levinson, & McKee, 1978). Time now enters the life experience in a sharp way. More of life is felt to be gone, less left. One begins to approach the limits of physical prowess, material acquisition, creativity, and of one's stay in this world. The fact of one's coming death can no longer be denied. This can cause considerable anxiety and stir up an 'asceticism–greed' dilemma' (see separate entry), with its regressive pull in the direction of either anhedonic withdrawal from life or a grotesque recourse to 'youthfulness'; the latter is often accompanied by extra-marital affairs and dramatic vocational changes. Under favourable psychoeconomical circumstances, however, the mourning of mute and unexpressed self-representations is better handled and there is a compensatory deepening of what one indeed has become. Independence of children is responded to by tenderness and pride rather than begrudging envy and bitterness. Identifications with one's own parents, now feeble and near death, are finally buttressed. Finally, during old age, as one approaches death oneself, a deep and post-ambivalent view of the world that one has lived in and is about to leave needs to be developed in order for this final transition to be smooth and the legacy one is leaving behind to be meaningful. This thumbnail sketch of 'adult development' can hardly do justice to the complexities of the issues involved, and the reader would benefit by looking up further material on this topic, especially the highly significant writings of Stanley Cath (1965, 1966, 1997); Calvin Colarusso and Robert Nemiroff (1979, 1981), Leo Madow (1997), and George Vaillant (1977).

Developmental tasks of early adulthood: see 'Developmental tasks of adult life'.

Developmental tasks of full adulthood: see 'Developmental tasks of adult life'

Developmental tasks of middle age: see 'Developmental tasks of adult life'.

Developmental tasks of old age: see 'Developmental tasks of adult life'.

Developmental work: implicit in the writings of Samuel Abrams (1978) and Calvin Settlage (1989, 1993), the concept of 'developmental work', has been most clearly spelled out by Fred Pine (1987, 1997). Essentially this involves (1) naming of affects, (2) helping the patient to find words for inner experiences, (3) confirming the patient's reality, (4) continuing to work with the patient in a matter-of-fact way even in the face of what, to the patient, might be reprehensible, (5) surviving the patient's assaults, and (6) maintaining hope over long periods of time when the patient might feel no reason to remain optimistic. Moreover, there needs to be a deep regard for the fact that psychic development is lifelong. The analyst might also benefit by recognizing that analytic process, like good parenting, includes both a context of safety and an exception of autonomous functioning. Indeed, it attempts to weave them together and uses both interpretive and relational interventions for this purpose.

Dialogue with oneself as a source of refuelling: a novel idea proposed by Joseph Sandler and Anne-Marie Sandler (1998), who stated that a growing child 'constantly and automatically scans and has a dialogue with his own self to get refueling and affirmation, through the perception of cues that his self is his old familiar self, that it is no stranger to him. He is normally constantly gaining a feeling of consonance from his own self-representation. If, on the other hand, he perceives a sudden chance in his own self-image, he may be exposed to dissonance or even a stranger panic in the same way as when confronted with a strange person' (pp. 97–98). While set in the child developmental context, these ideas might apply to adults as well. Dialogue with oneself can have ego-replenshing potential for them too. Elaboration of this idea can shed light on certain aspects of psychoanalytic process (e.g., pensive silences of the patient) as well as the potential overlap of psychoanalysis with Zen Buddhism (Coltart, 2000; Nichol, 2006; Rubin, 1995).

Differential use of the mother's and father's bodies by a growing child: it is Kyle Pruett's (1988, 2000) observation that a growing child uses the bodies of two parents for different psychological purposes. The mother's body is primarily used for seeking nourishment, soothing, and a haven from the menaces of external reality. The father's body is primarily used for horseplay, testing one's strength against, and enlarging one's receptive or motoric scope *vis-à-vis* external reality. A toddler's running to his or her mother for a caress after being hurt in play and a child sitting on his father's shoulder to be able to see further are analytic illustrations of this difference.

Differentiation subphase: from about 4–5 to 8–9 months of age; this is the first subphase of separation–individuation (Mahler, Pine, & Bergman, 1975). Inwardly propelled by autonomy strivings, the child begins to discern his psychic separateness through rudimentary exploration of the self, the mother, and the environment. The associated increase in alertness is called 'hatching', i.e., coming out of the common mother–child symbiotic membrane.

Direct analysis: a now-abandoned psychotherapeutic method that was evolved by John Rosen (1947, 1953) for the treatment of schizophrenia. Rosen acknowledged that he had named the method 'direct psychoanalysis', or simply 'direct analysis', at the suggestion of Paul Federu, a renowned psychoanalyst of that time. Essentially, Rosen's treatment consisted of three elements (1) the interpretative element aimed at communicating directly with the patient's unconscious, presumably with the id or with the ego states of infancy and childhood. The analyst made 'transference psychosis' (see separate entry) a tool of therapy and entered the patient's delusional world, after playing out the role of patient's imaginary tormentors, only with a benevolent twist. Interpretations were offered in a simple, blunt, and direct way ('you want to fuck your mother', 'you want to suck my cock') and were supposed to work like listening or reading to poetry does; (2) the supportive element was constituted by an offer to the patient of what he had supposedly lacked, namely, maternal love. Here, Rosen predated Donald Winnicott (1960) in suggesting that, for a growing child, mother equals environment, and it is the miscarriage of this early maternal environment that underlies severe psychopathology. Rosen, therefore, attempted to be kind, supportive, and exceedingly available to the patient, often spending up to sixteen hours a day with him; (3) the classical element comprised analysis conducted in the usual manner after the patient has been brought out of psychosis by the first two steps. Rosen's method appeared successful, at times dramatically so, but the results did not stand up to careful scrutiny. Whatever improvement did occur in his patient seems to have been a response to his charisma and enthusiasm and not to his treatment method. None the less, for a while, at least, he injected therapeutic zeal in the psychotherapeutic management of schizophrenia and his work was expounded and extended by Morris Brody (1959) and Spurgeon English,

William Hampe, Catherine Bacon, and Calvin Settlage (1961).

Direct countertransference: see 'Countertransference'.

Direct psychoanalysis: see 'Direct analysis'.

Disaggregation: see 'Disassociation'.

Disavowal: translation of *Verleugnung*, a German word Sigmund Freud (1924d) used, at first, for the little girl's refusal to acknowledge her lack of a penis, and later (1927c) to explain the fetishist's retaining two contradictory attitudes by which he simultaneously acknowledges and repudiates the absence of penis in women. The term 'disavowal' is often used interchangeably with 'denial' (Laplanche & Pontalis, 1973; Moore & Fine, 1990). However, subtle differences in their usage seem to exist. While both involve a refusal to accept painful aspects of reality, the use of this term 'denial' has been extended in the Kleinian tradition to include aspects of psychic reality, especially unacceptable self-representations. Additionally, 'disavowal' is consistently seen as leading to splitting of the ego (Freud, 1927c, 1940a [1938]), while no such connotation accompanies the term 'denial'.

Discharge: term used by Sigmund Freud (1900a, 1905a, 1915c) for the release of psychic energy into the external world. The resulting diminution of tension was associated with pleasure. Thus, 'pleasure principle' (see separate entry) involved quick and full discharge as against 'reality principle' (see separate entry), which inserted thought and judgement as intermediate steps in the path of instinctual pressure; resulting in a delayed or partial discharge.

Disclaimed action: Roy Schafer's (1973b) term for instances of masked activity as well as for passivity that appears, on closer examination, to be a rather determined form of activity. Slips of the tongue are prime examples of 'disclaimed action', where the individual disowns the intention to commit the act altogether. Another example is how some people refer to their mind (e.g., 'suicide entered my mind') as if they have no responsibility for it. Such statements imply that there is an agent who exists, or can exist, apart from the individual's own mind. The experience of conflict often shows a similar disclaimer, whereby one side of the two vectors in conflict is seen as not belonging to one's self.

Discriminating function of the ego: described by Frederick Hacker (1962), this aspect of the autonomous ego involves deciding 'which needs and tendencies should temporarily or permanently gain ascendancy, and whether at any given time superego, realistic, or id demands should be fulfilled, in what proportion, to what extent, and for what period of time' (p. 395). As a result, this function would determine the internal integrity as well as the behavioural coherence of the ego. Its failure, under-development, or malfunctioning would contribute to the manifestations of character pathology. Referring to such a situation, Hacker introduced the tongue-in-cheek phrase 'ego in the service of regression'.

Disgust: according to Otto Fenichel, 'disgust' is a feeling of revulsion with three levels (1) a physiological response to be repelled by certain tastes and smells, (2) its use by the ego for defensive purposes, especially for warding off oral and anal drives; overly intense disgust reactions, however, betray their character as a 'reaction formation' (see separate entry), where the suppressed interest in faeces, for instance, occasionally breaks through to the surface, and (3) 'neurotic attacks of disgust' (p. 139), in which the ego is completely overwhelmed by the affect, which was intended for defensive purposes. Here, disgust can become quite similar to guilt, especially when it is disgust with oneself.

Disidentification: term used to describe the shedding of the effects of an erstwhile identification. *Metapsychologically*, 'disidentification' implies decathexis of those aspects of self-representation that were derived from the introjection of an object's qualities. *Phenomenologically*, it implies change in the subjective experience and overt behaviour that emulated a particular object. 'Disidentification' is evident in the boy's development when, in order to consolidate his sense of masculinity, he moves away from mother (see 'Boy's dis-identification with the mother'). It is evident in full force, in both boys and girls, during adolescence, when disengagement with archaic ego and superego introjects occurs.

Disidentification with the aggressor: Glen Gabbard's (1997) term for the tendency on the part of some analysts to desperately avoid accepting the projection of patient's 'bad' internal objects and to act in an unrealistically kind and indulgent way towards the patient. This often results in heroic attempts at rescuing the patient, and can also cause serious boundary violations.

Disidentification with the mother: see 'Boy's disidentification with the mother'.

Dismantling: term coined by Donald Meltzer (1973) to describe a defensive process of transient suspension of mental activity in autistic individuals. 'Dismantling' differs from 'splitting' (see separate entry) in so far as it is more passive and involves less aggression. It allows the austic individual to disregard others' humanity and treat them as mere things.

Disorienting anxieties: a phrase coined by Leon Grinberg and Rebecca Grinberg (1989) to designate the inner and outer troubles resulting from a recent immigrant's failure to distinguish between the old and the new in the realm of his psychosocial existence.

Displacement: term originated by Sigmund Freud (1894a) to underscore the fact that psychic energy can be redirected from one idea to another. Characteristic of the 'primary process' (see separate entry) of mental functioning, 'displacement' underlies the formation of symbols, symptoms, and the manifest content of dreams (Freud, 1900a). A closer look at the literature reveals that the term 'displacement' subsumes four types of unconscious shifts: (1) *ideational displacement:* shifting of energy from one idea to another; 'displacement onto a little detail' (Fenichel, 1945, p. 285) is a special form of this dynamic process seen in compulsive neurotics; (2) *relational displacement:* changing an instinctual drive's object while retaining its aim (e.g., hating one person is changed into hating someone else); (3) *affective displacement:* relegating an affect that originated in one situation to a different situation; a common example of this is the fear of sexualized situations (e.g., a roller-coaster ride) instead of sexual situations; and (4) *temporal displacement:* assigning a different temporal location to an affect or an idea (e.g., an individual who is feeling angry towards the analyst might pronounce that some day he might get mad at him). Otto Fenichel's (1945) dictum that 'the advantage offered by displacement is that the original offensive idea does not become conscious' (p. 198) applies to all four situations mentioned above.

Disruption: the term does not appear in psychoanalytic glossaries (Eidelberg, 1968; Laplanche & Pontalis, 1973; Moore & Fine, 1968, 1990; Rycroft, 1968), even though it is a daily guest in the chamber of clinical discourse. It is used loosely for interruptions of treatment due to reasons in external reality (e.g., relocation, money) as well as for miscarriages of dialogue due to psychological reasons within the therapeutic dyad. Salman Akhtar (2007b) offered a tighter definition for the term, emphasizing three features: (1) a rupture of communication within the dyad; (2) sudden divergence in the agendas of the two parties; and (3) a threat to the safety or continuity of the ongoing clinical work. Such 'disruption' can be caused by unconscious guilt, anxious retreat, sadomasochism, separation anxiety, shift in the patient's structural organization, and empathic failures of the therapist. Akhtar described various manifestations of disruption and outlined therapeutic strategies to deal with such situations.

Disruptive attunement: see 'Homeostatic and disruptive attunements'.

Dissociation: a defensive mental mechanism originally described by Pierre Janet (1889), who used the term 'dissociation' interchangeably with 'disaggregation'. Employed in the context of constitutionally predisposed individuals who were severely traumatized, 'dissociation' referred to the keeping apart of psychic clusters, often with the aid of an amnesic barrier, for the purposes of avoiding mental distress. Though Sigmund Freud (1893a) incorporated Janet's ideas into his description of the 'splitting of consciousness', the fact that the term 'dissociation' did not originate with him perhaps contributed to its lack of 'popularity' in psychoanalytic parlance. In fact, four of the five major psychoanalytic glossaries (Eidelberg, 1968; Moore & Fine, 1968, 1990; Laplanche & Pontalis, 1973) do not mention it at all. The one that does (Rycroft, 1968) describes it in a rather fuzzy manner as 'the state of affairs in which two or more mental processes co-exist without becoming connected or integrated' and 'the defensive process' (p. 35) leading to the situation. 'Dissociation' is distinguished from 'splitting' on the grounds that the former affects processes and the latter affects structures (e.g., 'dissociation' of consciousness and 'splitting' of the ego). This distinction is hardly well-known or widely accepted. Matters are complicated further by the fact that a highly influential theoretician like Donald Winnicott (1960) used the term 'dissociation' almost synonymously with 'splitting'. Finally, it should be noted that, over the years, these terms have acquired a diagnostic 'buzz-word' significance; 'dissociation' is linked with multiple personality or 'dissociative character' (see separate entry) and 'splitting' with borderline conditions. A comprehensive and lucid review of the history of the term 'dissociation' is provided by Ira Brenner (2001).

Dissociative character: term introduced into psychoanalytic literature by Ira Brenner (1994) to highlight the fact that dissociation—a defensively altered state of consciousness—might lie at the core of certain character organizations. Most individuals with this type of character have been severely traumatized, and their psychic (and, at times, physical) survival depended upon the development and maintenance of sequestered pockets of psychological experience. In Brenner's view, there might actually be a hierarchical continuum of such dissociative character pathology. Dramatic forms of 'multiple personality' (dissociative identity disorder, in current psychiatric terminology) might represent one pole, and seemingly minor lapses of attention, unexplained sleepiness, and puzzling gaps in memory in the setting of an otherwise consolidated ego, might represent the other pole of this psychopathological continuum. Intermediate forms might exist with disturbances of 'object constancy' (see separate entry) and temporal continuity of the self-experience.

Disscociative identity disorder: see 'Dissociative character'.

Dissociative self: term coined by Ira Brenner (2001) for a psychic structure that is designed to keep mental contents separate from each other and inaccessible to synthesis. 'Affects, dreams, fantasies, perceptions, and somatic representations are all potentially subject to extrusion by this superordinate structure' (p. xii). Its main purpose is to disown mental contents with the help of 'negation' (see separate entry) and 'psuedo-externalized displacement' (Brenner, 2001, p. xi); the latter mechanism leads the patient to conclude that, since the subject experience is 'not me', it must be somebody else. That 'somebody' is what has been termed variously as an 'alter' (Kluft, 1984) or 'personification' (Fairbairn, 1931). Worth noting here is the overlap between these concepts and that of 'imaginary companions' (see separate entry).

Dissociopath: term coined by Ira Brenner (2009a) to designate those individuals with a 'dissociative character' (see separate entry) for whom identification with a brutal aggressor predominates over identification with rescuers or bystanders, or with their own role as the victim. The character of such 'dissociopaths' is suffused with sadism, superego pathology, and impulsivity. Their prognosis, even with treatment, is guarded.

Divergent conflicts: see 'Convergent and divergent conflicts'.

Double bind: a particular form of linguistic message which traps the one addressed by making contradictory demands upon him or her. First described by Gregory Bateson, Donald Jackson, Jay Haley, and John Weakland (1956) in connection with the communication patterns in the families of schizophrenic patients, a 'double bind' confuses and paralyses the individual. And, if the individual is strong, it infuriates him as well. It is, however, not restricted to the the families of schizophrenics, and can be found in other psychopathological settings as well. An illustrations of 'double bind' is constituted by a father yelling at his child and telling him to never listen to him when he is angry.

Dread to repeat: Anna Ornstein's (1974) phrase for the sense of helplessness a narcissistic patient feels when, after the establishment of a stable narcissistic transference which brings him peace, 'he is threatned with the need to repeat the old, self-defeating patterns' (p. 239). This 'dread to repeat' archaic patterns creates a conflict with the wish to maintain the improved mental functioning resulting from a well-established narcissistic transference.

Dream cowardice: term coined by Angel Garma (1966) for the fact that instinctual gratification in dreams lacks full blown realization of the wish in question. The wish to make love with a prohibited person might thus be manifested as merely rubbing against them. 'Dreams tend to be cowardly in attaining gratification' (p. 130).

Dream formation: according to Sigmund Freud (1900a), a dream is formed in accordance with the following steps; (1) an event in the day stirs up a wish that remains unexpressed or inoptimally expressed; (2) this trigger gains additional potency if it falls upon a similar unfulfilled wish of childhood; (3) the cumulative tension of the two sources of this wish pushes the mind to seek its discharge; (4) this cannot be done, because the wish is either morally reprehensible or dangerous in reality; (5) pressure for discharge is channelled into a hallucinatory wish fulfilment; (6) however, for this to acceptable, the wish and its accompanying fantasies and affects (collectively called 'latent dream thoughts') have to be transformed into palatable scenarios; (7) this is accomplished by 'dream work', or the processes of condensation, displacement, symbolism, and secondary revision; (8) the end product which invariably includes a reference to the precipitating event of the day (the 'day residue') is the 'manifest content' of the dream. While separate entries on each of these concepts help explain 'dream formation' better, this précis does not exhaust the mechanisms of dream formation. Dreams have been seen as the work of problem-solving aspects of the unconscious, for instance. There are still other hypotheses that merit consideration, especially when it comes to 'traumatic dreams', 'self-state dreams', 'dream within a dream', and so on. Separate entries on these concepts are also to be found in this dictionary.

Dream interpretation: the declaration by Sigmund Freud (1900a) that dreams constituted 'the royal road to a knowledge of the unconscious' (p. 608) led analysts to accord the analysis of dreams or 'dream interpretation' pride of place in clinical work. This enthusiasm reflected the lure of the 'topographic theory' (see separate entry) and what had come to be colloquially called 'id analysis'. With resurgence of 'ego psychology' (see separate entry) with its emphasis upon the defensive, deflective, and disguising functions of the ego and the variations in mental functioning in accordance with level of ego maturity attained by the individual, the interest in dreams diminished somewhat. None the less, understanding and interpretation of dreams remains an important aspect of a psychoanalyst's therapeutic armamentarium. A large body of work, including book-length discourses (Altman, 1969; Garma, 1966; Rothstein, 1987; Sharpe, 1949), has by now accumulated and is replete with 'rules', 'guidelines', and 'friendly tips' for conducting dream analysis. This vast literature can hardly be summarized here, but it might be possible to note areas of emphasis and dispute: (1) no dream can be fully understood; even after an exhaustive analysis, some elements elude the analytic grasp and vanish into the 'dream's navel' (Freud, 1900a); (2) the manifest content of a dream cannot be directly decoded to reveal the meaning of a dream; such an approach overlooks the complexity of 'dream work' (see separate entry); (3) a dream is 'exquisitely individual' (Rangell, 1987, p. 224) and cannot be understood without the help of the dreamer's associations to it; (4) that is why a far-reaching understanding of dreams is usually not possible in the beginning of an analysis; (5) the way of gathering such associations differs; sometimes an active invitation for the patient to associate in a piecemeal fashion to this or that aspect of the dream seems correct, while at other times simply treating what the patient has said before and after reporting a dream as associations to the dream is the way to go; (5) interpretation of dreams should not eclipse other aspects of analytic work; it 'should not be pursued in analytic

treatment as an art for its own sake' (Freud, 1911e, p. 94) ; (7) it is not mandatory to analyse each dream that the patient reports; 'countless times we have no choice but to let the dream drop and wait for better days' (Altman, 1969, p. 46) when therapeutic alliance would be stronger, emotions less strong, and associations more copius; (8) reporting of dreams can also serve as a resistance to analysis; this is especially true when the dreams are voluminous and fill up the entire session, or are typically reported at the very end of the session; in the words of Edward Weinshel (1984) 'a good deal can be learned by the way the dreamer reacts to or talks about the dream' (p. 84); (9) empirical reasearch (Bradlow & Coen, 1975) contradicts the clinical aphorism that the analyst's undisguised appearance in dreams early in analysis implies a negative prognosis for analysis; as a result, such an occurrence need not alarm the analyst; (10) changes in dream content and dynamics often reveal progress in analysis, and there are certain specific dreams that herald the approaching termination of treatment (see the entry on 'termination related dreams').

Dream resistance: a special type of transference resistance (Freud, 1911e) by which an analysand reports the manifest content of dreams endlessly without resolving a conflict or revealing transference details. 'Dream resistance' differs from ordinary resistances in so far as it does not serve as a countercathexis to repressed wishes, but serves rather to deflect attention from them during the analytic hour.

Dream screen: Bertram Lewin's (1946) term for the blank surface on which the contents of the manifest dream are projected. The 'dream screen' itself is only rarely visible to the dreamer. It stands for the wish to sleep while the visual images symbolize the wishes that are disturbing sleep. According to Lewin, the 'dream screen' also stands for the maternal breast (see also Abse, 1977). These ideas of Lewin were given a twist by Charles Rycroft (1951), who suggested that the 'dream screen' appears only in the dreams of people who are about to become manic. There, it symbolizes ecstatic fusion with the maternal breast and denial of hostility towards it.

Dream within a dream: according to Sigmund Freud (1900a), when someone sees a 'dream within a dream', the set aside segment (i.e., the one depicted as a dream within the dream) almost invariably represents an event that really took place. In fact, a 'dream within a dream' 'implies the most decided confirmation of the reality of the event' (p. 338).Austin Silber (1983) further elucidated this idea. He declared that a 'dream within a dream' belies a greater effort at disguise and at encapsulating the memory of one or more actual events with intense affects associated with them.

Dream work: refers to the set of ego operations that transform the raw material of the dream (e.g., wishes, thoughts, day residue) into its manifest content. Described by Sigmund Freud (1900a) in detail, such 'dream work' includes four mechanisms: (1) *condensation*, which allows the merger or transposition of disparate objects and ideas; (2) *displacement*, which permits the shift of an instinctual aim from one object to another; (3) *symbolism*, which allows the representation of a body part (e.g., breast), activity (e.g., sexual intercourse), feeling (e.g., love), or idea (e.g., patriotism) by a physical object; and (4) *secondary revision*, which shaves off rough edges and helps to reduce the coherent narrative of the manifest dream.

Dreams in pairs: idea proposed by Franz Alexander (1925) and enthusiastically received by Sigmund Freud (1933a) that two dreams occurring on the same night play a complementary role in wish-fulfilment in steps, a thing which each alone does not accomplish.

Dreams of convenience: Sigmund Freud's (1900a) designation for dreams that are undisguised wish-fulfilling responses to bodily needs of the moment. For instance, a sleeping person might dream that he is drinking water in response to thirst. Or, he might dream of urinating in response to the tension from a full bladder. Such dreams have a resemblance to children's dreams, which are also relatively simple and thinly disguised.

Dreams of resolution: see 'Termination related dreams'.

Dreams that mirror the session: described by Giuseppe Civitarese (2006), such dreams offer a glimpse of a significant and even traumatic event that has occurred in the previous or a recent session. By depicting the analytic scene with little disguise, such a dream serves as a defence against the historic reality of the disturbing event; 'a multiple and alternating game takes place between reinforcing and weakening the reality effect of psychoanalytic narrative' (p. 719).

Drive psychology: see ' Four psychologies of psychoanalysis'.

Drive theory: see 'Instinct theory'.

Dual instinct thory: see ' Instinct theory'.

Dual track theorem: expression used by James Grotstein (1997) to describe the interaction between 'autochthony' and 'cosmogony' on the one hand and 'alterity' on the other (see the entry on 'autochthony, cosmogony, and alterity'). In essence, the 'dual-track theorem' proposes the following. The individual, from birth onwards, attempts to give order to the random events of life by personalizing them ('autochthony') and placing them in an organized universe of his creation ('cosmogony'). Only later does he begin to realize the impersonal Otherness and disconnectedness of external objects; no longer do they appear under his omnipotent control. The earlier ownership, even creation, of the object gives way to accepting its separateness, experiential Otherness, and motivational autonomy. 'These two processes may seem sequential but may also occur simultaneously—or may even occur in reverse order. A realistic perception may initially occur that initiates a retrospective/retrospective autochthonous reworking of the reality of the perception so as to re-establish a personal cosmogonic sense of control i.e. a sense of agency and of responsibility' (p. 415). The autochthonous world seems self-created; the world of alterity accommodates the self–other distinction. The coexistence of these two modes constitutes the essence of the 'dual-track theorem', and psychopathology is, in essence, the loss of this perspective. Lacking a 'dual-track theorem', one feels trapped in a single-minded perspective. 'An important component of this theorem is that there is no psychopathology when a dual-track perspective is in operation because alternatives are possible i.e. one is not trapped' (p. 425). Grotstein states that viewed for this print of new psychoanalytic treatment is an attempt to establish a reconciliations between personal and impersonal perspectives on self and others.

Dual unity: term used by Margaret Mahler, Fred Pine, and Anni Bergmann (1975) to denote the infant's 'hallucinatory or delusional somatopsychic omnipotent fusion with the representation of the mother and, in particular the delusion of a common boundary between two separate individuals' (p. 45). The experience of 'dual unity' is characteristic of the 'symbiotic phase' of development and lasts from the second month to about the fourth or fifth month of life.

Dyadic conflicts: see 'Dyadic *vs.* triadic conflicts'.

Dyadic *vs.* triadic conflicts: intrapsychic conflicts about wishful scenarios involving the self and two other objects. Desired or feared relationships with both may be held in the consciousness, or the relationship with one may be conscious and with the other unconscious. The predominant affects associated with 'triadic conflicts' are rivalry, jealousy, feelings of exclusion, and hostile competitiveness. While these two objects can certainly be constituted by a sibling and a parent, customarily the term 'triadic conflicts' is used in the context of oedipal issues. The point is to distinguish the oedipal situation from the preoedipal one, which is characterized by 'dyadic conflicts'. In the latter, the struggles involve the self and one other object, and the capacity for experiencing a triangular situation does not exist; at times, the ambivalence towards the dyadic object is split and a third party is enlisted to contain one side of the conflicting feelings. This can give rise to an appearance of the conflict being 'triadic', but the lack of self and object constancy betrays their actual nature. (See the related entries on 'Oedipal pathology' and 'Preoedipal pathology'.)

Dynamic perspective: see 'Metapsychology'.

Dynamic unconscious: see 'Unconscious'.

Dysautomatization: term coined by Peter Glauber (1968) for the loss of smoothness in the execution of ego's autonomous functions. Under normal circumstances, these functions operate automatically; this is made possible by the maintenance of optimal connections and optimal barriers between the three topographic systems (unconscious, preconscious, and conscious). When such balance between the three systems is disturbed, 'dysautomatization' results, leading to a jerky execution of ego functions. Notably, such dysfunction, evident, for instance, in catatonia or stuttering, might itself acquire a 'secondary autonomy' (see separate entry).

┌─────┐
│ **E** │
└─────┘

Eating disorders: collective designation for the nosological entities of 'anorexia nervosa', 'bulimia', and other mixed forms of problems involving food intake. Studies of 'eating disorders' consistently show that about ninety to ninety-five per cent of patients are women (Garfinkel, 1995). Symptoms commonly associated with 'eating disorders' are morbid fear of becoming fat, body image disturbances, self-induced vomiting, laxative abuse, and cessation of menstruation. Sociocultural factors of prejudice against obesity and idealization of thinness play a role in the symptom choice, but the causation is ultimately psychogenic. Generally speaking, anorexia and bulimia are manifest phenomena which can have multiple and varied determinants. Otto Fenichel's (1945) words are telling in this regard. He declared that 'any conflict between activity and receptivity may result in eating disturbances' (p. 176), and went on to say the following about anorexia: 'It may be a simple hysterical symptom expressing the fear of an orally perceived pregnancy or of unconscious sadistic wishes. It may be a part of an ascetic reaction formation in a comp neurotic. It may be an affect equivalent in a depression, in which the symptom of refusal of food makes its appearance before other signs of depression are developed. It may be a sign of the refusal of any contact with the object world in an incipient schizophrenia' (pp. 176–177). Following Fenichel's astute observations, it is possible to conceive of 'eating disorders' as existing on three levels of psychic organization: (1) *lower level eating disorders* constitute but one aspect of repudiating pleasure; hateful attack on physical and mental enjoyment and the 'life instinct' (see separate entry) that shepherds them is at the heart of the matter. Libido is corrupted by the poison of paranoia, customary gender markers are obliterated, synthetic function of ego is interfered with, and esoteric beliefs govern the mind. Psychotic and near-psychotic character organizations are associated with 'eating disorders' at this level; (2) *intermediate level eating disorders* emanate from a problematic relationship with the mother; binging and purging are protosymbolic oscillations of closeness and distance from her (Guntrip, 1969) and betray what are now recognized as conflicts around separation–individuation (Fischer, 1989). Underlying the 'oral deadlock' (Bergman, Schwartzman, Sloate, & Wilson, 1983), however, are anal-sadistic struggles over control and autonomy (Bruch, 1978; Fenichel, 1945). A history of childhood sexual abuse often compounds the clinical picture. Diagnostically speaking, schizoid, borderline, and histrionic personalities are preponderant in this group; and (3) *higher level eating disorders* are derivative manifestations of powerful oedipal fantasies and defences against them (Schwartz, 1986). Themes of oral impregnation by incorporating the prohibited paternal phallus propel both binging (with the mouth–vagina equation in full bloom) and purging (to appease the maternal rival). Anxiety-laden efforts to undo the feminine contours of the body and maintain a childlike stance (by alarming thinness or obese blurring of curves) are frequent accompaniments (Lieberman, 2000). Other symbolic manifestations of yearning for the paternal phallus include sudden onset vegetarianism, kleptomania, inordinate love of horses, and delicate self-cutting. Diagnostically speaking, most such patients display hysterical personalities with obsessional features. Knowledge of these different levels of 'eating disorders' can help empathic attunement and guide interventional strategy with such patients. See also the two remarkable monographs on this topic by Kathryn Zerbe (2005, 2008).

Echo phenomenon: while conducting psychoanalytically informed unofficial political dialogues between high-level representatives of 'enemy' groups, Vamik Volkan (1987, 2006) noticed that the shadow of some recent military or political event falls over the work group, igniting emotions that cause resistance to adaptive situations. He called this an 'echo phenomenon'. It then becomes necessary to acknowledge and assimilate this 'shadow' (and its meaning for the opposing groups) before realistic negotiations can resume.

Ecological dimension of the self: see 'Ecological self'.

Ecological self: Marianne Spitzform's (2000) evocative term for the aspects of the self that develop in response to the specifics of one's childhood external environment. Thus an individual who has grown up in a rural environment would show subtle differences in the core representation from one who was born and raised in a large metropolitan area. This 'ecological dimension of the self' (Akhtar, 2001) might include differences in language, spatial organization, sense of the passage of time, and attitude towards nature at large.

The individual's relationship with the world of animals, plants, and inanimate objects would be greatly affected and the consequence of this would be likely to appear not only in the psychopathology he or she develops, but also in the events of the clinical session. These and other related matters are thoroughly discussed in Harold Searles' (1960) brilliant but lamentably forgotten monograph on non-human environment and Salman Akhtar's (2003, 2005) recent reviews of the role of 'things' in normal and pathological mental life. Also pertinent are Ashis Nandy's (2007) views on the rural–urban dialectics in the subjectivity of individuals from rapidly growing societies, especially India.

Economic perspective: see 'Metapyschology'.

Educational boundary violations: according to Stephen Sonnenberg and William Myerson (2007) a 'zone of privacy is supposed to surround the activities engaged in by faculty and students during analytic training' (p. 203). Faculty members' and supervisors' behaviours that invade or rupture the zone constitute 'educational boundary violations'. These authors provide fourteen varieties of such behaviours encountered by candidates-in-training, including attacks against another candidate, attacks against a present and past analyst, or efforts to seek support for an opposition faction within the institute, among others. See also Glen Gabbard's (1999) paper on how a candidate's idealization and loyalty can lead to collusion with a senior member of an institute who is sexually involved with a patient.

Efficacy experiences: these emanate from the 'awareness of having an initiating and casual role in bringing about states of needed responsiveness from others' (Wolf, 1994, p. 73). Efficacy experiences strengthen the ego and provide a sense of vitality to the self. Their lack results in a feeling of dejection and worthlessness. The feelings of depression seen in immigrants whose skills are not transportable across cultures seem based on this dynamic.

Ego: while scattered references to it existed in the early writings of Sigmund Freud (1894a, 1896, 1900a, 1911b), a thorough elucidation of 'ego' did not appear until his seminal monograph titled *The Ego and the Id* (1923b). A word of caution is, however, needed right here. The English word 'ego' is James Strachey's translation of Freud's German *das Ich* and contained two separate meanings: 'one in which the term distinguishes a person's self as a whole (including, perhaps, his body) from other people, and the other in which it denotes a particular part of the mind characterized by special attributes and functions. . . . It is not always easy, however, to draw a line between these two senses of the word' (editor's introduction, Freud, 1923b, pp. 7–8). It was Heinz Hartmann (1939) who emphatically separated the two implications by reserving the term 'ego' for a mental agency and 'self' for the individual himself. It is with this in mind that one ought to approach the following ten points about the 'ego': (1) the 'ego' is not present at birth; it arises out of an undifferentiated id–ego matrix. In Otto Fenichel's (1945) words, the outer surface of the early mental structure is 'differentiated gradually with respect to its functions of stimulus perception and discharge. The product of this differentiation becomes the ego' (p. 15); (2) the main function of the 'ego' is to receive stimuli from the external and internal worlds and to allow motility and discharge to instinctual impulses; (3) the 'ego' is in contact with reality and scans; selects, suppresses, filters, and organizes perceptions and stimuli using intelligence and judgement; it works in accordance with 'reality principle' and 'secondary process thinking'; (4) it is responsible for compromise formations between the demands of reality, instincts, and superego; (5) it has both conscious and unconscious aspects; the defences it deploys against physically unsafe or morally repugnant wishes especially operate on an unconscious level; (6) some of its functions (e.g., thinking, intelligence) are primarily 'autonomous' while other functions can acquire 'secondary autonomy'; the primarily autonomous functions are, however, far from sacrosanct and can be sucked into instinctual conflicts; (7) the 'ego', according to Freud (1923b) is 'first and foremost a bodily ego' (p. 26); its origins are intricately related to the constitutional capacities for anxiety tolerance, aggression, problem solving, assertiveness, and intelligence. However, an additional meaning of its being 'bodily' is that many of its operations are patterned after body functions (e.g., incorporation upon swallowing, projection upon spitting, negation upon turning the head away from an undesirable food or sight; (8) at the same time, it is true that 'the character of the ego is a precipitate of abandoned object cathexis . . . [and] . . . contains the history of those object choices' (1923b, p. 29). In other words, the elements of the ego are constituted by identifications; (9) in the treatment situation, one notices that the ego contributes to 'resistance', participates in 'therapeutic alliance' and becomes a vehicle for experiencing and expressing 'transference' related fantasies and affects. It is to the ego that the analyst directs his or her interventions; in Fred

Busch's (2004) words, the ego is at the centre of technique; and (10) finally, the purpose of psycho-analysis, according to Freud was to ascertain that 'where id was, there ego shall be' (1933a, p. 80). In other words, the instinctual pressure for discharge would have come under the dominance of rationality and all the vectors of 'secondary process' thinking (e.g., concerns for safety, awareness of time). It should be noted, in the end, that while Freud (1923b) enunciated his ideas about the ego early on, it took many years and contributions by many subsequent authors (A. Freud, 1936; Hartmann, 1952, 1956; Hartmann, Kris, & Loewenstein, 1946; Kris, 1951) to define and consolidate the above mentioned picture of the ego.

Ego automatisms: Heinz Hartmann's (1939) term for those functions of the ego that are performed without conscious thought though their origins can be made readily available to awareness. In other words, they operate at neither the conscious nor unconscious level; their execution happens at a 'preconscious' level. Examples include driving a car, typing on a keyboard, using a cell phone, and so on.

Ego boundaries: see 'Boundaries'.

Ego coverage: Donald Winnicott's (1956b) term for the mother's task of protecting her infant from 'annihilation' or 'psychotic' anxiety (see separate entry). This notion is very similar to the classical concept of the 'protective shield' (see separate entry); typically, however, Winnicott does not link the two ideas. His concept of 'analaytic management' (see separate entry) or the psychoanalytically orientated long-term care of severely ill patients is essentially based on the analyst's providing 'ego coverage' for the patient.

Ego defects: see 'Ego modification'.

Ego defences: see 'Defence mechanisms'.

Ego deviation: see 'Ego modification'.

Ego distortion: see 'Ego modification'.

Ego function of metaphorization: see 'Concretism'.

Ego functions: the functions performed by the ego can be divided into three basic categories: (1) *autonomous ego functions*, which are not derived from the ego's relationship to instincts and their objects; these include intelligence, thinking, perception, reality testing, learning, motility, synthe-sis, and speech; (2) *relational ego functions*, which include object seeking, attachment, internalization, and the development and sustenance of 'object constancy' (see separate entry), i.e., the capacity to maintain a positive tie to a love object even when it is not being need-satisfying; and (3) *defensive ego functions*, which ward off anxiety consequent upon the emergence into consciousness of unacceptable sexual and aggressive impulses and their attendant self- and object representations; these 'defence mechanisms' (see separate entry) have varied forms, but the essential goal of all these forms is the same: reduction of anxiety. Such categorization of 'ego functions' is, however, not water-tight. The primarily 'autonomous ego functions' (see separate entry) can get caught up in conflict and the 'relational ego functions' can be used for defensive purposes, and so on. Moreover, the linkage of thinking and synthesis with 'life instinct' (see separate entry) by post-Freudian theorists, especially Wilfred Bion (1967, 1970) has blurred the pristine 'autonomy' that these functions were earlier accorded by the great ego psychologist, Heinz Hartmann (1939, 1964).

Ego ideal: the inner image of oneself as one wants to become. This psychic structure tells us what is our path, what is it that we should do. It is derived from three sources: the separation of realistic from wishful self-images under the influence of ordinary childhood frustrations (Freud, 1914c; Jacobson, 1964), the 'forward projection' of narcissism upon the same-sex parent during the oedipal phase (Chassaguet-Smirgel, 1984) and the resolution of negative oedipal strivings during adolescence (Blos, 1985). As a psychic structure, the ego-ideal provides a yardstick for an individual's assessing how well he has met his expectations of himself. It is, thus, a counterpart of 'superego' or the conscience. The ego-ideal exhorts and pushes, striving to diminish the gap between the self as it is and as it is desired to be. The superego, in contrast, criticizes one for transgressing inner moral injunctions. Failure to meet superego demands causes guilt. Failure to approach the ego-ideal's demands causes dejection and shame.

Ego identity: see 'Identity'.

Ego in the service of regression: see 'Discriminating function of the ego'.

Ego instincts: while Sigmund Freud had contrasted the demands made by the sexual instinct with basic psychological needs in 1905a, it was not until 1910i that he explicitly proposed the concept of 'ego instincts' or 'self presevatory instincts'. His idea was that the 'sexual instinct' aimed at species propogation and the 'ego instinct' aimed at self preservation. 'Ego instincts' are (1) are aimed at self-preseval and self-seeking, (2) fulfil non-sexual aims, (3) operate under the reality principle, and (4) carry an energy of their own that was not libido but 'interest' (Freud, 1905a, 1910i, 1915c). In moving from his 'first dual-instinct theory' of sexual and ego instincts to his 'second dual-instinct theory' of 'life instinct' and 'death instinct', Freud began to view 'ego instincts' as a sub-category of 'life instinct' (see the entry on 'instinct theory' for greater detail). Regrettably, this move led to a gradual loss of conceptual zeal about ego instincts. Motivations, psychopathology, and transferences were now infrequently traced back to thwarted self-presevative tendencies. The wishes generated by sexual and aggressive drives took centre stage and the needs emanating from ego instincts were confined to the heuristic and clinical Green Room. The concept of ego instincts became repressed, as it were. Yet, like the repressed, which exerts a 'continous pressure in the direction of the conscious' (Freud, 1915d, p. 151), it kept seeking readmission into the main corpus of the psychoanalytic thought. Donald Winnicott (1960) spoke of 'ego needs'. Arnold Modell (1975b) argued for 'quieter' instincts, not associated with id functions and accounting for the development of attachment and object relations. Patrick Casement (1991) reformulated the concept as 'growth needs', distinguishing them from 'libindal demands'. Even Heinz Kohut's (1977) self-psychological motivations contain a remote echo of the 'ego instinct' concept. Not surprisingly, the thinking behind these diverse but overlapping concepts found a counterpart in a broadened view of psychoanalytic process (Akhtar, 1999a). This particular conundrum of having to 'rediscover' ego instinct-like concepts ('psychic needs', 'developmental needs', 'ego needs', 'growth needs', 'self-object needs', etc.) over and over again might have been avoided had Freud gone from his first dual-instinct theory not to his second dual-instinct theory, but to a 'triple-instinct theory' (sexual, aggressive, and ego instincts). Tongue-in-cheek though it may sound, this idea is not entirely devoid of seriousness.

Ego integrity *vs.* despair: the last among the eight psychosocial stages described by Erik Erikson (1950). Ego integrity involves many subsets of capacities. These include a post-narcissistic love of the human (not personal) self, a sense of spirituality, an acceptance of the actuality and inevitability of one's life, a deep acceptance of the character flaws and strengths of one's parents, pride in the dignity of one's life style, and what Erikson called 'the patrimony of one's soul' (p. 268), i.e., the seal of moral paternity of oneself. In the absence of such accrued wisdom, the individual keeps feeling that he or she could have lived a different life and, since no time is left to redo or undo life, experiences a deep sense of despair. Peaceful acceptance of the coming end of one's life is replaced by a deep fear of death.

Ego libido: see 'Narcissistic libido'.

Ego modification: Gertrude Blanck and Ruben Blanck's (1974) collective designation of four types of impairment of ego functions: (1) *ego defects*, which refer to the constitutionally determined compromise of autonomous ego functions (e.g., perception, control of motility, temporal ordering of events); (2) *ego deviations*, which involve developmentally induced departures of ego growth from its normally expected course (e.g., precocious independence due to neglect by parents who are busy taking care of a sick sibling of the subject); (3) *ego distortion*, which involves impairment of ego functions due to the internalization of faulty perceptions of the self by others (e.g., inhibitions of intellect and creativity because of being viewed as unintelligent by the parents, and (4) *ego regression*, which includes loss of ego functions under biopsychosocial stress (e.g., encopresis in a toilet-trained child following the birth of a sibling). While overlaps can and, most likely, do exist here, this classification remains appealing. It helps to organize empirical data, prompt useful lines of research, and, potentially, guide therapeutic strategies.

Ego needs: see 'Basic needs'.

Ego nuclei: term coined by Edward Glover (1956a) to highlight that the ego does not arise *de novo* as a fully formed entity. It consists, at first, of loosely arranged clusters which only gradually come together to form a coherent structure. According to Glover, any psychic system, however rudimentary, which can relate to objects, discharge tension, and reduce anxiety, qualifies to be called an 'ego nucleus'. Such a system might be affect-specific, task-specific, and even phase-specific. One can thus conceive of oral 'ego nuclei', anal 'ego nuclei', and so on. Under normal circumstances, the primitive polynuclear ego is increasingly organized into a composite whole. Fixation on oral ego nuclei paves the way for borderline and psychotic conditions, and fixation on anal and phallic ones lays the groundwork for obsessional and hysterical neuroses.

Ego passage: term coined by Eduardo Weiss (1957) for the fact that an object which has been introjected and whose qualities have turned into ego traits can be externalized again; this results in one's object-derived traits appearing as belonging to someone else. In the process of such introjection and projection, the original qualities of the object certainly undergo alterations. In other words, the re-externalized representations are not replicas of the original object. Weiss called this phenomenon 'passing of an object through the ego', or simply 'object passage'. The term is little used these days.

Ego psychology: a depth-psychological approach that addresses various mental phenomena (e.g., fantasies, dreams, ambitions, free-association during the clinical hour) from the vantage point of ego. The term 'ego psychology' is intended to distinguish this perspective from that of instincts, drives, energy, impulses, and tension discharge; the latter can be referred to as 'id psychology' or 'drive psychology'. The emergence of 'ego psychology' marks a shift in Sigmund Freud's theorizing, in the early 1920s (see, especially, Freud, 1923b), from drive to defence, from discharge to sublimation, from impulse to countercathexis, from revelation to resistance, and from the cauldron of instincts to the executive operations of the ego. Later, Anna Freud's (1936) categorization of ego defences and Heinz Hartmann's (1939, 1964) elucidation of principles of adaptation, fitting together, and synthesis 'formally' made study of ego central to the concerns of psychoanalysis. All this has clinical relevance. Fred Pine (1988), in his seminal paper on 'four psychologies of psychoanalysis' (see separate entry), has explicitly outlined the questions that arise from an 'ego psychology' perspective while listening to clinical material. Pine deftly compares these queries with those arising from approaching the clinical material from the perspective of the other three 'psychologies' (drive, self, and object-relations) of psychoanalysis. The Miami-based analyst, Peggy Hutson (2002), has, on the other hand, demonstrated how valuable tenets from 'ego psychology' can inform the conflicts involving problems of the self and object relations. The most prominent representatives of the 'ego psychology', however, include Jacob Arlow, Charles Brenner, David Beres, Martin Wangh, Humberto Nagera, Paul Gray, Steve Levy, Lawrence Inderbitzin, and Fred Busch in North America. In Europe and Latin America, less sharp demarcation of 'ego psychology' seems to exist. The followers of Anna Freud and the doyen of British psychoanalysis, Joseph Sandler, are exceptions in this regard. Sandler is especially outstanding among the ego-psychologists because he made concerted efforts to build bridges between ego psychology, the Kleinian approach, and the independent tradition of British analysis, represented, among others, by Michael Balint and Donald Winnicott.

Ego regression: see 'Ego modification' and 'Regression'.

Ego relatedness: see 'Object relating'.

Ego states: term coined by Paul Federn (1928, 1932) for organized clusters of experience and behaviour that are distinct and separated from similar other clusters. Federn used 'ego states' somewhat interchangeably with 'ego nuclei' (see separate entry); subsequent literature shows that some authors (e.g., Watkins & Watkins, 1997) prefer the former term and others (e.g., Abse, 1966) the latter. Essentially, an 'ego state' comprises a feeling, particular thought content, and the tendency to act in a certain way. While Federn focused solely on the ego aspect of the entity, John and Helen Watkins (1997), who have elucidated and employed this concept exhaustively, include object-cathected elements in it as well. In their view, 'ego states' can be sequestered or overlapping, organized at different levels of emotional sophistication, and have different languages, both literally and metaphorically. Created for coping with external and internal problems, 'ego states' tenaciously guard and perpetuate their existence. Such description makes one ask whether an 'ego state' is metapsychologically any different from a 'self-representation' (see separate entry) and experientially any different from a 'self state' (see separate entry). Or, whether the concept has an insular currency only among the investigators of dissociative disorders and multiple personality. Is it possible that the three concepts simply reflect the languages of psychoanalysts with differing persuasions? Or, do these terms address just very slightly different aspects of the same phenomenon, with 'ego state' underscoring executive powers, 'self-representation' highlighting awareness (even if at an unconscious level), and 'self state' emphasizing the affective colouring of the moment? The jury, as they say, is out.

Ego strength: a relative concept resting upon the following three considerations: (1) the capacity to resist immediate instinctual discharge, which is demanded by the pleasure principle and is incompatible with correct judgement, (2) the capacity to anticipate in fantasy the potential consequences of an action, hence the possibility of choosing to act or not, and (3) the capacity to avoid using regression as a pathway to defence against anxiety.

Together, the intactness of these three capacities suggests ego strength (Fenichel, 1945). Their absence, or pallor, suggests 'ego weakness' (see separate entry). A strong ego can tolerate anxiety well, does not show impulsivity, and contributes to sublimatory activities. While resistant to regression under instinctual pressure, it can occasionally allow transitory regression for the purpose of its own replenishment (see 'Regression in the service of the ego').

Ego weakness: refers to deficits in the capacity to negotiate between the demands of external reality on the one hand and instinctual urges and superego dictates on the other. Manifestations of ego weakness belong to two categories (Kernberg, 1975): those 'specific' to lower levels of character organization and those which are 'non-specific' signs of ego weakness. Among the former are blurring of boundaries and predominance of primitive defences. A weak ego has ill-defined boundaries, which result in shaky reality testing and difficulty in discerning whether one's affects, ideas, and impulses are originating from within oneself or in external objects. A weak ego is also characterized by the use of primitive defences such as splitting, projective identification, denial, and primitive idealization. Among the non-specific manifestations of ego weakness are lack of anxiety tolerance, poor impulse control, and impaired capacity for sublimation. Lack of anxiety tolerance is reflected by the extent to which any stress leads the individual towards regression, symptom formation, or discharge through action. Lack of impulse control manifests either as 'structured impulsivity' (focal, repetitive, and ego-syntonic specific acts) or a diffuse loss of restraint upon inner urges. Lack of well-developed sublimatory channels also suggests ego weakness. In assessing this, however, it is important to keep the individual's socio-cultural background in mind. The concept of ego weakness is significant for diagnostic purposes and for selecting a treatment strategy. Patients with ego strength are suitable for psychoanalysis, while those with ego weakness require more structured psychotherapeutic interventions.

Ego's sense of self disappearance: subsumed under André Green's (1999, 2005) broad rubric of the 'work of the negative' (see separate entry), this particular mechanism is related to traumatic abandonment by the mother or to experiences with the 'dead mother' (see separate entry). The syndrome that results from this mechanism includes (1) incapacity to tolerate frustration, (2) inconsolability, (3) hatred of the other sex, (4) fre-

netic sexuality, (5) great need for control, and (6) occasionally, 'very extreme sublimations' (Green, 2005, p. 224), which serve to please a harsh superego and create a sort of insulation around the self. Patients with this syndrome often have an aspiration which takes the form of self disappearance. At their core, they feel subject to maternal vampirism and, defensively, to powerful wishes to invade her.

Eight-month anxiety: see 'Stranger anxiety'.

Either-or dilemmas: see 'Convergent and divergent conflicts'.

Elation: an affective state characterized by happiness, high self-esteem, and optimism. 'Elation' usually results from three psychological sources. (1) approval by the superego, (2) diminution of the gap between ego and ego-ideal, and (3) indulgence by a highly cathected external object. Normal relations, therefore, follows doing a 'good deed', moving a step closer to what one wants to become, and receiving affection from a respected and loved person. Pathological elation occurs from 'manic defence' (see separate entry) against depressive or paranoid feelings. It also can be caused by the blurring of boundaries between the ego and superego. Society at large allows for such structural fusion at times of festivals (Freud, 1921c). The ego–superego fusion allows the id to run free and reproduces the blissful union with the maternal breast. A robust tendency to devour the external world (by excessive eating and drinking), to be 'eaten up' and consumed by it, and fall asleep at a bountiful breast then takes over the psyche (Lewin, 1950).

Electra complex: term introduced by Carl Jung in 1915 to denote the girl's erotic love for her father and the parallel jealousy of her mother. Derived from the Greek myth of a young woman who is enraged at her mother for betraying her father, the term did not gain Sigmund Freud's approval. This could be because, as the originator of psychoanalysis, Freud was reluctant to allow his disciples the pride of 'fathering' new concepts. The fact that Freud and Jung were at odds at that time might also have added to the former's lukewarm attitude towards the term. In fact, he is known to have stated, 'I do not see any advance or gain in the introduction of the term "Electra Complex" and do not advocate its use' (Freud, 1920a, p. 155). Such rejection on Freud's part might actually have foreclosed the investigation of a girl's erotic fixation upon her father and its potentially inhibiting impact upon her later, adult sexuality. The fact that the Greek word 'Electra' literally means 'unmarried', and the fact that Freud made it difficult for his own beloved daughter, Anna, to enter matrimony, makes one wonder (we are analysts after all!) about his anxious repudiation of Jung's fine concept.

Elusion: term coined by Ronald Laing (1964) to describe a process by which an individual bypasses a genuine encounter with others and even his own self by impersonating himself ,i.e., playing the very role that he has in reality. Helene Deutsch's (1942) concept of 'as-if personality' and Priscilla Roth's (1994) descriptions of those who are 'true to a false object' are phenomenological neighbours of Laing's intriguing idea. George Zavitzianos's (1972) notion of 'homovestism' also seems to have an echo of it.

Emergent self: see 'Sense of an emergent self'.

Emotional flooding: According to Vamik Volkan (1976), the first manifestation of emotional flooding 'is usually and accumulation of memories and fantasies (flooding in the ideational field) that support the same emotion. The patient can refer to these memories or fantasies only in a kind of "shorthand"—fragmentary sentences, or a single word. He may then begin stuttering and lose the power of intelligible speech altogether . . . The patient may scream and exhibit diffuse motor activity; he may seem to have lost his human identity' (p. 179). In contrast to 'abreaction' (see separate entry) where some observing ego is retained, emotional flooding is associated with loss of the capacity for self-observation.

Emotional refuelling: term originated by Manuel Furer (cited in Mahler, Pine, & Bergman, 1975, p. 69) for the tendency on the part of 7–10-month-old children, who have crawled away from the mother, to quickly crawl back to her and perk up instantly upon such return; Furer also called it 'libidinal refueling' (cited in Mahler, 1963, p. 11) The contact with mother might vary from the children righting themselves on her leg, touching her in other ways, or just leaning against her. It gives the child a new momentum and he or she can go back to his exploration of the outer world. As development proceeds, the circles of these explorations widen, but mother remains at the centre of them and children keep 'returning' to her, though in increasingly subtle forms. Physical contact gives way to visual contact and objects that stand for mother also begin getting used for refuelling purposes. Clearly, these developmental concepts have great relevance for understanding ana-lysands who lack object constancy and require 'emotional refuelling' during separations from the analyst.

Emotional reliving: see 'Abreaction'.

Emotionality as a defence: see 'Affectualization'.

Empathic reconstructive-interpretation: term coined by Paul and Anna Ornstein (1980) to designate analytic interventions that respond to the total self of the patient and not only to the isolated fragments of experience or deconstructed elements, such as drives and defences. In making an 'empathic reconstructive-interpretation', the analyst not only reconstructs the sequence of intra-analytic events but also the genetic mold of that sequence. Such an intervention conveys 'poignantly the perception by the analyst of the whole person of the patient, in his historic and genetic-dynamic continuity, thereby aiding the patient's ability to restore or make firm the cohesiveness of his self' (p. 207).

Empathy: derived from the German *Einfuhlung*, the term 'empathy' refers to the ego's capacity to transiently identify with someone else in order to grasp his or her subjective experience. An altruistic elimination of one's personal agenda—to the extent this is possible—and attunement to the other's affect and fantasy are hallmarks of 'empathy'. In an elegant and succinct statement, Daniel Stern (1985) describes empathy as comprising four distinct and probably sequential processes: (1) the resonance of feeling state; (2) the abstraction of empathic knowledge from the experience of emotional resonance; (3) the integration of abstracted empathic knowledge into an empathic response; and (4) a transient role identification (p. 145). Sigmund Freud's (1912e) exhortation that the analyst synchronize his ear to the mute rumblings of his patient's unconscious was intended to encourage these very processes. However, as analytic technique advanced, 'empathy' receded into the background and greater attention was directed at 'interventions' (see separate entry) made by the analyst. A related problem was that the 'intoxication' with the knowledge of unconscious dynamics led many analysts to become declarative, authoritarian, and, in essence, less empathic. Decoding of dream symbols without the help of patient's associations, 'direct analysis' (see separate entry) and 'deep interpretations' (see separate entry) which disregarded the patient's need for resistance, and the certainty that the analyst was the superior arbitrator of reality were all results of such departure from 'empathy'. The advent of 'self psychology' (see separate entry) refocused the spotlight. Set into motion by Heinz Kohut (1977), this perspective emphasized that listening with 'empathy' was not only important, but itself gave the patient a sense of consolidation and vitality that was superior to one resulting from interpretation alone. With a slightly different bent, Evelyne Schwaber's (1998, 2007) paper on listening from the patient's perspective carried the same message. Other analysts (Buie, 1981; Cooper, 1983; Wallerstein, 1983), however, noted that 'empathy' was a prerequiste, and not a replacement for interpretation, and that empathically derived data can have their own limitations. Still others (Akhtar, 2002; Killingmo, 1989) suggested that, while the demonstration to the patient that one is indeed listening empathically is soothing and stabilizing, it merely prepares the psychic structure to move 'upwards' when an interpretive handling of the same material becomes possible. Three other matters need mentioning: (1) empathy originates in the amalgamation of constitutional talents for attunement and identification with devoted and empathic parents, (2) it involves both cognitive and affective factors (Hojat, 2007); Arnold Goldberg's (1999) quip that 'the two Heinzes—Kohut and Hartmann—must be joined in this reconciliation of empathy and judgment' (p. 357) is pertinent in this context, and (3) it is unclear whether 'empathy' implies getting in touch only with what the patient is experiencing, or also with what the patient is unable to bear within himself. Tongue-in-cheek, the first propostion can be said to define 'Kohutian empathy' and the second 'Kleinian empathy'.

Emptiness: a disturbing state of subjective impoverishment whereby the inner world feels dead and no sustaining fantasies can be evoked. Behaviour loses anchor with emotional agency and acquires a mechanical quality. Emptiness is not the same as loneliness; the latter is associated with longing for objects that are not realistically available or morally permissible. Prominent among the North American psychoanalysts who have contributed to the understanding of emptiness are Otto Kernberg (1975), Melvin Singer (1977a,b) and Steven Levy (1984). These authors see emptiness as emanating from *six dynamic sources*: (1) defence against intense affects, especially those of the destructive type, (2) desperate appeal to be 'filled up' with emotional nourishment, (3) deterioration of good internal object relations, (4) self-fragmentation, (5) symbolically disguised demand to be made pregnant, and (6) identification with an unloving, 'empty' mother.

The view of these North American authors consistently portrays emptiness as pathologic and leaves no space for a positive state of emptiness. The so-called 'independent' tradition of British psychoanalysis picks up the thread here, and proposes that certain states of emptiness and non-relatedness to objects might actually be health-promoting and conducive to ego-replenishment. Some of Michael Balint's (1968) concepts (see 'Area of creation') and two of Masud Khan's enigmatic papers 'Infancy, aloneness, and madness' (1983a) and 'On lying fallow' (1983b) address this very point.

Empty circle: term introduced by Dori Laub (1998) in connection with the lives of adult children of Holocaust survivors, to denote 'the absence of representations, the rupture of the self, the erasure of memory, and the accompanying sense of void that are the core legacy of massive psychic trauma' (p. 507). The 'empty circle' is created, as it were, by the absence or breakdown of an empathic relationship that could contain the affects mobilized by trauma. The subject's later resistance (or inability) to integrate this 'unmentalized' (Fonagy & Target, 1997) psychic spot into the main body of his affective and ideational life results in the perpetuation of the 'empty circle'. This legacy—characterized by a sense of void, dread, and wordless inconsolability—can compound ordinary developmental conflicts.

Enactment: a term that is popular in contemporary psychoanalysis and seems to be used in five different ways: (1) the first refers to the analysand's putting his transference fantasies into actions rather than into words (Hirsch, 1998). Used this way, 'enactment' seems simply a 'new and improved' form of Meyer Zeligs' (1957) term 'acting in' (see separate entry); (2) the second use suggests that 'enactment' happens when a patient has unconsciously induced the analyst to live out the former's transference fantasy. Used this way, 'enactment' seems allied to 'projective identification' and 'role responsiveness' (see separate entries), both of which indicate that the analyst is pressured to behave in a manner consistent with the patient's internal fantasy; (3) the third use refers to an 'embedded series of often subtle, unconscious, interactive, mutually constructed dramas that are lived out' (Levine & Friedman, 2000, p. 73). Used this way, 'enactment' seems akin to 'intersubjectivity' (see separate entry) since the analyst is seen as a 'co-creator' of what happens between the two parties; (4) the fourth use takes the term to its other extreme by naming it 'countertransference enactment' (Jacobs, 1986b;

Gerrard, 2007). Used this way, 'enactment' is reduced to the analyst's acting out of a countertransference wish; and (5) finally, there is a concept of 'interpretive enactment' (Steiner, 2006), which subsumes the analyst's verbal communication that, given as interpretations, none the less contain countertransference feelings and attitudes. For the clinical overlap between 'enactment', 'play', and 'acting out' (see separate entries), see Adeline van Waning's (1991) evocative paper. For an elucidation of 'enactment' as understanding and as misunderstanding, see Arnold Goldberg's (2002) essay and for the transformation of what is enacted into mental representation, see Ilany Kogan's (2007) recent contribution. Nadine Levinson's (2003) report of a panel discussion on the topic, held at the 42nd Congress of the International Psychoanalytical Association in Nice, France, is also quite informative in this regard. A thorough and formidable review of the definitional ambiguities *vis-à-vis* the concept of 'enactment' and their technical implications is provided by Gavin Ivey (2008).

Encounter with limits: extending Erik Erikson's (1950) ideas and adding his own, Otto Kernberg (1980) suggested that coming face to face with limits is the main developmental challenge of midlife. These limits include those of material and financial acquisition, control over one's children's lives and aspects of one's own life, and, ultimately, limits of creativity, time, and life itself.

Endeavour and erotic excitements of the girl: two types of a girl's emotional reaction to her father described by Lora Tessman (1982). *Endeavour excitement* begins in the second year of life, and consists of the girl's looking up to the father for recognition of her burgeoning psychomotor skills. This becomes a mutually curious, affectionate focus of his helping her separate from the mother. *Erotic excitement* begins in the fourth year of life and is characterized by romantically charged wishes to look at and be looked at and admired by the father; vague and, at times, not so vague genital stirrings and fantasies also accompany such excitement. A nurturing father accepts these desires, but from a distance, which, paradoxically, intensifies the erotic mystery of the girl's body. The father's unique contribution is to accept both the girl's striving for competence and for physical attractiveness. If he denigrates the former element, the girl ends up inhibited about her intellect. If he overlooks the latter, the girl becomes conflicted about her sexuality.

Endeavour excitement of the girl: see 'Endeavour and erotic excitements of the girl'.

Entitlement: beginning with Sigmund Freud's (1916) description of 'exception' (see separate entry), i.e., individuals whose childhood misfortunes permit them an attitude of feeling exempt from ordinary societal expectations, the attitude of 'entitlement' has drawn the attention of psychoanalysts (Jacobson, 1959; Murray, 1964; Levin, 1970; Rothstein, 1977; Apprey, 1988; Coen, 1988; Volkan & Rodgers, 1988). 'Entitlement' is variously seen as (1) a manifestation of un-renounced infantile omnipotence, (2) a developmental consequence of parental neglect and abuse; (3) an ego defence against feelings of helplessness, separateness, and rage; and (4) a manoeuvre to repudiate perception and awareness of parental indifference. Maurice Apprey (1988) delineates a 'developmental line' of 'entitlement' with five nodal points: (1) an inchoate and instinct-ridden preoedipal stage, (2) a narrower sense of 'entitlement' which respects the oedipal boundaries, (3) a post-oedipal expansion of the feeling with reaction formations leading to an accompanying sense of humility; (4) a more mature sense of 'entitlement' with an increasingly realistic view of parents and now also of extra-familial objects; and (5) a fully mature sense of 'entitlement' that permits giving up the discrepancy between expressed 'entitlement' and felt non-entitlement. 'Now the sense of entitlement is acquiescent, accepts reality, and moves away from gross narcissim and the related rejection of one's existential situation of utter finiteness' (pp. 96–97). Stanley Coen (1988) emphasizes the superego placating facet of 'entitlement' which seeks to ward off or justify destructive urges. He sees it as combining 'attempts to seduce the superego and to express sadistic extractive drive derivatives. Entitlement involves a quality of (preverbal) misuse of others in exploitative or extractive ways; sadism, to varying degrees, is a central feature' (p. 410). Working with entitled patients poses serious countertransference challenges, and both Arnold Rothstein (1977) and Stanley Coen (1988) discuss the technical implications of this. This rich literature, however, pays less attention to 'lack of entitlement', which is also a frequently encountered phenomenon. This needs more study. Suffice to say, here, that in some individuals, who have not partaken in healthy and structure-building 'entitlement' during early childhood, the feeling of 'entitlement' might make its first appearance as a result of ongoing treatment (Kramer, 1987). This development is better handled by tolerance and waiting for it to automatically subside rather than by interpretive deconstruction.

Envelope of experience: Mark Gehrie's (1993) term for the psychological space in which an analysand is able to maintain the distinction between the transference experience and the analytic reality. 'This envelope varies in size, shape, and depth with the unique capacities of each analysand, and therefore the technique associated with maintaining it must be adjusted anew in every instance' (p. 1101).

Environment mother: see 'Environment mother *vs.* object mother'.

Environment mother *vs.* object mother: Donald Winnicott's (1962) distinction between two types of perceptions an infant and a growing child has of his mother. The 'environment mother' is experienced subjectively and during the states of instinctual quietude. The 'object mother' is experienced objectively during the instinctually needy states. The former provides the 'holding' and the latter the 'relating' functions for the child. Bringing these two mothers together is an achievement that facilitates the development of the 'capacity for concern' (see separate entry).

Envy: Sigmund Freud (1925j) located the origin of envy in the period when children discover the anatomical difference between the two sexes. His view was, however, quite restricted since it regarded envy to be the experience only of the female child (see separate entry on 'Penis envy') and not a ubiquitous human phenomenon. Melanie Klein (1957) rectified the situation by providing a most thorough and wide-ranging study of envy. She distinguished envy from jealousy, which aims at the possession of the love object and removal of a rival whereas envy is directed at the love object itself and seeks to acquire its good characteristics (see separate entry on 'Jealousy'). Jealousy involves whole objects and is triadic in nature. Envy, in contrast, involves part objects and a dyadic relationship. Klein traced the origins of envy to the earliest gratifiying experiences with the mother. Besides providing satisfaction, these experiences stir up in the child a wish to be the source of such 'goodness'. This wish is the psychic foundation of envy. If the gratification continues unabated, the experience of envy can be integrated with the parallel experience of love and gratitude. However, if the gratifying experiences with the mother are sporadic, their psychic value increases and so does the envy of her capacity to satisfy. Such intense envy cannot be interpreted with love. It fuses with greed, leading to 'a wish to exhaust the object entirely, not only in order to possess all its goodness but also to deplete the object purposefully so that it no longer contains anything enviable' (Segal, 1974, p. 41). Envy fuels

ambition, but strong feelings of envy can lead to despair and paralysis of effort (Spillius, 1993). The pain caused by envy is warded off by characteristic mental mechanisms (see 'Defences against envy'). See also the recent edited volume by Priscilla Roth and Alessandra Lemma (2008) titled *Envy and Gratitude Revisited*.

Epinosic gain: see 'Primary and secondary gain'.

Epistemophilia: see 'Epistemophilic instinct'.

Epistemophilic instinct: while both Sigmund Freud (1916–1917) and Melanie Klein (1924) had linked 'epistemophilia' to sexual curiosity and sadistic intrusion, respectively, Herman Nunberg (1931) emphasized the rational and ego-dominated aspects of man's 'need for causality'. Extrapolating this to a broader and more abstract level, Blema Steinberg (1993) proposed the notion of an 'epistemophilic instinct'. Essentially, this implies that human beings have a 'hard-wired', or, at least, psychologically 'hard-wired', desire to understand the meanings and causes of events that take place within and around them. In the clinical situation, the externalized version of this wish gives rise to questions about the analyst's ways of working (e.g., his silences, his anonymity). Frustration of this defensive and projected need for causality is, to a large extent, essential if the world of inner objects is to be called forth in a lively fashion into the transference context. However, when the analyst shows a striking departure from his usual manner of functioning, the patient's credulity is taxed and the resulting associations are coloured by iatrogenesis and false compliance. Under such circumstances (e.g., a sudden, long absence of the analyst), some explanation geared to the patient's ego level of affective tolerance has to be offered.

Eriksonian stages of psychosocial development: Erik Erikson (1950) proposed a sequence of developmental tasks that differed from the psychoanalytic models prevalent at that time in four important ways: (1) the stages were conceived in terms of polarities of success and failure in achieving a particular developmental milestone, (2) unfolding processes of development were not seen as resulting from instinctual forces, but from ego accomplishments, (3) the challenges faced and the rewards reaped by the ego in this process emanated not only from the individual, but also from the micro- (family) and macro- (school, workplace, society at large) communal realms, and (4) the tasks did not end with the so-called 'latency phase', or even 'adolescence' (see separate entries) but continued into adulthood until old age and the end of life. Erikson outlined eight such stages of development. These included (1) basic trust *vs.* basic mistrust, (2) autonomy *vs.* shame and doubt, (3) initiative *vs.* guilt, (4) industry *vs.* inferiority, (5) identity *vs.* role confusion, (6) intimacy *vs.* isolation, (7) generativity *vs.* stagnation, and (8) ego integrity *vs.* despair. These stages have been properly described in separate entries under their names.

Eros: Sigmund Freud (1900a, 1920g, 1921c) employed the name of the Greek god of sexual love almost synonymously with 'life instinct' (see separate entry). His choice of this metaphor was apt, since 'Eros' is the lover of Psyche, the Greek goddess of mind, and a force aimed at synthesis and harmony between disparate elements. Viewed this way, 'Eros' represents the energy of the sexual and self-preservatory drives, i.e., the two subsidiary aims of the life instinct.

Erotic desire: while Sigmund Freud (1910h) had defined romantic love as the result of a confluence between affectionate and sensual currents, full phenomenological explication of these two constituents evolved only gradually. Among the writings on the nature of erotic desire, the most detailed is that of Otto Kernberg (1991), who sees such desire as consisting of the following seven elements: (1) longing for pleasurable physical closeness with another person which has the quality of both forceful crossing of a barrier and of becoming one with the other person; (2) identification with the sexual excitement of the partner, with such intersubjective transcendence leading to a diminution of the envy of the opposite sex; (3) overcoming of shame (both one's own and that of the partner) and transgression of conventional morality; (4) desire for loss of all boundaries; (5) idealization of the partner's body and of objects that it symbolically represents; the body of the beloved thus becomes 'a geography of personal meanings' (p. 348); (6) wish for teasing and being teased, an element that draws attention to the intimate dynamic connections between exhibitionism and sadism, since sexual teasing is linked to exhibitionistic teasing; and (7) oscillation between the search for secrecy and exclusivity on the one hand, and a radical shifting from sexual intimacy on the other.

Erotic transference: described first by Sigmund Freud (1912–1913, 1915a) 'erotic transference' refers to the emergence of romantic feelings towards the analyst in the patient. This might be openly declared by the patient, or manifest itself through 'unmistakable indications' (p. 159) of love. Freud acknowledged that the experience is subjectively genuine, and the fact that it has infantile prototypes does not distinguish it from love in life outside analysis. However, such 'transference love' has certain special features: (1) it is stirred up by the analytic situation, (2) it is intensified by the resistance, and (3) it is less concerned with realistic situations and consequences than is love in ordinary life. Freud emphasized that it is 'as disastrous for the analysis if the patient's craving for love is gratified as if it is suppressed: the course the analyst must pursue is neither of these' (p. 166); it is one of analytic abstinence, transference interpretation, and reconstruction. An important matter to keep in mind in this context is the differential diagnosis of 'erotic transference'. Two other phenomena need to be ruled out. The first pertains to 'unobjectionable positive transference' and the second to 'erotized transference', or 'malignant erotic transference' (see separate entries on these entities). The former revolves around collaborative and affectionate feelings and does not contribute (at least, not significantly) to resistance, and the latter to demands for love that are far more desperate, coercive, and aggressively-tinged than is the case with 'erotic transference'. See also the discussion of 'erotic transference' by Stefano Bolognini (1994).

Erotized transference: in his paper 'Observations on transference love', Sigmund Freud (1915a) acknowledged that there is 'one class of women with whom the attempt to preserve the erotic transference for the purposes of analytic work without satisfying it will not succeed. These are women of elemental passionateness who tolerate no substitutes. They are children of nature who refuse to accept the psychical in place of the material' (pp. 166–167). This attitude received a comprehensive description by Harold Blum (1973) under the rubric of 'erotized transference'. Blum emphasized that underlying such erotic demands are intense object hunger, defective self- and object constancy, fears of depletion and engulfment, infantile omnipotence, and much sadomasochism. Condensation of the good-mother representation with that of the desired oedipal partner gives rise to intense longings experienced as unquestionable needs. However, the 'pre-eminent oral insatiability, the vulnerability to disappointment and detachment, the underlying sadomasochism soon become apparent' (Blum, 1973, p. 69).

Erotic excitements of the girl: see 'Endeavour and erotic excitements of the girl'.

Erotogenic masochism: see 'Primary masochism'.

Erotogenic zones: term introduced by Sigmund Freud in 1905a to designate those parts of the body which are especially capable of giving rise to sexual excitation. They are the sites of origin of 'component instincts' (see separate entry). Prominent among such 'erotogenic zones' are the mouth, anus, and genitals. However, 'erotogenicity is a general characteristic of all organs' (Freud, 1914c, p. 84). Whether a particular body part becomes erotogenic depends upon the increase or decrease in this potential. Later, Freud (1940a [1938]) emphatically declared that 'in fact the whole body is an erotogenic zone' (p. 151). While this seems true, even more important is the fact that 'erotogenic zones' do not operate in isolation from the overall developmental context; they unfold within a relational matrix and are imbued with memory, fantasy, affect, defence, and psychic elaboration.

Escapades: emphasizing that 'identity' (see separate entry) was a dynamic and ever-shifting configuration, Gustav Bychowski (1962) noted that ego-syntonic and ego-dystonic self-representations frequently coexist in one and the same person. The latter are usually handled by the mechanisms of repression, splitting, or disassociation. At times, however, transitory or permanent unshackling from the visual identity takes place; this can lead to episodic acts that are otherwise 'out of character', or to lasting breaks from one's profession, religion, ideology, and circle of friends. Dissociative features may or may not accompany such 'escapades', which discharge 'the inner tension created by the discrepancy and the conflict between antithetic images of the self' (p. 166).

Escape into reality: Bernard Robbin's (1937) phrase for the spontaneous disappearance of delusions one sometimes sees in hospitalized, mentally ill patients. Such 'social recovery' is not based upon the realization by the patient that his beliefs are fantastic. It is due to the patient accepting the dictates of external reality because they happen to serve more adequately the needs of certain internal emotional pressures at that time.

Eternal dilettante: a character type described by Kata Levy (1949) whose main feature is failure to consolidate a vocational identity. The individual dabbles in multiple and often contradictory professional interests. He enthusiastically takes up career tracks, only to drop them as the requirement for a deeper commitment becomes necessary. The result is that the person ends up knowing a little bit of this and a little bit of that while lacking in-depth knowledge of any field. He feels like a 'misfit' (see separate entry) everywhere. The aetiology of his confusion is multifold and involves (1) poor role models in early life and lack of direction from parents, especially the father, (2) inability to synthesize contradictory self-representations and, therefore, the syndrome of 'identity diffusion' (see separate entry), (3) a desperate object hunger that precludes closing doors on any vocational interest that comes one's way, and (4) blockage of aggression which makes such 'letting go' difficult. As a result, the individual drifts from one line of work to another; forlorn and empty, he yearns for identity but can find it nowhere. In Sø

ren Kierkegaard's words 'Condemned is the man to whom all options are open'!

Ethnic identity: this refers to an inner sense of belonging to a community that has persisted through passage of history and has common cultural characteristics. According to J. Anderson Thomson, Jr and colleagues (1993), 'ethnic identity' is both positive ('we can do this') and negative ('we do not do what they do'). It results from the exposure of a child to the family's cultural modes and its particular ways of conducting day-to-day life; identification with parents, especially during the oedipal phase, also enhances a sense of generational continuity, which is the cornerstone of later ethnic identity.

Ethnocentric identity: a term commonly found in the immigration literature that refers to the post-adolescent ethnocentricity that results in a feeling of comfort in the homoethnic milieu combined with discomfort in the sexual and vocational competitiveness of the culture at large.

Ethnocentric withdrawal: Salman Akhtar's (1999b) term for the tendency of some immigrants to lead a cloistered life and associate mainly or solely with people of their own ethnicity. Such individuals eat only their ethnic food and listen exclusively to their ethnic music. Their residences, replete with artefacts from 'back home', take an shrine-like quality. 'They become more nationalistic towards their country of origin than they were while living in it. To buttress such secondary nationalism, they often forge unlikely alliances and develop new prejudices' (p. 87).

Ethnocultural self-representation: a term introduced in the literature by Jennifer Bonovitz (1998) to link up the potentially overlapping ethnic and cultural aspects of identity and to keep it anchored in a metapsychological perspective. The 'ethnocultural self-representation' evolves from identifications with family members and with homoethnic extrafamilial figures, especially national heroes. It is 'negatively' buttressed by acquisition of the knowledge that one's ethnic group has interactional patterns, relational opportunities, history, myths, linguistic peculiarities (and, at times, an entirely different language altogether), and a group fantasy life that is different from individuals belonging to other groups. Such a self-representation is generally a source of silent pride, but it can be imbued with narcissism (leading to ethnic megalomania) or self-directed aggression (leading to feelings of inferiority).

Evacuation: term used by Wilfred Bion (1957, 1962a,b) for the proclivity of the psychotic part of the personality to expel split-off mental contents via different pathways in order to 'inoculate external objects' (Lopez-Corvo, 2003, p. 100) with them. The process of 'evacuation' is a method to get rid of bad internal objects, either in their totality or in their fragmented forms.

Evenly hovering attention: see 'Evenly suspended attention'.

Evenly suspended attention: Sigmund Freud's (1912e) phrase for the analyst's attitude of 'not directing one's notice to anything in particular' (p. 111) while listening to his patient. Such 'free-floating attention' assures that the analyst avoids prematurely selecting this or that bit of material, foreclosing the possibility of surprise and discovery. It also allows his 'unconscious memory' (p. 112) to capture important links from the seemingly less relevant aspects of the patient's associations. While Freud's dictate that the analyst maintain an 'evenly suspended' or 'evenly hovering attention' has become a cornerstone of psychoanalytic technique, the highly respected Charles Brenner (2000) has argued that Freud's views on listening changed. The position he took eventually was consonant with 'our current practice: in listening to a patient, one pays attention now to defence, now to what is defended against, depending on which is apparent in a patient's communications' (p. 548). Brenner concluded that 'those analysts who still believe that evenly hovering attention is the proper analytic attitude are, I believe, mistaken in citing Freud in support of that belief' (p. 549).

Evocation of a proxy: Martin Wangh's (1962) term for the use of another person by the ego for its defensive purpose. In doing so, not only the prohibited id impulses are induced in the other person, but certain ego experiences and ego functions can also be mobilized in them. The defence emerges in response to anxiety over loss of control of one's impulses and/or of unmanageable regression in reality testing. Individuals using this defence often betray a lack of dissolution of the early symbiotic tie to the mother and, with it, a weak and porus sense of identity.

Evocativeness: Stephen Appelbaum's (1966) concept referring to a feature of communication which tends to give the analyst's interventions a life-like and affectively charged quality in the therapeutic process. This contributes to a greater emergence of forgotten and latent aspects of the patient's psyche and to a more effective working through process. In a later, book-length elaboration of this idea, Appelbaum (2000) delineated what is fresh, deeply felt, authentic, and poignant in the analyst's communications and the ways such 'evocativeness' has impacts on the patient. This work is a most unusual confluence of ego psychology, British independence school, acting, poetry, linguistics, fiction, and many other unexpected ingredients.

Exaggeration as a defence: described by Otto Sperling (1963), this defence rests upon making a threatening id derivative or superego command into a gross caricature. This makes it tolerable to the ego, since it is not reflective of the actual psychic reality anyway. By overstating the issue at hand, an air of jocularity or maudlin sentimentality is injected into the situation. The id or superego impingement upon the ego is acknowledged, but its emotional significance (e.g., anxiety, remorse) is minimized. Otto Fenichel's (1945) earlier description of 'denial by exaggeration' is a related concept.

Examination dreams: see 'Universal dreams'.

Exceptions: a character type described by Sigmund Freud (1916d). Individuals who fall under this rubric display four characteristics (1) as children, they suffered from some illness or mishap which imposed 'an unjust disadvantage' (Freud, 1916d, p. 313) upon them, (2) they did not contribute to the occurrence of this problem and were truly guiltless, (3) due to such unearned suffering, they feel deserving to be spared of any further demands in life and are especially abhorrent of rules and regulations, and (4) their feeling of being an 'exception' often entitles them to immoral or illegal behaviour; their credo is 'I may do wrong myself, since wrong has been done to me' (p. 315). While these features are well recognized, some aspects outlined by Freud remain less known. He noted, for instance, that women in general have a tendency to claim privileges and treat themselves as exceptions since they unconsciously regard themselves as being 'damaged'. He also observed that the tendency to behave like an exception can arise for the first time in adult life as a consequence of learning one has been cheated by nature in the form of a late manifesting congenital disorder. Freud extended the notion of exception to group psychology as well, noting that 'the behavior of whole nations whose past history has been full of suffering' (p. 313) can also be exceptional; yesterday's oppressed can become today's tyrants. Freud's views have been given an additional twist by Selma Kramer (1987), who noted that each child goes through a normal, though transient, phase of being treated by his or her parents as special and an 'exception', so to speak, and those who have not had this experience might have it for the first time during their analyses. Such release of a thwarted developmental tendency by interpretive work is better handled by gentle support and, to use Daniel Patrick Moynihan's phrase from a different context, by 'benign neglect' rather than by interpretive deconstruction.

Exciting object: see 'Fairbairn's description of the endopsychic structure'.

Exhibitionism: the term is used in two different ways: (1) *in a narrow sense*, 'exhibitionism' refers to the male sexual perversion of exposing one's genitals to unsuspecting others, and (2) *in a broad sense*, 'exhibitionism' refers to any and all attempts at being looked at and admired by others. The former is usually a defence against castration anxiety' (see separate entry) and the associated feelings of impotence. The latter is a derivative of what Sigmund Freud (1905a, 1915c) called the 'component instinct' of exhibitionism. This instinct, along with its twin, 'voyeurism', succumbs to 'genital primacy' (see separate entries on these concepts) over the course of development. While this view of 'exhibitionism' remains respectable, contemporary psychoanalysis tends to conceptualize the character trait of exhibitionism less in terms of a partial instinct than in terms of pathological narcissism (which, in turn, is warding off feelings of inferiority and worthlessness).

Exit line: a popular theatrical device whereby a character who is leaving the stage utters a few words that give him the upper hand, since those left on the stage are robbed of the chance to respond; the latter must struggle with the emotional reverberations alone. Glen Gabbard (1982) has written a paper with this very title in which he notes that patients often convey highly important messages in the words they utter as they are leaving the office. Such 'exit lines' are of many types (e.g., cry for help, last minute questions) and often coloured by feelings derived from earlier separations. 'These 'last words' are saved for the hour's end to keep them out of the therapeutic process and to render the therapist impotent and unable to respond' (p. 597). Gabbard adds that the analyst need not despair since this material can be brought up in the next session, at times, with quite fruitful results.

Explicit and implicit memories: these terms refer to two different ways memories are acquired and stored, as well as two different deposits, as it were, in the memory bank. 'Explicit memory' is also called 'declarative memory' and 'implicit memory' is also called 'non-declarative ' or 'procedural memory'. 'Explicit memory' is acquired by focused attention, and coded in verbal constructs, and has 'content' as its end product. 'Implicit memory' is acquired by the accruing of subliminal cues, is coded in feeling tones and visual images, and has 'process' as its end product. 'Explicit memory' pertains to facts and stories; 'implicit memory' pertains to acts and lessons. Knowledge of a car's parts or of driving laws, for instance, are stored in 'explicit memory', but the habitual and unthinking driving itself is accomplished through 'implicit' or 'procedural' memory. 'Explicit memory' develops later than 'implicit memory'; there is some evidence (DeCasper & Spence, 1986) that the latter begins as early as in utero. In day to day adult functioning, and during the clinical work of psychoanalysis, both types of memories operate in unison. Interpretive handling of an 'enactment' (see separate entry) demonstrates the intervention-based transformation of 'implicit' into 'explicit' memory.

Externalization: term coined by Anna Freud (1936) to describe a particular sub-species of transference, but currently used rather loosely to denote a variety of psychological phenomena. In its original usage by Miss Freud, 'externalization' referred to an experience in the clinical relationship that resulted not from the unconscious repetition or re-creation of childhood experiences, but from the attribution of a fully formed part of the patient's personality to the analyst. Externalization is illustrated by a patient who, for instance, expects criticism from the analyst instead of experiencing the pangs of his or her own conscience. This is distinct from the usual meaning of transference, which, in a parallel case, would involve the unconscious attribution of a punitive father's traits to one's analyst. Such restricted use of the term 'externalization' has given way to it being employed for all sorts of events and perceptions, whereby an individual perceives his intrapsychic issues to be emanating from external reality. One or both sides of a conflict might thus be perceived as residing outside of oneself. A wife who is sick of her chronically uncommunicative husband might feel that, while she wants to leave him, it is their children who will object to this course of action; here her ambivalence is split, and the side that keeps her in a stifling marriage is attributed to their offspring. In an externalization of both vectors of a conflict, an administrator might see his followers split into two warring factions, which he desperately needs to bring into harmony. Finally, it should be noted that 'projection' (see separate entry) and 'projective identification' (see separate entry) are specific forms of externalization. Jack Novick and Karry Kelly Novick (1970) have elucidated the concept of 'externalization', noting that, essentially, it is the counterpart of internalization.

Externalizing transference: in a phenomenologically detailed application of Anna Freud's (1936) notion of 'externalization' (see separate entry) to the clinical situation, Morton Berg (1977) coined the phrase 'externalizing transference'. He distinguished it from the 'classical' transference on three grounds: (1) in 'classical' transference, it is infantile aims toward infantile objects that are displaced upon the analyst, whereas, in 'externalizing' transference, the emphasis is upon allocation of internal structures and their antecedent self and object representations to the analyst, (2) 'classical' transference involves object-libidinal and largely oedipal matters, whereas the 'externalizing transference' involves the revival of narcissistic pre-oedipal and pre-structural elements, and (3) the former rests upon repression and displacement, and the latter upon splitting and externalization.

Extimacy: neologism coined by Jacques Lacan (1959) for underscoring the dialectical closeness between what is inside and what is outside the psyche. Thus the 'real' (see separate entry) resides as much outside as inside and the 'Other' (see separate entry) is, in the end, as familiar to the self as it is foreign to it.

Extra-analytic contacts: while Sigmund Freud maintained a personal relationship with his patients that he often excluded from the treatment proper, later psychoanalysts began to be more rigid and almost phobic about encountering their patients outside of the clinical setting. In what is most likely the first paper exclusively dedicated to the topic, William Tarnower (1966) elucidated the significance of 'extra-analytic contacts'. He noted that there are good technical reasons to avoid a patient outside of his hour. Citing Edward Glover (1955), he suggested that if the psychoanalyst becomes aware that his patient is going to be present at a small gathering, he should decline to be there. This may protect the patient from over stimulation and gathering reality information that contradicts a particular transference that he or she needs to experience and work through. Tarnower acknowledged that chance meetings outside the clinical setting cannot be totally avoided, however. Such encounters might provide the analyst with an unusual opportunity to recognize hitherto unverbalized conflicts; the fact that a patient avoids talking about such a contact is often a giveaway sign for conflicts lurking underneath. This whole area received a further review and update by Herbert Strean (1981), who divided 'extra-analytic contacts' into three types: (1) those actively brought about by the patient, (2) truly accidental encounters, and (3) contacts anticipated by the analyst and not the patient. He emphasized that such meetings can stimulate secret wishes and and anxiety in both parties. Ultimately, though, it remains a matter of helping the patient explore his associations to such an encounter and to make these experiences a part of the analysis. The analyst should simply analyse their reverberations and neither encourage nor discourage their actual occurrence. When an 'extra-analytic contact' does occur, an attitude of informed naturalness on the analyst's part is the best. Helmut Thoma and Horst Kachele (1994) emphasize that 'it would be inappropriate for the patient to let himself freely associate in public, and the analyst would behave conspicuously if he refused to talk about the weather or vacation plans and instead remained silent or interpreted the conversation' (p. 298). Acting naturally can protect the patient from the potentially traumatizing effects of a stereotypically silent analytic attitude. To be sure, the patient can misunderstand and be burdened by the relative intermingling of roles as a result of seeing his or her analyst outside and within the clinical situation. However, lack of naturalness on the analyst's part can also hurt the patient. The special importance of these matters to training analyses is self evident. Here, too, Thoma and Kachele's recommendations are significant. 'It is essential that in their training candidates develop an uncomplicated relationship to the various roles they will play in and outside their professional lives. The degree of natural behavior by their analysts that candidates experience both in and outside psychoanalysis is an instructive measure for such tolerance toward the diversity of roles' (p. 299). See also the recent contribution by Janet Zuckerman and Lisa Horlick (2006) which highlights the potential for growth in moments when the analyst's 'falliblity and humanity' (p. 351) are unwittingly revealed.

Extraject: see 'Extrajection'.

Extrajection: described by Eduardo Weiss (1947) 'extrajection' is the transformation of a part of the ego into an object representation. It consists of the withdrawal of the ego cathexis from an aspect of one's self; the representation of this aspect thus falls outside the ego boundaries. The object representation which emerges as a result is called the 'extraject'.

Extrajective introjection: a concept proposed by Christopher Bollas (1987) as the converse of 'projection identification' (see separate entry). According to Bollas, this intersubjective process involves one individual 'stealing' an element of someone else's psychic life and assuming that the latter has no experience of that particular aspect of his or her inner life. The process of 'extrajective introjection' may last a short while or may extend over a lifetime. In the latter case, the psychic theft is undone only after a prolonged period of analytic treatment.

Extramural refuelling: Salman Akhtar's (1999a) term for the immigrant's seeking emotional sustenance and rejuvenation by phone contact with friends and relatives in the country of origin or by actually visiting the homeland. 'Extramural refuelling' strengthens those self-representations of the immigrant which are in close emotional contact with his original culture. Such strengthening, paradoxically, allows him greater freedom to explore and express his newly acquired self-representations that are in tune with his new, adopted land.

Extra-transference interpretation: in a comprehensive paper on this subject, Harold Blum (1983a) noted that the adult neurosis is never entirely mobilized within the transference and important conflicts and compromise formations appear outside the transference as well. Moreover, elements of transference neurosis can become displaced and enacted outside of the clinical setting. As a result, 'extra-transference interpretation' becomes necessary. This involves pointing out to the patient the situations in which he, for instance, has been timid or overly aggressive, based upon his confusing them with 'old' situations. Such observations may enlarge the analytic transference perspective. Blum warned that 'transference analysis only is an ideal fiction like the normal ego and would leave the analysis quite isolated from reality, with danger that the reality principle would not be strengthened but, in the long run, undermined' (p. 594).

F: see 'Act of faith'.

Face–breast equation: originally reported by Renato Almansi (1960), this phenomenon refers to the frequent equation of human face with the maternal breast. The two can symbolically represent each other, or one can serve as a screen for the other. Derived from the clinical observation that the longing for seeing the analyst's face increases when the analysand is experiencing a loss, the 'face–breast equation' posits that, at such moments, the longed-for visual contact has orally nourishing value for the patient. Almansi offered supportive evidence for this hypothesis from language, humorous drawings, and ancient artefacts. The ontogenetic root of such 'equation' might be that the infant-on-breast often has eyes fixed on mother's face, and when the nipple slips out of his mouth (due to infantile clumsiness) the visual cathexis of mother's face is intensified. Hence, in René Spitz's (1965) words, 'when the infant loses the nipple and recovers it, contact with the need-gratifying percept is lost and recovered. During the interval between loss and recovery of *contact*, the other element of the total perceptual unit, *distance perception* of the face, remains unchanged. In the course of these repetitive experiences, visual perception comes to be relied upon, for it is not lost' (p. 65, original emphasis). Visual cathexis of the face now draws energy originally invested in the tactile cathexis of the breast. This becomes the basis of the later mental equation of the face with the breast.

Face–genital equation: while the symbolic equation of parts of the face (e.g., nose, mouth) with the genitals of both sexes has been noted from the earliest days of psychoanalysis (Freud, 1900a), the phrase 'face–genital equation' was coined by Nathaniel Ross (1959). In his view, at times the entire face unconsciously represents the genitals. This is facilitated by the fact that both the face and genitals participate in the display of sexual feelings as well as in the discharge of libidinal tensions.

Factor C: Jacques Lacan's (1950, cited in Evans, 1996, p. 59) term for 'the constant characteristic of any cultural milieu' (p. 37). The only example he gave of this was the ahistorical and uncannily present-orientated nature of daily life in the USA. This, Lacan felt (echoing a sentiment voiced by Sigmund Freud long ago), meant that the culture of the USA was particularly unsuited to psychoanalysis. To the extent that such broad generalizations are possible, it is tempting to speculate that the West's rejection of the 'death instinct' (see separate entry) concept is related to the fact that the concept emanated from the 'Factor C' of the East (see 'Death instinct reformulated'), which incorporates stoicism, transience, and equanimity in the face of mortality as integral to human existence. Similarly, the West's puzzlement over the phenomenon of suicide bombing might have to do with its lack of comprehension of the Middle Eastern 'Factor C' of martyrdom.

Fairbairn's description of the endopsychic structure: taking the analysis of dreams and of schizoid withdrawal as his starting point, William Ronald Dodd Fairbairn (1944) came to discard the traditional structural model (comprising id, ego, and superego) in favour of a classification laid out in terms of an ego structure split into three parts (i) 'central ego' of the I, which is the seat of self observation and 'owned up' self experience, (ii) 'libidinal ego' which is highly endowed with libido, and (iii) a part which attacks the 'libidinal ego'; since such attack seems more vindictive than moral, this part is best termed 'antilibidinal ego' or the 'internal saboteur'. Libido is at the disposal of the 'libidinal ego' and aggression at that of the 'internal saboteur'. These ego structures are paired with corresponding internal objects. The 'libidinal ego' is attached to the 'exciting object' and the 'internal saboteur' to the 'rejecting object'. The 'central ego' observes and relates to both these units. It has conscious, preconscious, and unconscious elements. The two 'subsidiary egos' ('libidinal ego' and 'internal saboteur') are essentially unconscious. Fairbairn emphasized that, while these three structures have similarities with the Freudian ego, id, and superego, there exist important differences as well. 'Central ego' corresponds to the 'ego' of classical psychoanalysis, but it is not derived from something else (i.e., the undifferentiated ego–id matrix). Nor is it dependent upon for its activity upon the demands of id. The 'libidinal ego' resembles the id but is a derivative of the 'central ego' and not a reservoir of instinctual tension. The 'internal saboteur' resembles the superego, but differs in two important ways: (i) it is not an externalized object, but a split-off part of the 'central ego', and (ii) it is devoid of all moral significance. These fascinating, complex, and useful ideas of Fairbairn have been further elaborated by Harry Guntrip (1969), Otto Kernberg (1980), and Frederico Periera and David Scharff (2002).

Faith: the topic of 'faith' in the context of psychoanalysis is a tricky one. Sigmund Freud's (1927c) harsh debunking of religious belief and idealization of scientific rationality led his followers to be reticent in approaching 'faith'. Therefore, the first point needing emphasis here is that 'faith' does not necessarily stand for 'religious faith', though the latter can certainly come under this rubric. Defined by *Webster's Dictionary*, 'faith' denotes 'firm believing in something for which there is not proof' (p. 446). Given this, it would be perfectly fair to say that Freud had great faith in logic, science and, of course, in his discovery, psychoanalysis. Moving on to psychoanalytic perspectives on 'faith', one encounters three different accounts: (1) *Donald Winnicott's* (1953) delineation of the 'intermediate area of experience' (see separate entry), which owes its fragile aesthetics to the gentleman's agreement of not bringing questions of reality and unreality to bear upon it. The categorical separations between real and unreal, true or untrue, and actual or imaginary are set aside here; imagination is born and paradox reigns supreme. Play, metaphor, and creativity reside in this realm and so does 'faith'; one simply has to take it or leave it; (2) *Erik Erikson's* (1956, 1959) notions on 'basic trust' (see separate entry), especially when temporally extrapolated into the future, give rise to notions of hope and faith. Conscious hope promises the gratification of wishes. 'Unconscious hope' (see separate entry) holds the possibility of finding needed developmental objects in future. It is when both these hopes get delinked from self and human objects and come to be about all others and institutions and nature, repectively, that 'faith' is born. The feeling that future generations will be taken care of by the advancement of science, justice, democracy, and the arts is the essence of such 'Eriksonian faith'; (3) *Wilfred Bion's* (1967, 1970) views on 'O' (see separate entry) or the ultimate truth supremely coherent reality, or the thing in-itself, gives rise to a third, perhaps more 'spiritual', view of faith. Here 'faith' is not ontogenetically earned, nor is it courteously permitted by the dignity of others' restraint. 'Faith', for Bion, is leaving knowledge and experience behind and permitting oneself to see the truth of the movement as it exists. Did the Oedipus complex exist before Sophocles or Freud, a Bionian might ask? And, if so, where was it? And, in the same vein, wasn't

$E=mc^2$ in existence long before Albert Einstein's discovery of it? In essence, the three psychoanalytic perspectives on 'faith', even without going into matters of God or of religion, take one into an area of psychological experience that, by reason of being dimly lit, turns out to be scary and alluring at the same time. Stay tuned.

Falling asleep during the session: while the work of psychoanalysis demands much mental activity (more verbalized from the patient's side than that of the analyst's) and, therefore, a certain level of alert awakeness, the fact is that the degrees of alertness on the part of both parties tends to vary from sharply vigilant states through fuzziness of attention to drowsiness and falling asleep. When not related to physiological (e.g., extraordinary fatigue, hangover) or situational (e.g., dim light, reclining comfort, silence) factors, this is a clinical matter of considerable concern. Sleepiness during the session can affect both parties, though, curiously, almost never does it happen to them simultaneously: (1) *The patient's falling asleep* on the couch usually represents 'resistance' (see separate entry) against the emergence of disturbing themes, especially those involving aggression. It should be remembered, however, that somnolence of this sort can also be a hint that the childhood witnessing of the 'primal scene' (see separate entry) is being recalled by the patient. Masud Khan (1962) has described a growth-promoting type of sleep during the analytic session as well. In other words, the patient's falling asleep on the couch is multiply-determined (Waelder, 1936). (2) *The analyst's falling asleep* has also been reported in the literature. James McLaughlin (1975) suggests that obsessional patients (whose intellectualizations can have a mind-numbing effect), borderline patients (who mobilize countertransference hate), and patients whose conflicts are too similar to those of the analyst can allcause sleepiness in the analyst. Hyman Spotnitz (1979) added narcissistic patients to this category, since their solipsism and aloofness can push the analyst towards detachment and sleepiness. More recently, Ira Brenner (2004) has added patients who 'regularly utilize defensive altered ego states and manifest autohypnotic, dream-like phenomena' (p. 219) to those who can induce sleepiness in the analyst. He reviews the pertinent literature and provides detailed clinical material to illustrate how one such countertransference enactment, upon thorough self-analysis, yielded useful data for 'reconstructions' with a patient.

False object: term introduced by Joseph Sandler and Anne-Marie Sandler (1998) to denote the fact that, by using various intrapsychic and interpersonal manoeuvres (e.g., intense idealization), an individual can force an object into a tightly defined role. By distorting his perception, the individual can make the object safe and psychically useful, even though, in the process, its actual qualities have been banished into oblivion. This tendency is marked in the setting of pathological narcissism, religious cults, and sexual perversion. Sandler's concept offers an aesthetic as well as logical complimentarity to Donald Winnicott's (1960) well-known concept of 'false self' (see separate entry). See also Priscilla Roth's (1994) paper on being true to a 'false object'.

False self: Donald Winnicott's (1960) term for that aspect of psychosocial functioning that results from accommodating and responding to environmental demands and not one that comes from inner spontaneity. Some degree of false self is inevitable, and might even be necessary. Too much of it leads to a life lived only for others; a wistful and unrealized existence. The purpose of the false self is to 'search for conditions in which the true self can come into its own' (p. 138).

Falsified screens: see 'Screen'.

Familial self: a term used by Alan Roland (1988) to denote a psychic structure common in Asian Indians. This type of self is enmeshed with others and primarily experiences itself in relation to them. The degree of psychic separateness and of firmness of self-boundaries is less than is customarily seen in the West.

Family romance fantasy: term coined by Sigmund Freud (1909c) for a group of fantasies by which a child invents a new family for himself. Such scenarios include imagining that one is a foundling, that the parents are not one's real parents, and one was born in a noble or royal family, or that while one is their legitimate offspring, one's siblings are not. Generally transient, this fantasy serves four purposes: (1) compensates for the narcissistic deflation that results from an increasingly realistic view of parents who can no longer be idealized, (2) nostalgically links one to the 'perfect' parents of infancy and early childhood by creating a proxy image of them, (3) mitigates oedipal guilt, since those towards whom erotic and rivalrous feelings are being experienced are not one's 'real' parents anyway, and (4) repudiates kinship with envied siblings, who are now seen as the children of mere commoners. When persistent (and fuelled by the need for grandiosity emanating from severe trauma and deprivation in childhood), the family romance fantasy tends to contribute to the charming but fraudulent tales told by an imposter.

Fantasy: refers to the mental creation of personal scenarios that serve diverse psychic purposes. The topic of 'fantasy' is vast, and can be addressed from the perspective of the following binaries: (1) *conscious vs. unconscious:*' unconscious fantasy' (see separate entry) is generally a more organized and organizing psychic element than conscious fantasy, which is usually a derivative of the former; (2) *discursive vs. existential*: the former consists of stories with the subject as the active (e.g., 'I do such and such thing to him') or passive (e.g., 'She does such and such to me') agent while the latter involve states of being (e.g., 'I am so and so', 'I have become such and such'); (3) *simple vs. complex*: content-wise, fantasies can be relatively transparent (e.g., a child's imagining that her father will bring her a toy upon returning from work) or quite convoluted (e.g., a woman's fantasy that a man is having sex with her while a somewhat effeminate man is watching them and drinking a glass of milk); (4) *ephemeral vs. fixed*: passing fantasies in response to drive imbalances under the influence of environmental cues are to be distinguished from the more persistent and recurrent imaginary scenarios on the mind's stage; (5) *common vs. uncommon*: like 'universal dreams' (see separate entry), there are fantasies which are ubiquitous in human experience (e.g., themes of glory, fame, revenge, sexual encounters) and then there are those which are highly personal and idiosyncratic; (6) *culturally sanctioned vs. culturally dystonic*: there are fantasies which are sanctioned by the culture at large to the extent that the fact that they are fantasies is all but forgotten (e.g., the belief in a colonized race's inferiority by those belonging to the colonizing group) and then there are fantasies which are contrary to the beliefs held in the prevalent culture (e.g., a firm belief in reincarnation on the part of a Western individual) ; (7) *discharge vs. defensive function*: while the two aims are often simultaneously present, it is important to discern whether the predominant goal of a fantasy is instinctual discharge or ego defence, even in the seemingly adaptive form of trial action; and (8) *inherited or experientially derived origin*: while most fantasies draw their content from wishes, defences, slivers of memory, and current realities, some fantasies (see entry on ' primal phantasies) are viewd as inherently known and even phylogenetically determined. See also the related entry on 'phantasy'.

Fantasies of the imaginer and the imagined: described by Lucy Lafarge (2004, 2006), these pertain to the object relationship between the parent and the child engaged together in imagining the child's experience. The parent's capacity for, and attitude in, imagining the child has an impact upon the child's subjective experience of the parent. The two sets of fantasies are thus dialectically linked. These 'fantasies of the imaginer and the imagined' are ubiquitous, but often remain silent during the clinical work. They draw upon historical experience, but are also altered by wishes and defences against those wishes. With their emergence in treatment, the patient might remain in the imagined-child role and cast the analyst in the imagining-parent role. Or, the roles may be reversed. Discerning these fantasies helps to formulate object relation-based interpretations. In a later paper, Lafarge (2009) applied these ideas to the realm of lying and deception by patients in analysis.

Fascist state of the mind: Christopher Bollas's (1992) designation for a psychic state whose core characteristic is the total domination of the mind by an ideology and 'the operation of specific mental mechanisms aimed at eliminating all opposition' (p. 200). Such a state reduces complexity to simplicity, adamantly refusing to entertain any doubts about the convictions it holds. An intoxicated sense of purity prevails. 'The moral void created by the destruction of opposition begins to make its presence felt. At this point, the subject must find a victim to contain that void, and now a state of mind becomes an act of violence' (p. 205). Paula Heimann's (1952) essay on the intricate relationship between paranoia and hypomania, David Shapiro's (1965) description of paranoid cognition, and Eric Brenman's (1985) perspective on cruelty and 'narrow-mindedness' (see separate entry) are pertinent in this regard. Affective and cognitive propensities of the kind these papers describe are of great significance to applied psychoanalysis, as Vamik Volkan's (1988, 1997, 2004) psychopolitical work amply demonstrates.

Fate compulsion: term used by Sigmund Freud (1920g) for the unhappy life-pattern of some individuals which appears driven by a dark and demonic force. Such individuals repeatedly encounter similar mishaps and give the impression of 'being pursued by a malignant fate' (1920g, p. 21). The casualties they meet with over and over (e.g., betrayal by lovers, failures in business) seem to emanate from outside them. It is as if they are cursed. They have little access to the masochistic repetition and the unconscious wishes for suffering that actually lead to these soul-wrenching fiascos.

Fate neurosis: see 'Fate compulsion'.

Father hunger: term coined by James Herzog (1980, 2001) to denote the growing son's longing and need for contact (including physical contact) with his father or a father substitute in order to fully experience his own masculine sense of self. 'The father's sameness (non-motherness) is appreciated and needed' (p. 228) for the formation of the sense of self, the completion of 'separation–individuation' (see separate entry) and, the beginning of the modulation of instinctual drives, especially those pertaining to aggression. Herzog postulates that the father's careful use of aggression to modulate his son's management of aggressive and assertive behaviour is of profound significance to the boy's development. Not only does the father separate the boy from the mother, he also becomes an identification model that helps the boy regulate his aggression. In father's absence (Herzog, 2004), the boy lacks this experience and develops a life-long yearning for it; the resulting clinical picture often consists of an admixture of passivity and fearfulness on the one hand, and perverse sexuality and outbursts of bravado on the other. While Herzog acknowledges that such hunger might also exist in girls, this idea is further developed in the work of Lora Tessman (1982) and Jessica Benjamin (1988). Ruth Garfield (2004), in her careful review and extension of this literature, mentions that a 'sugar daddy fantasy' or a 'kept woman fantasy' often evolves in women who, despite their overtly accomplished lives, are somehow still stuck with unresolved idealization of the father; this persisted because of the unavailability of the father during childhood.

Father regression: term used by Ruth Stein (2006) to denote a 'downward' movement along the spectrum on which the father–son relationship exists. According to her, one pole of this continuum involves a son's loving and de-individuated connection to a kind and trustworthy father who is in need of protection. The next step is a son's bondage to an idealized and exalted father figure who is felt to be both protective as well as frightening. The last pole of this continuum consists of 'the most radical thralldom to a persecutory, Godly object, a regressive submission that banishes women and enthrones a cruel superego, and that ends in destruction and self-destruction' (p. 1005). Stein illustrates these three ideas with data from her clinical work with neurotic and transsexual men, and with speculations about Mohammed Atta's relationship with Osama bin Laden, respectively.

Father's blessing: phrase used by Peter Blos Sr. (1985) to describe the father giving a 'green signal' to his son around the time the latter is considering marriage. The father is pleased to do so, as he is now relieved by his son's oedipal competitiveness and also because his son is now entering the common fraternity of married men and, in that way, coming close to the father. His approval instils greater confidence in the son and his affirmation of the son's manhood encourages the latter to assume adult prerogatives. It should be noted that when the father is absent (via desertion or death), the son seeks similar 'blessing' from father substitutes (e.g., uncles, grandfathers, mentors) or visits his father's grave to have the latter help him achieve this developmental step by proxy (Akhtar & Smolar, 1998).

Favoured and repudiated selves: Rosemary Balsam's (1984) designations for two mental states that often characterize patients who seem 'perfect' for psychoanalysis. The 'perfect' patient operates within a 'favoured' mode; he moulds himself to what he imagines are the likes and preferences of the analyst. Sacrificing spontaneity, he none the less gives the appearance of being supremely co-operative with the analytic procedure; he free associates, reflects, catches his own slips, and reports frequent dreams. However, it gradually becomes apparent that all this is in the service of pleasing the analyst and denying separateness, differences, and aggression within the dyad. He insistently keeps his self-representations to the contrary—the 'repudiated self'—out of the discourse; this buried, but actually more spontaneous self, often emerges through 'negation' (see separate entry) i.e., in statements about the patient having behaved unlike himself in a given situation. Balsam likens the dichotomy to Domald Winnicott's (1960) 'true and false selves' (see separate entry) but states that these terms invite value judgements and tend to get used in oversimplified ways. Moreover, the 'favoured' self is not neccessarily 'false' and the 'repudiated' self , which the patient is likely to denounce as not really him, is actually quite 'true', so to speak. To call this construct 'repudiated' serves the purpose of underscoring the dynamics of suppressing spontaneity as a habitual defence against painful memories of the past and their dreaded re-creation in the present interpersonal situations.

Favoured self: see 'Favoured and repudiated selves'.

Fear: refers to an emotional response associated with anticipation or awareness of danger. 'Fear' needs to be distinguished from 'anxiety' as well as from a 'phobia'. The difference between 'fear' and 'anxiety' is that the former is a response to a danger that is actual and external, while the latter is a response to a danger that is imaginary and internal. The difference between 'fear' and 'phobia' is that the former is a legitimate response to a plausible external danger, while the latter is an exaggerated response to an external situation or object that may or may not be dangerous in reality. The extra quantum of emotion in 'phobia' is derived from the inner fantasy world. As a result, one can view 'phobia' as containing the elements of both 'fear' and 'anxiety'.

Fear of breakdown: in a posthumously published paper, Donald Winnicott (1974) spoke of the 'fear of breakdown' as a deep anxiety that the established unit self will fall apart. He proposed that the disaster the patient is afraid might befall him in the future has threatened him in the past as well. The fear felt in the present is therefore an old fear. Winnicott suggests that the patient 'needs to remember this, but is is not possible to "remember" something that has not happened yet because the patient was not there for it to happen to. The only way to "remember" in this case is for the patient to experience this past thing for the first time in the present, that is to say, in the transference' (p. 92).

Fear of death: also referred to as 'death anxiety', 'fear of death' has traditionally been viewed as an expression of unconscious infantile fears. Robert Stolorow (1973, 1979) has comprehensively reviewed the literature on this topic and discerned four unconscious fantasies mentioned in connection with 'fear of death'. These include: (1) fear of castration (Freud, 1923e), (2) fear of separation and object loss (Bromberg & Schilder, 1933), (3) fear of one's own overwhelming masochism (Fenichel, 1945), and (4) fear of talionic punishment by the superego for one's death wishes towards others (Freud, 1923b; Bromberg & Schilder, 1936). Such linkage of death with childhood fears has two consequences. On the one hand, it enriches our understanding of why human beings fear death and, on the other hand, it takes theoretical attention away from the concrete and literal fact of death. The same conundrum exists in the post-Freudian psychoanalytic literature on 'death instinct' (see separate entry; see also 'death instinct reformulated'), which avoids facing the fact that an internal pull towards non-existence (or at least, non-humanness) exists in all human beings. 'Fear of death' might be a result of this inner pull threatening to become conscious. In those individuals who have experienced childhood parental loss, there is an exaggerated 'fear of death' (Akhtar, 2001; Settlage, 2001) which, in part, emanates from the desire to merge with the lost object. 'The despair of dying without having joyously lived is far more than expecting death after having lived well' (Akhtar, 2001, p. 105). Finally, there is a cultural angle to all this. Individuals belonging to cultures which regard death as *a part* of life feel less fear of death than those belonging to cultures that regard death as *apart* from life.

Fees: setting a fee constitutes an important step in establishing that the analyst–patient relationship is a professional one. It can reveal useful information about the inner dynamics and external realities of the patient's life. Daniel Jacobs (1986) has discussed setting the fee in a lucid manner, offering the following guidelines: (1) the amount to be charged should be explicitly discussed between the analyst and patient; (2) how sustained the patient's resources are needs to be assessed, given the long-term nature of analytic treatment; (3) the analyst should mention his 'usual' fee only if he is going to stick to it or make only minimal reductions; to mention a 'usual' fee and then agree to a markedly lower fee can stir up a sense of being special or cause much guilt in the patient; and (4) in exceptional circumstances, the analyst might agree to a lower fee than is realistically possible for the patient to pay; this allows some patients a comfortable sense of separateness which they might need, at least until it comes under analytic scrutiny. Two other points need mention (1) the fee should be realistic for both parties in the clinical dyad; (2) in just the way the analyst explores the patient's claim that he cannot afford to pay the fee mentioned, he should explore a patient's quick readiness to pay the amount mentioned by the analyst; this is especially important with patients from cultures where reverence for authority is an important virtue.

Female genital dress rehearsal: Sallye Wilkinson's (1993) phrase for the young girl's manual stimulation of her genital folds in so far as it provides her with the possibility of enacting the role of both parents in the primal scene. 'She is at once both vaginal and phallic, receiver and giver, participant and observer, mother and father . . . by attributing phallic qualities to her hand (or toy, or swimsuit) in a genital dress rehearsal, the girl can express *both* a phallic identification *and* a disguised claim for her own genital maturation' (p. 320, original italics). Paradoxically, it is via a phallic identification that the girl elaborates and masters her unfolding sexuality.

Female homosexuality: while the detailed entry on 'homosexuality' covers women also, the topic of 'female homosexuality' deserves some extra attention because the literature on 'homosexuality' is preponderantly about male homosexuality. Sigmund Freud's (1905a, 1919h, 1920g, 1922b, 1933a) views on 'female homosexuality' include the following points: (1) the condition involves a bitter turning away from the father, and men in general, when a severe oedipal disappointment is felt; (2) the rivalrous rage at mother is disguised by resorting to an 'earlier' (preoedipal) love for her; (3) there is also the phenomenon of 'retiring in the favour of someone else' (1920a, p. 159) whereby men are left for mother to enjoy; (4) there develops an identification with the father and this results in masculine characterstics; (5) turning to women, the female homosexual enjoys homoerotic love but, at an unconscious level, also heterosexual love, since she is identified with men; (6) psychological precipitants involving oedipal defeat can occur at anytime in life and this 'temporal factor may turn out to be of great importance' (p. 158); (7) psychological factors mentioned above must operate in conjunction with factors of 'internal nature' (1920a, p. 168) to cause homosexuality; and (8) 'in general, to convert a fully developed homosexual into a heterosexual does not offer much prospect of success than the reverse' (p. 151). Freud's early followers largely replicated his ideas. Helene Deutsch (1925) posited that 'phallic phase' (see separate entry) conflicts are repeatedly activated in a woman's life and this makes her vulnerable to regression into homosexuality. Ernest Jones (1927) emphasized the role of the girl's anger at her mother and identification with the father. He also noted that sexual involvement with women also provides a vicarious opportunity to enjoy one's repudiated femininity. As psychoanalysis evolved further, preoedipal factors at the root of 'female homosexuality' began to be emphasized (Rado, 1933; Glover, 1939; Khan, 1962; Socarides, 1978). Frustration at the hands of a stern and depriving mother caused hatred for her which was defensively transformed into love. Still later, the father's lack of mirroring acceptance of the girl's attractiveness was seen as an additional factor leading to the turning away from men. With one or the other variation (see also Quinodoz, 1989), such object choice on a woman's part was regarded to be pathological. Recently, the trend has shifted and 'female homosexuality' is being seen as an expression of (1) hereditary tendencies, as attested by three times higher concordance rates in monozygotic lesbian twins than dizygotic lesbian twins (Baily & Benishay, 1993); (2) the long-term effect of prenatal maternal hormonal balance in favour of androgens (Friedman & Downey, 1993); and (3) the need for a different kind and/or greater intensity of emotional intimacy that women draw from women, as against from men (Kirkpatrick, 1989). For a thorough critique and update of theoretical perspectives in this realm, see the papers by Jennifer Downey and Richard Friedman (1998) and Ruth Fischer (2002).

Feminine genital anxieties: a set of concerns that are unique to the nature of the female genitals and to the the role feelings and fantasies about them in the course of early childhood development of girls. Described by Doris Bernstein (1990), such 'feminine genital anxieties' include: *(1) access anxiety:* having lesser visual and tactile access to her genitals makes it harder for her to form pertinent mental representations; this renders her vulnerable to anxiety; *(2) diffusivity anxiety:* since the sensation the little girl obtains upon touching her genitals spreads over other parts of her perineal region, the ego comfort of localization is not available to her; this makes her vulnerable to anxiety; and *(3) penetration anxiety:* the girl's inability to open and close her vaginal orifice at will renders her vulnerable to penetration, and harm from what this can do becomes a source of anxiety (see also Mayer, 1985 in this regard). Bernstein goes on to describe the specific developmental efforts a girl evolves, including experiencing 'penis envy' (see separate entry), in order to cope with these anxieties. The contributions of other investigators are also pertinent in this context. Ruth Lax (1994), for instance, distinguishes between 'primary' and 'secondary' genital anxieties in girls; the former involves the fear of losing access to the pleasure that she derives from her genitals and the latter to the fantasy that she was deprived of a penis. Denise Dorsey (1996) calls the fear of injury to the female genital 'female genital anxiety' and the loss of an illusory penis the female 'castration anxiety'. Arlene Kramer Richards (1996) includes the fear of painful penetration, fear of loss of pleasure, and fear of loss of procreative function under her description of 'female genital anxiety'. The need for terminological clarity and consensus is evident here, especially because the ideas involved are clearly very significant.

Feminine masochism: label assigned by Sigmund Freud (1924d) to the attitude that underlies sexually masochistic fantasies in *men* of being beaten, bound, debased, dirtied, and humiliated. While he acknowledged that such masochism revolves around the image of a helpless and guilty child, Freud none the less called it 'feminine masochism', claiming that such fantasies 'place the subject in a characteristically female situation' (p. 162). A phallocentric bias of theory and cultural denigration of women clearly underlie the unfortunate choice of this designation; it creates the impression that there is an inherent link between femininity and masochism.

Femininity: the views of Sigmund Freud (1925j, 1931b, 1933a) on 'femininity' are, frankly, rather dismal. He did give due importance to the girl's preoedipal attachment to her mother, but even this was viewed by him through the retrospective lens of phallic–oedipal concerns. According to him, before discovering the anatomical difference between the sexes, 'the little girl is a little boy' (1933a, p. 118) and after the discovery of her 'organic inferiority' (1931b, p. 232) she develops 'penis envy' (see separate entry) which 'will not be surmounted in even the most favourable case without a severe expenditure of psychic energy' (1933a, p. 125). The girl feels self-contempt for belonging to 'a sex which is lesser in so important an aspect' (1925j, p. 253); Freud, of course, talked of the 'inferiority of the clitoris' (1925j, p. 255) as a fact. His scheme of female psychosexual development included her repudiation of the lack of a penis, anger at mother for depriving her of it, fixating on the clitoris and developing a 'masculinity complex' (1933a, p. 126), reluctantly making a cathectic shift from clitoris to vagina, and changing the object of her affection from mother to father in the hope of obtaining a penis (or its substitute, a baby) from it. Not subject to castration threat like a boy, the girl held on to her oedipal feelings much longer. As a result, her superego lacked 'strength and independence' (1933a, p. 129) and she grew up to be an individual with a 'lesser sense of justice' (1925j, p. 257). Freud's negative portrayal of women stands in contrast to his profound attachment to his mother and to his welcoming women in his analytic circle (Gay, 1988). The disclaimer at the end of his 'femininity' lecture (1933a) that to learn more about women one should 'inquire from (one's) own experience, or turn to poets or wait till signs can give deeper and more coherent information' (p. 135) is endearing but, in the end, does little to undo his unfavourable depiction of the female psyche. Here, it is important to note that departures from his views had begun during his lifetime. Karen Horney (1926, 1933) suggested that Freud's ideas were reflective of his cultural bias. She proposed that the development of female gender identity has aligned entirely independent of male psychosexual development. Freud's masculinized version of the female 'castration complex' (see separate entry) is regarded by her as abnormal development. In her view, vaginal eroticism is primary and not a willy-nilly derivative phenomenon. Ernest Jones (1927, 1935) cited Horney approvingly and questioned the use of the term 'castration' in the context of female psychosexual development. He suggested that the basic fear in both sexes is that of total loss of the capacity for sexual enjoyment (see the entry on 'aphanisis') but this manifests differently in the two sexes. In the male, it appears as fear of castration, and in the female, it appears as fear of separation and desertion; the distinction is due to the greater dependence of female sexuality on object relations. Jones also emphasized that 'penis envy' is not a bedrock phenomenon and its 'autoerotic' (exhibitionistic–masturbatory–urinary) dimension is far less dynamically and clinically significant than its 'alloerotic' (object-related and fantasied) dimension. Since these early criticisms of Freud, a lot has happened. Psychoanalytic theory has moved from a body-based ('instinctual') to a relationship-based ('object relations') model. Data from infant and child observation has enhanced our grasp of developmental events and processes. Cultural norms have changed and have affected child rearing. And, finally, the femininist movement has vociferously challenged the Freudian view of girls and women (see the entry on 'feminist critique of psychoanalysis'). As a result, most of Freud's ideas have been put aside. Eleanor Galenson and her colleagues (Galenson, 1980, 1988; Galenson & Roiphe, 1976) have made major contributions to the understanding of early female development, and Harold Blum (1996) has summarized the major revisions of theory in the following statement: 'The female superego is not now regarded as weaker or deficient, and sex differences in structure and function are not given value judgments. Libido is not masculine, neither are passivity, narcissisism, and masochism regarded as essentially feminine traits. Penis envy is no longer considered the bedrock of a woman's disappointment and necessary renounciation but has been subject to major reinterpretation. Neither masochism nor envy is confined to women nor necessarily related to the absence of a penis' (p. 5). Instead of 'castration anxiety' in women, one now speaks of 'female genital anxieties' (see separate entry). Instead of the girl's 'oedipus complex', one now ponders her 'Persephone complex' (see separate entry). Instead of the purported weakness of the female superego, one advocates a greater relational anchor to moral judgement in women (Bernstein, 1983; Gilligan, 1982). Instead of a 'femininity' that is reluctantly arrived at, there is celebration of 'primary femininity' (Stoller, 1964; see

also Kulish, 2000); this emphasizes that the girl develops an ego-syntonic mental representation of her genitals at a very early age. The girl's entry into the oedipal phase is seen to follow a different pathway than that proposed by Freud (Parens, Pollock, Stern, & Kramer, 1976). Her wish for a baby is no longer reductionistically traced to the sole determinant of her oedipal fantasies, even if these do play a role in the genesis of that desire; this wish is now seen to be more complex and multiply-determined, with tributaries derived from consitutional givens, early identifications with maternal caregiving attributes, and developmentally forward longings to fill her inner space, etc. There is also the mention of 'negative femininity', based upon the experience of lack described by Freud, and 'positive femininity', arising out of specific experiences related to female organs and relational fantasies they give rise to (Birksted-Breen, 1996a; see also Schmukler & Garcia, 1990). Indeed, an enormous literature on 'femininity' and 'female psychology' has evolved, which deals not only with childhood development, but also with the specific challenges and ego accomplishments of women as they encounter loss of virginity (Holtzman & Kulish, 1996), adult sexuality, pregnancy (Balsam, 1996, 2003; Raphael-Leff, 1996), motherhood (Balsam, 2000; Furman, 1996), menopause (Lax, 1982; Notman, 1984; Harris, 1990; Bemesderfer, 1996), and old age. Katherine Zerbe's (1992) paper on creative collaboration in the lives of five Impressionist and Post-Impressionist women artists is a significant contributuion as well. The reader would also benefit by looking up the *Journal of American Psychoanalytic Association's* Supplement in 1976 and Special Issues on female psychology in 1996 and 2003, which have contributions from a large number of psychoanalytic luminaries, including Dana Birkstead-Breen, Harold Blum, Nancy Chodorow, Erna Furman, Leon Hoffman, Deanna Holtzman, Nancy Kulish, Joan Raphael-Leff, Shelly Orgel, Arlene Richards, Robert Stoller, and Phyllis Tyson, to name a few. See also the recent monograph on this topic by Leticia Glocer Fiorini (2009).

Feminist critique of psychoanalysis: although departures from Sigmund Freud's (1925j, 1931b, 1933a) views on female psychology—including women's tendency towards 'affectualization', 'penis envy', weaker superego, and lesser contributions to human civilization—had begun during his lifetime (Horney, 1926; Jones, 1935), it was the feminist movement (c. 1960) that made a frontal attack on the phallocentrism of 'classical' psychoanalysis. Helen Rosen and Elaine Zickler (1996) have provided an engaging and lucid discourse on how the feminist psychoanalytic theory in the USA and France differed in their revisions and modifications of Freudian biases regarding female development. According to them, the American feminist theorists (e.g., Jean Baker Miller, Nancy Chodorow, Carol Gilligan) and their French counterparts (e.g., Helene Cixous, Luce Irigary, and Julia Kristeva) respectively took the path of reversal of Freud and recourse to Lacan. The former consists of viewing what had been derided about women (e.g., greater emotionality, more permeable ego-boundaries, context-bound morality) as not only normal, but desirable; it also consists of attributing women's difficulties to internalized societal attitudes instead of the psychobiological imperatives of being female. The latter consists of questioning of the conflation of the biological and the cultural, celebrating feminine *jouissance*, reminding one and all of the inherently fragmented and polymorphic nature of the subject and its desire, and underscoring the fact that 'the mother is not completely renounced when the human subject enters into the symbolic and acquires language, but is always present as its enabling background, its space, its melodies and repetitions' (Rosen & Zickler, 1996, p. 89). This thumbnail sketch hardly does justice to the Rosen–Zickler paper, which should be read in its entirety. Indeed, there is a considerable literature on this topic, ranging from Betty Friedan's (1963) *The Feminine Mystique* through Nancy Chodorow's (1989) *Feminism and Psychoanalytic Theory* to Elizabeth Wright's (1992) *Feminism and Psychoanalysis: A Critical Dictionary*.

Fetish: see 'Fetishism'.

Fetishism: a sexual deviation where the interposition of an inanimate object (e.g., shoe, earrings) or some part of the body (e.g., foot, a lock of hair) becomes a mandatory requirement for achieving arousal, intercourse, or orgasm. Prototypically a male perversion, 'fetishism' is a response to intense 'castration anxiety' (see separate entry) and the specific object (the 'fetish') chosen invariably represents the penis. 'To put it more plainly: the fetish is a substitute for the woman's (the mother's) penis that the little boy once believed in and, for reasons familiar to us, does not want to give up' (Freud, 1927c, pp. 152–153). The fetishist thus maintains two incompatible mental attitudes: women do and do not have a penis. Three other points need mention: (1) excessive exposure of a boy to the sight of female genitals in childhood predisposes to the development of fetishism; (2) kleptomania in women seems to have psychodynamic kinship with male fetishism, and

(3) it was in the context of his study of fetishism that Sigmund Freud (1927c) first described the mechanism of 'splitting' (see separate entry), even though the current usage of this term is mostly in a different context. Among the later contributors to the understanding of 'fetishism' are William Gillespie (1940), who stated that the condition results from 'a specific form of castration anxiety, a form produced by a strong admixture of oral and anal trends' (p. 414,) and Charles Socarides (1960, 1988), who declared that 'fetishism' actually comprises aetiologically diverse conditions that range from those which derive from very archaic primitive levels to those which are a product of more highly differentiated ones. Also of interest is the controversial issue of fetishism in women (Raphling, 1989).

Filial piety complex: term coined by Ming Dong Gu (2006) for the culturally transformed derivatives of 'Oedipus complex' (see separate entry) in China. Drawing inferences from Chinese literature and films, Gu concluded that oedipal themes in China are reconfigured by Confucian morality and take the disguised form of parental demands for filial piety and children's commitment to the resulting duties. The manifestations of such 'filial piety complex' include (1) the mother's possessiveness towards her son coupled with a strong antipathy towards his wife, (2) the son's profound longing for a woman who is a surrogate mother or an aunt, with complete obliteration of the parricidal dimension of the usual oedipal complex, and (3) the daughter's fierce and blind loyalty to her father, often accompanied by an 'incomprehensible inhibition against love and marriage' (p. 189). In essence, the Oedipus complex is muted, fragmented, and couched in terms of family roles and moral duties; libidinal dimension is accentuated and aggression minimized, though it certainly lurks under the surface.

Filter screens: see 'Screen'.

First censorship: see 'Three-box model of the mind'.

First organizer of the psyche: see 'Organizers of the psyche'.

Fitting together: Heinz Hartmann's (1958) phrase for the fact that a state of mental equilibrium, in the face of constant disruptive stimuli, can exist only if there is a peaceful relationship with one's environment, lack of instinctual tension, absence of conflict between major psychic structures, *and* if these achievements are brought into an overall harmonious *gestalt* by the synthetic function of the ego. It is only with this 'fourth equilibrium' (p. 38) that the human being achieves proper adaptation and there is a 'fitting together' (p. 38) of outer and inner worlds.

Fixation: concept originated by Sigmund Freud (1905a) to denote the persistence of anachronistic sexual traits. Employed at its inception in the context of sexual perversions, the term referred to an adult's continued attachment to component instincts (e.g., voyeurism, exhibitionism, coprophilia) and certain properties of love objects that were traceable to the sexual life of his or her childhood. Gradually, however, 'fixation' acquired a broader connotation. With the development of theory of libidinal stages (e.g., oral, anal, phallic), for instance, the term came to mean a persistent attachment not only to the specific instinctual aims of a particular era, but, instead, to the entire complex of self and object relations (and their attendant affects and fantasies) of that specific stage of life. Another usage of the term that evolved was the context of trauma. In *Beyond the Pleasure Principle*, Freud (1920g) highlighted this usage and related it to the compulsion to repeat. All in all, therefore, it seems that fixation refers to the persistence of earlier developmental modes, pregenital instinctual aims, and effects of trauma on the mind. When fixation is strong, these persistent effects are overtly evident. When fixation is mild, it merely constitutes the point to which regression will occur under stress. Occurring in childhood, strong fixations result in 'developmental arrest' (A. Freud, 1965; Nagera, 1966) and mild onset in potential vulnerabilities and psychic 'weak spots'. The preconditions for developing a fixation are a combination of psychological factors (e.g., overindulgence, deprivation, trauma) and constitutional factors (e.g., the so-called 'adhesiveness of libido,' which create an intractable indolence *vis-à-vis* behavioural change).

Flight from insight: Allen Wheelis's (1949) term for a patient's inability to tolerate an increase in knowledge about themselves, especially if it is accurate. Under such circumstances, either the patient suddenly becomes very 'concrete', or escapes altogether from the treatment situation. Imparting insight prematurely, *in toto*, and without resolving pertinent resistances generally leads to such a situation. Charismatic analysts, novices, and analysts who feel compelled to 'interpret' their friends in social situations are especially likely to precipitate 'flight from insight'.

Flight into health: phrase coined by George Train in 1953 to denote the proclivity of some patients

to show dramatic improvement in their symptoms either soon after the recommendation of psychoanalysis or very early during the course of their analytic treatment. This usually signifies a powerful resistance to the exploration of their inner conflicts. Indeed, many patients with 'flight into health' refuse to start their treatment or abruptly terminate it.

Flight into illness: Sigmund Freud's (1909a) phrase for an individual's tendency to seek haven in symptomatic suffering in order to escape facing the underlying intrapsychic conflicts. Before settling on this succinct and yet broader expression, Freud used phrases like 'flight into psychosis' (1894a) and 'flight into neurotic illness' (1908e) to denote roughly similar phenomena. What all these terms highlight is that, in developing mental symptoms, one achieves the 'primary gain' (see entry on 'Primary and secondary gain') of avoiding an encounter with the conflict that is the actual cause of one's troubles.

Flight into neurotic illness: see 'Flight into illness'.

Flight into psychosis: see 'Flight into illness'.

Floating couch: an arrangement of the psychoanalytic setting where the couch does not rest against a wall. It is in the room, most likely in its centre, in a way that all four sides of it are unencumbered by walls and other furniture. The idea is that the wall along which the couch rests is a symbolic arm of the analyst, 'holding' (see separate entry) the patient; the removal of this auxiliary support leads to greater regression and taxes the analyst's holding capacity. It can, therefore, be anxiety producing for the analyst and the analysand alike.

Floating transference: term used by Edward Glover (1927, published in 1955) to describe the shifting and changing transference reactions typical during the initial stages of an analysis. These are to be distinguished from 'transference neurosis' (see separate entry), which is characterized by a more focused attention upon the fantasies, feelings, and fears involving the analyst, and is, therefore, more present than past-orientated.

Focal symbiosis: Phyllis Greenacre's (1959) term for an intense interdependence that, unlike the usual mother–child symbiosis (Mahler, 1952, 1955; Mahler, Pine, & Bergman, 1975), is restricted to one particular aspect of the body. The partners in 'focal symbiosis' are of uneven development i.e., parent and child, older and younger sibling, or even stronger and weaker twins. 'The focal symbiosis represents the special site of emotional disturbance in both members of the symbiotic pair. But it is ordinarily manifest in the weaker or smaller partner, who remains functionally dependent in this specific area on the active response of the older partner, far beyond the maturational period at which the special functions would become autonomous' (p. 146).

Foreclosure: term used by Sigmund Freud interchangeably with 'repudiation'. The latter, which he employed more frequently, appears to have *four connotations*: (1) the end point of repression, (2) the countercathectic pressure of the superego's judgement, (3) disavowal of reality, which can be partial (e.g., fetishism) or total (e.g., psychosis), and (4) elimination of an idea from consciousness and the elimination of the awareness that this has occurred. This last meaning is most evident in Freud's statement that 'the ego rejects the incompatible idea together with its affect and behaves as if the idea had never occurred to the ego at all' (1894a, p. 58). In Jacques Lacan's (1956, 1977) work, this connotation of 'repudiation' or 'foreclosure' is placed at the forefront. According to him, the mechanism of 'foreclosure' refers specifically to the exclusion from the mind of the 'name-of-the-father' (see separate entry) which leads to a psychotic character organization.

Forepleasure: according to Sigmund Freud (1905a), 'forepleasure' is the positive emotional response of increasing intensity associated with the stimulation of genitals or other diffuse erotogenic zones (mouth, breasts, buttocks, anus) preceding the act of sexual intercourse. Freud (1908e) extended the use of the term 'forepleasure' to the enjoyment derived from anticipation of the punch-line of a joke and from aesthetic experience in general. Ludwig Eidelberg (1954) underscored this expanded definition and added that it is 'the act of anticipation, rather than the localization of the sensation, that seems to be of more importance' (p. 19) to the concept of 'forepleasure'.

Fore-un-pleasure: term coined by Anna Freud (1936) to denote the unpleasant experience that is expected to occur with an increase or decrease of instinctual tension above or below a particular threshold. Such *Vor-Unlust* governs the ego's behaviour and can result from less than promising external circumstances as well as from internalized moral dictates which, in the absence of 'appropriate' modulation of instinctual life, threaten to cause subjective distress, remorse, and guilt.

Forgiveness: in the first paper exclusively dedicated to the topic of 'forgiveness', Salman Akhtar (2002) synthesized scattered bits of pertinence from evolutionary, developmental, literary, and phenomenological sources. He noted that 'forgiveness' comprises two mental operations: (i) resolution of an unpleasant angry emotion within oneself, and (ii) changed attitude toward an offending party, which is then allowed freedom from one's claims over it. The relationship between forgiving and forgetting is contestable. Forgetting too early in the course of mourning betrays defensive distortion of internal and external reality. On the other hand, once 'forgiveness' is granted, affective charge of the memory of the traumatic event diminishes; the memory may remain at a preconscious level, serving as a potential signal for the future risk of being traumatized. Akhtar quoted the Dutch novelist, Cees Nooteboom (1980), as having offered a deliciously paradoxical idea in this context. Nooteboom concluded that the injury that has been forgiven should be forgotten, but the fact that it has been forgotten should be remembered. Akhtar drew upon Melanie Klein's (1937) view of the infantile metabolism of aggression and Winnicott's (1962) ideas on the development of the capacity for concern and their parallels with 'peaceful post-conflict signals' (Silk, 1998) of non-human primates in order to present a rich theory of the origins of 'forgiveness'. He also outlined eight psychopathological syndromes in this realm: (i) inability to for-give, (ii) premature forgiveness, (iii) excessive forgiveness, (iv) pseudo-forgiveness, (v) relentless forgiveness seeking, (vi) inability to accept forgiveness, (vii) inability to seek forgiveness, and (viii) imbalance between capacities for self-forgiveness and forgiveness towards others. He also elucidated the significance of these ideas to the clinical work of psychoanalysis. A number of publications on the topic of 'forgiveness' followed, the most important among these being the papers by Henry Smith (2002b), Melvin Lansky (2001, 2005), Shahrzad Siassi (2004, 2007), Roy Schafer (2005), Madelon Sprengnether (2005), and Leonard Horwitz (2005). Isaac Tylim's (2005) paper on the power of apologies in transforming resentment into forgiveness also merits attention.

Formal regression: see 'Regression'.

Forward projection of narcissism: Janine Chassaguet-Smirgel's (1984) phrase for the fate of infantile narcissism during the oedipal phase. According to her, the child's acceptance of the chronological lag between his or her oedipal longing and the attainment of adult genital capacity deepens the acceptance of reality in general. The resulting narcissistic injury is compensated for by the projection of infantile narcissism on to the parents (especially the same-sex parent) and the formation of ego ideal. This structure implies hope and future and therefore facilitates the child's 'entrance into a temporal order' (p. 28). These developments are accompanied by the child's acquisition of generational filiations (being a son or a daughter, not merely a boy or girl) and, through that, a sense of historical continuity.

Four person psychology: see ' One, two, three, four, and multi-person psychologies'.

Four psychologies of psychoanalysis: according to Fred Pine (1988), psychoanalysis has produced 'four psychologies'. These conceptually separable perspectives include those of drives, ego, object relations, and self. They overlap, but each adds something new to the understanding of development, psychopathology, and technique. (i) *Drive psychology* views the individual in terms of instinctual forces, their overt and disguised viscissitudes, and the conflicts caused by them. Listening from this perspective makes the analyst ask: which wish is being activated: what is the associated fantasy? How conscious is the wish? And so on. (ii) *Ego psychology* views the individual in terms of reality testing, defence, and adaptation. Listening from this perspective makes the analyst ask: what defences are operative? How effective are these defences? Is there a capacity for anxiety tolerance and sublimation? And so on. (iii) *Object relations psychology* views the individual in terms of the internal drama derived from early relationships (even though coloured by memory distortions) and enacted in current situations. Listening from this perspective makes the analyst ask: what relationships are being played out? Whose role is the patient taking on? And so on. (iv) *Self-psychology* views the individual in terms of the continuity and vitality of the ongoing subjective state. Listening from this perspective makes the analyst ask: how coherent is the sense of self? Is the self valued? And so on. Pine discusses the developmental and technical overlaps, distinctions, and uses in much more detail in his 1988 paper and also in his other works (Pine, 1997, 2005).

Four senses of self in Daniel Stern's developmental scheme: see 'Sense of a core self', 'sense of an emergent self', 'sense of a subjective self', and 'sense of a verbal self'.

Four tracks of post-immigration identity change: Salman Akhtar's (1995) delineation of four dimen-sions along which the identity change following immigration occurs; these dimensions along with their metaphoric journeys include (1) drive and affects (from love or hate to ambivalence), (2) interpersonal and psychic space (from near or far to optimal distance), (3) temporality (from yesterday or tomorrow to today), and (4) social affiliation (from yours or mine to ours).

Fourth individuation: see 'Second adolescences and fourth individuations'.

Fourth object: phrase used by Christopher Bollas (2009) for the psychic structure that 'receives and transmits at the level of unconscious communication the differing unconscious interests of the family group' (p. 109). This structure stands for multilateral and multilayered relationships that ultimately form what is called a 'family'. It is regulated by a primitive law of love that wards off a primitive law of hate in children long enough for them to grow up and evolve a less primitive internal structure.

Fragmentation: though not included in five of the six psychoanalytic glossaries (English & English, 1976; Rycroft, 1968; Laplanche & Pontalis, 1973; Moore & Fine, 1968, 1990) 'fragmentation' as a term persists in the psychoanalytic lexicon. The Eidelberg (1968) encyclopedia of psychoanalytic concepts does include the term, defining it as a tendency to prevent the unification of contradictory psychic components to prevent anxiety. The origin of the term is attributed to Isidor Silbermann (1961), though its distinction from other ego methods of keeping things apart (e.g., repression, splitting, and dissociation) is not spelled out. Most likely, fragmentation differs from repression by the latter's rendering unacceptable wishes or self-representation unconscious; in fragmentation, the sequestered mental elements can both be conscious and unconscious. Fragmentation differs from splitting by involving smaller portions of psychic material than better organized self and object representations that are usually subject to splitting. Finally, it differs from dissociation by not necessarily involving memory disturbance. Fragmentation as a consequence of severe internal aggression leads to the disposal of minute segments of felt internal and perceived external reality. It is characteristically seen in association with psychotic levels of personality functioning.

Fragmented body: term employed by Jacques Lacan (1951) for the disjointed perception the infant has of his own body during the 'mirror stage' (see separate entry). While the later synthesis of body image glues the shards of the 'fragmented body' together, its memory remains and appears in the dreams, hallucinations, delusions, and conversion symptoms involving fantasies of castration, evisceration, mutilation, somatic implosion and explosion, etc. Lacan's notion of the 'fragmented body' seems to overlap with Donald Winnicott's (1945) sense of self before the stage of integration (see 'Integration, personalization, and realization).

Framing structure: André Green's (1993) term for the trace of maternal holding that is left after the actual contact with her body is broken.This 'framing structure' shelters the loss of the perception of maternal object in the form of a 'negative hallucination' (see separate entry) of it. It is against this background, and within the protective confines of the 'framing structure', that future object relations are experienced and registered.

Free association: taking his 'most momentous step' (1924f, p. 195), in the late 1890s Sigmund Freud abandoned hypnosis in favour of the treatment method based upon 'free association'. He relied upon 'free association' for his self-analysis and instructed his analysands to speak without censoring their thoughts. This requirement came to be known as the 'fundamental rule' (see separate entry) of psychoanalysis. According to Jean Laplanche and Jean-Bertrand Pontalis (1973), Freud's use of the prefix 'free' in 'free association' implied that there would be no fixed point from where the session begins and no steering of the thought chain by the analyst. The patient was to utter whatever entered his mind (e.g., ideas, feelings, body sensations, dreams) with as little restraint as possible. Such bypass of the censorship between the systems conscious and preconscious (see 'topographic theory') resulted in the emergence of concealed purposive ideas and links between them (for a history of the concept of association of ideas, see Rapaport, 1974 and also Gedo, 1975). The analyst listened with 'evenly suspended attention' and 'neutrality' (see separate entries) and made interpretations to create or enhance the patient's insight into the origins of his problems. If the patient hesistated or refused to collaborate, it was considered a 'resistance' (see separate entry) which has to be worked through. Freud's ideas were elaborated upon, expanded, modified, and challenged by a number of analysts, beginning with Sandor Ferenczi (1919a, 1921; Ferenczi & Rank, 1924), whose therapeutic zeal was a mismatch for the relative passivity of Freud's method; he advocated a more 'active technique' (see separate entry). Patrick Mahony (1979)

has summarized the literature of 'free association' from its beginnings until the mid 1970s, and Axel Hoffer (1991; Hoffer & Hoffer, 1999) has elucidated the Freud–Ferenczi tension *vis-à-vis* this and other aspects of technique. It is clear that recent advancements in psychoanalytic theory and technique have raised questions about the centrality of 'free association'. On one side are Thomas Ogden (1996) and Irwin Hoffman (2006), among others, who believe that the requirement of 'free association' stifles the patient's privacy, diminishes his personal agency, unduly empowers the analyst, and creates a process that is non-analytic in spirit. On the other side are Anton Kris (1982, 1992), Paul Gray (1994), Fred Busch (1997), and Axel Hoffer (2006), who ardently uphold the value of 'free association'. They believe that it is only by following the patient's 'free-association', and impediments to it that one can gain access to the unconscious meanings of the patient's anguish; without such deep understanding, the help rendered is not analytic in the proper sense of the word. Such divergence of opinion mobilized panel discussions on the topic at the 43rd Congress of the International Psychoanalytical Association in New Orleans (Youngren, 2004) and at the 2002 Annual Meetings of the American Psychoanalytic Association held in Philadelphia (McDermott, 2003). Polarizing arguments centred upon 'free association' leading to change via insight, and a deep relationship with the analyst leading to change via emotional experience. The sense was that elucidation of unconscious meanings work in tandem in the process material and in the interventional responses to it. Finally, two other things need mentioning. The first pertains to the enlarged purview of 'free association' (see Peter Fonagy's remarks in McDermott, 2003), which now seems to include visual images (Kanzer, 1958; Warren, 1961), non-verbal cues derived from body movements and postural changes on the couch (McLaughlin, 1987, 1992), and an occasional invitation for the patient to draw something that he or she is finding difficult to put into words (Brakel, 1993; Slap, 1976). The second matter involves the manner in which the analyst tells the patient about the 'fundamental rule'. Freud's (1913c) way was to say the following to the patient: 'act as though, for instance, you were a traveller sitting next to the window of a railway carriage and describing to someone inside the carriage the changing views you see outside' (p. 135). Joseph Lichtenberg and Floyd Galler (1987) have conducted a survey which reveals the great variability in the manner of analysts' instructing their patients *vis-à-vis* the use of 'free association'.

Free associations of the analyst: in a lucid discussion of the psychoanalyst's own free associations, Christopher Bollas (1992) delineated how a judicious sharing of these with the patient can be of clinical use. He noted that this practice is perhaps more widespread than ordinarily acknowledged, though such passing disclosure of the analyst's free associations are often mistaken for 'interpretations' (see separate entry). Bollas emphasized that such disclosure should not be made (1) while the patient's dynamic process is smoothly unfolding, (2) in the spirit of largesse and 'friendship', and (3) with an implicit requirement that the patient respond to it. Instead, the disclosure of the analyst's free association should be (1) selective, (2) related to the patient's material, (3) unformulated, raw data of the analyst's mind, (4) 'a pre-conscious link to the unconscious latent thoughts' (p. 116) of the analysand, and (5) followed up by a careful assessment of the patient use of it.

Free energy: see 'Psychic energy'.

Free-floating attention: see 'Evenly suspended attention'.

Free-floating responsiveness: Joseph Sandler and Anne-Marie Sandler (1998) suggests that not only does the analyst listen in a relaxed, open-minded manner, he responds similarly as well. In their own words, the analyst 'will, unless he becomes aware of it, tend to comply with the role demanded of him, to integrate it into his mode of responding and relating to the patient. He can often catch this counter-response himself, particularly if it is in the direction of being appropriate. However, he may only become aware of it through observing his behaviour, responses, and attitudes after these have been carried into action' (p. 550).

Free-swinging attention: David Carlson's (2002) term for the kind of attention required for psychoanalytic work, an attention that is characterized by (1) swinging between focused and 'free-floating' attention, (2) activity and not passivity, (3) being in rhythm with the patient, (4) accommodating shifting perspectives, (5) combining loving and aggressive undercurrents, (6) preparedness for surprise and for being surprised, and (7) pleasure mixed with mild apprehension. The concept underscores the role of the analyst as a child; this has mostly been overlooked in the psychoanalytic literature.

Freud's first dual instinct theory: see 'Instinct theory'.

Freud's second dual instinct theory: see 'Instinct theory'.

Friendship: Sigmund Freud (1921c) stated that 'friendship or friendliness is aim-inhibited sexuality or aim-inhibited love' (p. 102). Melanie Klein (1937) suggested that (1) unconscious homosexual trends often underlie friendships; (2) however, there is a de-linkage of affection and sex; (3) in childhood friendships especially, homosexual bonding serves as a defensive aim against heterosexual anxieties; (4) the love and admiration between friends is also a defence against their mutual aggression; (5) prototypes of mother–daughter and father–son, as well as those of real or wished for sibling relationships, underlie 'friendships'; and (6) the need to work through envy and aggression is essential for forming a stable 'friendship'. While these contributions were made in contexts other than 'friendship' *per se*, Leo Rangell's (1963b) paper on the topic was seminal in addressing the topic head on. Based upon his reading of psychoanalytic literature at large (*sans* Klein), non-analytic writings, and his extensive clinical experience, Rangell concluded that 'friendship' is a 'deep, kind, enduring affection, founded on mutual respect and esteem' (p. 11). He added that 'friendship is intellectual and less emotional than love. Friendship is more calm and quiet, love more fervent, often rising to intense passion. Friendship implies some degree of equality, while love does not' (p. 11). Rangell observed that people differ in their need for, and in their capacity to nurture and sustain, friendships. Drawing a 'developmental line' (see separate entry) for 'friendship', Rangell traced the epigenetic unfolding of such relationships from early childhood to adulthood. He also tackled the tricky matter of man–woman friendships, suggesting three possible dynamics underlying them (1) aim-inhibited heterosexual love, (2) 'aim-inhibited homosexual interest or link, deriving from the bisexuality of each' (p. 30), and (3) continuation of aim-inhibited and desexualized love of a mother–sister prototype. Rangell acknowledged that 'friendly' feelings exist within the analytic couple, but, owing to the asymmetry required by the nature of their work, the analyst cannot actually be a 'friend' of the patient. The topic of 'friendship' was not picked up by any analyst until the Montreal based analyst Rita Schulman edited a book on it; the book, despite the submission of its complete manuscript years ago, remains unpublished. Schulman (2009), however, has recently written a thoughtful commentary on Rangell's paper; this commentary appears in a book titled *Good Feelings* (ed. S. Akhtar, 2009b).

Frigidity: see 'Sexual dysfunction'.

From simplicity through contradiction to paradox: Salman Akhtar's (1998) delineation of a three-step process in the evolution of psychic reality of a borderline patient during analytic treatment. These steps include: (1) *simplicity*: experiencing and presenting disparate psychic states without the awareness of inherent contradictions, (2) *contradiction*: observing, acknowledging, and mending the splits responsible for the logical incompatibilities, and (3) *paradox*: developing a capacity for feeling and accepting the coincidence of multiple feelings at different levels of abstraction. This three-step movement *vis-à-vis* the associative material takes place first within the analyst's reverie and then in the patient's psychic reality. The analyst's holding, unmasking, bridging, and depth-rendering interventions (and the vicissitudes of the patient's identification with the analyst's work ego) make the patient's advance possible. Akhtar highlights the developmental *analage* of such interventions on the analyst's part. He adds that the practising analyst needs to traverse a 'simplicity–contradiction–paradox' sequence in his view of the divergent theoretical approaches to the analytic understanding and treatment of severe character pathology.

Frozen dreams: according to Vaimk Volkan (1981), in the early phases of grief over death, the bereaved often has dreams in which no movement takes place. The manifest dream is made up of still images. Such 'frozen dreams' are soon replaced by other dreams typical of the mourning period, e.g., seeing someone coming close to death and then being rescued back to life. The persistence of 'frozen dreams' beyond a few weeks or months suggests that the intrapsychic work of mourning is not proceeding well and a pathological grief reaction (see separate entry) is in the offing.

Frozen introject: Peter Giovacchini's (1967) designation of a particular sort of maternal introject seen in certain patients. Brought up by utterly 'non-maternal' mothers, or having lost mothers at a very early age, such individuals retain an internal percept of her that can neither be hypercathected (for that will give rise to immense rage) nor decathected (for that will mobilize unbearable pain of mourning). The introject is kept in a state of suspended animation. It interferes with the ego's inability to incorporate later adaptive experiences; any ego growth that does take place is largely on an 'as-if' (Deutsch, 1942) basis.

Functional phenomena: described by Herbert Silberer (1909a,b), these refer to those 'autosymbolic experiences' (see separate entry) which 'have to to do with the mode of functioning of consciousness and not with the content of thought-act' (p. 199). These phenomena most often represent feelings associated with tiredness and the struggle against it. In clinical context, a frequent 'functional phenomenon' is the patient's getting drowsy, nearly falling asleep on the couch, and having a dream or even a fragment of a dream. While earlier it was thought to represent merely an ego-alteration due to regression, such an occurrence is now viewed as also containing defensive meanings. For a thorough elucidation and update on the concept, see Austin Silber (1970).

Fundamental rule: also called 'basic rule', this precept pertains to the requirement that the patient eliminate all conscious censorship over his psychic contents and verbalize all that enters his mind. Stated explicitly by Sigmund Freud in 1900a, this rule emanated from the notions of psychic determinism, connectedness of all things in the unconscious, and the dynamic view of unconscious wishes seeking their fulfilment through preconscious and conscious derivative discharges. Following the 'fundamental rule' leads the patient to free associate and the analyst to glean a look into the patient's unconscious through the lattice of these scattered but ultimately connected thoughts. Such 'thinking aloud' allows the analysand some discharge of instinctual tensions which in itself may be of some therapeutic benefit. More importantly, putting inner experiences into words turns internal reality into a shared external reality. This, in turn, can be examined, deconstructed, and interpreted.

Fusion and defusion of instincts: in enunciating his final 'instinct theory' (see separate entry) that delineated the concept of 'life' and 'death instinct', Sigmund Freud (1924f) declared that 'we never have to deal with pure life instincts and death instincts but only with mixtures of them in different amounts. Corresponding to a fusion of instincts of this kind, there may, as a result of certain influences, be a defusion of them' (p. 164). Three things are important to note here: (1) 'fusion' of instincts does not mean that they get directed at the same object but that that they evolve a synthesized aim, and (2) the admixture of the two instincts is ubiquitous, though the proportion of each in these amalgams varies, and (3) since synthesis is the function of 'life instinct' and splitting apart a function of 'death instinct', fusion and defusion are, respectively, to be viewed as libidinal and aggressive outcomes of instinctual life.

Fusion of instincts: see 'Fusion and defusion of instincts'.

Fusion with the victim: phrase coined by Shelley Orgel (1974) for a mechanism that is characterized by (1) viewing the parental object not as omnipotent but as a victim, since it is still largely fused with the primary narcissistic self, (2) failing to turn passive into active; instead of externalizing the aggression or identifying with the aggressor, the subject turns the aggression upon himself, and (3) creating a vulnerability to regression in the face of instinctual upsurge. Orgel proposed that the failure of the primary love object to provide 'reliable aggressive resonance with the infant from about six months to fifteen months' (p. 532) makes it impossible for the child's immature ego to neutralize aggressive drives and to deflect their muted forms out for containment. He added that this situation is the earliest prototype for many pre-suicidal states in later life, and its regressive intensification contributes to actual suicidal tendencies.

G

Ganesha complex: originated by the Indian psychoanalyst Sudhir Kakar (1989a, 1989b, 2001), this concept relates to a particular culturally shaped facet of the boy's oedipal development. The designation of the 'complex' is derived from the story of Ganesha, the widely worshipped Hindu diety represented as a 'pot-bellied toddler with an elephant head and one missing tusk' (1989a, p. 135). According to Hindu mythology, Ganesha was created by Parvati, Lord Shiva's consort, all on her own. Shiva was away and she needed someone for her protection. Upon his return, Shiva, unaware of Ganesha's origin, finds him an obstacle to his intimacy with Parvati and decapitates him. When Parvati laments, Shiva quickly repairs the damage by giving the boy an elephant's head. The myth goes on to reveal that Shiva has another son, Kartikeya, who was born from his union with Parvati and is handsome, slender, and, in psychoanalytic parlance, phallic. Kakar notes that Ganesha and Kartikeya personify two opposing wishes of the boy *vis-à-vis* his mother. He is torn between the developmental push for autonomy and an equally strong pull towards return to the enveloping maternal fusion from which he has emerged. Kartikeya chooses growth but is banished from proximity from his mother. 'Remaining an infant, Ganesha's reward, on the other hand, will be never to feel the despair at her absence. That Ganesha's lot is considered superior to Kartikeya's is perhaps an indication of Indian man's culture reference in the dilemma of separation–individuation' (p. 137). Kartikeya's growth also owes itself to his 'acceptance' of being born of parental copulation, whereas Ganesha's continued symbiosis contains the fable of being only his mother's child. The painful reality of the oedipal situation is bypassed, but the price paid for it involves remaining childlike. Kakar extends this myth to suggest that, at his core, the Indian male wishes to remain emeshed with his mother while splitting off the more 'grown-up' sexual, triangular dimension of male–female relations (see also his concept of 'maternal enthralment'). His ideas have been critically evaluated and placed alongside more familiar Western psychoanalytic concepts by Manasi Kumar, who underlines the fact that, in Indian mythology, the motif of a father killing a son is far more prevelant than the other way around.

Gap: term used by Jacques Lacan (1950, 1957, 1964) in four different ways that included (1) the distance between the experience of psychotic phenomena and intellectual puzzlement over them, (2) the separation between man and nature, (3) the irreducible space between the sexes, and (4) the unbridgeable abyss between the subject and the Other. In all four realms, imagination sought, however haplessly, to minimize the gap and smooth things over.

Garmenzy's triad: see 'Resilience'.

Gaslighting: term introduced by R. Barton and J. Whitehead (1969) to designate situations where one individual is attempting to make others feel that a second individual is crazy. The expression is derived from the 1938 Patrick Hamilton play *Gaslight*, which was later made into an Oscar nominated movie (*Gaslight*, MGM, 1944) and showed a crafty and sociopathic husband's attempts to drive his rich wife insane in order to gain her wealth. Though unnamed, the concept was implicit in Sandor Ferenczi's (1933) ideas about the impact of sexual abuse upon children. It also appears repeatedly in the writings of Ronald Laing (1960) and Harold Searles (1965) on the interpersonal origins of schizophrenia. More recently, Victor Calef and Edward Weinshel (1981) concluded that 'gaslighting' is basically 'an introjective defence in which victim and victimizer join in expressing and defending themselves against oral incorporative impulses. The behavior permits the judgements and perceptions of one individual to be shaken by another and functions for the disavowal of anxiety by the latter. The accomplishment is an intrapersonal one (although instituted interpersonally) to rid the perpetrator of all manner of mental functions and contents, in his or her attempt to avoid anxiety and breaks with reality' (p. 64). Leonard Shengold (1975, 1989), too, underscored the role of 'gaslighting' in his description of 'soul murder' (see separate entry). While these descriptions pertain to individual psychopathology, the fact remains that 'gaslighting' is a frequent manoeuvre in politics, ethnic warfare, and colonial oppression. Powerful nations or groups supported by them can occupy others' lands and when the latter protest, declare them to be 'insurgents' and 'terrorists'.

Gender identity: this consists of three aspects: core gender identity (Stoller, 1968) or the awareness of having one or the other type of genitals and therefore being male or female, gender role (Green, 1975), or one's overt behaviour in relation to others with respect to one's gender, and sexual partner orientation. In 'classical' psychoanalytic view, the latter inevitably implied heterosexual object choice but this view has been mostly replaced by contemporary voices that have not only delinked sexual object choice from gender identity, but questioned the veracity of the latter concept itself. It is suggested that each individual evolves a uniquely specific view of masculinity and femininity for his or her own self, based upon a complex interplay of genital anatomy, secondary sex characteristics, family tradition, and cultural norms. Moreover, a certain fluidity ('gender multiplicity') persists and is selectively evoked for psychosocially beneficial purposes.

Generational boundaries: the inner awareness and acceptance of the differences in the rights and privileges of parents and children. Emanating from the supine infantile eye's experience of awe (Ostow, 2001), the parent–child distinction is strengthened by their physical disparity, the gradient of dependence in the dyad, and the laying down of shame and 'sphincter morality' (Ferenczi, 1925b) during the anal phase, and guilt and superego, which create and enforce the incest barrier, during the oedipal phase (Freud, 1900a, 1924d).

Generational continuity: the development of separateness and autonomy during childhood depends upon the internalization of parental ego skills, moral injunctions, and preferred ideals. Identification is the key here. The next step, during adolescence, involves disengagement from early parental mores (Blos, 1967; Erikson, 1956) and 'depersonification of the superego' (Jacobson, 1964). However, such disengagement is not total. It occurs 'in a way that simultaneously permits individual autonomy together with maintenance of valued traditional continuity' (Poland, 1977, p. 410). Thus, even with the pronunciation inherent in the mastery of the oedipus complex and with the passage through adolescence, family traditions persist in the ego and superego. This is called 'generational continuity'.

Generational filiation: refers to the emotional sense that one belongs in a chain of generations. In other words, rather than being merely a boy or a girl, one feels that one is the son or daughter of so and so. This sense is acquired during the passage through the Oedipus complex (Chassaguet-Smirgel, 1984) and consolidated in adolescence (Blos, 1967). This early sense of generation filia-

tions extends to grandparents and, later, to one's children. Though cultural variations exist, the feeling is often generalized to older and younger figures in one's immediate environment. Capacities for respect towards elders and tenderness towards younger people result from this structural achievement, as does a strengthening of the incest barrier.

Generative and malignant moods: Christopher Bollas's (1987) terms for affective states that are aimed at generativity and self-repair, or at influencing another person, respectively. 'In a generative mood, the person goes into himself to contact the mute, unknown child self' (p. 101), and in a 'malignant mood' he primarily aims to coerce another individual to perform some function. The former type of mood has much greater self-informative potential.

Generative empathy: Roy Schafer's (1959) term for sharing in an understanding the psychological state of another person for the latter's benefit. According to Schafer, 'generative empathy' is 'a sublimated act in personal relationships' (p. 370) with the following five characteristics: (1) it is not meant to discharge one's own tensions, (2) it involves a subtle and conflict-free interplay of introjective and projective mechanisms, (3) it enhances one's boundaries of awareness through discovery of new forms of experience, (4) it strengthens the empathizer's ego, and (5) it enhances communication with the object and the fruits of such empathy ultimately serve not oneself, but the other person.

Generative mood: see 'Generative and malignant moods'.

Generativity *vs.* stagnation: Erik Erikson's (1950) seventh psychosocial stage. This is the characteristic issue of midlife and involves the development of the capacity to nourish and guide the next generation. Merely having children, nephews and nieces, junior employees, or students is not enough. It is the intrapsychic capacity to treat them with benevolent care, to give them autonomy, to facilitate their growth, and to encourage them in their pursuits that constitutes 'generativity'. Also included here is the growing care one shows towards the animal and plant worlds, and the attitude (and practice) of supporting civic structures through selfless devotion and charity.

Genetic fallacy: Term coined by Heinz Hartmann (1955) to label the frequent, though mistaken, tendency to ascribe the origins of a particular behaviour in adult life to that phase of childhood during which the behaviour appears for the first time. An illustration of 'genetic fallacy' is to assume that manifest oral behaviour of an adult (e.g., smoking, drinking, nail biting) derives from an oral fixation. Such thinking is often incorrect because it overlooks that behaviours evolved in childhood undergo 'change of function' (see separate entry), i.e., acquire different aims and meanings as development proceeds and more life experience accrues. Earlier purposes become condensed with later purposes, or are abandoned altogether.

Genetic interpretation: analysts' interventions that are geared towards making conscious the hitherto unconscious ontogenetic origins of a given psychological phenomenon. Contrary to the portrayal of psychoanalysis in popular media, the 'genetic interpretations' are used in a cautious and sparing manner. Making such interventions requires (1) avoidance of formulaic reductionism, (2) extensive familiarity with the patient's childhood background, (3) corroborative associations that have prepared the ground for the analyst's remarks, (4) sifting through the confounding factors of 'screen memories' (see separate entry) and 'change of function' (see separate entry), and (5) patient's preparedness to hear and assimilate the insight given. 'Genetic interpretations' are to be distinguished from 'reconstructions' (see separate entry); the latter 'may be considered a special form of genetic interpretations, but are not identical. We reconstruct events but we interpret meanings' (Moore & Fine, 1968, p. 58).

Genetic immortality: see 'Illusion of genetic immortality'.

Genital love: while Sigmund Freud (1905a) did talk of 'genital phase' and 'genital primacy' (see separate entries), he did not refer to 'genital love'. The term first appeared in the writings of Michael Balint (1948), and its hybrid nature demonstrates the transition from the instinctual and body-orientated ('genital') foundations of early psychoanalytic theory to a more object-related ('love') perspective on human motivation and development. In essence, 'genital love' simultaneously refers four developmental achievements: (1) the unification of 'component instincts' (see separate entry); (2) fusion of 'affectionate and sexual currents' (see separate entry); (3) overcoming of the Oedipus complex, and (4) actualization, in late adolescence or young adulthood, of a deep romantic relationship (see the related entry on 'Mature love' also).

Genetic perspective: see 'Metapsychology'.

Genital primacy: term employed by Sigmund Freud (1905a) to denote the developmental achievement characterized by the genitals becoming the dominant source of sexual excitation and discharge. The sensual potential of pregenital erotogenic zones does not disappear and need no longer be dealt with by repressive countercathexis. Instead, it is organized under the reign of satisfaction through genital climax and discharge. This 'genital stage' has three other features: (1) it heralds the onset of adulthood, (2) it involves not only the shift of zonal excitement, but also a shift in the nature of the relationship established with a love object; full satisfaction is no longer possible without satisfying the partner, (3) not surprisingly, then, genital primacy and 'mature love' (see separate entry) reinforce each other. Early psychoanalysis held that the achievement of 'genital primacy' is impeded by the anxiety and guilt consequent upon unresolved oedipal strivings. However, the contemporary viewpoint will also include excessive amounts of unmentalized aggression, which have weakened the ego's capacity for a post-ambivalent, total object relationship and facilitated the substitution of full genital pleasure by regressive pregenital pleasures. Martin Brezin's (1967) report of the Panel Discussion on 'genital primacy' during the 1968 Fall Meetings of the American Psychoanalytic Association provides a charming glimpse into the discussions that preoccupied the North American ego psychologists in those days.

Genital phase: term introduced by Sigmund Freud (1905a) to denote the psychosexual events of development between the third and fifth year of life; 'genital phase', in this early sense, was the third psychosexual phase (after oral and anal phases) and subsumed 'phallic phase' and 'Oedipus complex' (see separate entries). Later, however, Freud (1933a) referred to 'genital phase' as the fourth and final phase of sexual development, equating it with the unification of pregenital 'component instincts' (see separate entry) under the influence of maturing genitals during puberty. Alongside this instinctual achievement, there are advances in the capacity for deeper object relationships.

Genital stage: see 'Genital primacy'.

Geography of transference: term introduced by Jill and David Scharff (2005) to denote the mapping out of the transference phenomena along the axes of 'what', 'how', 'where', and 'when'.

121

Essentially, this implies that one needs to understand what kind of transference one is dealing with, how that feeling is expressed, where it is located (e.g., inside the patient, inside the therapist, or in the space between), and when in time (past, present, or future) this feeling is felt to occur.

Geopolitical identity disorder: Ira Brenner's (2009b) wry designation of the psychological dimension of the Israeli–Palestinian conflict. Drawing a metaphorical parallel with 'dissociative identity disorder' (see separate entry) or the so-called multiple personality, Brenner notes the striking similarities between this malady and the Israeli–Palestinian conflict: (1) existence of separate selves, (2) constant friction between them to take control over the whole organization, (3) inability to accept their common fate, and (4) tendency to erupt in frequent mortal combat with each other.

Geopolitical space: term coined by Thomas Wolman (2007) to underscore the fact that psychological configurations of human space are deeply affected by the forces of history and politics. The concept of a 'nation' illustrates this point quite well. Seemingly self evident, it actually turns out to be elusive. Wolman points out that the concept raises many questions. 'Does a "nation" have to have territorial boundaries? What sort of symbolic significance do the borders of such a territory (Falk, 1974) come to acquire in the human mind? How does a redrawing of borders between countries affect the sense of nationhood of those affected by such seemingly arbitrary geopolitical acts? What is the relationship between "nation" and "state"? Is "nation" itself a conceptual monolith, or might it contain micro-nations within it? Can there be emerging "proto-nations" that are invalidated as misguided uprisings by a majority invested in cohesion? Clearly, one can go on and on with such queries, but the point is incontestable: "nation" is a slippery concept. And, once established, the instability of the concept produces daunting consequences, ranging from the extremes of maudlin sentimentality to vicious and divisive politics' (p. 41). Three other intersections between history, politics, and human space are to be noted: the flight of the persecuted; migrations of the colonized; and the grave impact of what is euphemistically called 'globalizations'.

Geopsychoanalysis: Jacques Derrida's (1998) ironic designation for 'the figure which psychoanalysis in its becoming-a-world, in its ongoing worldification, inscribes upon the earth, upon the surface of mankind's earth, upon the body of the earth and of mankind' (p. 66). Derrida wryly observed that the three regions constituting IPA (International Psychoanalytic Association) are North America, Latin America, and Europe, leaving out a huge chunk of this world, namely, Africa, Asia, and Australia; even when psychoanalysis exists in the nooks and crannies of such places, 'they are outposts of European or American psychoanalytic Societies in these regions' (p. 69), which raises few, if any, questions of their practice in its political and socio-institutional dimensions. Acknowledging Frantz Fanon (1994) to be a major exception, Derrida lamented the 'utter dissociation of the psychoanalytic sphere from the sphere of the citizen or moral subject in his or her public or private life' (p. 77).

Ghostline personality: term used by Christopher Bollas (1989) for a character organization where transitional activity and symbolization are stunted and the individual creates a make-believe world to live in. The characters in this world take on a life of their own, and the patient seems to be deeply involved with these 'lives'. He uses imagination as an alternative to reality and not for the purposes of reaching out to reality.

Gifts: while the history of psychoanalysis, from its earliest days until now, is replete with 'gifts' analysts have received from their patients, a taboo exists *vis-à-vis* this practice. Taking something from an analysand is regarded as a collusion with the latter's instinctual agenda and a gratification of his id pressures or superego commands. It is supposed to contaminate transference, since all sorts of unspoken wish–defence–fantasy constellations might get smuggled out (of analytic scrutiny) along with the 'gift'. The mainstream position is to decline the patients' offer of a 'gift' and instead analyse what gives rise to such a wish (ref). This is viewed as being loyal to the technical principle of 'abstinence' (see separate entry). 'Gifts' that are too instinctual (e.g., expensive, edible, sexual) and/or are likely to corrupt the analyst's 'work ego' (see separate entry) are especially to be declined. Gifts that are minor and understandable tokens of gratitude at termination, for instance, might pose less threat to the integrity of the analytic process. The overt 'magnitude' of a gift is, however, less important than its true meanings within the context of the real and transference relationship the patient has with the analyst. While it is generally better to err on the side of 'abstinence', it needs to be kept in mind that 'rejecting gifts can increase the asymmetry of the dyad to a painful extreme and the consequences might sometimes be irremediable' (Thoma & Kachele, 1994, p. 301). The considerable literature on this topic has been skilfully summarized by Andrew Smolar (2002, 2003), who also discusses the less frequently encountered (or acknowledged?) situation of the analyst giving a gift to the patient.

Glass bubble fantasy: described by Vamik Volkan (1982), this fantasy is commonly employed by narcissistic individuals to keep their illusory greatness intact. They feel that they are living by themselves in a glorious 'glass bubble' that offers them imperious but transparent protection. They can see others but cannot be meaningfully 'touched' by them. This protects their fragile self-esteem and keeps their aggression in abeyance, but it also leaves them lonely and isolated from others.

God complex: term coined by Ernest Jones (1913a) to designate the narcissistic attitude that often underlies undue self-effacement ('pseudo-humility'), social reserve, and pretended contempt for money in real life. Unlike the flamboyant, openly acquisitive, and assertive type of narcissistic personality, such individuals are characterized by a desire for aloofness, inaccessibility, mysteriousness, and modesty. They are happiest in their own home. They surround themselves and their opinions with a cloud of mystery, exert only an indirect influence on external affairs, never join in any common action, and are generally unsocial. They take great interest in psychology and have secret fantasies of power, especially the idea of possessing great wealth. They act as if they know everything and tend to reject all new knowledge.

God-representation: term proposed by Ana-Maria Rizzuto (1979, 1996, 2001) in order to underscore that psychoanalytic focus upon religious belief ought not to be upon whether God exists, but upon the pertinent intrapsychic construction. According to her, such 'God representation' is a developmental product derived from multiple sources to which experience with real parents of childhood contributes but one tributary. Fantasies of wished-for parents and imaginary constructs of feared parents also contribute to the 'God representation'. Moreover, formation of the internal image of God is an 'object-representational process marked by the emotional configuration of the individual prevailing at the moment he forms the representation' (1979, p. 44). Each individual's 'God representation' is psychi-

cally helpful in ways specific to him or her. It is 'a conglomerate of his or her preoedipal psychic situation, the beginning stage of the oedipal complex, the charcteristics of the parents, the predicaments of the child with each of his parents and siblings, and the general religious, social, and intellectual background of the household' (1979, p. 45). Of note here are the four significant departures from Sigmund Freud's (1927c) impassioned stance that God is a fantasy evolved to perpetuate infantile dependence upon a majestic father substitute. These include: (1) the argument as to whether God exists in actuality is put aside and rendered moot; (2) experience and fantasies involving *both* parents and not only the father are seen to contribute to the formation of this image; (3) additional vectors contributing to the genesis of this image are recognized; and (4) its potential usefulness is acknowledged. See also the important contributions of William Meissner (1992a,b) to the realm of religious belief. The recent IPA (International Psychoanalytic Association) sponsored update on Freud's ideas about God (O'Neil & Akhtar, 2008) elucidates the tension that continues to exist in the diverse psychoanalytic views on the place of religious faith in human life.

Godfather fantasy: Ethel Person's (2001) label for a secular version of the human need for transcendence, by which people either aspire to become powerful and generous figures for others or seek 'vicarious power through a connection to one or another mortal—a godfather or godmother, a titan of industry, a mentor, a totalitarian leader—whom they imbue with the mystique of power and to whom they pledge obeisance' (p. 1143). Person duly credits the novelist Mario Puzo, whose celebrated novel *The Godfather* (1969) became the source of her designation of this fantasy. She notes that this fantasy deftly brings together the human drive for omnipotence with the equally human 'propensity for obedience'

Going-on-being: Donald Winnicott's (1956b) phrase for the infant's constitution beginning to 'make itself evident, for the developmental tendencies to start to unfold, and for the infant to experience spontaneous (psychic) movement' (p. 304). Such 'going-on-being' is characterized by four elements: spontaneity, authenticity, agency, and continuity. All this is possible only if the mother is in the state of 'primary maternal preoccupation' (see separate entry) and can provide a non-intrusive holding environment for the infant.

Golden fantasy: described by Sydney Smith (1977), this fantasy refers to a simple wish: 'to have all of one's needs met in a relationship hallowed by perfection' (p. 311). The subject displays remarkable passivity and seems convinced that somewhere someone exists who can and someday will take care of all his needs. This belief is profoundly important, and to give it up is to give up on everything. Smith delineated the narcissistic and 'separation–individuation' (see separate entry) based foundations of this fantasy, though without citing Karl Abraham (1924b), who, long ago, said that 'some people are dominated by the belief that there will always be some kind of person—a representation of the mother, of course—to care for them and to give them everything they need. This optimistic belief condemns them to inactivity' (p. 399). See also the related entry on 'Someday and as if only fantasies'.

Good dream: in a paper titled 'Dream psychology and the evolution of the psychoanalytic situation', Masud Khan (1962) delineated the features of the sleeper's intrapsychic situation which makes it possible for him or her to have a 'good dream'. These included the following: (1) the availability of a secure and restful physical space which permits the ego to safely withdraw its external cathexes, (2) a certain amount of 'basic trust' (see separate entry), (3) the ego's capacity to be in touch with the wish to sleep, (4) an unconscious internal source of disequilibrium needing articulation through the dream work, (5) optimal availability of day-residues, (6) capacity for benign regression, (7) reliability of the integrative processes in the ego, (8) 'ego's narcissistic capacity for gratification from dream world in lieu of either the pure narcissism of sleep or of the concrete satisfaction of reality' (p. 34), (9) a healthy capacity for symbolization, (10) 'a capacity for benign distancing from primitive and sadistic superego elements so as to allow for relaxing of the repressive barrier' (p. 34), (11) a capacity for receptiveness to the id material with the confidence in the ability to resist being overwhelmed by it, (12) the availability of a reliable time–space unit to actualize and repeat all this at reliable intervals, (13) enough neutralized energy to modulate id impulses, and (14) the capacity to retain the manifest dream in the waking state should this be necessary and beneficial for the ego. Khan went on to state that the capacity to have a 'good dream' 'though a prerequisite for psychic health, is, however, not a guarantee of it' (p. 35).

Good enough hate: Harvey Rich's (personal communication, December 1994) phrase for the fact that a robust capacity for indignation, outrage, and even sustained dislike, is a hallmark of mental health. Pertinent, in this connection, is Richard Galdston's (1987) inclusion of 'those who are incapable of hating' among individuals displaying various psychopathological syndromes associated with hatred.

Good enough mother: Donald Winnicott's (1960) term for a mother who, while not being perfect, is devoted to her child, tries to understand the child's mind, survives his assaults, almost never fails in meeting the child's ego needs though frequently frustrates his id-wishes, and is able to leave him alone when he seems to require autonomous functioning.

Grandfather complex: see 'Grandparent syndrome'.

Grandiose self: term first used by Heinz Kohut (1971) to designate the grandiose and exhibitionistic image of the self in individuals with narcissistic personality. A common consequence of such a psychic structure is relentless pursuit of perfection and constant need for acclaim. A truly talented person's ego 'may well be pushed to the use of its utmost capacities, and thus to a realistically outstanding performance, by the demands of the grandiose fantasies of a persistent, poorly modified grandiose self' (p. 109). Less gifted individuals, however, can only manage a caricature of this situation. Kohut proposed that, under empathic developmental conditions, the grandiose self of childhood is gradually tamed and becomes integrated into the adult personality. It then supplies the force behind realistic ambitions. However, if the child suffers narcissistic traumas, the grandiose self persists unaltered, constantly striving for the fulfilment of its primitive aims. In contrast to Kohut, Otto Kernberg (1975) uses the term 'grandiose self' not to describe the normal narcissism of childhood, but for a psychic structure that is pathological to begin with. He proposes that the grandiose self is formed by the fusion of (1) the actually praiseworthy aspects of the self, (2) an idealized self-image that protected the child against feeling frustrated and angry, and (3) an ideal object representation i.e., the fantasied, everloving parent. At the same time, the aggressively tinged self- and object representations are split off and externalized. There are two distinctions between Kohut's and Kernberg's views on the grandiose self. Kohut regards it as a fixation upon a normal structure of childhood. Kernberg believes that it reflects a pathological structure distinct from normal childhood narcissism. Kohut believes the rage of such persons to be a response to their grandiose selves being injured, whereas

Kernberg sees their rage as the inciting agent for the formation of the grandiose self.

Grandparent syndrome: the significance of grandparents in the development of a child was recognized from the earliest days of psychoanalysis (Abraham 1913a; Ferenczi, 1913, Jones, 1913b). Sandor Ferenczi even coined the term 'grandfather complex'. This referred to the complexity of the child's feelings towards the grandfather. On the one hand, these involved the awareness that the grandfather was 'higher' than the father, whom the child respected and feared. On the other hand, the encounter with the grandfather made the child aware of ageing and death. Both sets of feelings had deep reverberations inside him. Ferenczi stated when the grandfather is the master of the house, then 'the child in his phantasy goes beyond the powerless father and hopes to inherit the whole of the grandfather's power directly' (p. 324). Elaborating on these ideas and adding extensive clinical material, Ernest Rappaport (1958) described a psychopathological constellation in which a child places the grandparent in the place of the parent while relegating the parent to the status of a sibling. This is more likely to happen if the grandparent lives in the same household with children and grandchildren. Such a 'grandparent syndrome' implies the child's identification with grandparents and not the parents, and upon a fantasized reversal of generations. If the identification is with a powerful grandparent, a self-indulgent attitude coupled with irreverence towards parents results. If the identification is with a weak and hypochondriacal grandparent, significant ego-inhibitions, especially in the realm of sexual assertiveness, tend to develop. Landrum Tucker (2006) has provided a more recent exposition of this syndrome.

Gratitude: Melanie Klein (1957) made the most significant contributions to the developmental and phenomenological understanding of 'gratitude'. According to her, 'a full gratification at the breast means that the infant feels that he has received from his love object a unique gift which he wants to keep. This is the basis of gratitude' (p. 188). The emotion is closely linked to trust in others and contributes to consolidation of good relations with them. Klein added that 'gratitude is closely bound with generosity. Inner wealth derives from having assimilated the good object so that the individual becomes able to share its gifts with others' (p. 189). Lest all this appear idealized in and of its self, it should be noted that Klein distinguished generosity prompted by guilt from that mobilized by love. The former has a rigid quality and is accompanied by praise-seeking exhibitionism (see the related entry on the various types of 'altruism' also).

Greed: while earlier writings on the anally-determined interest in money had touched upon it, the topic of 'greed' got the most concerted psychoanalytic attention from Melanie Klein (1931, 1937). In her view, the infant's 'greed', or an insatiable hunger, arose from an unsatisfactory oral tie with the mother and had two aims: (1) 'to get hold of "good" substances and objects (ultimately, "good" milk, "good" feces, "good" penis and "good" children) and with their help to paralyze the action of "bad" objects and substances inside the body, and (2) to amass sufficient reserves inside itself to be able to resist attacks made upon it by external objects, and if, necessary, to restore to its mother's body, or rather to its objects, what it has stolen from there' (1931, pp. 246–247). The insatiability component of 'greed' emanates from the fact that internalization of 'good' objects is soon followed by their destruction or functional diminution by internal aggression. Mrs Klein observed that 'greed' in adult life could lead to collecting and hoarding physical objects, 'devouring' knowledge and facts, and fierce clinging to desired others with little empathy for them. Defences against such inclinations could lead to indiscriminate ejection of objects and pseudo-generosity. Moreover, since hostility lurks underneath their dependence, greedy individuals constantly need the loved person to demonstrate by his or her overt affection that 'they are not bad, not aggressive, and that their destructive impulses have not taken effect' (1937, p. 322) (see also the entry on 'analyst's greed')

Grid: a complex arrangement of conceptual axes evolved, over many years, by Wilfred Bion (1963, 1965, 1970, 1977) in order to organize the ways in which understanding and thinking takes place. The horizontal axis contains six named columns (definitory hypothesis, falsehood, notation, attention, research, and action) and one 'open' one at their end. The vertical axis contains eight columns (beta elements, alpha elements, dreams thoughts, preconception, conception, concept, scientific–deductive system, and algebraic calculus). At the risk of oversimplification, the horizontal axis can be seen as comprising elements of how to think and the vertical axis about what kind of material is being offered to be thought about. The former is the 'usage axis' and the latter a 'genetic axis'. The purpose of the 'grid' is to bridge the gap between the events of analysis and their interpretation *and* to serve as an instrument for better recording of the analytic material.

Grief: while the term 'mourning' (see separate entry) is used in many different ways, 'grief' is generally restricted for the reaction that follows the loss of a loved one. Sigmund Freud's (1917e) seminal paper 'Mourning and melancholia' elucidated the sequential dynamics of grief as involving the steps of mental pain, defensive idealization of the lost object, its gradual decathexis, and its replacement by a substitute object. The subsequent works of George Pollock (1961, 1970), Elisabeth Kubler-Ross (1969), Colin Parkes (1972), and Vamik Volkan (1981) refine these 'stages' while noting that the anguish of grief invariably comes in waves; the so-called 'stages' are not necessilary clear-cut. It should also be noted that the death of a child, especially an adolescent, is very hard, if not impossible, to mourn. In general, there is little one can do to hasten the resolution of grief (with a major loss taking about two years to overcome), and the following factors can lead to its prolongation: (1) sudden or unexpected death, (2) suicide or homicide, (3) special relationship with the deceased, (4) major reality change as a result of the death, and (5) unresolved emotional business between the deceased and the bereaved (see also 'Pathological grief reaction').

Group psychology: in a monograph titled *Group Psychology and the Analysis of the Ego*, Sigmund Freud (1921c) attempted to bridge the gap between individual and 'group psychology'. He traced the origins of the 'herd instinct' back to the growing child's experience with his family of origin and suggested that a group is formed when a number of individuals take one and the same person as a replacement of their ego ideals. The authority of the powerful oedipal father then comes to reside in this leader. Critical judgement of one's own is sacrificed at the altar of such submission. Two other features characterize the situation: 'intensification of the affects and inhibition of the intellect' (p. 88). Freud's ideas in this regard remained unquestioned until subsequent investigators, especially Vamik Volkan (1988, 1997, 2004), declared that it was a fallacy to apply the model of individual dynamics to 'large group psychology' (see separate entry) which has rules and patterns of its own.

Growth needs: see 'Ego needs'.

Guilt: inadequately distinguished from 'remorse' (see separate entry) in psychoanalytic literature, 'guilt' is a dysphoric experience felt at breaking rules (familial, religious, national, etc.) or even at the thought of such transgression. Within psycho-analysis, 'guilt' has received two major explanations: (1) *according to Sigmund Freud* (1916d, 1924d), 'guilt' is traceable to the childhood wishes for committing 'the two great human crimes, namely incest and parricide' (1916d, p. 321). 'Guilt' is quintessentially oedipal in origin, and is felt at the behest of the superego's critical and admonishing response to the upsurge of prohibited instinctual desires. Consequently, 'guilt' leads to the 'need for punishment' (see separate entry) which, in turn, is fulfilled by 'moral masochism' (see separate entry), being 'wrecked by success' (Freud, 1916d, p. 316), and, in the course of treatment, by 'negative therapeutic reaction' (see separate entry); (2) *according to Melanie Klein* (1935, 1940), the origin of 'guilt' is traceable to the infant's dawning awareness of his attacks (real and phantasied) on the mother who 'survived' them and continued to give him love and attention. In this view, 'guilt' is preoedipal and signals the beginning of the capacity for concern for the object. The Freud–Klein difference in the genesis of guilt is not devoid of technical implications, as lucidly demonstrated by Desy Safran-Gerard (1998). An analyst with the former orientation might conduct 'superego analysis' (see separate entry), which runs the risk of exacerbating patients' manic defence against depressive anxiety. An analyst of the latter orientation might help patients bear the guilt but run the risk of appearing to collude with the patient's harshness towards himself. A balanced approach aims at unmasking the origins of guilt and enhancing the capacity to bear guilt. The Freud–Klein divergence, however, does not exhaust the aetiology of guilt. Note the following three types of guilt: (1) 'survivor's guilt' (Niederland, 1968), which results from having outlived loved ones; (2) 'induced guilt' (Asch, 1976), which results from parents, especially the mother, repeatedly telling the child of the hardship in her pregnancy and labour and/or overall raising of the child; and (3) 'separation guilt' (Modell, 1965), which results from the narcissistic and needy parents discouraging the child's age-specific movement towards autonomy and independence; this is often seen in the children of immigrants (Akhtar & Choi, 2004). These aetiological variations have technical implications, as do the defences that are characteristically deployed against guilt. Prominent among the defences with a pathological outcome are blaming others, irritability, and the subsequent hatred and fear of them (Jones, 1929). A healthier outcome is constituted by consciously bearing guilt and making affective and material 'reparation' (see separate entry) to the object one has hurt in reality and/or phantasy.

Guilty Man *vs*. Tragic Man: during the final and 'radical' phase of his relationship to mainstream psychoanalysis (following 'classical' and 'transitional' phases), Heinz Kohut (1982) declared that 'self psychology has freed itself from the distorted view of psychological man expoused by traditional analysis' (p. 402). It was at the dawn of this phase that he proposed the dichotomy of 'Guilty Man *vs*. Tragic Man' (Kohut, 1977). The former was battling with his prohibited sexual and aggressive drives. The latter was struggling to maintain cohesion of his fragmenting self. A careful look, however, reveals that such a dichotomy is largely quantitative and not qualitative. After all, 'the Tragic Man is no less guilty than the Guilty Man; the Tragic Man's guilt emanates from his pre-genital sadism towards the parental objects and from the sense of having taken too much from the mother and depleted her. Similarly, the Guilty Man is no less tragic than the Tragic Man insofar as the source of his guilt is his incestuous and patricidal fantasy (not acts), wishes that emanated from within him with the unfolding of a constitutional blueprint beyond his control and a family structure not of his choosing' (Akhtar, 1988, p. 344). The dichotomy of Guilty and Tragic Man oversimplifies human experience, ignores genetic spirality, overlooks the 'principle of multiple function' (see separate entry), separates pre-oedipal and oedipal development, and produces duplicity in psychoanalytic technique.

H

H: see 'L, H, and K'.

Hallucinatory wish fulfilment: Sigmund Freud (1895d) proposed this term for the infant's attempt to satisfy his unmet instinctual needs and wishes by simply imagining their gratification. He held the same mechanism responsible for the creation of dreams (Freud, 1900a). Such wish fulfilment, however, does not provide actual gratification and therefore, paradoxically, contributes to the onset of reality-testing.

Hand–mouth–ego integration : See 'Body ego'.

Hanuman complex: phrase originated by the renowned Indian psychiatrist, Narendra Nath Wig (2004) to denote an individual's incapacity to know his strength unless reminded of it by someone older and wiser. The complex is named after the 'monkey god' character, Hanuman, in the ancient Indian epic Ramayana (*c.* 400 BC). Hanuman was the son of Pawan (the God of Wind) and possessed the ability to fly. However, as a child, he used this ability for all sorts of mischievous pranks and was cursed by *Rishis* (holy men) to lose his power to fly. Deeply upset, Hanuman told his mother, Anjana, who pleaded with the holy men for forgiveness. They relented and modified the curse such that Hanuman would not lose his divine power to fly, but would lose the knowledge of this power until reminded about it by some wise man. Later, in the fable, when Rama's wife, Sita, is kidnapped and taken to Sri Lanka, Hanuman is reminded of his power by an aged and wise bear, Jambavan, and flies to rescue her. Wig uses this parable to help a patient 'shake off diffidence and realize his true potential' (p. 27) and to help psychotherapy trainees to realize that the potential of change ultimately lies within the patient who, like Hanuman, has temporarily lost this awareness.

Harmonious interpenetrating mix-up: Michael Balint's (1968) term for a subjective state of mind where the self is in peaceful oneness with its environment. Under such circumstances, objects are few, and those which might exist are utterly non-demanding. Environment and individual penetrate into each other. Balint illustrated such 'harmonious interpenetrating mix up' (p. 66) by three instances: (1) the 'relationship' between the foetus, amniotic fluid, and placenta, or, in other words, between the foetus and its environment mother, (2) the fish in the sea; Balint stated that 'it is an idle question to ask whether the water in the gills or in the mouth is part of the sea or of the fish' (p. 66), and (3) the sort of smooth indifference to others' demands that a periodic drinker seeks; what the alcoholic desires most is that no one disagrees with him or makes demands upon him. Balint proposed that the severely regressed patient in analysis also needs a similarly undifferentiated, undemanding, and unobtrusive atmosphere in order to arrive at a 'new beginning' (see separate entry).

Hatching: Margaret Mahler's (1954, cited in Mahler & Gosliner, 1955) term for an infant's breaking out of the symbiotic mother–child common membrane to begin the process of 'separation individuation' (see separate entry). 'Hatching' takes place around 4–5 months of age. Its occurrence depends on both the infant and mother; the infant must give psychomotor cues for his rapidly evolving drive for self discovery and separateness, and the mother must discern these cues and respond to them in an optimally available, flexible manner.

Hatred: a complex, characterologically anchored, chronic affective state that involves much cognitive elaboration and rationalization. It angrily and relentlessly demands the destruction of a specific internal object and its externalized forms. However, it is more than an affect. It is invariably accompanied by tenaciously held unconscious fantasies as well as distortions of ego and superego functioning. The unconscious fantasy underlying hatred consists of a belief that one has been wronged, betrayed, and injured by others. Accompanying this is a peculiar narrowing of cognitive functions that shapes but distorts reasoning capacities. This prevents the alteration of sadomasochistic beliefs by benevolent, corrective knowledge. Corruption of superego function is also usually present in the form of blindness to ethical barriers in the path of one's destructiveness. The myriad manifestations of hatred, going from the most severe to the mildest, include planned murder, psychosocial ostracization, physical torture, sadomasochistic sexuality, psychological abuse, emotional domination, intellectual control, and unrelenting demonstration of one's moral superiority over others. Major contributions to the psychoanalytic understanding of hatred have been made by Melanie Klein (1933, 1948b), Ping Ne Pao (1965), Wilfred Bion (1967), Herbert Rosenfeld (1971), John Maltsberger and Dan Buie (1974), Eric Brenman (1985), Otto Kernberg (1992, 1995b), Jerome Winer (1994), Harold Blum (1995), and Fred Pine (1995). See also *The Birth of Hatred*, a slim but highly informative volume edited by Salman Akhtar, Selma Kramer, and Henri Parens (1995).

Headline intelligence: phrase coined by Christine Olden (1946) for a cognitive style characterized by 'gathering catchwords or headlines in one dashing glance' (p. 263). Individuals with 'headline intelligence' 'combine the few and superficially collected bits and apply these pieces of knowledge in a skillful way so that they appear to be profundities' (p. 263). Such individuals are often incapable of thorough learning in any one field. While Olden emphasized the oedipal anxieties related to acquiring deeper knowledge, the shallowness of such individuals perhaps also results from pathological narcissism (which makes learning difficult) and pervasive use of manic defence (which precludes sustained attention on a single topic).

Healing transformations of later life: phrase coined by David Guttman (1980) to denote the positive and ego-enriching alterations that take place in old age. According to him, old age relieves one of the necessity to exercise visible and pragmatic social power. The individual is now free to explore and utilize powers that are split-off from the body, i.e., powers that come from the historical, political, and 'sacred perimeter of the community' (p. 501). The older woman can boldly step into the arena of politics (directly or through her sons) and the older man becomes a 'fit vessel for sacred power' (p. 508); his blessing is sought and can be uplifting. Guttman emphasizes that such experiences are not merely social. Older individuals can convert them into internalized objects and these psychocultural objects perform for older individuals the ego supportive functions that children perform for younger adults.

Herd instinct: see 'Group psychology'.

Heterosexuality: refers to a psychosocial constellation in which 'gender identity' (see separate entry) is consonant with the given biological sex and the choice of love object involves the opposite sex. Like its counterpart, 'homosexuality', it is an end product of complex and multilayered biopsychosocial processes. Constituional predisposition, anatomical integrity of genitals, proper sex assignment and gender appropriate ego socialization lead to the consolidation of 'gender identity' during the late second year of life. Passage through the 'Oedipus complex' (see separate entry) and a 'positive' resolution of it in the form of identification with the same sex parent and libidinal investment in the disguised and displaced representations of the opposite sex parents lays the ground work for 'sexual identity'. Later, during adolescence, three developments help to consolidate heterosexuality: (1) deeper resolution of close internal ties with primary objects; (2) renunciation of 'negative' oedipal strivings and consolidation of ego ideal, and (3) synthesis of 'affectionate and sensual currents' (see separate entry) in the realm of love and romance. The stage of 'genital primacy' (see separate entry) is aimed at, and pleasure derived from component instincts becomes subservient to genital sexual activity; foreplay does, however, permit the emergence of oral, anal, phallic, exhibitionistic, and autoerotic aims. With the sustained capacity to direct affection and 'erotic desire' (see separate entry) towards a roughly similar chronological, socioeconomic and intellectual level, 'heterosexuality' acquired a more mature flavour; this reaches its zenith with parenthood. However, this is perhaps a bit too smooth and idyllic a portrayal of 'heterosexuality'. The fact is that this developmental achievement is no guarantee of mental health, which is a broader concept involving a large number of variables (e.g., reality testing, capacity for genuine attachment and mournful separation reactions, incest barrier, generational boundaries, genetivity, and so on). Indeed, many psychopathological forms of 'heterosexuality' exist. (1) *Conditional heterosexuality:* where sexual consummation with the opposite sex is contingent upon certain conditions (e.g., only at night, with lights off); 'fetishism' is an example *par excellence* of this situation. (2) *Perverse heterosexuality:* which involves sexual relations with a member of the opposite sex but within the structure of a 'sexual perversion' (see separate entry); an example of this is constituted by sadomasochistic sexual practices. (3) *Promiscuous heterosexuality:* where an insatiable, mostly orally determined hunger for flirtation, seduction, and sexual activity with members of the opposite sex characterizes the picture. (4) *Paedophilic heterosexuality:* where sexual activity is restricted to children and adolescents. Such association of 'heterosexuality' and psychopathology is important to keep in mind in order to avoid idealizing 'heterosexuality' and upholding it against 'homosexuality'. Pertinent in this context is Sigmund Freud's (1905a) reminder that 'the exclusive sexual interest felt by men for women is also a problem that needs elucidating and is not a self-evident fact' (p. 145). See also Nancy Chodorow's (1992) paper 'Heterosexuality as a compromise formation'.

Hierarchy of interpretation: while Wilheim Reich's (1927) recommendation that one should not simply interpret what the patient is talking about, but interpret at the point where the economically decisive characterological resistance appears, and Otto Fenichel's (1941) recommendation that 'analysis starts always from the surface of the present' (p. 19), laid the groundwork for this idea, the evocative phrase 'hieracrchy of interpretation' was first used by Rudolph Loewenstein (1951). He emphasized that it is preferable to give interpretations in a certain sequence. In Loewenstein's own words: 'under this heading can be placed the preparation for an interpretation, the rules of analyzing the resistances or the defenses before the id derivatives, as well as the choice between the interpretations of the transference as opposed to that part of the material which is not included in the patient's relations to the analyst' (pp. 6–7). He added two other 'rules' about the sequence of interpretation: (1) one should avoid analysing an important neurotic symptom in the beginning, and (2) one should interpret the relatively fluid defences before those which are rigid and fixed. However, Loewenstein acknowledged that analytic work rarely proceeds in such a schematic fashion, and that intuitive evaluation decides the choice of intervention on a moment to moment basis. This 'softening' comment captures the essential paradox that lies at the heart of psychoanalytic work: clinical psychoanalysis is a peculiar amalgam of experience, knowledge, deliberateness, and 'strategy' (Levy, 1987) on the one hand, and a warm personal relationship which one approaches 'without memory or desire' (Bion, 1967) and where spontaneity is one's ally and surprise one's reward. Michael Parsons (2000) has elucidated this multifaceted paradox better than anyone in his elegant book *The Dove that Returns, the Dove that Vanishes* (see also the related entry on 'Strategy in technique').

Historical truth: see 'Narrative truth and historical truth'.

Histrionic personality: see 'Hysterical and histrionic personalities'.

Higher level of character pathology: one among the three levels (the other two being 'intermediate' and 'lower') of character pathology described by Otto Kernberg in 1970. At this level, the patient has a relatively well-integrated but rather punitive superego. Self-concept is stable and identity is well established. Defensive operations against conflicts centre on repression, which is buttressed by inhibitory and avoidant ego operations. Social adaptation is good, but at the cost of ego restriction. Object relations are deep and stable. However, expression of aggression and sexuality is hesitant. Most well-functioning hysterical and obsessional personalities are thus organized.

Holding: see 'Holding environment'.

Holding environment: term coined by Donald Winnicott (1960) in connection with the ordinary function of a mother holding her infant. Holding in this context meant 'not only the actual physical holding of the infant, but also the total environmental provision' (p. 43). Winnicott believed that the psychotherapeutic situation represents a similar 'holding environment'. Such an environment meets physiological needs and is reliable. It does not abandon, nor does it impinge. It facilitates growth. Moreover, such 'holding' extends beyond the infantile period to the broader caretaking functions of the parents in relation to the older child. The holding environment concept has an impact on three aspects of psychoanalytic technique. (1) *Physical aspects:* a therapist mindful of the holding environment would make his office comfortable, noise free, and authentic, without undue self-revelation. He would avoid frequently altering the décor and safeguard the physical integrity of this environment. (2) *Psychological atmosphere:* he would provide an ambience of trust, acceptance, safety, and containment of affects while helping the patient's growth potential to be activated. (3) *Environmental interpretations* (see separate entry also): he would interpret the patient's experience and use of the therapist as a much-needed environmental provision (in contrast to a specific human object). Winnicott's ideas have been further developed by Masud Khan (1963b, 1983a), Patrick Casement (1991), Arnold Modell (1976), Roger Lewin and Clarence Schulz (1992), Jeffrey Applegate and Jennifer Bonowitz (1995), and Joyce Slochower (1996).

Holocaust culture: term coined by Judith Kestenberg and Yolanda Gampel (1983) to denote the psychosocial ambience in which the child survivors of the Holocaust grew up. Splitting of identity, precocious ego-growth, and, at times, lying in order to save one's own life and the lives of others were typical developments under such circumstances. Rarely, one also came across instances of 'identification with the aggressor' (see separate entry), where some adolescent boys emulated the cruelty of the Nazis and inflicted suffering on Jewish inmates. Mostly, however, these children adopted an attitude of concern and helpfulness towards others, especially their own younger siblings. For poignant details of the impact of such 'Holocaust culture' upon children, see Judith Kestenberg and Ira Brenner's (1996) impressive book, *The Last Witness*. Ilany Kogan's (1995) monograph *The Cry of Mute Children*, with its detailed clinical accounts of the second generation of Holocaust survivors, is also pertinent in this context.

Homeostatic and disruptive attunements: through video-monitored child-observational studies, James Herzog (1984) has elucidated two types of parental attunement to young children. Mothers usually join in with a toddler in his or her ongoing play, thus giving the child a 'continuity of being' (Winnicott, 1965, p. 54), validity, and harmony with the environment. This is 'homeostatic attunement'. Fathers typically disrupt the toddler's equilibrium by cajoling him into joining in a new activity. This is 'disruptive attunement'. Homeostatic attunement has affirming qualities necessary for the sustenance and consolidation of self-experience. Disruptive attunement has enhancing qualities necessary for the broadening and deepening of self experience. The influence of the two attunements is addictive and contributes to the 'fluid solidity' (Akhtar, 2003, p. 195) of a healthy self experience. Herzog further observed that fathers create disruptive attunement only when the mother is with the child. In her absence, they, too, offer homeostatic attunement to the child. Homeostatic attunement thus seems to be an experiential prerequisite for disruptive attunement. This has clinical relevance. The analyst's 'holding' and affirmative functions seem akin to the maternal homeostatic attunement, and his unmasking and interpretive functions to the paternal disruptive attunement. Extrapolating Herzog's observations suggest that the analyst's holding ('homeostatic') functions must be securely in place for his interpretive ('disruptive') attempts to be fruitful. The patient must posses or be helped to posses a 'safety feeling' (Sandler, 1960, p. 4) before the risk of encountering the repudiated aspects of his self experience.

Homeostatic attunement: see 'Homeostatic and disruptive attunements'.

Homeostatic instinct: Douglas Orr's (1942) term for a biologically rooted human tendency that strives to maintain the dynamic balance within certain limits which are variously known as health, safety, satisfactory adjustment, and the like. At the psychological level, it manifests through various derivatives found in such activities as earning a living, saving for future needs, and seeking group affiliation. These derivatives make for 'conservatism, order, repetition of the familiar, and in times of crisis or threat, regression to what has proved successful in the past' (p. 335).

Homophobia: see 'Internalized homophobia'.

Homosexual genital primacy: see 'Homosexuality'.

Homosexuality: refers to an individual's romantic and sexual interest in a person of the same sex. Such inclination might be conscious, ego-syntonic, and accompanied by pleasurable fantasies, emotions, and sexual acts. Or, it might be repressed, suppressed, ego-dystonic, and lack behavioural expression. The latter might represent true intrapsychic conflicts or stem from the internalization of social prejudice against 'homosexuality' (see 'internalized homophobia'). Psychoanalytic views on 'homosexuality' have had a chequered history. Sigmund Freud (1905a, 1908d, 1919h, 1920a, 1921c, 1922b, 1933a) held markedly ambivalent views on it. On the one hand, he placed 'inversion' (his preferred term for 'homosexuality') as one among the three 'deviations in respect of the sexual object' (1905a, pp. 136–149), with the other two being paedophilia and bestiality. And he stated that 'homosexuality' betrays 'a certain arrest of sexual development' (1935, p. 786). On the other hand, he emphatically declared that: 'homosexual persons are not sick' (1903), 'all human beings are capable of making a homosexual object choice' (1905a, p. 142), 'inversion is found in people who exhibit no other serious deviation from the normal' (1905a, p. 138), and 'homosexuality' 'cannot be classified as an illness' (1935, p. 786). This contradiction, according to Ralph Roughton (2002), arose from Freud's strong commitment to two opposite perspectives on life: radical opposition to sexual conventionality and prudishness on the one hand, and a conservative Darwinian commitment to seeing reproduction as the main goal of sexuality on the other hand. Freud's views on the causation of 'homosexuality' were restrained, and accommodated both innate predisposition and childhood experience. Here, it should be noted that a certain amount of 'psychic homosexuality' (Bokanowski, 1995) is an integral aspect of psychic 'bisexuality' (see separate entry) and exists mostly on an unconscious level; it is part of oedipal structure and carries with itself a strand of the so-called 'feminine masochism' (see separate entry). Returning to Freud, it can be added that he did not fall prey to the naïve equation of 'homosexuality' and gender dysphoria. He stated that 'in men, the most complete masculinity can be combined with inversion' (1905a, p. 142). Talking of 'female homosexuality' (see separate entry), Freud leaned towards viewing lesbians as having masculine characteristics, though here, too, he tempered his views by adding that 'a closer knowledge of the facts might reveal a greater variety' (1905a, p. 145). Regarding psychoanalytic treatment of 'homosexuality', Freud was not very hopeful. His ambivalence, restraint, and open-mindedness were not replicated in the subsequent psychoanalytic literature. Contribution after contribution (Ferenczi, 1914, 1925b; Sachs, 1923; Bibring, 1940; Fenichel, 1945; A. Freud, 1951; Bychow-ski, 1954; Bergler, 1944, 1956, 1959; Ovessey, 1969) emphasized that 'homosexuality' was pathological and elucidated the various genetic and structural constellations underlying it. Charles Socarides (1960, 1962, 1970, 1978), who became the chief advocate of this vantage point, classified 'homosexuality' into the following six types: *preoedipal* (inflexible, ego-syntonic, and associated with gender disturbance); *oedipal* (anxiety-laden and ego-dystonic); *situational* (due to non-availability of heterosexual objects); *variational* (ego-syntonic, occasional, and co-existent with heterosexuality); *latent* (repressed preoedipal or oedipal forms), and *'schizo homosexuality'* (a psychotic state with homoerotic object choice). Socarides felt that some homosexual individuals can be helped to become heterosexual by analysis and his vision is reflected in the current 'reparative therapy' for homosexual individuals. However, a survey of 285 psychoanalysts reporting on their clinical experience with 1215 homosexual patients (MacIntosh, 1994) demonstrated that most analysts do not hold 'a conviction that homosexual patients in analysis can and should change to heterosexuality' (p. 1197), even though 23% of patients in this survey did change their sexual orientation. How such a dramatic change of opinion regarding the nosological status of 'homosexuality' has come about is an interesting story in itself. The intensity of both its 'pathologization' and 'depathologization' seems quintessentially American, even though the two perspectives themselves arise from a combination of theory, clinical experience, and sociocultural factors. A particular theoretical model which gave premium to heterosexual 'genital primacy' (see separate entry), clinical experience shaped by that model, and 'American moralism, medical diagnosis, and

zest for cure' (Roughton, 2002, p. 745) led to the 'pathologization' of 'homosexuality'. A different set of theoretical notions, largely proposed by gay and lesbian psychoanalysts based upon their experiences on both sides of the couch, coupled with the American gay activism, resulted in the 'depathologization' of 'homosexuality' (Bayer, 1981; Socarides, 1992, 1995). These details, and the role played by the pioneering gay psychoanalyst, Richard Isay (1985, 1987, 1991) in the move towards 'depathologization', have been described in engaging, if somewhat one-sided, detail by Ralph Roughton (2002). His paper also summarizes the recent developments in the study of 'homosexuality', especially those added by gay and lesbian analysts themselves. These new insights include (1) a shift away from viewing the strained father–son relationship as the cause to viewing it as the result of the son's homosexuality (Isay, 1987, 1989); (2) in light of an ego-syntonic developmental line of normal gay development, one might now talk also of 'homosexual genital primacy' (Roughton, 2002, p. 736); (3) modifying the concept of narcissistic object choice by stating that 'loving that is termed narcissistic is not about whom one loves but how one loves' (Frommer, 2000, p. 203), (4) viewing the so-called negative Oedipus complex of the boy as a normal phenomenon for the gay boy (Goldsmith, 1995, 2001); (5) the effect of constant overstimulation on the gay teenager by his having to associate with objects of his sexual desire (Philips, 2001); (6) the finding that indicators of a good marriage (e.g., shared ego ideal, continued sexuality, and puttng greater premium on the newly formed family than upon the family of origin) are the same in homosexual couples as they are in heterosexual couples (Heanares-Levy, cited in Roughton, 2002); and (7) the emergence of defensive heterosexual fantasies during the psychoanalytic treatment of lesbians (Vaughan, 1999). Clearly, the psychoanalytic perspective on 'homosexuality' has come a long way from its origins. See also Bertram Cohler and Robert Galatzer-Levy's (2000) *The Course of Gay and Lesbian Lives*.

Homovestism: decribed by George Zavitzianos (1972), 'homovestim' is a condition closely related to 'transvestism' (see separate entry) and 'fetishism' (see separate entry). 'Homovestim' involves drawing sexual excitement by wearing clothes of one's own gender. Like the transvestite, the individual with homovestism is involved in a denial of the female genitalia in order to avoid castration anxiety. Like the fetishist, the homovestite relates to clothes of the same sex in a manner to deny castration. The 'dressing up' of the homovestite shows some peculiarities. The man wears clothes that are just a bit over-sized and hypermasculine; the woman is always a bit over-dressed and well made-up. They experience themselves as boys and girls, respectively, who, at an unconscious level, are carrying on a homoerotic relationship with the man and woman they are dressed as. This negative oedipal scenario, fuelled by factors of narcissism and exhibitionism, is the key dynamic of 'homovestisim'.

Hope: early psychoanalytic literature treated the topic of 'hope' with benign neglect or, at best, normative platitudes. This tendency was set into motion by Sigmund Freud's (1917b) renowned correlation of confidence and success with being 'mother's undisputed darling' (p. 156), and Karl Abraham's (1924b) linking 'imperturbable optimism' (p. 399) with an overly gratifying oral phase. Subsquent analysts (Glover, 1925; French, 1945; Menninger, 1959) echoed this formulation. In an exception to such thinking, Amy Angel (1934) noted that excessive hope is often a defensive development against the anxiety and sadness consequent upon castration related fantasies. Among other significant views subsequently voiced are the following: (i) Harold Searles (1977) distinguished realistic hope from denial-based, manic repression of loss and despair. (ii) Jacqueline Amati-Mehler and Simona Argentieri (1989) described 'pathological hope' as the 'last and unique possible tie with the primary object, giving up of which would mean the definite downfall of the illusion and the admission that it is truly lost' (p. 302). (iii) Salman Akhtar (1991b, 1994, 1996) delineated the 'Someday . . .' and 'if only . . .' fantasies (see separate entry) as interrelated structures of undue optimism and idealization. (iv) Anna Potamianou (1992) asserted that excessive hope can serve as a character armour, keeping reality in check, and (v) Steven Cooper (2000) offered a comprehensive discussion of the tension that invariably exists between the so-called timelessness of the unconscious and the hope of change resulting from the analytic process. Besides these descriptions of excessive hope being pathological, there exist the views of the British independent analysts which offer a converse formulation: psychopathology is a manifestation of hope. Donald Winnicott's (1956a) declaration that 'the anti-social act is an expression of hope' (p. 309) is the most dramatic example of such thinking. Finally, Patrick Casement's (1991) distinction of 'conscious hope' and 'unconscious hope' needs mention. The former seeks the realization of wishes and the latter pertains to the search for development-facilitating objects and

experiences. 'Unconscious hope' can, therefore, be seen to underlie 'repetition compulsion' (see separate entry) in so far as the recreating of traumatic experiences is undertaken with the aim of mastering them.

Horizontal split: see 'Horizontal and vertical splits'.

Horizontal and vertical splits: terms employed by Heniz Kohut (1971) to denote the two ways in which a narcissistic individual's 'grandiose self' (see separate entry) is kept separated from his otherwise reality-orientated ego. His concepts of horizontal and vertical splits are akin to 'repression' (see separate entry) and 'disavowal', respectively. *Horizontal split* forces archaic grandiosity to go underground, leaving the reality ego filled with feelings of inferiority and shame. *Vertical split* maintains a wall between the weakened reality ego and a conscious tendency towards grandiosity and exhibitionism. Kohut proposed that the psychoanalytic treatment of narcissistic personality should proceed by first 'taking down the vertical barrier' (p. 185) and then working to dissolve the horizontal barrier.

Hospitalism: syndrome first described by René Spitz (1945) in infants who are raised in institutions without the warmth of maternal care. Such children show weak immunity against infections, appear depressed, have vacuous facial expressions, and show marked impairment of cognitive functions. If physical nutrients are available, they might grow, but tend to be disaffiliated and antisocial. Spitz's pioneering descriptions established, once and for all, the fundamentally essential role of maternal care in early childhood. Extending Spitz's ideas to the impact of profound maternal neglect occurring within the family setting, Leon Kreisler (1984) has coined the phrase 'intrafamilial hospitalism'.

Hostile destructiveness: term coined by Henri Parens (1979, 1989) for a particular strand of aggression which plays a crucial role in the development of individual and group hatred. Based upon his longitudinal child observational studies, Parens detected four categories of aggressive behaviour: 'unpleasure related destructive behaviour' (eg., rage reactions of infancy), 'non-affective destructive behaviour' (akin to the 'prey aggression' of animals), 'non-destructive aggressive behaviour' (eg., assertion), and 'pleasure-yielding destructive behaviour' (e.g., teasing). This led him to propose three fundamental trends of aggressive drive: (1) 'non-destructive aggression', (2) 'non-affective destructiveness', and (3) 'hostile destructiveness'. This last mentioned variety had the most significant repercussions. While infantile rage reactions were its prototype, 'hostile destructiveness' emerged only gradually and in the context of greater ego maturity. It required excessive unpleasure for its activation. This meant that 'hostile destructiveness' should be avoidable if one can reduce unpleasure faced by an individual. This deduction is one of enormous preventive potential *vis-à-vis* child rearing (Parens, Scattergood, Singletary, & Duff, 1987) as well as the larger cultural arena of ethnic prejudice and violence (Parens, Mahfouz, Twemlow, & Scharff, 2007).

Hot places: Vamik Volkan (1997) uses this term to describe physical locations that induce immediate and intense feelings among the members of an ethnic, religious, national or ideological large group. Typically, these are places where people have been recently killed and/or humiliated by others. 'Hot places' (e.g., Paldiski in Estonia, 'Ground Zero' in New York) induce shared feelings of sadness, rage, and victimization, as well as a desire for revenge. Visiting hot places is to large-group psychology what recounting dreams is to an individual undergoing psychoanalysis.

Hypercathexis: see 'Cathexis'.

Hyperconfidentiality: term coined by Andrea Celenza (2007) to denote a situation that develops in the course of sexual boundary violations by the analyst. Explicitly or implicitly, such an analyst encourages the patient to keep what is happening secret from others; the patient, who is being victimized, complies, and contributes to the perverse secrecy. Drawing an analogy to a family's silence about incestuous sex, Celenza notes that the analyst–analysand compact of such sort leads to a treatment bubble that deprives both the transgressor and the victim of the potentially corrective influence of others. She distinguishes 'hyperconfidentiality' from the ordinary confidentiality that is integral to conducting psychoanalytic treatment; the latter's psychic periphery is selectively porous in so far as it permits supervisory input and/or peer consultation.

Hyphenated identity: an expression frequently used to denote the immigrant's sense of himself as belonging partly to one culture and partly to another; it results in mixed and, at times, contradictory behaviours and attitudes.

Hypnoid hysteria: see 'Hysteria'.

Hypnosis: a somnolent state in which the critical faculty of the mind becomes compromised, rendering the individual vulnerable to suggestions of the hypnotist. Before settling on the method of 'free association' (see separate entry), Sigmund Freud (1891), inspired by Hippolyte Bernheim and Jean-Martin Charcot, used 'hypnosis' to remove conversion symptoms associated with hysteria. Freud noted that the hypnotized person adopts a passive attitude towards the hypnotist and allows the latter to become a substitute for his conscience. Sandor Ferenczi (1909) elaborated on this, and declared that the hypnotic state was, in essence, a transference phenomenon; some aspects of the hypnotist was paternal (e.g., authoritative position, forceful suggestions) and others (e.g., soothing voice) maternal in nature. Over the subsequent course of psychoanalysis, recourse to hypnosis was given up, due, in part, to the fact that Freud was not very good at it (see also 'Autohypnosis').

Hypnotic evasion: see 'Autohypnosis'.

Hypnotic facilitation: see 'Autohypnosis'.

Hypochondriasis: even a cursory look at how this term has been interpreted over the history of psychoanalysis is enough to prove how far the theory has evolved from its early physicalistic origins. 'Hypochondriasis', or a morbid preoccupation with bodily functioning, fear of illness and disease, and a tendency to exaggerate symptoms that might actually exist, has been viewed in ways that have kept up with the refinement of psychoanalytic theory: (1) Sigmund Freud (1892) at first regarded it as a symptom of anxiety neurosis which, in turn, was a type of 'actual neurosis' (see separate entry); (2) later, he added a paranoid element to it by suggesting that the hypochondriac prefers an external (i.e., toxic) over an internal (i.e., degenerative) aetiology for his symptoms; (3) still later, Freud (1895d) elevated 'hypochondriasis' to be an independent 'actual neurosis', and (4) in his paper on narcissism (Freud, 1914c), he proposed that it was the draw of libido from objects and excessive investment in the ego that led to megalomania and 'hypochondriasis'; this could be seen at the outset of a psychotic regression also. This understanding of 'hypochondriasis' was deepened by later contributors to the subject. David Rosenfeld (1984) based his ideas on the development of body image and delineated subtypes of 'hypochondriasis' that included diffuse psychotic type and encapsulated autistic type, alongside neurotic preoccupations with health and clear-cut somatic delusions. Heinz Kohut (1977) regarded 'hypochondriasis' as a concretized allusion to the disintegrating anxieties of the self. Robert Stolorow (1977) offered a sophisticated reading of Freud's ideas in this regard, and concluded that 'just as a neurotic anxiety signals anticipated danger emanating from object-instinctual investments, hypochondriacal anxiety signals dangers threatening in the narcissistic sector of the personality' (p. 245). Stanley Coen (2002) elucidated that pathological modes of relatedness and affect intolerance underlay 'hypochondriasis'. The reader would also benefit by looking up Arlene Richards' (1981) paper comparing and contrasting conflict theory and self-psychology perspectives on hypochondriasis.

Hypomania : see 'Mania'.

Hypomanic character: The issue of characterlogical hypomania was first addressed by Helene Deutsch (1933), who suggested that a persistent denial underlies such a state. Such individuals depreciate what they have lost and quickly find substitute objects. However, 'we note the hollowness of their success in comparison with the energy expended, how the love relationships lack warmth, in spite of their apparent passion, how sterile the performance in spite of continuous productivity. This results from the monopolization of psychic energy in service of the goal we have described: the silencing of the narcissistic wound, of aggression, and guilt reactions' (p. 215). Melanie Klein's (1935) and Donald Winnicott's (1935) ideas about 'manic defence' (see separate entry) are also pertinent in this context. More recently, Salman Akhtar (1984) has provided a comprehensive review of psychoanalytic writings on hypomanic character.

Hysteria: recognized from times immemorial, the puzzling and often unexplained symptoms of 'hysteria' formed the focus of Sigmund Freud's earliest investigations. His encounter with Jean Martin Charcot, the great French psychiatrist and hypnotist, in part spurred him in this direction. Collaborating with his senior colleague, Joseph Breuer, Freud (1893a, 1895d) strove to unmask the psychological aetiology of 'hysteria'. On the phenomenological level, the symptoms of this condition were clusterd into 'conversion' and 'dissociation' type. The former consisted of somatic disturbances and the latter consisted of alterations of consciousness; often the two coexisted. On dynamic grounds, the cause of 'hysteria' was traced to psychic trauma and two mechanisms were proposed for its impact. The first refered to 'hypnoid hysteria', suggesting that the mind was unable to integrate the trauma when it happened and went

into an altered or 'hypnoid state' as a result, the traumatic memory remained sequestered and exerted pathogenic effects. The second hypothesis refered to 'defence hysteria', emphasizing that it was not traumatically altered consciousness but active psychological processes of defence that were responsible for the symptoms of 'hysteria'. With passage of time, the concept of 'hypnoid hysteria' dimmed as increasing light was shed upon 'defence hysteria'. In 1905, Freud drew attention to conversion symptoms having roots in the oedipal conflict. Later analysts (Fenichel, 1945; Marmor, 1953; Rangell, 1959) noted that preoedipal conflicts can also be involved in hysterical symptomatology (see 'Pregenital conversions'). 'Hysteria' became a popular psychiatric diagnosis which, along with obsessional neurosis and phobia, made up the triumvirate of 'classical neuroses' i.e., symptom clusters derived from the Oedipus complex. By the early 1980s, however, the nosological revolution in psychiatry demolished the term 'hysteria'. Forces of feminism (protesting that the association of the word 'hysteria' with the uterus rendered it antiquated and pejorative) and the new found fervour for descriptive psychiatry (which took glee in Freud bashing) were, in part, responsible for this. The contemporary culture's widespread familiarity with the unconscious and with the basic concepts of anatomy and physiology also led to a dramatic drop in the incidents of gross hysterical symptoms. Other diagnostic categories (e.g., somatoform disorder, body dysmorphic disorder) subsumed what little might have been left of the original 'hysteria'. Curiously, the concepts involving 'hypnoid hysteria', which had been more or less set aside, re-emerged forcefully as interest in dissociative disorders (Kluft, 1985; Brenner, 1994, 2001; Shengold, 1989) grew. For the rich history of the syndrome and for the varied phenomena associated with it, the reader might not find a better book than *Hysteria and Related Mental Disorders*, by David Wilfred Abse (1987).

Hysterical personality: see 'Hysterical and histrionic personalities'.

Hysterical and histrionic personalities: while attempts at a deeper understanding of hysterical symptoms led to the birth of psychoanalysis, Sigmund Freud himself did not refer to a specific hysterical personality. The first psychoanalytic description of it was provided by Franz Wittels (1930). According to this description 'hysterical personality' displayed strong dependency needs and vulnerability towards depression, addiction, and even suicide. In the following year, Sigmund

Freud (1931a) published his paper 'Libidinal types' and his category of the 'erotic type' resembled what Wittles had termed 'hysterical personality'. Both these authors emphasized the preoedipal substrate to this type of character. Wilhelm Reich (1933), however, emphasized the hysteric's oedipal fixation and outlined the following traits: (1) coquettishness, (2) bodily grace, (3) suggestibility, (4) excitability and what would today be called 'affectualization' (see separate entry), (5) pathologic lying, and (6) a perplexing withdrawal when sexual seductiveness seemed close to achieving its goal. This description became widely accepted, and so did the view that a hysterical personality was largely oedipally fixated. Then, in 1953, Judd Marmor brought back the early emphasis on oral fixation in such characters. Since then a large number of phenomenological binaries in this realm have cropped up. These include 'hysterical *vs.* hysteroid' (Easser & Lesser, 1965), 'true *vs.* good-enough hysterics' (Zetzel, 1968), 'hysterics *vs.* hysteriform borderline personalities' (Abse, 1974), 'hysterical *vs.* infantile' (Kernberg, 1967), and 'hysterical *vs.* histrionic' (Kernberg, 1984) personality disorders. Careful recording of this literature (Lazare, 1971; Akhtar, 1992b) suggests that 'hysterical personality' refers to a relatively well-integrated character organization with intact identity, a solid repressive barrier, reasonably good superego, mild affectualization, oedipally-derived and trangulated seductiveness coupled with sexual inhibition, and little vulnerability to depression and addiction. 'Histrionic' (or 'infantile') personality, in contrast, refers to a pre-oedipally fixated personality constellation with a poor sense of identity, weak repressive barrier, powerful oral dependent longings, crude sexual seductiveness, marked suggestibility, pervasive affectualization, and vulnerability to corruption, addiction, depression, and suicidal crises.

Hysteriform borderline personality: see 'Hysterical personality'.

Hysteroid personality: see 'Hysterical personality'.

Id: as Sigmund Freud (1923b) shifted his conceptualization from the 'topographic model of the mind' (see separate entry) to the 'structural model of the mind' (see separate entry), the concept of 'id' came into being. Freud borrowed the expression *das Es* (rendered as the 'id' by his English translators) from Georg Groddeck (1923) who had employed it for the internal, 'unknown and uncontrollable forces' (p. 10) that determine much of our behaviour; Groddeck's translators have retained the more impersonal and darker 'it' as the English version of *das Es*. Freud juxtaposed the 'id' and the 'ego' (see separate entry), portraying them as agencies of passion and reason. The id is governed by the 'pleasure principle' and the ego by the 'reality principle'. The id sees no contradictions and operates on the basis of 'primary process', and the ego on the basis of the logical, 'secondary process'. In a famous analogy, Freud described the relation between the id and the ego as that between a horse and its rider. 'Id' contained 'everything that is inherited, that is present at birth that is laid down in the constitution—above all therefore, the instincts, which originate from the somatic organization' (Freud, 1940a [1938], p. 145). The concept of id was thoroughly elucidated by Max Schur (1966). Some of his points, as well as a few later elaborations, need emphasis: (1) the overlap between the 'id' and the system 'unconscious' (see separate entry) of the topographic model at first appears indistinguishable, but in *The Ego and The Id* (Freud, 1923b), it becomes clear that aspects of the ego are also unconscious. As a result, 'id' and the unconscious no longer seem synonymous; (2) the boundary between the id and the ego is not rigid; the lower part of the ego merges into the id; (3) the same is true of the id–superego boundary. Forces of the id contribute to the ferocity of the superego which, in turn, can serve instinctual aims; (4) whether id has some organized form remains unclear. On the one hand, it is viewed as 'a chaos, a cauldron full of seething excitement' (Freud, 1933a, p. 73) which has no organization. On the other hand, the fact that it contains the life and death instincts implies a dialectical structure; (5) is id the source of all psychic energy? Are the forces of the ego merely neutralized forms of id energy? Or, does ego have its own energy? The former is the position mostly taken in connection with the id. However, concepts such as 'ego instincts' (Freud, 1905a, 1915c, see separate entry), 'autonomous

functions of the ego' (Hartmann, 1939, see separate entry), and the various ego pleasures described by George Klein (1976) suggest otherwise. (6) Finally, it should be noted that, while the shift of psychoanalytic theory from instinctual drives to ego psychology and object relations theory has led to an eclipse of id study, the forces of id remain integral to any broad-based conceptualization of human motivation. Fred Pine's (1988) inclusion of id based vectors as one among the 'four psychologies of psychoanalysis' (see separate entry) is a recent testimony to this.

Id resistance: see 'Resistance'.

Ideal hungry personalities: see 'Narcissistic personality types'.

Ideal object: in elaborating his earlier ideas on the concept of 'ideal self' (see separate entry), Joseph Sandler, along with Anne-Marie Sandler (1998), stated that such a wished-for self-representation actually includes a wished-for self-object interaction. 'So the prescence of an "ideal object" may be as much a part of the ideal state as the ideal self' (p. 13). In simpler words, one can hardly envision an ideal state of self-experience without conjuring an object that is perfectly attuned and responsive to one's self.

Ideal self: term coined by Joseph Sandler, Alex Holder, and Dale Meers (1963) for a view of the child that is upheld by the parents as ideal and accepted by the child himself, since at any given time it provides the greatest narcissistic satisfaction, evokes least superego censure, and closes the gap between ego and ego-ideal.

Ideal spouse representation: a term coined by Calvin Colarusso (1997) to denote the mental image of a future husband or wife evolved by an adolescent. This image is influenced by infantile omnipotence and heavily coloured by childhood attachments to parents. As a result, the expectation to find such a person in external reality almost always fails. A certain amount of structural modification and mourning are necessary to renounce this image. Only then, the capacity for entering marriage in a meaningful way develops.

Idealization: the tendency to exaggerate the 'good' qualities of a specific person, an organization, a place, an ideology, or a temporal era in one's personal life or one's national history. This tendency can also be directed at one's self. 'Idealization' is associated with feelings of euphoria, confidence, and optimism. Sigmund Freud (1914c), traced the origin of 'idealization' to the loss of primary narcissism; disillusioned in his own powers, the child assigned omnipotence to his parents, especially the father. Disillusionment with the latter led to the search for a universal father, in the form of God (Freud, 1927c). A similar mechanism was evident when one was falling in love (Freud, 1921c). Freud's ideas were given a different slant by Melanie Klein (1935, 1940) and Otto Kernberg (1975, 1984). They noted that idealization results from the incomplete integration of primitive love and hate during development. What was a developmental inability in early childhood can later be used for the purposes of ego defence. As a result, 'all-good' self- and object representations are actively kept apart from 'all-bad' self- and object representation. Idealization thus becomes a defence against aggression. Behind gushing enthusiasm for this or that object lies critical feelings and even hostility towards it. In contrast to this conceptualization is Heinz Kohut's (1971, 1977) view emphasizing the developmentally necessary and growth-promoting role of idealization. The two views (i.e., those of Kernberg and Kohut) have significant technical implications, with the former putting a premium on resolving idealization by interpreting its defensive functions, and the latter on leaving it unquestioned and letting it undergo a spontaneous 'transmitting internalization' (see separate entry). Finally, idealization is also responsible for the '"Someday . . ." and "If only . . ." fantasies' (see separate entry) which perpetuate pathological optimism and inordinate nostalgia, respectively (Akhtar, 1996).

Idealized parent imago: Heinz Kohut's (1971) term for the narcissistically invested and exalted view of the parents that a growing child develops as he struggles with disillusionment in his own imagined omnipotence. Such overvaluation can exist alongside a more realistic and genuine object relationship with parents. Under normal circumstances, the child experiences gradual disappointment in the 'idealized parent imago' too, and withdraws the narcissistic cathexis. Internalization of this overvaluation then leads to the 'acquisition of permanent psychological structures which continue, endopsychically, the functions which the idealized self-object had previously fulfilled' (p. 45). Under abrupt and traumatic loss of the 'idealized parent imago', however, such optimal internalization and the

resultant faith in one's superego and ego ideal does not develop. Narcissistic hunger for validation by idealized others persists and, in clinical situations, contributes to the development of an 'idealizing transference' (see separate entry).

Idealizing transference: term introduced into the psychoanalytic literature by Heniz Kohut in 1971 to denote 'the revival during psychoanalysis of the state in which, after being exposed to the disturbance of the psychological equilibrium of primary narcissism, the psyche saves a part of the lost experience of global narcissistic perfection by assigning it to an archaic, rudimentary (transitional) self-object, the idealized parent imago' (p. 37). Kohut described two types of idealizing transference. The first is based on the activation of the archaic state in which the idealized mother image is almost completely merged with the self. The second emanates from later developmental phases, where a traumatic disappointment in parents has led to impaired deidealization of them and insufficient idealization of the superego. Individuals of the latter type are forever attempting to achieve a union with an idealized object. They view the analyst as omnipotent and feel whole, safe, and strong as long as they can maintain such idealization. They respond to disappointments in the analyst by denial or by despondency and rage. Indeed, it is the repeated occurrence of such disruptions and their affirmative–reconstructive handling that, in Kohut's view, leads to transmuting internalization of idealization and enhances ability to regulate self-esteem. Other viewpoints also exist regarding the technical handling of idealization. Otto Kernberg (1975), for instance, views such idealization as a defence against transference hatred of the analyst and recommends a shaper focus on the negative transference in the treatment.

Identificate: Leslie Sohn's (1985) term for the change in the self that comes about by a certain form of narcissistic identification. This leads one to 'becoming the object, which is then felt to be within the possession of the self . . . it has all the chameleonic satisfaction of being anew and wishes to stay that way. It is, however, done destructively and can never be used constructively—the destruction being to the state of the ego, and to the object which is consequently devalued' (pp. 277–278). Sohn prefers to call such a structure 'identificate' rather than 'identification' (see separate entry) because there is little introjection here and the ego continutes to be split.

Identification: see 'Internalization'.

Identification with the aggressed: see 'Atonement–forgiveness dyad'.

Identification with the aggressor: a defence mechanism described by Anna Freud (1946), 'identification with the aggressor' leads a harshly treated subject to take on the attribute of his abuser. Consequently, a subject himself becomes harsh and abusive towards others. While originally described in the context of child development, especially the preliminary stages of superego formation, 'identification with the aggressor' also seems to underlie the functioning of those large groups who, having faced persecution by one group, begin to persecute other, more vulnerable groups. This seems to be a counterpart of Sigmund Freud's (1916d) idea that the psychology of being an 'exception' (see separate entry) can involve both individuals and nations.

Identification with the doer: Nathan Segal's (1969) phrase for a defensive ego activity aimed at mastering a passively imposed over-stimulation by actively repeating role aspects of the original disturbing experiences. These usually involve primal scene exposure or a credible threat of abandonment. 'Identification with the doer' differs from 'Identification with the aggressor' (see separate entry) by its being more generalized, by its involving objects other than those responsible for the original trauma, and by its being directed to both aggressive and sexual impulses.

Identification with the hater: phrase coined by Bernhard Berliner (1958) for an individual's identification with the parent who hated and rejected him or her as a child. This results in a tendency towards masochism, a libidinized defensive reaction to the parental sadism. The 'pain-giving love object' (p. 44) now becomes a constituent of the superego. The resulting libidinization of trauma makes suffering ego syntonic. 'Suffering, repressed in its original form, reappears as the price to be paid for obtaining a little bit of love or the imagination of it' (p. 45).

Identification with the humiliator: Arnold Rothstein's (1984) phrase for a sadistic mechanism seen in certain narcissistic personalities who externalize their humiliating superego introjects and treat others with vicious contempt. Such components of the superego are often derived from actual experiences with parents who enjoyed humiliating the narcissistic individual during their childhood.

Identification with the introject: Joseph Sandler's (1960) term for the step in superego formation that follows 'compliance with the introject' (see separate entry). 'Identification with the introject' diminishes reliance on external sources of praise and admonition. The standards and demands of the object-turned-introject are now assimilated into the core self-representation. Consequently, the child begins to fear more the loss of love from his own self than from his parents. A newly emergent superego is therefore clearly evident. Phyllis and Robert Tyson (1984) have further elucidated this concept in their writings on the development of superego.

Identification with the lost object: described by Anna Freud (1984), this is one among the various reactions to losing an object. According to her, the loser's emotions, at times, extend to the feelings the lost object is allegedly experiencing. One who has lost a wristwatch, for instance, might say 'oh, how lonely my poor watch must be feeling'. One may now sob for the forlorn watch, as it were. Clearly, the mechanism of projection has here led to personification, which is followed by identification. Such projection of affect from the loser to the lost object is more obvious when the lost object is human. In the end, the sad experiences felt on behalf of the lost object 'reveal themselves as based upon early childhood events when the loser was himself "lost", that is, felt deserted, rejected, alone, and experienced in full force as his own all the painful emotions which he later ascribes to the objects lost by him' (p. 15).

Identification with the persecutor: term coined by Otto Fenichel (1945) to denote a defensive manoeuvre against guilt. This consists of accumulating power so that one can free oneself of the need to justify one's actions. Feelings of guilt that accrue under such circumstances are warded off by 'stressing the point: I alone decide what is good and what is evil' (p. 500). However, struggle against guilt through power often sets up a vicious cycle, whereby power leads to ethical violations and subsequent guilt, and guilt leads to greater need for power (see entry on the related concept of 'malignant narcissism' also).

Identity: this term was introduced into psychoanalytic literature by Victor Tausk (1919), who examined how the child discovers itself and asserted that man, throughout life, constantly finds and experiences himself anew. Sigmund Freud (1926e) referred to the concept of identity once and this was in his address to B'Nai B'rith. The fact that identity was a two-sided term with intrapsychic as well social ramifications contributed to its lack of acceptance in the subsequent psychoanalytic literature (for a comprehensive review of writings in this area, see Akhtar & Samuel, 1996). In the 1950s, Erik Erikson resurrected the term as 'ego identity'; he later dropped the prefix 'ego', in part to accommodate Heinz Hartmann's (1950) differentiation between ego and the self. All in all, the current view is that a well established identity consists of: (1) a sustained feeling of self-sameness displaying roughly similar character traits to varied others, (2) temporal continuity in the self-experience, (3) genuineness and authenticity, (4) a realistic body image, (5) a sense of inner solidity and the associated capacity for peaceful solitude, (6) subjective clarity regarding one's gender, and (7) an inner solidarity with an ethnic group's ideals and a well-internalized conscience.

Identity crisis: Erik Erikson's (1950, 1956) term for the phase-specific and expectable resurgence of doubts, regression in behaviour, and reorganization of self-image that occurs during adolescence. Subsequent contributors, including James Masterson (1967), Daniel Offer (1969, 1971), and Otto Kernberg (1978) distinguish this sort of disturbance from the more serious syndrome of 'identity diffusion' (see below) that characterizes severe personality disorder. They emphasize that adolescents undergoing identity crisis do not display deep-seated pathology of object relations. Their idealizations, though intense, are based upon surprisingly deep knowledge of their heroes and their devaluations are largely defensive in nature. Their conflicts involve their psychosocial roles, not the totality of their self-experience. They do not display gender identity disturbances and, while often lonely, do not experience the emptiness associated with identity diffusion.

Identity diffusion: term first used by Erik Erikson (1950) to denote the failure during adolescence to integrate earlier identifications into a harmonious psychosocial identity. In a later paper (1956), he described the clinical manifestations of identity diffusion, towards conventional roles, and pronounced conflicts regarding one's ethnic origins. Otto Kernberg (1967, 1978), elaborated on this concept and distinguished it from ordinary crises of identity during adolescence. According to him, identity diffusion suggests severe pathology originating in chronic frustrations during early childhood. As a result, splitting predominates over repression, and self continues to contain unintegrated introjection and identifications. In reviewing the pertinent literature and adding his own perspective, Salman Akhtar (1984) concluded that the 'syndrome of identity diffusion' comprises

(1) markedly contradictory character traits, (2) subtle body-image disturbances, (3) feelings of emptiness, (4) lack of authenticity, (5) temporal discontinuity in the self-experience, (6) gender dysphoria, and (7) inordinate ethnic and moral relativism. Indeed, identity diffusion is a hallmark of severe character pathology and, in an overt or covert manner, invariably associated with severe personality disorders (Kernberg, 1984; Akhtar, 1984, 1992b).

Identity theme: term given by Heinz Lichtenstein (1963) to the particular theme of life imparted to the child by his or her mother during early infancy. According to Lichtenstein, 'the mother imprints upon the infant not an identity, but an identity theme. This theme is irreversible, but it is capable of variations, variations that spell the difference between human creativity and a "destiny neurosis"' (p. 208).

Identity *vs*. role confusion: this is the fifth among the eight stages of psychosocial development outlined by Erik Erikson (1950). This stage typifies the conflicts of adolescence. Like the other stages (see 'Eriksonian stages of psychosocial development'), this stage, too, is conceived in terms of two potential outcomes that are polar opposites of each other. The fortunate outcome of this stage is the consolidation of ego identity. This is 'the accrued confidence that the inner sameness and continuity prepared in the past are matched by the sameness and continuity of one's meaning for others, as evidenced in the tangible promise of a career' (pp. 261–262). The danger of this state is role confusion. This is manifested as the inability to settle on a vocational choice, and continued vulnerability to the whims of cliques and crowds. A tendency towards delinquent behaviour and psychotic-like episodes may also be evident.

Idolization: Masud Khan's (1979) term for a particular kind of treatment by the mother of her child, in which she lavishes intense body care on the latter but in a rather impersonal way, treating the child as her 'thing-creation' rather than as an emergent person with his or her subjectivity. 'Idolization', often lurking in the developmental background of perversions and perverse characters, is distinct from 'idealization' (see separate entry). Idealization is an intrapsychic process. Idolization, in contrast, is 'an explicit over-cathexis of an external actual object and is sustained by elaborate ego attitudes' (p. 12) on the mother's part.

If-only fantasy: see '"Someday . . ." and "If only" fantasies'.

Illusion–disillusion: according to Donald Winnicott (1953), the transition from illusion to disillusion is a fact of childhood development. 'The mother's adaptation to the infant's needs, when good enough, gives the infant the illusion that there is an external reality that corresponds to the infant's capacity to create' (p. 239). The next step is disillusionment, which is a gradual process with no definite end point. This corresponds with the mother's graduated de-adaptation and is essential because 'a too perfect adaptation to need, continued too long is tantamount to magic, and inhibits the capacity to separate' (p. 238). Winnicott emphasized that the task of reality-acceptance is never completed and 'no human being is free from the strain of related inner and outer reality, and that relief from this strain is provided by an intermediate area of experience which is not challenged (arts, religion, etc.)' (pp. 240–241).

Illusion of genetic immortality: Calvin Colarusso's (1997) term for the subjective sense of exhilaration people feel upon the birth of grandchildren. It is as if a grandchild assures us of going on despite mortality. What actually happens is this: by midlife, we can sense our mortality and by late life we can even envision our children's mortality, but at no point can we think of a grandchild's death. As a result, we feel as if we have defeated death after all. A magical repair of the most fundamental threat to narcissism thus takes place, and one begins to feel as if one has defied the limits of life, as if one would go on forever. This sense produces equanimity and bliss and is called the 'illusion of genetic immortality' by Colarusso.

Imaginary: see 'Real, symbolic, and imaginary'.

Imaginary companions: beginning with Otto Rank's (1914) early work on the 'double' and its later elaboration by Sigmund Freud (1919h) in his paper on the 'uncanny', the theme of 'imaginary companions', 'imaginary twins' and 'doubles of the self' (*Doppelganger*) has repeatedly arrested the attention of psychoanalysts. The most prominent contributions to the topic are those of (1) Donald Winnicott (1945), who regarded imaginary companions to be 'other selves of a highly primitive type' (p. 151) magically created as a defence against anxieties of integration; (2) Wilfred Bion (1950), who viewed an 'imaginary twin' to be a device used as an obstacle to understanding splitting and projective identification; (3) Selma Fraiberg (1959), who emphasized the development-facilitating role of imaginary companions of

childhood, and (4) Sheldon Bach (1977), who shed light on the phenomenon from the perspective of narcissistic disturbances of consciousness. A different, but none the less important and overlapping vantage point, is evident in the literature on dissociative disorders; the concepts of 'alter' or 'personification' are especially pertinent in this context (see entry on 'dissociative self').

Imaginary twin: see 'Imaginary companions'.

Immediacy: the case for the need of 'immediacy' in an interpretation to be meaningful was made most clearly by James Strachey in 1934. He stated that 'every mutative interpretation must be emotionally "immediate"; the patient must experience it as something actual (and) of a certain intensity' (p. 218). This well-accepted idea has found its clearest explication in Stephen Appelbaum's (2000) work on 'evocativeness' (see separate entry). More recently, Warren Poland (2002a) has highlighted that 'immediacy' refers to something more than present tense; 'it suggests a present tense that carries emotional vividness' (p. 114). Poland goes on to add that 'immediacy speaks of the present, but with the intrinsic implication of a context of hidden affective meanings that transcend the manifest here and now; and those meanings are born out of urges, feelings, fantasies, and experiences alive from the past' (p. 115).

Impasse: according to Judy Kantrowitz (1993), intense resistances occupy centre stage in analysis when an analysand sees the analyst as having confimed 'a pre-existing belief that is central to, and possibly the basis of, the patient's primary conflict or primary area of difficulty' (p. 1022). If such resistances can be worked through, a crucial piece of analytic work gets accomplished. However, if they remain unanalysed, a situation of an 'impasse' develops; often the patient drops out of treatment at this juncture. Such a predicament usually results from 'our insufficient knowledge about the patient, limitations in our theory or technique, or countertransference interference' (p. 1022). The patient's own intolerance of strong affects mobilized by resolving resistances around core conflicts can also contribute the development of an impasse.

Impingement: Donald Winnicott's (1960, 1962) term for environmental acts and events that disrupt the infant's (and, later, the child's) authentic 'going-on-being' (see separate entry). Not all 'impingement' is bad. A small amount can be assimilated and lead to ego growth. Premature and intense 'impingement', however, causes the infant to become reactive and thus leads to the formation of 'false self'. Sustained impingement can lead to fragmentation of the personality.

Implicit relational knowing: psychoanalytically-informed child observation has revealed that infants employ a sort of relational knowledge of anticipation in interacting with their caregivers (Sander, 1988; Tronick, 1989). These configurations of adaptive strategies constitute the foundations of subsequent 'implicit relational knowing' (Stern et al., 1998). Such knowledge is not symbolically represented in the mind and pertains to what is called 'procedural' or 'implicit memory' (see the entry on 'explicit and implicit memory'). In the intersubjective view of the analytic dialogue, the patient's 'implicit relational knowing' is as important a source of data for the analyst as are his free associations.

Imposture and fraudulence: Karl Abraham (1925b) wrote the first psychoanalytic paper on the psychology of the impostor. He regarded the underlying problem here to be a lack of development of genuine object cathexis since the individual, as a child, had himself been hated by others. Such an individual had also failed to develop and master the ordinary feelings characteristic of the Oedipus complex. A 'regressive narcissistic charge of the ego' (p. 299) along with a tendency to seek revenge developed instead. The urge to demonstrate that one was 'lovable' to everybody led to glibness and charm, and the wish for revenge led to betraying others. A cycle of seduction and betrayal was thus established. Subsequent psychoanalytic study of fraudulence, inauthenticity, and imposture has evolved along three lines which associate these character traits with (1) antisocial character, with emphasis upon disturbance of identity and associated superego defects (Eissler, 1949; Lampl de Groot, 1949; Kernberg, 1975, 1984) (2) narcissistic character where 'forward projection of narcissism' (see separate entry) has failed to occur due to the over-seduction by the mother and the associated devaluation of the father (Chasseguet-Smirgel, 1984; Lafarge, 1995), and (3) defensive repudiation of authenticity due to castration anxiety (Gediman, 1985). See also the related entry on 'Transferences of deception'.

Impotence: see 'Sexual dysfunction'.

Impulse: see 'Instinctual impulse'.

Impulse neurosis: does not refer to the generalized impulsivity seen in association with border-line, antisocial, and infantile characters, but to the repetitive break-through of a specific impulse in an otherwise integrated personality. This may involve gambling, drinking, sexual promiscuity, lying, and stealing apparently useless objects ('kleptomania') on impulse. However, repeated acts of generosity and of saying 'yes' to anything asked might also represent an 'impulse disorder'. These impulses are (1) ego syntonic, (2) irresistible, (3) pleasurable, and (4) relatively unmodified expressions of what remains repressed at other moments. Their leaping into action is because of selective weakness of regulating mechanisms and not the result of a tedious compromise formation on the ego's part. Thus, they differ from compulsive acts, although the prefix 'compulsive' is often—erroneously—applied to such acts of gambling, promiscuity, lying, etc. In the words of Sir Aubrey Lewis, the doyen of descriptive psychiatry in England, 'the more enjoyable an act, the less likely it is to be compulsive in origin' (1936, p. 326). Finally, impulsive actions are distinguished in Burness Moore and Bernard Fine's (1990) glossary on the grounds that the former lack an organized fantasy, while the latter result from 'dealing with an organized fantasy through substitutive action' (p. 95).

Inactment: Jessica Benjamin's (2007) term for 'those enactments that are still born, because their content is hidden by inaction, deliberate avoidance of the clash or rupture' (p. 61). The ebb and flow of attunement within the clinical dyad at times reaches the bank of 'enactment' (see separate entry) and at other times the shore of detachment, boredom, and 'inactment'.

In-and-out programme: Harry Guntrip's (1969) designation of the 'chronic dilemma in which the schizoid individual is placed, namely that he can neither be in a relationship with another person nor out of it, without risking the loss of both his object and himself' (p. 36). The origin of this problem is preoedipal. Its result is that the individual feels utterly lost when separated from his love object and enslaved when reunited with it. Therefore he oscillates between seeking security through attachment and autonomy through breaking off that very attachment. Notably, Guntrip's eloquent description preceded by six years the delineation of 'separation–individuation' (see separate entry) by Margaret Mahler (1958); it is conflicts around this developmental task that seem to underlie the 'in-and-out programme'.

Incest: refers to sexual acts between family members especially those closely linked on a biological basis. While the outer limit up to which the taboo against such sexuality extends and the number and kind of relatives susbsumed under it varies with different religions, eras, and legal systems, there seems to be a universal prohibition on sexual activity between parents and children, and between siblings. The fact, however, is that such acts occur, and do so with alarming frequency (Fischer, 1991; Kramer & Akhtar, 1991). They occur in dysfunctional families and often in a setting of multiple traumatogeneic factors (e.g., emotional neglect, physical abuse, parental alcoholism). From Sandor Ferenczi's (1933) pioneering observations on the deleterious impact of the sexual abuse of children, through the poignant and clinically instructive early contributions by Marvin Margolis (1977, 1984), Leonard Shengold (1980), Brandt Steele (1991), and Austin Silber (1979), to the more recent papers by Glen Gabbard and Stuart Twemlow (1994), and Howard Rudominer (2002), a voluminous literature has grown in this realm. The following picture emerges as a result. 'Incest' is inimical to healthy psychic development. It leads to profound disturbances, including life-long guilt, whereby the abused child takes on the responsibility of the parental misdeed; Sandor Ferenczi's (1933) 'confusion of tongues' and William Ronald Fairbairn's (1940) 'moral defence' are concepts highly pertinent to this development (see separate entries). Victims of incest are filled with dread and hatred, not only for their abuser, but also for the parent who, by his or her silence, absence, or active refusal to acknowledge the abuse, colluded with the perpetrator. Their lives are often replete with sadomasochistic tendencies, defects of self esteem, sexual dysfunction, and vulnerability to psychosomatic phenomena, accidents, rape, injuries, depression, and even suicide. Some victims display a certain self-reliance, ambition, vigilance, perseverance and tenacious pursuit of knowledge. Much psychic pain lurks underneath, however. Treatment-wise, there is no uniform approach for incest victims, since their psychopathology, level of character organization, life narrative, and transferences vary. However, there does seem to be the need for an explicit validation of the patient's trauma; the usual analyst explanation of defensive repudiations and distortions, and the intermingling of fantasy and reality must take place with the joint acceptance of the veracity of the patient's actual trauma. More than ordinary vigilance towards the potential for boundary violations and countertransference enactments in general also seem needed here. One countertransference problem that often crops up is the analyst's inability to recognize, or even suspect, that incest has occurred in the patient's childhood. This is more marked when the perpetrator was the patient's mother (Kramer, 1991). To be sure, mother–son incest is rare, and only four cases of actual sexual intercourse between them have been reported in the psychoanalytic literature (Margolis, 1991; Shengold, 1989; Gabbard & Twemlow 1994; Rudominer, 2002). But subtle forms of sexual overstimulation of children by mothers are not uncommon; these might go unrecognized due to countertransference blind spots (Kramer, 1991). See the related entry on 'object-coercive doubting'.

Incest barrier: safeguarding the survival-related necessity of bonds with close family members (especially the mother) and accepting the harsh, but ultimately useful, realities of the oedipal situation, children—and, later adults—develop a psychic fence, so to speak, which forever bars them from choosing incestuous (actually or symbolically via displacement) objects as sexual partners.

Incestuous failure: Michael Conran's (1976) term for the maternal incapacity to enjoy the sensual pleasures of the bodily care of her infant. Such failure on the mother's part to take sexual possession of her infant leads, paradoxically, to the child's difficulty to assume control of his body later on. According to Conran, before a child 'can claim ownership, there has to be a sense of something to own, which arises, in part at least, from successful stimulation by mother in the course of attachment' (p. 480).

Inconstant object: Harold Blum's (1981a) term for an ambivalently loved object that is felt to be both persecutory and highly needed. Such an object cannot be allowed to have an independent existence. The threat of betrayal by it must be tenaciously maintained. This constant fear of abandonment is the aggressive reciprocal of 'libidinal object constancy' (Mahler, Pine, & Bergman, 1975) and a desperate effort to preserve an illusory constant while unremittingly fearing betrayal and loss. Indeed, it is the very relentlessness of such dread that becomes a psychological constant of sorts. In the clinical setting, this translates into a rigid paranoid transference (see entry on 'Transferences of hatred'), which secretly provides structural stability to the patient. In a related spirit, a character in Harold Pinter's play *No Man's Land* (1975) says 'I have never been loved. From this, I derive my strength' (p. 30).

Incorporation: see 'Internalization'.

Indirect countertransference: see 'Countertransference'.

Individuation: see 'Separation–individuation'.

Industry *vs.* inferiority: this is the fourth of the eight stages of psychosocial development described by Erik Erikson (1950). It typifies the consolidation (or otherwise) of a sense of workmanship and, through it, a feeling of efficacy. Like the other stages (see 'Eriksonian stages of psychosocial development'), this stage, too, is conceived in terms of two potential outcomes that are polar opposites of each other. The fortunate outcome is that the child learns to apply himself to tasks at hand and can become 'an eager and absorbed unit of a productive situation' (p. 259). Erikson evoked Ives Hendrick's (1943a,b) description of work-related pleasure of the ego to buttress his ideas in this regard. He also noted that the stage of 'industry *vs.* inferiority' is comparable to the psychosexual phase of 'latency' (see separate entry). It is decisive in laying down the foundations of a work ethic. Problems negotiating this stage result in inability to devote sustained attention to projects assigned by others or chosen by oneself. The result is a sense of inferiority.

Inexact interpretation: Edward Glover (1931) noted that while a patently inaccurate interpretation is usually rejected by the patient, a slightly 'inexact interpretation' might have a positive therapeutic impact. He distinguished 'inexact interpretation' from 'incomplete interpretation' on the grounds that the former was content with not unearthing the pertinent unconscious fantasies, while the latter merely postponed that work after meeting a strong resistance. The 'inexact interpretation', based as it was on the understanding of derivative phenomena alone, created the possibility of the patient using such 'interpretation' as 'ego-sytonic displacement system' (p. 410). In other words, it helps the patient to form a new compromise formation that is healthier than his original symptoms.

Infancy: variously described as incorporating 'the oral stage and the beginning of the anal stage' (Eidelberg, 1968, p. 191) and the period 'from conception to three years of age' (Moore & Fine, 1990, p. 96), 'infancy' refers to the earliest period of childhood. Its main characteristics are a slow and progressive move from total dependence, poor reality testing, rudimentary self-awareness, weak ego controls, and reliance upon sensori-motor cognition to relative dependence, well-developed reality testing, self and object differentiation, emergence of a coherent self, strengthening of the ego and the development of defences, and increasing dominance of representational intelligence.

The psychological tasks of 'infancy' are too numerous to list here, and their description is scattered through out this glossary. See, especially, the entries on 'dependence', 'dual unity', 'infantile amnesia', 'infantile omnipotence', 'mother–infant symbiosis', 'mother–infant synchrony', 'object constancy', 'organizers of the psyche', 'separation–individuation', 'smiling response', 'stranger anxiety', and so on.

Infantile amnesia: term used by Sigmund Freud (1905e, 1924d) to denote the ubiquitous 'forgetting' of early childhood events. Such elimination from consciousness (1) is not based upon functional immaturity of the brain, (2) is caused by repression of the ideas and affects associated with traumatic events of that era, (3) is a bedrock for all later amnesia, and (4) extends from the earliest infancy to the dissolution of the oedipus complex and the beginning of the latency period. Subsequent authors have quibbled about the precise age up to which such infantile or 'childhood amnesia' extends, with Franz Alexander (1948) restricting it to six and Ludwig Eidelberg (1968) to eight years of age. They agree, however, that the 'infantile amnesia' allows some fragmentary recollections to survive and that such residues frequently become the nidus of 'screen memories' (see separate entry). The contemporary view (Levin, 1995; Zimmer, Bookstein, Kenny, and Kraeber, 2005) also holds that the inability of the developing brain to record events so they can be properly recalled later is also, at least partly, responsible for 'infantile amnesia'.

Infantile catastrophe: term coined by Wilfred Bion (1962b, 1963) to denote the overwhelming of the rudimentary ego by a trauma that cannot be brought under the omnipotent organizing control of thinking. This differentiates it from 'infantile neurosis' (see separate entry) which is an organized construction of compromises between the child's wishes, fantasies, and fears involving his primary objects. The 'infantile castastrophe' lacks ego participation, which the 'infantile neurosis' does not.

Infantile dependence: see 'Dependence'

Infantile neurosis: term introduced by Sigmund Freud (1909b, 1918b) to subsume the universal fantasies stirred up by a child's encounter with the 'Oedipus complex' (see separate entry) and the conflicts attendant upon them. These consist of the child's puzzlement and curiosity about the nature of the parental relationship and his or her position *vis-à-vis* that relationship. Rivalry with the same-sex parent and jealousy of the opposite sex parent follow and are associated with castration anxiety. Internalization of parental authority moves the conflict from outside to inside the psyche. Fear of parental punishment is now felt as guilt, or the superego's rejecting attitude towards the ego. Sexual and hostile wishes involving parents are renounced and what remains of them undergoes repression. This nuclear conflict, with its psychically structuralizing aspects, is called the 'infantile neurosis'. While generally it is not a symptomatic condition but an internal state of affairs, exceptions in this regard do exist (Kolansky, 1960), the precise constellation of which gives shape to later, adult neuroses as well as to character traits. During analytic treatment, 'infantile neurosis' is reactivated in transference and is then resolved to a greater degree. While Freud emphasized only its oedipal origins, later contributors (Tolpin, 1970; Khan, 1971; Loewald, 1974; Ritvo, 1974; Mahler, Pine, & Bergman, 1975) suggested that 'infanitle neurosis' also draws tributaries from preoedipal development.

Infantile omnipotence: while Sigmund Freud had noted the omnipotence of thought in obsessional neurosis and religion (1912–1913), it was Sandor Ferenczi (1913, 1923) who first elucidated the omnipotence that accompanies the infantile lack of perception of objects. The ego, at this stage, is not separated from the external world and views it as a part or extension of its self. With the arousal of need tensions which cannot be relieved by one's self, existence of external objects can no longer be denied. 'Infantile omnipotence' is punctured. This is a gradual process, however. Among the subsequent contributions to this topic, the following six appear to be the most prominent: (1) the elucidation of 'primary narcissism' (see separate entry) and its impact on object choices (Freud, 1914c), (2) the displacement of omnipotence from self to parents and then to God (Freud, 1927c), (3) the fear of omnipotent destructiveness via 'phantasy' (see separate entry) and its subsequent impact on psychic structure and defensive constellations (Klein, 1935, 1940), (4) the role of the mother in allowing a child to emerge from his 'primary omnipotence' at his own pace and with the aid of 'transitional objects' and 'transitional phenomena' (Winnicott, 1953), (5) the regressive emergence of megalomania in psychotic states (Fenichel, 1945; Arieti, 1974; Searles, 1960), and (6) the developmentally necessary aspects of feeling omnipotent in early childhood and the finding of such bliss in 'mother–infant symbiosis' (Mahler, Pine, & Bergman, 1975). All these contributors agree that there is such a phenomenon as 'infantile omnipotence', that it gradually recedes, that its sudden rupture is dramatic, and that recourse to it is evident in states of psychopathological regression. Defensive use of omnipotence against envy and dependence (Klein, 1935; Kernberg, 1975, 1984) is also noted. Less well known is the ego-sustaining role of transient and benign pockets of omnipotence in creativity (Kris, 1952) and healthy optimism (Akhtar, 1996).

Infantile personality: see 'Hysterical personality'.

Infantile psychotic self: see 'Psychotic core'.

Infantile sexuality: in his renowned monograph *Three Essays on the Theory of Sexuality*, Sigmund Freud (1905a) delineated the concept of 'infantile sexuality'. Also referred to as 'pregenital sexuality', it differs from adult sexuality in five ways; (1) excitement is not primarily located in the genitals but in other erogenous zones (e.g., mouth, anus), (2) excitement and satisfaction are not clearly demarcated, (3) autoerotism is an integral aspect, (4) energic rise of any kind (e.g., muscular activity, exercise of intellect, pain) can become a source of sexual excitement, and (5) the instinctual aim is not sexual intercourse but activities (e.g., sucking, looking, smelling) that would later play a role in the adulthood foreplay. The concept of pregenital or 'infantile sexuality' is an encompassing one and subsumes a large number of meta-concepts, separate entries on which can be found in this glossary. Most prominent among these are 'component instincts', 'erogenous zones', 'oral phase', 'anal phase', 'urethral eroticism', 'phallic phase', 'pregenital conversions', and 'forepleasure', though the concepts of 'fixation'and 'regression' also have links with the theory of 'infantile sexuality'.

Inhibition: psychoanalytic term for the inability to perform a psychomotor act owing to unconscious psychic conflicts. Sigmund Freud's (1926d) pathbreaking monograph *Inhibitions, Symptoms, and Anxiety* underscores six features of such 'restriction of ego function' (p. 89). According to Freud, an 'inhibition' (1) can affect any area of functioning, including love, sex, work, creativity, play, and so on, (2) may or may not have pathological consequences, (3) may represent the negative side of a symptom, (4) may reflect the relinquishment of a function because its exercise produces anxiety, (5) is often caused by the increase in the erogenicity of the organ involved in that particular function (e.g., hand in the act of writing), and (6) can serve the purpose of self-punishment and, through this, the appeasement of a superego opposed to the smooth execution of that particular function. Freud left the possibility open that 'generalized inhibitions of the ego' (p. 90) can result from quantitative factors alone. When the ego is overwhelmed (e.g., during grief), it can accomplish little else and appears to be inhibited. Freud's ideas about the aetiology of 'inhibition' have stood the test of time and later additions, including, for instance, the role of 'castration anxiety', 'separation guilt', and 'shame' (see separate entries) in casuing 'inhibitions', have been mere refinements of his fundamentally solid proposals in this regard.

Initiation fantasies: described by Milton Jucovy (1976), these fantasies occur in the setting of male transvestism and involve being tutored by seductive and glamorous women in the art of dressing and make-up so that one could achieve a truly feminine appearance. Ethel Person (1976) added that there are actually two versions of this fantasy. In one, initiation into cross-dressing is forced upon the protagonist by a dominant, big-breasted, booted phallic woman. In the other, a kindly woman dresses him in women's clothes to disguise him and save him from members of the Mafia who wish to kill him. The fantasy of performing sexual intercourse with a woman while dressed as a woman often accompanies 'initiation fantasies'.

Initiative *vs*. guilt: this is the third of the eight stages of psychosocial development described by Erik Erikson (1950). It typifies the consolidation (or otherwise) of a sense of agency and executive power. Like the other stages (see 'Eriksonian stages of psychosocial development'), this stage, too, is conceived in terms of two potential outcomes that are polar opposites of each other. The fortunate outcome is that the child develops a capacity for planning and undertaking a task for the sake of being active, and not merely as a gesture of defiance. 'In the boy, the emphasis remains on phallic-intrusive modes; in the girl it turns to modes of "catching" in more aggressive forms of snatching or in the milder form of making oneself attractive and endearing' (p. 255). Failure to negotiate this developmental stage manifests in a sense of guilt over one's goals and actions. A long-term consequence of this is ego inhibition or defensive over-activity.

Injustice collecting: see 'Oral triad'.

Innate knowledge: Melanie Klein (1927) proposed that the infant possesses 'innate knowledge' of certain basic human facts, especially those pertaining to sexual difference and childbirth. While others took exception to this, Klein's followers not only agreed with her, but advanced her ideas in this regard. Two prominent examples of this are Susan Isaacs' (1948) formulation of unconscious 'phantasy' (see separate entry), which implied an innate and somatic knowledge of aims and objects of instincts, and Wilfred Bion's (1962b) notion of 'pre-conception' which is ripe to be actualized by its encounter with a matching external object.

Inner sustainment: concept introduced by the Philadelphia-based analyst Leon Saul (1970) to describe how the continuance in the mind of positive early object relations (and their accompanying affects) helps in maintaining dignity, self-esteem, and perseverance under difficult circumstances. In the 'unsustained' individual, the fight/flight reactions to threats are tinged with negativity: fight becomes sadomasochistic and flight turns into apathetic withdrawal. In the individual with 'inner sustainment', the same reactions show a healthy attitude: fight leads to sublimation and flight to immersion in creativity. Saul's paper was based upon the analysis of Henri Parens, the well-known child analyst, who contributed a metapsychological essay on 'inner sustainment' to the same volume. Parens (1970) stated that at the core of 'inner sustainment' lay the internalization of early relationship with a benevolent mother; constitutional factors also played a role here. The 'collaboration' between Saul and Parens became explicit a few years later in the form of a co-authored book (Parens & Saul, 1971) on the vicissitudes of human dependence. More pertinent to the context of 'inner sustainment' is the fact that Parens (2007b) went on to write a poignant autobiographical account of his resilience as a child survivor some 36 years after his 'silent' elaboration of his analyst's ideas!

Insight: a metaphorical term for seeing 'with the eyes of the mind' (*Oxford English Dictionary*, 1980, p. 5337) or 'seeing intuitively' (*Webster's Ninth Collegiate Dictionary*, 1987, p. 626). Sigmund Freud used the word *Einsicht* or 'insight' for a patient's acknowledgement of the existence, severity, and significance of his problems. This is the way the term came to be used in general psychiatry, even though the concept was found to be far from simple. Distinctions between 'intellectual insight' and 'emotional insight' (with the former being cold and cerebral and the latter affectively meaningful) were soon added. The expression 'unconscious insight' also gained popularity for a while, but was regarded as tautological since 'insight' was conscious and the system Unconscious was supposed to know what it contains anyway (Zilboorg, 1952); more recently, André Green (2005) has revived the concept of 'unconscious insight' under the title of 'unconscious recognition' (see 'Recognition and misrecognition'). It was also debated whether psychoanalysis restores or creates insight. Anna Freud (1981b) took the latter position, and noted that those who have undergone a successful analysis often find themselves a bit apart, even isolated, from their unanalysed peers since they have acquired a new and deeper way of looking into themselves. In her characteristically lucid style, Miss Freud delineated how ego defences hamper insight, how latency is a missed opportunity to gain insight into infantile conflicts, and how adolescence is an intellectual flirtation with insight. She noted that, while the capacity for deepening insight into oneself ceases with adulthood (except with the help of analysis), poets, creative artists, and 'some rare individuals driven by the wish for discovery and regard for truth' (p. 249) can overcome this obstacle. Other developmental and phenomenological aspects of 'insight' have been elucidated in a special section in 1981's *Psychoanalytic Study of the Child*, with contributions from Samuel Abrams, Charles Mangham, George Pollock, Leonard Shengold, and Arthur Valenstein. Harold Blum (1979), Paul Meyerson (1965), and Warren Poland (1988) are among others who have made contributions to the concept of insight. Together, these contributions regard 'insight' to be an evolving process which is the 'condition, catalyst, and consequence of the psychoanalytic process' (Blum, 1979, p. 66). All in all, there are three shifts discernible in the place of insight within clinical psychoanalysis over time (1) the view that insight is imparted by the analyst has given way to the view that the patient's insights and the analyst's insights are in constant interaction and the ultimate insight is the result of this interaction, (2) insight is no longer considered the end-point, but its assimilation and integration is, and (3) insight is certainly regarded to be very important, but it is no longer felt to be the only, or perhaps even the main, curative agent in the clinical work of psychoanalysis (see also the panel report by Blacker, 1981).

Insight addiction: see 'Analyst induced termination'.

Insight-orientated psychotherapy: see 'Psychoanalytic psychotherapy'.

Instinct: Sigmund Freud (1905a, 1915c) employed the term *Treib* (rendered by his pre-eminent translator James Strachey as 'instinct') 'as a concept on the frontier between the mental and the somatic, as the physical representative of the stimuli originating from within the organism and reaching the mind, and as a measure of the demand made upon the mind for work in consequence of its connection with the body' (1915c, pp. 121–122). Four important facts to keep in mind regarding this concept are the following: (1) the term 'instinct', as it is used in psychoanalysis, has a connotation quite different from its usage in biology, especially in the study of animal behaviour. In psychoanalysis, 'instinct' refers to the psychic representation (mostly through wishes) of the stimuli arising from somatic processes. No specific behavioural response is assigned to an 'instinct'. This sharply contrasts with the ethological use of the term, which invariably implies a specific and reflexive behavioural pattern; (2) an instinct has four aspects: source (somatic foundation), impetus (psychic energy invested in it), aim (the action that will lead to its discharge), and object (the provider of its gratification); (3) while the term 'instinct' pervades the *Standard Edition* of Freud's works, later theoreticians (e.g., Hartmann, 1948; Schur, 1966) substituted it with 'instinctual drive' (see separate entry) noting the latter's better capacity to integrate the biopsychological features of the concept; (4) Freud's (1915c) 'first dual instinct theory' proposed 'sexual instinct' and 'self-preservatory' instinct to be the two instincts, but his 'second dual instinct theory' changed this to the formulation of 'life instinct' and 'death instinct' (see separate entries on each and also on 'instinct theory').

Instinct for mastery: first proposed by Sigmund Freud in 1905a, the 'instinct for mastery' is a non-sexual force whose aim is to seize control of, or dominate, objects in external reality. It can, secondarily, get caught up in other instinctual agendas and serve sadistic purposes. Freud (1912–1913) later related 'instinct for mastery' with the concept of 'activity' (see 'Activity and passivity'), while extending its scope to inner states and excitements. These ideas found a most enthusiastic exponent in Ives Hendrick (1943a, 1943b), who suggested that the 'instinct for mastery' (1) reflects an inborn need to control the environment, (2) is non-sexual but can become sexualized, and (3) yields a special kind of pleasure, i.e., that derived from a task well performed (see also George Klein's 1976 work in this context).

Instinct theory: over the course of many papers, Sigmund Freud (1900a, 1905a, 1915c) enunciated what retrospectively came to be known as

'Freud's first dual instinct theory'. This 'dual instinct theory' proposed that there were two fundamental motivating forces: 'sexual instinct' and 'self-preservatory instinct' (also called 'ego instinct'). The former sought erotic pleasure and served the goal of species propagation. The latter sought safety and growth and served the goal of self-preservation. Some years later, Freud (1920g) revised his views. 'Freud's second dual instinct theory' classified instincts into 'life instinct' and 'death instinct' categories. The former subsumed the prior two categories of 'sexual' and 'self-preservatory' instincts. The latter was a radical and new concept involving a 'daemonic force' (Freud, 1920g, p. 35), which searched for psychosomatic quiescence and, at its deepest core, sought to reduce the animate to its previous inorganic state. Three important shifts happened as a result of Freud's move from the first to the second theory: (i) aggression, which has been seen as a subsidiary of 'sexual instinct', in the first theory came to be viewed as the outward manifestation of the 'death instinct' in the second theory; (ii) the earlier formulation that sadism was primary and masochism its inverted and secondary form was reversed, with the concept of 'death instinct' placing masochism to be the primary phenomenon and sadism its externalized consequence; and (iii) the resulting brou-ha-ha about the 'death instinct' and whether 'aggression' was or was not an instinct *per se* (see Akhtar, 1995 for details of this controversy), coupled with the ongoing enthusiasm about 'sexual instinct', led to the unfortunate neglect of the study of 'ego instincts'. Yet, like repressed material, the concept of 'ego instincts' kept seeking readmission into the main corpus of psychoanalytic thought; its re-emergence is most obvious in the views of the British independent analysts (e.g., Balint, Winnicott) and the self-psychology of Heinz Kohut (1977). In a tongue-in-cheek statement, Salman Akhtar (1999b) concluded that 'had Freud gone from his first dual instinct theory not to his second dual instinct theory but to a "triple instinct theory" (sexual, aggressive, and ego instincts), all this theoretical conundrum might have been avoided' (p. 200).

Instinctual drive: although James Strachey, the main translator of Sigmund Freud's work, rendered the latter's concept of *Trieb* as 'instinct' (see separate entry), later analysts, especially Heinz Hartmann (1948) and Max Schur (1966), preferred to use the term 'instinctual drive'. To them, 'instinct' and 'drive' used in isolation appeared too biological and too psychological, respectively. 'Instinctual drive' seemed a good compromise. It retained the somatic underpinnings of *Trieb* while

delinking the concept from its reflexive and behavioural connotations. The next step was to employ 'libidinal instinctual drive' and 'aggressive instinctual drive' in the place of corresponding 'instincts'. A legacy of this conceptual and linguistic shift is evident in the fact that Fred Pine's (1988) 'four psychologies of psychoanalysis' include a 'drive psychology', not an 'instinct psychology'. Matters, however, go further than this. The greater 'psychologization' of *Trieb* also contributed to the controversy over the origins of 'instinctual drives' with some theorists (e.g., Brenner, 1982) regarding them as inborn while others (Kernberg, 1982) proposed that affects 'are the building blocks, or constitutes of drives' (p. 908). Finally, the label 'instinctual drive' served to restrict the range of motivations that could be considered to constitute a 'drive'. Those derived purely from experience; for instance, the seeking of power and fame could not be accorded the status of a 'drive' even though it might be fuelled by instinctual sources. The fate of motivations originating from 'ego instincts' (itself a concept eclipsed by sexual and aggressive drives) became questionable within this classical metapsychological paradigm.

Instinctual energy: see 'Psychic energy'.

Instinctual impulse: Sigmund Freud's (1915c) term for a single unit of an instinct's action, a unit that carries an ideational representation and content. This distinguishes 'instinctual impulse' (*Triebregung*) from 'instinct' (*Trieb*) which is the fundamental source of such an impulse. However, Freud used the terms interchangeably at times (Laplanche & Pontalis, 1973, p. 223).

Integration: see 'Integration, personalization, and realization'.

Integration, personalization, and realization: three processes that, according to Donald Winnicott (1945), start soon after birth and constitute the psychic development of early infancy. (1) *Integration* involves bringing together of scattered bits and pieces of experience into a composite whole. This transforms experiences into personality, however rudimentary that might be at such an early stage of life. (2) *Personalization* happens when 'the person of the baby starts to be linked with the body and the body functions, with the skin as the limiting membrane' (p. 57). (3) *Realization* is said to have taken place when this psychosomatically anchored self begins to appreciate time, space, and other features of external reality. A good-enough mother–infant relationship is necessary for these processes to evolve. Lack of integration is evident in fragmented states of the self, lack of personalization in persistent psyche–soma split, and lack of realization in disorientating and psychotic anxieties.

Intellectualization: the term is used in three different ways in psychoanalysis. (1) the first is in the context of adolescence, during which the resurgence of instinctual (especially sexual tensions) is often channelled into mental activities and philosophical ruminations; a situation of what is colloquially called 'mental masturbation' thus prevails; (2) the second use of the term 'intellectualization' is in the context of psychoanalytic treatment, whereby the patient either always appears reasonable and refuses to allow emotionality to take over, or employs psychoanalytic jargon to explain away the emotions that are getting mobilized; and (3) finally, the term is used in connection with obsessional character style, whereby a preference for logic and rationality leads to a constriction of affective life and spontaneity. Seen this way, 'intellectualization' is the exact opposite of 'affectualization' (see separate entry) seen in hysterical personalities.

Interactional field: see 'Bipersonal field'.

Intergenerational transmission of trauma: see 'Transgenerational transmission of trauma'.

Interject: term coined by Christopher Bollas (1999) to distinguish a particular type of object representation in the subject's psyche. Unlike the usual 'introject' (see separate entry), which is the result of gradual and 'willing' internalization of an object representation, 'interject' arises out of a forcible and traumatic insertion of parental projections or highly disturbing external realities.

Intermediate area of experience: see 'Potential space' and 'Transitional space'.

Intermediate level of character pathology: designation used by Otto Kernberg (1970) to distinguish a group of personality disorders from the 'higher level' (including hysterical and obsessional personalities) and 'lower level' (including borderline, antisocial, paranoid, and schizoid personalities) of character pathology. At the 'intermediate level', the superego is more punitive but less integrated than it is at the 'higher level' character pathology. Thus, vulnerability to paranoid trends, contradictions in the value system, and severe mood swings appear on the clinical horizon. Defensively, reaction formations predomi-nate and there is some defensive splitting of the ego in limited areas. Pregenital conflicts dominate the scene but, to a considerable extent, are regressive escapes from unbearable oedipal anxieties. Object relations are more or less like the 'higher level' pathology, i.e., capable of tolerating ambivalence and of deep involvement with stress. Kernberg included sadomasochistic, passive aggressive, narcissistic, and some of the better functioning infantile or 'hysteroid' (Easser & Lesser, 1965) personalities in this group. He added that many patients with a well-crystallized sexual deviation that remains within the confines of a stable object relationship also belong in this category.

Intermittent decathexis: described by Robert Furman and Erna Furman (1984) 'intermittent decathexis' is a particular type of family dysfunction involving a frequent and sudden loss of all interest in the child on the part of the parent. Occurring on an unconscious level, such withdrawl of investment is shockingly complete. There are other characteristics to it as well: 'it occurs in the span of a moment; it is not associated with pain; it does appear to be adaptive; it is not undertaken at the behest of reality, and of furthering healthy development' (p. 340). The result of it is reactive hostility and depression in the child. An occasional reversal of roles in the form of 'mothering in order to be mothered' (p. 341) also is witnessed in older children.

Internal developmental conflict: see 'Developmental conflict'.

Internal objects: Melanie Klein (1932, 1935, 1940, 1946) proposed that the infant, under the pressure of his drives, 'creates' and 'discovers' objects in external reality that correspond to his needs. Thus, hateful feelings create persecutory objects and loving feelings create idealized objects. These structures are then brought inside the psyche by the processes of 'incorporation' and 'introjection' (see entry on 'Internalization') and become 'internal objects'. Now their cognitive and affective memory can be readily evoked and manipulated. Four aspects of such intrapsychic prescences are: (1) they can be 'all good' or 'all bad', i.e., exist as 'part objects', or they can be integrated into a composite, post-ambivalent configuration; (2) they carry on emotional dialogue with parts of the self and can have impact upon self-esteem; 'good' internal objects make one feel pride and 'bad' internal objects make one feel remorse, guilt, and shame; (3) they can come into conflict with each other and can be re-projected outwards, and finally (4) they can have impact upon external behaviour of an individual. While these Kleinian ideas regarding 'internal objects' have become the most significant in the use of this term, the fact remains that William Ronald Fairbairn (1944) had elaborated a somewhat different theory of 'internal objects'. The key feature of this theory is that objects are not internalized alone, but in association with the fragment of ego that is involved in interaction with them (see 'Fairbairn's description of the endopsychic structure'). In today's terminology (Jacobson, 1964; Kernberg, 1975), these units will be known as internal self- and object representations (see related entry on 'Introjects' also).

Internal saboteur: see 'Fairbairn's description of endopsychic structure'.

Internalization: an inclusive term referring to processes that lead to the psychological contents of significant others being brought inside one's mind and, to a greater or lesser degree, made part of it. Three separate concepts are subsumed under the term 'internalization'. These include (1) *incorporation*: expression first used by Sigmund Freud (1915c) in the context of what he called the 'oral phase' of development. 'Incorporation' meant bringing objects from the external world inside oneself in order to achieve mastery over them, make them a part of oneself, and thus destroy them. The term had a developmental anchor in the infant's tendency to put things in his mouth. It gradually developed a metaphorical reign over all forms of taking objects in (e.g., visual incorporation, anal incorporation); (2) *introjection*: term introduced by Sandor Ferenczi (1909) for a process opposite of projection and later adapted by Karl Abraham (1924) and Melanie Klein (1937). This term had lesser somatic foundations and involved taking the whole or part object in. Its end products ('introjects') could reside in different parts of the psychic structure (e.g., ego introjects, superego introjects). However, the organized cluster of memory traces consequent upon introjection remained unassimilated into the total self image; (3) *identification*: a process which brings into the psyche less concrete and more role-orientated aspects of significant others in relationship to oneself. Identifications, unlike introjects, do not feel like a 'foreign body' in the self and are more likely to be ego-syntonic and in harmony with the individual's self-image. Matters in this realm are far from simple, though. There are four sources of confusion: (1) processes and their results are often ill-demarcated. Thus, the world 'identification' is used for both a process of internalization and the psychostruc-tural change it causes ; in a brief but theoretically rich essay, Robert Knight (1940) elucidates such confusions and underscores that 'identification' is 'an accomplished fact, not act, and may result from several different mechanisms acting separately or together' (p. 341); (2) some authors (e.g., Kernberg, 1975; Meissner, 1979) consider the various internalization processes as categorically distinct from each other while others (Behrends & Blatt, 1985) hold internalization to be one and same process, which appears different at different levels of development and self and object differentiation, (3) some authors (Rycroft, 1968) reserve the use of 'incorporation' for oral fantasies and 'introjection' for the psychically altering impact of object relations, (4) there is disagreement over the extent to which internalization reflects actual experiences of childhood; Melanie Klein (1937, 1940) and Harry Stack Sullivan (1953) represent two extreme poles here, with the former emphasizing drive-impelled 'phantasy' (see separate entry) and the latter parent–child interaction in reality. Occupying an intermediate place in this theoretical spectrum are Edith Jacobson (1964) and Otto Kernberg (1975), who propose that while actual relationships of the child do give rise to them, the shape of internal object relations is also affected by the state of ego apparatus and the economy of drives.

Internalized conflicts: see 'Conflict'.

Internalized homophobia: the term 'homophobia' was introduced by Kenneth Smith (1971) to designate rational and negative attitudes and beliefs about homosexual individuals. Donald Moss (1997) refined the definition to include 'the entire spectrum of conscious and unconscious fantasy–feeling–idea–sentiment through which persons structure and are structured by an avoidant–perverse relation to all things sensed as homosexual' (p. 203). He added that the HIV epidemic has led to an increase in 'homophobia'. When such prejudicial attitudes are incorporated by homosexual men and women themselves, the condition of 'internalized homophobia' (Maylon, 1982; Friedman & Downey, 1998) results. Self doubt and self hatred then develop and impede psychosexual functioning and interpersonal adjustment.

Interpersonal psychoanalysis: refers to the psychoanalytic school originated by the quintessentially American psychiatrist–psychoanalyst, Harry Stack Sullivan. The fact that Sullivan did not present his ideas in a final and systematized form, worked in defiance of the conservative norms of North American psychoanalysis, and created his own terminology contributed to his lack of acceptance. His dense style of writing (Sullivan, 1947, 1953), which would have hardly deterred the French, also proved a liability in his homeland. At the same time, his views were valuable and most probably contain the roots of the 'relational' and 'intersubjective' approaches in vogue today. Essentially, the proposals of 'interpersonal psychoanalysis' are (1) striving for security and the satisfaction of drives are indissolubly linked; (2) the integrated force of these impact upon the evolving interpersonal relationships and is affected by them in return; (3) what is called the 'self' is nothing but a collection of 'reflective appraisals' by early caretakers; (4) anxiety, a result of threat to safety and satisfaction, can only occur in an interpersonal context; (5) the self maintains its integrity by 'selective inattention' to those aspects of behaviour which stir up anxiety; (6) the foundation of moral concepts lies in the perceptions by the child of parental approval or disapproval; (7) sexuality is important, but not the central motivating force in life; (8) psychopathology results from the eruption of self states that were dissociated and the expression of which causes anxiety; (9) treatment ought to focus on the relational context of anxiety; and (10) as a result, active participation of the therapist is more desirable than his laid-back anonymity; countertransference plays a central informative and guiding role in treatment.

Interpretation: among the various 'interventions' (see separate entry) made by the analyst, 'interpretation' occupies the most important position. It refers to the analyst's verbally conveying to the patient his understanding of the patient's material. Central to this message is helping the patient become aware of some aspect of his mind (e.g., a feeling, fantasy, thought, impulse, inhibition) which was hitherto unconscious. 'Interpretation' is an unmasking and deciphering activity. Not surprisingly, Sigmund Freud (1900a) began using this term in the context of understanding dreams. Later contributors (Fenichel, 1941; Loewenstein, 1951; Shapiro, 1970; Brenner, 1976; Gill, 1982; Sandler & Sandler, 1983; Levy, 1984) refined the concept of 'interpretation' and added significant nuances. These include (1) formulating an 'interpretation' happens in steps; the analyst listens, collects information, pools the data, evolves patterns in his mind, comes up with 'conjectures' (Brenner, 1976) and 'inferences' (Ramzy & Shevrin, 1976). These lead to interventions that are best called 'preparations for interventions' (Loewenstein, 1951, p. 4); these include confrontation,

encouragement to elaborate upon what is coming to mind, and, above all, 'clarification' (see separate entry); (2) interpretation must proceed from surface to depth; what is known to the patient and what is currently on his mind must form the beginning point of the interpretive sojourn towards the depth (see the related entry on the 'three-box model of the mind'); (3) other variables contributing to such 'hierarchy of interpretation' (see separate entry) are the rules of addressing defence before the drive, fluid defences before rigid defences, transference over extratransference, and dynamic over genetic issues; (4) interpretation may be short or long, prosaic and routine or 'inspired' (Meltzer, 1979) and evocative; at times an action on the analyst's part might also have the effect of an 'interpretation' (see 'interpretive action'). During his days as a candidate in training, John Gedo (1997) is known to have asked Rudolph Loewenstein whether one can interpret by whistling; (5) 'interpretation' is a gradual, oft-repeated, and increasingly deepening process; 'a single interpretation, however, precise, inclusive, well phrased and well-timed can not produce a permanent beneficial alteration' (Brenner, 1976, p. 50); (6) correct interpretations enhance the knowledge of both the patient and the analyst; (7) symptomatic improvement is not a reliable indicator of correctness of 'interpretation' since the patient may get better from noninterpretive effects of analysis also, and a correct interpretation may lead to worsening via 'negative therapeutic reaction' (see separate entry); (8) the same applies to the patient's agreeing or disagreeing with the 'interpretation'; neither confirms or refutes its correctness'; (9) responses that do confirm the correctness of an 'interpretation' include the patient's recognition of what is conveyed with surprise, recall of a new memory that substantiates what has been said, a significant emotional reaction, a confirmatory dream in the subsequent days, outpouring of corroborative associations, and discovery of extra-analytic evidence supporting the 'interpretation'; (10) interpretations are of many types including 'transference interpretations', 'anagogic interpretation', 'extra transference interpretation', 'deep interpretation', and so on (see separate entry on each); Wilfred Bion (1974) also speaks of 'pure interpretation', which is free of contaminates of countertransferences, and (11) 'interpretations' can have the effect of 'suggestion' (see separate entry); this needs to be looked for and interpretatively handled itself.

Interpretive actions: Thomas Ogden's (1994) concept referring to the 'analyst's use of activity to convey specific aspects of his understanding of the transference–countertransference that can not be communicated to the patient in the form of verbally symbolic speech alone' (p. 135). Interpretive action differs from the analyst's use of action as a stop-gap measure to establish (or re-establish) optimal conditions for analytic work. It is a non-verbal intervention aimed at putting the analysand in contact with the unconscious goings-on in his mind at the moment.

Interpretive attitude: Warren Poland's (2002b) term for the analyst's ongoing stance of curiosity which serves as a background mental activity that gives rise to formal interpretations. This attitude is a constant, and is unconsciously communicated to the patient. Such persistent, even though silent, 'aiming towards understanding and insight is the essential factor that shapes the psychoanalytic situation and makes possible the psychoanalytic value both of non-interpretive, non-insight-oriented activities, and of formal declarative interpretations' (p. 817).

Interpretive enactment: see 'Enactment'.

Interpretive neutrality: see 'Neutrality'.

Inter-racial analysis: an expression involving Black and White clinical dyads that appeared in the North American psychoanalytic literature of late 1960s and early 1970s and then disappearred. This in itself raises questions behind which lurk several untold stories. Why did the term originate in North America and remain restricted in its use to American authors? Was it quintessentially American candour or provincial surprise that made the fact that the 'Negro' could be analysed, or even conduct an analysis, reportable phenomena? And, does the rapid disappearance of the term from the literature reflect that such clinical dyads are now commonplace and need little mention separately? Leaving such sociopolitical matters aside, a review of papers on this topic (Schachter & Butts, 1968; Fischer, 1971; Goldberg, Meyers, & Ziefman, 1974) reveals that the contribution of racial stereotypes to transference and countertransference phenomena were analysable. In fact, the racial disparity proved, at times, to be a catalyst for the evolving analytic process. It is also clear that obscuring or overestimating racial stereotypes by the analyst or patient complicates the analysis. Finally, it should be noted that, while the term 'inter-racial analysis' has vanished from analytic literature, there is a resurgence of interest in the impact of racial, ethnic, and cultural difference upon the analytic process and technique. In contrast to the literature of three or four decades ago, which was predominately written by white analysts, the current contributions have been made by African-American analysts (Holmes, 1992; Leary, 1995, 1997, 2006; Hamer, 2007). For further explanation of these contributions, see entries on 'Race and transference' and 'Racial fantasies'.

Intersubjectivity: while it was implicit in the writings of Harry Stack Sullivan (1953), Frieda Fromm-Reichman (1950), and Harold Searles (1965, 1979), the perspective of 'intersubjectivity' has been brought to prominence by Stephen Mitchell (1988, 1993), Thomas Ogden (1986, 1994), and Robert Stolorow and George Atwood (1978). In the USA especially, the intersubjective critique of the 'classical' psychoanalytic model's positivistic tradition has created quite an excitement. Jonathan Dunn (1995) has provided a succinct and sophisticated overview of this tension. Essentially, the intersubjective approach asserts that psychic phenomena cannot be understood in isolation from their interpersonal matrix. Far from being discrete entities within the patient's psyche, mental events are dialectically constructed experiences, specific and idiosyncratic to a particular interpersonal situation or clinical interaction. Each glimpse of a patient's psychic reality is therefore contextual. It is inevitably coloured by the analyst's subjectivity, which, in turn, is open to influence by the patient's inner experience. Viewed this way, countertransference is not merely a reaction to the patient's experience, but the totality of the analyst's subjective state, which works as an active constructing force of the analytic material as whole, including the transference. The analyst is not a blank screen for the patient's projections, nor is the patient a tabula rasa for the analyst's interpretive dictates. The subjectivities of the two are interlinked and any attempt to unmask a psychic reality of the patient that is independent of a particular interaction is epistemologically misguided.

Intersystemic conflict: see 'Conflict' and 'Structural conflict'.

Interventions: a generic term for all sorts of active endeavours on the analyst's part to facilitate and conduct the work of analysis. Broadly speaking, there are four types of interventions: (1) *Preparatory* (these include instructions regarding the 'fundamental rule' of free association, explanations regarding the overall framework of the analytic setting, acknowledging that it is an unusual type of dialogue, asking questions and gently confronting the patient with his or her contradictions), (2) *Affirmative* (these include facilitation of abreaction, empathic remarks, plausibility-rendering statements, validations of prejudice and misfortune), (3) *Interpretive* (these include comments that help to decipher concealed meanings in the patients' communications and can refer to genetic past, transference, or real current relationships) and (4) *Reconstructive* (these include attempts to create narratives for what might have taken place in the remote past and especially what escaped the patient's conscious attention and knowledge at the time of its occurrence). The work of an ongoing analysis employs these four types of intervention in as needed basis.

Intimacy *vs.* isolation: this is the sixth among the eight stages of psychosocial development described by Erik Erikson (1950). It typifies the consolidation (or otherwise) of young adulthood. Like the other stages (see 'Eriksonian stages of psychosocial development'), this stage, too, is conceived in terms of two potential outcomes that are polar opposites of each other. On the fortunate side is the development of the capacity for committing oneself to 'concrete affliations and partnerships and to develop the ethical strength to abide by such commitments, even though they may call for significant sacrifices and compromises' (p. 263). The solidarity of closed friendships, the experience of being inspired by mentors, and the pleasure of romantic and sexual union offer the individual opportunities for experiencing genuine intimacy. However, such experience tests the ego's resilience and, if the fear of ego loss is great, may lead to defensive withdrawal and self-absorption. The unfortunate outcome of this developmental stage is a deep sense of isolation.

Intimate edge: Darlene Ehrenberg's (1992) poetic designation for the ever-shifting, moment-to-moment mutual impact of the analyst and the patient upon each other that forms the fundamental unit of psychoanalytic data and its primary locus of intervention. Judicious 'self disclosure' (see separate entry) is often necessary in Ehrenberg's proposed method to unravel the knots of transference-countertransference impasses and confusions. It is only with a truthful focus on the relational foundations of the current affective experience that its earlier prototypes can be discerned, explicated, and mastered.

Intrafamilial hospitalism: see 'Hospitalism'

Intramural refuelling: Salman Akthar's (1999b) designation for the emotional sustenance immi-

grants draw from their contact with a homoethnic community. Comfort of such sort can be obtained from homoethnic friendships and by visiting homoethnic enclaves that are often bustling with familiar sounds, attires, and culinary aromas. Encounter with them symbolically brings one close not only to one's motherland, but, at the deepest layer of the psyche, to one's mother.

Intrapsychic terrorist organization: like a terrorist organization that seeks an idealized and impossible goal by violent means, an intrapsychic structure in some patients demands a total undoing of the effects of their childhood trauma, or even erasing its occurrence in the first place. This 'intrapsychic terrorist organization' (Akhtar, 1997) demands absolute devotion, exquisite empathy, and perfect love from the analyst and, lacking that, it attacks the latter. It also seeks to destroy those parts of the patient's own self that are aligned with the analyst and retain the capacity for mourning and compromise formation.

Intrasystemic conflict: see 'Conflict'.

Introject: term used for the end-product of the process of 'introjection' (see separate entry). An 'introject' comprises an organized cluster of memory traces, including a self representation, an object representation, and an affective tone of their connection. Introjects are less assimilated in the self-image than identifications; they tend to feel like 'foreign bodies' in the psyche and are vulnerable to externalization (see also 'Internal objects').

Introjection: see 'Internalization'.

Introvision: see 'Insight'

Inversion: see 'Homosexuality'.

Irony: defined as 'the use of words to express something other than, and especially the opposite of, their literal meanings' (*Merriam Webster's Collegiate Dictionary*, 1998, p. 619), 'irony' drew the attention of the two of the finest North American psychoanalysts: Roy Schafer and Martin Stein. Schafer (1970) included the 'ironic vision' among the four major perspectives on reality (the other three being the comic, romantic, and tragic). He characterized it by a readiness to seek out inconsistencies, ambiguities, and paradoxes. Yet, the 'ironic vision' is not cynical or mocking of the world at large. It keeps things in perspective and takes little for granted. By readily spotting the antithesis to any thesis, it 'tends to limit (not minimize) the scale of involvement in human difficulties of human existence' (p. 293). Stein (1985) elucidated the finer details of 'irony', especially as it pertains to the clinical encounter. He separated 'verbal irony' (i.e., use of one set of words to convey the meaning that is opposite) from 'situational irony' (i.e., the ambiguities and contradictions inherent in the psychoanalytic situation *per se*). With the help of evocative and convincing clinical material, Stein elucidated the defensive uses of 'irony' by the patient. He warned that, while an ironic stance on the analyst's part is helpful, even necessary, for understanding and interpreting transference, it can be used by him for defensive purposes as well.

Isakower phenomena: designation applied to a set of perceptual experiences that largely involve hands and mouth, and mostly occur at the time of falling asleep. First described by Otto Isakower in 1938, these experiences included a sense that something round and soft was coming nearer and nearer to one's face, one's hands were becoming limp, skin was turning soft, something was in the mouth, and/or one was entirely enveloped by a round, big object. This sort of experience can at times occur during analysis when the patient is recumbent on the couch. It is seen as a regressive reactivation of the infantile experience at the maternal breast. When it appears soon before falling asleep, it might represent a wishful return to blissful merger with the object world. When it appears in the clinical situation, it is often a regressive defence against the anxiety of oedipal impulses and, more significantly, the recall of having witnessed the primal scene. See also the important contribution to this topic by Arnold Richards (1985).

Isolation: this term has had many different meanings and usages over the course of psychoanalytic history. Of these, the following seven meanings seem most prominent: (1) Sigmund Freud (1926d) used the term 'isolation' as a defence which, after a painful event has taken place, 'interpolates an interval during which nothing further must happen . . . .the experience is not forgotten but instead is deprived of its affect, and its associative connections are suppressed or interrupted so that it remains as though isolated' (p. 120); (2) Freud also used the expression 'isolation' for the capacity to keep irrelevant details away from the mind while concentrating on a task; (3) Otto Fenichel (1939b) used the term 'isolation' for the tendency on the part of some patients to carry on their whole analyses in a peculiar non-conjunction with the rest of their lives; (4) he also employed the term for the occasional delinkage between affectionate and sensual currents of love seen in oedipally fixated neurotics (p. 155); (5) the tendency to keep libidinal and aggressive feelings apart was also subsumed under the rubric of 'isolation' by Otto Fenichel (1945, p. 156); (6) Anna Freud (1946) introduced the term 'isolation of affect', emphasizing that severing the links between an idea and its affective accompaniment also constitutes a form of isolation; and (7) Kurt Eissler (1959) used the term for this purpose but also for ego's keeping two related and conscious ideas apart, since putting them together would cause anxiety and suffering. Most of these usages have fallen by the wayside and the term 'isolation' is currently used most often in Anna Freud's (1946) sense of 'isolation of affect' (see below).

Isolation of affect: a particular subtype of the mechanism called 'isolation' (see above). This unconsciously operative manoeuvre consists of the ego separating a disturbing or painful event or idea from the feelings that accompany it. As a result, the individual is left only with an intellectual awareness of the event with no apparent emotion. Thus, aggressive thoughts (e.g., stabbing someone with a knife) or erotic impulses (e.g., having sex with someone) might appear in consciousness as meaningless (i.e., feeling-less) thoughts. Anxiety and guilt consequent upon such desires is thus held in abeyance. 'Isolation of affect' is frequently seen in obsessional personalities and in obsessive–compulsive disorders.

154

$$\boxed{\text{J}}$$

Jealousy: a painful affect involving the sense that someone else is receiving more attention and affection from one's love object. Sigmund Freud (1911c, 1922b) described three types of jealousy: *competitive* (involving the desire to outdo the fortunate rival), *projected* (involving the attribution of the desire to betray one's lover to her and then feeling suspicious of an imagined rival) and *delusional* (involving a man's unconscious assignment of homosexual impulses to his female partner and then fearing her betrayal). The latter two forms were subsumed under 'pathological jealousy'. These distinctions do not draw much attention nowadays, especially since paranoia is increasingly viewed as a primary response to childhood mistreatment and as projection of masochistic (rather than homosexual) wishes. Three things, however, can confidently be said about jealousy: (1) it pertains to its origins in the sibling experience and in passage through the Oedipus complex; both these situations create triangles, making the child vulnerable to feeling less affectionately treated than someone else; (2) it pertains to an admixture of love (of the desired person) and hate (of the rival) in the emotion of jealousy; and (3) jealousy has to be distinguished from envy and rivalry. No one has provided more succinct descriptions of the three emotions, as they exist in the context of family relationships, than Peter Neubauer (1983). According to him, '*Rivalry* is the competition among siblings for the exclusive or preferred care from the persons they share. *Envy* refers to the wish for the possession of attributes that a parent or sibling has, such as penis, strength, breasts. *Jealousy* is the competition with sibling or parent for the love of the person whom they share' (pp. 326–327, original italics). In the specific context of romantic relationships, the regressive pulls and torments associated with jealousy have been recently deconstructed by Marcianne Blevis (2008).

Jettisoned object: term coined by Judith Mitrani (2001) for an object that has become violently separated from the self with which it had been fused before; it now retains only one quality, that of being distinct from the subject. Citing Julia Kristeva (1982), who termed it the 'abject', Mitrani linked the emergence of such an object to ruptured omnipotence in the setting of 'adhesive pseudo-object relations' (see separate entry). Under such circumstances, a total collapse of the self occurs and the object, instead of eliciting desire or hate and thus forging a link between itself and the subject, creates a pull towards the dreadful and mocking void between them.

Joint acceptance of reality of the Holocaust: in the treatment of the surviviors of the Holocaust and their offspring, it is essential that the analyst demonstrate his acknowledgement of the reality of this great tragedy. 'The analyst's silence may approximate too closely the silences of the survivor's Holocaust world, the absence of any response to his or her messages of need' (Auerhahn & Laub, 1987, p. 57).

Jokes: Sigmund Freud (1905c) concluded that the essential nature of a joke consists of (1) aesthetic pleasure yielded by a temporary weakening of repression and the discharge of sublimated energy, (2) greater importance of form in which the story was told than its content, (3) use of condensation, displacement, reversal, and fusion of instincts, (4) bypass of the censorship owing to the disguise of instinctual aims. Noting the similarity between the mechanisms responsible for creating jokes and dreams, Freud felt it necessary to underscore their difference. 'Dreams serve predominately for the avoidance of unpleasure, jokes for the attainment of pleasure' (p. 180). Moreover, dreams involve a more passive ego than do jokes. Freud (1927) declared humour to be a victory of self-assertion. Further contributions to the psychoanalytic understanding of jokes and humour have been made by George Christie (1994), Warren Poland (1990), Janine Chasseguet-Smirgel (1988), and Alessandra Lemma (2000).

Jouissance: a French word meaning 'enjoyment' but also having a slight sexual connotation. The word was frequently used by Jacques Lacan (1957, 1958) to refer to the enjoyment of a sexual object and even for orgasm. Later on, however, Lacan (1960) began to distinguish between 'jouissance' and pleasure. He suggested that the subject constantly attempts to exceed the 'pleasure principle' (see separate entry) though this does not lead to more pleasure, but to pain. This 'painful pleasure' is exactly what Lacan referred to as 'jouissance'. Marcianne Blevis and Judith Feher-Gurewich (2003) have elaborated these ideas further and demonstrated the intricate links between the 'jouissance' of the other and prohibition of incest.

K: see 'L, H, and K'.

Kore complex: described by Susan Fairfield (1994), this complex refers to certain anxiety-laden aggressive fantasies of preoedipal children. These fantasies involve condensation of generational and gender roles and of oral and genital themes. According to Fairfield, preoedipal children experience themselves as 'kore' (Greek for girl) in primary identification with the mother. Hence this developmentally earlier counterpart of the Oedipus complex is termed the 'kore complex'.

L

L: see 'L, H, and K'.

L, H, and K: Wilfred Bion's (1963) designations for the fundamental human motivations of love, hate, and desire for knowledge. 'L, H, and K' share four features: (1) each links the self with its own self and with the world of objects, both animate and inanimate; (2) each exists in an active and a passive form (to love and be loved, to hate and be hated, and to know and be known); (3) each has a positive (L, H, and K) and a negative (−L, −H, and −K) form; these imply loving and not loving, hating and not hating, and knowing and not knowing, respectively; and (4) each has a counterpart in the classical 'instinct theory' (see separate entry) with 'L, H, K' corresponding, roughly, to 'life', 'death', and 'ego instincts', respectively.

Lack: in an elegent elucidation of Jacques Lacan's (1955, 1956) concept of 'lack', Dylan Evans (1996) has discerned four uses of this term: (1) lack of being, which has an existential ring to it, (2) lack of having, (3) lack of object, and (4) lack of a signifier (see separate entry) in the Other. The first gives rise to 'desire' (see separate entry), the second to 'demand' (see separate entry), the third to the hunger for an object, and the fourth for the search for meaning.

Laius complex: term coined by John Munder Ross in 1982 (Ross, 1994, p. 10) to denote the paternal counterpart to a son's Oedipus complex, which impels urges to commit pederasty and filicide in the father. 'Repressed from consciousness, the existence of these aggressive impulses helps to explain religious sacrifice and submission, authoritarianism, child abuse, and war, in all of which the older generation threatens sons with exile and death and now and then actually sends them to their death' (p. 10).

Large group identity: building upon Erik Erikson's (1956) idea about the group dimension of individual 'identity' (see separate entry), Vamik Volkan (1997, 1999b, 2004) proposed the concept of 'large group identity'. Instead of focusing upon an individual's sense of solidarity with his group's ideal, it emphasizes the group's own view of itself. Volkan delineated *seven components* of it: (i) shared reservoirs for images associated with positive emotion, (ii) shared positive identi-

fications, (iii) absorption of 'bad' qualities deposited into the group by others, qualities that actually belong to those 'others', (iv) absorption of the transformative leader's internal world, (v) 'chosen glories' (see separate entry), (vi) 'chosen traumas' (see separate entry) and (vii) symbols that might evolve from any of the six vectors above, but sooner or later acquire their own autonomous stance. Volkan has elaborated the role of such 'large group identity' plays in the generation and sustenance of inter-ethnic conflicts.

Large group psychology: distinguishing his views from those of Sigmund Freud's (1921c) on 'group psychology' (see separate entry), Vamik Volkan (1988, 1997, 1999b, 2004) proposed the concept of 'large group psychology'. The former focuses upon the individual's regressive submission to a leader (who replaces the powerful, oedipal father) and the dominance of emotionality over logic and reason. The latter regards the characteristic of the large group (comprising thousands and millions of people) itself as the central issue at stake. The leader–follower relationship is but one aspect of it. The use of historical, literary, economic, legal, and military means to maintain and protect the 'large group identity' (see separate entry) are central to 'large group psychology'.

Latency phase: the period of childhood from six to twelve years that follows the oedipal phase and extends until the onset of puberty. It is characterized by diminution in drive energy, increasing relationships with peers, growth in ego functions, especially skills and sublimations, and by conformity to the rules of the family and community. The intense attachment to the parents is resolved and repressed. Adults outside the family (e.g., school teachers) and other children, especially those of the same sex, assume a greater role in the child's life (Pearson, 1966). There is also 'a sublimation of sexual curiousity into intellectual curiousity' (Kramer & Rudolph, 1980, p. 111), leading the child to become 'calm, pliable, and educable' (Sarnoff, 1976, p. 43). Formal as well as improvised games preoccupy the child. Though largely in the service of ego mastery, the insistence on rules and fairness in such games betrays their elaborate defensive nature. Struggle against masturbation also plays an important role in latency. Berta Bornstein (1951) divided latency into early (from 6–8 years) and late (from 8–12 years).

Miriam Williams (1972) divided 'latency phase' into early latency, latency proper, and late latency subphases. However, neither of these schemes imply a strict categorization, though they do imply differences in the structural consolidation of the personality. For further details on the normal and pathological developments during latency, see the contributions of Erna Furman (1980), Robert Furman (1980), and Ann Smolen (2006), but most importantly, Charles Sarnoff (1976, 1987).

Latent content of the dream: see 'Dream work'.

Law of suspicious cultural intensity: phrase coined by Salman Akhtar (1999b) to underscore the fact that intensely felt cultural concerns during analysis frequently turn out to be unconscious covers for deeper intrapsychic conflicts.

Lay analysis: it was Sigmund Freud's (1926e) impassioned defence of the non-physician psychoanalyst Theodore Reik, who was facing a legal suit by a disgruntled analysand, that introduced the phrase 'lay analysis' into the psychoanalytic lexicon. The history of non-medical professionals in analysis actually begins from Otto Rank's admission into Freud's inner circle in 1907, and extends through the pioneering contributions of Hans Sachs and Anna Freud to the luminous works of Ronald Fairbairn, Harry Guntrip, Erik Erikson, Ella Freeman Sharpe, and James Strachey, to name but a few (Meisels & Shapiro, 1990; Akhtar, 1995; Wallerstein, 1999). Psychoanalysis in Europe never became strongly identified with academic medicine. Consequently, non-physicians have continued to form a sizable group among analysts practising there. While it is not possible to list even the most shining stars in this galaxy, it would be a 'psychoanalytic sin' to not mention Christopher Bollas, Elizabeth Bott Spillius, Janine Chasseguet-Smirgel, Peter Fonagy, Jacques Lacan, and David Tuckett, among others. Even in the USA, where psychoanalysis acquired a strong medical identity, non-medical professionals have played a prominent role in all four 'generations' of psychoanalysts. An admittedly incomplete list of these individuals includes (1) among the immigrants: Erik Erikson, Ernst Kris, David Rapaport, and Robert Waelder; (2) in the 'first generation': Peter Blos, Sr, Margaret Brenman-Gibson, Selma Fraiberg, Marjorie Harley, Robert Holt, George Klein, Herbert Schlesinger, Roy Schafer, Donald Spence, and Ernst Ticho; (3) in the 'second generation': Stephen Appelbaum, Henry Bachach, Jennifer Bonovitz, Fred Busch, Dorothy Holmes, Judith

Kantrowitz, Nancy Kulish, Frederic Levine, Jack Novick, Fred Pine, Nadia Ramzy, John Munder Ross, Howard Sherwin, and Phyllis Tyson; and (4) the 'young Turks': Andrea Celenza, Kimberlyn Leary, Susan Levine, Monisha Nayar, Shahrzad Siassi, and Sharon Zalusky. In addition, there are prominent non-medical psychoanalysts in the USA who have been trained outside the American Psychoanalytic Association. These include Sheldon Bach, Erna Furman, Helen Gediman, Jay Greenbeerg, Stephen Kurtz, Ruth Lax, and Stephen Mitchell. All together, this is an impressive cadre of professionals that has made profoundly significant contributions to psychoanalysis.

Lay analyst: refers to a psychoanalyst who is not medically trained. With the cadre of analysts tilting increasingly in the direction of recruiting such individuals, the term is becoming somewhat dated and redundant. See also the entry on 'lay analysis'.

Libidinal ego: see 'Fairbairn's description of endopsychic structure'.

Libidinal investment: see 'Libido'.

Libidinal object: see 'Libido'.

Libidinal object proper: see 'Organizers of the psyche'.

Libidinal phases: see 'Psychosexual stages of development'.

Libidinal refuelling: see 'Emotional refuelling'.

Libidinal stages: see 'Psychosexual stages of development'.

Libidinal types: Sigmund Freud's (1931a) categorization of individuals based upon the differences in the distribution of libidinal energy to the main parts of the psychic apparatus: (1) *erotic type:* where libido is mostly allocated to id; the main interest of such persons is loving and being loved and their main dread is loss of love; (2) *obsessional type:* where libido is mostly allocated to the superego; perfectionism, guilt, and self-reliance characterize such people; (3) *narcissistic type:* where libido is mostly allocated to the ego; such individuals readily impress others and can become leaders 'to give a fresh stimulus to cultural development or to damage the established state of affairs' (p. 5). Mixed types, with features of more than one category, also existed. Ludwig Eidelberg

(1957) added 'sensuous' and 'athletic' types on the grounds that 'narcissistic' type did not adequately cover the libidinal investment of ego.

Libidinization: a term denoting the infusion of 'libido' (see separate entry) into aims and objects cathected with aggressive energy or into autonomous ego functions. Libidinization is different from 'libidinal investment', which means putting 'sexual' energy into an object or activity pertaining to love. In contrast, libidinization means placing 'sexual' energy in a sphere ordinarily divorced from love. (1) The *first* type of 'libidinization' is implicit in Sigmund Freud's (1920g) ideas about 'primary masochism', which results from the binding of a portion of death instinct by libido. Otto Fenichel's (1934) discussion of human beings finding 'pleasure in pain' (p. 308), and Betty Joseph's (1982) concept of 'addiction to near-death' (see separate entry) also rests upon the notion of such libidinization of aggression. And Salman Akhtar's (2000) list of defences against mental pain includes 'libidinization' by name. (2) The *second* type, i.e., the investment of libido in autonomous ego functions leads to 'libidinization of thinking' (Bach, 1977), seen in narcissistic individuals and in the extreme passion creative artists display while doing their work.

Libido: Sigmund Freud first used the term 'libido' in 1894 (Laplanche & Pontalis, 1973, p. 239). Initially, it stood for sexual desire, but over time came to denote the psychic energy of the sexual instinct. Thus, in the 'first dual instinct theory' (Freud, 1905a, 1915c), libido was opposed to the energy of life preservatory instinct and in the 'second dual instinct theory' (Freud, 1920g), it was opposed to 'destrudo' (see separate entry), or the energy of the death instinct. Thus, the following adjectival forms of the word arose: 'libidinal investment' (placement of sexual energy in a love object or loving activity), 'libidinal drive' (instinctual drive pertaining to sexual and loving aims), 'libidinal attachments' (object relations of a loving kind), and so on.

Libido theory: Sigmund Freud (1905a, 1914c, 1915c, 1920g, 1931a, 1937c) evolved a complex model of distribution of mental energy that is subsumed under the rubric 'libido theory'. *Seven fundamental propositions* of this theory are (1) libido is a form of mental energy, (2) libido may be discharged via instinctual activities or get 'dammed up' and give rise to neurotic symptoms, (3) libido may be invested in objects ('object libido') or in the self ('ego libido' or 'narcissistic libido'), (4) libido may be pliable and shift from object to object or it can be 'adhesive' and show rigidity in its attachments, (5) libido may be directed towards loving investment in self and others or be used to 'bind' aggression and infuse ego-activities (see 'libidinization'), (6) libido follows erotogenic zones as they become psychically ascendant over the course of development; hence, there are 'libidinal stages' or 'libidinal phases' parallel to psychosexual stages of development, and (7) libido might be distributed in patterns that are specific to various character organizations ('libidinal types').

Lichtenberg's motivational systems: according to Joseph Lichtenberg (1989), human beings are basically motivated by a series of systems that seek to assure the fulfilment of certain essential needs. Each system pertains to a specific need. Each has psychological, behavioural, and, perhaps, neurophysiological foundations and correlates. Each is discernible from the neonatal period onwards. Lichtenberg's scheme includes five such motivational systems: '(1) the need for psychic regulation of physiological requirements, (2) the need for attachment-affiliation, (3) the need for exploration and assertion, (4) the need to react aversively through antagonism or withdrawal, and (5) the need for sensual enjoyment and sexual excitement' (p. 1). These systems evolve and mature with the unfolding of the life span. They interact with each other and have conscious and unconscious operations and representations. One particular system may be dominant at one moment and a different system at another moment. It is from initiating, organizing, and integrating these systems under a central locus of agency that the 'self' (see separate entry) arises. See also the report on the application of Lichtenberg's systems to mother–infant observational data by Kay Campbell, Donald Silver, Kerry Kelly Novick, Jack Novick, Mary Mittlestaedt, and Anne Walton (1995).

Lies: broadly-speaking, 'lies' can be grouped under the following six categories: (i) *social lies*, which involve the innocuous excuses and pretences of daily life, (ii) *narcissistic lies*, which include omissions and exaggerations for avoiding shame, (iii) *psychopathic lies*, or misrepresentations deliberately aimed at obtaining sensual or material gratification, (iv) *pathological lies*, which betray pervasive inability to tell the truth with no material gain; these arise out of a fundamental hatred of reality, (v) *life-saving lies*, which have to be spoken in situations of being held hostage or tortured, and (vi) *occupational lies*, or deceits that are integral to being a spy or undercover agent. To be sure, admixtures between these categories exist. Within psychoanalysis, Wilfred Bion (1962a) has given most thought to this topic, looking at the pathological as well as the creative aspects of lying. Bion concluded that truth, being self-evident, does not require a thinker, but a lie, being a manufactured thought, does. Alessandra Lemma (2005) has also made a significant contribution to the psychoanalytic understanding of 'lies'. According to her, there are three psychic and relational configurations associated with lying : (1) *sadistic lying*, where the object is duped and humiliated in an effort to reverse earlier humiliations of the self, (2) *self-preservative lying*, where a false and embellished picture of the self is presented in order to seduce someone perceived to be disinterested, and (3) a different form of self-preservative lying which could be called *self-protective lying* (though Lemma herself does not employ this expression) and is intended to protect oneself from an intrusive object. The question of whether a liar can be psychoanalysed has also preoccupied analysts, with the initial discouragement giving way to a tempered optimism (O'Shaughnessy, 1990; Lemma, 2005). See the entry on 'transferences of deception' for further clinical elucidation of this matter, and also Salman Akhtar's (2005, pp. 137–154) discourse on the psychosocial dynamics of forgery, especially in the world of art and antiques.

Life and death narcissism: André Green's (1983, 2001, 2002) terms for two forms of narcissism, one that shapes a certain manner of living and the other that fuels cynicism and withdrawal. Life narcissism results in living that is restricted to illusory relationships without genuine involvement with others. Death narcissism embodies 'a culture of void, emptiness, self-contempt, destructive withdrawal, and permanent self depreciation with a predominant masochistic quality: tears, tears, tears' (p. 645).

Life goals *vs.* treatment goals: see 'Treatment goals *vs.* life goals'.

Life instinct: term used by Sigmund Freud (1920g) in his 'second dual instinct theory' for one of the two major motivational forces of mental functioning. 'Life instinct' operates in ways that lead to the protection, sustenance, and enhancement of the self and to species propagation. On a more sublime level, it is responsible for evolving finer solutions for the problems of psychological and social life, and for arriving at better synthesized gestalts of experiencing and relating to

onself and others. Integrating ideas, establishing links in diverse realms, firming up connections between self and others, and facilitating personality growth, all result from the functioning of the 'life instinct'. In Freud's (1920g) words, Eros (the psychic energy of 'life instinct') is 'the preserver of all things' (p. 52). In Freud's move from his 'first dual instinct theory', to his 'second dual instinct theory', 'life instinct' came to subsume the 'sexual instinct' and 'ego instinct' (also called 'self-preservatory instinct'), though, at this time, the term 'life instinct' was used synonymously with 'sexual instinct' alone. More importantly, 'life instinct' was juxtaposed with its counterpart, the 'death instinct'. Together, these magisterial forces determined how the human life unfolded. Their interactions ranged from staunch opposition to varying degress of mutual 'binding' and amalgamation; these scenarios have found futher explication in the writings of many subsequent theorists, especially Heinz Hartmann (1939, 1956), Max Schur (1966), Melanie Klein (1923, 1929, 1932, 1935), Wilfred Bion (1967, 1970), and André Green (1999, 2005), to name a few (see the related entries on 'instinct theory', 'death instinct', 'fusion and definition of instincts', 'binding' and 'life and death narcissism').

Life narcissism: see 'Life and death narcissism'.

Lines of exploration: see 'Therapeutic strategy and psychoanalytic technique'.

Linking objects: concept described by Vamik Volkan (1981) to denote a physical object that is 'actually present in the environment that is psychologically contaminated with various aspects of the dead and the self ... the significance of this object does not fade as it does in uncomplicated mourning. Rather, it increasingly commands attention with its aura of mystery, fascination, and terror' (p. 101). A noticeable linking object, such object can neither be rationally used nor discarded. They are usually hidden away in the house and might remain so for years. Looking at them stirs up pain as well as a vague sense of fear. Pain is caused by the physical object's reminding one of the original loss. Fear results from the mechanism of projective identification that endows the physical object with menacing and accusatory qualities.

Linking phenomena: described by Vamik Volkan (1981), such phenomena include fantasies, sensations, songs, musical tunes, and behaviour patterns that perpetuate the possibility of contact between a bereaved individual and the deceased for whom the former is mourning. No tangible objects, like mementos or 'linking objects' (see separate entry) are involved in such a scenario. Prolonged persistence of 'linking phenomena' suggests an unresolved grief reaction.

Links: see 'Attacks on linking'.

Listening cure: phrase coined by Salman Akhtar (2007d) to match the celebrated label 'talking cure' given to psychoanalysis by Sigmund Freud's early patient Anna O. (Breuer & Freud, 1893–1895). Essentially, the former phrase serves as a reminder that psychoanalysis is a listening *and* talking cure. The fact is, Freud knew this well and, unlike his patient, emphasized both elements as integral to clinical work. In a characteristically pithy remark, he stated that the analyst 'must adjust himself to the patient as a telephone receiver is adjusted to the transmitting microphone' (1912e, pp. 115–116). The idea of psychoanalysis as a 'listening cure' was taken to its zenith by Leopold Nosek in his keynote address at the 45th IPA Congress held on July 29–August 1, 2009, in Chicago.

Little man phenomenon: originally described by Paul Kramer (1955), this phenomenon involves the sequestering of an ego segment at the occurrence of premature and traumatic discovery of separateness from the mother. The 'little man' (so named because that's how Kramer's patient referred to this self-representation) represents an area of condensed narcissism. Its function is to make available to the rest of the ego a mother substitute from which separation would never be required. The 'little man' remained in the ego as an alien 'presence', separated from its more advanced elements. 'In this fashion, there came to exist a house divided with the ego itself, and the total effect was that of a weak, helpless, impoverished ego, even though actually a part of it, the "little man", gave every evidence of possessing great power' (p. 71). Kramer's observations were later 'confirmed' by William Niederland (1965) and Vamik Volkan (1976).

Location of cultural experience: see 'Potential space' and 'Transitional space'.

Locomotor anxiety: see 'Agoraphobia'.

Loss complex: term used by Gregory Rochlin (1959) for a highly organized psychological constellation resulting from childhood experience of loss. The final texture varies with the age at which the loss occurred but as a generalization it can be said that the earlier the loss the greater are the chances of ego alteration. Vulnerability to regression, increased narcissism, animistic beliefs, and a depressive proclivity are typical of this syndrome. All sorts of defences are mobilized to protect oneself from a recurrence of the loss trauma; clinging to objects is commonplace in the setting of 'loss complex'. 'Unlike other conflicts, it appears never to be actually resolved. At best it is satisfactorily defended' (p. 315). The echoes of Rochlin's paper are to be found in Calvin Settlage's (2001) essay titled 'Defenses evoked by early childhood loss'. Settlage portrays the inner world of individuals with a history of early childhood loss as comprising excessive dependency on external objects, turning of aggression against the self, inordinate separation anxiety, and an exaggerated fear of death.

Love: see 'Mature love'.

Low-keyedness: term used by Margaret Mahler, Fred Pine, and Anni Bergman (1975) to describe a specific affectomotor state seen in 'practising phase' (see separate entry) toddlers when separated from their mothers. This state is characterized by slowing down of motility, diminution of interest in the external world, and shifting of attention towards inner experience. The child bursts into tears if comforted by someone other than their mother. His 'low-keyedness' rapidly disappears upon mother's return, though even then not before a short crying spell has released the accumulated tension. Mahler, Pine, and Bergman proposed that this state reflects the child's effort to inwardly hold on to an ideal state of the self, especially as it was experienced in a pleasant closeness with the mother.

Lower level of character pathology: one of three (higher, intermediate, and lower) levels of character pathology described by Otto Kernberg (1970). Diagnostic categories of borderline, antisocial, paranoid, hypomanic, and schizoid personalities belong in this group. Although they differ in surface presentations and, to a certain extent, in developmental backgrounds and psychostructural characteristics, these personality disorders share many features. Descriptively, such individuals exhibit chronic restlessness, unstable emotions, vacillating relationships, unrealistic goals, excessive self-absorption, defective empathy, egocentric perception of reality, impaired capacity for mourning, inability to love, sexual difficulties, and moral defects of varying degrees. Dynamically, splitting or active dissociation of mutually contradictory self and object representations is a major defensive operation in these conditions. This is accompanied by the subsidiary mechanisms of denial, primitive idealization, and projective identification. Psychostucturally, at this level of character organization there is a restriction of the conflict-free ego, poor superego internalization and integration, blurring of the ego–superego delimitation, and, most importantly, the lack of an integrated self-concept, resulting in the syndrome of identity diffusion (Erikson, 1959; Kernberg, 1980; Akhtar, 1984).

Lying fallow: a state of alert quietude described by Masud Khan (1983b) that has *four characteristics*: (1) slowing down of mental activity, (2) reduced relatedness to the environment, (3) peaceful acceptance of the self, and (4) enriching and replenishing effect on the ego. Such a state seems to replicate the infantile calm after a good feeding. Not surprisingly, then, it can only be reached in the presence of a loving but unintrusive person, or even a pet.

M

Male and female elements: Donald Winnicott's (1971) independent reformulation of the earlier psychoanalytic notion of 'psychic bi-sexuality' (see separate entry). In his view, the 'female element' is the earlier one and emerges in relation to the developmental phase, when mother and infant are psychically merged. It gives tone and texture to the way of being one has in life. The 'male element' appears later and denotes a capacity for differentiation. Its development occurs parallel to that of the 'capacity for concern' (see separate entry). It regulates doing. In the words of Jan Abram (2007), the pre-eminent exponent of Winnicott, 'creative living is associated with a bringing-together of male and female elements with the ability to both be and do, and this has to appear in a sequence' (p. 129).

Malignant erotic transference: Salman Akhtar's (1994) designation for the intense and seemingly erotic transference that actually hides marked aggression towards the analyst and the internal object he stands for. Such transference is more common among female analysands. Its *four features* are (1) predominance of hostility over love, (2) intense coercion of the analyst to indulge in actions, (3) marked inconsolability, and (4) the absence of erotic counterresonance in the analyst. In the throes of such transference, the patient can become convinced that the analyst should, or will actually, consummate their relationship and marry her.

Malignant hysteric: Christopher Bollas's (2000) designation for a type of hysteric who is far more distressed, desperate, and evocative than the ordinary patients of hysteria. The 'malignant hysteric' is intensely dramatic and coerces the environment to listen and respond. 'Unlike the borderline patient, who seeks effectively to bond with the analyst in a fusion of turbulence, thus constituting the primary object, the malignant hysteric seeks to impose an inequality upon this dyad, in which a helpless and paralysed self is further enervated by the passing by of powerful visual scenes' (p. 131). As a child, such a patient has been the recipient of violent projections on the mother's part, which have crowded out his or her self; it is these internal objects that the patient desperately ejects through enactment and by depositing them into the analyst. All this gives the clinical picture a confusing and dream-like quality.

Malignant masochism: term coined by Edmund Bergler (1961) in order to distinguish ordinary, neurotic forms of masochism from the one encountered in a setting of schizoid and schizophrenic conditions. According to Bergler, 'malignant masochism' is characterized by (1) replacement of a game-like quality to the behaviour by absolute seriousness and literalness; (2) lack of fear of consequences of one's destructive actions; (3) unpredictability of sadomasochistic outbursts; and (4) absence of rational fear, which serves a self-protective function. Individuals with 'malignant masochism' hold on to 'the masochistic and provocative pseudo aggressive solution because in itself it is an active defence against a deeper danger, the total and absolute helplessness of being totally and absolutely manipulated by the mother' (p. 46).

Malignant mood: see 'Generative and malignant moods'.

Malignant narcissism: it was Edith Weigert (1967) who first coined the terms 'benign narcissism' and 'malignant narcissism'. The former stood for the enhanced self-esteem that results from successful sublimations and having endured adversities in creative ways. The latter stood for regressive escape from frustration by distortion and denial of reality. She emphasized that there is no sharp division between the two forms of narcissism and they exist in various degrees of admixture. The term 'malignant narcissism' was used in a considerably different manner by Herbert Rosenfeld (1971). He described a disturbing form of narcissistic personality where grandiosity is built around aggression and the destructive aspects of the self become idealized. Such patients seek to destroy whatever love is offered them in order to maintain their superiority over others. Developing these ideas further, Otto Kernberg (1984) introduced the term 'malignant narcissism' to denote the co-existence of the following *four features*: (1) a typical narcissistic personality disorder, (2) antisocial behaviour, (3) egosyntonic sadism, and (4) a deeply paranoid orientation toward life. Their paranoid beliefs fuel their antisocial behaviour and the societal retribution for such actions lend justification to their mistrust. Individuals with malignant narcissism consistently attempt to destroy, symbolically castrate, and dehumanize others. Their sadism is often expressed in ideological terms. They can become leaders of religious cults. They can also have ego-syntonic suicidal tendencies that do not reflect sadness and inner guilt, but a megalomaniac triumph over the ordinary fear of pain and death.

Malignant prejudice: see 'Benign and malignant prejudice'.

Malignant regression: see 'Benign and malignant regression'.

Management: see 'Analytic management'.

Mania: refers to a mental state characterized by elated mood, psychomotor excitement, distractability, impulsivity, and impairment of social judgement. The manic individual displays pressured speech, flight of ideas, and exalted self esteem; in more severe 'mania', grandiosity can turn delusional and give rise to secondary paranoid ideas. Sigmund Freud (1917c, 1930a) viewed 'mania' as a forceful reversal of depression and an individual psychopathological counterpart to the societally sanctioned group celebration of festivals: in both circumstances, there was a fusion of superego and ego, releasing a huge amount of energy and permitting uninhibited behaviour. Further understanding of 'mania' was provided by Karl Abraham (1924), Melanie Klein (1935), Bertram Lewin (1950), and the Washington based psychoanalytic investigators Mabel Cohen, Grace Baker, Robert Cohen, Frieda Fromm-Reichmann, and Edith Weigert (1954). They pointed out at that 'mania 'is characterized by (1) fusion of ego and superego; (2) fusion of the self and the object in an oral symbiotic union; and (3) regaining of infantile omnipotence. However, the defensive nature of all this is betrayed by the thinly veiled melancholic tinge to the manic's desperation; his object hunger is an insatiable 'orgy of cannibalistic character' (Abraham, 1924, p. 474). The same is true of the manic's hypersexuality, which is predominantly narcissistic and oral with little concern for his partners. Significantly, while Freud's aligning mania with the celebration of a festival by the ego involved a denial of the primal crime of killing and eating the totemic father, later authors, beginning with Karl Abraham (1924), posited that the murderous fantasies of the manic are primarily directed against the mother.

Manic defence: a term first used by Melanie Klein (1935) to describe a set of mental mechanisms aimed at protecting the ego from depressive and paranoid anxieties. Omnipotence, denial, and idealization are the three constituents of manic defence. Omnipotence is utilized to control objects but without genuine concern for them. Denial is aimed at erasing the awareness of dependence upon others. Idealization is meant to retain an 'all good' view of the world which defends against guilty recognition of one's aggressive impulses. Donald Winnicott (1935) noted that the use of manic defence is typical of individuals who dread sadness and are unable to mourn. He outlined *four components* of manic defence: (1) denial of internal reality, which involves a repudiation of internalized bad objects but might also send the good internal forces into psychic exile, thus diminishing the individual's faith in his own goodness; (2) flight to external reality involves frequent daydreaming, which interposes fantasy between the internal and external reality, and an exploitation of sexuality and other bodily sensations; (3) suspended animation: in this aspect of manic defence, omnipotent control of the bad internal objects stops all truly good relationships. The individual feels dead inside and the world appears still and colourless; (4) denial of depressive feelings and use of exalted opposites (e.g., full as against empty, moving as against still, fast as against slow, light as against heavy, etc.) for reassurance. This last aspect of manic defence can also affect symbolism.

Manic depressive illness: see 'Bipolar affective disorder'.

Manic reparation: see 'Reparation'.

Manifest content: term used by Sigmund Freud (1900a) as a counterpart to 'latent content' of a dream. The 'manifest content' or the 'manifest dream' is the result of 'dream work' (see separate entry) consisting of condensation, displacement, symbolism, and secondary revision. In practice, the 'manifest dream' consists of the verbal report of a dream by the analysand; this might not be an exact replica of what was 'seen' during sleep. Not surprisingly, there has been ambivalence regarding the 'manifest dream', beginning with Freud himself; it is derided as mere surface phenomenon, but also regarded as providing valuable clues to what lies underneath it. Erik Erikson's (1954) discourse on deconstructing the texture of 'manifest dream' is seminal, but significant contributions have been made after it as well (Brenneis, 1975; Palombo, 1984; Renik, 1984; Coen, 1996). The appearance of early childhood trauma in undisguised form (Pulver, 1987) and the relatively transparent depiction of recent immigration (Akhtar, 1999b; Grinberg & Grinberg, 1989) in the 'manifest dream' have been especially noted.

Manifest dream: see ' manifest content'.

Manipulation: one among the five therapeutic interventions (the other four being 'suggestion', 'abreaction', 'clarification', and 'interpretation') delineated by Edward Bibring (1954) as being typical of psychoanalysis and psychodynamic psychotherapies. Used in a non-pejorative sense, 'manipulation' refers to 'the employment of various emotional systems existing in the patient for the purpose of achieving therapeutic changes either in the technical sense of promoting the treatment or in the curative sense' (Bibring, 1954, pp. 750–751) of reducing some aspect of the patient's pathology. 'Technical manipulation' can be directed at producing a favourable attitude towards the treatment situation (e.g., by telling a patient forced into treatment that it is entirely up to him to talk or not, or by telling a patient who is afraid of being influenced that he must never accept any explanation unless he himself is fully conviced of its validity). 'Therapeutic manipulation' is intended to produce 'adjustive change' (p. 751), for instance, by raising questions that encourage the patient to move from a submissive to a more autonomous stance. A subtype of 'therapeutic manipulation' is what Bibring called 'experiential manipulation'. Containing echoes of Franz Alexander's (1948) 'corrective emotional experience' (see separate entry), this intervention consisted of exposing the patient to a new experience from which he learnt more adaptive ways of responding to inner and outer conflicts. Despite Bibring's sanitizing of it, the term 'manipulation' never lost its 'denigrating implications' (Kernberg, 1984, p. 159) and therefore did not gain popularity in psychoanalytic parlance.

Masculinity: while early psychoanalysis did help in understanding the boy's phallic–oedipal development (Freud, 1910h, 1912a, 1923e, 1924d, 1925j), a thorough study of what it truly means to be a boy and, later, a man, began much later. Three pioneering contributors to this topic were: (1) *Ralph Greenson* (1968), who proposed that a boy must disidentify with his mother in order to consolidate his masculine identity (see the entry on 'boy's dis-identification with the mother'); (2) *Ernest Abelin* (1971, 1975), who underscored the role played by the 'preoedipal father' (see separate entry) *vis-à-vis* the boy's growing sense of separateness, assertiveness, and modulation of aggression; and (3) *John Munder Ross* (1975, 1979, 1992, 1994), who emphasized that a split father image ('good father' to be loved and emulated and 'bad father' who is punishing and has to be rebelled against) exists from very early on and both these images affect the boy's emerging masculinity. Ross also noted the role played by the mother in helping her son respect his father and uphold him as a model for identification. These early contributions were respected, but not followed up with further investigation. The topic of 'masculinity' was eclipsed by the psychoanalytic interest in 'femininity' (see separate entry). Then, in 2006, the *Journal of the American Psychoanalytic Association* brought out a special issue devoted to this topic. An introduction by Janice Lieberman and commentaries by Jane Flax and Donald Moss sandwiched original papers by Richard Reichbart, Michael Diamond, Gerald Fogel, and Ethel Person. Pooling the ideas in this special issue with the literature mentioned above reveals the following 'developmental line' (see separate entry) of 'masculinity': (1) being born with intact male anatomy and physiology; (2) proper sex assignment; (3) gender-specific ego socialization in terms of the name, clothes, and toys given to the child; (4) empathic affirmation by a mother who shows 'the capacity to support her son's journey towards the world of his father—the world of males' (Diamond, 2006. p. 1119); (5) interactions with father that pull the boy out from the symbiotic orbit; (6) the boy's encounter with the mother's endorsement of the father's authority; (7) resolution of the Oedipus complex and internalization of an early genital–father imago; (8) later, in adolescence, the boy's sensing the father's capacity to let go of him, same sex peer group identifications, exercise of sexual prowess, and pride in the ability to endure pain; (9) still later, ego expansion and enhanced social mastery with the help of a 'mentor' (see separate entry); (10) further refinement of 'masculinity' with deep and committed romantic intimacy and with becoming a father (Colarusso, 1990; Ross, 1975); (11) merger of phallic assertivness and genital ego ideal; and (12) a shift of identity towards increased 'generativity' (Erikson, 1950) with a less grandiose and more nurturant lifestyle. While the contributions mentioned above are all outstanding, Diamond's paper is truly a gem!

Masochism: term coined by von Krafft-Ebing (1892) as a generalization for the erotic role of pain and humiliation in the novels of Von Sacher Masoch; 'masochism' consisted of being dominated, controlled, hurt, and humiliated by a person of the opposite sex for the purpose of erotic gratification. This narrow definition led to Sigmund Freud's (1905a, 1915c, 1919h, 1920g, 1924d) wide-ranging ideas about 'masochism'. The trajectory of these speculations dovetails the evolution of his instinct theory in general and the oedipal situation in particular. To begin with, Freud (1905a) regarded 'sadism' and 'masochism' as 'component instincts' of sexuality and declared that they invariably coexisted; it was thus heuristically better to speak of 'sadomasochism' than of 'sadism' and 'masochism' alone. In his first dual instinct theory (see 'instinct theory'), Freud (1905a, 1915c) regarded 'sadism'—a pleasurable infliction of pain upon others—as primary and masochism as secondary (being a deflection of 'sadism' upon the self). In his second dual instinct theory (see 'instinct theory'), however, Freud (1920g) proposed that 'masochism' was a manifestation of 'death instinct'; it was 'primary', and 'sadism', its outward deflection, was secondary. In these and other papers (e.g., 1919h, 1924d), Freud related masochism to the fantasy of being beaten by the father and saw it as providing both sexual satisfaction and punishment for one's forbidden wishes. He thus introduced the intricate relationship 'masochism' has with 'guilt' (see separate entry) and divided 'masochism' into three types: (1) *primary* (which was the somatic substrate of 'death instinct' bound with the libido of 'life instinct'; the pleasure in pain came from the latter source); (2) *erotic or feminine* (which was the attitude underlying sexually exciting fantasies in men of being bound, beaten, and humiliated); and (3) *moral* (which emanated from an unconscious sense of guilt and led to chronic self depreciation and self punishment). Analytic investigators following Freud (e.g., Berliner, 1958; Brenner, 1959; Bergler, 1961) elaborated, elucidated, and expanded the meanings of the term 'masochism'. This led, on the one hand, to increasing sophistication of understanding, and, on the other hand, to the term 'masochism' acquiring 'a confusing array of meanings and connotations drawn from varied levels of abstraction . . . . [which] may falsely suggest underlying similarity between fundamentally different phenomena' (Maleson, 1984, p. 325). The related entry on 'masochistic character' in this glossary should also help to clarify some of these issues.

Masochistic character: a natural corollary of the evolving psychoanalytic ideas on 'masochism' (see separate entry) was the concept of 'masochistic character'. While a large number of analysts have contributed to its understanding; the views of following five seem most prominent: (1) *Wilhelm Reich* (1933) proposed that 'masochistic character' arose out of severe childhood frustrations; much aggression was mobilized, but, instead of being discharged on the frustrating others, was defensively directed at oneself; individuals with a 'masochistic character' were passive–aggressive,

guilt-inducing, and coercive in their demand for love; (2) *Edmund Bergler* (1961) saw masochism as 'a desperate attempt to maintain infantile megalomania' (p. 18). The masochist unconsciously provokes and enjoys rejection but consciously reacts with righteous indignation. This helps him deny his responsibility in the rejection and his unconscious pleasure in it. After the outburst of pseudo aggression, he indulges in self-pity and unconsciously enjoys the wound-licking; (3) *Bernhard Berliner* (1958) sidelined the instinctual basis of masochism and emphasized its object-relational value. Masochism, for him, was a child's way to cope with his sadistic parents. The masochist mistreated himself and sought mistreatment by others because his superego was patterned after his cruel parents; love of suffering was an adaptive response to an abnormal childhood environment; (4) *Charles Brenner* (1959), in contrast, declared that masochism represented the acceptance of a painful penalty for forbidden sexual pleasures associated with oedipal fantasies; and (5) *Arnold Cooper* (1988a), who highlighted the coexistence of narcissism and masochism, proposed the concept of 'narcissistic–masochistic character' (see separate entry). For more details pertaining to 'masochistic character', and 'masochism' in general, see the highly informative book *Masochism: Current Psychoanalytic Perspectives*, edited by Robert Glick and Donald Meyers (1988); the chapters by Herbert Rosenfeld (1988) and Helen Meyers (1988) are especially pertinent to the technical handling of masochistic patients.

Masochistic contract: Victor Smirnoff's (1969) designation for the agreement that exists between two parties involved in masochistic sexual enactments. Their contract arranges an immutable setting in which the victim actually lays down the rules. 'The conditions imposed are clear enough: the tormentor's panoply only underlines his role; he must wear a 'uniform' to remind him that he is merely an employee, a slave of the self-styled victim' (p. 666). According to Smirnoff, it is neither the physical torment nor the moral degradation that constitutes the essence of masochistic pleasure; it is the 'casting' of the play that is the main source of delight here.

Masturbation: while Sigmund Freud (1905a, 1908c) had described childhood masturbation and its displaced forms leading to 'masturbatory equivalents' (e.g., hair pulling, playing with the ear lobe or nose), it was Victor Tausk (1912) who provided a formal definition of 'masturbation'. According to him, masturbation is constituted by 'that kind of sexual manipulation of genitals or of an erogenous zone which has no partner as an indispensable prerequistite, and the aim of which consists in the direct discharge of sexual excitation' (p. 62). A number of subsequent analysts made important contributions to the understanding of such autoerotic sexuality. Prominent among these are Sandor Ferenczi (1925b), Ludwig Eidelberg (1945), Otto Fenichel (1945), Annie Reich (1951), Jacob Arlow (1953), Berta Bornstein (1953), Steven Hammerman (1961), Virginia Clower (1976), Moses Laufer (1982) and Theodore Shapiro (2008). Insights derived from the works of these contributors are wide-ranging and include: (1) disappointments in early object relations lead to narcissistic withdrawal and this, in turn, accentuates the ordinary self-exploratory and masturbatory activity into its more driven forms; (2) direct genital masturbation is less apparent than rocking movements and even faecal play in object-deprived children; (3) the rhythmicity typical of sucking movements at the breast lays down the somatic prototype of the to-and-fro movement of masturbation and of sexual acts in general; (4) fantasies attached to masturbation involve early object ties, but are subject to transformations that are both defensive and phase-specific; in general, adult masturbation with conscious fantasies involving parents belies a guarding prognosis; (5) defences against masturbation might involve compulsive rituals and scrupulousness as well as the splitting apart of the masturbatory organ and the masturbatory method for the purpose of disguising the actual intent; (6) displacement of masturbation can involve non-genital bodily activities, but also contact with animals and inanimate objects (including cigars!); (7) the actual act of masturbation, and even the accompanying fantasy, might be used as a defence against more regressive aims; (8) with greater 'ownership of the body' (see separate entry), guilt regarding masturbation diminishes; in adolescence a 'normalization' (Shapiro, 2008, p. 123) of the central masturbation fantasy occurs. 'The path towards airing these private fantasies is facilitated by chumship relationships as a step toward further exposure to the social surround' (p. 123); (9) a thorough analytic treatment should include a careful analysis of the total masturbatory process; and (10) 'the reappearance of direct masturbation during the course of an analysis is frequently an indicator of beginning therapeutic improvement' (Hammerman, 1961, p. 291).

Material: analytic colloquialism for clinical data, especially as it is presented in supervisory sessions or academic seminars or reported in publications. Thus, one hears colleagues say that 'the material he presented was actually quite convincing', 'let us hear some material', and so on.

Maternal and paternal modes in technique: designating two poles of therapeutic technique as maternal and paternal, Kenneth Wright (1991) traces their respective origins to Sigmund Freud and Donald Winnicott. According to Wright, 'Freud stands for the father with his forbidding and fulfillment; Winnicott stands for the mother and her caring, nurturing, and loving. Freud is the mediator of reality principle to which the child must adapt; Winnicott is the protector of a kinder, more lenient space, which keeps reality, to some extent, at bay' (p. 280). In Wright's view, analysis involves a renewal of the process of psychic formation. It provides the space within which new forms or symbols of the self may be created. However, for fully separated and representative symbols as well as less separated and iconic symbols in the human discourse to emerge, be understood, and coalesce, the analytic technique requires both maternal and paternal elements. The maternal element (holding, facilitating, enabling, and surviving) 'posits faith in the background process. Things will happen if you wait' (p. 283). The paternal element (searching, confronting, deciphering, and interpreting) underlies the analyst's scepticism, his struggles with the patient's resistances, and his confrontations with the turbulent world of intrapsychic conflict. The two modes of intervention might be appropriate at different times and foster different modes of symbolizing. However, maternal holding of the psychically banished elements has to precede a meaningful looking at them for self-understanding. In essence, the maternal and paternal elements of technique 'provide a point and counterpoint in analysis between two styles and two visions and neither wins the day completely' (p. 300). See also the related entry on 'classic and romantic visions of psychoanalysis'.

Maternal enthralment: term coined by the Indian psychoanalyst Sudhir Kakar (2001) for the iridescent and luminous feelings of love that a boy feels just when he begins to discover his and his mother's sexuality and before a potential rival (the father) has entered into this experience. Such a love is a brief interlude of *jouissance*, a period when mother, for once, is experienced as overarchingly sexual. The wish to stay in this state contributes to the formation of an unconscious fantasy of eternal sexual excitement. In elucidating Kakar's complex ideas, Manasi Kumar (2005) states that 'what makes this idea interesting is the notion that hate or badness is projected onto the act of expericing orgasm. In effect, one seeks to get back to the original erotic play with the mother (her physical, bodily, and mental prescence), where intense sexual arousal and excitement were generated; but sexual intercourse with a woman would amount to an unconscious attempt to have intercourse with the mother—it is that which appears incestuous and this disables pleasurable unity with the mother' (p. 572). The Indian male, then, remains in a state of 'maternal enthralment' by adoring women's sensuality but splitting-off or fearing adult genital female sexuality. The sexual woman seems demonically powerful and becomes the depository of the man's own split-off phallic self-representations. Surrender to a woman thus acquires a 'feminine' and masochistic tinge as well. The threat posed by women's sexuality to the male identity under such circumstances is warded off, according to the New Delhi based analyst, Ashok Nagpal (2000), by drawing strength from a life-long dependence upon spiritual gurus and family patriarchs.

Maternal reverie: Wilfred Bion's (1967) term for the mother's capacity to hold, contain, elaborate, and transform her baby's unspoken and unspeakable thoughts and affects into thinkable and understandable ideas. The existence and sustenance of this capacity is a sign of mother's love. A counterpart of such transformative 'daydreaming' on the other's behalf is to be seen in the 'analyst's reverie' (see separate entry).

Mature ego defences: while ego defences associated with a high level of functioning have been described by a number of authors (Kernberg, 1970; Jacobson et al., cited in Vaillant, 1992), the term 'mature defences' is generally associated with the work of George Vaillant (1992). Included among these are the following: (1) *altruism*, which involves constructive and gratifying service to others, (2) *humour*, which permits playful acknowledgement and expression of feelings that would otherwise have been uncomfortable, (3) *suppression*, which facilitates postponing action and thus permits further thinking, (4) *anticipation*, which helps in planning for the future, including how to deal with difficult situations in inner and outer reality, and (5) *sublimation*, which makes attenuated and socially acceptable expression of instincts possible (see separate entries on 'Altruism' 'Suppression' and 'Sublimation'.

Mature dependence: see 'Dependence'

Mature love: according to Otto Kernberg (1974a,b, 1995a) two developmental achievements are necessary for the capacity for 'mature love': (1) the early capacity for sensuous arousal must be integrated with the later capacity for total object relations, and (2) early body-surface eroticism must be brought under the dominance of full genital enjoyment in the context of a total object relation that includes a complementary sexual identification. The preoedipal tasks of integrating love and hate, acquiring 'object constancy' (see separate entry), and developing the capacity for sustained and in-depth relatedness with others must be achieved. Also necessary is the mastery of the oedipal tasks of (1) mending the 'affectionate and sensual currents' (Freud, 1912d, p. 180) of psychic love life, (2) developing and abiding by the incest barrier, and therefore finding extrafamilial partners for romantic love, and (3) consolidating the dyadic boundaries of the romantic couple in identification with the experience of unity between parents during the oedipal phase. Martin Bergmann (1971) adds that in order to achieve 'mature love', the ego (1) has to realistically assess the qualities of love object, though too much reliance upon reality can spoil love, (2) must integrate aspects of many childhood love objects into the love object of adult life, (3) integrate its own bisexual identifications, (4) counteract the superego so that the inevitable similarity of the love object with parental figures of childhood does not become incestuous in the mind, and (5) counteract the inner pressure of 're-finding the impossible, the replica of longed-for symbiosis'. However, as Janine Chasseguet-Smirgel (1984) noted, the pain over remnant longings for oneness with primary objects and incestuous gratifications is compensated for by the attachment to the love object and its sustained availability. All in all, 'mature love' integrates the passionate character of the 'three aspects: the sexual relationship, the object relationship, and the superego investment of the couple' (Kernberg, 1995a, p. 32.).

Mechanisms of defence: see 'Defence mechanisms'.

Medication and psychoanalysis: while published statements to the effect are difficult to locate, the commonly held view until recently has been that the use of psychotropic medications is contraindicated in conjunction with psychoanalysis. These drugs were seen to siphon off the anxiety that motivates the patient, alter ego functions, and dampen the sadness and mourning consequent upon letting go of infantile psychosexual aims. All this has undergone a change. Recent surveys indicate that nearly 30 per cent of patients in analysis are also on medications and nearly 60 per cent of analysts have at least one such patient in their practice (Roose & Stern, 1995; Donovan & Roose, 1995; Michels, 1995; Yang et al., 2004). A new generation of psychoanalysts trained in the era of psychopharmacological revolution in psychiatry, pressures of the changed health insurance environment in the USA, and the arrival on the analyst's clinical doorstep of patients who are already on medications are among the factors responsible for this change (Gottlieb, 2006). A recent set of papers by Susan Bers (2006), Robert Glick and Steven Roose (2006), Wendy Olesker (2006), Adele Tutter (2006), and Josephine Wright (2006), in a special issue of the *Journal of the American Psychoanalytic Association*, address this topic from various perspectives. Setting finer nuances aside, five important conclusions can be derived from pooling the ideas proposed in these contributions with those proposed earlier (Ostow, 1962; Awad, 2001): (1) psychoanalytic treatment is compatible with the use of psychotropic medications; (2) medications can acquire myrid symbolic significance, affect transference (by becoming a stand-in for the analyst or by becoming a third object), stir up fantasies, and elicit countertransference reactions; (3) the introduction and use of medications should, therefore, be handled as any other intervention, i.e., with the usual analytic oscillation (Killingmo, 1989) between the poles of credulous listening, leading to affirmative interventions, and sceptical listening, leading to interpretive interventions; (4) both 'split treatment' (where medication is prescribed by someone other than the analyst) and 'combined treatment' (where the analyst does both) can be effective; the former needs a good collaborative alliance between the three parties; and (5) since prescribing and analysing require different types of conversation, 'the analyst must be "bi-lingual". All conversations about the "medications" and "psychoanalysis" must be simultaneously translated in the mind of the analyst' (Glick & Roose, 2006, p. 761). See also Gregg Gorton and Salman Akhtar's (1990) paper on the use of medications in the treatment of personality disorders, and the recent book by Allan Tasman, Michelle Riba, and Kenneth Silk (2000) for the converse dynamics: i.e., the use of psychoanalytic ideas in managing pharmacotherapy to improve treatment effectiveness.

Memory trace: using it interchangeably with 'mnemic trace' and, at times, with 'mnemic image', Sigmund Freud (1895d, 1900a, 1923b, 1925a) defined 'memory trace' as the recording and topographical storage of a perception of later recall. 'Memory traces' could be classified according to their (1) associative links, (2) chronological sequence, and (3) accessibility to consciousness. While active effort at recall could only bring forth pre-conscious memory traces, environmental triggers to a pertinent chain of associations could mobilize memory traces that were unconscious.

Mental energy: see 'Psychic energy'.

Mental health: see 'Normality'.

Mental pain: while poets and writers from around the globe had written about 'mental pain' for hundreds of years, a 'scientific' exposition of it was first provided by Sigmund Freud in 1926. He acknowledged that he knew little about *Seelenschmerz* (literally, soul-pain) and fumbled in describing it. He referred to a child's crying for his mother and evoked analogies to bodily injury and loss of body parts. He also mentioned a sense of 'yearning' and mental helplessness as being components of mental pain. Subsequent analysts continued to use words such as 'pining' (Klein, 1940, p. 360) and 'longing' (Joffee & Sandler, 1965, p. 156) in association with mental pain. They also resorted to somatic analogies and metaphors. Alan Wheelis (1966) referred to the 'furtive pain around the mouth' (p. 161). Betty Joseph (1981) noted the frequency with which physical allusions appear in associations to mental pain stating that it is 'experienced as on the border between mental and physical' (p. 89). Reviewing these and other (e.g., Kogan, 1990) writings on the topic, Salman Akhtar (2000) concluded that 'mental pain' consists of a wordless sense of self-rupture, longing, and psychic helplessness that is vague and difficult to convey to others. It usually follows the loss of a significant object or its abrupt refusal to meet one's anaclitic needs. This results in the laceration of an unconscious, fused self-object core of the self. Abruptly precipitated discrepancies between the actual and wished-for self-states add to the genesis of mental pain. Issues of hatred, guilt, moral masochism as well as fantasies of being beaten can also be folded into the experience of 'mental pain'. The feeling is highly disturbing and is warded off by characteristic defences (see 'Defences against mental pain').

Mental representation: term denoting the 'relatively permanent image' (Rycroft, 1968, p. 142) of something that has been previously perceived. The term 'mental representation' is used synonomously with 'psychic representation', 'mental image', 'memory image', and 'mnemic image'. It underscores the distinction between external reality and 'psychic reality' (see separate entry) by reminding one that the mental imagos of self and objects are just that, i.e., mental constructs. All objects are, therefore, only 'object representations', and so is the self which, at its base, reflects nothing but an amalgam of diverse 'self representations'. The construction of 'mental representation' is affected by the degree of drive activity and the level of ego maturity at the time when the representation is formed, the prevalent sociocultural idiom, and the objective qualities of the object. See also the related entry on 'thing presentation and word presentation'.

Mentalization: although this term had been used in a different context (Baron-Cohen, 1995), its psychoanalytic use began with the work of Peter Fonagy and Mary Target (Fonagy, 1998, 1999; Fonagy & Target, 1997; Target & Fonagy, 1996). Also calling it the 'reflective mode' of psychic functioning, these authors define 'mentalization' as the capacity to reflect upon one's own thoughts and to experience mental states as representations. 'Mentalization' evolves from the integration of the earlier mental operations called 'psychic equivalence' and 'pretend mode' (see separate entries); the former of these implies a conflation of intrapsychic and external realities and the latter a splitting-off of the two. 'Mentalization', in contrast, allows for linking up the internal and external realties. Its emergence and consolidation depends heavily upon the reflection of one's mental states in the context of secure play during childhood. In other words, the growing child needs the help of parents and older siblings in order to achieve the capacity for 'mentalization'. The importance of 'mentalization' is evident in the following ways: (1) it enables the child to see people's actions as meaningful, since they seem based upon feelings and thoughts; (2) it creates the possibility of distinguishing between 'inner and outer truth' (Target & Fonagy, 1996, p. 462). In other words, the child becomes able to conclude that simply because someone is behaving in this or that fashion does not mean that things *are* that way; this has prophylactic value against taking over the responsibility for being maltreated; (3) it facilitates communication, since keeping others' perspective in mind improves listening, and guides responding; and (4) it enhances 'inter-subjectivity' (see separate entry) and therefore deepens life experience. All this readily indicates the importance of 'mentalization' for psychotherapy and psychoanalysis. See also 'mentalization-based therapy'.

Mentalization-based therapy: refers to a set of psychotherapeutic interventions evolved from the work of Peter Fonagy and colleagues (Fonagy & Target, 1996, 1997; Target & Fonagy, 1996; Allen & Fonagy, 2006; Bateman & Fonagy, 2006). Such treatment pays focused attention to facilitating 'mentalization' (see separate entry) which, at the risk of oversimplification, can be seen as the capacity to understand how behaviour and feelings are both related to underlying mental states, not just in oneself, but also in others. While it was developed for the treatment of borderline patients, 'mentalization-based therapy' is now being incorporated in family therapy, child and adolescent therapy, and work with hospitalized patients. Regardless of the context, the interventional strategy is aimed at enhancing self-reflective capacities (Allen, 2006; Holmes, 2006).

Mentalized affectivity: extending the work of Peter Fonagy and colleagues (Fonagy & Target, 1996; Fonagy, Gergely, Jurist, & Target, 2005), Elliott Jurist (2005) proposed the concept of 'mentalized affectivity'. This refers to a particular kind of affect regulation which entails evalutating and not just regulating affects. Three elements of such affectivity include (1) identifying affects (naming and distinguishing feeling states); (2) processing affects (modulating and refining feelings); and (3) expressing affects (including both outward and inward expression and communication of feelings). Each of these elements exists on a basic and a complex level.

Mentor: a development-facilitating object of young adulthood that helps consolidate and advance one's work-related identity. A 'mentor' has similarities with the roles of a teacher, parent, lover, and psychotherapist, and yet is different from each (Akhtar, 2003). Like a teacher, he imparts knowledge, but, unlike him, he develops a special relationship with the protégé and facilitates the latter's growth by more than didactic means. Like a parent, he offers himself as a role model and encourages links with his name and prestige. Unlike a parent, he is free of distortions derived from early instinctual investments and is also not responsible for the real life issues of his mentee. Like a lover, he has an intense bond with his mentee; the two also strive to create a mutual product, rather like a baby. Unlike a lover, the mentor does not enter into a romantic relationship with the protégé and prevents the latter's 'respect crushes' (Eleanor Ainslie, personal communication, September 2007) from becoming sexualized. Like a psychotherapist, he knows, or attempts to know, the personality functioning of the young one in his care. However, his focus remains upon the outer rind of the latter's ego and his knowledge of the personal background helps him tran-scend it by wit, cajoling, and light-hearted con-frontation.

Merger fantasies: psychic elaborations whereby an individual envisions a state of oneness with another person. Three different contexts have elicited the description of such phenomena: (1) the blissful fusion with the universe in the state called ' oceanic feeling' (see separate entry), (2) the permeability of boundaries during 'mother–infant symbiosis'(see separate entry), and (3) the re-establishment of archaic identity with a self-object of early childhood during a 'merger trans-ference' (see separate entry). Regardless of the vantage point, all 'merger fantasies' seem to hark back to the early mother–infant relationship. The questions that remain unanswered include the following: when are such fantasies ego-replenish-ing and what circumstances turn them into the dread of engulfment? Are there developmental phases that intensify 'merger fantasies' or at least heighten the emotional response to them? Are such fantasies normal during sex? What is the dif-ference between a peaceful religious mendicant who feels at one with the cosmos and a borderline who is desperate to lose his self and merge with the other? While the answers to these questions are far from clear, developmental phase-speci-ficity, degree of object hunger, intensity of aggres-sion, and the extent of ego consolability seem to play an important role here.

Merger hungry personalities: see 'Narcissistic personality types'.

Merger transference: described by Heinz Kohut (1977), this type of transference reflects the re-establishment of oneness with a self object (see separate entry) of childhood via extension of the self to include the analyst. The analysand does not perceive the analyst to have a separate and auton-omous psychic life. Instead, he experiences the analyst to be in perfect unison with his psychic events and processes.

Messianic sadism: Salman Akhtar's (2007c) term for cruelty towards others that in the internal world of the perpetrator seems morally justified. 'Messianic sadism' is a facet of extreme ethno-racial and religious prejudice. As the extreme end of hateful prejudice is approached, the raw aggression of the id begins to flow in the veins of the superego. An idealized self-image and an ego syntonic sadistic ideology begins to rationalize antisocial behaviour. Thinking becomes danger-ously stilted and all capacity for empathy with

others is lost. When such a state of mind receives encouragement from politico–religious exhorta-tions, violence appears to be guilt-free and even 'divinely' sanctioned. Killing others becomes a means of buttressing one's own callous megalo-mania and also merging with an idealized deity or leader who comes to embody an archaic and omnipotent superego.

Metamorphosis: Heinz Lichtenstein's (1963) term for an inherent pull (evident from infancy and extending through the entire life span) or a long-ing to abandon the human quality of identity alto-gether. This can be anxiety producing or blissful. It underlies the capacity for 'self-dehumaniza-tion', which can have a variety of psychological antecedents and consequences (Akhtar, 2003).

Metapsychology: term first used by Sigmund Freud in 1898 to designate a psychology that he hoped would lead behind consciousness. The pre-fix 'meta' in 'metapsychology' had a connection with 'metaphysics' as well for Freud, since he viewed the latter as dealing with issues (e.g., superstition, speculations about life after death) that illustrated nothing but psychology projected outwards upon the matters of nature. However, it was not until his paper 'The unconscious' (1915e) that Freud proposed the operational definition of 'metapsychology' as an approach that takes 'dynamic, topographical, and economic aspects' (p. 181) of psychological phenomena. As the work of subsequent analysts, especially Heinz Hart-mann, Ernst Kris, and Rudolph Loewenstein (Hartmann, 1939, 1950, 1952; Hartmann, Kris, & Loewenstein, 1946) accrued, more 'perspectives' were added to this list. David Rapaport's (1960; see also Rapaport & Gill, 1959) seminal synthesis described a metapsychological approach to con-sist of the following five perspectives, with their paradigmatic questions regarding the psychologi-cal phenomenon at hand: (1) *topographic perspective* (what is conscious, preconscious, and unconscious in this material?); (2) *dynamic perspective* (what forces are involved in the compromises that are evident here?); (3) *economic perspective* (what is the energic distribution here? Is something in this experience 'too much' or 'too little'?); (4) *genetic perspective* (what is the childhood prototype or determinant of this experience?); and (5) *adaptive perspective* (how is this fantasy or behaviour useful to the individual? What purpose is it serving?). While many contemporary psychoanalysts have moved away from this rigorous manner of con-ceptualization and taken a phenomenological and 'literary' (Green, 2005, p. xviii) path, the fact is that 'metapsychology' remains the heuristic backbone of what is central to psychoanalysis. See also Arnold Modell's (1981) well-reasoned defence of this position.

Methods of listening in psychoanalysis: see 'Analytic listening'.

Methods of observation in psychoanalysis: James Spencer and Leon Balter (1990) have classified methods of 'psychoanalytic observation' into two types: the 'introspective' and 'behavioural'. In the former, the analyst puts himself in the position of the analysand and derives clinical understanding from his perspective. In the latter, the analyst adopts the 'view of a spectator, without regard to the subject's own thoughts or feelings' (p. 402). The two methods, often yielding different sets of information, are complementary, each modifying the other in the service of deepening the grasp of the analysand's mental functioning (see also the related entry on 'Analytic listening').

Mid-life crisis: A number of psychoanalytic investigators, especially Erik Erikson (1950, 1959), Elliott Jaques (1965), Theodore Lidz (1968), George Vaillant (1977), Stanley Cath (1965) and Otto Kernberg (1980), have described the developmental tasks specific to the period of middle age. These include coming to grips with external aggression, acceptance of limits, acknowledgement of bodily changes, assimilation of a shift in time perspective, renegotiation of oedipal challenges, and creation of ego-integrity. Such pressures on the ego can and do lead to some regression, some denial, and an occasional acting out. In fortunate circumstances, when internal and external objects remain supportive and available, a subtle but profound reconfiguration of character takes place in the direction of equanimity, dignity, and wisdom. Under less fortunate circumstances, when persecutory and depressive anxieties cannot be worked through, the regression is severe. Major ruptures in the continuity of personal and professional life now happen, leading to chaos and destabilization all around oneself. This is what is called a 'midlife crisis'.

Middle phase: although it is not listed in psychoanalytic glossaries (Moore & Fine, 1968, 1990; Rycroft, 1968; Eidelberg, 1968; Laplanche & Pontalis, 1973), the term 'middle phase' is frequently used in the discourse about psychoanalytic technique. Sigmund Freud's (1913c) oft-quoted remark that, in conducting psychoanalysis, 'only the openings and end game admit of an exhaustive systematic presentation' (p. 133) accomplished the dual task of creating, as it were,

a 'middle phase' as well as stirring up some intrigue about it by leaving it undefined. Of course, Freud wrote about matters pertaining to it in his guidelines about working with transference (1912e) and in his paper on working through (1914g), but he never gave a systematic description of the 'middle phase', with the clear beginning and end points of it. This is perhaps because the 'middle phase' is exquisitely unique for each treatment. Should it then suffice to say that 'middle phase' subsumes all that happens between the end of 'beginning phase' and beginning of 'termination phase' (see separate entries)? If this is correct, the onset of 'middle phase' would be indicated by the crystallization of fleeting transference reactions into 'transference neurosis' (see separate entry). The 'middle phase' would last until transference pressures on the analyst diminish, the patient's attention shifts towards the future, and reasonable evidence of major transferences having been worked through is demonstrated; in other words, when 'termination' is in the air. Analytic work during the 'middle phase' (e.g., Fenichel, 1941; Greenson, 1967) is characterized by consistent resistance analsysis, deepening of transference–countertransference experience, dream analysis, interpretive handling of enactments, reconstructions, and, above all, the tedious process of 'working through' (see separate entry), by which the patient gains insight into how many different ways and with what self-deceptive ease he still remains vulnerable to his infantile longings; trying new ways of acting, maintaining vigilance towards the potential for regression, and increasingly self-observant building up of core childhood conflictual issues with their adult life, and transferential re-creations are all tasks of the 'middle phase'. In essence, the most important work of analytic treatment takes place during the 'middle phase', though both 'opening' and 'termination' phases have their own special therapeutic value as well.

Militarization of identity: in most societies, the attitudes, preoccupations, and language of civilian life remain at a distance from those of the army. In certain other societies, where ethnic warfare is a matter of daily occurrence, this gap collapses, resulting in a 'militarization of identity' (Awad, 2007). Civilian and army mentalities begin to overlap and the individual identity acquires a militant quality.

Mini countertransference: see 'Countertransference'.

Mirror complimentary of the self: phrase first used by Sheldon Bach (1977) for describing a split-off self-representation which harbours personality attributes contrary to those consciously presented to oneself and others. 'Someone who feels physically weak and powerless may harbor a grandiose and dangerous powerful split-off image, while someone who presents with arrogance and grandiosity may be fearful of the dangerously vulnerable and dependent little-child self' (p. 16). Such sequestering of self-representations is usually defensive. However, it can also represent a developmental failure to achieve self-coherence. In the clinical situation, the repudiated self-representation is often deposited into the analyst, who is then controlled and manipulated by projective identification.

Mirror dreams: fascinatingly, the dreams of seeing oneself in a mirror find little mention in Sigmund Freud's (1900a) seminal treatise on dreams. The first description of them was provided by Milton Miller in 1948. Since then a considerable literature, with all sorts of fulfilment ideas, has accrued on this topic. For instance, a phenomenological nuance was added by Stanley Coen and Paul Bradlow (1985) by distinguishing 'common mirror dreams' (where the dreamer sees himself looking into a mirror) from 'uncommon mirror dreams' (where some other dream character looks into a mirror). These authors regard only the former as bona fide 'mirror dreams'. The dynamic significance of such dreams has varied explanations. Miller (1948) regarded them as the evidence of the ego's enhanced ability to integrate hitherto repressed parts of the personality. Alan Eisnitz (1961) concluded that 'mirror dreams' represented an attempt to undo narcissistic mortification or castration threat emanating from the superego; the threatening part of the superego was projected on to the mirror and mastered and re-internalized through omnipotent voyeurism. Heinz Kohut (1971) related 'mirror dreams' to 'mirror transference' (see separate entry) and a continued search for an empathic and affirming selfobject. Coen and Bradlow (1985) observed that every dreamer of 'mirror dreams', in their experience, had felt enjoined by the mother not to see her or reflect her back clearly. A 'mirror dream' represented 'the wish that the analyst–mother counter a feared injunction against accurate visual perception and evaluation so as to correct the distorted perceptions of self and objects and provide visual affirmation of the value and, perhaps, the integrity of the self representation' (p. 798).

Mirror hungry personalities: see 'Narcissistic personality types'.

Mirror phase: described by Heinz Kohut (1977), this is the developmental period during which the gleam in the mother's eye mirrors the child's exhibitionistic display and thus helps to consolidate his phase-specific 'grandiosity'. Mother's responses to her child's narcissistic–exhibitionistic enjoyment range from verbal affirmations to empathic and enthusiastic participation in the child's activities. Kohut emphasized that such maternal 'mirroring' confirms 'the child's self-esteem and, by a gradually increasing selectivity of these responses, begin to channel it into realistic directions' (p. 116). See also the views of Malcolm Pines (1984) on mirroring.

Mirror stage: described by Jacques Lacan (1949) as the developmental period between the age of six months and eighteen months. The importance of this stage lies in the fact that the baby begins to recognize the image he sees in a mirror (the 'specular image') as his own. However, this image stands in contrast to his unco-ordinated, 'fragmented body' (see separate entry). As a result, the child feels rivalrous towards his image, which seems more whole. In order to overcome this tension, the child identifies with his own image. The ego is thus born. However, it is the product of a misunderstanding which, despite its jubilant affect, lays the ground for the subject's 'alienation' (see separate entry) from himself. In later work, Lacan (1956, 1977) shifted the emphasis from the chronological to the structure-giving aspect of the 'mirror stage'.

Mirror transference: although the metaphor of the mirror has been used by various psychoanalytic theorists (e.g., Donald Winnicott, Jacques Lacan, Margaret Mahler), the concept of 'mirror transference' owes its origin to Heinz Kohut (1971). According to him, 'mirror transference' reflects the therapeutic reactivation of the narcissistic patient's grandiose self. Furthermore, there are three types of mirror transferences. (1) *Merger type*, in which the patient experiences the analyst as an extension of his grandiose self. It is as if the analyst were a part of him with no mind of his own. (2) *Alter-ego type*, in which the patient feels that the analyst is just like him, that is, they are psychological twins; another name for this type of transference is 'twinship transference'. (3) *The true mirror transference*, where the patient does experience the analyst as a separate person, but one whose significance is restricted to reflecting the patient's grandiose self. This mirror transference is the therapeutic reinstatement of that normal 'mirror phase' (see separate entry) of childhood.

Mirroring: see 'Mirror phase'.

Misfit: Arnold Goldberg's (1983) term for a character type with sustained subjective feeling of not belonging to any group and of not being able to fit in with others. One with such a character is usually a person in 'transition from one developmental stage to another, unable to forge ahead or to adapt successfully through retreat' (p. 293). Unlike 'exceptions' (Freud, 1916d), who insist upon standing apart from the crowd, 'misfits' desperately long to lose themselves in a larger group.

Misrecognition: see 'Recognition and misrecognition'.

Missed appointments: undergoing psychoanalysis requires a regular attendance at four to five times per week sessions with one's analyst. This needs discipline. While pre-arranged absences that have been realistically discussed and interpretively explored cause less disturbance to the flow of the analytic process, it is the unexpected, sudden, and impulsive absence from the session that draws greater analytic attention. Purposes of resistance, acting-out, and transference-based enactments can all be served by such 'missed sessions'. Clearly all this has to be analytically handled i.e. by acknowledgment, exploration, interpretation, and reconstruction. However, the aspect that becomes quite 'charged' (pun intended) for the novice is whether to bill the patient for a missed session or not. In one of his technique papers, Sigmund Freud (1913c) emphasized that the patient is liable for his hour even if he does not make use of it. This gradually became the standard practice, or, at least, the practice that is upheld as the desirable one. Adherence to it is defended by the rationalization that charging for all missed sessions keeps the analytic frame intact and the analyst clear of making 'good absence–bad absence' sort of quasi-moral decisions. However, this overlooks the fact that the 'classical' guidelines were developed in the early twentieth century, when life's pace was slower, analyses were shorter, and authoritarian models of clinical work prevailed. That all this has changed must be considered *vis-à-vis* the charging or not charging policy. Moreover, there might be special groups of patients (e.g., children, college students) whose attendance either depends upon others or upon developmentally appropriate, out of town interludes (for visiting parents, study abroad). A rigid policy, however idealized, hardly seems appropriate under such circumstances. Adam Limentani's (1989) solemn observation that 'psychoanalysis is an art and for this reason it needs discipline' (p. 260) is pertinent in this context.

Mnemic image: see 'Memory trace'.

Mnemic objects: term coined by Christopher Bollas (1992) for 'a particular form of subjective object that contains a projectively identified self-experience, and when we use it, something of that self-estate stored in it will arise' (p. 21). A garden swing set, a grandfather clock, and an old sewing machine may all serve as depositories of unverbalized childhood experiences. Subsequently, they become capable of evoking the early affects simply by coming into sight. Harold Searles' (1960) monograph on the developmental role of non-human environment and Salman Akhtar's (2005) book on the diverse roles 'things' play in human mental life are pertinent is this regard.

Mnemic trace: see 'Memory trace'.

Mobile energy: see 'Psychic energy'.

Mockery through caricature: phrase introduced by Warren Procci (1987) to denote a particular twist to the phenemenology and dynamics of 'moral masochism' (see separate entry). Using this mechanism, the individual emulates a harsh parent to an extreme. Like the usual cases of masochistic character, this allows the individual to maintain an ongoing tie with the primary object. However, the element of excess in patterning one's behaviour after a cruel parent accomplishes another purpose. It exposes to the world the unfairness and absurdity of the parent. Pseudo-compliance with the anti-instinctual attitudes of the parent to the extent of caricature ends up mocking the parent and thus covertly discharging the otherwise repressed aggression towards him or her.

Moment of meeting: described by Daniel Stern and co-authors (1998), this is a 'now moment' (see separate entry) that is 'therapeutically and mutually realized' (p. 913) by both the partners in the clinical dyad. It is highly specific in nature and represents a co-creation of authentic contributions of the analyst and patient. A 'moment of meeting' is hardly routine and technical; it is a 'newly created dyadic state . . . . [and] the point at which the intersubjective context gets altered' (p. 913). Interpretations can lead to a 'moment of meeting' and a 'moment of meeting' can lead to an interpretation. Darlene Ehrenberg (1992) has also emphasized the mutative impact of such moments during the course of an hour.

Moment of hesitation: see 'Spatula game'.

Money-related psychopathology: while speculations abound when it comes to the symbolic significance of money (Freud, 1908b; Ferenczi, 1914; Jones, 1918; Fenichel, 1938, 1945; Krueger, 1986), it is only recently that a succinct discourse on 'money-related psychopathology' has become available. Bringing a considerable body of literature together, Salman Akhtar (2008) has delineated six syndromes in this realm. These include (1) *chronic miserliness*, which is a Janus-faced problem; internally, the miser is filled with dread that spending money will diminish his sense of safety but, interpersonally and out of his own awareness, he is identified with a depriving and sadistic mother; (2) *inordinate generosity*, which is the inverse of miserliness and emanates from an identification with a wished-for bountiful mother; (3) *characterological overspending*, which reflects a 'manic defence' (see separate entry) aimed at sustaining a fragile self, denying felt inferiority, and purchasing relationships; (4) *monetary masochism*, whereby an individual turns financial opportunities away, squanders resources, and fails to enjoy the money he or she has; (4) *bargain hunting* of the type where the sadomasochistic haggling and the desire to outsmart the seller becomes more important than whether one actually needs the pursued object or not (Bergler, 1947); and (6) *pathological gambling*, which draws its lure from the conscious desire for omnipotence via great sums of quickly earned money and from the unconscious desire to lose, suffer, and derive masochistic pleasure from such self-destruction.

Moral defence: this mechanism was described by William Ronald Fairbairn (1940) in connection with schizoid individuals. Its origin is in childhood abuse. The child takes the blame for abuse upon himself and 'forgives' the perpetrator. This has two reasons: the child's egocentric perception, which precludes an awareness of others' independent motivations, and the child's attempts to preserve some hope and optimism. In other words, if the child allows himself to feel that his parents are 'bad', then the situation becomes hopelessly unbearable since he has no other place to go. However, if he feels that it is he who is 'bad', then, by behaving better, he can hope that his parents might treat him better.

Moral masochism: Sigmund Freud's (1924c) designation for the tendency on the part of some individuals to seek suffering and act against their own interests. Such individuals enter into unhappy relationships, fail in business ventures, and have frequent accidents. They are haunted by 'conscience anxiety' or an 'unconscious sense of guilt'. This propels them to chronically need punishment while unconsciously drawing pleasure from their suffering. 'Thus moral masochism becomes a classical piece of evidence for the existence of fusion of instincts' (p. 170). Freud traced the guilt underlying moral masochism to unresolved oedipal issues. Later authors (Asch, 1976; Modell, 1965; Niederland, 1968) noted that guilt derived from other sources (e.g., separation guilt, survivor guilt) can also lead to life-long need for punishment.

Moral masochist: see 'Moral masochism'.

Moral narcissism: like the narcissistic over valuation of the body (resulting in exhibitionism and hypochondriasis) or intellect (resulting in libidinization of thinking about a tendency to dominate others by intellectual prowess), one's conscious can also become an avenue for self-aggrandization, albeit a covert and subtle one. Such 'moral narcissism', a term coined by André Green (1986), gives rise to a yearning to be pure, above ordinary human needs, and free of attachment to others. Green distinguishes the resulting aesceticism (which might be a more frequent presentation of narcissistic personality in oriental cultures) from masochism on two grounds. First, the moral narcissist suffers from shame over his needs, while the moral masochist (see separate entry) suffers from guilt over the nature of his wishes. Second, the moral narcissist seeks to impoverish his true object-relations (love of humanity not being the same as love as human beings) in order to restore his infantile megalomania of self-sufficiency, while the moral masochist retains a tormented but rich tie to his objects. An illustration of moral narcissism comes from Gandhi (1940) who, in attempting to become 'absolutely passion-free' concluded: 'I must reduce myself to zero' (pp. 504–505).

Moral sadism: term introduced into the psychoanalytic literature by Judith Butler in 1998. However, to grasp its essence, one has to take a step back and consider the psychoanalytic theory of melancholia. Extending the well-recognized dictum that the rage against a lost object becomes rage against oneself (Freud, 1917e), Melanie Klein (1934) proposed that with the introjection of a lost object, the ego enters into a moral relationship with it. The sadism that could not have been (and can no longer be) directed at the object is now experienced as guilt towards it. This causes further depletion of the ego's capacity to remain related to the object's 'good' qualities. Judith Butler (1998) furthered these ideas by stating that 'in this act of moralization, the critical voice, which Freud identifies in melancholia, is at first the voice of another berating the ego subsequently uncovered as the voice of the ego as it would have spoken to the lost other if it could have spoken; the voice of moral sadism is essentially equivocal, a rendering reflexive of rage that constitutes the surviving subject's self-annihilating soliloquy' (p. 177). In a recent contribution, Cordelia Schmidt-Hellerau (2009) has used the term 'moral sadism' in a different way, however. In her view, such sadism arises from one's repudiation of oedipal guilt and the externalization of a bad conscience, which makes one 'feel morally superior, even flawless, while enacting the unconscious erotic fantasy of intercourse as a sadistic subjugation and penetration of the object' (p. 236). Schmidt-Hellerau's ideas contain a remote echo of Otto Kernberg's (1992) view that moralizing is a manifestation of 'hatred' (see separate entry) but her emphasis is upon the guilt-relieving functions of 'moral sadism'. See also the related entry on 'messianic sadism.'

Morning ruminative state: John Frosch's (1977) designation of the somewhat hazy period between waking up in the morning and actually beginning the day with clarity. This period is characterized by continued drowsiness interrupted by a flash of an idea pertaining to the anticipated problems of the day and, from then on, a bit of restlessness that finally gives way to clarity. Frosch proposes that the 'morning ruminative state' represents the working over of a problem which appeared, in a disguised form, in the previous night's dream. See also the related entry on 'Day precipitate'.

Morris hypothesis: see 'Day precipitate'.

Mortido: see 'Mortudo'.

Mortudo: a term coined by Eduardo Weiss in early 1920s (Gay, 1988) and rendered as 'mortido' by Paul Federn (1934) to denote the psychic energy of the death instinct. The idea was to create a concept analogous to 'libido' (the psychic energy of the life instinct). Niether version of the term was liked by Sigmund Freud, and therefore they never gained popularity in psychoanalytic literature.

Mosaic transference: Ira Brenner's (2001) term for the feelings patients with 'dissociative identity disorder' (see separate entry) develop towards their therapists. Since the psyche of these patients is splintered, their transference also takes the form of 'separate tiles fitted into a large and complex mosaic' (p. 136). Sudden shifts from one relational paradigm to another, mutual contradictions between various self- and object configurations, and variable degrees of instinctual and affective discharge characterizes such 'mosaic transference' (p. 131).

Mother–infant symbiosis: implicit in the related concepts of 'primary maternal preoccupation', 'symbiotic phase', and 'dual unity' (see separate entries on each) is the idea that a neonate and his mother exist in a state of merger and that this relational configuration takes precedence over their individual interests. There is a 'mother–infant symbiosis', so to speak. At best, such conceptualization is metaphorical, since the infant does not have a differentiated self at this stage and the mother is not really dependent upon him. At worst, it is wrong. Indeed, the notion of the infant–mother symbiotic merger has come under criticism by contemporary child analysts (e.g., Stern, 1985), who view the infant as possessing a greater degree of separateness, intentionality, and agency from the very beginning of life than was previously assumed to be true.

Mother–infant synchrony: described by a number of psychoanalytic infant observers (Stern, 1977; Beebe & Stern, 1977; Sander, 1980; Brazelton, 1980; Lichtenberg, 1982, 1996), 'mother–infant synchrony' refers to the mutually corresponding exchange of eye-to-eye contact, non-verbal vocalizing, and other body language signalling between mother and infant. There is a dance-like quality to such exchanges, with the infant and the mother both taking active part in it. 'With split-screen photography, mother and infant can be observed to perform a repertoire of eye widening, mouth opening, and vocalizings with temporal gradients of speeding up and slowing down. These synchronous actions build up and collapse, to build again, in patterns suggesting a neurophysiologically based behavioral mode of "being with" mother—a type of "we" rather than "you and I"' (Lichtenberg, 1996, p. 58). It is this reciprocity and synchrony that forms the substrate of the deepest level of empathic contact underlying later verbal communication (Stern, 1977).

Mother within the mother: Rosemary Balsam's (2000) phrase that subsumes the internalization of mothers as manifested by their daughters when they become mothers themselves. At times, the new mother finds herself utilizing affective and behavioural constellations that, to her surprise, come directly from her mother. Her emotional response to this might be positive or negative. What seems inevitable, however, is that a new mother would internally encounter 'the intimate actions and attitudes of her primary caretakers as they have imprinted themselves within her' (p. 483). Balsam acknowledged that the earlier concept of 'motherhood constellation' (see separate entry) overlaps with her ideas, but disputed that the internal dialogue of a mother with her own mother is something entirely new. In her view, the new mother's inner discovery of her own mother represents the 'psychodynamic development of a continous inner evolution of mother–daughter' (p. 484) relationship. Pratyusha Tummala-Narra's (2009) observations regarding the difficulties faced by immigrant women as they face motherhood in their adopted countries are also pertinent in this context.

Motherhood constellation: Daniel Stern's (1995) term for the new and unique state of being that a woman discovers upon becoming a mother. This state of being brings forth 'the mother's discourse with her own mother, especially with her own mother-as-mother-to-her-as-a-child; her discourse with herself, especially with herself-as-mother; and her discourse with her baby' (p. 174).

Mourning: Beginning with Freud's (1917e) classic paper 'Mourning and melancholia', through Melanie Klein's (1940, 1946) impressive contributions, to the work of George Pollock (1980) and Vamik Volkan (1981), the role of mourning in human life has been recognized as a paramount one. Regardless of whether the term 'mourning' is used in a 'narrow' sense (i.e., referring to reactions to a loved one's death) or in a 'broad' sense (i.e., referring to reactions to all losses—big or little—and changes in oneself and one's environment), mourning is an ego capacity necessary for peaceful passage through life. It helps us to renounce what can no longer be had and, even though it requires the interpolation of denial and idealization of the lost object as intermediary steps, the work of mourning ultimately releases us from the bondage to earlier objects and earlier relational configurations. It is akin to the healing of a wound. A scar might be left, but the pain certainly diminishes. In this connection, Freud's early idea that a lost object is replaced by a new object once mourning is complete has become questionable. The lost object is not entirely given up. It acquires a quantitatively dimmer and qualitatively different psychic position in the heart and mind of the mourner.

Mourning-liberation process: a term coined by George Pollock (1989) for the Janus-faced nature

of response to trauma: on the one hand it causes grief, and on the other it opens up new vistas of life experience by freeing the person from early objects.

Multideterminism: see the 'Principle of multiple function'

Multi-person psychology: see 'One, two, three, four, and multi-person psychologies'.

Multiple personality: currently termed 'dissociative identity disorder' (*DSM-IV*, 1992, p. 526), the syndrome of 'multiple personality' has long been an object of fascination for psychiatrists and psychoanalysts. Sigmund Freud (1923b) declared that 'the secret of the cases described as multiple personality is that different identifications seize hold of consciousness in turn' (p. 30). He speculated that this happens especially when the ego's object identifications are 'too numerous, unduly powerful, and incompatible with one another' (p. 30). Current literature, however, emphasizes the role of severe child abuse as the main aetiology of multiple personality disorder. Under these circumstances, the self undergoes a defensive fragmentation that is typically associated with elaboration, naming, personification, and dramatization of the sequestered self-representations; an amnesic barrier keeps the various identities apart. Other dissociative phenomena (e.g., fugues, trance-like states, physiognomic alterations) are also common features of the syndrome. A large body of popular and professional literature on the topic exists. Here it will suffice to note the psychoanalytic contributions of Irene Fast (1974), Wilfred Abse (1983), Richard Kluft (1984, 1985, 1986, 1993), and Ira Brenner (1994, 2001).

Multisensory bridges: a concept evolved by Ira Brenner (1988) to describe a response to traumatic loss in which early developmentally appropriate sensory experiences are revived in memory and used to re-create the illusion of being with lost loved ones. While originally introduced in the context of children who survived the Holocaust and were traumatically separated from their parents, the concept can be extended to explain certain psychosomatic aspects of the experience of nostalgia in general.

Mutative interpretation: phrase originated by James Strachey (1934) for interpretations which demonstrate to the patient how his or her harsh superego has been projected upon those around him, especially the analyst. The two essential ingredients of a 'mutative interpretation' are (i) its addressing matters that are emotionally active in the 'here-and-now' of an analytic session, and (ii) its softening impact upon the patient's super-ego which, in turn, allows for greater emergence of wishes and the possibility of their modulation and expression by the ego. The first of these two ingredients has been commonly misunderstood to mean solely 'transference interpretations' (see separate entry). While such interpretations are extremely useful, the fact is that not all transference interpretations are mutative and not all mutative interpretations pertain to the transference. Extra-transference interpretations (see separate entry) can also be mutative. A psychodynamically naïve patient, for instance, can derive great benefit by being shown that his reactions to his boss emanate from the unconscious attribution of his own inner harshness to him; the impact of such an interpretation is especially powerfully felt if it is given while the patient is recounting a clash with his boss in an emotionally charged manner.

Mutual analysis: as Sandor Ferenczi (1929, 1932) became increasingly convinced that actual experience in the analytic relationship held greater therapeutic value than interpretation, he took the step of sharing his own thoughts and feelings with his analysands. The growing openness in the dyad led his patients to see and address his limitations. One patient insisted that she should have the right to analyse him, since his conflicts were impeding her treatment. 'Mutual analysis' thus began. Ferenczi felt that such bilateral analysis (1) diminished the patient's fear of the analyst and thus loosened repression; (2) reduced the patient's sense of inferiority, since he or she could now see the analyst's conflicts and limitations, and (3) made things 'real'; the analyst's disclosures made the patient give up unrealistic expectations. Alongside these advantages, there existed serious problems including (1) the impossibility of having an analysis with each patient, (2) the difficulty in titrating self-disclosures in accordance with the patient's preparedness at a given moment and ego structure in general, (3) the possibility that clinical attention might shift entirely away from the patient's problems, and (4) the difficulty in assuring confidentiality in regard to the analyst's self-disclosures. Keenly aware of the double-edged nature of the mutual analytic scalpel, Ferenczi struggled throughout his clinical career with this challenging innovation of technique, sometimes restricting and at other times expanding its scope. Today, the practice hardly exists, but the shadows of it can be seen in the relational perspective (e.g., Ehrenberg, 1974; Mitchell, 1993; Ogden, 1994) that regards the clinical material as 'co-constructed' by the dyad and also in the renewed vigour about candour and self-disclosure on the part of the analyst (Renik, 1995, 1998, 1999).

Mutual cueing: term used by Margaret Mahler, Fred Pine, and Anni Bergman (1975) to describe a circular process of interaction between mother and infant by which they intuitively read each other's signals and react accordingly to each other. Such attunement forms the most fundamental substrate of the later development of 'empathy' (see separate entry) and of feeling understood by others.

Mutual regression: Karen Maroda's (1991) term for the need for merger and shared madness that some patients require to feel truly engaged in analytic work. Extending such narrow use of the term to the larger principle of relational intersubjectivity, Lewis Aron and Annabelle Bushra (1998) propose that regression, during analysis, always affects both the analysand and the analyst. The analyst does not remain 'normal' while the patient regresses. Both parts move through a wide range of states, including some that are regressive.

$$\boxed{\text{N}}$$

Name-of-the-father: expression used by Jacques Lacan (1955, 1977) to underscore three aspects of the father's role in the child's mind: (1) his role in establishing the incest barrier, (2) his role in laying down the law, so to speak, in general, and (3) his role in imparting a historical dimension to the child's sense of identity.

Nameless dread: term coined by Karin Stephen (1941) to denote an intense form of infantile anxiety which is coupled with a feeling of powerlessness in the face of inner instinctual tension. This concept was further elaborated by Wilfred Bion (1962a) who suggested that 'nameless dread' happens when the child's mother is unable to transform his inchoate tension into meaningful, even if unpleasant, experience through her reverie.

Naming and containing: in a paper by this very title, Ronald Britton (1998) noted that the psychoanalytic situation functions as both a sanctuary and as a space where meaning can be found. The latter is facilitated by 'naming' affects and other psychic experiences. 'If a name enshrines a psychic quality—like love, for example—the word provides a container for the emotional experience, putting a semantic boundary around it. It also places it in a ready-made context of significance provided by the place in human affairs of love and the place of the word in an existing language' (p. 21). In turn, the experience of the emotion provides meaning to the word for that person.

Naming and taming: extrapolating Annie Katan's (1961) observation that, during early childhood, 'verbalization leads to an increase of the controlling function of the ego over affects and drives' (p. 185), Vamik Volkan (1976) suggested that simply naming the emotion overwhelming a patient at a particular moment is often helpful in calming him down. Volkan added that patients in a state of 'emotional flooding' (see separate entry) might also be helped by being addressed by their name. Naming the emotion provides a cognitive handle for ego dominance, and naming the person restores identity and slows down the diabolical transformation intense affects, especially rage, tend to cause. Volkan used the phrase 'naming and taming' collectively for such interventions.

Narcissism: Sigmund Freud (1914c) first used this term in a 1910 footnote to his earlier written monograph *Three Essays on the Theory of Sexuality* (1905a). He then elaborated upon the concept in a number of subsequent essays, most notably 'On narcissism' (1914c). Essentially, his views on narcissism can be seen as consisting of the following ideas: (1) *primary vs. secondary narcissism:* the former is the original libidinal investment in the self and the latter is the result of withdrawal of cathexis from objects; (2) *narcissistic object choice:* this consists of loving only those who reflect the attributes of oneself; (3) *narcissistic foundations of the ego ideal:* the psychic structure that contains the ideal version of ourselves and propels us towards actualizing that image is based upon the shifting of narcissism from a psychic today to a psychic tomorrow; (4) *relationship between love and narcissism:* Freud (1914c) noted that 'a person who loves has, so to speak, forfeited a part of his narcissism, and it can only be replaced by his being loved' (p. 98); he also noted that in the state of love 'the object has been placed in the place of the ego ideal' (1921c, p. 113) and is thus idealized; (5) *narcissistic character type:* Freud (1931a) described a character organization with aggressiveness, leadership qualities, and fascinating impact upon others as related to great libidinal cathexis of the ego. Many subsequent analysts have made major contributions to the study of narcissism. Sydney Pulver (1970) and Salman Akhtar (1992b) have reviewed this literature in detail. Hossein Etezady (1995) has elucidated the distinctions between 'primary' and 'secondary' narcissism and Isaiah Share, Shirley Rashkis, and Bertram Ruttenberg (1995) have shed further light on the developmental aspect of 'narcissism'. However, it is the work of four individuals that stands out in bold relief. These are Heinz Kohut (1971, 1977), Otto Kernberg (1975, 1976a,b, 1984), Sheldon Bach (1977), and André Green (1983, 1986, 1999, 2001, 2002). Separate entries in this glossary describe the important concepts described by them. These include 'grandiose self', 'narcissistic personality types', and 'narcissistic rage', 'normal and pathological narcissism', 'malignant narcissism', and 'narcissistic personality disorder', 'narcissistic state of consciousness' and 'narcissistic fantasies', and 'life and death narcissism' 'positive and negative narcissism', and 'moral narcissism' . See also the entry on Judith Kestenberg and Ira Brenner's (1995) concept of 'tertiary narcissism'.

Narcissism of minor differences: phrase originated by Sigmund Freud (1918a, p. 199) to describe the fact that often trivial differences between people who are otherwise alike form the basis of feelings of hostility between them. A close look at the ethnic conflicts in Sri Lanka and the erstwhile Yugoslavia, for instance, testifies to the validity of of this idea.

Narcissism of minor similarities: Andreas Kraeber's (personal communication, January 21, 2004) playful alteration of Sigmund Freud's (1918a) celebrated phrase 'narcissism of minor difference'; Kraeber's phrase can shed light on the compromises of logic and mindless loyalty that often accompanies homoethnic idealizations.

Narcissistic boundary violations: Howard Levine's (2005) term for a particular form of misuse of the analyst's power. Such misuse is motivated by the drive for self-aggrandizement and can emanate from the analyst's character pathology or from a specific countertransference stimulated by the patient. Such 'narcissistic boundary violations' also tend to occur in organizational settings where analysts in leadership roles and with educational responsibilities can control and subjugate candidates and younger colleagues, stifling their intellectual freedom and professional advancement. The far-reaching consequences of such misuse of power can hardly be overlooked. (Coen, 1995).

Narcissistic countertransference: term used by Hyman Spotnitz (1979) to denote the analyst's affective response to 'narcissistic transferences' (see separate entry). The analyst's reaction might reflect an objective response to the patient's self-absorption (with the analyst feeling bored, drowsy), over-idealization (with the analyst feeling exalted or burdened), or twinship experience (with the analyst feeling as if he and the patient are kindred spirits). The presence of such emotions in the analyst should alert him to the patient's excessive narcissism.

Narcissistic fantasies: Sheldon Bach (1985) noted that, in contrast to the ubiquitous object-related fantasies (e.g., a bountiful mother, phallic woman, castration, and primal scene), there exist a set of fantasies that are self-related; they have to do with the origins and vicissitudes of the self-directed drives, needs, and wishes. Among these are the scenarios involving (1) *the 'wise baby'* which pertains to the origins of the self's perfection and uniqueness; this fantasy was inherent in Sandor Ferenczi's (1923) description of the 'wise-baby' dream and Bertram Lewin's (1968) description of the 'erudite nursling'; (2) *death of the self,* which concerns loss of infantile omnipotence; (3) *doubles*

and imaginary companions, which perpetuate narcissistic love; and (4) *the ladder, tree or rope to another world,* which sustains the search for transcending earthly limitations. Bach underscored that all these fantasies imply some unification of opposing concepts and contain a longing for the lost paradise of symbiotic unity, if not that of the 'purified pleasure ego' (see separate entry). While not included in this scheme, Ernest Jones' (191a) 'God complex', Helen Tartakoff's (1966) 'Nobel Prize complex', and Vamik Volkan's (1982) 'glass bubble fantasy' (see separate entries on each of these) also constitute what Bach has labelled 'narcissistic fantasies'.

Narcissistic libido: Sigmund Freud's (1914c) term for the investment of 'libido', or the psychic energy of the life instinct, in the self. Also called 'ego libido', this energic investment was original, so to speak, since, at the onset of life, all psychic energy was invested in the self. Later, some of this energy was invested into objects, creating 'object libido'. This last mentioned energy could, however, be withdrawn and re-invested into the self; this reflected 'secondary narcissism'. In Freud's view, there was an inverse relationship between narcissistic and object libido; it was a u-tube theory of available energy. The greater the object investment, the lesser the narcissism, and vice versa. Thus, the state of falling in love led to feelings of humility, and having toothache, for instance, diminished one's capacity for concern for others (Freud, 1914c). Contrary to this established view, Heinz Kohut (1971) proposed a time to development of narcissism that was independent of object relations and thus proposed an entirely different conceptualization of 'narcissistic libido' with its own line of development from primitive to more advanced forms.

Narcissistic masochistic character: described by Arnold Cooper (1988a), this personality type is characterized by (1) pursuit of rejection or disappointment by others, (2) drawing of secret pleasure from the predictability of rejection, which is invariably greater than that of love, (3) obtaining secondary pleasure from exhibiting one's hurts and from self-pity, (4) excessive harshness of superego, (5) a constant sense of envy, (6) an unshakeable conviction of being wronged, and (7) 'a hypersensitive self-esteem alternating between grandiosity and humiliation' (pp. 128–129). In some cases, the narcissistic features are more overt, and in some others the masochistic features are more overt. However, both features are sooner or later found in one and the same individual. The unconscious aim of such character organization is 'not a fantasied reunion with a loving and caring mother; rather it is fantasied control over a cruel and damaging mother' (p. 128).

Narcissistic–masochistic position: noting the inherent contradiction in the proposition that the masochist 'feels pleasure in pain' (for, if it is pleasurable, where is the pain?), Daniel Lagache (1968) suggested that one needs to view the masochistic pleasure differently. He said that 'the passive, dependent, submissive child must experience some satisfactions at being submitted to the beneficent omnipotence of the other' (p. 103) and thus replaced 'pleasure in pain' by 'a state of well-being by submission'. Lagache's stance emphasizes that the essential component of masochism might not be suffering *per se*, but the position taken by the masochist in the masochistic relationship. Since this assures him a sense of safety and well-being, it is appropriately called the 'narcissistic–masochistic position'.

Narcissistic neurosis: term from the earliest days of psychoanalysis when neuroses were divided into 'actual neuroses' (see separate entry) and 'psychoneurosis' (see separate entry). The former were caused by disturbances in contemporary sexual life and the latter by childhood conflicts and trauma. Psychoneurosis was divided into 'transference neurosis' (Jung, 1907), where libido was displaceable and the possibility of developing transference existed, and 'narcissistic neurosis', where libido turned back to the ego and a clinically meaningful transference did not develop. Owing to its intensely self-centred nature, this condition was not amenable to psychoanalysis. In today's terms, the category of 'narcissistic neurosis' would encompass severe narcissistic personalities, psychotic character, and psychoses.

Narcissistic object choice: Sigmund Freud (1914c) distinguished two types of object choices made by human beings: (1) anaclitic and (2) narcissistic. In the former (see separate entry), an individual chooses someone who represents a childhood parent and provides psychic sustenance via gratification of dependent longings. In the latter, the individual chooses someone who is either like oneself, or like what one wants or imagines oneself to be, or one who has been a part of oneself (i.e., an offspring, and, one would think, by extension a grandchild, a student, supervisee, or employee). Given this perspective, homosexuality came to be viewed as narcissistic and heterosexuality anaclitic. While this has become disputed, Freud's notion of narcissistic object choice

remains pertinent in understanding the object relations and transference of those with a narcissistic personality disorder. The 'alter ego personalities' (Kohut & Wolf, 1978)—persons who need a relationship with someone conforming to their own values and thus confirming the veracity of their selves—give the most dramatic example of narcissistic object choices.

Narcissistic personality disorder: while Sigmund Freud's (1931a) description of the 'narcissistic character type' is considered the pioneering portrayal of this disorder, the fact is that Ernest Jones (1913a) and Robert Waelder (1925) offered elegant descriptions of such phenomenology long before Freud. Under the designation 'God complex' (see separate entry), Jones described individuals who displayed excessive confidence in their own powers and yet had an exaggerated need for praise and admiration. He also made the sophisticated observation that narcissistic grandiosity is often masked by an 'unusually strong series of opposing tendencies' (p. 244) including caricatured modesty and pretended disinterest in money. Waelder added lack of empathy, self centred morality, and over-valuation of mental processes to the list of narcissistic symptoms. Reviewing the subsequent psychoanalytic literature, especially the contributions of Otto Kernberg, (1975, 1976b) and Heinz Kohut (1971, 1977), Salman Akhtar and James Anderson Thomson, Jr (1982) concluded that 'narcissistic personality disorder' consists of overt and covert manifestations in six areas of psychosocial functioning. These include (1) self concept, (2) interpersonal relations, (3) social adaptation, (4) love and sexuality, (5) ethics, standards, and ideals, and (6) cognitive style. The individual with a narcissistic personality disorder is overtly grandiose, scornful of others, successful, seductive, and often strikingly articulate. Covertly, he is doubt-ridden, envious, bored, incapable of genuine sublimations, unable to love, corruptible, forgetful, and impaired in the capacity for genuine learning.

Narcissistic personality types: many analytic investigators have attempted to subdivide narcissistic personality into subtypes. Ben Bursten (1973) subclassified the disorder into 'craving', 'paranoid', 'manipulative', and 'phallic' subtypes. Others (Gabbard, 1989; Masterson, 1993; Hunt, 1995; Akhtar, 2000) created sub-categories based upon how overt and unconflicted *vs.* how hidden and morally conflicted was a narcissistic individual's grandiosity and ambitiousness (for a delineation of these sub-categories, see entry on 'Shy narcissist). Yet another classification of considerable phenomenological and psychodynamic interest was offered by Heinz Kohut and Ernest Wolf (1978). According to them, there were five subtypes of narcissistic personality: (1) *mirror-hungry personalities*, who are constantly impelled to display themselves and seek admiration to counteract their inner sense of worthlessness; (2) *ideal-hungry personalities*, who are forever searching for others they can admire for their prestige, skills, or power and from whom they can draw emotional sustenance; (3) *alter-ego personalities*, who need a relationship with someone conforming to their own values and thus attesting to the veracity and significance of their selves; (4) *merger-hungry personalities*, who have a relentless desire to control others in an enactment of their need to buttress their own psychic structure; (5) *contact-shunning personalities*, who avoid social contact to combat their powerful and frightening need for others. While not made explicit by Kohut and Wolf (1978), the last two types seem to overlap borderline and schizoid personalities, respectively.

Narcissistic rage: term coined by Heinz Kohut (1972) for the profoundly angry reaction that follows an injury to self-esteem in the setting of a narcissistic personality. Such rage differs from the anger that is defensive against feelings of guilt (Jones, 1929) or the consequence of distress at separation from love objects. It is a direct response to threatened omnipotence; the latter is sorely needed by the narcissist to ward off his covert sense of inferiority and worthlessness. Narcissistic rage fuels 'the need for revenge, for righting a wrong, for undoing a hurt by whatever means; and a deeply anchored, unrelenting compulsion in the pursuit of all these aims' (Kohut, 1972, p. 380). Herman Melville's (1851) classic novel *Moby-Dick* is a story *par excellence* of narcissistic rage despite the castration-related imagery in its overt content.

Narcissistic scar: phrase used by Sigmund Freud (1920g) for the permanent, though subtle and dormant, injury to self-esteem that results from the fact that infantile sexual wishes are doomed, since they are 'incompatible with reality and with the stage of development which the child has reached' (p. 20). The narcissistic scar can be turned into a wound by a major heartbreak or a highly significant vocational setback; this is especially so when such situations evoke feelings of inferiority and exclusion.

Narcissistic state of consciousness: a particular type of mental state described by Sheldon Bach (1977) that seeks, through selective alterations of reflective awareness or though an interference with the development of such awareness, to establish or recapture an ego state of psychophysical wholeness and well-being. Such a subtly altered state of consciousness is seen in association with narcissistic character pathology. It involves disturbances of (1) self and body-self, (2) language and thought, (3) volition, (4) mood, and (5) time sense (see also Kernberg's 2008 paper on the destruction of time in pathological narcissism). According to Bach, the narcissistic self-disturbances include the existence of split-off contradictory representations, constant self-stimulation, peculiar thermal and boundary sensitivities, and hypochondriasis. Disturbances of language and thought include a highly autocentric use of speech (directed at regulating self-esteem rather than actually communicating with others), 'soft' learning difficulties, and 'a loss of flexibility in perspective, leading to over-abstraction or concreteness, or fluctuations between these extremes' (p. 23). Disturbances of volition include restriction of spontaneity, a felt limitation of choice, and, occasionally, the tendency to allow all decisions to rest on an omen or potent of some sort. Disturbances of mood include affective swings resembling classical cyclothymia (see also Akhtar & Thomson, 1982). However, these 'ups' and 'downs' are transient, environmentally triggered, and occur in the setting of an integrated personality. Finally, the time sense also shows peculiarities with a subjective sense of temporal uncertainty, undue personalizing of time markers, and attempts to make time stand still.

Narcissistic transferences: in his book, *The Analysis of the Self* (1971), Heinz Kohut proposed a line of development for narcissism that was independent from that of object-relations. It was from this vantage point that he proposed two types of 'narcissitic transferences', namely 'mirror transference' and 'idealizing transference' (see separate entries). However, as he took a more radical position *vis-à-vis* 'classical' psychoanalysis and founded 'self psychology' (see separate entry), Kohut (1977) dropped the term 'narcissistic transferences' in favour of 'self-object transference'.

Narrative truth: see 'Narrative truth and historical truth'.

Narrative truth and historical truth: according to Donald Spence (1982), the facts brought forth by the patient during the analytic hours do not reproduce the objective realities of his current or childhood experience. They are approximations and might even be generated by the hypotheses in the patient's and analyst's mind. Pereceptual experience undergoes subtle but important alterations upon being reported in ordinary language. The incorporation of a remembered experience into a narrative structure especially alters the former to fit into the latter's organizing pattern. Based upon these ideas, Spence contrasted 'narrative truth' with 'historical truth'. The former was constructed in the clinical encounter and the need for coherence and significance added to both embellish and discard various objective realites. The latter pertained to the objective realities of the patient's experience as they existed before the psychoanalytic exploration. He buttressed these ideas by underscoring that the language in which the patient records and reports his experience is his own and carries a particular associative context which is hardly possible for the analyst to share on an exquisitively attuned basis. For a thorough discussion of the criteria for establishing 'truth ' in psychoanalysis (including coherence and correspondence), see the contributions by Charles Hanly (1990, 1992), and, for a specific critique of the contemporary hermeneutic slant to psychoanalysis, see the paper by Louis Sass and Robert Woolfolk (1988).

Narrow-mindedness: according to Eric Brenman (1985), love tames cruelty in the course of normal development. In order to maintain the practice of cruelty, one involves the mechanisms of 'narrow-mindedness'. 'This has the function of squeezing out humanity and preventing human understanding from modifying cruelty' (p. 273). The sharp restriction of cognition and attention facilitates overlook the redeeming features of those who are hated. Personal omnipotence is placed above love and forgiveness and is used as a defence against depression. There is simultaneously a moral sanctification of grievance and revenge-seeking. See also the related entries on 'fascist state of mind', 'revenge', and 'vengeance'.

Necrophilia: a perversion characterized by sexual acts with a corpse. At times, the acts performed are not overtly sexual but have an unmistakable 'instinctualized' (i.e., pressured, cyclical, and discharge-seeking) quality. Such acts might include cruelty, cannibalism, and, via displacement and symbolism, 'agoraphilia' (see separate entry). Their fundamental aim is to preserve a relationship with a lost object at any cost (Brill, 1941). A reversal of 'primal scene' (see separate entry) by attacking a defenceless parental figure (Tarachow, 1960) might also play a role here. The object of such hostile and frozen mourning is usually an ambivalently held dead mother. Alfred Hitchcock's movie *Psycho* (Paramount Pictures, 1960) captures some of these of themes in a powerful, if highly dramatized, way.

Need: while a wish was the paradigmatic motivational concept in classical psychoanalysis, later models (e.g., object relations, self psychological, attachment theory based) introduced optional models of motivation which placed the role of 'needs' as comparable to (if not greater than) that of 'wishes'. Various labels, including 'psychic needs', 'developmental needs', 'ego needs', 'growth needs', and 'self-object needs' made their appearance in this context. The fact is, however, that such a motivational force was implied by Sigmund Freud himself, who, early on, talked about the ego's 'need for established causes' (1908c, p. 212) as well as a child's 'need for help' (1909b, p. 47), 'need for affection' (1905a, p. 227) and 'need for a father's protection' (1930a, p. 72). The definition of 'need', however, was not clearly spelled out until Salman Akhtar (1999a), in a comprehensive review of the literature on this topic, concluded that a 'need' is a psychic requirement that (1) arises from a sense of lack, mentalized as a consequence of ego inability in the face of instinctual pleasure or external frustration; (2) is not experience-bound but common to all human beings; (3) if fulfilled, helps in the development and sustenance of mind; (4) if unfulfilled, leads to a structural disintegration of the mind; and (5) has a certain freedom from intentionality which, in turn, confers on it an aura of justifiability.

Need–fear dilemma: phrase coined by Donald Burnham, Arthur Gladstone, and Robert Gibson (1969) to denote the schizophrenic's intense dependence upon external objects as well as his deep dread of them. According to Burnham and colleagues, the schizophrenic lacks internal structure and, therefore, is inordinately reliant upon routines and schedules as well as external objects, both human and non-human. This excessive need, however, makes him fear objects, since they can make or break him. The threat is compounded by the fact that his ego is ill-structured and vulnerable to merger with others. Burnham and his co-authors outlined three strategies used by the schizophrenic to handle this 'need–fear dilemma': (1) the patient abandons all effort at differentiation and gives in to the need side of the equation; he clings to objects, (2) the patient recoils and seeks refuge in solipsistic withdrawal, and (3) the patient redefines the object, changing its form and function under the sway of his internal drives and affects. While Burnham and colleagues' delineation of 'near-fear dilemma' is dynamically elegant and phenomenologically convincing, their restriction of it to the schizophrenic is questionable. Such approach-avoidance conflicts are also witnessed in the setting of borderline and schizoid personalities. Indeed, Harry Guntrip's (1969) description of the schizoid individual's 'in-and-out programme' (see separate entry) has remarkable overlaps with Burnham's (1919) 'need–fear dilemma'.

Need for enemies and allies: extrapolating Sigmund Freud's (1900a) personal 'confession' that he always needed a close friend and a hated enemy in his life, Vamik Volkan (1988, 1999a,b) states that all human beings have a need to have societal allies and enemies. He sees the preoedipal child's externalization of his or her 'good' unintegrated self and object images into 'suitable reservoirs' (see separate entry) as the beginning of a need to have societal allies. He also describes how the externalizations of 'bad' unintegrated self and object images prepare the child to have a need for societal enemies.

Need for punishment: Sigmund Freud's ideas about what he called 'need for punishment' evolved in four steps: (1) in 1909d, he noted that the self-reproaches of the obsessional neurotic were forms of self-punishment; (2) in 1916d, he described a character type called 'criminal from a sense of guilt' (see separate entry); this constellation involved committing outrageous and socially unacceptable, even criminal, acts in order to elicit punishment and relive 'unconscious guilt'; (3) in 1923b, he described the phenomenon of 'negative therapeutic reaction' (see separate entry), whereby the analysand responds adversely to a correct interpretation, thus betraying his difficulty with improvement; this, too, is an evidence of 'unconscious guilt'; and (4) in his 1924c paper 'The economic problem of masochism', Freud talked about how the 'need for punishment' can become sexualized. What was an attempt to seek superego retribution now turns into an instinctual gratification itself. Later analysts elaborated upon the myriad forms such unconscious need for punishment can take. Two prominent examples are Ernest Jones (1929), who observed that the need for punishment frequently becomes transformed into relentless proving others to be wrong, and Otto Fenichel (1945), who emphasized that the 'need for punishment is a special form of the need for absolution: the pain of punishment is accepted or even provoked in the hope that after the punishment the greater pain of guilt feelings will cease' (p. 105). He said the 'need for punishment

is subordinate to the need for forgiveness' (p. 293).

Need gradient: expression intended to underscore that, in the clinical setting, the patient's psychic needs should almost always be more important than those of the analyst. This derives from the prototypical situation of the mother–infant dyad and speaks for the fundamentally generative and growth-promoting attitude of the psychoanalyst.

Need satisfying object: Anna Freud's (1965) designation of the object sought by the infant solely for the purposes of gratifying the drive-related tensions of his body. When needed, the object is cathected with psychic energy. When not needed, it is psychically dropped. Developmentally, this type of object-relationship precedes the stage of 'object constancy' (see separate entry), where an inner tie to the object is retained regardless of its being instinctually 'needed' and/or being gratifying or not.

Need–wish distinction: based upon a comprehensive review of pertinent literature, Salman Akhtar (1999a) noted the two motivational concepts have a complex relationship with each other. They are not easily distinguishable in adult life, where motivations are usually multidetermined and it is difficult to separate them out on a phenomenological basis alone. A narcissistic person exalts his wishes as needs and a masochist derides his needs as wishes. The concept of need and wish perhaps exist on somewhat different levels of abstraction as well. Need arises from lack and leads to yearning. Wish, by contrast, is an individual's specific way of fulfilling needs. Need is universal; wish is experience-bound. A wish invariably has 'a uniquely personal history, a uniquely personal form, and a uniquely personal content' (Brenner, 1982, p. 22). A need, unlike a wish, is not subject to repression. Also, a wish can be replaced by another wish, but a need cannot be replaced by another need. A need is psychically represented (via a demand) only when it is not fulfilled. A wish, on the other hand, has a persistent psychic representation with memory, fantasy, and affect. Frustration of a need results in urgent demands which, if unmet, are followed by a structural regression. Frustration of a wish causes dynamic shifts and compromised formations. Needs and wishes can be in harmony (e.g., the desire to sleep) or in opposition to each other. Examples of the latter involve 'a toddler's wish to follow a lost ball into the street and yet need protective restraint' (Lichtenberg, 1992, p. 112) or a patient's 'wish' to make love with the analyst while having the 'need' to be denied such indulgence.

Needs: see 'Basic needs'.

Negation: term coined by Sigmund Freud (1925h) to denote a defence mechanism which allows the repressed material to emerge in consciousness until the time it remains in its negative form. A disavowed acknowledgment of this sort marks the beginning of something repressed becoming available for analytic investigation. In Freud's words, there is no stronger evidence 'that we have been successful in our effort to uncover the unconscious than when the patient reacts to it with the words "I didn't think that" or "I didn't (ever) that of that"' (p. 239). The concept has received considerable attention from later analysts, especially Bonnie Litowitz (1998) who has traced the developmental pathways that lead to the ego capacity for 'negation'. André Green's (1999) notion of the 'work of the negative' (see separate entry) is, however, the most outstanding extension of this idea.

Negative: see 'Work of the negative'.

Negative acting in: term coined by Cecilio Paniagua (1997) for the contribution an analysand makes to the analytic material by a 'behavioral omission' (p. 1209). Such failure to act in the session when some motor reaction seems appropriate requires the analyst's attention, just as his 'acting in' (see separate entry) does. The most common form of 'negative acting in' is the absolute stillness shown by some patients on the couch.

Negative and positive femininity: see 'Femininity'.

Negative and positive narcissism: terms coined by André Green (1999, 2001, 2002) for the forms of narcissism that are combined with self-destructive drives and that are free of such 'contamination', respectively. In 'negative narcissism', it is the individual who feels worthy and, in fact, desirous of universal contempt, while in 'positive narcissism' it is the object world that is seen as vulgar and useless. 'Negative narcissism is the result of the combination of narcissism with an orientation towards psychic death' (Green, 2002, p. 645).

Negative hallucination: concept elaborated upon by André Green (1999) to describe a psychological phenomenon with the following five characteristics: (1) it is the converse of hallucination and constitutes a non-perception of an object or perceptible psychic phenomenon, (2) it involves a wish to reject a distress-inducing perception, (3) it plays an important role in repressing and repudiating aspects of external reality, (4) it is not limited to external objects and can affect internal perceptions (e.g., memories, images) also, and (5) it plays a role in normalcy via the retention of mother's holding functions in the form of the psyche's 'framing structure' (see separate entry).

Negative hallucination of thought: described by André Green as a special form of 'negative hallucination' (see separate entry), this pertains to the repudiation of a thought that is about to become conscious. Unlike 'negation' (see separate entry), which permits the thought to emerge in its inverse form, 'negative hallucination of thought' leads to its complete erasure. The statement that one's mind has suddenly gone blank is a illustration *par excellence* of this mechanism.

Negative narcissism: see 'Negative and positive narcissism'.

Negative nostalgia: see 'Poisoning of nostalgia'.

Negative Oedipus complex: while Sigmund Freud's (1910h) description of the 'Oedipus complex' (see separate entry) initially focused on its 'positive' or heterosexual dimensions, later it began to include a 'negative' dimension also. In 1923b, for instance, Freud stated that 'a boy has not merely an ambivalent attitude towards his mother, but at the same time he also behaves like a little girl and displays an affectionate feminine attitude to his father and a corresponding jealousy and hostility towards his mother' (p. 33). A similar development in the girl can happen. In both sexes, constitutional factors and specific childhood experiences (especially the preoedipal relationship with mother) determine the intensity of negative oedipal feelings (Fenichel, 1945). Three main differences between the 'positive' and 'negative' oedipal complex are (1) the former pushes towards a heterosexual and the latter towards a homosexual object choice, (2) the former is mostly resolved in childhood (though requires reworking during adolescence), the latter is resolved mostly during adolescence, and (3) while the superego is the heir to the positive Oedipus complex (though certainly deriving its might and content from other sources as well), ego-ideal is the heir to the negative Oedipus complex (Blos, 1967). In the unfolding of clinical material, the two oedipal constellations can serve as defences against each other and both as 'upward' defences against the emergence of preoedipal material.

Negative self-object: Christopher Bollas's (1987) term for the creation by some analysands of an irritated and even hateful presence in the analyst in order to feel themselves in rapport with the latter. Such patients attempt to convert a differentiated object, with which they feel no connection, into an undifferentiated (even though hateful) object.

Negative therapeutic alliance: Jack Novick's term (1980) for an unconscious collusion between the therapist and the patient to bring about a failure of treatment. Such a situation results from the confluence of 'negative therapeutic motivation' (see separate entry) on the patient's part and issues of 'omnipotence, magical expectation, failure, and externalization blame' (p. 314) on the analyst's part.

Negative therapeutic motivation: term coined by Jack Novick (1980) for entering psychoanalysis or psychotherapy with an unconscious wish to make the treatment a failure. In so far as change is taxing, 'negative therapeutic motivation' is a part of all treatments. However, it is more prominent 'in certain types of patients, such as those with severe masochistic disturbances, and at certain ages, such as adolescence' (p. 318).

Negative therapeutic reaction: this term was coined by Sigmund Freud in 1923 to denote the paradoxical worsening of some patients after a successful piece of therapeutic work is accomplished. Referring to such patients, Freud (1923b) stated 'every partial solution that ought to result, and in other people does result, in an improvement or a temporary suspension of symptoms produces in them for the time being an exacerbation of their illness' (p. 49). Among the causes for negative therapeutic reaction, the following four are the most prominent: (1) *unconscious guilt:* this derives from childhood fantasies of having committed a 'crime' and therefore deserving, even needing, punishment. Such imaginary crimes frequently involve the dual oedipal transgressions of incest and murder. (2) *problematic identifications:* identification with a masochistic parent who idealized a life of suffering can also lead to negative therapeutic reaction. Becoming healthy, under such circumstances, is tantamount to betraying the suffering parent. (3) *separation-related issues:* even more pernicious negative therapeutic reactions are based on guilt in having an autonomous

and separate existence from the mother (Gruenert, 1979). A narcissistically needy mother who cannot let go of her child renders him vulnerable to unconsciously equating separation with causing injury to her, even killing her. Stuart Asch (1976) notes that certain 'separation accusations by mother (your birth was so difficult, I almost died; I was so torn up inside) often add fixating elements of historical "reality"' (p. 392) to such fears. Subsequent separations from primary objects (and later, from their transferential recreations) provoke anxiety and are dreaded. With each progressive movement in their treatment, such patients develop a fear of abandonment by the therapist and therefore regressively lose the newly acquired insights. (4) *envy:* yet another cause of negative therapeutic reaction is the patient's envy of the therapist's ability to soothe him. That the therapist does not appear to be as unfortunate as the patient, seems free of psychic turmSoil, and appears to possess patience and creativity, lead the patient to feel hateful envy of him. This, in turn, propels the patient to undo the benefit received from the therapist's interpretation.

Nemesis: Albert Chapman's (1959) concept for the psychological presence of a deceased relative that compels an individual to repeat the life pattern of the dead individual. The 'nemesis' feeling may be conscious or may surface into awareness for the first time in the course of treatment. The person whose life one feels doomed to repeat is most often a parent who has died during the patient's life.

Neo-generational objects: the forging of identity during adolescence uses inanimate objects in two different ways. One is for the purposes of disengaging from parental mores and the other is for creating new ego ideals. The former include cutout jeans, nose and tongue rings, T-shirts with outrageous declarations, painting the room's furniture over with flowers and Eastern motifs, and so on. The latter include the ever-growing CD collection, the inevitable guitar, and the posters of various athletes or musicians that adorn the walls of the adolescent's room. Together, these 'neo-generational objects' (Akhtar, 2003) help in disengagement from the earlier parental dictates internalized in the form of a strict superego and express the parallel reliance on the value of one's peers.

Nested dream or work of art: in Leon Balter's (2005, 2006) terminology, a 'nested dream or work of art' is something that is contained within a work of art. Its defining characteristics include: (1) its being a well-defined element of the containing work of art; (2) its having a distinct boundary that separates it from the containing work of art; and (3) it is both an integral element as well as a complete entity within the containing work of art. Such 'nested dream or work of art' can also be found within dreams. Akin to Sigmund Freud's (1900a) explanation for 'dream within a dream' (see separate entry), such 'nested ideation' is an unsuccessful attempt to deny a painful reality by its psychic encapsulation.

Nested ideation: see 'Nested dream or work of art'.

Neuraesthenia: see 'Actual neurosis'.

Neuropsychoanalysis: term jointly coined by Edward Nersessian and Mark Solms— at the New York apartment of Arnold Pfeffer—in the Spring of 1998 while planning to bring out a journal devoted to the interface between brain functions and psychoanalytic ideas (Edward Nersessian, personal communication, 30 April 2008). The journal that was subsequently founded by them is called *Neuropsychoanalysis: An Interdisciplinary Journal for Psychoanalysis and Neurosciences*. It embodies and reflects a newly emergent, though rapidly burgeoning, subspeciality in the field of psychoanalysis. Or, perhaps it is inaccurate to call it that, since the conceptual striving is rigorously aimed at integrating contemporary advances in neurophysiology and psychoanalytic hypotheses, not letting the latter colonise the former. Themes such as consciousness, dream formation, memory, affect, attachment, and even the theories of transference are at the centre of attention in 'neuropsychoanalysis'. While some (Kunstadt, 2001; Pulver, 2003; Blass & Carmelli, 2007) question the relevance of neuropsychoanalytic findings to the day to day clinical practice, others (Levin, 1995; Reiser, 1997; Schore, 1997; Pally, 2000) believe that the field would enrich the analyst's technical armamentarium. While this is awaited, a deeper mind–brain linkage and its consequent enrichment of psychoanalytic theory is already evident. The rewards of 'neuropsychoanalysis' in terms of informing treatment strategies and studying psychodynamic hypotheses and change processes are also beginning to surface (Beutel, Stern, & Silbersweig, 2003).

Neurosis: see 'Psychoneurosis'.

Neurotic exogamy: Karl Abraham's (1913c) term for the compulsion some individuals feel (even if they are not consciously aware of it) to have romantic, sexual, and marital relationships outside of their own religious, racial, and ethnic group. This happens because individuals of their own group come to stand too closely for early familial objects and therefore arouse incestuous anxieties and the inhibitions consequent upon them. An important consideration here is to remember that love, sexuality, and marriage outside of one's race, religion, or ethnicity are not pathological in themselves, especially if the capacity for romantic love with a partner from within one's group is retained. In other words, the exercise of choice is compatible with mental health while a restriction of the ego and a resulting compulsion is not.

Neutral energy: see 'Psychic energy'.

Neutrality: as pointed out by Axel Hoffer (1985), 'neutrality' is James Strachey's translation of *Indifferenz*, the German word used by Sigmund Freud (1914c) in describing the proper analytic attitude towards a patient's transference. While Freud did not use *Neutralitaet*, the actual word for 'neutrality', Strachey's expression gained wide acceptance. Its association with a detached and aloof stance was spurred by Freud's use of 'mirror' (1912e, p. 118), and 'surgeon' (1912e, p. 115) metaphors. Not only was such complete neutrality impossible to achieve in a prolonged and intimate dialogue, it was not truly desirable (Glover, 1955; Greenson, 1958a, 1974; Kris, 1982; Bornstein, 1983; Shapiro, 1984; Gill, 1994). It was certainly not what Freud practised. 'Neutrality', characterized by a non-judgemental and non-critical attitude, was always coupled with earnest interest, compassion, and 'sensitivity to the patient's developmental potentialities' (Blum, 1981b, p. 66). Terms such as 'technical neutrality' (Kernberg, 1976b) and 'interpretive neutrality' (Gill, 1994) emphasized one pole of this dialectic and 'compassionate neutrality' (Greenson, 1958) and 'benevolent neutrality' (Stone, 1961) highlighted the other pole; a more inclusive term that struck a compromise between these two poles was 'psychoanalytic neutrality' (Hoffer, 1985). It was conceded that departures from 'neutrality' might be necessary in situations that constitute '(1) emergencies for the patient—suicidality, psychosis, toxic state, etc.; (2) emergencies for someone potentially vulnerable to the patient's destructiveness e.g. the analysand's children; and (3) emergencies for the analyst e.g. physical or psychological threats' (Hoffer, 1985, p. 786). Two other points need mentioning. The first pertains to Anna Freud's (1936) comment that, in conducting his work, the analyst 'takes his stand at a point equidistant from the id, the ego, and the super-ego' (p. 776). This widely-quoted definition was questioned by Otto Fenichel (1945), who said that the analyst is always on the side of the ego. It has been extended by Axel Hoffer (1985), who proposed that the variable of the analyst's view of reality and indeed his own intrapsyhic conflict be added to Anna Freud's definition of 'neutrality' (see also Levy & Inderbitzin, 1992 in this regard). The second and final point pertains to the exact purview of 'neutrality'. Here again, Axel Hoffer's (1985) proposal that 'neutrality' involves three realms is highly pertinent. These include (1) neutrality with respect to feeling, (2) neutrality with respect to the patient's conflicts, and (3) neutrality with respect to power differential in the dyad.

Neutralization: a somewhat ambiguous term arising out of the economic perspective of psychoanalytic metapsychology, 'neutralization' has two overlapping connotations: (1) it is the *result* of 'aim inhibition' (see separate entry) and represents a type of sublimation (Freud, 1923b), and (2) it is the *process* by which libidinal and aggressive impulses lose their instinctual (i.e., cyclic, urgent, and discharge seeking) qualities (Hartmann, 1958). Viewed this way, 'neutralization' appears synonymous with 'deinstinctualization' (see separate entry). 'Neutralization' leads to 'neutral energy' as opposed to 'instinctual energy' and this energy fuels ego functions, especially sublimation. However, 'neutral energy' can also be derived from the undifferentiated id–ego matrix at birth and becomes available as the ego becomes more demarcated from the id (Hartmann, Kris, & Loewenstein, 1946).

New beginning: Michael Balint's (1932) phrase for the psychic advance consequent upon experiencing a regression that has occurred in the presence of the analyst and has been unobtrusively 'accepted' by the latter. The following five features are characteristic of a 'new beginning': (1) at first, there is an urgent demand and, following this, there is a sudden change resulting in a feeling of tranquillity and quiet well-being; (2) intensity of such 'newly begun' activities does not reach end-pleasure level, (3) all 'new beginnings' happen in the transference, (4) 'new beginnings' can lead to character change, and (5) their underlying mechanism is regression to a pre-traumatic, early stage and, from that psychic vantage point, the discovery of new ways of dealing with oneself, others, and life in general. In a later reconsideration of these matters (1959), Balint called the sum total of these phenomena 'regression in the service of progression'.

New object: while the implication that the analyst is internalized as a 'new superego' (Strachey, 1934, p. 144) was inherent in early psychoanalysis, the specific concept of 'new object' emerged in the work of Hans Loewald (1960). In a through elucidation of this concept, Ronald Baker (1993) underscored its elusive nature, noting that 'it is easier to define what it is not, than what it is. For instance, it is not a transference object; it is not a corrective emotional experience; it is not an empathic self-psychologist. Nor is it an alliance or real relationship that reflects a conscious working together and collaboration of patient and analyst' (p. 1228). It is an experience related to unmet developmental needs. Unlike the spontaneous, even if gradual, experience of the analyst as a re-creation of early internal objects, the 'new object' experience becomes available to the patient largely as a result of interpretive resolution of transferences. Analytic 'neutrality' (see separate entry), rather than any special indulgence on the analyst's part, plays an important role in the resumption of ego development consequent upon encountering a 'new object' (Chused, 1982).

Night residue: Alan Leveton's (1961) term for a drive-derivative arising in sleep because of a reduction in repression which persists into waking life. Most often, the night residue is simply the manifest dream of that night. However, other night residues also exist. These include drive forces which do not create imagery or affect, but may be noted by their effects on waking life. These effects can range from belief in the prophetic nature of dreams, acting out of repressed impulses, morning depression, and newly acquired and transitory compulsive rituals.

Nirvana principle: Sigmund Freud (1920g) used this expression to denote a most fundamental human tendency, which strives to reduce all instinctual tension to zero. Used in this way, 'nirvana principle' seems equivalent to the 'principle of inertia' that Freud (1895d) had proposed much earlier. However, there seems to be something more to Freud's 'nirvana principle'. Two evidences for this are: (1) it is his only concept with an Eastern word in its title; indeed, Freud (1920) acknowledged that he got this term from Barbara Low, an English analyst and a Sanskrit scholar, and (2) the Hindu notion of 'nirvana' refers to the soul's release from life's tension and fusion with supreme Godhead, the collective soul (*paramatama*) of the universe. Freud's employment of this term in the paper where he first articulated the concept of 'death instinct' (see separate entry) is telling. Indeed he explicitly said that 'Nirvana principle expresses the trend of the death instinct' (p. 160). Thus, this principle may go above and beyond the elimination of instinctual tension to the human striving for non-existence. It has been suggested that 'the word *nirvana* evokes a profound link between pleasure and annihilation; this is a link that always remained problematic for Freud' (Laplanche & Pontalis, 1973, p. 273). Both parts of this statement are, however, misleading. Nirvana is above both pleasure and unpleasure; it is extinction of the self and its absorption into the cosmic order. And it was not problematic for Freud—he embraced the concept—but it *was* and has remained problematic for the Western mind in general, which abhors non-existence, not to say longing for it.

Nobel Prize complex: phrase coined by Helen Tartakoff (1966) for a particular character constellation seen in some highly gifted individuals. The main features of this syndrome are its (1) frequent occurrence among the first-born children, (2) co-existence with actual intellectual or artistic talent of outstanding proportions, (3) background of precocious ego-development, (4) manifestation through all sorts of highly ambitious goals (e.g., to be the President, win an Oscar, receive a Nobel Prize), (5) accompaniment by the active fantasy of being the 'powerful one' and the passive of being the 'special one', and (6) psychic substrate of 'a circumvention of the resolution of the oedipal conflict' (p. 237). Individuals with 'Nobel Prize complex' differ from the 'exceptions' (Freud, 1916d) since they have not had physical defects or great misfortunes in their childhood. Tartakoff emphasized that individuals with this complex are not borderline or psychotic, but are generally well-integrated and high functioning. In today's terminology, they would most likely belong to the 'narcissistic personality disorder' (see separate entry) category.

No-entry defences: term proposed by Gianna Williams (1997) for mechanisms of refusal evolved by patients of anorexia nervosa. The 'no-entry defences' comprise intention to reject food intake as a displaced repudiation of the unbearable feelings projected into the patient by his or her parents during childhood. Food is not the only object refused entry, however. Sexual fantasies are not allowed to enter the mind from within and interpretations are not allowed to enter the mind from outside. In a further elaboration of these ideas, Julian Stern (personal communication, March 2008), has observed that the very patients who deploy 'no-entry defences' are the ones who invite all sorts of intrusions (including medical and surgical procedures) into their bodies.

Noisy phase: expression used in two different contexts. In the clinical context, some analysts (Boyer, 1971; Volkan, 1987) report that they themselves grunt more in the early phases of treating sicker patients, in order to assure them of the continued involvement of the analyst. In the developmental context, Louis Leaff (1991), among others, have noted that some phases (e.g., adolescence, mid-life) are more turbulent or 'noisy', while others (e.g., latency, young adulthood) are marked by a relative quiescence of instinctual pleasures.

Non-humanness experiences: these involve a subjective sense of being nothing, a thing, an animal, or a part of nature (e.g., vegetation, landscape, celestial bodies) at large. Such experiences can emanate from (1) psychotic or near psychotic states, whereby inadequate self–non-self discrimination persists at the core of the psyche and is regressively reactivated under states of anxiety (Searles, 1960). While delusions of zoophilic transformation (e.g., lycanthropy) and catatonic fusion with the surroundings are better known, milder versions of these also exist; (2) borderline organizations, where massive splitting and projection are buttressed by experiencing oneself as empty or as nothing. This 'reverse animism [is utilized] to deny and reverse totally insufferable passions' (Singer, 1988, p. 54); and (3) severely traumatized states whereby a child who is mercilessly beaten by a parent identifies with the parent's loss of humanity and the loss of his own humanity in the parent's eyes during the violent moments; this leads to a non-human quality being a part of self-experience (Pine, 1995). While these are the most frequent genetic–dynamic constellations associated with 'non-humanness' experiences, fleeting mergers with nature and cosmic forces can also be witnessed in drug induced states and even otherwise in healthy individuals. Whether such states would be viewed as narcissistic regression or as spiritual ascendance boils down, in the end, to the perspective one brings to bear upon them. See also the related entry on 'dehumanization'.

Non-verbal elements of psychoanalytic process and technique: besides the verbal communication between the patient and the analyst, psychoanalytic work also includes all sorts of non-verbal exchange between them. On a global level, the regularity of appointments, time limits, payment of fees, couch, the analyst's anonymity and neutrality are all non verbal facilitators of the analytic process. They constitute the relatively unsung part of analytic technique. On a micro level, 'non-verbal elements of psychoanalytic process and technique' include: (1) *from the patient's side*: a pause reflecting resistance, silent contemplation upon receiving an interpretation, gross and fine gestures and movements (Steere, 1982; McLaughlin, 1987, 1992; Jacobs, 1994), evocative 'acting in' (see separate entry), bodily sensations and noises, and adherence or non-adherence to the analytic frame; and (2) *from the analyst's side*: the rigorous allegiance to the attitude of 'neutrality' and 'abstinence' (see separate entries), the altruistic restraint in not objectively rectifying transference distortions, the 'interpretive' attitude (see separate entry), the carefully thought out 'interpretive actions' (see separate entry), and his survival as well as sustaining hope when the patient has little reason to be optimistic. Together, these elements, along with moments of acute affective attunement, create the 'something more' (Stern et al., 1998) than interpretation.

Normal and pathological narcissism: Otto Kernberg was the first to make a clear distinction between 'normal' and 'pathological' forms of narcissism (1975) and to delineate their respective impacts upon the developmental tasks of middle age (1980). *Normal narcissism* is characterized by a coherent sense of self, relatively conflict-free ambitiousness, realistic goals, and retention of capacity for love as well as for enjoying the success of one's relatives, friends, and offspring. During middle and old age, normal narcissism helps one bear the age-specific losses and anxieties. *Pathological narcissism*, in contrast, emanates from the desire to bury one's hidden feelings of inferiority deeper. It results in an insatiable search for glory and success. The underlying feelings of self-doubt fuel the envy of others and make their successes intolerable. Contemptuous devaluation of others and withdrawal into 'splendid isolation' often becomes habitual under such circumstances. Craving for more and more fame and power robs one of the capacities for mutuality and peaceful solitude, and can also lead to unethical conduct. During middle age, pathological narcissism leads to difficulty in tolerating age-specific losses and can contribute to severe 'mid-life crises', manifesting in depressive asceticism or grotesque attempts at youthfulness.

Normal narcissism: see 'Normal and pathological narcissism'.

Normality: according to Daniel Offer and Melvin Sabshin (1974), psychoanalytic notions about 'nor-

mality' can be grouped in three categories: (1) *normality as an ideal fiction* or a goal which can never really be achieved. Sigmund Freud's (1937c) statement that 'a normal ego is like normality in general, an ideal fiction' (p. 235) summarizes this point of view. Ernest Jones (1931) also concluded that a 'normal' mind does not actually exist. However, he went on to suggest that adaptation to reality, friendly relationships, capacity for work, a certain degree of internal freedom, and, above all, a more or less stable sense of happiness, constitute 'normality'. Kurt Eissler (1960) concurred; (2) *normality as optimal integration* was delineated by Melanie Klein (1960). She proposed that 'normality' consists of renunciation of infantile longings, capacity to bear ambivalence, emergence of balance between internal life and external adaptation, and integration of various aspects of personality into a harmonious gestalt; (3) *normality as adaptation within context* was elucidated by Heinz Hartmann (1939), Karl Menninger (1945), Lawrence Kubie (1954), and Edward Glover (1956b). Hartmann stated that existence of vitality and ego robustness in the setting of adaptation that is optimally balanced between alloplastic and autoplastic trends (see 'adaptation') is the hallmark of 'normality'. Menninger equated 'normality' with 'mental health' regarded them as 'the adjustment of human beings to the world and to each other with a maximum of effectiveness and happiness' (p. 2). Glover agreed with this, but warned against idealizing conformity. He stated that the external adaptation of an individual must be in tune with the inner melodies of his self. While these models are elegant, four caveats need to entered: (1) the idea of 'normality' can be used as a narcissistic defence involving a powerful identification with the society as an aggressor (Gittleson, 1954); (2) while it is imperative to keep statistical, cultural, and moral dimensions of the concept away from its psychoanalytic conceptualization, this is not an easy task; (3) the idea that the ego's benevolent dominance over the demands of id, superego, and reality constitutes 'normality' (Freud, 1923b; A. Freud, 1965) must be tempered by the fact that this is not a once and for all occurrence. Erik Erikson's (1950, 1959) stages of psychosocial development that cover the entire life span make this point clear; and (4) finally, to Freud's (cited in Erikson, 1959, p. 96) aphoristic statement that mental health involves the capacity to love and work, a third component of play (Winnicott, 1971) needs to be added. However, this element is not in the same plane as love and work. It subsumes them. In other words, it is not the capacity to love, work, and play but the capacity to love and work in a spirit of play that constitutes the evidence of 'normality' in so far as it is equated with 'mental health'. See also the report of a panel discussion (chaired by Arthur Valenstein and with presentations by Samuel Abrams, Sibylle Escalona, and Daniel Offer) held during the 1976 Fall Meetings of the American Psychoanalytic Association (Sachs, 1977).

Normalization: see 'Masturbation'.

Normotic character: Christopher Bollas's (1987) term for a character organization where the deletion of subjective factors and a genuine intrapsychic life is central. Such an individual is abnormally normal. He cannot introspect and is merely concerned with the materialness of external objects. However, he is not devoid of identity and does not reflect a 'false self' (see separate entry) character. His actions define his identity.

Nostalgia: a characteristically 'bitter-sweet pleasure' (Kleiner, 1970, p. 11), nostalgia is a mixed affective state of pain and joy associated with the wish to recapture an idealized past. Pain is evoked by the awareness of separation from old objects and joy by a fantasized reunion with an idealized version of them through reminiscences. While often attributed to a loss during adult life, nostalgia actually emanates from incomplete mourning of disruption of the early mother–child relationship. Edith Sterba (1940) was the first to correlate homesickness with a longing for the maternal breast. Otto Fenichel (1945) also explained nostalgic yearning with a deep-seated longing for the undisturbed prenatal state. However, such references seem largely metaphorical. Much takes place between a traumatic rupture of infantile bliss and its alleged counterparts in adulthood. Heinz Hartmann's (1964) warning regarding 'genetic fallacy' must be heeded here. Awareness of the 'screen' functions of nostalgia has led to the distinction between 'normal and pathological' (Werman, 1977) and 'true and false'

(Sohn, 1983) types of nostalgia. The former is supposed to reflect a continuation of mourning and the latter its idealized blockade.

Nostalgic relationship: described by Daniel Geahchan (1986), this type of bond keeps an idealized lost object in psychic limbo; the object is neither given up through the work of grieving nor assimilated into the ego via identification. If an object corresponding to the nostalgic desire should appear, 'it is promptly rejected, it becomes demythologized; it is not what it promised to be: the subject's projection of what it should be. The subject can thus only enjoy the search and never the possession' (Werman, 1977, p. 391).

Now moments: term introduced by Daniel Stern and his colleagues (1998) to denote special points in the present time 'that get lit up subjectively and affectively, pulling one more fully into the present. They take on this subjective quality because the habitual framework—the known, familiar intersubjective environment of the analyst–patient relationship—has all of a sudden become altered or risks alteration' (p. 911). Such moments force the analyst into action. Stern and co-athors describe five fates of 'now moments': (1) 'missed now moment', where the possibility for deeper understanding is lost; (2) 'failed missed moment,' where a 'now moment' ends up being destructive; (3) 'repaired missed moment', where a 'failed' moment is revisited, explored, and understood; (4) 'flagged now moment' or a 'now moment' that is named and stored in memory for future references; and (5) 'enduring now moment', where a 'now moment' is not momentary but longer in duration, often lasting over many sessions until it is resolved.

Nuclear ambitions: see 'Bipolar self'.

Nuclear goals: see 'Bipolar self'.

$$\boxed{\text{O}}$$

O: term used by Wilfred Bion (1965, 1967, 1970) to denote the ultimate truth of the moment or for the thing-in-itself, which is immeasurable. This truth is out there, waiting to be found by a receptive mind that has emptied itself of preconception, memory, and desire. Acquired knowledge can prepare the platform from which the leap of faith is taken, but it is leaving knowledge and experience behind that actually constitutes a step towards 'O'. Take, for instance, the Oedipus complex, or, for that matter. the mathematical equation, $E=mc^2$; these truths existed long before Sophocles', Sigmund Freud's and Albert Einstein's discovery of them. In other words 'O ' is the absolute truth and the supreme godhead of pure veracity. Moreover, 'O' is constantly becoming; therefore, 'O' of one moment may not be the 'O' of the next moment. Within the analytic situation, 'O', is common to both the patient and the analyst. Finally, there is the mystery of Bion's choice of the letter 'O' for this idea. At least three explanations have been offered: (1) Rafael Lopez-Corvo (2003) thinks that the letter 'O' is taken from the word 'origin' and is 'related to the same term used to designate the centre of the Cartesian coordinates that correspond to the point where the X and Y axes intercept; however, it could have also been taken from the concept of "origin" in Zen Buddhism' (p. 197); (2) Neville Symington (2008) believes that 'O' stood for Ontos in Bion's mind, since he often used Greek letters to designate psychological realities and both 'O' and Ontos denote ultimate reality and absolute truth; and (3) Salman Akhtar (2008) proposes that Bion's 'O' is a truncated form of Om, the Sanskrit word for the Omnipresent Creator; this is likely in light of the fact that Bion grew up until the age of eight in India, where he was taken care of by a Hindu maid who presumably took him to many Hindu temples and exposed him to the chants of the word Om.

Obituary addition: see 'Pathological grief reaction'.

Object: since the term 'object' had two, almost independent, origins in Sigmund Freud's writings, the term has been saddled with some confusion. The first sense of the term 'object' is derived from Freud's (1891) use of *Vorstellung* (object-representation) in connection with internal registration of perception of a thing which is richer and more complex than the thing itself; it can be evokedin the thing's absence as a memory. This conceptualization of Freud's anticipated Jean Piaget's (1937) concept of 'object permanence' and was later picked up by Heinz Hartmann (1952) and Edith Jacobson (1964), among others. The second sense of the term 'object' is evident in Freud's (1905a) early adumbration of the 'instinct theory' (see separate entry). In this context, he stated: 'Let us call the person from whom sexual attraction proceeds the sexual *object* and the aim towards which the instinct tends the sexual *aim*' (pp. 135–136). Of note is the distinction between these two connotations of the term 'object'. The first refers to an intrapsychic structure, and the second to a person in real life. This, however, is not the only source of ambiguity in the use of the term 'object'. An admittedly incomplete list includes the following areas: (1) informal discourse, external objects are simply referred to as 'objects', while their intrapsychic constructions are called 'internal objects'; (2) the term 'object', for some (Spitz, 1965; Mahler, Pine & Bergman, 1975) refers to human beings, while others (Klein & Tribich, 1981) include animals, things, plants, and elements of nature in it as well; (3) though most analysts agree that an amalgamation of external reality, drive-based fantasy factors, and the degree of ego maturation gives shape to internal objects, some (e.g., Klein, 1935, 1940) emphasize the intrapsychic and others (Fairbairn, 1952; Winnicott, 1960) the reality-based contribution; (4) while the establishment of the capacity for self–non-self discrimination is the ego's earliest task (Kernberg, 1975; Stern, 1985) and the failure to accomplish this leads to a propensity towards self–object fusion and psychotic-like states, the fact is that the boundaries between self and object always remain a bit porous. Self can be taken as an object by the libido, as in 'secondary narcissism' (Freud, 1914c) and the object can come to contain aspects of the self via 'projective identification' (Klein, 1935). Even mental processes themselves can be turned into 'objects' (Green, 2005). Then there is the 'intermediate area of experience' (Winnicott, 1953) and the realm of 'intersubjectivity' (Stern, 1985; Dunn, 1995), where a smooth confluence of self and non-self is amply evident; and (5) 'whole objects' refer to a perceptually complete and emotionally balanced view, and 'part objects' result from fragmented perception and affectively unintegrated use. All this goes to show that the ambiguities and confusions regarding the term 'object' are myriad. The various terms used in this passage can be looked up in this glossary for further clarification. Other pertinent entries include 'anaclitic object choice', 'narcissistic object choice', 'object constancy', 'object permanence', 'object relations theory', and 'use of an object'.

Object a: in contrast to the 'Other' (see separate entry) which represents a 'radical and irreducible alterity' (Evans, 1996, p. 125), 'Object a' (Lacan, 1955) is intricately coupled with the ego itself. Also referred to as 'Object petit a', it is the cause of desire. According to Lacan, the analyst must situate himself in the psychic position of the 'Object a' and thus be the object of the analysand's desire.

Object choice: Sigmund Freud introduced the term 'object choice' in 1905a. 'Object' here stands for a love object (or, in common parlance, a person in whom positive emotions are invested) and 'choice' means the developmentally and emotionally determined selection of such a love object. It is not a matter of intellectual choice but of irrevocable selections made on the basis of developmental fixations, instinctual wishes, and ego needs. In a later paper, Freud (1914c) distinguished between two types of object choice, namely 'narcissistic' and 'anaclitic' types (see separate entry).

Object coercive doubting: a clinical phenomenon described by Selma Kramer (1983) in connection with sexual overstimulation of children by their mothers. It is characterized by (1) the child engaging the mother in endless arguments in which she is coerced into taking the opposite side of what the child feels is true at a given moment, (2) such coercive doubting 'often ends in orgasm-like fury for both, thus reenacting the sexual play between them' (p. 345), (3) the coercion also represents a hostile tormenting of the mother, and (4) the child forces the mother alternately to tell him the truth and set him free from the burden the mother's earlier dishonesty had placed upon him and to continue maintaining the earlier denial. 'Object coercive doubting' is distinct from obsessional doubting, which is derived from conflicting feelings within a tormented self; the former is experienced as emanating from the mother (or a maternal substitute) since the sexual stimulation in question has often occurred when adequate self and object boundaries were not formed.

Object constancy: term introduced by Heinz Hartmann (1952) to denote a stage when the growing child's tie to its love object becomes a stable and enduring inner relation independent of need satisfaction. Elaborated and refined in the developmental observations of Margaret Mahler (1965, 1968; Mahler, Pine & Bergman, 1975). According to her, this is an open-ended process ('on the road to object constancy') and becomes discernible by about 24 months of age. It is characterized by the establishment of a more realistic and less shifting internal maternal representation. Such a developmental achievement assures the mother's lasting presence in the child's mental structure, enhances his or her capacity for tolerating ambivalence, and reduces dependence upon the actual mother to a certain degree.

Object construction: David Guttman's (1980) term for the older individual's capacity to draw emotionally meaningful sustenance from those matters which are seemingly insubstantial but actually fundamental. 'This special talent would seem to rest upon two bases: the later life diminution of the instincts and the motivated search for the ultimately trustworthy object' (p. 492). The aged person is set free to search for those objects that will be finally security-giving even if such objects themselves are intangible (e.g., cultural institutions, history, ethical principles). In fact, because they cannot be 'lost', such intangible objects might be even more satisfying to the elderly, who are already facing losses of all varieties.

Object having: see 'Other having'.

Object mother: see 'Environment mother *vs.* object mother'.

Object permanence: term proposed by Jean Piaget (1937) to denote the child's capacity to know and remember that physical absence of objects does not mean their having disappeared totally; the child learns that they might be existing somewhere else at this time. In other words, a capacity arises to internally hold on to an object in its absence.

Object petit a: see 'Object a'.

Object-relating: Donald Winnicott (1969) distinguished two types of ego–object relationship. One he called 'object-relating' and the other 'object-usage' or the 'use of an object' (see separate entry). 'Object-relating' occurs when the baby and mother are psychologically merged. The mother is in the state of 'primary maternal preoccupation' (see separate entry) and the baby perceives the mother subjectively rather than as someone outside of his omnipotence. 'Object-relating', for which Winnicott had earlier (1956b) used the term 'ego-relatedness', is a precursor to 'object usage', which requires a greater self-object differentiation.

Object-relations conflicts: term proposed by Theodore Dorpat (1976) to describe a type of internal conflict that involves a psychic structure that is less differentiated and antecedent to id–ego–superego differentiation. The individual with an 'object relations conflict' experiences opposition between his own wishes and his internalized representations of another person's wishes. He says 'I want to do this but my mother's soul would be hurt', for instance. This is in contrast to a 'structural conflict' (see separate entry), in which both vectors of the quandary are experienced as belonging fully to his own self. As a result, the person says that 'I want to do this but I should not do this', or that 'I want to do this but I also want to do its opposite'. Since Anna Freud (1965) referred to 'structural conflicts' as 'internalized conflicts' (because these can only come into existence after the child identifies with external powers and introjects their authority), it is possible to view 'object-relations conflicts' as 'partially internalized conflicts'. See also the related entry on 'conflict'.

Object-relations theory: the term, coined by William Ronald Fairbairn (1943, 1944), refers to a set of psychoanalytic developmental and structural hypotheses which place the child's need to relate to others at the centre of human psychological motivation. This is in contrast to the 'classical' psychoanalytic theory, which conceptualizes human motivation in terms of instinctual tension and discharge. The main proponents of 'object-relations theory', besides Fairbairn himself, include Michael Balint, Donald Winnicott, Harry Guntrip, Masud Khan, John Sutherland, Christopher Bollas, and Patrick Casement. In North America, there is a tendency to include the views of Melaine Klein, Edith Jacobson, Margaret Mahler, and Otto Kernberg under the rubric of 'object-relations theory' as well. However, these theorists remain largely loyal to the classical instinct theory. Strictly speaking, they cannot be considered pure object-relations theorists.

Object-representation: while the British analysts of both the Kleinian and Independent traditions continue using the term 'object' in regard to intrapsychic constructs, the North American analysts tend to follow the lead of Heinz Hartmann (1950) and Edith Jacobson (1954, 1964) in using the metapsychologically precise term 'object representation'. This term establishes that an 'object' in its actual three-dimensional nature and in its autonomous subjectivity might be quite different from its internalized presence in the subject's world. The latter is not a cent–per cent reproduction but a representation built under variable ego capacities and changing drive pressures. Contradictory 'object-representations' built under libidinal and aggressive drive derivatives coalesce over time (Kernberg, 1967, 1976a), especially if the libidinal representations are predominant over those tinged with aggression. This contributes to the emergence of 'object constancy' (see separate entry), enhances the capacity to bear ambivalence, and diminishes the need for an external object to support the coherent functioning of the self.

Object usage: see 'Use of an object'.

Objectalizing and disobjectalizing functions of the ego: terms used by André Green (2005) to denote processes that govern the ego's relationship to external and internal objects and their evolving transformations as well as to its own psychic functions. The 'objectalizing function' is manifested via 'binding' and the 'disobjectalizing function' via 'unbinding activities'. The 'objectalizing function' is what helps the ego relate with objects or, to put it more precisely, create objects for relating. It can turn parts of the ego itself into an object, as happens in state of melancholia, where ego identifies with a lost object (Freud, 1917e). And it can elevate psychic functions to the status of object (note the expression 'my creativity', 'my dedication', and so on). 'Objectalizing function' 'can also manifest itself during sublimation or in the production of the transitional objects energizing for the intermediate space' (Green, 2005, p. 119). The 'disobjectalizing function', in contrast, attacks the ego's ties with objects and, in the end, the very propensity to have such ties in the first place. It is a manifestation of the 'death instinct' (see separate entry). Negative narcissism is its ally and its aim is total disinvestment. The overlap between Green's 'disobjectalizing function' and Wilfred Bion's (1967, 1970) 'attacks on linking' is obvious, and Green clearly acknowledges it.

Objectivation: Eduardo Weiss's (1947) term for an individual's locating the traits of a disowned aspect of the self (which reverts to feeling like an object within the psyche) in an actual object. Weiss distinguished this process from 'projection' (see separate entry), which implies an incorrect externalization of mental contents. 'Objectivation', however, implies finding the actual representation of an 'extraject' (see separate entry) in a real, external object.

Obscene words: while the current works on analysis of bilingual (Amati-Mehler, Argentieri, & Canestri, 1993) and immigrant (Akhtar, 1999b) patients have brought this issue into focus, it was actually Sandor Ferenczi (1911) who long ago pointed out that using obscene words in one's mother tongue offers more powerful id discharge and hence meets with greater superego admonition than saying the same things in a later acquired language. The reason for this is that, lacking lexical substitutes, the originally acquired obscene words stay close to the acts they describe; the word becomes the thing or the act. For instance, to an English-speaking person, uttering the word 'fucking' feels almost akin to doing the act itself. A second reason, not explicit in Ferenczi's paper, is that one learns such words at a time when the only adults in one's life are family members. Hence, these words come to have an incestuous tinge at their base. As a result, the immigrant enjoys cursing in his original language but, in general, prefers speaking of genitals and sexual acts in a later acquired language. Such defensive use of a 'foreign language' is also evident in Sigmund Freud's (letter to Fliess, 3 October 1897, in Masson, 1985, p. 268) use of Latin *matrem nudam* while describing, at age 41, the childhood memory of his having seen his mother naked during a train journey.

Observing ego: coined by Otto Fenichel (1938), the term designates that part of ego which scans itw own experience and enters into a collaborative compact with the analyst. Fenichel emphasized that it is only by separating the reasonable, 'observing ego from the automatic, defensive, and experiencing element' (p. 425) that the analyst is able to engage the patient in genuine self-scrutiny and self-understanding. It is fascinating to note that, while his ideas bore close resemblance to those already enuciated by Richard Sterba (1934), Fenichel, ordinarily a comprehensive scholar, did not refer to the latter in his paper!

Obsessional character: also known as 'compulsive' character, this personality constellation has the triad of orderliness, parsimony, and obstinacy (Freud, 1908b) as its chief manifestation. Intolerance of dirt and disorder, meticulous record keeping, punctuality, desire for control, and a tendency towards perfectionism are also typical of 'obsessional character'. While some of these features create an overt resemblance to 'narcissistic personality disorder' (see separate entry), the two conditions differ in important ways. The obsessional seeks perfection; the narcissistic claims to have it. The obsessional loves details, which the narcissist casually disregards (Reich, 1933). The obsessional respects authority and is highly moral, while the narcissist values only himself and can easily cut ethical corners. Developmentally, the obsessional character is derived from anal fixation (see 'anal character') while the narcissistic character arises as a defence against earlier frustrations and oral rage.

Obsessional reparation : see ' Reparation'

Obstinacy: among the cardinal traits of 'anal character' as described by Sigmund Freud (1908b), 'obstinacy' involves rigidity of thought and behaviour patterns as well as negativism and defiance *vis-à-vis* others' input. The underlying dynamics of this trait includes (1) anal fixation, (2) self esteem regulation, (3) orally-determined lack of generosity; the obstinate person cannot give others the gratification of having influence over him, and (4) add a bit of 'adhesive libido' (see separate entry), to bring in an old psychoanalytic concept. Christine Olden (1943) has addressed the technical challenges posed by obstinacy and suggested that 'the attitude of the analyst is of greater importance than the content of his interpretations' (p. 255). The analyst must avoid counter-obstinacy and ironical remarks about the patient's attitude while occasionally praising the patient's effort to collaborate in the analytic work.

Oceanic feeling: a term employed for a sense of expansion of the self beyond its customary temporal–spatial limits, leading to a feeling of merger with the universe at large. The feeling is believed to recall very early infantile states of being where all experience of time and space is coextensive with the subject's ego. Hence, in adult life, the experience of oceanic feeling is considered a regressive phenomenon. Oneness of the self and its object world is regarded as a narcissistic illusion underneath which lurks split-off hostile destructiveness. Less comfortable to the Western mind is the possibility that recapturing the infantile bliss of oneness with the universe might be a positive and transcendental occurrence. In the context of such an 'Eastern' perspective on the oceanic feeling, it should be remembered that Sigmund Freud was introduced to the concept by Romain Rolland (cited in Freud, 1930a), the French biographer of Bengali mystics Sri Rama Krishna Paramhansa and Swami Viveakanada.

Ocnophilia: see 'Ocnophilia and philobatism'.

Ocnophilia and philobatism: in 1959, Michael Balint proposed two fundamental attitudes about distance from objects. These he termed the 'ocnophilic' (hesitant, clinging) and the 'philobatic' (thrill-loving) attitudes. Balint described the ocnophilic world as consisting of objects separated by horrid empty spaces, and the philobatic world as comprising friendly expanses dotted with unpredictable objects. The ocnophile lives from object to object, cutting short his travels through empty spaces. The philobat lives in friendly expanses, avoiding contact with potentially dangerous objects. The ocnophile feels safe as long as he is in touch with his objects, while the philobat lives in the illusion that he needs no objects. The ocnophile must please others. The philobat has no such need, since he feels able to conquer the world without relying on potentially untrustworthy objects. The ocnophile likes to stay home; the philobat loves to travel. The two tendencies, however, never exist in isolation and most individuals show some admixture of both.

Oedipal pathology: while this hardly ever exists in isolation from 'preoedipal pathology' (see separate entry), the psychic and behavioural consequences of a problematic and unmastered oedipal phase do have certain specific features of their own. Such 'oedipal pathology' affects generation boundaries, the incest barrier, the capacity to wait and respect time as an important dimension in life, and, most significantly, the supergo formation. The resulting symptomatic constellations are generally of two types: (1) *neurotic*, involving undue fear or bristly combativeness towards authority figures, nervousness about sex, undue jealousy, and tendency to seek unavailable and prohibited romantic partners, and (2) *perverse*, involving cockiness, destructive attitudes towards others' couplehood, breach of the incest barrier, and failure to enter the temporal order of life, manifesting in the character trait of being chronically hurried.

Oedipal phase: the period of childhood, usually from three and a half or four years to about six years of age, when the 'Oedipus complex' (see separate entry) comes into full bloom.

Oedipal sibling triangles: according to Sheila Sharpe and Allan Rosenblatt (1994), there are sibling triangles that exist outside of parent triangles and contain an unmistakable oedipal flavor. Competitivenss and hostility towards a sibling who is felt to be more loved by the opposite sex parent is coupled with affectionate concern towards the rival. As a result, feelings of guilt accompany this ambivalence. Projection of hostility upon the rival can give rise to fears of retaliation. Alongside these similarities with the usual parent-directed 'Oedipus complex' (see separate entry), 'oedipal sibling triangles' show four differences from: (1) the sexual element in them is less blatant, (2) the 'rival' may comprise more than one sibling and may be of the same or opposite sex, (3) the 'complex' usually begins with negative feelings and is then complicated by the development of positive feelings; this is the opposite of what generally happens in the usual oedipal situation involving parents, and (4) conflicts attendant upon 'oedipal sibling triangles' are harder to resolve than those related to the usual Oedipus complex.

Oedipal triumph: while phrases like 'oedipal triumph' and 'oedipal victory' are part and parcel of psychoanalytic language (appearing in nearly 1,000 journal articles, according to the PEP Disc), the number of times they appear in the title of a paper is astonishingly small. There are only two papers with 'oedipal winner' (Simo, 1983; Lasky, 1984), one each with 'oedipal triumph' (Gill, 1987) and 'oedipal victor' (Kieffer, 2004), and none with 'oedipal victory' in their titles. While it is tempting to speculate that this, in itself, is defensive against the pleasant intoxications and castrating horrors of 'oedipal triumph', the line of thinking might, in the end, be tantamount to 'wild analysis' (see separate entry). It is more important to understand what is meant by the synonymous expressions of 'oedipal triumph' and 'oedipal victory'. Essentially, these denote the experience of a child whose rival parent of the same sex has buckled under and appeared as defeated, removed from his or her position of authority, and vanquished. This can happen due to the same sex parent's death (Fenichel, 1931; Gill, 1987) or absence owing to other reasons (e.g., divorce, desertion). Undue seduction by an opposite sex parent who visibly devalues the same sex parent can also have a similar impact upon the psyche of the growing child (Chasseguet-Smirgel, 1984). All such occurrences give rise to the perception in the child's mind that his or her oedipal wishes have been fulfilled and this, in turn, arouses powerful feelings of guilt. Children who have experienced 'oedipal triumph' grow up to be adults who tend to be cocky, irreverent, hurried, and unable to abide by the 'incest barrier' (see separate entry). At a deeper level, however, they feel imposturous and replete with guilt (Freud, 1900a). As far as gender differences in such phenomena are concerned, there seem to be two different views. Janine Chasseguet-Smirgel (1984) proposed that maternally seduced boys develop 'perverse character' (see separate entry) while paternally indulged girls become hysterics; the reason for greater pathology in boys was that the source of over-stimulation was the primary object and this led to an idealized and merged self-object representation. More recently, Christine Kieffer (2004) has proposed that a boy who is favoured by the mother over his father is more likely to internalize this sense of privilege than a daughter in a similar position *vis-à-vis* her father. Kieffer states that 'for the female "oedipal victor", the recognition may not be authentic and may be won at the expense of her autonomous development. That is, the admiration and idealization she receives is contingent upon her ability to serve as a mirror to her father and provide self object functions for him' (p. 78). This impedes her growth as an independent human being.

Oedipus complex: Sigmund Freud's (1908c, 1924d) designation of the broad and confusing set of feelings, curiosities, and fantasies that a child of four or five years of age develops upon contemplating the relationship between the two parents and his or her role *vis-à-vis* that relationship. Among the complex set of feelings are sexual rivalry (with the same sex parent, usually), erotic longing (for the opposite sex parent, usually), and attempts to understand the mysteries of pregnancy and childbirth. Successful negotiation of passage through the Oedipus complex results in the creation of the incest barrier, acceptance of generational boundaries, entry into the temporal dimension of life, respect for the value of waiting and effort, and formation of the superego. However, when the negotiation of this conflict is inoptimal, psychopathological symptoms result (see 'Oedipal pathology').

Older patients: Sigmund Freud stated that patients over 50 years of age were not suitable for analytic treatment due to their excessive 'accumulation of material' (1898a, p. 282) and 'inelasticity of mental processes' (1905c, p. 264). Karl Abraham (1919), in a rare dissent from the Master, stressed that this was not always true and 'older patients' can indeed benefit from analytic treatment. The subsequent course of psychoanalysis has borne out Abraham's cautious optimism. Three reasons seem to account for this: (1) increase in life expectancy has pushed what is called 'old age' farther and farther ahead in the human life span; (2) refinements in analytic theory and technique, especially the shift from a strictly drive-based model to object relations models, have also facilitated conceptualization of problems faced by older patients; and (3) the gradual accruing of encouraging data from clinical work with 'older patients' (Wylie & Wylie, 1987; Cath, 1997; Settlage, 1996; Plotkin, 2000; Valenstein, 2000; Lax, 2007). A special clinical population is constituted by older psychoanalytic candidates; in 2006, fifteen per cent of individuals beginning analytic training in the United States were above 55 years of age (Sandra Taub, personal communication, 12 February 2008). The formation of analytic identity in older candidates and the special experiential and technical challenges in their training analyses are certainly worthy of attention.

Olfactory repression: George Wilson (1948) observed that chronic and non-infectious nasal congestion can, at times, represent the negation of interest in smells either as a form of fetishism or related to tendencies towards transvestitism. Such congestion 'markedly lowers the threshold of olfactory sensitivity and serves as an efficient deodorant, particularly in people who retain strong olfactory sensitivity' (pp. 338–339). In effect, it constitutes a 'somatic compliance' (see separate entry) with the defensive inverse of the underlying perversions. See also the related entry on 'smell'.

One person psychology: see 'One person *vs.* two person psychology' and 'One, two, three, four, and multi-person psychologies'.

One person *vs.* two person psychology: a current North American psychoanalytic euphemism intended to underscore the essential difference between classical 'ego psychology' (see separate entry) and the relational (Bromberg, 1980, 1988; Mitchell, 1993) and intersubjective (Stolorow & Atwood, 1978; Ogden, 1994) approaches. The former regards psychic phenomena, including pathologic formations and transferences, as contained within the patient's mind. The latter views all psychic activity to be contextual and dialectically constructed within an interpersonal matrix. While a tendency has arisen to denigrate the former and exalt the latter perspective, the fact is that both remain important; indeed Jonathan Dunn (1995) has convincingly demonstrated the complimentarity of the two vantage points. Fascinating to note in this war of euphemisms is that the contemporary labels 'relational' and 'intersubjective' themselves studiously avoid the dreaded 'interpersonal', associated with the work of that quintessentially American psychiatrist–psychoanalyst, Henry Stack Sullivan (1947, 1953). See also the related entry on 'One, two, three, four, and multi-person psychologies'.

One, two, three, four, and multi-person psychologies: long before the current North American uproar over 'one person *vs.* two person psychology' (see separate entry), the British analyst, John Rickman (1951) had divided psychology into five types: (1) one person psychology, which deals with 'what goes on inside one person in isolation' (p. 150) and addresses matters like sensation, reaction time, imagery, hallucinations, memory, etc.; (2) two person psychology, which concerns itself with actual or fantasied reciprocal relationships and deals with phenomena like love, hate, transference, and so on; (3) three person psychology, which deals with triangular psychic constructs, whether these pertain to the mother–infant–father (or the examining physican in place of the father) triad or the more familiar oedipal triangle (within the actual family or re-created in transference); (4) four person psychology, which pays attention to sibling rivalry and the role of the two parents in that situation; and (5) multi-person psychology, which is the domain of 'group psychology' (see separate entry). Rickman emphasized that the data of one psychology inform that of the other only to a limited extent. Thus, he laid down the groundwork for the conceptual and utilitarian criss-cross of these paradigms, which at the first and the last, fade into neurosciences and anthroplogy, respectively.

Onymy: see 'Self naming'.

Opening phase: see 'Beginning phase'.

Opposite wishes: see 'Theory of opposite wishes'.

Optimal disillusionment: phrase coined by John Gedo and Arnold Goldberg (1973) for the fact that undergoing psychoanalytic treatment requires that the analysand learn to give up magical thinking. Ordinarily, this happens gradually over the course of an analysis. However, in the case of patients who are stubbornly fixated on pathological optimism, it may come down to explicitly 'having to state that neither analysis nor the analyst is an omnipotent rescuer, as the patients in their illusion need to believe' (Amati-Mehler & Argentieri, 1989, p. 301).

Optimal closeness: see 'Optimal distance'

Optimal distance: concept introduced into psychoanalytic literature by Maurice Bouvet (1958) and later elaborated by Michael Balint (1959),

Margaret Mahler (1971, 1975), and Salman Akhtar (1991b, 1992a). A Janus-faced concept with both interpersonal and intrapsychic referents, 'optimal distance' can be defined at two levels: (1) *at the pre-oedipal level* it is the distance between the maternal psyche and that of her child which best facilitates the latter's growth. More specifically, it is a psychic position that permits intimacy without loss of autonomy and separateness without painful aloneness, (2) *at the oedipal level*, it can be viewed as the capacity to renounce primary objects in a way that (on the aggressive side) permits individuality without sacrifice of family continuity and (on the libidinal side) establishment of the incest barrier without total obliteration of aim-inhibited, cross-generational eroticism. Sexual and aggressive drive derivatives can often be encoded in conflicts that superficially involve matters of distance. There might be some gender difference here, as well, with men liking a greater distance in relationships than women; in this connection it is interesting to note that Joyce Edwards, N. Ruskin, and Patsy Turini (1981) prefer the term 'optimal closeness' over 'optimal distance'. Either way, the matter of distance has profound implications for the technique of psychoanalysis (Akhtar, 1992a; Escoll, 1992) and psychoanalytic supervision (Haesler, 1993).

Optimal frustration: see 'Optimal responsiveness'.

Optimal gratification: see 'Optimal responsiveness'.

Optimal responsiveness: phrase coined by Howard Bacal (1985) to subsume the notions of 'optimal frustration' and 'optimal gratification'. Essentially, this means that the analyst must titrate the degree of his 'abstinence' (see separate entry) to match the patient's ego state at any given moment during the analysis. Such a decision cannot be made once and for all; it must be constantly revisited and guided by empathy towards the patient.

Oral character: though infrequently used today, the term 'oral character' was quite popular in the early days of psychoanalysis. Sigmund Freud (1917b) correlated life-long 'confidence in success' with being mother's 'undisputed darling' (p. 156). Karl Abraham (1924) made the link between optimism and a gratifying oral phase explicit. Edward Glover (1925) repeated that profound oral gratification leads to an 'excess of optismism which is not lessened by reality experience' (p. 136). Conversely, excessive frustrations during oral phase result in depressive tendencies and an overall pessimistic outlook on life. It should, however, be noted that optimism and pessimism can be deployed as defences against each other (Bergler, 1961). Moreover, there are other character traits that seem to betray similar 'orality' of origin: excessive or inhibited eating, curiosity and intellectual appetite, visual hunger and intensified pleasure in looking, excessive generosity or miserliness (the latter also has anal roots), dependency, impatience and hurry, and so on.

Oral deadlock: see 'Eating disorders'.

Oral dependence: see 'Oral phase'.

Oral eroticism: see 'Oral phase'.

Oral gratification: see 'Oral phase'.

Oral phase: while Freud (1905a) had earlier noted the existence of oral sexual pleasure, it was not until 1915c that he described the 'oral phase' to be the first stage of libidinal development; curiously this was seven years after his description of the 'anal phase' (see separate entry). Extending from birth until about 18 months of age, 'oral phase' is characterized by intense libidinal investment of the mucous membrane of the mouth. Sucking on the breast, licking, swallowing, biting, spitting, and all other activites involving the mouth are deeply cathected. These activities provide opportunities for the gratification of both libidinal ('oral eroticism') and aggressive ('oral sadism') drives. The diminution of oral drive tensions causes 'oral gratification' and their build-up without satisfactory discharge leads to 'oral deprivation'. Energic investment during this phase shows a gradual evolution from autoerotism to part object relations to full object relations. In other words, the maternal breast is at first felt to be a part of oneself, then cathected as an object itself, and only later does the comprehension of mother as a total and separate person develop. Karl Abraham (1924) divided the 'oral phase' into an earlier 'oral–erotic phase' and a later 'oral–sadistic phase'. The former was concerned primarily with sucking and was devoid of ambivalence. The latter emerged when biting became possible and gave rise to ambivalence. While the later ascendancy of other erotogenic zones (e.g., anal, phallic) eclipsed the oral phase; its impact upon personality development was persistant. Excessive indulgence or undue frustration during this phase, for instance, gave rise to life-long tendencies towards optimism and pessimism as well as conflicts over longings for attachment ('oral

dependence'). Moreover, conflicts derived from oral phase issues could complicate subsequent psychosexual development and become condensed with anal or oedipal phase agendas.

Oral sadism: see 'Oral phase'.

Oral stage: see 'Oral phase'.

Oral triad: Bertram Lewin's (1950) concept consisting of the wish to eat, the wish to be eaten, and the wish to sleep; he deduced this triad from his discovery of the 'dream screen' (see separate entry), which is the visual representation of the breast as the satiated infant blissfully falls asleep. In undisturbed sleep, the active and passive oral wishes (respectively, the desire to eat, and the desire to be 'eaten', or passively incorporated into the mother's body) are realized by a fantasied reunion with the maternal breast. Joseph Kepecs (1957) later elucidated the pertinence of Lewin's 'oral triad' to the understanding of psychosomatic disorders. Interestingly, the same term was used by the prolific analyst, Edmund Bergler (1961), for the entirely different purpose of describing a three layered mechanism underlying masochism: arranging refusal of needs, feeling self-righteous indignation and pseudo-rage at the refusing object, and then drawing unconscious pleasure from the juicy defeat and accompanying self-pity.

Orality: see 'Oral phase'.

Ordinary devoted mother: like Sigmund Freud, who received the term 'Nirvana principle' (see separate entry) from the English analyst and Sanskrit scholar Barbara Low (Freud, 1920g), Donald Winnicott received the term 'ordinary devoted mother' from the BBC producer Isa Benzie, who suggested it to him during a walk on the streets of London in 1949. However, it was almost two decades later that Winnicott (1966) published a paper with this title. Essentially, the term stands for the devotion and preoccupation that develops in a woman soon after, or even before, childbirth, and from which she ordinarily 'recovers' over the subsequent weeks or months. An intense identification with her infant underlies this affective state (see also 'Primary maternal preoccupation').

Organ neuroses: term used by Otto Fenichel (1945) to collectively designate four types of somatic symptomatology resulting from psychological conflicts: (1) affect equivalents, (2) results of bodily changes secondary to repressed affects, (3) physical results of unconscious attitudes, and

(4) combination of the above. The non-inclusion of conversion symptoms here reflected Fenichel's conceptual loyalty to Sigmund Freud, who had distinguished between conversion symptoms, which were somatic 'translations' of specific fantasies, and an unnamed category of bodily symptoms that resulted from physical changes in an organ due to non-specific exaggeration of its erotogenic value.

Organ pleasure: expression used by Sigmund Freud (1905a) to underscore that instinctual excitation in a particular erotogenic zone is satisfied by the exercise of that very organ regardless of any object relation or any reality benefit form the act. For instance, relief for the tension in the erotogenic zone of lips and mouth is provided by sucking, despite there being no nutritional value or object relationship (e.g., the infant's sucking of a spatula or toy). Over the course of development, all sorts of zone-based 'organ pleasures' come together to create the composite, object-related pleasure of mature genitality.

Organizers of the psyche: borrowing the term 'organizer' from the field of embroyology, where it refers to a tissue centre radiating its influence, René Spitz (1950, 1957, 1963, 1965) came up with the concept of 'organizers of the psyche' or simply 'psychic organizers'. His knowledge of celluar mechanisms had informed him that, before the emergence of an 'organizer', transplanted tissue tends to assume the characteristics of surrounding tissues, but once an organizer has emerged, the transplanted tissue retains and reproduces its own strain. Extrapolating these notions to child development, Spitz proposed three nodal occurrences of great significance. These included (1) the 'first organizer of the psyche', or the level of development manifested by the appearance of 'smiling response' (see separate entry), which indicates the beginning capacity for object relations; (2) the 'second organizer of the psyche', or the level of development manifested by the appearance of 'stranger anxiety' (see separate entry), which suggests that the infant has become capable of specifically recognizing the mother and has established her as a 'libidinal object proper' in his internal world; and (3) the 'third organizer of the psyche', or the level of development manifested by the appearance of the child's capacity to say 'no'. Not only does this imply an 'identification with the aggressor' (see separate entry), which, in this case, is the limit-setting and frustrating parent, but it constitutes a psychic bedrock of 'agency' (see separate entry). Saying 'no' is also the first abstraction in the sense of adult mentation. With this gesture, action is

replaced by message, making newer and more complex forms of semantic communication possible.

Ostow's triad: see 'Religious instinct'.

Other: the term 'Other' appears in the contemporary psychoanalytic discourse with ever increasing frequency and the reasons for this might themselves shed some light on the term. Before speculating on these, it seems proper to locate the three contexts in which this term appears. (1) *Lacanian psychoanalysis:* Jacques Lacan (1955) distinguished between the 'big Other' ('Other') and the 'little other' ('other'). The former is not really other, but a reflection of the ego (see 'Object a') and is recorded in the 'imaginary' (see separate entry) order of the mind. The latter represents a radical alterity with which identification is not really possible. In the clinical situation, the analyst offers himself as the 'little other' for the analysand to develop desire and transference, but he makes interventions from his position of the 'big Other'. (2) *Contemporary intersubjective movement:* 'Other' from this vantage point is an object that is dialectically created in the matrix self–object relation and, in turn, contributes to the creation of the self. (3) *Psychoanalytically informed ethnography of the immigrant experience:* Here the term 'Other' is used largely in the phenomenological sense of underscoring difference and difficulty in communication (Akhtar, 1999b; Elovitz & Kahn, 1997; Grinberg & Grinberg, 1989). This brings up the point raised earlier: what might be the explanation of the term 'Other' being so popular these days? Could it represent the encounter psychoanalysis is now having with a clinical population that is ethnoculturally more diverse than ever before? Could it suggest that the capacity for empathy and actual repect for difference has diminished so much that everyone now appears an 'Other'? Or, could it herald a dawning awareness on the part of psychoanalysis that the discipline itself is an 'Other' in the chamber of human discourse?

Other having: Susan Levine's (2004) phrase for an individual's sense of a continuous presence of others in mind and of the psychic freedom to use them productively in fantasy or reality. This is a necessary building block of mental structure and an assurance against the despair of inner emptiness. 'The initial sense of object having is related to the establishment of object permanence, that is, to the sense of Others and things continuing to exist while they are physically absent; more mature object having, though comes into being with achievement of object constancy' (p. 951).

The implication for 'having an analyst' (p. 950) and 'having a patient' (p. 954) are also elucidated by Levine.

Overdetermination: Sigmund Freud (1895d) introduced the term *Überwertigkeit* (translated into English as 'overdetermination') to denote the fact that psychic phenomena are caused by multiple factors operating in unison. Thus, forces of constitution and trauma, scenarios of past and present, and pressures by different psychic agencies converge into the final common pathway leading to a given phenomenon. Freud's later study of dreams (1900a) and parapraxes (1916–1917) gave strong support to this idea. Still later, his delineation of a tripartite psychic structure (1923b) led to the conclusion that neurotic symptoms were not simply breakthroughs of instinctual impulses but a compromise between the demands of id, ego, and superego. Ludwig Eidelberg (1954) and Heinz Hartmann (1958) later added the aetiological vector of external reality, stating that not only neurotic symptoms but all psychic phenomena reflect a compromise between the demands of the id, ego, supergo, and external reality.

Over-interpretation: term used by Sigmund Freud (1900a) in the context of dream analysis. According to him, 'over-interpretation' refers to a new interpretation of a dream that has seemingly been adequately interpreted already. Jean Laplanche and Jean-Bertrand Pontalis (1973) suggest that Freud's term can be seen to have two meanings: (1) a fresh interpretation of the dream arising as a result of new associations by the patient, and (2) a deeper interpretation of the dream that becomes possible only after the initial understanding of it.

Ownership of the body: Moses Laufer's (1968) phrase for the achievement, during adolescence, of the capacity to experience one's body as belonging to oneself and not to one's mother who first cared for it. Failure to develop this capacity results in severe conflicts around masturbation. Such adolescents hate their bodies for 'forcing' erotic desires upon them. They also feel helpless in the face of regression fantasies that invariably intrude into their masturbatory experience and cause them feelings of worthlessness and guilt.

P

Pairs of opposites: Sigmund Freud (1905a) declared that 'impulses to perversion occur regularly as pairs of opposites' (p. 160). Thus, voyeurism is invariably accompanied by exhibitionism, sadism with masochism, and so on. While the statement was made in relation to sexual practices (and accompanying fantasies), it also came to apply to the existence of opposing tendencies in character organization. Jean Laplanche and Jean-Bernard Pontalis (1973) note that the idea also 'appears at various levels of conceptualization: in the three antitheses which define the successive libidinal positions of the subject, namely active/passive, phallic/castrated, and masculine/feminine, in the pleasure–unpleasure opposition; and, at a more radical level, in the instinctual dualism (love/hunger, life instincts/death instincts)' (p. 295).

Panic attacks: refer to bouts of intense apprehension and feelings of impending doom that are accompanied by physiological symptoms including shortness of breath, dizziness, choking, palpitations, trembling, and chest pain or discomfort. Fear of dying and fear of going crazy are also frequent. The attacks seem to come from out of the blue. However, careful investigation invariably reveals that stressful events have actually precipitated the outburst of anxiety. The nature of these events is, at times, subtle. Physical and emotional separations from loved ones often precipitate 'panic attacks'. More important, perhaps, are sudden changes in expectations involving the subjects being asked to assume increased responsibilities in their occupations (Milrod, Busch, Cooper, and Shapiro, 1997). Such career advances can become linked with hostile competitiveness with parents and thus stir up unconscious fantasies of attacking, hurting, or even killing them. This, in turn, becomes the source of anxiety.

Panic disorder: see 'panic attacks'

Parallelism phenomena in psychoanalysis and supervision: a number of psychoanalysts have noted that psychoanalytic candidates unconsciously enact with their supervisors the very problems with which they are struggling with their patients. The supervisee who talks of an analysand's seductiveness, for instance, acts seductively towards the supervisor, and the one who complains about the patient's rambling on

and on himself goes on with an out-pouring of minute details about the case. While the occurrence of such 'parallel process' or 'parallelism' is agreed upon, some things about it remain unclear: (1) does this sort of thing happen more often in novice therapists facing difficult clinical situations (Sachs & Shapiro, 1976), or this is a reporting artefact and experienced analysts are also subject to it?; (2) does the theme being enacted originate in the patient and then enter the supervisory situation (Arlow, 1963; Ekstein & Wallerstein, 1958; Searles, 1955), or does the supervisor's behaviour towards the supervisee (or, at least, how it is experienced by the supervisee) also get enacted in the latter's clinical work (Doehrman, 1976)?; and finally (3) whether such enactments on the supervisee's part can be explained on the basis of transient identifications with the patient and countertransference collusions (Searles, 1955; Sachs & Shapiro, 1976), or do they derive from a complex conscious and unconscious interactional system to which all three participants (i.e., the patient, analyst, and supervisor) contribute (Gediman & Wolkenfeld, 1980)? This last question is addressed from a contemporary relational perspective by Lawrence Brown and Martin Miller (2002). These authors emphasize that affects arising in either the analyst–patient or the supervisor–analyst dyads both impact upon the ongoing treatment of the patient. The personalities of the supervisor, analyst, and patient come into play with each other and create a 'triadic intersubjective matrix' which, not unlike the 'analytic third' (see separate entry), has a significant impact upon both the supervision and the treatment. See also the sophisticated elucidation by Eva Lester and Brian Robertson (1995) of the multiple interactive processes that go on during the analytic supervision, and Germano Filho, Antonio Pires, Gerson Berlim, Raul Hartke, and Sergio Lewkowicz's (2007) description of the 'supervisory field' which is formed from the transposition of the two fields between the candidate and patient and the candidate and supervisor.

Parameters of technique: Kurt Eissler's (1953) term for 'a deviation, both quantative and qualitative, from the basic model technique, that is to say, from a technique which requires interpretation as the exclusive tool' (p. 110). While acknowledging that it was often difficult to maintain the standard technique and modifications of clinical approach were necessary, Eissler was clearly of the view that there was, in fact, a 'standard technique'. This was reflective of his fierce loyalty to Sigmund Freud's ideas and of the tenor of North American psychoanalysis during the 1950s. A 'parameter of technique', or simply a 'parameter', according to Eissler, was a deviation that had to meet the following four conditions: (1) it was to be introduced only when it was proved that the basic technique would not suffice, (2) it must never transgress the basic minimum, (3) its impact upon the transference relationship must not be so great that it cannot be dissolved by interpretation, and (4) it should be self-eliminating over time, i.e., 'the final phase of the treatment must always proceed with a parameter of zero' (p. 111). After nearly three decades of wide acceptance in the North American psychoanalytic circles, the concept of 'parameters' was eclipsed by a more inclusive view of psychoanalytic technique in general. This view regarded empathy, mild educative comments in the beginning, non-verbal exchanges, clarifications, remarks preparatory for making interpretation, and post-interpretative work as integral to analytic technique. With 'interpretation' (see separate entry) losing its regal centrality, the concept of 'parameters' fell by the wayside. What was deemed exceptional turned out to be commonplace and a shining originality was revealed to be a transitional link in the evolving history of psychoanalytic technique.

Paranoid personality disorder: while Sigmund Freud (1922b) traced paranoid tendencies to repressed homosexuality, most contemporary analysts hold the paranoid individual's hostility to be primary and not merely a defence against latent homosexual impulses. Harold Blum (1980b, 1981a) notes that a complex interplay of innate disposition, actual threats to survival during childhood, impaired object relations, and subsequent structural defects and defensive elaborations underlie the ultimate paranoid picture in adulthood. Lack of basic trust, weak object constancy, and persistence of splitting of self and object representations, along with severe sadomasochism (Meissner, 1978) pervade the psyche. Corruption of ego's perceptual functions (Shapiro, 1965) is also in evidence. A triumphant feeling, while convicting others of disloyalty or incompetence, links the paranoid and manic states (Heimann, 1952). All in all, 'paranoid personality disorder' consists of 'overt' and 'covert' manifestation in six areas of psychosocial functioning (Akhtar, 1990). These include: (1) self-concept, (2) interpersonal relations, (3) social adaptation, (4) love and sexuality, (5) ethics, stan-

dards, and ideals, and (6) cognitive style. The individual with a paranoid personality disorder is overtly arrogant, mistrustful, suspicious of others, driven, at times successful in solitary professions, moralistic, and sharply vigilant toward the external environment. However, covertly, he is frightened, timid, gullible, chronically experiencing interpersonal difficulties, corruptible, vulnerable to erotomania and sadomasochistic perversions, and cognitively unable to grasp the totality of actual events in their proper context.

Paranoid position: Melanie Klein's (1940) designation of the psychological stance when the infant is dominated by the struggle to achieve and maintain an optimal deflection of the 'death instinct' (see separate entry) since it is only with such deflection that he can feel confident of not falling into pieces. Typical of early infancy, such a 'paranoid position' involves expelling all 'badness' and projecting it into the mother. At the same time, the 'all-good' object is greedily incorporated directly into the ego, giving it a sense of omnipotent solidity. Such internalization differs from 'the introjection of the good object in depressive position, which is loved and worried over by an ego in relation to it' (Hinshelwood, 1991, p. 161). The externalization of aggression creates 'bad objects' and persecutory anxiety. The emotional consequences of these developments include fear, greed, envy, hate, and arrogance. Defences against such paranoid fears are usually in the form of obsessional and manic defences. It should be noted that Klein did not refer to this constellation as the 'paranoid stage'. Instead she called it the 'paranoid position'. This underscores that the propensity to perceive the world and oneself from such a perspective remains 'available' throughout life. An individual reacting from the 'paranoid position' feels good, smugly certain of himself, thinks that others are 'bad', and is dominated by the above mentioned affects. Such 'mentality' stands in sharp contrast with that emanating from the 'depressive position'; the latter is associated with a realistic self view, concern for others, gratitude, humility, and desire for reparation. For further understanding of these issues, see the elegant two-volume set on Klein's work edited by Elizabeth Bott Spillius (1988a,b).

Paranoid–schizoid position: see 'Paranoid position' and 'schizoid position'.

Paranoid transference: see 'Transferences of hatred'.

Paranosic gain: see 'Primary and secondary gains'.

Paraphilias: see 'Sexual deviations'.

Parapraxis: refers to a consciously unintended faulty action that replaces or compounds the intended behaviour. Slips of the tongue, slips of the pen, forgetting otherwise known names, and other momentary laspes of memory are all examples of a 'parapraxis'. Sigmund Freud (1901b) included them in the 'psychopathology of everyday life' and viewed them as a partial breakthrough of repressed impulses or a 'compromise formation' (see separate entry) between the interfering impulse and the interfered-with intention. Depending upon the balance between these two factors, such errors can be harmless (Freud, 1901b) or quite disturbing and hurtful to self and others (Eidelberg, 1948).

Parasitic doubles of the superego: expression used by Sigmund Freud (1919d, p. 209) to denote the usurping of superego functions by the introjection, during adulthood, of dictates that are quite different from the moral codes acquired from one's parents. Freud noted that this could happen under the influence of mass suggestion during times of political conflict and war. Values acquired under such circumstances sharply conflict with the genuine superego and permit the expression of otherwise forbidden impulses (e.g., those towards violence). Rado (1925) included the superego alterations under hypnosis also under this rubric. It is possible to conceive of immediate post-immigration superego disturbance (Akhtar, 1995) in the same vein.

Part objects: term introduced by Melanie Klein (1935) to describe the infant's relations with his early environment and caretakers, especially the mother. Two connotations can be discerned in her usage of the term 'part objects': (1) the first pertains to the fact that the limited visual perception of the tiny infant allows him to perceive the mother only in parts, with a special focus, understandably, on her breast. 'Part objects' thus comes to mean literally an object in parts. Only gradually does the child begin to perceive the mother *in toto*, i.e., as a 'whole object' (see separate entry). (2) The second meaning involves the world of emotions. 'Part objects' here means objects at whom only one or the other form of feeling (e.g., love, hate) and not an admixture of feelings are directed. Such objects frequently contain projected parts of the self; as a result, they are not 'allowed' independent affects and motivations. At first, such 'splitting' and 'projective identification' (see separate entries) are developmentally determined. Later, these come to serve defensive purposes.

Deployment of 'part objects' then serves as a protection against the anxiety of ambivalence. This characteristic 'paranoid position' is given up in the 'depressive position' (see separate entries) where the capacity to succeed and sustain 'whole objects' prevails. In Otto Kernberg's (1970) 'update' of this scheme, the existence of 'part objects' is typical of borderline personality organization, while the capacity to relate to 'whole objects' characterizes neurotic and mature personality organizations.

Partial instincts: see 'Component instincts'.

Partially internalized conflicts: see 'Object-relations conflicts'.

Passive primal repression: see 'Primal repression'.

Passivity: see 'Activity and passivity'.

Past unconscious: see 'Three-box model of the mind'.

Paternal identity: while Sigmund Freud did mention the little boy's wish to have children, it was in connection with his negative oedipal strivings (1909b) and equation of faeces with the penis and, in turn, with a baby (1911c, 1918b). Subsquent analysts (Abraham, 1925a; Horney, 1932; Jacobson, 1950) persisted in this line of thinking and traced a man's wish to have a baby to his negative oedipal orientation and his unconscious envy of women. It was not till 1950 that Erik Erikson recognized that parental ambitions in a boy might arise out of healthy and generative identification with the father. In a comprehensive review of literature on this topic, John Munder Ross (1975) carefully delinates how the post-Freudian generations of analysts have gradually discovered the active and progressive dimensions of a boy's procreative strivings, emphasizing that 'parental aspirations are organic, indeed organizing components in the evolution of male identity' (p. 812). Recently, Calvin Colarusso (2005) has elucidated the vicissitudes of becoming a father during late adulthood, noting that intrapsychic experiences of fatherhood at this point cannot be divorced from the challenging developmental tasks of the period.

Pathological attractor sites: extrapolating from cognitive neuroscience, which suggests that frequently used neural networks create 'attractor sites' for perception and comprehension, Fred Busch (2007) proposed the psychoanalytic concept of 'pathological attractor sites'. These refer to foci of high psychic activation 'due to the experience of trauma, and the resulting viligence for similar situations, along with the ongoing pressure from unconscious fantasy and gratification' (p. 428). Such sites exert a strong pull on how the individual experiences psychological events. They are kept intact by deep unconscious fears of change and, in turn, contribute to rigid and stereotypic responses to environmental stimuli.

Pathological grief reaction: unlike ordinary 'grief' (see separate entry) over the loss of a loved one, which undergoes certain recognizable steps (Freud, 1917e), 'pathological grief reaction' acquires a chronic and unchanging form. Metapsychologically, denial of loss is pervasive and the work of mourning is stalled. According to Vamik Volkan (1981), the following features characterize the resulting clinical picture: (1) prolonged duration of emotional disturbance, often lasting for years and even for an entire lifetime, (2) long term persistence of dreams that are typical of early grief; these include 'frozen dreams', 'life-in-death dreams', and rescue dreams, (3) inability on the bereaved's part to properly and in a timely fashion dispose of the deceased's physical possessions, (4) the deployment of 'linking objects' (see separate entry), which permits the shifting of ambivalence originally directed at the deceased to inanimate objects, and (5) 'obituary addiction', whereby the bereaved develops a habit of compulsively reading newspaper death notices in an unconscious effort to demonstrate to himself that the dead person's name is not there and therefore he is still alive. Recognition of 'pathological grief reactions' has therapeutic implications, since specific forms of psychoanalytically informed interventions have been evolved (Volkan, 1981) for its treatment (see 'Re-grief therapy').

Pathological hope: see 'Hope'.

Pathological jealousy: see 'Jealousy'.

Pathological narcissism: see 'Narcissism'.

Pathological weeping: Phyllis Greenacre (1945) regarded the tendency to cry at the drop of a hat to be more common in women. According to her, it represented an 'upward displacement' from urination to crying. Greenacre described two types of 'pathological weeping'. In one, the woman weeps in anger because she cannot approximate male urination and in the other, the woman weeps as a substitute for urinating. Her views reflected the somatocentric orientation of early

psychoanalysis which often ignored the object-related scenarios underlying psychopathological formations. Later authors (Lacombe, 1958; Yazmajian, 1966; Sachs, 1973) have discussed 'pathological weeping' from the latter perspective.

Penis awe: see 'Awe'.

Penis envy: concept originated by Sigmund Freud in 1908, extended to include the wish for a child in accordance with the symbolic equation of penis and child in 1917, and thoroughly elucidated in his 1925 paper 'Some psychical consequences of anatomical distinction between the sexes'. Freud's assertion was that the little girl becomes aware of lacking a penis upon noticing the genital anatomy of the two sexes. She feels inferior, 'lesser in so important a respect' (1925j, p. 253), and wants to have a penis. She thinks that she did possess a penis and has been castrated as a punishment for masturbation and/or imagines that she was deprived of a penis by her unloving and neglectful mother. She envies the penis for its size, masturbatory ease, and its manipulation of the urinary stream. Lacking it, she turns away from the mother to the father to obtain one from him; the wish to have a baby is thus born. The wish for possessing a penis is never fully given up by the girl; it always persists in the unconscious and might be impervious to analysis (Freud, 1937c). Such 'penis envy' is a 'fundamental element' (Laplanche & Pontalis, 1973, p. 302) and 'primary organizer' (Moore & Fine, 1990, p. 140) of the female psyche. It underlies many character traits (e.g., competitiveness with men, preferring a weak and 'castrated' male for a partner) and neurotic symptoms (e.g., kleptomania, vaginismus) in adult women. Freud's early followers elaborated his ideas in this regard. Karl Abraham (1919) discerned anal sadism in 'penis envy' and Ernest Jones (1933) expanded the concept to include: (1) wanting a penis to swallow, retain, and perhaps, make a baby out of it; (2) wanting a penis instead of a vagina; and (3) wanting a penis to give pleasure in adult sexual intercourse. More importantly, he emphasized that the 'autoerotic' (exhibitionistic–masturbatory–urinary stream related) basis for 'penis envy' was far less significant than its 'alloerotic' (object-related, fantasied) basis. Gradually, however, the early Freudian ideas came under increasing criticism along the following lines: (1) the entire concept of 'penis envy' and Freud's use of the expression 'superior organ' for the penis represented the phallocentricism of a narrative written by and for men; (2) the portrayal of female psychosexual development as 'disappointed masculinity' (Moore & Fine, 1990, p. 140) was not only theoretically biased and implicitly pejorative, but empirically untenable in the light of child-observational studies (Galenson & Roiphe, 1976); (3) even when 'penis envy' was discernible in girls, it was subtle, phase-specific, and transient, and not pronounced and life-long as Freud had proposed; (4) rather than emanating from auto-erotic and narcissistic factors, 'penis envy' arose from object-relations; it was a manifest content that hid all sorts of affects and longings; (5) maternal masochism and self-neglect contributed to the girl's feelings of inferiority more than the 'lack' of a penis; (6) overvaluation of males by the family of origin and culture at large played a prominent role in the genesis of 'penis envy'; (7) prominent 'penis envy' betrayed psychopathology, not normal development; (8) the girl's wish for a baby antedates the phallic phase and is not the product of a penis–baby equation (Parens, Pollock, Stern, & Kramer, 1976); (9) 'penis envy' may be but one manifestation of 'envy' (see separate entry) at large, and thus can also be encountered in men; and (10) such issues may not be impervious to analysis; these do not form the 'bedrock' of female psyche.

Penis-in-link: asserting that the word 'phallus' (see separate entry) is not appropriate for an important symbolic function attributed to it, Dana Birksted-Breen (1996b) introduced the concept of 'penis-in-link'. This 'links mother and father, underpins oedipal and bisexual mental function and hence has a structuring function which underpins the process of thinking' (p. 656). The introjection of the 'penis-in-link' promotes mental space. Lack of its internalization leads to a compulsive search for the 'phallus' in the hope of buttressing psychic structure.

Perceptual bath: a term coined by George Awad (cited in Akhtar, 1999b, p. 176) for the holding function of smells, sounds, and visual texture of the early environment; its relatively silent internalization provides a background screen for all subsequent perceptions.

Perceptual identity: see 'Perceptual identity and thought identity'.

Perceptual identity and thought identity: terms used by Sigmund Freud (1900a) to denote two different forms of seeking instinctual satisfaction. 'Perceptual identity' refers to the mind's insistence upon finding, again and again, that very object which provided a truly satisfactory discharge of tension; it is as if the sense of gratifica-

tion had become identical with the perception of that object. 'Thought identity', in contrast, freed mental processes from being ruled by the 'pleasure principle' (see separate entry) and created the intellectual option that different objects might provide the same instinctual gratification. The two concepts anticipate Freud's (1895d) formulation of 'primary and secondary processes' (see separate entry) and are more or less akin to these later concepts.

Perennial mourning: see 'Pathological grief reaction'.

Performance: term introduced by Joachim Danckwardt and Peter Wegner (2007) for a particular form of interaction between the patient and analyst which differs from 'enactment' (see separate entry). Unlike 'enactment', which involves the analyst being pulled in through countertransference, 'performance' involves the analyst's being recruited as a spectator and hence losing his analytic function. 'In a performance, the analysand borrows from the analyst those component parts which the analyst normally requires for his functioning—and to that extent the analyst is annihilated' (p. 1121). 'Performance' does not involve the analysand's living out of an intrapsychic fantasy; it involves the transference of that which is not yet represented symbolically. 'Performance', therefore, seems to have the creative function of bridging internal and external realities.

Perils of neutrality: phrase originated by Owen Renik (1996) in the context of his questioning the validity and usefulness of the concept of analytic 'neutrality' (see separate entry). Calling adherence to neutrality a misguided pursuit, Renik declared that 'patients benefit from knowing what we think about matters that are of greatest importance to them' (p. 507) and a disinterested understanding is neither possible or desirable. He acknowledged that his suggestion could mean that fears of becoming advice-giving counsellors and embarking on the slippery slope of exploitation are stirred up by his theoretical stance. In rebuttal, he asserted that 'by advocating for his or her personal beliefs, an analyst does not necessarily claim authority for those beliefs' and that 'we are best off by acknowledging that non-neutrality lies at the heart of our clinical method precisely because doing so encourages us to decline authority to which we are not entitled' (p. 513). Moreover, neutrality is not what prevents ethical transgressions; a responsible sense of morality, that is independent of technique, does. Renik concluded that the concept of 'neutrality' needs to be put aside and better ways found to conceptualize the analyst's helpful influence.

Persephone complex: Nancy Kulish and Deanna Holtzman's (1998) term for the female Oedipus complex; the latter designation, derived from the saga of a male protagonist, is regarded as an oxymoron by these authors. According to them, the Greek fable of Persephone's straying from her mother to pick flowers and her subsequent abduction by the king of the underworld is a better metaphor for the dynamics and concerns of the girl during the triangular conflict phase of development. Persephone's mother's mournful search for her daughter especially underscores the prominence of separation themes in the girl's so-called oedipal phase. These authors (Kulish & Holtzman, 1998; Holtzman & Kulish, 2000) state that the very person, i.e., the mother, with whom the girl experiences rivalry at this time is her source of her security and 'home base' for nurturance. This makes separating from mother difficult. However, these triangular phase separation issues are neither synonymous with, nor recreations of, anxieties arising out of 'separation individuation' (see separate entry) of earlier childhood. None the less, the the divided pull towards the caretaker–mother and lover–father takes its toll. The tendency, in many adult women, to feel that passionate sexuality is somehow opposed to their mothers owes its origin to this conflict. 'Misunderstanding how these separation conflicts tie into triangular "oedipal" relationships can lead to a "preoedipalization" of the dynamics of girls and women' (Holtzman & Kulish, 2000, p. 1413) and a stalemated and endlessly regressive treatment.

Personal myth: introduced by Ernst Kris (1956), this concept refers to an emotionally invested and relatively harmonious version of one's biography evolved by the individual for self-stabilizing purposes. The remarkable coherence and the firm conviction that characterize such an autobiographical memory indicate that it is a defence against discordant aspects of one's life history and unacceptable fantasies that one carries within one's self. The 'personal myth' supports repression on the one hand, and expresses wishful scenarios regarding the self on the other hand; it can also serve as a defence against internal primitive aggression (Beratis, 1988).

Personal relationship: see 'Real relationship'.

Personality: a term that refers to an individual's habitual and ego-syntonic way of negotiating between the inner pressures of his desires and morality on the one hand, and the outer demands of reality on the other. Such 'negotiation' results in a sense of subjective sameness and a consistent pattern of behaviours. Under normal circumstances, this pattern remains more or less predictable. The concept of 'personality' subsumes both the genetically received affectomotor propensities (*temperament*) and the behavioural style derived from the actual and imagined childhood interactions with parents (*character*). Personality may be well-adjusted or maladjusted. Collectively, the latter types of personality are termed 'Personality disorders' (see separate entry).

Personality disorders: a group of conditions characterized by chronic, repetitive, egosyntonic, and maladaptive patterns of behaviour that lead to interpersonal strife and social maladjustment. Broadly speaking, such disorders belong to three categories (Kernberg, 1970): higher, intermediate, and lower levels. The first category includes phobic, hysterical, obsessional, and mild self-defeating or depressive characters. The second category includes narcissistic and masochistic characters. The third category includes borderline, infantile ('histrionic'), paranoid, hypomanic, antisocial, as-if, schizoid, and schizotypal characters. One extreme is close to mild neurotic constellations of everyday life, though certainly in a rigid and exaggerated form. The other extreme is close to severe ego dysfunction, including psychosis.

Personalization: see 'Integration, personalization, and realization'.

Personification: Ronald Fairbairn's (1931) term for the tendency on the part of some individuals to anthropomorphize various aspects of their psyche. In describing a patient who evolved 'the mischievous boy' and 'the critic' as two such 'personifications', Fairbairn noted that these occurred in both her waking life and in dreams. 'There occurred dreams in which the "I" of the dream was herself represented as playing the part of "the mischievous boy", and that there were also frequent teaching dreams, in which "I" of the dreamer played the part of the critic. Usually, however, the dreaming consciousness played the part of an independent onlooker, whose sympathies were sometimes on the one side, sometimes on the other' (p. 127). While acknowledging that such 'personifications' can represent various psychic stucutures (id, ego, superego), Fairbairn asserted that they might also stand for chronologically earlier or later images of the self. He declared that 'the personifications have something in common . . . with the phenomena of multiple personality' (p. 219) and, thus, laid the foundation of later studies of this syndrome (e.g., Brenner, 2001; Kluft, 1985, 1986, 1993).

Perverse character: Janine Chasseguet-Smirgel's (1984) designation for a personality whose main features are precocity, cockiness, disregard for generational boundaries, failure to enter into the temporal order of life, and weakness of the inner barrier against incest. Though superficially charming, such individuals are actually inauthentic and hollow. The syndrome is more common in men, and ostensibly results from the over-idealization of the son by a seductive mother who prefers him over his father. The father is either absent or has abdicated his responsibilities. Given this scenario, 'forward projection' of boys' narcissism does not occur. Pre-genitality is placed above genitality and the 'anal universe' (see separate entry) lurking underneath is hidden by inordinate enthusiasm about matters close to creativity, aesthetics, and beauty. See also the related entry on 'character perversion'.

Perverse defences: although a remote echo of Melanie Klein's (1935) concept of 'manic defence' and Janine Chasseguet-Smirgel's concept of 'perverse character' (see separate entries on the two) can be heard here, the term 'perverse defences' owes its origin to Lee Grossman (1996). According to him, these are defences that, instead of inhibiting or disguising a troublesome wish, facilitate a disavowal of the significance of reality. The wish in question is acted out, but the significance of such action is denied and discordants aspects of reality are ignored. Stanley Coen (1998) extended the term to include 'states of excitement, distraction, and pomposity, as well as sadomasochistic relations with others, in an attempt to ward off the unbearable: intense affects, painful ideas, and loving, committed need of a valued, distinct person' (p. 1171). Such tenacious refusals to be reasonable provoke 'perverse countertransference', characterized by the analyst's becoming judgemental, angry, and even sadomasochistic.

Perversions: see 'Sexual deviations'.

Phallic mother: see 'Phallic woman'.

Phallic narcissism: idea derived from Sigmund Freud's (1925j) observations regarding the emotional consequences of children's discovery of anatomical differences between the two sexes. 'Phallic narcissism' or 'phallic pride' (Reich, 1933) refers to the euphoria and self-infatuation that

boys show in 'discovering' their penises. Soon their interest in the penis is displaced to elongated objects (e.g., toys in the form of cars, planes, and guns) and activities and fantasies that involve the phallus. The near-manic excitement also celebrates the escape from symbiotic engulfment (since the penis confirms being different from the mother) and serves as a defence against castration anxiety. The essentially autoerotic 'phallic narcissism' gradually becomes more object-related as the child moves into the oedipal phase proper. However, remnants of it might persist on a life-long basis, giving the adult character a 'cocky' and exhibitionistic slant.

Phallic narcissistic character: Wilhelm Reich's 1933 designation for an individual who is arrogant, energetic, often promiscuous, and reacts to any offence to his vanity with 'cold disdain, marked ill-humor, or downright aggression' (p. 218). Reich regarded this character pathology to be more common among males, and felt that it was largely a defence against a deep-seated feeling of inferiority (see also 'Narcissistic personality disorder'). He distinguished the phallic narcissistic character from the compulsive character by the former's lack of reaction formation against his openly aggressive behaviour and his tendency to be less thorough with respect to details. See also the paper titled 'Phallic narcissitic personality' by William Meissner (1985).

Phallic patheticness: Moshe Halevi Spero's (1993) designation for the character trait of being pitiable, which, despite its oral qualities, arises from complex phallic wish-defence structures. The pessimism and neediness of such individuals does indicate oral fixation; however, 'the more subtle nuances of ironical self-defeat, miscarried ambitiousness and failed sexual negotiation of triangular ensnarement suggest urethral–phallic and oedipal conflict' (p. 528).

Phallic phase: the psychosexual phase that follows the 'anal phase' (see separate entry) of development. First described by Sigmund Freud in 1923e, this phase is characterized by intense libidinal investment in the penis and clitoris. It begins with the child's discovery of anatomical differences between the sexes and ends with the onset of 'oedipal phase' (see separate entry). Chronologically, this generally translates into the period between two and half to three and a half or four years of age. According to Freud (1923e, 1924d, 1925j), the boy feels pride and excitement about his penis while the girl, comparing her clitoris to the penis, feels inferior and wishes to have the bigger organ. 'Phallic pride' (Reich, 1933) and 'penis envy' (Freud, 1925j) designate these emotional dispositions. These proclivities play a decisive role in the subsequent oedipal development. The boy renounces his oedipal wishes for the mother under the threat of castration by the father, a threat made more potent since it undermines his 'phallis pride'. This renunciation under the threat of castration leads to the formation of the superego. The girl resents the mother for not giving her a penis and turns to the father for receiving his penis or its symbolic equivalent, the child. Since the girl does not fear castration, the superego she develops is weaker. These developmental postulates of Freud, and especially his notion about the girl's development, have been seriously disputed on three grounds: (1) Freud did not recognize that the girl has an intuitive knowledge of her vagina and therefore her sexual feelings are different from the boy from the very beginning (Horney, 1926, 1933; Jones, 1927, 1935); (2) the girl's desire for a baby emerges long before the oedipal phase (Parens, Pollock, Stern, & Kramer, 1976) and (3) the female superego is not weaker, though it might be different from the male superego in embodying a greater relational perspective (Bernstein, 1983; Gilligan, 1982).

Phallic stage: see 'Phallic phase'.

Phallic woman: term used by Robert Bak (1968) to underscore that the fantasy of the maternal or female phallus is ubiquitous in human psyche and is regressively revived, dramatized, and acted-out in sexual perversions. Differing from Sigmund Freud (1925j), who had suggested that the sight of female genital leads to a split in the ego whereby two contradictorary attitudes (women have a penis; women do not have a penis) are retained in the mind, Bak introduced the idea that the child is actually uncertain of whether women do or do not have a penis and later puts this uncertainity to defensive uses. 'This "uncertainty" helps maintain an oscillatory identification with either parent, prevents the clear demarcation of the two sexes that would lead to "certainty" of sexual identity, and sustains a bisexual position by fused self-representation' (p. 29). According to Bak, all sexual perversions in men are ritualized denials of castration and rest upon the fantasy of a 'phallic woman'. In women, the fantasy of possessing a secret or illusory phallus might coexist with relatively normal sexual functioning, accompany masochistic inclinations (Freud, 1919h; Rado, 1933), or become pressing and severe, leading to transvestite and transsexual tendencies (Stoller, 1973).

Phallus: in psychoanalysis, the term 'phallus' is used literally for the penis (and, occasionally, the clitoris), and metaphorically for power, prowess, assertion, etc. 'Phallus' therefore represents many things and, in turn, can itself be represented by many symbols. At times, the individual as a whole can represent the 'phallus'. Given the largely metaphorical nature of the concept, it is not surprising that objectival forms of it ('phallic narcissism', 'phallic phase', 'phallic woman', etc.; see separate entries on each) are more often to be found in the psychoanalytic literature than its nominal form. A major exception in this regard is Sigmund Freud's (1923e) declaration that 'for both sexes, only one genital, namely the male one, comes into account. What is present, therefore, is not the primacy of genitals, but the primacy of the phallus' (p. 142). Jacques Lacan (1977), too, employs 'phallus', in its 'real, symbolic, and imaginary' (see separate entry) forms as a central concept in his discourse on the oedipus complex and sexual difference. Such 'phallocentrism' of psychoanalytic theory has fuelled the legitimate feminist critique of its developmental postulates. To complicate matters, the choice of the term 'phallus' has, at times, created serious mishaps in the enterprise of applied psychoanalysis. The recent uproar by Hindu nationalists (who could hardly find a Hindi equivalent for 'phallus' that was not lewd) over the Emory University professor, Paul Courtright's (1985) psychoanalytic speculations regarding the elephant-headed god, Ganesha, is one unfortunate example of this cross-cultural confusion of tongues.

Phantasy: term associated with the work of Melanie Klein (1921, 1923) and her followers (e.g., Issacs, 1948; Segal, 1981). The focus of heated debate during the 'controversial discussions' (see separate entry) between the Kleinians and Anna Freudians during the early 1940s, 'phantasy' differs from the usual, ego psychological notion of 'fantasy' (see separate entry) in six important ways: (1) 'fantasy' is a wish-fulfilling imaginative mental content evolved in response to frustration (Sandler & Nagera, 1963) in contrast, 'phantasy' is an incessant accompaniment of all mental activity; (2) whereas 'fantasy' is an ego function, 'phantasy' is a mental corollary of instinctual urges; (3) 'fantasy' may be conscious or unconscious, but 'phantasy' is always unconscious; (4) 'fantasy' is juxtaposed to reality so that there is either 'fantasy' or reality. However 'phantasy' accompanies all experience of reality; (5) 'fantasy' depends upon synthetic functioning of the ego and thus develops later than 'phantasy', which is present from birth onwards; and (6) 'fantasy' is derived from thinking, while thinking is derived from 'phantasy'. For a lucid and historically grounded discussion of these matters, see Anne Hayman's (1989) paper 'What do we mean by "phantasy"?' and, for the Freud–Klein divergence in this realm as well as for further refinements of the Kleinian concept of 'phantasy', see Elizabeth Bott Spillius's (2001) contribution.

Pharmacothymia: see 'Addiction'.

Phase of joint acceptance of the Holocaust reality: Ilse Grubrich-Simitis's (1984) phrase for the period in the analytic treatment of Holocaust survivors when the analysand develops a lasting conviction that his or her analyst does not deny the reality of concentration camps. The analysand also comes to believe that the analyst can endure the intense feelings that the description of Holocaust related realities can arouse. 'In other words, the analyst is perceived by the patient as a person with stable ego boundaries who can distinguish between nonmetaphorical and metaphorical thinking. It is precisely with these ego functions of the analyst that the patient now begins to identify in the developing working alliance' (p. 316).

Philobatism: see 'Ocnophilia and philobatism'.

Phobia: a psychiatric condition characterized by inordinate fear of a specific object that is animate (e.g., dogs, cats, bats, snakes) or inanimate (e.g., knives, masks). Excessive fear evoked by specific situations (e.g., fear of heights, flying in a plane, crowded or open spaces) also qualifies to be called a 'phobia'. Mechanisms of symbolism and displacement play a major role here; the feared object stands for a projected part of the superego and, within that projection, the image of a castrating father or mother. Sigmund Freud's (1909b) celebrated case history of Little Hans, a five-year-old boy with an intense fear of horses, elucidated these mechanisms for the first time. Situational phobias involve activation of unconscious impulses that are deemed morally abhorrent or physically dangerous by the conscious ego. Fear of heights, for instance, often stems from unconscious narcissistic impulses to fly or guilt-driven impulses to jump and commit suicide.

Phobic character: Otto Fenichel (1945) coined this term for individuals 'whose reactive behavior limits itself to the avoidance of the situations originally wished for' (p. 527). Roger Mackinnon and Robert Michels (1971) also pointed out that more common than symptomatic phobia is the use of fearful avoidance as a character defence, adding

that such an individual is 'constantly imagining himself in situations of danger while pursuing the course of greatest safety' (p. 49). While resembling schizoid individuals in their restricted life-style, phobic characters are different in important ways. They avoid situations, not people. Outside of their feared situation, they can have empathic and meaningful relationships with others.

Physical contact between analyst and patient: while the regression inherent in psychoanalytic treatment frequently mobilizes longings in the patient to be touched, held, hugged, kissed, and made love to, the gratification of such desires is prohibited (see the entry on 'abstinence'). The rationale for such proscription rests upon viewing such desires as essentially transference-based and not directed at the analyst *per se*; even if a modicum of 'reality' exists in the object-choice of such instinctual aims, it is not deemed sufficient to warrant their gratification. This stoic ethic seems to have its origin in the Victorian prudishness of early Vienna, where psychoanalysis originated, and in the need felt by the nascent discipline to distinguish itself from various magical, hypnotic treatments, including the so-called 'pressure technique' (see separate entry). As psychoanalysis evolved, it also became clear that the desire for physical contact with the analyst is multiply-determined; it carries tributaries from id impulses, unconscious fantasies from various psychosexual phases, long-lasting effects of childhood trauma, including sexual abuse and emotional neglect, and defensive warding off of still other agendas, including mourning for the ontogenetically earlier and current deprivations. This justifies the abstinent stance *vis-à-vis* such longings. At the same time, the history, especially the early history, of psychoanalysis contains dramatic episodes of 'physical contact between the patient and analyst'. Most such occurrences constitute what would today be called 'boundary violations' (see separate entry). Others (e.g., during Donald Winnicott's treatment of Margaret Little; see Little, 1990, and also Balint, 1968) appear to be heroic measures that somehow ended up having therapeutic benefit. Still others, while less heroic, none the less appeared clinically useful (Mintz, 1969). Putting these historic 'blips' aside, it can be safely said that 'physical contact between the patient and analyst' is a matter riddled with conceptual and ethical complexities, though, by and large, it is something to be avoided. However, it is worthwhile to keep the following variables in mind: (1) *age of the patient*: while physical contact with adult patients remains undesirable, it is, at times, unavoidable with child patients, especially during play and/or for protecting them from injury; (2) *nature of contact:* erotic contact is never appropriate, given the patient's regressed and dependent state, but protective and affectionate contact that is 'within the ethical and legal guidelines of one's community' (Breckenridge, 2000, p. 2), under certain circumstances, might be permissible. However, such distinctions are never easy. A 'slippery slope' exists in this realm that can readily transform the innocent and benevolent to the transgressive and harmful; (3) *nature of the patient's psychopathology:* those with severe childhood frustrations and sexual abuse are more likely to develop 'malignant erotic transference' (see separate entry) with desperate coercion to actualize their demands. Preparedness on the analyst's part can serve as a prophylactic against 'boundary violations'; and, finally (4) *societal norms and cultural context:* in some countries (e.g., Germany), it is customary for the patient and analyst to shake hands before and after each session. And the nature of such handshake (e.g., firmness, duration, difference in skin temperature, or moisture before or after the session) can itself be a rich source of psychologically important information. That the practice is part of the 'frame' does not preclude it from getting caught up in conflict and thus becoming a topic for analytic exploration (Danckwardt & Wegner, 2007). However, where such custom does not exist (e.g., in the USA), a handshake might acquire a much greater symbolic value and contain more that is of psychic valence. The level of paranoia and litigiousness in a particular society can also regulate matters in this context. As the foregoing makes evident, the whole issue of 'physical contact between the patient and analyst' is far from simple. Patrick Casement's (1982) celebrated paper 'Some pressures on the analyst for physical contact during sessions' elucidates the deeper issues and technical dilemmas involved here in captivating detail. See also the special issue of *Psychoanalytic Inquiry* (2000) which is edited by Ellen Ruderman, Estelle Shane, and Morton Shane and has contributions from a number of distinguished analysts, including Ann Appelbaum, Herbert Schlesinger, James Fosshage, Alex Holder, and James McLaughlin, among others. While differing in nuance, almost all these authors agree that non-sexual, non-aggressive physical touch might at times be therapeutically appropriate. One author (Holder, 2000) gives an example where the mere offer of a hand to be held was soothing, though the patient never actually held the analyst's hand. Another author (Fosshage, 2000) suggests that when the analyst concludes that the discomfort in touching is primarily his, 'an open acknowledgement of

that discomfort, rather than pathologizing the patient's desire for physical contact will facilitate the analytic interaction' (p. 40). Referring again to Holder's contribution (Holder, 2000), his comment, taken with due caveats, summarizes it all: 'Rules are a good thing to have for general guidance, but they should not stop us from being flexible, from trusting our intuitive feeling and occasionally breaking such rules when it feels right to do so' (p. 45).

Placental paradigm: concept introduced by Joan Raphael-Leff (1996) for the fact that the 'bidirectional placental system can serve as a metaphor for the imagined give-and-take within the affectively colored exchange' (p. 380) between a pregnant woman and her foetus. The experience of being pregnant and thus being united with another being can activate fantasies of merger the nature of which varies with the maternal emotional state. At one moment, such blurring of boundaries may seem ecstatic, and at another time suffocating and dangerous. The 'placental paradigm', therefore, involves representations of the woman herself as mother and her fantasy baby linked through affective states. Raphael-Leff proposes that a benevolent relationship between mother and foetus is only possible 'if the expectant mother is able to tolerate her ambivalence towards the pregnancy as a source of both joy and discomfort' (p. 380).

Play: while Sigmund Freud's (1920g) celebrated observations on the 'fort-da' game that his eighteen-month-old grandson was playing and Melanie Klein's (1923) introduction of 'play technique' in the psychoanalytic treatment of children form the early foundations of the discipline's interest in 'play', the subject was truly rendered intriguing, exciting, and profoundly meaningful by Donald Winnicott (1942, 1946, 1953, 1968b, 1971, 1989). He took playing seriously, considered it a developmental achievement, and located it in the 'intermediate area of experience' (see separate entry). In Winnicott's view, 'play' was an imaginative elaboration of thoughts and feelings about body, object relations, and anxieties. Play enriches life, and enjoyment of playing is a hallmark of the growing child's mental health. Playing was the result of acting from the centre, so to speak, and fearlessly being imaginative and innovative. It depended upon the capacity to enter a spirit which would not torment itself with questions of reality and unreality; instead, it will peacefully accept the paradox that some activities are neither real nor unreal. 'Play' shared this characteristic with creativity in general. Winnicott recognized that formal games did provide an opportunity to 'play', but he also knew that such operationalized activities could also stifle playfulness. In a posthumously published and undated essay (Winnicott, Shepherd, & Davis, 1989, pp. 59–63), he described seven types of pathology of 'play' and playfulness, including (1) loss of capacity to play associated with mistrust, (2) stereotypical and rigid play, (3) flight into day-dreaming, which he felt was a midway state between dream and play; (4) excessive sensualization of play; (5) dominating play; (6) playing as compliance to authority; and (7) flight to strenuous physical exercise. Play, and especially children's games, drew the attention of other analytic contributors as well (Erikson, 1950; Balint, 1959; Kleeman, 1967; Phillips, 1960; Waelder, 1933; Glenn, 1991). Together these contributors elucidated the ego replenishing aspects, strivings for mastery over inner conflicts and external dangers, and epistemophilic impetus to children's play while also underscoring the transformations a child's play undergoes with unfolding psychic development and ego growth. The role of 'play' in evaluation and treatment of children was also noted (though with less than full consensus over its equivalence with the adult's free association); see the entries on 'spatula game' and 'squiggle game'. Few analysts, however, wrote about the element of 'play' and playfulness in the course of working with adult analysands. Here again, Winnicott (1967) stands out. Note his statement that 'psychotherapy has to do with two people playing. The corollary of this is that when playing is not possible then the work done by the therapist is directed towards bringing the patient from a state of not being able to play into a state of being able to play' (p. 38). See also Linda Hopkins (2000) paper on Masud Khan's applications of these ideas to adult analysis.

Play technique: introduced by Melanie Klein (1923, 1926) for the treatment of very young children, the 'play technique' consisted of letting them play with small toys. The underlying assumption was that freedom to play could become a substitute for 'free association', used in the treatment of adults. Mrs Klein allotted separate toys and separate lockers to each child under treatment. She watched the child's play with great interest and occasionally joined the child in playing. Unlike other child analysts of the era, like Hermine Hug-Hellmuth and Anna Freud, she interpreted the unconscious aspects of the child's play directly, talking simply but explicitly about sexual and hostile 'phantasies' (see entry on 'phantasy'). Today the 'play technique' is integral to the therapeutic armamentarium of child ana-

lysts. However, the technique is no longer restricted to work with very young children and is frequently used with older children and, at times, even with adolescents. Board games are often used. Interpretation is generally not as direct and instinctually geared as was employed in the early Kleinian approach; it takes the ego's defensive aims also into account.

Pleasure principle: see 'Pleasure–unpleasure principle'.

Pleasure–unpleasure principle: first described by Sigmund Freud (1911b, 1915–1916 [1917], pp. 243–462), this principle proposes that the mind avoids pain or 'unpleasure' and seeks 'pleasure'. 'Unpleasure' results from accumulation of instinctual tension and 'pleasure' from the discharge of this tension. The concept of 'pleasure–unpleasure principle' can be seen from many vantage points: (1) *conceptual perspective*: avoiding 'unpleasure' is more basic than seeking 'pleasure'; indeed Freud had originally named it 'unpleasure principle' and only later referred to it as 'pleasure–unpleasure principle' (the term 'pleasure principle' appeared even later in his lexicon); (2) *developmental perspective*: while the 'pleasure–unpleasure principle' dominates psychic functioning during infancy and childhood, with growth it is tempered by the 'reality principle' (see separate entry); (3) *structural perspective*: the id is totally governed by the 'pleasure–unpleasure principle' but the ego is subject to the 'reality principle' as well; and (4) *dynamic perspective*, since it is anxiety or a sense of perceived danger that mobilizes defences, the 'pleasure–unpleasure principle' is involved in warding off the threat. Further points pertaining to the concept of the 'pleasure–unpleasure principle' include (1) accumulation of instinctual tension (e.g., during foreplay) is not always unpleasurable (Freud, 1920g); (2) the 'reality principle' is not in principle (pun unintended) opposed to 'pleasure–unpleasure principle' and might, in fact, expedite the aims of the latter; (3) it is also questionable whether the 'reality principle' emerges later in development (Hartmann, 1939) or, in some larger sense, it precedes the 'pleasure–unpleasure principle', (4) the 'pleasure–unpleasure principle' is more closely related to the 'constancy principle' (see separate entry), which means that the mind seeks to maintain energy at a constant level, than to the 'Nirvana principle' (see separate entry), which declares that the mind seeks to reduce instinctual tension to zero (Laplanche & Pontalis, 1973); and (5) the possibility, suggested by Heinz Kohut (1977), that the 'pleasure–unpleasure principle', far from being ubiquitous, emerges only when the child's age-specific reality functioning is not met with empathic care; the 'pleasure–principle' is a degradation product, not the fundamental element in this perspective.

Plural Oedipus complex: Bhaskar Sripada's (2005) term for the fact that, in the context of Indian society, where psychic bisexuality is less repressed and widely accessible to consciousness through androgynous mythological tales, both father and mother can be sources of a boy's masculinity, just as both can be a source of a girl's feminity. This casts doubt upon the mainstream psychoanalytic notion that the oedipal boy gains masculinity exclusively from identification with his father and the oedipal girl gains feminity exclusively from identification with her mother. In Indian culture, both parents offer pathways for homosexual and heterosexual identifications. Clearly, this has implications for the shape of the Oedipus complex, with both parents potentially becoming the objects of the positive and negative oedipal desires. This is what Sripada calls the 'plural Oedipus complex'. Clearly, this has an effect upon post-oedipal developmental vicissitudes and also upon the transference Indian analysands develop during their analyses.

Poisoning of nostalgia: term coined by Salman Akhtar (1999b) for the retrograde spread of inner aggression which blocks access to prior good memories. This is commonly seen in traumatized refugees and exiles who, unlike ordinary immigrants, experience no yearning for their lost homelands. Or, they experience 'negative nostalgia', i.e., a preoccupation with how bad their country of origin was. An alternative hypothesis about the absence of nostalgia in exiles is suggested by Ruth Lax. According to her, 'nostalgia can only be for something one loved and where one was loved' (personal communication, January 1999), and this was not the case with Jews in Poland, for instance. One way to reconcile these divergent views is to be found in Vamik Volkan's (1999d) division of such experiences into three categories: lack of nostalgia, poisoned nostalgia, and healthy nostalgia. See also Honey Oberoi's (2009) monograph on the psychology of Tibetan refugees in India.

Pollakiuria nervosa: Carel van der Heide's (1941) term for abnormally frequent urination of psychogenic aetiology. The symptom is multiply determined and seems somewhat more common among women. Early psychoanalytic literature (Alexander, 1933; Menninger, 1941) underscored 'urinary envy', competition, and hostility towards men as the main causes of the symptom. Patho-

logical erotization of urination can turn the symptom of frequent urination into a masturbatory equivalent. A different sort of dynamics was shown by individuals who use frequent urination to assure themselves of being full of something and thus not empty (Agoston, 1946).

Polycratism: term coined by Sandor Ferenczi (1915) for the superstitious avoidance of good things coming to one lest they be followed by a proportionate punishment from God. Much unconscious guilt lurks behind the attitude.

Polymorphous perverse sexuality: Sigmund Freud's (1905a) designation of the infant's 'sexual' life, which lacks the aim specificity of adult, genital pleasure. 'Infantile sexuality' (see separate entry), in contrast, is driven by relatively fluid and interchangeable play of various 'component instincts' (see separate entry) such as desires to suck, bite, smell, and so on. Comparing them to interlinked canals, Freud emphasized that these pleasures can be replaced by each other and their active and passive aims are readily reversed. Nothing is sacrosanct. He therefore referred to 'infantile sexuality' as essentially 'polymorphously perverse' in nature.

Positive narcissism: see 'Negative and positive narcissism'.

Positive projective identification: see 'Projective identification'.

Post-oedipal transformations: in elucidating the impact of latency and adolescent experiences on refinement and reshaping of the preoedipal and oedipal psychic substrate, Kerry Kelly Novick and Jack Novick (1994) emphasize that 'earlier is not necessarily more important and that there can not be pure recapitulation, revival, or "reanimation" (Freud, 1925) of the past in the present' (p. 143). Adult memories of latency and adolescence are not merely defensive screens, but are genuine in themselves and contain 'postoedipal transformations' of earlier material. Keeping this in mind increases the specificity of 'genetic interpretation' (see separate entry) and enhances the credibility of 'reconstruction' (see separate entry).

Post-parental crisis of narcissism: David Guttman's (1980) phrase for the disturbance in narcissistic equilibrium that takes place within the lives of parents once their children become independent and leave home. Deprived of narcissistic mirroring and feeling 'needed', parents often are traumatized by this development. Moreover, they are now thrown into greater intimacy with each other. They also do not have to sustain the hitherto demarcated roles they had. This post-parental period gives back to women their covert masculinity and to men their covert femininity. Each recaptures repudiated aspects of their self-representation with consequent shifts in intrapsychic and interpersonal dynamics of not insignificant proportions.

Post-interruption contacts : see ' Analyst's relocation'.

Post-termination contacts: despite Sigmund Freud's (1937c) observation that 'not every good relation between an analyst and his subject during and after analysis was to be regarded as a transference: there were also friendly relations which were based on reality and which proved to be viable' (p. 222), and despite the fact that analysts themselves remain in touch with their own training analysts, there evolved a tendency to look down upon or avoid 'post-termination contacts' with one's analysands. Inviting or initiating such contact was regarded as intrusive, undermining of the patient's autonomy, encouraging infantile dependence, and potentially undoing the gains made during the analysis (Kubie, 1968; Firestein, 1978). Revisiting the issue recently (Calef, 1982; Schacter, 1990, 1992) has challenged these assumptions. Expectations of adverse impact have not been borne out. On the contrary, 'post-termination contacts' have been found to enhance the patient's self-analysis (Schlessinger & Robbins, 1974), minimize the loss of earlier gains (Luborsky, 1988), and facilitate seeking further treatment if that seems needed (Wallerstein, 1986; see also 1992). Joseph Schacter (1990, 1992) , the strongest advocate for this intervention, delineates the following guidelines for its use: (1) a one session, face-to-face meeting in the analyst's office should be proposed by the analyst during the 'termination phase' (see separate entry) but the patient should have freedom to accept or decline it without being 'grilled' about his response; (2) its purpose—namely, to assess how the treatment has fared and how the patient's life is going since ending treatment—should be made clear ; (3) the patient should be given a choice; (4) the patient should be asked after what length of time following termination he would like to have such a meeting; generally speaking, a lapse of six months to a year seems good; (5) following termination, it should be left entirely to the patient to initiate setting up such a meeting and, if he does not, the analyst should drop the matter; (6) if the meeting does take place, the patient should be charged the customary fee; and (7) at the end of the session, the patient should be asked if he would like to have a similar session six months or a year later. Schacter firmly believes that 'iodic post-termination contacts as extensions of the analytic situation provide the analyst with an improved perspective for evaluating the prior analytic work and provides the patient with evidence of the analyst's continuing physicianly concern for his/her well being. The latter extends the therapeutic alliance which had supported the earlier analytic work and which probably enhances the maintainence of analytic gains and facilitates continued self-analytic work' (p. 149).

Post termination phase: it was Leo Rangell (1966) who first described a set of three events (further and deeper resolution of transference neurosis, dissolving the analytic situation both externally and internally, and mourning the actual loss of the analyst) as constituting a 'post-termination phase'. The literature on the topic since then has been masterfully summarized by Heather Craige (2002); she notes the following salient points: (1) a mourning process lasting for about six months to a year is frequent; (2) how the balance between feeling deprived and feeling emancipated at termination determines how well the patient mourns the analyst in the 'post-termination phase'; (3) this mourning pertains to the loss of the analyst as an analyst as well as a real object; (4) over time, the analyst's imago becomes more abstract and his analysing functions become absorbed in the patient's ego; (5) sorting out transference residues while holding on to the analyst as a good internal object is a most important task of this phase; and (6) complications arise when latent negative transference and unanalysed selfobject transference emerge for the first time or with an unprecedented intensity after termination, and when the actual separation from the analyst becomes a trigger for deep preverbal trauma. Under these circumstances, the patient often returns for further help. The interested reader would benefit by reading from the extensive bibliography of Craige's paper and also by looking up Jack Novick and Kerry Kelly Novick's (2006) meaningful discourse on this topic.

Post traumatic dreams: see 'Traumatic dreams'.

Post traumatic stress disorder: contemporary psychiatric term for a syndrome that (1) develops as a consequence of exposure to a shocking event (e.g., violence, automobile accidents), (2) comprises intrusive and troubling memories of that event (flashbacks), startle reponses, and phobic avoidance of stimuli associated with the trauma, and (3) leads to impairment of personal and social functioning (*DSM-IV TR*, 2000, pp. 463–468). The related psychoanalytic concepts are 'traumatic neuroses' and 'war neuroseis' (see separate entries).

Potential space: term used by Donald Winnicott (1971) somewhat interchangeably for the space between (1) the subjectively perceived environment mother and objectively perceived object mother, (2) the child's experience of unity with and separateness from the mother, and (3) the ego's perception of reality and unreality. 'Potential space' is actualized by the mother's provision of an appropriate 'holding environment' (see separate entry). It contains 'transitional phenomena', play, and creative imagination. The concept of 'potential space' seems akin to what Winnicott described as the 'intermediate area of experience', the 'third area', and the 'location of cultural experience'. These concepts are additionally subsumed under the rubric of 'transitional space' (see separate entry).

Practical psychoanalysis: declaring that psychoanalysis, as it is generally practised, 'has become, deservedly, the stuff of *New Yorker* cartoons' (2006, p. 2), Owen Renik laid out a blueprint for what he called 'pratical psychoanalysis'. The ingredients of this conceptualization and technical approach included (1) emphasis on symptom relief, (2) rejection of technical 'neutrality' (see separate entry), (3) an ambiance of 'bilateral candor' (p. 59) between the analyst and analysand, (4) the provision of novel perspectives by the analyst, and (5) consistent demystification of the treatment process. While these recommendations can mislead the novice into a path away from the unconscious, their impact upon the experienced analyst might be in the form of a useful corrective against caricatured neutrality and abstinence.

Practising subphase: the second subphase of separation–individuation (from 9 to 16 months or so) in which the crawling child, and later, the walking toddler, elatedly asserts his newfound psychomotor autonomy and freedom. Although the child frequently looks for 'emotional refueling' (Manuel Furer, quoted in Mahler, Pine, & Bergman, 1975, p. 69), his main preoccupation is to exercise his ego apparatuses and widen the orbit of his explorations.

Preadolescent drive organization: described by Peter Blos (1958), 'preadolescent drive organization' shows considerable variation in boys and girls. In the boy, the upsurge of instinctual drives leads to a relatively indiscrimate cathexis of pregenital aims. Thus, one sees fidgetiness, oral greediness, minor sadistic pleasures, and anal activities (e.g., disregard of cleanliness, fascination with body odours). The boy feels castration anxiety in relation to the phallic mother and employs a homosexual defence before successfully turning to full masculinity. The girl shows less anality and exaggerates her heterosexual desires in a defence against the regressive pull to the preoedipal mother. There is an aggressive quality to her 'femininity', however. In Blos' words, 'the phallic quality of her sexuality is prominent at this stage and affords her, for a brief period, an unusual sense of adequacy and completeness' (p. 52).

Pre-conception: see 'Preconception and pre-conception'.

Preconception: see 'Preconception and pre-conception'.

Preconception and pre-conception: terms used by Wilfred Bion (1963, 1967) to describe two types of thought processes. The first refers to a theory or a sentiment that something is taking place, though one is not fully aware of what it is. The second refers to a state of expectation, a sort of desire awaiting its fulfilment in the form of 'realization' (see separate entry).

Preconscious: one of the three components of Sigmund Freud's (1900a) 'topographical model of the mind'; the other two components are 'conscious' and 'unconscious'. According to this 'topographical theory' (see separate entry), there are six features of the system called 'preconscious': (1) it lies between the 'conscious' and 'unconscious' systems; (2) it is separated from 'conscious' by a 'secondary censorship', which scans and selects information rather than actively repressing it; the latter is characteristic of 'censorship proper' (see entry on 'censorship') that lies between 'preconscious' and 'unconscious'; (3) it is mostly, though not exclusively, governed by 'secondary process' (see 'primary and secondary processes') and operated by bound psychic energy; (4) its contents are out of the conscious of awareness but can be readily brought into awareness; they are descriptively but not dynamically unconscious; and (5) when introduced, 'preconscious' was seen to perform the functions that were assigned to the 'ego' (see separate entry) with the inception of 'structural theory' (see separate entry); still later, it became clear that some aspects of superego functioning are also 'preconscious'.

Predepressive idealization: see 'Primitive idealization'.

Pregenital conversions: Otto Fenichel's (1945) term for those symptoms whose dynamics centre upon the unconscious transformation of unacceptable impulses into symbolic symptoms but whose origin lies not in the Oedipus complex, but in pregenital aims. While pregenital erogenous zones (e.g., mouth, anus) more readily lend themselves to the symbolic expression of pregenital conflicts, all conversion symptoms involving pregenital zones are not pregenital in origin; oedipal conflicts can also be expressed by conversion symptoms involving pregenital zones. It is not the surface manifestation that determines whether it is 'pregenital conversion' or not; it is the overall character organization (e.g., increased ambivalence, unresolved bisexuality, sexualization of talking, magical thinking) and discernment of the underlying aim of the symptom that decides this. Among the common 'pregenital conversions', Fenichel included stuttering, psychogenic tics, and bronchial asthma, the last mentioned is now more likely to be placed under psychophysiological or psychosomatic disorders than under conversion disorder, pregenital or otherwise.

Pregenital sexuality: see 'Infantile sexuality'.

Premotion: credit must go to Rafael Lopez-Corvo (2003) for pursuing the potentional meanings of this term of Wilfred Bion (1963), since the latter left it undefined. Lopez-Corvo, in his schlolarly treatise on Bion, allows, on the one hand, for the possibility that 'premotion' might simply have been a typographical error. On the other hand, he doggedly pursues it in his dialogue with other Bion scholars and, with their help, concludes that 'premotion' might stand for emotions (of the analysand) that can be intuitively grasped by the analyst (through his 'premotion').

Prenatal stage of development: while Sigmund Freud (1918b) declared fantasies involving intrauterine life as 'retrospective phantasying' (p. 103), the notion that foetal 'psychological life' affects the neo-natal and later psychological development has never left the psychoanalytic field. Margaret Little's (1960) concept of 'basic unity' (see separate entry) was largely based on such an assumption. Ivan Milakovic's (1967) went to the extent of proposing a specific 'deglutitive' or prenatal stage of libidinal development. He felt that this stage leaves memory traces which can be experienced to a certain degree and can be decoded at later periods of a person's life. It is

essentially a 'pre-stage of omnipotence' (p. 78) whose leitmotif is the maintenance of homeostasis. Alessandra Piontelli's (1987, 1988) 'infant' observations from before birth and reconstructions from the analysis of a two-year-old psychotic girl also speak to this point.

Preoedipal colouring of the Oedipus complex: the developmentally appropriate and chronologically well-timed manifestations of the Oedipus complex, as well as its derivates and residues in adult life, are generally muted, aim-inhibited, and disguised. When oedipal conflicts appear in intense, acted-out, and 'noisy' forms, however, a suspicion arises that remnants of preoedipal hunger and aggression are the source of their intensification. Five constellations of preoedipally distorted conflicts are highlighted by Otto Kernberg (1967): (1) an excessively aggressive tinge to oedipal conflicts, (2) undue idealization of the heterosexual object in the positive oedipal relation and the homosexual love object in the negative oedipal relation, (3) a highly unrealistic quality to the fantasied relations with either of these objects, (4) a pregenital agenda to seemingly oedipal desires, and (5) a premature 'oedipalization' of preoedipal conflicts. Lingering influence of unresolved preoedipal conflicts and self and object constancy are also evident in a split oedipal 'resolution', in which one side reflects mastery (well established incest barrier, clear generational boundaries, capacity to wait, etc.) and the other side reflects defiance (via cross-generation sex, irreverence, etc.) of oedipal conflicts, and both sides are alternately acted out.

Preoedipal development: the term refers to the psychological tasks and achievements of the period extending from birth until about three or three and half years of age. These developments have been delineated by various theoreticians in different 'languages', though overlaps exist in their descriptions. (1) Sigmund Freud (1905a, 1915c, 1920g) decribed the evolution of libido through 'oral', 'anal', and 'phallic' phases, each of which also involved specific type of object relations with the caretakers, especially the mother. His emphasis, however, was upon the shifting somatic foundations of the evolving psyche and the dominance of the 'pleasure principle' over the 'reality principle' during this stage of life. (2) Melanie Klein (1935, 1940, 1945) focused upon the advance from a developmental position, where the self and its objects were split along the libidinal and aggressive lines to one where the objects were seen in their totality and capacity for ambivalence arose. Rather than attacking and/or greedily incorporating the primary object, the child now began to feel gratitude for having received love, remorse over his aggression, and reparative impulses arising out of this remorse. Naming these 'paranoid' and 'depressive' positions, respectively, Klein underscored that the essential movement here was from grandiosity, greed, and destructiveness to empathy, guilty recognition of one's aggression, and attempts to mend the situation. (3) Donald Winnicott (1953, 1960, 1962), focused upon the 'illusion–disillusion' sequence, whereby the infantile omnipotence (co-created by the devoted mother) came to be replaced by greater reality testing and the capacity to locate needed objects outside of subjective control. 'Capacity for concern' then evolved from the mother's survival of infantile ruthlessness in taking all sorts of things (e.g., love, attention, physical indulgence, tolerance) from her. Winnicott also noted that the development of authenticity occurred in an environment that safeguarded the child's spontaneous 'going-on-being' without much 'impingement'. (4) Margaret Mahler (1955, 1958, 1971) described a sequence of 'mother–child symbiosis' and 'separation–individuation' which eventually consisted of the emergence of the child from a fused state with the mother to progressively increasing degrees of autonomy and separateness. The end point of this process was 'object constancy', or, to be more accurate, in Mahler's own words 'on the road to object constancy', which implied the consolidation of a sustaining internal image of the mother alongside a less shifting and drive-dependent view of oneself. Dependence upon the external presence of the mother diminished and a greater confidence in the self emerged. While differences in these models do exist and they use different terminology (see separate entries for all the terms mentioned above), collectively all of them underscore certain basic points which are central to preoedipal development. These are (1) emergence of a coherent self with a sense of agency, (2) renunciation of infantile omnipotence, (3) capacity for deeper object relations, with objects being sensed in their totality, (4) integration of pregenital drives under a pathway leading to genital primacy, (5) submergence of the 'pleasure principle' under the 'reality principle', (6) capacity for muted affects such as concern and affection, which signify a synthesis of libidinal and aggressive drives, and (7) an advance from involvement in dyadic relationships to the capacity to experience triadic relationships and the conflicts attendant upon them. *Vis-à-vis* this last mentioned point, it should be noted that Jacques Lacan (1977) viewed the preoedipal development to also be

triadic in nature, since the child struggled to become or defy the 'phallus' or what he felt to be the object of mother's desire besides him. This, however, is a 'minority opinion', to use a phrase from legal discourse.

Preoedipal father: Dorothy Burlingham (1973), Ernest Abelin (1971, 1975), James Herzog (1980, 2001) , Ralph Layland (1981) , Kyle Pruett (1988, 2000) and Peter Blos Sr (1985) are prominent among those who have pointed out that the father's role in the development of the child begins long before the 'Oedipus complex' (see separate entry). The 'preoedipal father'serves as an additional or alternative attachment figure during early infancy. He offers himself, to a somewhat older child, as an ego-orientated new object during the latter's struggles over autonomy and separateness from the mother. While helping to modulate the aggressive drive in both the boy and girl, the 'preoedipal father' especially helps the former achieve a measure of 'disidentification with the mother' (see separate entry). Contrasting with such a direct role in the consolidation of the boy's gender identity, the 'preoedipal father' plays an indirect role in the girl's gender identity formation; this is accomplished through his admiring glance that persists despite the gradually increasing physical distance between them. Father's role during the Oedipus complex continues to embody these early modes of relating; however, by visibly appearing as the mother's romantic partner, the father mostly helps to consolidate the child's capacity to experience, bear, and benefit from the triangular familial relationship and the conflicts attendant upon it.

Preoedipal fixation: see 'Preoedipal pathology'.

Preoedipal mother: expression used in two senses: (1) the actual person of the mother during her child's 'preoedipal development' (see separate entry), with an emphasis upon the maternal functions of holding, protecting, nourishing, containing, and helping the child differentiate and separate from her; and (2) the internal construct of the mother, which can be externalized on to other objects in reality or transferentially reactivated in the analytic situation. The latter is a much needed, dyadically experienced, ambivalently held, though often idealized, sexually sanitized (or regressively hyper-instinctualized), and rather fantastic internal image that is discernible in transferences of abject but hateful dependency. It also fuels 'malignant erotic transference' (see separate entry), though in such situations the longing for 'preoedipal mother' is tightly condensed with that of a sexually seductive parent from a somewhat later phase of development.

Preoedipal pathology: to begin with, there is no such thing as purely preoedipal or purely oedipal pathology. The two themes invariably coexist. They might be condensed into each other, or one might serve as a defence against the emergence of the other. Manifest symptomology, therefore, is not a good enough guide to distinguish between them. More helpful is to discern whether object constancy and a coherent sense of identity exist. Stanley Greenspan (1977) has outlined *seven areas of functioning* that should be scrutinized to distinguish preoedipal from oedipal pathology: '(1) capacity for distinguishing internal v. external reality; (2) cohesion, organization, and resistance to fragmentation under stress of the self and object representations; (3) capacity for experiencing and perceiving a variety of affect states; (4) level of defences; (5) capacity to modulate impulses appropriate to external situation; (6) capacity for genuine attachment and separation, and for the experience of sadness and mourning; and (7) capacity for integration of love and hate (fusion of good and bad, aggression and libido)' (p. 385). Individuals whose characters are organized predominately around preoedipal levels carry an intense emotional conviction about the reality of their 'fantasies'. They tend to stubbornly maintain a particular view of themselves or the therapist, failing to see either in any other way. They might superficially acknowledge them as fantasies, but are reluctant to modify their ideas. Their affects are limited, though intense. They show a predominance of primitive ego defences and have poor impulse control. They think in 'either-or' terms (e.g., your way or my way, now or never, all or none, love or hate, good or bad) and lack the capacity for mourning and genuine sadness.

Preoedipal phase: see 'Preoedipal development'.

Prerepresentational self: term used by Robert Emde (1983) to denote the earliest core of the self that evolves around the general biological principles of 'self regulation,' 'social fittedness', and 'affective monitoring' (see separate entries). This core is essentially affective and remains continuous amid change as life unfolds and proceeds from infancy through childhood and adolescence to adulthood. The notion of 'prepresentational self' is intended to underscore the workings of these processes before the age of fifteen months or so, i.e., before the capacity for self-recognition appears in the child, and self, in the traditional sense of the word, emerges. This serves as a reminder that the 'self' (see separate entry) is a process with a 'vital set of synthetic functions which increase in complexity as development proceeds throughout the life span' (p. 167).

Present unconscious: see 'Three-box model of the mind'.

Pressure technique: with the abandonment of hypnosis as a way of reaching the depths of his patients' minds, Sigmund Freud moved on to placing his hand on patients' foreheads and asking them to report the thought or image that came to mind in response to a question. Freud soon gave up this 'pressure technique' in favour of the wholly non-directive methods of 'free association' (see separate entry).

Pretend mode: Mary Target and Peter Fonagy's term (1996) for an operational feature of the yound child's psyche which has the following characteristics: (1) knowledge that internal experience might not reflect the facts and events of external reality; (2) separation of internal and external realities with the accompanying assumption that an internal state has no impact upon external reality; and (3) selective incorporation of facets of external reality in the unfolding inner experience. The 'pretend mode' of mental functioning is most clearly evident when the child is playing; he can readily entertain a belief useful for his play activity while in reality knowing it to be false. According to Target and Fonagy the 'pretend mode of functioning gives access to processes and knowledge which would not otherwise be consciously available . . . thus playing or pretending at times reveals surprising abilities, while at other times it offers opportunities for regression and the expression of unconscious cries' (pp. 465–466). Over the course of development, the 'pretend mode' becomes integrated with the earlier 'psychic equivalence mode' (see separate entry), giving birth to the capacity for 'mentalization' (see separate entry).

Primal cavity: term first employed by René Spitz (1955) for the interior of the mouth, which he regarded as the bodily zone where internally present and externally introduced perceptions encounter each other. The inherent perceptual endowment of the 'primal cavity' renders it an instrument *par excellence* for the comprehension of the environment.

Primal horde: see 'Primal horde theory'.

Primal horde theory: Charles Darwin (1859) had speculated that primitive man lived in small groups ruled over by a dominating and powerful father who appropriated all women and kept them from his sons and other younger males. The latter then rebelled, killed the 'primal father', and cannibalized him. Sigmund Freud (1912–1913) elaborated these ideas and suggested that the guilty memory of this primal murder was phylogenetically transmitted and became the foundation of a more civilized social order. This new order precluded the guilt over primal killing by prohibiting murder and incest. It encouraged exogamy, or finding sexual partners from outside the family, and substituted the primal father with a totemic animal which could be revered, eaten, and mourned. The essence of Freud's 'primal horde theory', whose phylogenetic dimension does stretch credulity, is that 'the development of totemism as a practical solution to the oedipal problem marked the beginning of ethical restrictions, religion, and social organization' (Moore & Fine, 1990, p. 147).

Primal masochism: see 'Primary masochism'.

Primal parathymia: Karl Abraham's (1924) term for the infantile substrate for the depressive proclivity of later, adult life. According to him, the depressive's self-reproaches were not only directed at the abandoned love object of contemporary life, as proposed by Sigmund Freud (1917e), but against his primary object(s) as well. The disappointments faced by the depressed individual derive their importance from being representations of his original one. Abraham viewed adult depression to be a reactivation of this early disappointment and the resulting affective turmoil called 'primal parathymia'. While Abraham's term fell into disuse, his notion that depressive tendencies of adult life in part reflect the activation of their childhood prototypes became reasonably accepted. Edward Bibring's (1953) and Margaret Mahler's (1966) papers on the development of depressive affect is especially pertinent in this context.

Primal phantasies: term used by Sigmund Freud (1915f) for three scenarios commonly imagined by children: parental sexual intercourse, seduction by an adult, and castrastion. Curiously, all three are related to origins of things. 'In the primal scene, it is the origin of the subject that is represented; in seduction phantasies, it is the origin or emergence of sexuality; in castration phantasies, the origins of the distinction between the sexes' (Laplanche & Pontalis, 1973, p. 332). Freud posited that 'primal phatasies' are built around hints provided by external reality. However, a phylogenetic predisposition, whereby actual events in the pre-history of the human species have been transmitted to the modern mind as analogies of memory, also explains their existence. Here, Freud seems to have borrowed from Carl Jung's (1916) notion of the 'collective unconscious', which contained archetypal imagos that went beyond childhood sexual curiosities to include existential and cosmological dilemmas.

Primal psychophysiological self: term used by Edith Jacobson (1964) to describe the undifferentiated psychosomatic matrix which forms the earliest foundation of the self. At this stage, instincts are largely directed at the self and the predominant expression of the infant's emotional and fantasy life is psychophysiological; it is an 'affective organ language' which encompasses 'not only the silent inner physiological processes but also visible vasomotor and secretory phenomena and manifestations in the realm of oral and excretory functions' (p. 11). This 'language' persists to some extent throughout life, and is evident during the regressive 'resomatization' (see separate entry) of affects.

Primal repression: process described by Sigmund Freud (1895d) to account for the presence of elements in the unconscious that have neither been pushed down there by the superego countercathexis nor have been pulled by previously existing elements. These mechanisms apply to 'repression' (see separate entry) proper. 'Primal repression' is different. Freud described it as 'a first phrase of repression, which consists in the psychically (ideational) representative of the instinct being denied entrance into the conscious' (p. 148). He noted three other features of 'primal repression': (1) its conceptual closeness to 'fixation' (see separate entry), (2) its permanence, and (3) its origin in 'quantative factors such as an excessive degree of excitation and the breaking through of the protective shield against stimuli' (Freud, 1926d, p. 94). Freud's ideas on 'primal repression' have been reviewed and updated by later analysts (Frank & Muslin, 1967; Frank, 1969; Kinston & Cohen, 1986). These authors make five interesting points: (1) Freud's view on the concept evolved. His original view can be termed 'passive primal repression' and his later (1926d) view (which mentioned the unpleasure associated with overstimulation of the immature mental apparatus among the causes of the mechanism) 'active defensive primal repression'. (2) The former view held that there was no preconscious representation of material under 'primal repression' and the latter view implied that such representation might have existed but was subsequently lost. (3) The term 'primary repression' and 'primal repression' are often used interchangeably. However, the prefix 'primal' underscores not only the early, but the ubiquitous, nature of the phenomenon in human experience. (4) 'Primal repression' has close links with 'deferred action' (see separate entry) since the dynamic impact of such material is evident only much later. (5) 'Primal repression' is associated with the non-verbal period of infantile life; the elements under it cannot be remembered but only be relived. Alvin Frank (1969) called them 'the unrememberable and the unforgettable' (p. 48).

Primal sadism: Sigmund Freud's (1924c) term for the original aim of the death instinct. 'Primal sadism' is identical with masochism 'if one is prepared to overlook a little inexactitude' (p. 164), since the original object of the death instinct is none other than the self. 'Primal sadism' is the function of 'pure' death instinct while 'primal' or 'primary masochism' results from an admixture of death and life instincts.

Primal scene: expression first used by Sigmund Freud in 1918 to designate the universal childhood imagination of parental sexual intercourse. Such imagination can derive from actually having witnessed the occurrence or be based upon fantasies alone. The extent of its vividness and the degree to which it is imbued with aggression is variable. From Freud's (1918b) detailed elucidation of it in the celebrated case history of Wolf Man to his other scattered views on the topic, one concludes that Freud held the following to be the important aspects of the primal scene. (1) exposure to animals in coitus also propels the child's imagination in this regard, (2) the primal scene excites the child, but also induces fears of parental retribution, (3) the child frequently regards the act to be violent and thinks that the father is beating the mother, (4) the child interprets what is going on according to the framework of his limited knowledge and concludes it to be anal coitus, (5) it is only through 'deferred action' or *nachtraglicht* (see separate entry) that the essence of primal scene is grasped, and (6) the primal scene is a universal mental construction and perhaps even a phylogenetically given endowment prior to any personal significance attributed to it. While Freud thought them to be inevitably traumatic, primal scene fantasies are no longer viewed as such, though they might still hold an important place in one's unconscious mental life. For a recent update on the primal scene, see Danielle Knafo and Kenneth Feiner (1996).

Primary and secondary gain: also known as 'paranosic' and epinosic' gains, respectively, 'primary' and 'secondary' gains refer to the advantages that can result from having mental illness. 'Primary gain' refers to the relief from intrapsychic conflict and anxiety acquired by the formation of symptoms. 'Secondary gain' refers to the social benefits one receives because of being ill. The distinction is important in separating factitious disorders from malingering: the former centre upon 'primary gain' and the latter upon 'secondary gain'.

Primary and secondary guilt: see 'Guilt'.

Primary and secondary processes: two forms of mentation outlined by Sigmund Freud (1895d). 'Primary process' is the developmentally earlier and 'secondary process' the developmentally later one. 'Primary process' is governed by the 'pleasure–unpleasure principle' and seeks immediate discharge of tension through hallucinatory 'wish fulfilment' (see separate entries). Its cathectic energy is mobile and allows one object to be replaced by another ('displacement') and one idea to merge with others ('condensation'). Constraints of negatives, time, and contradictions do not apply to it. 'Secondary process', in contrast, has bound cathexis, verbal representations, loyalty to Aristolean logic, and subservience to the 'reality principle' (see separate entry). 'Primary process' is dominant in the formation of dreams and symptoms. 'Secondary process' is dominant and rational and scientific thought. In actuality, the two exist in varying degrees of admixture in all forms of mental activity. In poetry, especially, the proper proportion of the two is crucial. Profusion of 'primary process' makes poetry idiosyncratic, and excess of secondary process makes it didactic.

Primary and secondary shame: see 'Shame'.

Primary autonomy: see 'Autonomous functions of the ego'.

Primary communication: term coined by Marco DuPont (1984) for a regressive type of communication made possible by 'projective identification' (see separate entry). An example of this is the sudden appearance of a patient's thought, without it ever having been verbalized, in the analyst's consciousness. Within the framework of the theory of language, this is meta-language, which precedes the development of symbolic–verbal communication.

Primary femininity: see 'Femininity'.

Primary identification: Otto Fenichel (1945, pp. 36–49) regarded the infant's primitive reactions of imitating what is perceived and putting objects into his mouth as the two related prototypes of what would later evolve as a capacity for 'identification' proper. At this earlier stage, however, the 'instinctual behavior and ego behavior are not differentiated' (p. 37) and identification, rather than being an ego process *per se*, is in the service of building the ego in the first place. Fenichel credited Sigmund Freud (1917b, 1921c, 1923e) and Siegfried Bernfeld (1928) as having come up with important notions in this context, with the former declaring that 'primary indentification' is the 'original form of emotional tie with an object' (Freud, 1921c, p. 107). While this makes one think of 'primary identification' in connection with the early infant–mother relationship, Jean Laplanche and Jean-Bertrand Pontalis (1973) make the following observation: 'It is interesting to note that Freud, on the rare occasion when he in fact uses the expression 'primary identification', does so in order to designate an identification with the *father* in the individual's own personal prehistory' (p. 336, original italics).

Primary love: Michael Balint's (1937) phrase for underscoring the fact that the infant is object related from the very beginning of psychic life. The notion was intended to refute the earlier concept of 'primary narcissism' (Freud, 1914c), which proposed that originally all libido was invested in the ego itself; only later it found its way to objects. Balint regarded 'primary love' or 'primary object relationship' to be a pre-ambivalent state of relatedness with the primary object, i.e., the mother.

Primary masochism: Sigmund Freud's (1924c) term for the ubiquitous human potential to obtain pleasure from pain and suffering; this potential is derived from the portion of death instinct that is not externalized, but remains inside the organism and is bound there by libido. Also referring to it as 'primal' or 'erotogenic' masochism, Freud regarded the phenomenon as a form of 'taming of the death instinct by the libido' (p. 164). He distinguished it from 'secondary masochism', which results from the turning inwards of sadism.

Primary maternal preoccupation: Donald Winnicott's (1956b) term for a maternal state of mind which is characterized by 'heightened sensitivity during, and especially towards the end of, pregnancy. It lasts for a few weeks after the birth of the child. It is not easily remembered by mothers once they have recovered from it' (p. 302). Winnicott regarded this state as a 'normal illness' which enables the mother to delicately and sensitively adapt to the infant's needs. Not all mothers are able to achieve such absorption with the infant's interests to the exclusion of other concerns. They have to then make up for this early lack of attunement and, perhaps, can never fully mend the distortion resulting from it.

Primary narcissism: see 'Narcissism'.

Primary object relationship: see 'Primary love'.

Primary omnipotence: see 'Infantile omnipotence'.

Primary paradox of individuation: phrase originated by John Kafka (1989) to denote the fact that healthy mother–child symbosis, by its very nature, permits the child to grow and step away from its mother. 'Primary paradox of individuation' implies that 'love and mutual acceptance of separateness become subjectively equivalent' (p. 33).

Primary process: see 'Primary and secordary processes'.

Primary psychic creativity: Donald Winnicott's (Winnicott & Khan, 1953) term for what he saw as the infant's innate tendency to grow and strive towards health. This tendency finds strength by the fact that the meeting of his needs by his mother gives him the illusion that he has 'created' the object himself. Such 'creative drive' (Abram, 2007, p. 114) arises from an area that lies outside psychic conflict. 'Primary psychic creativity' is not synonymous with artistic creativity; it pertains to living authentically. Clearly the earlier concepts of 'self seeking' (Freud, 1908c, p. 212) instincts and 'conflict free sphere of the ego' (Hartmann, 1939) have overlaps with Winnicott's ideas in this regard, but he was not one to 'succumb' to theoretical integration of this sort.

Primary repression: see 'Primal repression'.

Primitive ego defences: the word 'primitive' is applied to ego defences in three different contexts. (1) *Developmental context:* this proposes that certain ego defences are utilized early in life, while others do not appear until a greater degree of ego organization is evident. Such chronological hierarchy was first noted by Anna Freud (1936), who stated that 'each defence mechanism is first evolved in order to master some specific instinctual urge and so is associated with a particular phase of infantile development' (p. 51). Denial, regression, and turning against the self appear earlier than repression and rationalization. Projection and introjection are also later in the developmental hierarchy, since their working depends upon the differentiation of the ego from the outside world. Melanie Klein's (1940) and Margaret Mahler's (Mahler, Pine, & Bergman, 1975) analytic work with children lent further support to the idea of such a hierarchy. (2) *Motivational context:* this differentiates between primitive and mature defences on the basis of the type of psychic danger that necessitates their use. John Frosch (1964), for instance, proposes that separation anxiety, castration anxiety, and guilt mobilize defences such as repression, reaction formation, rationalization, conversion, and displacement. Threats to self constancy or loss of identity, however, mobilize splitting, regressive loss of boundaries, projective identification, denial, and somatization. (3) *diagnostic context:* Here, Otto Kernberg's (1970) scheme of the hierarchical levels of character organization is pertinent. In this view, individuals with a lower level of character organization use different defences than are used by those at a higher level of character organization. These primitive defences include splitting, projective identification, denial, primitive idealization, omnipotence, and devaluation. While this seems generally accepted, a contrary sentiment also exists. According to this view (Willick, 1983) there are no specific primitive ego defences. All kinds of defences can be used by all kinds of people, and it is more important to have a broader assessment of ego functioning than to look for specific defences suggesting more or less severe psychopathology.

Primitive denial: Otto Kernberg's (1975) term for the borderline patient's tendency to wipe out the emotional significance of an area of consciousness that is contradictory to the one being experienced at the moment. 'The patient is aware of the fact that at this time his perceptions, thoughts, and feelings about himself or other people are completely opposite to those he has had at other times but this memory has no emotional relevance; it can not influence the way he feels now' (p. 31). Kernberg emphasizes that in 'primitive denial', emotions that have actually been experienced at one time are denied at another time. This differentiates it from the higher levels of 'denial' or 'negation' (see separate entries) where the emotional relevance of what is refuted has never been present in the consciousness. 'Primitive denial' is a mechanism to support splitting while the higher levels of denial are elated to repression.

Primitive idealization: Otto Kernberg's (1975)

term for a tendency to see external objects as totally 'good', in order to make sure that they can protect one from other objects that are seen as totally 'bad'. This mechanism, earlier labelled 'pre-depressive idealization' (Kernberg, 1967), differs from the more advanced form of idealization born out of guilt over aggression towards an object. The latter is akin to 'reaction formation' (see separate entry). 'Primative idealization', in contrast, is a direct manifestation of an infantile protective fantasy in which there is neither any conscious or unconscious aggression towards the object nor any genuine concern for it. A primitively idealized object serves as a recipient of omnipotent identification and thus provides direct gratification of narcissistic needs. The mechanism of 'primitive idealization' is typically seen in association with a borderline personality organization.

Primitive splitting: see 'Splitting of self and object representations'.

Principle of inertia: see 'Nirvana principle'.

Principle of maintaining a psychological border: Vamik Volkan (1988, 1997, 1999a) described that large groups in conflict often need to maintain a border, gap, or tangible space between them. Although the demarcation of borders has always been vital to international and large-group relationships, closer examination indicates that it is far more critical to have an effective psychological border than simply a physical one. In a regressed society, political or territorial borders begin to symbolize the canvas of the large-group 'tent'. In other words, borders become highly 'psychologized' and ordinary citizens, leaders, and official organizations become preoccupied with their protection. Physical borders are successful only when they represent a sufficient psychological one.

Principle of maintaining non-sameness: According to Vamik Volkan (1988, 1997, 1990a) an unalterable principle in large-group relationships is the 'principle of maintaining non-sameness'. One large group cannot be the same as, or even closely similar to, a neighbour who is perceived as an enemy and dangerous. Although antagonist groups usually have major differences in religion, language, and historical or mythological backgrounds, the 'narcissism of minor differences' (Freud, 1921c) between them can become a major problem. When large groups regress, any signal of similarity is perceived, often unconsciously, as unacceptable; differences between the two parties are then over-emphasized.

Principle of multiple function: according to Robert Waelder (1936), the ego attempts to solve problems which are placed before it by the id, the superego, the compulsion to repeat, and the external reality. In addition, the ego assigns to itself the task of actively relating to these four agencies. As a result, there are 'eight problems whose solution is attempted by the ego: four of these are assigned to the ego and the other four the ego assigns to itself' (p. 47). It is in this setting, that the 'principle of multiple function' is seen to operate. This principle states that 'no attempted solution of a problem is possible which is not of such a type that it does not at the same time, in some way or the other, represent an attempted solution of other problems. Consequently, each psychic act can and must be conceived in every case as a simultaneous attempted solution of all eight problems, although it may be more successful as an attempted solution of one particular problem than of another' (p. 48). In other words, each psychic act reflects a 'compromise formation' (see separate entry) and is an expression of the collective function of the total organism. Such a perspective enhances the understanding of the origins and aims of neurotic symptoms, character pathology, and the material of a clinical hour by encouraging one to see it from diverse angles (see also 'overdetermination'). Ishak Ramzy (1963) has further elucidated the plurality of determinants that is integral to psychoanalytic theorizing.

Principle of neuronal inertia: see 'Project for a Scientific Psychology'.

Principle of stability: see 'Constancy principle'.

Procreative container: extending the Bionian metaphor of 'container' (see separate entry), Joan Raphael-Leff (1996) proposed the concept of 'procreative container'. Essentially, this refers to the mind–body receptacle of the pregnant woman in which the protopsychic life of her child unfolds. Factors playing a role here include maternal physiological and emotional states, father's genetic and direct emotional input as well as his indirect psychic impact through his presence in the mother's mind, and the foetus's own active utilization of the intrauterine environment. Although the mother's 'idea of the baby has its roots in her own infancy, and although the actual social relationship with her baby becomes operative only postnatally, an interactive systemic exchange begins during pregnancy as the woman unwittingly receives and metabolizes her baby's products while transmitting bodily and psychic products of her own—investing her own

unknown inmate with derivations of her life-blood and her innermost feelings' (p. 378). See also the remarkable monograph on the psychological impact of intrauterine life by Alessandra Piontelli (1992).

Project: see 'Project for a Scientific Psychology'.

Project for a Scientific Psychology: like the word 'cathexis' (see separate entry), this title of a monograph by Sigmund Freud is the brainchild of James Strachey, the chief translator of Freud's complete works. Written in 1895, the 'Project' was not published until 1950. It contains a detailed neurophysiologically inclined model of the mind and proposes that the nervous system tends to divest itself of excitation; this is called the 'principle of neuronal inertia'. Discharge of tension causes pleasure and accumulation of tension causes unpleasure. Some tension, however, always remains within the system, which attempts to keep it at a low level. The mental system is, thus, governed by the 'constancy principle' (see separate entry). Moreover, there are separate systems to account for perception, consciousness, and memory. Freud discussed the specific characteristics of each system in detail. He also elucidated the nature of affect, the concepts of 'primary and secondary process' (see separate entry), dream formation, and psychopathology of hysteria in the 'Project'. Despite its vast scope and its depth, the book is actually imcomplete, since it is based upon two of three notebooks containing the entire manuscript; the third and final notebook remains undiscovered to date. There is also controversy over the significance of this early work of Freud's. Some regard it as a fanciful and failed piece of speculation while others (e.g., Pribram & Gill, 1976) see it as a neurophysiologically prescient and pioneering contribution.

Projection: concept originated by Sigmund Freud (1911c) in connection with the paranoic's disownment of an unacceptable impulse or idea and its subsequent attribution to an external object. Freud traced the origin of this tendency to the earliest periods of life when everything pleasurable was felt to belong to the 'purified pleasure ego' (see separate entry) and everything painful as being external to it. In consonance with the somatocentric foundation of early psychoanalytic theory, spitting was seen as the prototype for projection; excretory functions later got condensed with this psychophysical template. While using projection during early childhood was expectable, its persistence suggested a weak demarcation between ego and non-ego. Paranoid disorders clearly illustrate the operation of this mechanism. At times, however, tidbits of external reality also contribute to such misperceptions; 'the monster of paranoid delusion may be a distortion of a microbe of reality' (Fenichel, 1945, p. 147). Four other aspects of projection need to be mentioned: (1) projection can be seen in the setting of relative normalcy; childhood animistic beliefs about nature and superstitions that persist during adulthood are illustrations of this; (2) the ubiquitousness of projection in infancy was emphasized by Melanie Klein (1932, 1940). She saw 'introjection' (see separate entry) and 'projection' as developmental processes of regulating inner instinctual pressures that lead to the formation of 'good' and 'bad' internal objects which become the earliest building blocks of the psyche; (3) the concept of 'projection' was further refined by Joseph Sandler (1987), who, in building bridges between ego psychology and object relations perspective, defined projection as the shifting of the attributes of an unconscious self-representation to a conscious object-representation; (4) projection can involve the depositing into others of an *affect* ('I hate him' becomes 'He hates me'), an *instinctual aim* ('I want to hurt him' becomes 'He wants to hurt me'), or even an *internal object* ('I am like my cruel father' becomes 'You are like my cruel father'). However, 'since introjected objects may themselves be the depositions of projection, projection of internal objects may lead to endowing the recipient with aspects of one's past objects but also of one's past self' (Rycroft, 1968, p. 126). This brings up the phenomenological and dynamic overlap between projection and 'projective identification' (see separate entry); in general, the latter mechanism has a greater interpersonal component than the former.

Projective counter-identification: Leon Grinberg's (1962) term for a situation where excessive use of 'projective identification' (see separate entry) on the patient's part leads the analyst to behave 'as if he had really and concretely acquired, by assimilating them, the aspects that were projected on to him' (p. 437). The fact that he is under the sway of the patient's projection is not recognized by the analyst.

Projective identification: a term introduced into psychoanalytic literature by Melanie Klein in 1946. She described it as a process that begins in early infancy and consists of parts of the self being split off and projected into an external object. The latter then becomes identified with the split-off part as well as internally controlled by it. While starting as a developmental process, projective identification can come to serve many defensive

purposes. These include attempted fusion with an external object to avoid separation control of internal bad objects that cause persecutory anxieties, and preservation of endangered good elaborated by Klein's followers, and Otto Kernberg's (1967) seminal work on borderline personality organization rejuvenated the concept. Projective identification differs from 'projection' (see separate entry), which does not involve blurring of ego boundaries and causes a lesser need to manipulate the external object. Projective identification, in contrast, is a hybrid defence, involving both intrapsychic and interpersonal aspects. Essentially these consist of the repudiation of a self-representation, its attribution to another individual who can emotionally experience such induction, and an unconscious manipulation of the latter so that he or she lives out the deposited aspect in reality. While a repudiation of unwanted aggressive self-representations has received more attention, Klein's notion that endangered good aspects can also be deposited into others for safekeeping still remains valid. Gregory Hamilton's (1986) elaboration of this idea under the title of 'positive projective identification' and Roy Schafer's (2002) delineation of 'defences against goodness' (see separate entry) are also pertinent in this context. Also important is Betty Joseph's (1987) extension of Klein's ideas by emphasizing that while 'projective identification' is typical of 'paranoid position', it is never totally given up. With the achievement of 'depressive position', the mechanism of 'projective identification' becomes 'less absolute, more temporary, and more able to be drawn back into the indidivual's personality and thus the basis of empathy' (p. 140).

Projective objects: according to Christopher Bollas (1992) different types of objects possess different processional potential and invite the projective disownment of different parts of the self. 'Projective objects' 'serve to think the self (and its internal objects) by the projection of parts of the self in the here and now of everyday life' (p. 35). Bollas illustrates this type of object by pointing to one's reading a book on Margaret Thatcher to process the harsh part of one's own personality!

Projective transformation: term used by Wilfred Bion (1965) for that degree of alteration caused in an object by 'projective identification' (see separate entry) that makes it hard or impossible to discern its original qualities. This process is more commonly seen in association with psychosis.

Projective transidentification: James Grotstein (2005) proposed the term 'projective transidentification' in order to bring together Melanie Klein's (1946) unconscious and largely intrapsychic view of projective identification with Wilfred Bion's (1962a,b) communicative and intersubjective view of it. Grotstein proposed that the metapsychological aspects of 'projective identification' (see separate entry) were only one aspect and not the totality of this mechanism. There were actual and experiential components to it as well. He pointed out that projective identification also involves: (1) a sensori-motor process of gesturing and prompting on the part of the one doing the projecting, and (2) an empathic resonance on the part of the one receiving the projection. To this enriched view of projective identification, Grotstein gave the name of 'projective transidentification'.

Prolonged adolescence: this developmental protraction allows the individual to consolidate his identity and synthesize the contradictory challenges of transformation and continuity over a period of time that extends well over into seeming adulthood. Perpetually remaining a student and avoiding commitment in romantic relationships often are manifestations of such prolongation of adolescence.

Propaganda addiction: Salman Akhtar's (2007c) term for the voracious appetite that some prejudiced individuals develop for published or broadcasted material that supports their biased worldview. Spiralling downward into an abyss of rage towards minorities, they find such material exalting. It diminishes their inner aloneness and enhances their narcissism. By mirroring their prejudice, it makes their distorted beliefs seem rational, consensual, and even normal.

Propensity to obedience: see 'Godfather fantasy'.

Protective rite of farewell: phrase used by Leon Grinberg and Rebecca Grinberg (1989) to underscore the fact that the opportunity to say 'goodbye' to loved people and places lessens the trauma of leaving. The immigrant has access to such a privilege while the exile, leaving his land of origin in fear and hurry, does not. As a result, the exile's trauma of departure becomes greater and more difficult to mourn.

Protective shield: a notion implied in the earliest speculations regarding mental trauma by Sigmund Freud (1895) but not fully elucidated until his much later work, *Beyond the Pleasure Principle* (1920g). Using the term *Reizchutz*, Freud proposed the existence of a threshold of stimulation by the external environment, the exceeding of which becomes psychologically traumatic. Later analysts (Mahler, 1958; Khan, 1963a; Gediman, 1971; Esman, 1983) expanded Freud's view to include the regulation of internal stimuli also among the functions of the 'protective shield'. Moreover, they traced the origins of such a 'stimulus barrier' (see separate entry) to mother–infant interactions, whereby the mother regulates the extent of stimulation the infant has to face. This function of the mother is then internalized by the child, who, as a result, develops self-regulatory functions especially with regard to the tolerable amount of excitement and stimulation. This ego attribute is called the 'protective shield'.

Proto-altruism: see 'Altruism'.

Proto-masochism: Eleanor Galenson's (1988) term for the precursors of masochism that evolve in the latter part of the first year and particularly during the second year of life. Under ordinary circumstances at this time, oral aggression is transformed into anal and urethral patterns of instinctual discharge. However, if there is too much hostility in the mother–child relationship, then the child identifies with the aggressor and turns the aggression upon its own self. Passivity and regression follow and impede the consolidation of the early genital phase. Such 'proto-masochism', while more common in girls, is less damaging to their sexual identity. However, 'boys who become excessively passive during the early anal phase, in the face of intense hostile maternal conflicts, suffer a serious blow to their sense of masculine identity with the advent of early genital phase; their object relationships assume a truly masochistic character with oedipal development' (p. 203).

Proto-phallic phase: see 'Proto-phallic and deutro-phallic phase'.

Proto-phallic and deutro-phallic phase: Ernest Jones' (1927) division of 'phallic phase' (see separate entry) into two subphases: (1) 'proto-phallic phase', where the child innocently assumes that everyone has a penis, and (2) 'deutro-phallic phase', where the child begins to suspect that the world is made of penis-possessing and penis-less people which, in his mind, are still not squarely equated with boys and girls, respectively. With the relative eclipse of the early instinctual theory and especially the descriptions of the 'phallic phase' by object relational and feminist advances in psychoanalysis, these terms gradually fell into disuse.

Proxy-base for refuelling: term coined by Salman Akhtar (1995) for a place or country that can stand for the lost home and therefore provide emotional sustenance to those who have lost their original sources for refuelling. Such 'proxy bases' can exist within the country of adoption (e.g., London's Southall district for Indians, New York's Little Italy for Italians, and so on) or they might be constituted by nations that are newly founded (e.g., Israel for the displaced European Jews) for more or less this purpose.

Pseudo-externalized displacement: see 'Dissociative self'.

Pseudo-homosexual anxiety: see 'Pseudo-homosexuality'.

Pseudo-homosexuality: term introduced by Lionel Ovessey (1969, 1976) for the distressing feeling on the part of heterosexual men that they might be homosexual at the time when they are experiencing failure in what they feel to be a test of their masculinity; a hapless first sexual performance is especially notorious in stirring up such fears (Nasser Harvani, personal communication, 22 June 2008). The feeling that 'I am a failure as a man' is translated into the sequential steps of feeling castrated, feminine, and homosexual. However, the anxiety experienced under such circumstances it is 'not a true homosexual anxiety since it is not motivated by the homosexual wish nor is it accompanied by homosexual arousal. It is simply the result of the masculine failure which has been symbolically misinterpreted as homosexuality; hence the anxiety is pseudo-homosexual anxiety and the man experiencing it is said to be suffering from pseudo-homosexuality' (1976, p. 147).

Pseudo-humility: see 'God complex'.

Pseudo-imbecility: term used by Margaret Mahler (1942) to describe the fact that compromise of intellectual functions can be used by a child 'to restore or maintain a secret libidinous rapport with the family' (p. 154). Reporting on children who were incestuously abused or overstimulated, Mahler suggested that their seeming stupidity served as a device to enable both them and their parents to deny such goings-on on the one hand, and maintain the knowledge of them on a non-verbal level on the other hand. Mahler used the expression 'pseudo-imbecility' (p. 149) interchangeably with 'pseudo-stupidity' (p. 163); the latter subsequently was used by other analysts with a different formation (see 'Arrogance, curiosity, and pseudo-stupidity').

Pseudo-sexuality: term first used by Otto Fenichel (1939b) to describe the sexual acts performed for motives other than erotic; these motives include counterphobic measures, narcissistic needs, and orally determined hunger for contact with others. Amusingly, in this context, Fenichel quoted Georg Groddeck as having said 'a glance, a touch can be the highest point in a human life. It is not true that sexual intercourse reflects the culmination of erotic life. People are really bored with it!' (p. 168).

Pseudo-speciation: concept originated by Erik Erikson (1975) to denote the pervasive tendency among human beings to divide themselves into an in-group that is created superior to all others and 'others' who are inferior and who must be subjugated by periodic warfare or conquest, stringent legislation, or local customs. This turns man, who is obviously one species, into a 'pseudo-species', whereby one group is claimed to lack any similarity or affinity with the other. Commenting upon some unexplored overlaps between Gandhi and Freud, Erikson stated that 'the insides and methods created by the young Hindu lawyer in South Africa and those created about the same time by the young Jewish doctor in Vienna promised to rate high among the century's correctives of the untruths adhering to the pseudo-species mentality' (pp. 180–181).

Pseudo-stupidity: see 'Arrogance, curiosity, and pseudo-stupidity'.

Pseudo-sublimatory potential: Otto Kernberg's (1975) term for the narcissistic individual's capacity for sustained hard work for obtaining 'greatness' and admiration from others. However, there is a peculiar lack of depth and sustained inquiry to such work. 'Quite frequently, these are the "promising" geniuses who then surprise other people by the banality of their development' (p. 230). Pseudo-sublimation differs from true 'sublimation' (see separate entry) in so far as the work in the former is instinctualized and in the latter is not; creativity that results from true sublimation is not primarily motivated by the desire for external acclaim.

Pseudo-symbiosis: Klaus Angel's (1967) term for merger fantasies and extreme dependence of patients, which differs from true symbiotic relationships on two counts: (1) in symbiosis, merger is the reflection of the actual state of ego; self- and object-representations are fused (Mahler, 1958). In 'pseudo-symbiosis', merger fantasies serve as defences against painfully separated self- and object representations, and (2) in true symbiosis, there is fixation upon infantile states, whereas in pseudo-symbiosis the scale is weighted heavily on the side of defensive regression from conflicts that often emanate from unresolved oedipal longings.

Pseudo-tact: see 'Tact'.

Pseudo-twinning: see 'Twining reaction'.

Pseudo-vitality: Heinz Kohut's (1977) term for the overly enthusiastic and intense lifestyle of certain narcissistic patients, which must be understood as an attempt to counteract inner feelings of futility, depression, and deadness.

Psychic apparatus: expression used by Sigmund Freud (1900a) in order to assign different mental functions to separate components of the mind. In the context of his 'topographic theory' (see separate entry), Freud used the term 'agencies' or 'systems' to denote the three parts (conscious, preconscious, and unconscious) of the 'psychic apparatus'. With the shift to 'structural theory' (see separate entry), the expression 'systems' nearly disappeared and the newly described parts of the mind (id, ego, superego) were referred to as 'agencies' and, more often, as 'structures'. In current usage, the term 'psychic apparatus' is almost synonymous with this latter tripartite structure of the mind.

Psychic bisexuality: see 'Bisexuality'.

Psychic creationism: see 'Autochtony, cosmogony, and alterity'.

Psychic determinism: this is a most fundamental tenet of psychoanalytic theory and it holds that nothing in the mind happens on a random or arbitrary basis (Brenner, 1955). All psychic acts and events have causes and meanings. All are determined by, and can be understood in light of, the subjective events that preceded them. This applies to seemingly incomprehensible mental phenomena and apparently 'accidental' occurrences as well. Dreams, obsessions, and phobias, delusions and hallucinations, and parapraxes (unintended actions such as slips of the tongue and pen) are all subject to such understanding. While this attitude is central to psychoanalytic thinking, it should not preclude the practising analyst from retaining the capacity to believe that some occurrences can still be purely accidental and random. David Werman's (1979) paper on chance occurrences addresses this very point. It echoes the earlier

quip by Sigmund Freud that 'sometimes a cigar is just a cigar'.

Psychic energy: Sigmund Freud's (1894a) term for a hypothethical force that is 'spread over the memory traces of ideas, somewhat like an electric charge is spread over the surface of a body' (p. 60). In his 'first dual instinct theory', Freud (1900a, 1905a, 1915c) divided instincts into 'sexual' and 'self-preservatory' types and called the 'psychic energy' of the former 'libido'; he did not give a name to the psychic energy of the latter. In his 'second dual instinct theory', Freud (1920g) divided instincts into 'life' and 'death' instincts and called the former's energy 'libido' but gave no name to the latter's energy. He rejected names like 'destrudo' and 'mortudo' (see separate entries on these terms) suggested to him by others. Four other considerations need mention: (1) 'psychic energy' or 'mental energy' may be 'mobile' (or 'free') or 'bound'. 'Mobile energy' is typically associated with 'primary process' and 'bound energy' with 'second process'; (2) 'psychic energy' might be 'instinctual' (i.e., attached to instincts) or 'neutral' (i.e., divested of its instinctual charge due to the fusion of instincts); (3) 'psychic energy' serves both motivational and instrumental purposes; in other words, it can originate mental events or simply carry them; and (4) 'psychic energy' is regulated by many principles, including the 'principle of neuronal inertia' or the 'Nirvana principle' and 'pleasure–unpleasure principle'. All in all, the concept of 'psychic energy' is central to the 'economic perspective' and constituent of the 'dynamic perspective' of classical 'metapsychology' (separate entries in this glossary exist on all the terms mentioned in quotation marks here).

Psychic equivalence mode: Mary Target and Peter Fonagy's (1996) term for a particular operational feature of a two–three-year-old child's psychic reality, whereby the internal world of feelings and imagination is expected to correspond to external reality. Subjective experience is often distorted to match the information coming from outside. To hold reality and appearance simultaneously in mind, especially when there is a discrepancy between the two, seems difficult. Moreover, it is not possible, at this stage, to conceptualize others' minds as separate; indeed, their minds, too, are deemed loyally reflective of reality. Over the course of development, the 'psychic equivalence mode' becomes integrated with the later emerging 'pretend mode' (see separate entry) which underlies the capacity for play in the true sense of the word; this results in the birth of 'mentalization' (see separate entry).

Psychic genera: according to Christopher Bollas (1992) there exist reception-based unconscious elements in tandem with the more familiar repression-derived unconscious elements. The aim of such 'reception' is to allow unconscious development without the impingement of consciousness. With reception, the 'ego understands that unconscious work is necessary to develop a part of the personality, to elaborate a phantasy, to allow for the evolution of a nascent emotional experience, and ideas or feelings and words are sent to the system unconscious, not to be banished but to be given a mental space for development which is not possible in consciousness' (p. 74). Like the repressed material, the contents of the received unconscious also return to consciousness, but they do so as acts of self-enrichment. To this structure, Bollas applies the term 'psychic genera'. While he does not mention them, Jean Piaget's (1937) ideas about accommodation and assimilation and Joseph Weiss's (1988) work on unconscious problem solving seem to be of pertinence to his concept.

Psychic homosexuality: see 'Homosexuality'.

Psychic reality: concept derived from the psychoanalytic premise that the individual's subjectivity is as 'real' in its experience and impact upon behaviour as are the facts and events of his external environment. Sigmund Freud (1906a, 1916–1917) discovered this as he moved from the 'seduction hypothesis' (see separate entry), which proposed that neurotic patients had been sexually seduced as children, to the idea that such events had not taken place in actuality and only represented the child's wishes. At this point Freud declared that 'in the world of neuroses, it is psychical reality which is the decisive kind' (p. 368). Seen from the reverse angle, neurotic symptoms emanated from a certain sort of reality; there was a rationale for them. 'Psychic reality' is juxtaposed with 'external reality'. It contains wishes, fears, fantasies, and, indeed, all mental activities. 'Psychic reality' has conscious, preconscious, and unconscious existence. And, it can evolve and change both with the unfolding of development and with psychoanalytic treatment. Finally, three other points should be noted: (1) in psychotic states, the distinction between psychic and external reality breaks down; (2) in perversions, the capacity to distinguish between the two remains intact but is selectively jettisoned to keep certain psychosexual, sadistic, and narcissistic fantasies alive; and (3) there exists a realm of confluence between external reality and 'psychic reality' in the form of the 'intermediate area of experience' (see separate entry); this is the location of play, imagination, faith, and creativity. Clearly, this thumbnail sketch of psychic reality can hardly do justice to the complexities in this realm. To wit, an entire panel was devoted to the topic of 'psychic reality' at the 1982 Fall Meeting of the American Psychoanalytic Association in New York with contributions from such luminaries as Robert Michels, Jacob Arlow, Roy Schafer, and Robert Wallerstein. Moreover, the proceedings of the 39th Congress of the International Psychoanalytic Association, held in San Francisco (1995), were devoted almost in their entirety to the topic of 'psychic reality', with presentations from the likes of Joseph Sandler, Horacio Etchegoyen, Claudio Eizirik, Paul Williams, Elizabeth Spillius, Clifford Yorke, James Herzog, and Anna Ornstein, to name a few. Their papers, as well as the reports of a number of panels on diverse aspects of psychic reality, have been published in the 1996 issues of the *International Journal of Psychoanalysis*. See also the report of the International Panel by Claudio Laks Eizirik (1996).

Psychic representation: see 'Mental representation'.

Psychic retreats: term coined by John Steiner (1993) to denote withdrawn states of mind that provide 'relative peace and protection from strain' (p. 1) when interpersonal contact seems painful and threatening. When transient, such states pose little difficulty and might even be ego-replenishing. However, turning to 'psychic retreats' habitually and tenaciously can pose a serious challenge to conducting analysis. Among the forms such retreats can take are aloof superiority, prolonged silences, and avoidance, not only of the analyst (and the implicit interpersonal contact) but of reality in general. 'The retreat then serves as a area of the mind where reality does not have to be faced, where phantasy and omnipotence can exist unchecked and where anything is possible. This feature is often what makes the retreat so attractive to the patient and commonly involves the use of perverse and psychotic mechanisms' (p. 3). Steiner eloquently discusses the technical aspects of handling the impasses caused by such developments in his monograph titled *Psychic Retreats*.

Psychic structure: see 'Structure'.

Psychic trauma: according to Sigmund Freud, 'any experience which calls up distressing affects—such as those of fright, anxiety, shame, or physical pain—may operate as a trauma' (Breuer & Freud, 1895d, p. 6). This early definition got refined over the later course of Freud's (e.g., 1916–1917, 1920g, 1926d) thinking and in the light of further advancements in psychoanalytic theory (Glover, 1929; Kris, 1956; Khan, 1963a; A. Freud, 1965; Krystal, 1985; Furst, 1967, 1978, 1995; Blum, 1987b; Parens, Blum, and Akhtar, 2008). The resulting contemporary view holds that: (1) 'psychic trauma' can occur on an acute or slowly evolving basis; the two types are called 'shock trauma' or 'strain trauma' (Kris, 1956) or 'cumulative trauma' (Khan, 1963a), respectively; (2) acute trauma results from an internal or external event that stimulates the mind to an unbearable degree; the 'protective shield' (see separate entry) is ruptured, affects generated are hard for the ego to cope with, and a state of helplessness results; (3) trauma is a double-edged sword: it can cause 'fixation', 'traumatic neurosis', and long-lasting weak spots in character (see separate entries) but it can also lead to vigilance, self-protectiveness, perseverance, curiosity, and altruistic tendencies; (4) the outcome of trauma does not depend solely upon its severity; constitutional factors, including those pertaining to 'resilience' (see separate entry), pre-existing character structure, psychic states at the time of trauma, and the presence or absence of supportive and ameliorative input from family and society at large determine whether positive or negative effects of trauma will predominate; (5) the effects of the trauma are, to a certain extent, phase-specific; thus, physical injury at age one or two might have consequences for body image formation and separation tolerance while the same injury at four or five years of age might intensify castration related fantasies; (6) trauma is ubiquitous and no childhood is free of it; only its extent and severity differs; (7) generally speaking, adults are less susceptible to trauma owing to their greater ego resourcefulness; however, matters of marriage, parenting, retirement, diminution of sexual potency, ageing, failing health, and expectation of death do constitute potentially traumatic situations in adult life; (8) massive trauma (e.g., that of the Holocaust, other genocides, earthquakes, and famines) tends to linger and is not metabolized in one generation; its effects are passed on to subsequent generations; (9) 'screen trauma' (Glover, 1929) refers to events that are recalled vividly as traumatic but in actuality hide other traumatic events behind them; and (10) clinical treatment of traumatized individuals, especially those who have been sexually and physically abused as children, poses special challenges and requires special techniques (Furst, 1978; Kluft, 1984, 1985; van der Kolk, 1987; Kramer, 1991; Brenner 1996, 2001, 2004; Schmidt-Hellerau, 2006b; Nayar, 2008).

Psychoanalysis: a particular depth-psychological discipline founded by Sigmund Freud. While he had earlier used the terms 'psychical analysis' and 'psychological analysis' (Freud, 1894a), the German term *Psychoanalyse* was introduced by him in 1896. According to Freud (1923a) himself 'psychoanalysis is the name (1) of a procedure for the investigation of mental processes which are almost inaccessible in any other way, (2) of a method (based upon that investigation) for the treatment of neurotic disorders and (3) of a collection of psychological information obtained along those lines, which is gradually being accumulated into a new scientific discipline' (p. 235). This definition is still held valid and subsumes all the core aspects of the discipline. At the same time, it remains true that, in almost all its facets (e.g., developmental hypotheses, clinical technique, and social applications), 'psychoanalysis' has grown in leaps and bounds since its inception by Freud. This mushrooming of ideas has resulted in the conceptual split between those who view 'psychoanalysis' as an umbrella term for diverse and often contradictory theories and those, like the theoretical stalwart Leo Rangell (2006), who assert that all these perspectives can be subsumed under a composite 'unitary theory' (see separate entry.

Psychobiography: see 'Psychohistory'.

Psychoanalytic candidate: see 'Analytic candidate'.

Psychoanalytic love: in a careful reading of the psychoanalytic literature on this topic, Lawrence Friedman (2005) suggests that an actual loving feeling on the analyst's part might indeed emerge in all analyses. This happens as a result the paradoxical features of 'taking of distance, and immersion in the patient's experience' (p. 371) during analysis. Friedman notes the earlier stances taken towards this matter, paying special attention to the contributions of five of his predecessors (1) *Heinrich Racker* (1968), who believed that correct interpretation is an evidence of love and that the analyst does love the patient as a parent and might even want the patient's love in return. Recognizing the potential risks in such a stance, Racker none the less declared that the analyst who cannot allow himself this parental wish will not feel entirely comfortable in pushing the project of the patient's analysis as needed. (2) *Hans Loewald* (1960, 1970), who felt that the analyst's love was evident in his perceiving the patient's potential, pursuing the patient's truth, and facilitating the patient's growth as a separate and worthy individual, (3) *Roy Schafer* (1983), who implied that the analyst's affirmative and generative construction of the patient itself awakens a love-like feeling in the analyst; (4) *Irving Steingart* (1995) who emphasized that real love is evoked by the analysand, since he is the subject of intense study. However, this understanding 'includes—and is not just derived from—the personal impact of patient and analyst on each other, and some degree of meshing of their movements' (Friedman, 2005, p. 363), who essentially locate love within the therapeutic alliance, with the analyst feeling love for his patient who allows him successful exercise of his analysing function. (5) *Jack Novick and Kerry Novick* (2000), who describe a sort of analytic love that is freeing and emerges from collaborative work over long periods of time. They declare that such love fits into none of the ordinary social scenarios and is unique in its nature. Following this review, Friedman returns to underscore the role of diverse factors—understanding, collaboration, wholeheartedly and yet from a distance experiencing the patient's appeal, and, perhaps, a re-experiencing of the joy of spontaneous discovery that characterized the early mother–child bond—in the genesis of the so-called 'psychoanalytic love'. See also the pertinent contributions of Stanley Coen (1994) and Otto Kernberg (1994).

Psychoanalytic neutrality: see 'Neutrality'.

Psychoanalytic object: Wilfred Bion's (1970) term for what he regarded as the proper object of observation and investigation during the psychoanalytic hour. This object has seven characteristics: (1) it manifests through verbal associations and non-verbal gestures of a patient in contact with himself; (2) it has its genetic history in the way the patient's thinking has evolved; (3) it is, in part, integral to the patient's character; (4) it contains and displays patient's expectations; (5) it has a direction; (6) it is 'discovered' by the analyst's intuition; and (7) it changes after interpretation. Bion's 'psychoanalytic object' is not related to the word 'object' (see separate entry) as it is generally used in psychoanalysis; instead, 'it is an object of knowledge' (Grinberg & De Bianchedi, 1977, p. 111).

Psychoanalytic observation: see 'Methods of observation in psychoanalysis'.

Psychoanalytic psychotherapy: called by various other names (e.g., 'analytic psychotherapy', 'psychodynamic psychotherapy', 'insight-orientated psychotherapy'), 'psychoanalytic psychotherapy' refers to a form of treatment whose definition, methodology, boundaries, and aims remain open to controversy. Sigmund Freud's (1919a) early warning not to 'alloy the pure gold of analysis freely with the copper of direct suggestion' (p. 168) and Edward Glover's (1931) view that essentially any therapy short of full and deep analysis was largely a work of suggestion set the ground for the desire to distinguish psychoanalysis proper from psychotherapy in general and from psychotherapy derived from psychoanalytic ideas in particular. The American Psychoanalytic Association (Johnson & English, 1953; Eidelberg, 1954; Rangell, 1954, 1981; Chassell, 1955), as well as the International Psychoanalytic Association (Wallerstein, 1969), held panel discussions to sort out the similarities and differences between treatments called 'psychoanalysis' and 'psychoanalytic psychotherapy' but the exchange of ideas between the distinguished panellists left the matters mostly unresolved. To some, the preoccupation appeared a peculiarly North American phenomenon where psychoanalysis, until recently, was largely in the hands of medical practitioners who sought to protect the boundaries of their discipline and profession by declaring that the lay analysts were practising 'psychoanalytic psychotherapy'. Even without this variable, the distinction is more relevant for some (e.g., Kernberg, 1984) than for others (Pine, 1997). Still others have shifted their position over the long course of their careers (see Gill, 1954 and Gill, 1994, for instance). What it boils down to is essentially this. 'Psychoanalytic psychotherapy' and 'psychoanalysis' are similar in so far as both rest on the conviction of unconscious, psychic determinism, transference–countertransference developments, and, by and large, the five perspectives of 'metapsychology' (see separate entry). However, their differences are more murky. Robert Wallerstein (1969), in a comprehensive essay on the subject, has proposed nine variables on which it might be possible to distinguish the two treatment modalities: (1) therapeutic goal, with psychoanalysis aiming at re-structuring of personality and psychoanalytic psychotherapy seeking to stabilize the psyche; (2) therapeutic aim, with psychoanalysis exploring the unconscious and psychotherapy more directly therapeutic towards the symptoms; (3) techniques, with psychoanalysis centring upon interpretation and psychotherapy upon clarification; (4) methods, with psychoanalysis resting upon free association and psychotherapy upon free communication. which. none the less. remains organized around topics; (5) locus of therapeutic concern, with analysis occupying itself with the analytic situation and psychotherapy with life situation; (6) treatment values, with psychoanalysis putting a premium on self-knowledge and psychotherapy on self-improvement; (7) degree of discovery, with psychoanalysis aiming at radically new discoveries about the self and psychotherapy doing that to a much lesser extent; (8) relationship to time, with psychoanalysis being 'timeless', as it were, and psychotherapy being a time bomb; and finally (9) patient population, with psychoanalysis being more suitable for higher level neurotic individuals and psychoanalytic psychotherapy being more suitable for lower level narcissistic borderline and schizoid patients. Merton Gill (1954) offered a simpler scheme with the three variables of neutrality, establishment of transference neurosis, and its resolution by interpretation alone as the hallmarks of psychoanalysis; 'psychoanalytic psychotherapy' departed from all these variables to a greater or lesser extent. This definition, while later abandoned by Gill (1994) himself, formed the centrepiece of The Psychotherapy Research Project of the Menninger Foundation (Wallerstein & Robbins, 1956) and also of Otto Kernberg's (1984) more recent views. Gill's (1994) revised view is reflected in Fred Pine's (1997) statement that he does as much psychotherapy as needed so that he can practise as much psychoanalysis as possible. In essence, all analyses include interventions that are essentially psychotherapeutic, and all significant psychotherapies done by an analyst have elements of psychoanalysis. It is a continuum of dimensions that one is dealing with here, and not a cubicle of categories

Psychoanalytic training: see 'Analytic training'.

Psychoanalytic treatment of schizophrenia: see 'Schizophrenia'.

Psychoanalytically informed advice: mindful of the complex determinants of human behaviour and seeking to resolve psychological dilemmas by unearthing their deeper meanings, psychoanalysts are averse to giving advice. It appears mostly useless, transient in its impact, and can, at times, cause harm by prematurely tilting the balance of a conflict in one or the other direction. However, it is also true that a seasoned analyst's advice can, at times, be quite useful. Indeed, Sigmund Freud's (1909b) 'treatment' of Little Hans, largely conducted by telling the boy's father what to say or do, is an example *par excellence* of such 'advice' giving. And the same happens to a greater or lesser extent in child analysts' meetings with the parents of a child that they are analysing. Anton Kris (1981) has noted that giving advice might be necessary and ethically imperative in situations

where an analysand is talking about his or her child who is in acute distress. Salman Akhtar (1999b) extended the scope of giving such 'psychoanalytically informed advice' (pp. 147–151) to parents who ask for 'informal' help (e.g., in social settings) for problems their children are experiencing. However, the following criteria must be met for making such intervention: (1) the analyst must be quite experienced, (2) advice must have been solicited, (3) the likelihood of seeking 'proper' help must be limited, owing to resistance, or actual unavailability of child therapists or analysts, (4) mild and short duration symptomology, and (5) the existence of the possibility of a follow-up 'conversation' with the parental couple.

Psychohistory: term used somewhat interchangeably for (1) psychoanalytic interpretation of historical events and their impact, and (2) psychoanalytic perspectives on how history gets recorded in the first place, and on the way reality and fantasy intersect in the register of historical accounts. Peter Loewenberg's (1995) outstanding book *Fantasy and Reality in History* addresses these matters in depth. The term 'psychohistory' is at times used synonymously with 'psychobiography', and in that case refers to psychoanalytic writings on the lives of individuals of historical importance. Prominent examples of such 'psychohistory' are Erik Erikson's (1958, 1969) essays on Martin Luther and Gandhi, John Mack's (1976) Pulitzer Prize winning book on Lawrence of Arabia, Vamik Volkan and Norman Itzkowitz's (1984) biography of Kemal Atatürk.

Psycholingiustics: refers to the psychoanalytically informed study of the structure, nuance, layering, aims, and uses of language. While this designation is of recent origin, interest in language has been central to psychoanalysis from its inception; after all, it was called the 'talking cure' by Sigmund Freud's (1893a) patient, Anna O. An admittedly incomplete list of the areas of language psychoanalysis has engaged with includes free association, transposition of words in parapraxes, obscene words' capacity to mobilize anxiety, representation of things by words and vice versa, concretization of language via symbolism in dreams, the poetics of interpretation, the dilemmas of bilingual analytic dyads, and, indeed, the very structuring of the system unconscious. Theodore Shapiro's (1979) book *Clinical Psycholinguistics* and Jacqueline Amati-Mehler, Simona Argentieri, and Jorge Canestri's (1993) book *The Babel of the Unconscious: Polylingualism and Polyglottism in Psychoanalysis* are two outstanding contributions to this realm of psychoanalytic discourse. See also Jorge Canestri's (1994) thought-provoking paper on the meta-levels of linguistic discourse during a session and the role that holding and understanding them plays in the formulation of the analyst's interpretations.

Psychological mindedness: refers to a person's ability to see relationships between feelings, thoughts, and actions with the purpose of learning the causes and meanings of one's behaviour. Morton Reiser (1971), Stephen Appelbaum (1973), Daniel Werman (1979), and Nina Coltart (1988) have written meaningfully on this subject. In summarizing their views and adding his own, Salman Akhtar (1992b, pp. 292–296) concluded that psychological-mindedness is manifested in a capacity for reflective self-observation (as evident in the individual's giving a coherent history and being or becoming aware of inner conflicts), interest in one's mental life (as evident in having kept journals, and thinking about one's dreams), belief in psychic causality (as evident in the individual's offering a childhood explanation for his or her adult life behaviour), a readiness to see symbolic meanings (as evident in interest in art and poetry or in a welcoming response to a trial interpretation), and, paradoxically, the retention of the capacity to accept chance experiences in the external reality.

Psychological twinning: see 'Twinning reaction'.

Psychoneurosis: term used by Sigmund Freud (1894) for mental conditions (anxiety hysteria, conversion hysteria, and obsessional disorder) caused by childhood conflicts and trauma. 'Psychoneurosis' was different from 'actual neurosis' (see separate entry), which resulted from disturbances in adult sexual life. Two categories of 'psychoneurosis' were later recognized: 'narcissistic neurosis' (see separate entry), where libido turned back on to the ego, and 'transference neurosis' (see separate entry) where libido remained mobile and the possibility of developing a clinically meaningful transference existed. The former were not suitable for psychoanalytic treatment, the latter were.

Psychopathic personality: see 'Antisocial personality disorder'.

Psychopathic transference: see 'Transferences of hatred'.

Psychophysical downsizing: Salman Akhtar's (2003) notion about the diminution of acquisitiveness during late mid-life, especially discernible if

the development is proceeding well. Three manifestations of this internal process are a noticeable reduction in the number of new material acquisitions, renunciation of previously valued possessions via donation or gifts, and, frequently, a change of residence to smaller living quarters. Psychological counterparts of such altered material attitudes include letting go of old grudges, owning up to one's misdeeds and failures, and revealing hitherto long-held secrets. The process is evident by one's late fifties and is at its peak by one's late sixties in the West; in regions of the world where life expectancy is lesser, psychophysical downsizing might set in earlier.

Psychosexual stages of development: Sigmund Freud's (1905a) delineation of an unfolding series of libidinal configurations through which a child passes before reaching the 'latency phase' (see separate entry). These psychosexual phases (also referred to as 'libidinal phases' or 'libidinal stages') consist of oral, anal, phallic, and oedipal phases. Together, the first three are called 'pre-oedipal' phase. Libidinal excitement centring upon mouth and lips, anus, and genitals characterized these phases. Such 'erotogenic zones' impelled the actions of mouthing, sucking, biting, expelling and retaining faeces, and manipulating the genitals ('infantile masturbation'). Later developments in psychosexual theory (Abraham, 1925a; Jones, 1957;) led to (1) the division of oral phase into 'oral–erotic' and 'oral–sadistic' subphases, (2) the division of anal phase into 'anal–erotic' or 'anal–retentive' and 'anal–sadistic' subphases, and (3) the addition of a 'urethral' dimension to the phallic phase. These pre-oedipal phases were followed by the oedipal phase, during which sexual curiosities, rivalries, and jealousies involving the parents occupied the centre stage. This next step was 'latency' (see separate entry), a period of instinctual quiescence and attention shift to mastery of external reality. Still later was 'adolescence' (see separate entry) where the instinctual resurgence found its ultimate path to the mature adult sexual configuration of genitality. Freud's pre-oedipal theory was largely a drive theory with inoptimal attention to object relations of that period. Contemporary psychoanalysis has made up for this by reformulating the first three years of development via a prism of complex interactions between constitution, attachment patterns, parental attitudes and behaviours, object-related fantasies of the child, and the variable consolidation of self experience at any given time. In this contemporary framework, libidinal phases (oral, anal, and phallic) and their corresponding drive pressures do figure, but as a constituent of the entire scenario, not as its main plot. The play has indeed been re-written!

Psychosexual theory: refers to Sigmund Freud's (1905a, 1915c, 1923e, 1924d) proposal that 'infantile sexuality' and its epigenetic unfolding through the various 'psychosexual stages of development' (see separate entries) determine the form and texture of adult personality in both its psychopathological and relatively healthy aspects. This idea occupied a central position in early psychoanalytic theory and Freud's pupils, especially Karl Abraham and Ernest Jones, laboured day and night to fortify its observational substrate. However, with the later shift of attention to ego functions (Freud, 1923b; A. Freud, 1936; Hartmann, 1939), and with the advent of 'object-relations theory', 'attachment theory', and 'self psychology', the perspective of 'psychosexual theory' lost its centrality. In contemporary psychoanalysis, it occupies a place that is parallel to these other perspectives (see 'Four psychologies of psychoanalysis').

Psychosis: a generic term for conditions (e.g., schizophrenia, mania, drug induced severe mental disorders) that have a break from reality as their common characteristic. In day-to-day clinical discourse, however, this broad connotation is often lost and the term 'psychosis' becomes synonymous with 'schizophrenia'. While the contributions of descriptive psychiatrists far outweigh those of psychoanalysts, the latter none the less remain important. Sigmund Freud (1924e) distinguished neuroses from psychoses by declaring that in the former, the ego, in the light of its allegiance to reality, suppresses part of the id , while in the psychoses, the ego, in the service of the id, withdraws itself from a part of reality. Melanie Klein (1928, 1930, 1946) emphasized the role of constitutional aggression, especially the 'death instinct' (see separate entry), severe annihilation anxiety, and of paranoid defences in psychosis. Later analysts, especially Wilfred Bion (1957) questioned the completeness of the break from reality in psychoses suggesting that psychotic and non-psychotic parts of the personality often exist together. He also underscored the psychotic's hatred of reality and of the mechanisms that remind him of reality. Among others who have made significant contributions to this realm are Hanna Segal (1950), Herbert Rosenfeld (1965), Gustav Bychowski (1953, 1954), Harry Stack Sullivan (1947, 1953), Harold Searles (1960, 1965), Ronald Laing (1960, 1971), and Ping-Ne Pao (1977, 1979), to name a few. See the related entries on 'psychotic and non-psychotic personalities', 'psychotic anxiety', 'psychotic character', and 'schizophrenia'.

Psychosomatic disorders: while sporadic speculations regarding these conditions (Fenichel, 1945; Garma, 1950; Sperling, 1955; Strauss, 1955) existed before him, Franz Alexander, along with his colleagues Thomas French and George Pollack (1968), systematized the study of 'psychosomatic disorders' into a distinct subspeciality. In tandem with the work of Flanders Dunbar (1954), Alexander's views became the established psychoanalytic perspective of the day. Seven conditions were recognized as core psychosomatic disorders (hypertension, bronchial asthma, peptic ulcer, rheumatoid arthritis, thyrotoxicosis, and ulcerative colitis) and a 'specificity theory' (which traced each of these conditions to particular childhood antecedents) was advanced. Despite its dramatic appeal and initial 'popularity', the model did not hold up to scrunity, however. The growing mass of information about these conditions (including studies from epidemiology, neurophysiology, endocrinology, genetics, and celluar biology) began to indicate that a 'biopsychosocial' (Engel, 1977) aetiology was responsible for these disorders. To be sure, the distinction of 'psychosomatic conditions' from 'conversion hysteria' (see separate entry) on the grounds of the former's involving the autonomic nervous system and the latter's involving the central nervous system remains valid. However, the symbolic significance of somatic symptoms was found to be restricted only to hysteria; in 'psychosomatic disorders,' physical symptoms were not symbolic of underlying conflict nor did they magically relieve the conflict (Thompson, 1991). There was no *la belle indifference* associated with these disorders, therefore. These 'old time' distinctions continue to be valuable. What has come into question is whether a specific childhood trauma leads to this or that psychosomatic disorder. Or, is it that individuals with low expressive capacity for affect, 'alexithymia' (see separate entry) and hereditary vulnerabilities of enzyme regulation develop these conditions when facing environmental stress? Such complexities have led to a bit of diminution in psychoanalytic interest in 'psychosomatic disorders'. However, this might be more true for the USA than for other regions of the world, where psychoanalytic interest in this area persists to a considerable degree. The French analyst, Joyce McDougall (1974, 1982, 1989a) has especially made significant contributions to this realm, proposing that early trauma that cannot be represented psychically tends to get expressed through the body. None the less, she expressed optimism regarding treatment of psychosomatic patients and stated that analysis can overcome their affect intolerance, dissolve bodily symptoms, and replace them with transference affects. More recently, an impressive contribution to this area has been made by Barbara Shapiro (2003), who, in discussing the analytic treatment of an adolescent with chronic pain, elucidates the technical principles of working with psychosomatic conditions. She advocates 'respecting the mind–body split as a primary defence, speaking the language of the body with the language of the mind, and developing the verbal sphere around the non-verbal symptoms' (p. 547).

Psychotic and non-psychotic personalities: according to Wilfred Bion (1957), 'psychotic and non-psychotic personalities' can be distinguished on the grounds of the former displaying the following four characteristics: (1) preponderance of destructive feelings; (2) hatred of internal and external reality and of all those processes that make one aware of those realities; (3) dread of imminent annihilation, and (4) tendency towards sudden and premature formation of object relations, especially transferences 'whose thinness is in marked contrast with the tenacity with which they are maintained' (p. 216). Although Bion used the term 'personalities', a reading of his paper makes it clear that he was talking about two aspects of personality. Thus, he stated that in the severe neurotic 'there is a psychotic personality concealed by neurosis as the neurotic personality is screened by psychosis in the psychotic' (p. 275). See also the entry on 'psychotic character'.

Psychotic anxiety: term associated with the work of Kleinian analysts and, to a lesser extent, with those of the British independent tradition, especially Margaret Little (1990). The term is often used in its plural form, especially by Melanie Klein (1927, 1930). Following Sigmund Freud's suggestion (1923b, 1926d), that neurotic anxiety in childhood was a rule rather than an exception, Mrs Klein suggested that the same applied to 'psychotic anxieties' during early infancy. Constitutional aggression, compounded by frustrating experiences, threatened to implode the self. Projection of this resulted in phantasies of retaliation from objects and a partial or total cessation of internal life altogether. There was dread that any and all 'good' internal objects would be drowned and aggression would destroy the mental capacities for synthesis and symbolization. Defensive mechanisms of splitting, denial, idealization, and projection were deployed against this level of anxiety. However, even these ego operations became suffused with omnipotence and were carried out with great violence in phantasy. Klein's ideas were further elaborated by Wilfred Bion (1957) who emphasized the hateful destruction of reality and of the cognitive functions that could register such reality in the psychotic sector of the mind. See also the related entries on 'annihilation anxiety', 'psychotic and non-psychotic personalities' and 'unthinkable anxieties'.

Psychotic character: term coined by John Frosch (1960, 1964, 1970) to designate a personality organization characterized by (1) disturbed relationship to reality (e.g., illusions and bizarre deviations in social manners) and disturbed feeling of reality (e.g., depersonalization) in the setting of intact reality testing; in other words, these perceptual disturbances are correctible by firm confrontation with reality; (2) infantile object relations; (3) pervasiveness of 'primitive ego defences' (see separate entry); and (4) vulnerability to micropsychotic episodes that are time-limited and reversible. Frosch emphasized that individuals with a 'psychotic character' may go through life without breaking down into overt psychosis. See also the entry on 'psychotic and non-psychotic personalities'.

Psychotic core: the 'psychotic core' (Bychowsky, 1953) or the 'infantile psychotic self' (Volkan, 1994) refers to a central psychic structure (developed during infancy and childhood) that is filled with hatred for self and others, with chronic disgust with reality, and with vulnerability to autistic regression. It is constituted by an admixture of features, that include hereditary and constitutional factors (e.g., excessive anxiety, potential for abnormal thinking, impaired visual–proprioceptive integration, neuropsychological disharmony), environmental contributions (e.g., problematic object relations, inadequate differentiations, deficient ego skills, unassimilable contradictions, family xenophobia, etc.) and intrapsychic fantasy (e.g., retrospective fantasizing, bizarre objects, etc.). It can have varied fates, ranging from psychic calcification to florid psychosis, with intermediate forms between the two extremes (Volkan, 1995).

Publication anxiety: concept delineated by Ronald Britton (1994) to address the near ubiquitous sense of nervousness when it comes to putting one's ideas on paper for others to see. Such anxiety can lead to writing and publishing inhibition as well as symptomatic disorders of the text. According to Britton, 'a profound fear of rejection by the primary intended listener' (p. 1214) underlies such inability to write. Matters are complicated by the fact that, on the one hand, the author wishes to communicate something novel to a receptive audience and, on the other hand, he wishes to remain loyal to his professional 'affiliates and ancestors' (p. 1215). This creates a triangular situation which can activate unresolved oedipal issues. To publish is to know and possess a subject. This is aimed to please the readership, but can create distance from one's teachers and colleagues. Fears of retaliation are stirred up and lead to anxiety about writing and publishing.

Punishment dreams: termed as such by Sigmund Freud (1920g) 'punishment dreams' 'replace the forbidden wish-fulfilment by the appropriate punishment for it' (p. 32). Themes of insult, humiliation, and corporeal discipline dominate the manifest content, while pleasure-seeking desires lurk in the latent thoughts behind the dream. Also called 'superego dreams', such dreams have overlaps with the typical 'exmination dreams' (Renik, 1980), in so far as both contain similar disguise and an admixture of moral and self-interested motives.

Pure and abstract interpretation: see 'Interpretation'.

Purification rituals: After a nation or large group emerges from a crisis such as war, the break-up of a political system, or drastic revolutionary change, a period of restabilization typically ensues. During this time of reassessment, attempts at group 'cleansing' often occur. Like a snake shedding its skin, a large group tends to cast off certain elements such as symbols or ideologies that no longer seem useful or appropriate, or those things that seem to impede growth and the revitalization of large-group identity. Such 'purification rituals' (Volkan, 2006) involve a spectrum of practices, policies, and ideologies, ranging from benign (return to more formal and 'original' forms of language) to malignant (ethnic cleansing).

Purified pleasure ego: the expression refers to a primitive ego state 'which places the characteristic of pleasure above all others' (Freud, 1915c, p. 136). All sources of pleasure are co-opted and those of unpleasure projected. Ego and pleasure thus become equated though eventually the necessity of external objects for obtaining gratification leads to frustration; 'reality testing' (see separate entry) sets in and the ego begins to mature. The possibility of aggression to the 'purified pleasure ego' however remains; this is especially evident in the state of hypomania.

$$\boxed{Q}$$

Q: see 'Quantity'.

Qualified agreement: phenomenon described by Sander Abend (1967), whereby certain analysands agree with the interpretation their analyst has just given them but do so in a characteristically conditional manner. They say 'yes' but promptly pile up additional explanations for the behaviour, fantasy, or feeling which was being interpreted. Calling such behaviour 'an analogue of negation' (p. 631), Abend underscored that 'these patients as a rule are quite unaware of the strength of their wish to disagree with interpretations' (*ibid*.).

Quantity: a term used by Sigmund Freud (1895) in his *Project for a Scientific Psychology* (see separate entry) to denote that which differentiates neuronal activity from neuronal rest or inertia. Used in its abbreviated form, 'Q', 'quantity' was seen as being capable of shifting from one neuron to the other and thus intensifying or diminishing their charge; this was a precursor to Freud's later concept of 'psychic energy' (see separate entry).

Quasi-autistic phase: see 'Autistic phase'.

Quasi-independence: according to William Ronald Fairbairn (1943), the transition from 'infantile dependence' (see separate entry) to the indepent stance of mature adulthood is hardly ever smooth. Even under favourable conditions, there remains a conflict between the progressive wishes to renounce the reliance on parents (since it is limiting) and the regressive urge to cling to it (since it is safe). Under unfavourable circumstances, this conflict is heightened. The intensified longing for infantile dependence is then compensated for by its denial via 'quasi-independence' and 'counter-phobic bravado'.

Questions as analytic interventions: while asking questions forms an integral part of initial assessment, it is the questions that the analyst explicitly asks his patient during the analytic hour that form the focus of attention here. Stanley Olinick (1954) has elegantly discussed this topic and concluded that questioning should be resorted to only when the following five conditions are fulfilled: (1) the patient has had ample opportunity to talk freely; (2) the analyst has scrutinized his psychic state thoroughly; (3) resistance has cropped up and interpretation requires preliminary validity;

(4) patient's level of anxiety is high and he needs support and direction; and (5) patient's ego structure is such that it needs reality testing. In contrast to this judicious allowance is Theodore Dorpat's (1984) categorical rejection of questioning on the grounds that it merely produces intellectualization and adds to resistance. Dale Boesky (1989) acknowledges this possibility, but does not grant it the power to eliminate the use of questioning altogether. He adds that the analyst's questions can be heard as suggestions, advice, requests, and even masked interpretations. 'During the darkest times of the unavoidable silence of the analyst, the seemingly simple question the analyst asks can be a reassuring beacon from the lighthouse on shore. It may be a caress, an admonition, a rebuke, a scopophilic intrusion, a compliment, a manipulation, an invasion of privacy—the list is endless' (p. 592). Mostly, however, the analyst's questions are repertory to interpretation and insight. Boesky states that 'the enlighted ignorance of the analyst is often communicated with a question that the patient has never thought of asking' (pp. 581–582). In general, there is nothing inherently bad or good about the analyst's asking a question; it is the dynamic impact of such an intervention on the analytic process that matters in the end.

Questions asked by the patient: these belong to two types: (1) questions that the patient directs at himself, and (2) questions that the patient directs at the analyst. The former (e.g., 'Why did this movie upset me so much?') indicate the patient's readiness to deal with new psychological material that is on the cusp of emerging; such questions do not require an answer from the analyst. The latter pose a greater challenge, especially when these involve the analyst's personal life. One knows the fewer factual details the patient has about the analyst, the greater are the chances of his filling up the blanks with externalizations and projections which provide the fodder for clinical work. However, to apply a strict policy of not answering any question is a caricature of the proper analytic attitude. The analyst can take pride in such 'discipline' and the patient might comply with it or masochistically enjoy the deprivation, but their work would suffer in the end. With these considerations in mind, it is safe to say that no hard and fast rule can be evolved here. Some guidelines do, however, exist: (1) a distinction should be made between answering a patient's question and responding to it (Schlesinger, 2003); the former may or may not be correct, but the latter is always essential. How, when, and why the question is asked by the patient needs exploration; (2) analytic process can be impeded or faciliatated by both answering and not answering the patient's question; (3) some selectivity in answering is inevitable: questions about the analyst's sexual life or religious beliefs, for instance, can hardly be answered, while questions about schedule changes, for instance, can be tackled on a factual basis. This is not to say that the latter might not conceal matters of fantasy and transference, but only that they seem exempt from the firm restriction on highly personal disclosures; (4) it is better to respond factually and quickly 'when the question is realistic and the answer will save a lot of irrelevant explaining' (Greenson, 1967, p. 342) on the patient's part; (5) when deciding not to answer, the analyst should explain to the patient his reasons for doing so; this is especially true in the early phases of the treatment. In the end, it boils down to balancing the tension between facilitating the unfolding of the analytic process and maintaining optimal interpersonal distance. Curiosity about the patient's questions and encouraging him to associate further are important. Work along these lines often leads to deeper insights into the patient's inner workings. Herbert Schlesinger's (2003) wise reminder in this regard that 'a quick answer can ruin a good question' must be kept in mind.

Quota of affect: a metapsychological concept used by Sigmund Freud (1894a) to denote that element of affect which remains invariable despite any transformation of affect; the latter might include isolation, displacement, repression, and so on.

$$\boxed{\textbf{R}}$$

Race and transference: unlike the literature of 1960s and 1970s, which mostly consisted of White analysts writing about their work with Black patients, the recent literature is mostly the product of African-American analysts (Holmes, 1992, 2006; Leary, 1995, 1997, 2006; Tang & Gardner, 1999; Hamer, 2006, 2007). They note that racial difference in the clinical dyad tends to pull forth a variety of projections and stereotypes; the resulting associations can become useful 'points of access to a patient's transferences' (Holmes, 1992, p. 8). The choice of a racially different analyst itself may be laden with deep meanings which become evident only after the analysis is well under way. However, this gentle scepticism about the patient's choice must be tempered by recognition that, at times, such choice may have no 'deep' significance at all. At other times, an early and seemingly mundane reference to racial themes might give the first hint of major transferences lying in wait. The analyst should scan the associative material for disguised and displaced references to the racial difference while remembering that every such utterance on the patient's part might not be transferentially significant. See also the related entries on 'inter-racial analysis' and 'racial fantasies'.

Racial identity: refers to that aspect of an individual's self-perception which involves his or her sense of sharing similar racial characteristics and heritage with a particular group of people (Helms, 1990). Development of 'racial identity' involves an interaction of personal identity, reference group orientation, and ascribed identity. The vectors of transgenerationally transmitted family myths and ego organization and drive-based fantasies also contribute to the manner in which individuals organize racial information about themselves, others, and institutions. Issues involving 'racial identity' can play a significant role in the psychotherapeutic relationship, the supervisory relationship, and in individuals' self concept and psychological adjustment (Helms & Cook, 1999; Neblett, Shelton, & Sellers, 2004; Tummala-Narra, 2004). Psychoanalysts (Altman, 2004; Leary, 1995) have explored the concept of racial identity primarily through an intersubjective lens, emphasizing the influence of societal realities of race and inter-racial relationships upon transference and countertransference dynamics within the clinical dyad. See also the entry on 'Inter-racial analyses'.

Racialized sexual fantasies: while prejudice, originating from the projection of warded-off drives and unacceptable self-representations, leads to the creation of fantasies whereby a racial, ethnic, or religious group other than that of the subject is looked down upon, Luz Calvo (2008) has recently described two 'racial fantasies' that are closely tied with ordinary psychosexual development of White individuals living in a racist culture. Calvo labels these fantasies as: (1) the primal scene of miscegenation (i.e., inter-racial sexual relations), and (2) 'a black man is being beaten'. Combining the reading of Sigmund Freud's (especially 1918b, 1919e) perspective on childhood witnessing (or imagining) of the primal scene in the Wolf Man case and the punishment-seeking submission to the father in his 'A child is being beaten' paper with Frantz Fanon's (1994) theories of colonial and post-colonial racialized desire, especially his desconstruction of the fantasy 'a Negro is raping me', Calvo highlights that 'the subject is constituted through fantasy scenarios in which difference is conceived as a tangled web of sexual, racial, and class positions' (p. 57). In 'racial fantasies' (perhaps, more properly called 'racialized sexual fantasies'), the object of racism is constructed as not only inferior and primitive, but also highly sexual.

Rage: an extreme, almost psychosomatic, outburst of anger. Rage is different from hatred in six ways: (1) rage is acute, hatred chronic; (2) rage has physiological concomitants which hatred lacks; (3) rage is mostly directed at an external object, hatred at an internal object (and its externalized versions); (4) rage aims to unshackle oneself from the frustrating object while hatred ties one to it in abiding ways; (5) rage implodes the capacity to think logically while hatred sharpens reasoning, though at the cost of narrowing its focus; and (6) finally, rage plays little role as an ego defence while hatred can serve as an important shielding measure against the emergence of guilt, sadness, dependence, and love. While most papers cited in the context of 'hatred' (see separate entry) address the topic of 'rage', that by Ping-Ne Pao (1965) does so most specifically. One other area of concern is that of 'rage' leading to violence. The disorganizing impact of 'emotional flooding' (see separate entry) upon the ego's ordinary restraining functions is obvious under such circumstances. Donald Campbell and Henrik Enckell

(2005) note that the breakthrough of violence is often preceded by the perpetrators' use of metaphors that fail to function as containing linguistic devices and become concretized.

Rapprochement crisis: term coined by John McDevitt (cited in Mahler, 1971, p. 177) to describe an intensification of the 'rapprochement subphase' (see separate entry) of the separation–individuation process. The child's oscillations between closeness and distance from the mother, typical of this subphase, become pronounced and desperate. The toddler shows a heighten sensitivity to disapproval. There is a concomitant increase in aggression and negativism. According to Margaret Mahler (1971) the outcome of 'rapprochement crisis' depends upon: '(1) the development towards libidinal object constancy, (2) the quantity and quality of later disappointments (stress traumata), (3) possible shock traumata, (4) the degree of castration anxiety, (5) the fate of the Oedipus complex, and (6) the developmental crises of adolescence—all of which function within the context of the individual's constitutional endowment' (p. 179).

Rapprochement subphase: the third subphase of separation–individuation (from about 16 to 24 months) in which the child senses that his autonomy and psychomotor freedom have their limits and that the external world is more complex than he imagined (Mahler, Pine, & Bergman, 1975). Narcissistically wounded, the child regresses in the hope of refinding symbiotic oneness with the mother. This return is, however, an ambivalent one, since the drive of individuation is at work with great force and the child becomes familiar with the ego pleasure of autonomy. The child therefore shows 'ambitendency' (Mahler, 1974, p. 161), clinging to mother for reassurance at one moment and darting away from her the next. This is the so-called 'terrible twos'. While turbulent, this phase is highly significant because its successful resolution leads to self-and object constancy, replacement of splitting by repression, tolerance of ambivalence, and diminished dependence upon mother in external reality.

Rationalization: term originated by Ernest Jones in 1908 for a process by which the ego selects and offers to itself and other the most palatable of the multiple explanations underlying a behaviour. A rationalization is not a lie; it is a partial truth. In preferring a 'realistic' rationale for behaving this or that way, the ego wards off the anxiety that might surface if more conflictual and primitive reasons for the behaviour were allowed into conscious awareness.

Reaction formation: a particular form of defence mechanism in which (1) the aim of an instinctual drive (e.g., to destroy, to mess up) is transformed, at the behest of the superego, into its opposite, and (2) the resulting change is generalized over the ego's attitude towards all objects in the external reality. In other words, 'reaction formation' leads to a definitive change of personality, the newly formed character traits ensure the 'once-and-for-all' success of repression (Fenichel, 1945). Reaction formation is to be distinguished from three related mechanisms: (1) *undoing*: the relationship between 'reaction formation' and 'undoing' is the same as that between season and weather; reaction formation works by altering character, and undoing by reversing temporary increases in instinctual impulses; (2) *displacement*: in reaction formation, it is the instinctual aim that is changed, while in 'displacement', it is the object of that aim which is replaced, and (3) *sublimation*: behaviours resulting from sublimation are devoid of instinctual (pressured, rigid, and emotional) quality, whereas those caused by reaction formation do have this quality, best captured by Salman Rushdie's (1989) phrase 'pitiless hospitality'.

Real: see 'Real, symbolic, and imaginary'.

Real relationship: besides their connections due to 'transference', 'countertransference', and 'therapeutic alliance' (see separate entries), the analyst and analysand also have a 'real relationship' with each other. Constituents of these are manifest in their loyalty to the frame (e.g., punctuality, regularity, payment of fees) as well as the spirit (e.g., respect for complexity, quest for knowledge, and a fundamental attitude of decency and affection towards each other). While noted by a number of authors (A. Freud, 1954; Stone, 1954, 1961), this aspect of the analyst–analysand relation has received the most clear exposition by Ralph Greenson (1967). The word 'real' in this context signifies, for him, both 'realistic' and 'authentic'. This distinguishes it from transference and countertransference, which are authentic but unrealistic, and from therapeutic alliance, which is realistic but an artefact of the treatment situation. More often than not, however, the three relationships (i.e., transference–countertransference, therapeutic alliance, and real relationship) coexist in admixtures of various degrees. Each can be used as a defence against the other. The tension between recognizing this on the one hand and acknowledging the existence of a 'real relationship' on the other guides the analyst's response to major events in the patient's life, to his own errors in technique, and to the occasional impediment that socio–political differences pose in under-taking or continuing an analysis (Greenson, 1967, pp. 223–224). One particular clinical population that is more hungry for such a 'real relationship' and, at the same time, least capable of observing and mentally retaining the objective qualities of the therapist is made up of severe borderline patients. Using the alternate term 'personal rela-tionship', Gerald Adler (1985) has discussed in detail the importance of authenticity, demon-strated concern and patience, and unmistakable helpfulness in the treatment of such patients with-out minimizing the much-needed interpretive dimension and without ignoring the potential risks of therapeutic over-activity in this regard.

Real, symbolic, and imaginary: according to Jacques Lacan (1956, 1977), all psychoanalytic phenomena can be categorized under one or the other of three psychic orders: 'real', 'symbolic', and 'imaginary'. Dylan Evans (1996) has master-fully elucidated Lacan's evolving, elliptical, and elusive usage of the three terms. Here, it will suf-fice to say that (1) *real* pertains to that which lies outside of representability, especially by the means of language; it is linked to physicality and corporeality; (2) *symbolic* pertains to what is most crucial to psychoanalysis, namely representation and communication (with the self and/or the Other) by literal (e.g., a gift) or abstract (e.g., words) means; (3) *imaginary* pertains to the ego's identification with its specular image during the 'mirror stage' (see separate entry) and is thus the locale of both narcissism and identification. Hence, it is also the source of the subject's 'alien-ation' (see separate entry) from himself. Accor-ding to Lacan, psychoanalysis should penetrate the 'imaginary' order and get down to the 'sym-bolic', which is where the possibility of authentic growth resides.

Reality: while psychoanalytic theory and tech-nique have the world of instinctual drives, inter-nal objects, imagination, wishes, fantasies, and defences as their main concern, recognizing the existence and role of 'reality' is also integral to them. By 'reality', psychoanalysis means what is actually out there, can be objectively perceived, and consensually agreed upon. What is subjec-tively significant constitutes 'psychic reality' (see separate entry); this may or may not be congruent with the 'objective reality', or simply 'reality'. Evidence of the latter's significance in psycho-analysis is to be found via the concepts of 'reality constancy', 'reality principle', 'reality testing', 'de-realization', and 'alloplastic adaptation' (see sepa-rate entries). Other concepts that indirectly reveal

the recognition of objective 'reality' by psycho-analysis include 'average expectable environ-ment' (see separate entry) which is deemed neces-sary for the optimal psychic development to unfold, the role of actual parental behaviour in a child's psychic structure formation, 'transference' (see separate entry), which, by implication, sug-gests that something from the pre-existing inner world is being transposed in the current 'reality' and the 'disorienting anxieties' (see separate entry) consequent upon immigration and geo-graphical dislocation. All this should not, how-ever, distract one from the fact that matters of 'reality' can, and, often are, used defensively dur-ing clinical work by both the analysand and ana-lyst. The various subtle and often unrecognized ways this occurs have recently been highlighted by Lawrence Inderbitzin and Steven Levy (1994).

Reality constancy: John Frosch's (1964) term for the ego capacity which enables the child 'to per-ceive his identity and tolerate alterations and changes in environment without psychic disrup-tions and adaptational dysfunctions' (p. 350). In situations of major environmental change (even during adulthood), such as those during immi-gration and exile, the loss of predictable and familiar topographical surroundings becomes a source of chronic, often life-long distress.

Reality principle: juxtaposed to the 'pleasure–unpleasure principle (see separate entry) by Sig-mund Freud (1911b), 'reality principle' differs from the former in three important ways: (1) it is acquired rather than innate, (2) it seeks gratifica-tion in external reality and not merely by halluci-natory wish-fulfilment, and (3) it takes into account the availability of gratifying objects, safety of discharge, and potential benefits of post-ponement of instinctual gratification. Later ana-lysts refined, elaborated, and, in some cases, modified the concept of the 'reality principle'. Ludwig Eidelberg (1954) emphasized that 'reality principle modifies but does not eliminate the orig-inal pleasure principle' (p. 51). Heinz Hartmann (1956, 1964) distinguished 'reality principle in broad sense' from 'reality principle in narrow sense'. The former antedated the 'pleasure princi-ple' and was responsible for the infant's pre-paredness for, and 'realistic' responses to, mater-nal care. The latter involved specific ego modali-ties of assessing the environment, finding appro-priate objects, and delaying gratification for the sake of safety and escape from superego retribu-tion. Heinz Kohut (1977) preferred the broader usage of 'reality principle' suggested by Hart-mann, and carried the argument further by suggesting that it is the breakdown of such 'reality principle' that yields 'pleasure principle' as an alternative pathway and a sort of degradation product.

Reality testing: though implied in the earliest writings of Sigmund Freud (1895), the term 'reality testing' itself was first used by him in 1911. According to him, 'reality testing' refers to an ego function that distinguishes thought from perception and, by implication, the inner world from external reality. As result, it helps to define 'ego boundaries' (see separate entry) as well. The developmental line of 'reality testing' has four nodal points (Freud, 1911b, 1917d, 1925h, 1937c): (1) absence of distinction between the subjective and objective world; (2) emergence of such distinction, but with the proviso that only the pleasurable is assigned to the ego and whatever is unpleasurable is relegated to the outside world; (3) appearance and consolidation of the capacity to genuinely distinguish fantasy from reality and conception from perception regardless of the drive-based economy of such judgements; and (4) development of a finer capacity to scan how one's inner biases have an impact upon the perceptions and the relationships with people in one's life. Finally, it should be noted that impairment of 'reality testing' has many gradations. In dreams, this function is temporarily suspended. In psychosis, it is lost. In perversions, the ego shows a contradictory attitude towards reality with one part of it accepting and the other part denying what is real (see entry on 'fetishism', for instance). And, then, there are 'transitional phenomena' (see separate entry) where reality and non-reality coexist and the issue of 'reality testing' does not arise.

Realization: term used in considerably different ways by Donald Winnicott (1945) and Wilfred Bion (1967). For Winnicott, 'realization' occurs when the psychosomatic self of the baby begins to experience and accept time, space, and other features of external reality (see entry on 'Integration, personalization, and realization'). For Bion, 'realization' occurs when a 'pre-concepeion' (see separate entry) finds its longed-for object in the external reality. A baby's innate 'pre-conception' of the breast finds 'realization', for instance, when it encounters the actual breast in external reality.

Reanalysis: in 'Analysis terminable and interminable', Sigmund Freud (1937c) declared that analysis is complete when it has succeeded in placing the ego in the position of dominance so that it can arrive at the best possible compromises between the patient's wishes, moral dictates, and reality. At the same time, Freud felt that no analysis is ever complete, due to tenacity of instincts and to the fact that life events subsequent to termination can always stir up new conflicts. This was made emphatically clear to him as his now renowned patient, Wolf Man, returned for further treatment with him; indeed, he needed even more treatment later on (Brunswick, 1928; Gardiner, 1964, 1983). Much psychoanalytic literature revolves around the 'reanalysis' of Wolf Man. However, what actually comes under the purview of 'reanalysis' remains unclear. The term can be applied to: (1) an analysis which was moderately successful and mutually terminated with the understanding that some conflicts had not been adequately handled; (2) a failed or stalemated analysis; (3) a very satisfactory analysis, after which some powerful life events (e.g., a death of a loved one, major professional success or setback) stirred up 'newer' conflicts; and (4) an analysis interrupted due to the analyst's death or relocation of the analyst or analysand. Some analysts reserve the term 'reanalysis' only for the situation number three of those listed above. Others use the term more broadly. Two panel discussions (McLaughlin, 1959; McLaughlin & Johan, 1985) held at the Meetings of the American Psychoanalytic Association include the views of many distinguished analysts, including Paul Dewald, Ruth Eissler, Ralph Greenson, Daniel Jaffe, Carol Adatto, Earle Silber, and Julio Morales, among others. The prominent notes contained within this symphony are (1) the first analysis may have prepared the patient for a 'real' analysis; (2) the first analysis may have been successful and thus made the patient more attentive to his intrapsychic life as it unfolded later on; (3) no analysis fully resolves the transference, so that to find evidence of 'unresolved transference' in the patient is not an indication of the failure of the first analysis; (4) the patient may idealize or devalue the first analyst and split the transference to the second one; (5) actual neurosis of the patient can become intermingled with the transference neurosis to the first analyst; the presentation to the second analyst brings this 'carried over transference'; (6) information given by the patient regarding his first analysis is not totally reliable; some, if not all, of it is in the nature of a 'screen memory' (see separate entry); (7) the temptation on the second analyst's part to compete with the first analyst and to achieve a perfect outcome this time around contributes major problems in 'reanalysis'; (8) however, this should not preclude his validating egregious errors of commission, especially these involving 'boundary violation' (see separate entry); (9) different methodology or frame (e.g.,

241

lesser frequency, not using the couch) might be needed in 'reanalysis'; and (10) at times, it is better to have an analyst of different gender than the first analyst for 'reanalysis'. Besides these thought-provoking nuances in considering the 'reanalysis' of adults, there are special issues in the reanalysis of children (Ritvo & Rosenbaum, 1983); this is often indicated due to the continued interference in development caused by the lingering effects of the early disruptions of formative relationships.

Reassurance: ordinarily understood as remarks made by a friendly person or an authority figure that diminish the subject's anxiety and restore his confidence. 'Reassurance', in this sense, does not constitute an analytic intervention, though it is occasionally employed in psychotherapy and crisis intervention. In psychoanalytic work, the patient may indeed draw 'reassurance' from the solidity of the therapeutic frame (e.g., regularity of sessions, punctuality), the analyst's non-judgemental attitude and his 'survivng' the patient's assaults. A deeper understanding of 'reassurance' has been provided by Michael Feldman (1993). According to him, the patient may find illusory 'reassurance' from the use of splitting, which helps him to maintain an acceptable self-view. Within the clinical situation, the patient's disavowal of any third party (standing for the oedipal rival), and regarding his and the analyst's relationship as total and exclusive, provides such false 'reassurance'. Feldman declares that true 'reassurance' is only derived from the patient's 'belief that he has not succeeded in replacing the oedipal triangular relationship with one in which he and the analyst are exclusively involved with one another' (p. 284).

Recall residue: Robert Langs' (1971) term for those reality events in the day following a dream which trigger the recall of a previously forgotten dream. According to Langs, 'recall residues highlight the role of reality in the subtle alterations of ongoing intrapsychic balances which ultimately determine the level of defensive countercathectic barriers' (p. 509).

Recognition: see 'Recognition and misrecognition'.

Recognition and misrecognition: terms employed by André Green (2005) to denote phenomena that appear akin, respectively, to 'insight' (see separate entry) and its lack. Green's focus is on the former, which he also calls 'introvision'; he does not equate it with consciousness, though acknowledges that conscious awareness consti-

tutes an aspect of 'recognition' of the unconscious. At the same time, he proposes the notion of 'unconscious recognition', which seems paradoxical, since, if 'recognition' refers to grasping what was erstwhile unconscious, how can there be 'unconscious recognition'? Green suggests that such a process typifies the artist who, in sublimating (hence disguising) the unconscious material, shows an awareness of it that is not available to his own consciousness. This constitutes 'unconscious recognition'.

Reconstruction: see 'Construction'.

Referral-related boundary violations: Diana Siskind (1997) presents a significant reminder that making referrals of patients requires a certain restraint and respect for the patient's boundaries. Giving too much information, too personal information, information that the patient might not be prepared to reveal to the receiving therapist in the first encounter, and trying to control the form and frequency of the treatment of the patient being referred all constitute 'referral-related boundary violations'.

Refuelling dialogue: phrase coined by Joseph Sandler and Anne-Marie Sandler (1998) by melding René Spitz's (1965) description of early mother–infant 'dialogue' with Margaret Mahler's (1968) concept of 'refuelling' that the toddler gets from his ever-available mother. By putting these two ideas together, the Sandlers emphasized that a growing child needs not only the continued availability of visual and physical contact with the mother, but a resumption of mutual cueing and affecting interchange with her as well in order to feel safe in being relatively independent of her.

Re-grief therapy: a special type of short-term, psychoanalytic psychotherapy devised by Vamik Volkan (1981) for helping patients resolve their 'pathological grief reactions' (see separate entry). Its various steps include (1) offering an initial explanation to the patient that his symptoms arise from his inability to mourn and the treatment is aimed to address this inability, (2) recommending three to four sessions per week, (3) conducting some early 'demarcation exercises' (Volkan & Showalter, 1968), which stimulate the patient's secondary process and help him separate his own self-representations from those of the lost love object, (4) facilitating such 'demarcation of the introject' (Volkan, 1981, p. 206) with the help of the patient's free associations pertaining to the relationship with the dead person, (5) encouraging the patient to recall the relationship with the deceased, the circumstances of the final illness or the fatal accident, the conditions under which the news of the death was received, the reactions to seeing the dead body, and the events of the funeral, (6) with the help of thus increased knowledge of the patient's inner world, clarifying his ambivalence towards the dead person, (7) tolerating the anger and sadness that now emerge and recognizing that these reflect a recommencement of mourning, (8) making 'bridging interventions' (see separate entry) to mend the split 'dead' and 'alive' representations of the lost object, (9) employing the 'linking objects' (see separate entry) of the patient to evoke emotions and to decipher (and interpret) how the patient has been maintaining omnipotent control over contact with the image of the dead person and has thus been postponing grief, (10) containing the subsequent emotional storms, (11) interpreting the pre-existent death wishes towards the deceased, (12) remending the now more fully evolved hostile side of ambivalence with love and pain of loss, (13) containing further sadness, and (14) respecting the patient's newly emergent need to put a secondary process graft over the now better healed wound by re-visiting the grave, having a memorial service, writing an essay or poem about the dead person, and so on.

Regression: while Sigmund Freud had invoked this notion in his theory of dream formation (1900a) and sexual perversions (1905a), it was not until 1913 that he used the term 'regression' *per se.* Understandably, this happened only after an epigenetic sequence of libidinal stages was mapped out. Freud's first use of the term 'regression' was in his paper 'The disposition to obsessional neurosis' (1913i), where he distinguished between libidinal fixation and 'regression' to the anal phase dynamics. In 1914, Freud distinguished three kinds of regression (1900a, p. 548): *(1) topographical regression:* whereby the characteristics of the system unconscious become dominant over those of the system conscious and discharge of excitation changes its direction from action to perception and wish-fulfilling hallucination; *(2) formal regression:* where primitive methods of expression take over more advanced ones; in contemporary language, this is called 'ego regression', though the latter rubric also involves diminished impulse control and lowered anxiety tolerance; *(3) temporal regression:* implies a return to an earlier mode of existing and relating; this could involve the emergence of libidinal pleasures and object-relations already renounced. While ubiquitous, such regression is seen with special clarity in association with the post-migration turmoil (Grinberg &

Grinberg, 1989; Akhtar, 1999b). Freud's ideas on regression have been extended in many directions and led to concepts (each separately defined in this compendium) as diverse as 'anaclitic regression' (Khan, 1960), 'benign and malignant regression' (Balint, 1968), 'regression in the service of the ego' (Kris, 1952), 'regression in the service of development' (Blos, 1968), 'regression in the service of progression' (Balint, 1968), and 'regression in the service of of the other' (Olinick, 1969).

Regression in the service of development: phrase originated by Peter Blos, Sr (1968) for describing the fact that regression during adolescence brings the more advanced ego of this period into contact with infantile drive positions, early object relations, and old solutions to central conflicts. This revisiting of early psychic positions with the help of a more resourceful ego facilitates the working through of them and helps the adolescent come out of the family envelope to the degree that he or she can form the largely autonomous character of young adulthood. Regression during adolescence thus advances the cause of development.

Regression in the service of progression: see 'New beginning'.

Regression in the service of the ego: concept described by Ernst Kris (1952), who proposed that, in resilient individuals, transient, circumscribed, controlled, and reversible regressions might not be pathological, but constitute a way of replenishing the ego. Such 'regression in the service of the ego' makes id-derivatives, in their primary process form, accessible to consciousness without submerging the ego altogether. This sharpens intuition, enriches imagination, and aids creativity.

Regression in the service of the other: Stanley Olinick's (1969) phrase for the softening of ego boundaries and the increased permeability to trial identifications that occurs in the analyst during his or her clinical work. Such ego regression is a pre-condition for 'empathy' (see separate entry) and is based upon the prototype of the mother's capacity to transiently merge with her infant and thus discern his needs and desires (see also 'Primary maternal preoccupation' in this regard).

Regret: an emotion that is frequently encountered in clinical work and yet has received little psychoanalytic attention.. No entry on 'regret' exists in the index to the *Standard Edition* of Sigmund Freud's works, Alexander Grinstein's (1956) index of psychoanalytic literature, and the five major dictionaries (Eidelberg, 1968; Rycroft, 1968; Moore & Fine, 1960, 1990; Laplanche & Pontalis, 1973). Putting this puzzling omission aside, one resorts to the *Webster's Dictionary*, which defines 'regret' as 'sorrow aroused by circumstances beyond one's control or power to repair' (p. 992). 'Regret' shares many features with its twin sister, 'remorse' (see separate entry). Both are about the past. Both are about one's own actions. Both can involve acts of commission or omission. Both lead to a wistful rumination to somehow erase or undo the events of the past. Both can, therefore, underlie the 'if only . . . fantasy' (see entry on 'Someday . . . and if only . . . fantasies'); This fantasy assumes that, in the absence of this or that 'calamity', everything would have turned out all right. Both 'regret' and 'remorse' can impoverish the ego and contribute to anhedonia, depression, and suicidal tendencies. Finally, both 'regret' and 'remorse' can serve screen functions and both can be put to secondary (e.g., sadomasochistic) uses. However, there is one very important difference between the two emotions: 'remorse' involves feelings about how one's actions have affected others, while 'regret' involves feelings about how one's actions affected oneself. In other words, 'remorse' is more object related, 'regret' more narcissistic. For a sociological and literary perspective on 'regret', see Janet Landman's (1993) magisterial book.

Relational psychoanalysis: a relatively recent 'movement' in North American psychoanalysis that is spearheaded by Stephen Mitchell and Lewis Aron (1999). Drawing its armamentarium from the innovations of Sandor Ferenczi, Harry Stack Sullivan, Heinz Kohut, Thomas Ogden, and the social constructivist and intersubjective theorists (e.g., Irvin Hoffman), 'relational psychoanalysis' places 'two-person psychology' (see separate entry) and the 'co-created' nature of psychoanalytic data at the centre. The definition and scope of what is ordinarily understood as 'countertransference' (see separate entry) is thus enhanced. The rubric 'relational', in this context, is, however, a bit amusing and also a little sad. This is because it implies the existence of a 'non-relational' psychoanalysis as a counterpart. Perhaps that is what psychoanalysis in North America had been until the 1970s, when the contributions of Otto Kernberg and Heinz Kohut and the burgeoning infant observation studies gave it a rejuvenating jolt.

Relaxation technique: clinical approach devised by Sandor Ferenczi (1930) after he had abandoned

his 'active technique' (see separate entry). In contrast to the latter, which comprised injunctions and prohibitions, 'relaxation technique' involved gratification of the patient and overt demonstrations of tenderness and affection by the analyst. Soon, however, Ferenczi realized that 'he had merely erected a reaction formation against his sadistic propensitites by masochistically submitting to the propensity of many patients to abuse their analyst' (Bacon & Gedo, 1993, p. 134). He then arrived at a more or less appropriate midpoint between the two enactments ('active' and 'relaxation' techniques) of his countertransference vulnerability. Echoes of Ferenczi's 'relaxation technique' are to be found in the 'harmonious interpenetrating mix-up' (see separate entry) described by his pupil, friend, and successor, Michael Balint (1968), but with finer checks and balances upon which gratification can be offered and what sort of acting out tolerated.

Religious instinct: wryly 'confessing' at the outset that 'of course there is not religious instinct', Mortimer Ostow (2001) goes on to state that he coined the term 'as a metaphor for the almost universal readiness of individuals to cohere into social units in which all participate in cultic practices and shared beliefs in a supernatural entity with parent-like functions' (p. 199). Deftly combining ontogenetic roots, hard-wired brain functions, and societal messages, Ostow sheds light upon both the need for, and seeming veracity of, religious experiences, especially the triad of awe, mysticism, and apocalypse. Thus, he provides a deeper and broader explication for Sigmund Freud's (1927c) proposition that man's need for God emanates from childlike dependency and the replacement of father (in whose 'greatness' one was disappointed) by an omnipotent, universal father. Avoiding the trap of proving or refuting God's existence, 'Ostow's Triad' (Escoll, 2001, p. 238) facilitates the understanding of 'religious instinct' by breaking it down into its component parts.

Remorse: Sigmund Freud (1930a) distinguished between 'guilt' (see separate entry) and 'remorse' by declaring that the former refers to wishes to do what is prohibited and the latter to having done that act. This meaningful distinction got lost over the subsequent course of psychoanalytic theorizing. 'Guilt' and 'remorse' came to be used interchangeably, with little phenomenological rigour. Even Melanie Klein (1940), whose ideas about 'reparation' (see separate entry) are directly related to the undoing of 'remorse', used the word 'guilt' in its place. To be sure, there are overlaps in the two experiences. For instance, the distinction between wanting to do something and having done it might be blurred in the unconscious. At the same time, it is also true that 'guilt' and 'remorse' differ in many ways: (1) guilt is about wanting to do something and remorse about having done it, (2) guilt therefore involves the future, and remorse the past, (3) guilt is about transgressing a rule or law, while remorse is about having hurt a loved object, (4) guilt can exist on both conscious and unconscious levels, whereas remorse is invariably conscious, (5) guilt pushes for confession, remorse for reparation, and finally, (6) guilt's twin is shame and remorse's twin is regret. In light of these important distinctions, it is a pity that more attention has not been paid to sorting out the concept of 'remorse' in finer, thoughtful ways.

Reparation: concept introduced into the psychoanalytic literature by Melanie Klein (1940) in connection with the growing child's awareness that his aggression against his love objects has damaged them and that he needs and wants to redress this damage. Moving on from the earlier 'paranoid position' (see separate entry) of development to the later 'depressive position' (see separate entry), the child becomes capable of concern for his love objects and of feeling remorse for his earlier ruthlessness towards them. From this realization arises the wish for 'reparation'. Mrs Klein distinguished three types of reparation: (1) *manic reparation*, which reverses the parent–child relationship and is therefore contemptuous at its core; it is also belittling the seriousness of the situation by employing magical means to repair the damage done (see also Segal, 1981). The Hindu mythological tale of Shiva cutting off the head of Ganesha (the child his wife, Parvati, had singlehandedly made to protect herself in Shiva's absence) and then, realizing his mistake, quickly replacing the severed head by that of an elephant (since the animal happened to be passing by) is an example of 'manic reparation' *par excellence*; (2) *obsessional reparation*, where repeated acts of 'undoing' (see separate entry) are employed to reverse the aggressiveness unconsciously directed at objects; and (3) *creative reparation*, where genuine concern for love objects is evident and the transformation of guilt into repair finds sublimated and artistic pathways. All in all, reparation is 'a force for constructive action in the external world. It supplements or supplants the positive attitudes of a simple love relationship, since it is concerned with the troubles or difficulties of the loved object, and it is so in a way which approaches more realism than the simple love

relationship with an idealized uncontaminated loved one' (Hinshelwood, 1991, p. 416).

Reparative therapy: see 'Homosexuality'.

Repetition compulsion: term introduced by Sigmund Freud (1920g) in the course of explaining children turning passive traumatic experiences into play, analysands returning over and over again to painful past experiences, the behaviour of those who go through similar calamities repeatedly, and the dreadful preoccupations of war veterans. Freud suggested that that there might be a self-destructive 'daemonic force' (p. 35) at work in them; this force worked in opposition to the 'pleasure principle' (see separate entry). It is as though these individuals never comprehend the futility of their repetitions; often, they are unaware of their role in it and regard themselves a victim of 'bad luck'. Freud argued that the force underlying 'repetition compulsion' was aligned with a fundamental attribute of mind which involved a search for reduction of all excitation to quiescence, even to the extent of reducing the organism to its previous, inorganic state. 'Repetition compulsion' thus reflected the conservatism of instincts in general and the operation of the 'death instinct' (see separate entry) in particular. Subsequent analysts added other significant insights to this realm, emphasizing that 'repetition compulsion' was largely in the service of mastering a trauma. Prominent among these contributors were the following three: (1) *Edward Bibring* (1943) distinguished between id's 'repetitive' and ego's 'restorative' tendencies, noting that the former creates the traumatic situation again and again while the latter seeks to create the pre-traumatic situation; the clinical phenomena associated with 'repetition compulsion' often show an admixture of the two tendencies (see the related entry on 'resilience'); (2) *Hans Loewald* (1971) distinguished between passive repetitions and active re-creations; the former are evident in the infantile prototypical experiences being reproduced in neuroses, and the latter in the transferential re-creation of 'infantile neurosis' (see separate entry) during the course of analysis; and (3) *Patrick Casement* (1991) highlighted the role of unconscious hope (of finding development-facilitating objects and experiences) in 'repetition compulsion'.

Replacement child: Albert Cain and Barbara Cain's (1964) label for a child that is conceived soon after the loss of a significant person in the mother's life. Such a child is unconsciously equated in the maternal psyche with the deceased, especially if the mother has not been able to resolve her grief. The newborn's psyche becomes the recipient of the 'deposited representations' (Volkan, 1987) of the mother's earlier love object; this makes him 'special'. At the same time, the fact that he is *not* the deceased one fosters maternal neglect towards him. The result of such split attitudes on the mother's part is that the child develops a dichotomous identity with grandiose and unworthy self representations; these make contradictory demands upon the ego throughout his life. Many world-renowned individuals have been 'replacement children' (Cain & Cain, 1964; Poznanski, 1972), with lives full of self-doubt and glorious achievements.

Representation: see 'Mental representation'.

Representational world: concept introduced by Joseph Sandler and Bernard Rosenblatt (1962) in order to explain the internal organization of self and object representations and their corresponding affects and fantasies. These 'representations', or psychic reproductions, assist in sorting out the sensations and perceptions arising out of interpersonal experience. Together with Edith Jacobson's (1964) metapsychological mapping out of the inner psychic structure, Sandler and Rosenblatt's work helped to establish links between the early energic models of the mind and the later object relational ones. Thus, defences came to be seen with a finer theoretical lens. For instance, 'projection' (see separate entry) became a shifting of the attributes of an unconscious self-representation to a conscious object representation. Other concepts were similarly refined. Primary narcissism, for instance, was now viewed as the libidinal cathexis of the self-representation and object love as the shifting of this cathexis to an object representation. In essence, the concept of representational world provided the underpinnings of psychodynamic processes in the context of object relations.

Repression: mechanism of defence first mentioned by Sigmund Freud in 1893 and elaborated upon in a series of papers (e.g., 1906a, 1909d) and most notably in a paper (1915a) devoted solely to this topic. Originally used synonymously with 'defence', 'repression' gradually came to be recognized as but one, even if highly important, form of defence. Among the central ideas proposed by Freud about 'repression' are the following: (1) it consists of keeping some aspect of mental contents out of conscious awareness; (2) it can only come into being when a distinction between conscious and unconscious mental activity has

occurred; (3) there is 'primary repression' (see separate entry), where the instinctual derivatives have never been allowed entry into consciousness and there is 'repression proper' (Freud, 1915a, p. 148), which is an after-pressure or counter-cathexis, i.e., an active removal of mental contents from the conscious; (4) the 'success' of repression depends on the vehemence with which the material is pushed down and the attraction the material under 'primal repression' offers it; (5) it requires a constant expenditure of force since 'the repressed exercises a continous pressure in the direction of the conscious' (1915a, p. 151); and (6) while secondary defence mechanisms (conversion, displacement, reaction formation) determine the overt manifestations of neurotic conditions, 'repression' underlies all of them. Indeed, Freud (1914d) declared that 'the theory of repression is the cornerstone on which the whole structure of psychoanalysis rests' (p. 16). The centrality accorded by him to 'repression' has hardly been questioned, though it is now felt (Kernberg, 1970) that 'repression' as an organizing defence is typical only of neurotic or of 'higher levels of character pathology' and not of the borderline or 'lower levels of character pathology' which are organized around splitting-related mechanisms (see separate entries on these two concepts). Finally, it should be noted that while, generally speaking, 'repression' blocks the discharge of prohibited and dangerous impulses, it can facilitate such occurrence as well. The example of a jealous husband who 'forgets' to unload his gun and shoots his unfaithful wife dead by mistake shows the work of 'repression in the service of instincts'.

Repression in the service of instincts: see 'Repression'.

Repudiated self: see 'Favoured and repudiated self'.

Repudiation: see 'Foreclosure'.

Rescue fantasy: first described by Sigmund Freud (1910h) in connection with the child's wish to give back to the parents the life which he or she owes to them, by rescuing them from danger and death. When directed at the mother, such a fantasy also rests upon the childish belief that, in the act of parental sexual intercourse, the father is beating the mother. This gives rise to a desire to 'rescue' the mother and lays the groundwork for a lifelong tendency, more marked in men, to get romantically involved with partners who are in need, have a 'faint breath of scandal' (Freud, 1910h, p. 166) about them, and are 'unsuitable in reality' (Freud, 1912a, p. 181). To this well-reorganized oedipal aetiology of the syndrome, further impetus is occasionally given by sadomasochistic trends consequent upon childhood exposure to an actually depressed mother. When directed at the father, the 'rescue fantasy' contains an attitude of defiance in so far as it denies the fact that one has to thank one's father for one's life. Richard Sterba (1940) elaborated on the potentially aggressive aspects of the rescue fantasy. He underscored that 'the object to be rescued must first have been brought into the danger from which the producer of the fantasy is to save it' (p. 505). Transferences based upon such fantasies give rise to the wish to help, nourish, and financially support the analyst (Grinstein, 1956). Aaron Esman (1987) has provided an update on the topic of rescue fantasies, noting that, in contemporary usage, this term often refers to the analyst's conscious or unconscious desires to save his patient. Esman notes that such desires are more common in the course of child analytic work.

Resilience: a contemporary incarnation of Herman Nunberg's (1926) 'will to recovery' and Sigmund Freud's (1933a) 'instinct for recovery' (p. 106), the concept of 'resilience' refers to the ego's capacity to metabolize psychological trauma to the extent that resumption of the original level of psychic functioning becomes possible. In reality, a literal return to pre-trauma 'innocence' is niether possible nor, perhaps, desirable. The resumption of functioning typical of 'resilience' is actually an ego advancement; it assimilates the psychological consequences of trauma and is accompanied by deeper insights into the self and its interpersonal and socio–political context (Akhtar & Wrenn, 2008). Needless to add, such advance is inwardly supported by a strong constitution, unimpeded functioning of ego instincts, the achievement of libidinal object constancy, a benevolent and kind superego made up of good internal objects, and familial and societal support systems. The so-called 'Garmenzy's triad' (Garmenzy, 1985), which includes positive constitutional, familial, and societal factors as the basis for human 'resilience' speaks to this very point. For greater details see the contributions of Boris Cyrulnik, Henry Krystal, Henri Parens, Ira Brenner, and Harold Blum, among others, in the recent volume on the topic, evocatively titled *The Unbroken Soul: Tragedy, Trauma, and Resilience* (Parens, Blum, & Akhtar, 2008).

Resistance: term used by Sigmund Freud (1895d) to denote all verbal material and action that blocks the analysand's access to his or her uncon-

scious. Originated in the context of treating hysterical symptoms, 'resistance' was at first considered to be conscious; one overcame it by insistence and persuasion. Soon, however, Freud discovered that 'resistance' was not merely hiding the unconscious material; resistance was itself unconscious. The same forces that gave rise to repression were responsible for 'resistance'. Freud (1920g) declared that 'resistance during treatment arises from the same higher strata and systems of mind which originally carried out repression' (p. 19); this idea was sharpened years later by Merton Gill (1982), who stated that resistance is defence expressed in transference. Going back to Freud, we note that in 1926 he identified five types of resistance: (1) *repression resistance*, (2) *transference resistance*; here it is important to note that, while transference can be used as resistance, resistance is not restricted to transference, (3) *id resistance*, which represents the pull of repetition compulsion upon repressed instinctual processes, (4) *superego resistance*, expressing the need for punishment and continued suffering; and (5) *epinosic resistance*, or the difficulty in renouncing symptoms because of the 'primary and secondary gain' (see separate entry) provided by them. Freud came to the conclusion that the interpretation of resistance and the transference are the hallmarks of psychoanalytic treatment. This is well-established now and is accepted by psychoanalysts world-wide. However, with further accumulation of knowledge, it has become evident that resistances in the clinical situation do not emanate solely from the patient. The analyst's failures of tact and empathy, his or her ill-timed interpretations, and overall countertransference problems can also contribute to the cropping up of resistances (Krause, 1961; Stone, 1973; Rangell, 1983; Dewald, 1982b). Moreover, resistance is not restricted to hiding (consciously or unconsciously) unconscious material. It has communicative value as well.

Resistance analysis: the view at the inception of psychoanalysis that 'resistance' (see separate entry) has to be overcome by suggestion and persuasion (Freud, 1895d) gradually gave way to the understanding that resistance has to be interpreted (Freud, 1920g). While many subsequent analysts (Stone, 1961; Brenner, 1976; Rangell, 1983; Stark, 1994) have written about this piece of analytic work, none has approached the lucidity of Herbert Schlesinger (2003, pp. 81–101). Five attitudes and interventions can be distilled from his writing on the issue: (1) keeping in mind that resistance conveys information as well; (2) empathizing with the patient's need for resistance, i.e., his sense of danger in proceeding further; (3) 'normalizing' the blockage by suggesting potential reasons why it makes sense for the patient to feel unsafe at that moment; (4) 'going along with the resistance' and letting the patient communicate through the resisting behaviour; and (5) exploring the transference fantasy inherent in resistance.

Resomatization: see 'Somatization'.

Retention hysteria: see 'Hysteria'.

Retrogenetic phases: the tendency to traverse through modified forms of early developmental phases in reverse towards the end of life (Cath, 1990). It should be emphasized that such adult experiences are not literally akin to the infantile oral, anal, or symbiotic phases. Much ego structuralization has taken place and an entirely different set of instinctual and reality pressures is in evidence. None the less, one can sometimes discern the echo of early development—in reverse—at the end of life.

Retrospective self-envy: Otto Kernberg's (1980) proposition that, in pathologically narcissistic individuals, the tendency to envy the other spreads to involve their own youthful self from 'old times'. As a result, they develop a bitter wistfulness towards what they themselves used to be and used to accomplish. To defend themselves against such 'self envy' they might resort to ridiculing their own earlier, energetic selves.

Return of the repressed: phrase first used by Sigmund Freud in 1896 to denote the appearance of seemingly inexplicable symptoms or parapraxes that symbolically express repressed psychic contents. In contrast to the emergence of repressed material as a result of analytic work, 'return of the repressed' is involuntary in nature; unlike the former, which enlarges the scope of ego-dominance over problematic areas of the mind, 'return of the repressed' creates symptoms and, hence, more suffering. It betrays a partial failure of repression, though secondary defences can certainly be erected against it, in turn. In a later paper, Freud (1915d) posited that 'return of the repressed' comes about by the means of 'condensation'; 'displacement' and 'conversion' (see separate entries on each). He also described three pre-conditions for the repressed to return: (1) weakening of countercathexis, (2) upsurge of drives, and (3) environmental events that touch upon the repressed themes. The role played by the 'return of the repressed' in the adult survivors

of childhood sexual abuse has also been noted, especially via odd somatic sensations (Greer, 1994). Gagging during sexual intercourse , for instance, might reflect a bodily memory of forced oral sex during childhood.

Revenge: while deemed morally reprehensible and 'politically incorrect', the taking of some revenge by the victim of a trauma might actually be psychologically beneficial. Noting this, Salman Akhtar (1995, 2003) stated that taking revenge puts the victim's ego in an active position and changes the libido–aggression balance in the self–object relationship. The victim no longer remains passive, pure, and innocent; the perpetrator no longer remains the sole cruel party. These shifts can lead to reduction of hatred and create the possibility of a dialogue between the two parties. All this applies to revenge in fantasy, only a small portion of which should be allowed to appear in action. Massive retribution rationalized as 'revenge' and getting 'addicted' to revenge are, however, pathological, and can hardly be seen as providing psychological benefits. Such tendencies to seek 'vengeance' (see separate entry) are often based upon the conflation of a current trauma with early childhood deprivations and 'narrow-mindedness' (see separate entry) that facilitates overlooking the redeeming qualities of those who are hated. In contrast to the active revenge seeking, this gives rise to the tendency on the part of some individuals to hide their hate. John Steiner (1996) argues that 'when revenge is felt to be unacceptable, it is transformed into grievance and forms the focus of a psychic retreat' (p. 434). Another important contribution to the psychology of revenge has also been made by Lucy Lafarge (2006). In her view, the wish for revenge is a ubiquitous response to narcissistic injury, especially when such injury is combined with oedipal defeat. Fantasies accompanying the wish for revenge contain and express rage while seeking to 'restore the disrupted sense of self and internalized imagining audience that has resulted from injury' (p. 447). See also the important recent paper on the topic by Irwin Rosen (2007), report of a panel discussion (Beattie, 2005) on the topic of 'revenge' held at the 2004 Fall Meetings of the American Psychoanalytic Association, with Warren Poland as the Chair and Nancy Chodorow, Peter Dunn, Irwin Rosen, and John Munder Ross as the main presenters. Besides noting the various psychopathological constellations and consequences, the role of sublimated 'revenge' in writings of memoirs and pursuit of justice was also underscored.

Reverberation time: term coined by Dana Birksted-Breen (2009) to denote a primitive temporal sense arising from the earliest to-and-fro internalized exchange between the infant and his or her mother. The auditory dimension plays a significant part in the genesis of 'reverberation time'. Disturbances in its consolidation are reflected in pathological 'arresting' of time, which, in turn, impedes the negotiation of the depressive position and the oedipal situation. 'Reverberation time is also the building block of psychoanalysis, leading to "unfreezing" psychic time and enabling the reconnection of "here and now" with "there and then" in a flexible way which promotes open possibilities and this takes place via the analyst's reverie, or time of reverberation' (p. 35).

Reverie: see 'Analyst's reverie'.

Reversal in external and internal rates of change: Otto Kernberg's (1980) reminder that, unlike childhood, adolescence, and young adulthood, in midlife and later years, changes in external reality occur at a greater speed than those in internal reality. As a result, one is humbled, feels small, and becomes aware of the ephemeral nature of the human life in a convincing and concrete manner.

Reversal into the opposite: among the dynamic processes described by Sigmund Freud (1915c) in 'Instincts and their vicissitudes', two are intricately linked: 'reversal into the opposite' and 'turning round upon the self'. The former pertains to an instinct's aim and the latter to its object. They represent two sides of the same coin. The change of sadism into masochism, for instance, involves the alteration of an active aim (drawing pleasure from hurting someone) into its passive counterpart (drawing pleasure from being hurt by someone) *and* the self becoming the recipient of an object's aggression rather than vice versa. 'Reversal into the opposite' can also include the shift from passivity to activity. Thus, the transformation of masochism into sadism is also an illustration of it, though, clearly, here the mechanism parts company with 'turning round upon the self'. However, 'there is no difference in principle between an instinct turning from an object to the ego and its turning from the ego to the object' (Freud, 1920g, p. 54).

Reversed oedipal constellations: during midlife, oedipal conflicts that had been earlier worked through can be reactivated. The roles are, however, reversed. What had been the erotic desire (and attendant anxieties) towards the parent of the opposite sex now appear as the erotic desire (and attendant anxieties) towards the offspring of the opposite sex. And what was the hostile envy and competitiveness towards the parent of the same sex now appears as similar feelings towards the offspring of the same sex. Working through their feelings is integral to the developmental challenges of midlife and leads to further deepening and refinement of the incest barrier developed during the original oedipal phase.

Reversible perspective: term introduced by Wilfred Bion (1963) and elaborated upon by others (Grinberg, Sor, & Bianchedi, 1972; Etchegoyen, 2005). It refers to thought processes that aim to destabilize and destroy the analytic situation. These processes, relying heavily on splitting, seek to avoid 'mental pain' (see separate entry) at any cost. 'To negate psychic pain, reversible perspective relies on a permanent modification of the mental structure' (Etchegoyen, 2005, p. 767). In subtle forms, such cognitive–relational style is evident from the onset of treatment.

Review dreams: see 'Termination related dreams'.

Ritualization: while Julian Huxley (1966) had coined this term for certain phylogenetically preformed ceremonial acts in the so-called social animals (e.g., greeting ceremonies of some birds), Erik Erikson (1980) adopted it for the special form of everyday human behaviour which consists of 'an agreed upon interplay between at least two persons who repeat it at meaningful intervals and in recurring contexts' (p. 602). Such interplay has an adaptive value for the respective egos of both participants in the behaviour. Erikson proposed the way a mother and her baby greet each other upon waking up each morning as the basic prototype of 'ritualization'. He noted that 'ritualization' unites the two parties in practical as well as symbolic actuality. It is highly personal, yet group bound. It is playful, yet formalized. Erikson traced the ontogeny of 'ritualization' for this early prototype to more complex behaviours of childhood, adolescence, and adult life. In the clinical situation, the analyst and analysand's way of observing the ground rules of forms a sort of 'ritualization'

Role responsiveness: concept originated by Joseph Sandler (1976) in the context of his exploration of the play between transference and countertransference during the clinical hour. Sandler proposed that transference attempts to gratify a wishful fantasy by eliciting a corresponding

249

response from the analyst. The patient tries to actualize an unconscious scenario in which both he and the analyst are enacting a particular role. The latter's reflexive acceptance of the assigned role and his more or less acting it out is called his 'role responsiveness'. Sandler proposed that often it is after such 'countertransference enactment' (see separate entry) that the analyst becomes aware of what is going on and thus becomes able to interpret the transference.

Romantic vision of psychoanalysis: see 'Classic and romantic visions of psychoanalysis'.

Rotten core: Ruth Lax's (1980) designation of a self pathology consisting of the following five features: (1) recurrent depression, (2) chronic discontentment with the self, (3) a sense of being doomed, (4) a feeling of having two selves: a well-functioning outer self and a 'rotten' inner self, and (5) as a corollary to this split, a pervasive sense of inauthenticity about their actual lives. According to Lax, the 'rotten core' originates as a reaction to a depressed mother's lack of availability during his or her toddler years. The internalization of interactions with her results in a specific kind of identification with the aggressor. 'This identification leads to the formation of a rotten core which on the most primitive level represents the fusion of the "bad" (angry–rejecting) maternal introject with the "bad" (rejected) aspects of the self' (pp. 454–455).

Ruthless love: according to Donald Winnicott (1945), the infant shows a certain kind of ruthlessness in his relatedness to the mother. This consists of taking (attention, feeding, etc) from the mother in an entitled manner without regard for her feelings. Such 'ruthlessness of the baby', however, is not hate; there is little intent to hurt in it. Mother's surviving such 'ruthless love' of her child gives rise to the 'capacity for concern' (see separate entry) in the child. Winnicott also proposed that a similarly 'ruthless self' can be seen to operate in the creative artist who merrilys destroys order in the aim of creating it according to his own vision.

Ruthless self: see 'Ruthless love'.

Ruthlessness of the baby: see 'Ruthless love'.

S

Sachs' mechanism: a dynamic configuration described by Hans Sachs (1923) as being central to sexual perversions. It is characterized by a separation or split 'in which one piece (of infantile sexuality) enters into the service of repression and thus carries over into the ego the pleasure of a pre-oedipal stage of development, while the rest falls victim to repression' (p. 179).

Sadism: used in a *narrow sense*, the term 'sadism' refers to a sexual perversion where inflicting pain upon the partner is mandatory for achieving excitement and orgasm. This usage was initiated by Richard von Krafft-Ebing (1892) who named the cruel perversion after the deranged writings of the Marquis de Sade. Used in a broad sense, 'sadism' refers to the characterological tendency to enjoy hurting others; this is seen in association with 'malignant narcissism', paranoid personality disorder, antisocial disorder, and, in its most macabre form, serial killing. Sigmund Freud (1905a) extended the connotation of 'sadism' by pointing out that (1) it invariably occurs in tandem with 'masochism'; (2) it plays an important role in psychosexual development; (3) its intrapsyhic elaborations range from neutralization and sublimation on the one hand to the formation of a harsh superego and submissive ego on the other; and (4) finally, it should be noted that Freud's views on 'sadism' changed in accordance with his 'instinct theory'. In his 'first dual instinct theory', Freud regarded 'sadism' to be primary and viewed masochism as sadism turned around upon the subject's own self. However, in his 'second dual instinct theory', he turned this postulate on its head and suggested that 'masochism' was primary and 'sadism' resulted from an outward deflection of 'primary masochism' (see separate entries on the concepts with quotation marks around them).

Sadomasochism: see 'Masochism' and 'Sadism'.

Safety feelings: see 'Background of safety'.

Sanderian activation waves: term coined by Edward Tronick (2002) for the 'wave-like pattern of the sensitivity of the mood to activating affective input over time' (p. 82). Tronick traces the origin of such a pattern to the self-organizing brain and bodily processes ('biological clocks'). He named the phenomenon after Louis Sander (1980, 1983), who has convincingly demonstrated the powerful impact of the recurrence of caregiving events for the infantile psychosomatic regulation. The repetition of an interactional pattern increases the probility of the related affective state becoming ingrained and needing less external activation for its emergence. Joseph Lichtenberg (2005) provides a thoughtful evaluation of Tronick's proposal, comparing it with the clinically based ideas that he, along with Frank Lachman, and James Fosshage (1996), has developed.

Satellite state: Vamik Volkan and Robert Corney's (1968) term for the psychological state in which an individual fears both progression and regression in the realm of autonomy and exists as a captive body orbiting within the gravitational field of an intense, though ambivalent, dependency. Unresolved conflicts involving 'separation–individuation' (see separate entry) usually underlie such a state.

Schema model: proposed by Joseph Slap (Slap & Saykin, 1983, 1984; Slap, 1987; Slap & Slap-Shelton, 1991), the 'schema model' states that: (1) the mind is an organized depository of past perceptions and affective reactions; (2) these psychic organizations, called 'schemas', function as a unified structure; (3) 'schemas' are representational structures, but also provide the basis for action; (4) new perceptions are recruited to already existing 'schemas' in a process called 'assimilation'; (5) the 'schema' adapts to this new information and changes accordingly; this process is called 'accommodation'; (6) while the conscious 'schemas' incorporated in the ego are open to such influence, repressed 'schemas' only assimilate but not accommodate, i.e., they do not change as a result of feedback; (7) analytic treatment seeks to render repressed 'schemas' conscious and, thus, susceptible to the modifying influence of the ego.

Schizohomosexuality: see 'Homosexuality'.

Schizoid fantasies: see 'Schizoid personality disorder'.

Schizoid personality disorder: more than any other psychoanalyst, Ronald Fairbairn (1940) delved into the phenomenology and dynamics of schizoid personality. He viewed schizoid individuals as displaying an attitude of omnipotence, emotional detachment, and preoccupation with inner reality. As children, such individuals had felt unloved and deprived of maternal attention. Their dependent longings thus grew intense and became threatening to the ego; a defensive withdrawal was instituted to deal with this threat. Social contact taxed the ego and was felt as exhausting. There also developed fear of one's own love. To hide their love and to protect themselves from others' love (rendered dangerous by projection of one's hunger), schizoid individuals erect defences against loving and being loved. They feel compelled to distance others by indifference and even hate. This substitution of loving by hating has two motives: one immoral, the other moral. 'The immoral motive is determined by the consideration that, since the joy of loving seems hopelessly barred to him, he may as well deliver himself over to the joy of hating and obtain what satisfaction he can out of that. The moral motive is determined by the consideration that, if loving involves destroying, it is better to destroy by hate, which is overtly destructive and bad, than to destroy by love, which is by rights creative and good' (p. 37). Fairbairn's ideas were elaborated by others, especially Harry Guntrip (1969). In a thorough review of these works and the views of other analysts, especially Melanie Klein (1946) and Donald Winnicott (1960), Salman Akhtar (1987) concluded that 'schizoid personality disorder' consists of overt and covert manifestations in six areas of psychosocial functioning: (1) self-concept, (2) interpersonal relations, (3) social adaptation, (4) love and sexuality, (5) ethics, standards, and ideals, and (6) cognitive style. The schizoid individual is overtly detached, self-sufficient, absentminded, uninteresting, asexual, and idiosyncratically moral. Covertly, the person is exquisitely sensitive, emotionally needy, acutely vigilant, creative, often perverse, and vulnerable to corruption. Mention should also be made of Norman Doidge's (2001) description of 'schizoid fantasies' including being skinless, being buried alive, having hidden identities, animating the inanimate, and finding everything good to be imaginary.

Schizoid position: term coined by William Ronald Fairbairn (1940) to denote the mental state that preceeds the infantile 'paranoid position' (see separate entry). In Fairbairn's view, the term 'schizoid' represents certain overt personality traits (e.g., attitudes of omnipotence, detatchment, and introversion) but, more importantly, it refers to splitting of the ego. Since this is invariably true,

to a certain extent, at the deepest mental level, 'the basic position in the psyche is a schizoid position' (p. 8). Fairbairn stated that this idea is supported by the fact that most normal people experience, from time to time, a sense of looking at themselves, *déjà-vu*, and a strange feeling of calm in the face of a serious crisis. Dreams that everyone has on a nightly basis also testify to the split nature of the ego, since the various characters in the dream ultimately represent the dreamer's personality anyway. Fairbairn went on to elaborate the effects of the 'schizoid position' on development, and to demonstrate that the 'Oedipus complex' was actually a child's way of dealing with the split object relations by assigning the two sides to the two parents. He also added that hysterical and obsessional constellations were actually 'upward' defences against the schizoid split of the ego. His suggestion that it was the intensity of the 'schizoid position' that determined whether the guilt typical of the 'depressive position' (see separate entry) will be tolerable or not was liked by Melanie Klein, who changed the name of her 'paranoid position' (see separate entry) to the more accurate, though clumsy, 'paranoid–schizoid position'. See also the entry on 'Fairbairn's description of the endo-psychic structure'.

Schizoid transference: see 'Transferences of hatred'.

Schizophrenia: diagnostic entity originated by the great Swiss psychiatrist Eugen Bleuler (1911). Bringing a diverse group of severe mental illnesses (e.g., catatornia, hebephrenia, dementia praecox, dementia paranoides) and adding categories of his own (e.g., simple and latent), Bleuler created the umbrella term, 'schizophrenia' or, to put it the way he named the condition, 'the group of schizophrenias'. Central to this illness were disturbances of association, autistic withdrawal, ambivalence (in the sense of contradictory thoughts), and affective inappropriateness. From this core arose a diversity of symptoms, both of 'positive' (e.g., hallucinations, delusions) and 'negative' (e.g., apathy, anhedonia) types. Over the subsequent decades, descriptive psychiatry became engrossed with refining the concept of 'schizophrenia', categorizing its subtypes, and demarcating its boundaries with other severe mental disorders. Psychoanalysis took less interest in the condition, partly because overtly psychotic patients were hardly treatable by its method. None the less, the contributions it made remain significant. Sigmund Freud noted that (1) unbearable ideas can give rise to hallucinatory psychoses (1894a); (2) paranoid tendencies emanated from the projection of unacceptable homosexual impulses (1896, 1911c); (3) withdrawal of libidinal cathexis of external objects and consequently increased secondary narcissism underlies the megalomania and hypochondriasis of schizophrenia (1914c); (4) this loss of contact with reality was then defended against by massive re-cathexis of it; as a result, everything began to have meanings (1924a); and (5) whereas in neurosis the ego pledges allegiance to reality and represses portions of id, in psychosis the ego withdraws from reality and gives itself over to id (1924b). Subsequent psychoanalysts who made important contributions to the understanding of 'schizophrenia' include Otto Fenichel (1945), Harry Stack Sullivan (1953), Silvano Arieti (1955, 1974), Harold Searles (1960, 1965), Ronald Laing (1960, 1971), Bryce Boyer (1961, 1971), Thomas Freeman (1962, 1963, 1977, 1981, 1982, 1985), Donald Burnham, Arthur Gladstone, and Robert Gibson (1969), Theodore Lidz (1973), Vamik Volkan (1976, 1995), James Grotstein (1977a,b), Michael Robbins (1993, 2002a,b), Peter Giovacchini (1997), and Johannes Lehtonen (1997). Together, their work highlighted the formal structure of 'schizophrenia', including disturbances of ego functioning, primitive and magical forms of thinking, concretization of thought, and regressive fusion of self and object representations. Family dynamics and patterns of upbringing which led to poor affect differentiation, brittle ego skills, disturbed body image, xenophobia, longing and dread of object relationships, and muddled thinking were also highlighted. The ebb and flow between the dynamic processes generated by constitutional vulnerabilities (Karlsson, 1966; Bleuler, 1968; Fish & Hagin, 1972) early environmental peculiarities, and the child's own intrapsychic contributions were seen to be the ultimate determinants of the psychotic core that lay at the heart of schizophrenia. Such in-depth understanding led to dramatic attempts at treating schizophrenics with psychoanalysis. While it is certainly possible that some ambulatory patients benefited, it remains unclear to what extent such outcome was due to analytic intervention as against the personal devotion of a thoughtful individual. Over time, however, such approaches dwindled. This was in part due to the rapid advances in psychopharmacology and in part based upon the fact that such treatment was a monetary nightmare. Medical insurance companies would not pay for a treatment that had little hard research to demonstrate its efficacy. Shrinking its base to the highly affluent, the 'psychoanalytic psychotherapy' of schizophrenia gradually bowed out of the scene,

especially in North America. The current positon holds that 'the treatment approach needs to be biopsychosocial since the fundamental nature of this pathology is biopsychosocial. Pharmacologic and social interventions therefore deserve a place of importance in the treatment approach. At the same time, it cannot be overlooked that these modalities are most effective only when psychotherapeutic help is available on an ongoing basis' (Akhtar, 1997, p. 196). See also the UK–USA differences *vis-à-vis* the relationship between psychoanalysis and schizophrenia as highlighted in the 'debate' between Richard Lucas (2003a, 2003b) and Robert Michels (2003).

Scierneuropsia: decribed by Peter Martin (1960), this psychogenic visual symptom consists of a sensation that one is seeing objects as if through a screen. On an infrequent basis, 'scierneuropsia' can occur in normal individuals as a transitory phenomenon upon awakening from sleep. When persistent, it usually suggests serious character pathology, if not ambulatory schizophrenia. The symptom is a consequence of narcissistic disequilibrium. 'The physiological dysfunction in the eyes has resulted from pathological, emotional investment in a visual hallucination, a waking screen. This screen expresses a wish to relax into sleep in order to prevent a disruption of distructive impulses or a psychosis from becoming overt. It also symbolizes the cold hostile separation from the world' (p. 80).

Scopophilia: see 'Voyeurism'.

Screen: the term 'screen' is used in two different ways in psychoanalysis: (1) *as a suffix*, to convey the seemingly contentless but important surface upon which the perception of internal or external stimuli takes place; terms such as 'dream screen' and 'waking screen' (see separate entries) arise out of such usage ; and (2) *as a prefix*, to convey the idea that a particular manifest phenomenon is hiding a deeper and troubling phenomenon behind it; terms such a 'screen affects', 'screen defences', 'screen hunger', 'screen identity', 'screen trauma', and 'screen reconstructions' (see separate entries on each) arise out of such usage. It should also be noted that the surface phenomena in all these instances might be plausible and innocuous, or manufactured and bizarre. The former are called 'filter screens' and the latter 'falsified screens' (Simmel, 1925; Kennedy, 1950).

Screen affects: coined by Bertram Lewin (1950, p. 72) and further elucidated by Ralph Greenson (1958b) and Dale Boesky (1973), 'screen affects' denote the use of certain moods, especially pleasant ones, to ward off more painful and distressing emotions. The concept has overlaps with the aspect of 'manic defence' (see separate entry) pertaining to the denial of depressive feelings and use of exalted opposites (e.g., full as against empty) for reassuring an inwardly troubled self.

Screen defences: Norman Reider's (1953) term for the use of psychic phenomenon of a given class to ward off psychic phenomena of the same class. In other words, a feeling evoked in order to avoid another feeling, a thought entertained in order to cover up another thought, and so on. This constitutes the essence of 'screen defences' and separates them from other defences where a feeling can ward off a thought, thinking suppresses feeling, and moral injunctions help to restrain an instinctual impulse.

Screen hunger: term introduced by Otto Fenichel (1927) for the desperate, urgent, and repetitive quest of certain individual's for new experiences. These experiences not only offer instinctual gratification but also help to deny inner misery and aloneness. And yet, they somehow leave the individual unfulfilled. Old anxieties and morose self doubts persist beyond the transient titillation of novelty.

Screen identity: Ralph Greenson's (1958) term for a character constellation driven by 'screen hunger' and dominated by the use of 'screen defences' (see separate entries on each). Individuals with such a character are generally well-orientated to reality and might even be socially successful. Their ego functions are problematic only in ways that include subtle disturbances of body image, memory, and the sense of time. They show an uncanny closeness to the past which gives them a youthful quality. They are 'memory collectors' (p. 251). They regard themselves as lucky, or favoured. However, their sense of identity is far from coherent. They carry multiple self images on an unintegrated level. Each of these identities serves as a cover-up for the other.

Screen memories: term coined by Sigmund Freud (1899a) to denote the fact that the consciously recalled insignificant details of childhood often stand for emotionally significant experiences that have undergone repression. Such memories are almost invariably visual, and one sees oneself in them. Though vivid and convincing, they are actually the result of 'a process of displacement: they are substitutes, in mnemic reproduction, for other impressions that were really significant . . .

[and] owe their preservation not to their own content but to an associative relation between their content and another which is repressed' (1901b, p. 43). A 'screen memory' is therefore a 'compromise formation' (see separate entry) between a wish to remember and a wish to forget (Greenacre, 1949; Greenson, 1958). An important feature, added by Edward Glover (1954) to the original description of 'screen memories', was that traumatic memories can also serve 'screen' functions if they hide even more serverely traumatic events.

Screen perceptions: term coined by Otto Fenichel (1939a) for the tendency of some individuals, especially children, to focus upon and react to selective aspects of a traumatic situation in order to conceal the more terrifying perceptions that were simultaneously taking place on a preconscious or unconscious level. Phyllis Greenacre (1949) later elaborated upon this idea in her paper on 'screen memories' (see separate entry).

Screen reconstructions: Michael Good's (1998) designation for analytic 'reconstructions' (see separate entry) which are felt to be valid by both the patient and analyst, but are mostly untrue and defensive in nature. 'Screen reconstructions' may contain elements of truth, but also tend to weave 'screen memories' (see separate entry) into them. They evolve due to suggestive influences and a strong wish to see what happened in the past. They act as resistances against intense erotic, sadomasochistic, or narcissistic themes in the transference–countertransference axis.

Screen sensations: described by Herbert Fingarette (1960) and James Anthony (1961), these sensations refer to intense feelings and bodily phenomena experienced under certain regressive conditions; 'screen sensations' mask traumatic and dissociated genetic events.

Screen trauma: while the idea that a traumatic memory can serve screen functions was originally proposed by Edward Glover (1929), the term 'screen trauma' was originated by Sydney Furst (1967). According to him, a 'screen trauma', like 'screen memories' (see separate entry) can shield against the recall of a more severe trauma or even a cluster of traumatic events. In further elaborations of this idea, Jean Cournut (1991) and Dianne Casoni (2002) emphasized that even the repetition of a trauma for the purposes of mastery can serve to keep the unconscious content linked to it out of awareness.

Sculpted creativity: Elliott Jaques' (1965) term for the burgeoning capacity during midlife to improve upon and refine one's life work on the one hand and to give up the hope of having a perfectly rounded end product on the other. One simply keeps 'sculpting', chiselling away on one's blemishes, and yet one is not loath to accept one's imperfections. Unlike the creativity of youth, which was more passionate and instinctive, the creativity of midlife is thoughtful and disciplined. This applies to creativity in the artistic and scientific sense as well as to creativity of day to day life.

Second adolescence: see ' Second adolescences and fourth individuations'.

Second adolescences and fourth individuations: extending Margaret Mahler's (1958, 1967, 1972) childhood 'separation–individuation' paradigm, as well as its application to adolescence under the title of ' second individuation' (Blos, 1967) and parenthood under the title of 'third individuation' (Colarusso, 1990), John Munder Ross (1996), proposed the concept, a bit playfully, one suspects, of 'second adolescences and fourth individuations'. According to Ross, this happens in men who have ben married for a long time and have gradually developed a deferential, paternal transference towards their wives. Death of their fathers and/or the adolescence of their children often precipitates the process. Encountering such losses, these middle-aged men 'plunge into last-ditch efforts, consciously defiant and even deliberately regressive, at "second adolescences" and "fourth individuations". However destructive may be the results or primitively misguided the whole enterprise at times, the agendas involved have a progressive impetus behind them, namely some final stab at finding something new in a state of renewed abandon and at becoming even more of an individual' (pp.113–114). In a discussion of Ross's ideas, Lawrence Blum (1996) notes that preoedipal maternal injunctions, incorporated in the superego, might also contribute to men's so-called 'paternal transference' to their wives.

Second censorship: see 'Three-box model of the mind'.

Second individuation process of adolescence: described by Peter Blos, Sr (1967), this process refers to the emotional disengagement from the internalized object relations with one's parents during adolescence. While psychological separateness during childhood depends upon a secure internalization of the parental homeostatic functions, acquisition of such separateness during adolescence requires a reverse process. This, coupled with the characteristic drive upsurge of this period, results in certain ego instability. Progressive and regressive trends alternate, at times with disturbing rapidity. Regressive trends cause clinging to earlier modes of self-expression. Progressive trends, both defensive and autonomous, herald new self-configurations. On the one hand, there is insistent disengagement from the earlier parental dictates internalized in the form of superego; on the other, there is an equally tenacious reliance upon the values of the peer group. Trial indentifications and role experimentations within the latter context gradually broaden ego autonomy and impart a greater sense of inner solidity, constancy, and abstract morality.

Second organizer of the psyche: see 'Organizers of the psyche'.

Second symbiosis: Leo Madow's (1997) term for the psychologically anticipated experience of death in old age. He states that 'as we age, we slowly move psychologically towards a symbiotic state, passing in reverse through modified forms of rapprochement and practicing subphases culminating in an observable and well circumscribed event—death ... This second symbiotic phase might repel us despite its promise of soothing our life-long hurts, because it represents giving up the autonomy we have struggled to achieve throughout our lives' (pp. 166, 167). Madow's notion is an extrapolation of Margaret Mahler and colleagues' (1975) 'symbiotic phase' of early infancy to the other end of life. Madow also asks the provocative question, 'could this second symbiosis be the psychological equivalent of Freud's death instinct?' (p. 166), and turns Freud's (1920g, p. 8) dark remark that 'the aim of all life is death' into the more optimistic statement that 'the aim of all life is a return to symbiosis' (p. 166). The unmistakable confluence here of psychoanalysis and Hindu mysticism, especially the teaching of Vedanta, opens new pathways for psychoanalytic theorizing.

Secondary autonomy: see 'Autonomous functions of the ego'.

Secondary elaboration: Austin Silber's (1973) addition to the concept of 'secondary revision' (see separate entry); this consists of embellishment of dream contents, increased involvement with its images, and a certain quality of aggressiveness which works as a resistance. 'Secondary elaboration' tends to rupture therapeutic alliance.

Secondary gain: see 'Primary and secondary gains'.

Secondary narcissism: see 'Narcissistic libido'.

Secondary process: see 'Primary and secondary processes'.

Secondary revision: Sigmund Freud's (1900a) term for the ego's attempt to bring seemingly incomprehensible and disjointed elements of a dream by connecting and unifying them in a quasi-rational manner. Such 'revision' can also be used by the superego for further censoring the instinctual wishes that gave rise to the dream.

Secrets: while psychoanalysts constantly hear material that their patients wish to keep 'secret' and gradually discern the 'secrets' of the child within their adult patients, the literature on 'secrets' *per se* is meagre. Sigmund Freud (1901b) said that 'no mortal can keep a secret. If his lips are silent, he chatters with his finger tips; betrayal oozes out of him at every pore' (p. 71). However, it was not until the 1950s that papers specifically addressing the topic of 'secrets' and 'secrecy' appeared in print. Alfred Gross (1951) defined 'secret' as that which is known by one person and not by others around him. He noted that a 'secret' is invariably associated with powerful impulses to retain it as such and to reveal it as well. While anal phase derivatives are evident here, Gross emphasized that secret keeping (and tyring to pry open parental secrets) reaches its developmental zenith during the oedipal phase. Carl Sulzberger (1953) underscored the phallic–exhibitionistic qualities of secret keeping and observed that women are more likely to reveal others' secrets and men their own. Even more far-reaching papers on 'secrets' and 'secrecy' were written by Gerald Margolis (1966, 1974). Comprehensively reviewing the literature and encompassing the developmental (psychosexual and identity-related), literary, and technical realms, Margolis concluded that 'whatever is eventually rendered unconscious involves aspects of life that are first kept secret from parents or others and that therefore the formation of neurosis proceeds from conscious secret keeping by the child to keeping things secret from its own superego and ego' (p. 292). Margolis pointed out that exactly the reverse occurs in psychoanalytic treatment. 'The patient is encouraged to reveal all of his conscious secrets to the non-condemning analyst and, after he is able to do so, to no longer hide unconscious secrets for his own ego and superego' (p. 292). Others who have made contributions to this topic include: (1) Salman Akhtar (1985), who has made the statement that 'a secret is an intrapsychic cul-de-sac which not only disrupts life's experiential

continuity but also sets into motion defensive processes to guard its own existence' (p. 82); and (2) Andrea Celenza (2007), who, in the course of studying the sexual boundary violations by therapists, has noted the problems caused by a treatment getting too impervious to input, that the shift from 'confidentiality' to 'hyperconfidentiality' and secrecy heralds trouble and sets the ground for ethical misconduct.

Seduction hypothesis: term applied to Sigmund Freud's (1895d, 1896) proposal that psychoneuroses (obsessive compulsive and hysterical disorders) result from sexual 'seduction' by adults during childhood. This could range from verbal and visual overstimulation to actual sexual abuse. The 'seducers' were mostly parents, but sometimes older siblings and other caretakers as well. Freud proposed that, at the time of their occurrence, such sexual events only caused unease and fear; it was their later revival in memory, due to an environmental trigger, that became truly traumatic, mobilized repression, and led to symptom formation. However, Freud soon began to doubt this theory and gradually replaced it by the decisively intrapsychic theory involving 'psychic reality', 'infantile sexuality' and the 'Oedipus complex' (see separate entries). In 1914d, for instance, he wrote that hysterics 'create such scenes in phantasy' (p. 17) and in 1925d that 'these scenes of seduction had never taken place and that they were only phantasies which many patients had made up or which I myself had perhaps forced upon those' (p. 34). This shift is viewed as monumental in the growth of psychoanalytic theory, and indeed it is so. This has led some people (e.g., Masson, 1984; Ahbel-Rappe, 2006) to conclude that Freud turned away from his recognition of the reality of child abuse. The fact, however, is that Freud never totally abandoned the 'seduction hypothesis'; he continued to regard it as one possible factor in the genesis of adult psychopathology (Freud, 1940a [1938]) alongside the more prevalent one energizing from oedipal fantasies. The fact is that seduction of children by parents does occur (Kramer & Akhtar, 1991; Margolis, 1977, 1991; Shengold, 1980; Silber, 1979; Steele, 1991) and can reinforce the effects of the child's independent fantasy life (Greenacre, 1956; Sachs, 1967). See also Michael Good's (1995) historical elucidation of Karl Abraham's (1907a,b) continued investigation of childhood sexual trauma despite Freud's turning away from it and preventing him from further developing ideas in this regard.

Seduction of the aggressor: In playful activities of adults with children, the threat and its pleasurable removal often coincide in the same act, such as the parents' facetiously attacking and frightening the child. Children never tire of such games and endlessly ask for their repetition. This behaviour was labelled 'seduction of the aggressor' by Rudolph Loewenstein in 1957. It contains elements of future, actually masochistic behaviour: the seeking for situations that entail danger, fear, and unpleasure, and their attenuation through a loving, erotic complicity of the threatening person. It is true that the pleasure in these situations is not derived from the pain itself, but from its removal and from a loving reunion with the parent. Soon, however, the unpleasure of the threat and the pleasure of its removal become intimately tied together. Although this normal behaviour pattern in children does not always lead to masochism, it has elements of the prototype for a masochistic perversion in later, adult life.

Seduction of the humiliator: phrase applied to the tendency on the part of masochistic individuals to defend against their fear of humiliation by actively seeking humiliation (Eidelberg, 1959; Loewenstein, 1957). They do so to gain the unconscious narcissistic gratification of controlling the insult they feel to be inevitable.

Seductive superego: term proposed by Lawrence Josephs (2001) for a kind of superego that rationalizes the gratification of prohibited impulses and renders them ego syntonic. This, however, is followed by humiliating punishment. The 'seductive superego' thus inflicts a betrayal trauma upon the self and repeats similar betrayals by parents during the childhood. An additional aspect is that the superego is actually split into two parts, with the 'seductive' part inhibiting the healthier part by shaming pressure.

Selected fact: from a mass of verbal and affective data offered by the patient, the analyst picks up one fact, focusing upon which gives coherence to the rest of the data up to that moment. Wilfred Bion (1967) termed this the 'selected fact'.

Self: a colloquial term for decribing one's own person as opposed to others in the external world. Its psychoanalytic use can be traced to Sigmund Freud's (1923b) term *das ich* (translated as the 'ego' in English), which had a dual implication: 'one in which the term distinguishes a person's self as a whole (including, perhaps, his body) from other people, and the other in which it denotes a particular part of mind characterized by special attributes and functions' (editor's introduction, Freud, 1923b, p. 7). Since Freud's use of

das ich alternated between these meanings and the term 'ego' was increasingly operationalized as a part of the tripartite psychic structure (along with id and superego), the concept of 'self' was eclipsed. Then, in 1950, Heinz Hartmann emphasized the distinction between the 'ego' and the 'self'; the former stood for a particular mental agency and the latter for the whole person. Erik Erikson's (1950, 1959) concept of 'identity' (see separate etnry) came close to Hartmann's 'self' but did not gain wide acceptance in the purist culture of Freudian psychoanalysis due to its hybrid nature (with admixture of intrapsychic, interpersonal, and socio-cultural dimensions). Still later, Edith Jacobson (1964) and Otto Kernberg (1967, 1975) revived the concept of 'self', emphasizing that what one was dealing with was essentially 'self-represention' and not 'self' *per se*; one's objective characteristics did contribute, but were not the sole determinant of how one perceived oneself. Drive activity and level of ego-maturity also affected the 'self-representation'. Indeed, the early self-representations were clustered around libidinal and aggressive drive derivatives and only gradually coalesced to form a core self representation. Even this structure was not monolithic, and subsets of self-representation (some close to action, others to contemplation) continued to exist in a loose confederation of psyche (Eisnitz, 1980; Ghorpade, 2009). Such developmental considerations were furthered by child observational studies of Margaret Mahler, Fred Pine, and Anni Bergman (1975), Stanley Greenspan (1980), Robert Emde (1981, 1983), Daniel Stern (1985), Greenspan and Wieder, (2005), and Joseph Lichtenberg (1989), among others, though, certainly, the models they proposed differed in significant ways. Another important development in the study of 'self' was that of Heinz Kohut's (1977) 'self psychology' (see separate entry), which had echoes of Donald Winnicott's (1960) earlier ideas regarding the formation of self. In contemporary parlance, 'self' is used as a juxtaposition to 'object' (see separate entry) and the two are seen to be dialectically influencing each other from the earliest periods of life down to the subtle and gross interactions within the clinical dyad.

Self analysis: while psychoanalysis owes its origin, at least partly, to Sigmund Freud's 'self analysis' (see Anzieu, 1986 for a thorough discourse on it), its stance on such an undertaking is an ambivalent one. Freud himself made contradictory statements in this regard, stating, at one place (1914d), that self analysis might 'suffice for anyone who is a good dreamer and not too abnormal' (p. 20) and declaring, at another place (1892–1899), that 'genuine self analysis is impossible' (p. 271). The tension between these views has persisted since Freud's days. This is understandable in the light of inherent contradiction between the analyst's need to honestly understand his inner dynamics and his narcissistic resistances to such uncovering (Ticho, 1967; De Ekboir & Lichtmann, 1982; Mallard, 1987; Brakel, 1990). The issue therefore boils down to the distinction between three different uses of 'self analysis': (1) as a replacement of being analysed by a psychoanalyst; (2) as a resistance during analysis; this is often seen among narcissistically inclined and analytically informed patients; and (3) as a reinstatement of one's analyst's analysing function into one's own ego and the continuation of one's analysis following termination. The last mentioned is the only acceptable form of 'self analysis'. Scrunity of one's dreams, parapraxes, affective responses to books and movies, experiences during religious rituals and travel (Poland, 1977), and unexplained shifts of mood and attention are valuable aids in conducting such work. However, self-flattering by-passes of genuine self-examination can always mar the exercise. The aphorism that 'the only problem with self analysis is posed by countertransference' is popular for this very reason.

Self constancy: emerging around 20 months of age, a more realistic and less shifting view of the self (Mahler, Pine, & Bergman, 1975); this combines the dependent 'lap baby' self image with the triumphant 'conqueror of the world' self image, as well as the libidinally derived self-representations with the aggressively derived self-representations (Kernberg, 1976a).

Self-disclosure: the issue of self-disclosure is more complex than whether to reveal a piece of information about oneself to one's analysand or not. It involves other questions—what to disclose? How much to disclose? When? To whom? To what end? And, finally, how to determine whether one's decision has been appropriate. Moreover, it appears that there are three forms of self-disclosure: (1) *Integral:* some self-disclosure is inevitable in the analyst's being with the patient. His or her name and skin colour betray ethnic and racial identities. The office décor reveals the analyst's cultural dimension. While all this can undergo transference elaboration, it is naïve to maintain a belief in the analyst's total opacity. (2) *Situational:* this involves the therapist's departing from anonymity because it seems essential for protecting the therapeutic framework or for shielding the patient's ego from severe pain and regression. For instance, when the therapist sud-

denly has to take considerable time off (e.g., for major surgery) or when he is under severe strain (e.g., illness, mourning), he might need to give some actual information to the patient. However, the degree and timing of such disclosure has to be tailored to each specific patient's life history and ego asset. Consultation with a trusted colleague is helpful in such circumstances. (3) *Technical*: as a carefully chosen strategy, limited self-disclosure can be useful. Christopher Bollas (1992), for instance, describes the analyst's occasionally sharing his own free associations with the patient: 'You know, as you are speaking, I have a picture of a little girl of three . . .' (p. 121), and so on. Bollas discusses the risks of such an intervention and provides guidelines for its use. All in all, self-disclosure appears correct if it is followed by the patient's feeling peaceful and able to better co-operate with the treatment. Self-disclosure is incorrect (in nature, timing, or dosage) if it results in further demands, ego regression, or guilty reactions on the patient's part. Unfortunately, one can determine this only in retrospect. The decision to disclose information about one's self is risky, and the novice would do better to err on the side of caution. See also the important recent contributions on self-disclosure by Darlene Ehrenberg (1995), Fred Busch (1998), Steven Cooper (1998), Charles Hanly (1998), Theodore Jacobs (1999), William Meissner (2002), and Merton Shill (2004).

Self disorders: a phenomenological by-prduct of Heinz Kohut's (1977) 'self psychology' (see separate entry) is the description and classification of 'self disorders'. These conditions are viewed as emanating from pathogenic self object experiences and to betray either an arrested development or trauma to the self. Essentially, there are three types of 'self disorders': (1) *pre-emergence disorders*, resulting from an injury occurring before a coherent self has emerged; their phenomenological picture is akin to borderline or psychotic disorders; (2) *consolidation disorders*, resulting from traumatic occurrences after a somewhat cohesive self has been formed but before the final consolidation of a vigorous and balanced self; their clinical picture is akin to highly sensitive narcissistic personality; and (3) *life curve disorders*, resulting from internal or external interferences with the actualization of self's life aims; their clinical picture is in the form of midlife depression. Ernest Wolf (1994), who has provided detailed descriptions and clinical illustrations of these disorders, states that 'one can conceptualize the psychopathological effects originating in these phases, respectively, as those of the deformed self, the fragile self, and the unfulfilled self' (p. 83).

Self envy: in an attempt to integrate Melanie Klein's (1957) work with Margaret Mahler's (Mahler, Pine, & Bergman, 1975) ideas on separation–individuation, Neil Maizels (1985) proposed that the tendencies to remain fused with the primary object and to separate continue to coexist on a life-long basis. Most individuals find a balance between them. In some individuals, however, one or the other tendency becomes more dominant. In them, the manifest part of the self tends to become envious of the part that exists on a covert basis. One who has given in to his dependent and passive side will be envious of his active and aspiring self representation. On the other hand, one who is autonomous and ambitious on the surface might secretly envy his own dependent and retiring self. A different slant to 'self envy' was given by Otto Kernberg (1980) in his description of a pathologically narcissistic individual facing middle age. Suffering from 'the painful awareness that the narcissistic gratifications of youth and past triumphs are no longer available, and in order to avoid painful envy of his own past, the narcissistic patient is forced to devalue his own past achievements' (p. 138).

Self naming: although David Forrest (1973) mentioned the phenomenon of one's own 'onymy', and Dennis Farrell and Michael Hoyt (1982) reported in detail on a patient who often referred to himself by his first name while talking to his analyst, it was Mardi Horowitz (1982) who coined the crisp phrase 'self naming' in his discussion of that case. According to him, individuals with narcissistic vulnerability are more liable to exhibit this phenomenon. The use of one's name acts as a kind of 'orienting arousal that aids self-stabilization' (Horowitz, 1982, p. 623).

Selfobject: although the term 'self-object' was coined by Arnold Modell (1963), greater popularity was gained by its lexically transformed reincarnation i.e., 'selfobject' (Kohut, 1971, 1977). In this latter self psychological view, a 'selfobject' refers to any object that is (1) not felt as having intentionality and agency separate from oneself, and (2) primarily useful in supporting the cohesion and vitality of the self. Ernest Wolf (1994) categorized 'selfobjects' into mirroring, idealizable, alter-ego, and adversarial types. All of them help to sustain the vitality of the self though by the differing means of affirmation, offering glory to bask in, twinship, and invigorating opposition, respectively. The need for such experiences is not restricted to formative years and extends over the entire life span. In the clinical situation, the activation of such needs gives rise to 'selfobject transferences.

Self-object: see 'Selfobject'.

Self-object transferences: see 'Narcissistic transferences'.

Self preservatory instinct: see 'Ego instincts'.

Self psychology: a perspective on personality development and functioning evolved by Heinz Kohut (1971, 1977). In his own words, the designation 'self psychology' can be used in a 'narrow sense' or 'broad sense' (1977, p. 207). The former usage refers to his views in *The Analysis of the Self* (1971). The innovations introduced there were still within the framework of classical theory. Some conceptual discomfort was, however, palpable. The concept of a 'narcissistic libido' that is totally independent of 'object libido' was, on the one hand, an accommodation of the traditional drive model and, on the other, a departure from it. While employing energic concepts, it bifurcated the classical libido theory into two independent developmental lines, one leading to object love and the other to healthy self-regard. This 'psychology of the self in the narrow sense of the term' (Kohut, 1977, p. 207) regarded self as a content of the mental apparatus, that is, as mental representations within the id, ego, and superego. The concept of the Oedipus complex, the central shibboleth of 'classical' analysis, was retained, though with diminished emphasis; it was seen as a parallel development to the narcissistic consolidation of the self. In a subsequent monograph titled *Restoration of the Self* (1977), Kohut proposed his self-psychology in the 'broad sense' (p. 207), and this is the manner in which the term is currently used. In this perspective, self is viewed as a superordinate constellation with its own developmental aims and objectives. Tripartite structure of the mind is discarded and so is the Oedipus complex. With this shift, Kohut's language also underwent a dramtic change. He labelled instinctual drive as 'a vague and insipid biological concept' (1982, p. 401) and triumphantly declared that 'self psychology has freed itself from the distorted view of psychological man espoused by traditional analysis' (1982, p. 402). All this had technical implications. A noticeable shift from sceptical listening and interpretation to credulous listening and affirmation resulted. Empathy was elevated from being a necessary tool for analytic work to its main intervention. In Arnold Rothstein's (1980) clever play on the title of the two Kohut monographs, 'analysis' turned into 'restoration'. With these developments, there was a threatened break of Kohut and his followers from the mainstream psychoanalysis. However the contemporary vulnerability of the profession could ill afford such a major split within its ranks. A growing spirit of theoretical pluralism also facilitated a conciliatory stance (Bacal, 1987; Bach, 1985; Pine, 1988, 1997; Wallerstein, 1983) towards the latter-day Kohut. Some tempering of his ideas by his own followers (e.g., Wolf, 1994) also helped. Currently, the self-based perspective, with its focus on coherence, agency, efficacy, and vitality, forms one among the other vantage points (e.g., drive-based motivation, ego psychology, object relations) in clinical and theoretical aspects of psychoanalysis.

Self regulation: according to Robert Emde (1988), 'self regulation' is one of the 'basic motives of infancy'; the other three being 'activity', 'affective monitoring', and 'social fittedness' (see separate entries on each). 'Self regulation' refers to the tendency and capacity for maintaining or restoring the baseline functional integrity during environmental perturbations. The capacities for 'arousal, attentiveness, and sleep-wakefulness cycles, and in the long-term sense, for growth and vital developmental functions' (p. 29) are thus maintained admist change. Clearly the notions of 'resilience' and 'self-righting' are of pertinence in this context (see separate entries on each).

Self representation: coined by Heinz Hartmann (1950) and elucidated in detail by Edith Jacobson (1954, 1964), the term 'self-representation' is meant to denote the 'unconscious, preconscious, and conscious endopsychic representations of the bodily and the mental self in the system ego' (Jacobson, 1964, p. 19). By definition, a 'self-representation' is a subjective view of the self which may or may not correspond with the other's more objective assessment of the subject's self. During early infancy, 'self-representation' is fleeting and ill-synthesized. However, within increasing ego consolidation and drive-differentiation, 'self-representations' become organized as clusters under libidinal and aggressive drives. Still later, 'pooled self-representations' (Spiegel, 1959) yield composition and unified identity; this structure of 'self constancy' (see separate entry) shows minimal fluctuations under drive pressures (Kernberg, 1967, 1976a; Mahler, Pine, & Bergman, 1975). However, the coalescence of different self-representations does not mean that they cannot come apart under states of aggression or that, at a deeper level, some self-representations continue to exist closer to affect and action potential than others (Eisnitz, 1980).

Self-righting: borrowing the term from the renowned embryologist, Conrad Waddington

(1947), Joseph Lichtenberg (1989) elucidated the concept of 'self-righting' in the context of child development. According to him, 'self-righting refers to an inherent tendency to rebound from a deficit with a developmental advance when a positive change in an inhibiting external condition occurs' (p. 328). Once the environmental conditions have become friendlier, children try to make up for lost time by seeking and creating positive experiences and interactions. Lichtenberg (1989) emphasized that, although most illustrations of 'self-righting' are selected from child observational studies, the fact is that 'self-righting' continues to be an important psychic attribute throughout out life. Pertinent to this conceptualization are Donald Winnicott's (1956a) seeing the 'antisocial tendency'; (see separate entry) as a sign of hope, Marian Tolpin's (1986) regarding the evocation of useful responses from needed selfobjects as integral to self-improvement, and Patrick Casement's (1991) emphasizing that 'repetition compulsion' (see separate entry) invariably contains a modicum of hidden optimism in it. Together, all these notions underscore that, given a chance, human beings will seek to rectify deficits and resume the proper course of development. Sigmund Freud's statement that the 'ego instincts' (see separate entry) were 'self-seeking' (1908c, p. 212) and 'self preservative' (1909b, p. 44) was an early declaration of the same sort.

Self state dreams: see 'State-of-affairs dreams'.

Self seeking instinct: see 'Ego instincts'.

Semi-circle of mental health: phrase coined by Heniz Kohut (1982) in the context of distinguishing his proposed nuclear conflict of human psyche from the centrality of the Oedipus complex in 'classical' psychoanalysis. Kohut derived the phrase 'semi-circle of mental health' from the ancient Greek tale of Odysseus, who was feigning insanity to avoid serving in a war. When the officials came to enforce his compliance, they found him ploughing a field dressed outrageously and behaving in an odd manner. One of the officials picked up Odysseus' infant son and threw him in the way of the former's advancing plough. Upon this, Odysseus immediately made a semi-circle to avoid injuring his child. This showed the officials that he was not 'crazy'. Kohut found this to be a fitting symbol for the joyful human awareness of generational continuity and the tenderness that ensues from it. Juxtaposing the emblem of 'semi-circle of mental health' with Sigmund Freud's (1910h, 1912a, 1924d) Oedipus complex, Kohut declared that 'it is the primacy of the support for the succeeding generation which is normal and human and not intergenerational strife and mutual wishes to kill and destroy' (p. 404). He then underscored that even the actual beginnings of the story of King Oedipus contained his rejection by his parents. The parricide and incest which have been taken to be the central elements of this tale are actually tragic byproducts of the failure of the parents of Oedipus to have the generosity and affection towards a child that is typified by the 'semi-circle of mental health'.

Sense of a core self: according to Daniel Stern (1985), this forms the second step in the formation of the infant's self; the first being the 'sense of an emergent self' (see separate entry). The 'sense of a core self' begins at two to three months of age and is manifest via a greater sense of ownership and agency of one's action and a more active and coherent engagement with the interpersonal surroundings. Stern challenges the view that, from the second to seventh or ninth month, the infant is in a state of symbiosis with the mother and only slowly emerges from that enmeshment (Mahler, Pine, & Bergman, 1975). He proposes that forming a 'core self' is the infant's first order of business, and emergence of such a self happens earlier. His timetable 'reverses the sequencing of developmental tasks: first comes the formation of self and other, and then is the sense of merger-like experience possible' (p. 70). Stern goes on to delineate the four axes around which an organized 'sense of a core self' emerges. These include (1) *self agency* (a growing sense of authorship of one's actions and non-authorship of those of others); (2) *self-coherence* (an experience of being whole and centred); (3) *self-affectivity* (experiencing patterns of emotions); and (4) *self-history* (feeling a sense of continuity in one's experience, a sense of the enduring nature of subjectivity). According to Stern, the 'sense of core self' results from the 'integration of these four basic self-experiences into a social subjective perspective' (p. 71). Besides such consolidation of the self as opposed to other, there are also developments *with* others that contribute to the sense of core self. Interactions with others that evoke a sense of aliveness, excitement, and vitality, both as an object of their gaze, so to speak, and as a subject with changing feelings which, owing to their repetition, become increasingly familiar. Such 'core relatedness' and the rapidly developing bridges between the infant's and mother's subjective worlds also enrich the infant's 'sense of core self'.

Sense of an emergent self: according to Daniel Stern (1985), the human infant shows a qualitative change from a 'presocial, precognitive, preorganized lfe phase' (p. 37) at about two months of age. The infant begins to make direct eye to eye contact, smile responsively, coo, and visually scan the environment on a more alert basis. Stern proposes that, before this shift takes place, the infant is actively forming a 'sense of an emergent self'. This includes both the product and the process of establishing links between isolated and scattered experiences. The mental processes involved in such construction are (1) *a-modal perception* (an innate capacity to receive information in one sensory modality and translate it into another); (2) *physiognomic perception* (direct emotional conclusions drawn in relation to the human face); and (3) *vitality affects* (emotional experiences associated with the daily processes of living and interactions with caretakers). Together, these processes contribute to a global subjective world of emerging organization.

Sense of a subjective self: this contributes the third step in Daniel Stern's (1985) delineation of the formation of the infant's self; the first and second being the 'sense of an emergent self' and the 'sense of a core self', respectively (see separate entries). Stern places the occurrence of this third step somewhere between the seventh and the ninth month of life. The essence of this development is the 'momentous realization that inner subjective experiences, the "subject matter" of the mind, are potentially sharable with someone else' (p. 124). From this point onwards, the infant's relationships are no longer restricted to his or other's behaviour, but also include the subjective experience of the two partners as well. A new domain of 'intersubjective relatedness' is thus born. Core-relatedness and intersubjective relatedness now coexist and interact. Capacity for genuine psychic intimacy arrives on the horizon. 'What is ultimately at stake is nothing less than discovery of what part of the private world of experience is sharable and what part falls outside the pole of commonly recognized human experience. At one end is psychic human membership, at the other psychic isolation' (p. 126). Needs for security—itself derived from attachment—reinforce the intersubjective dialogue typical of this phase of development.

Sense of a verbal self: this constitutes the fourth and final step in Daniel Stern's (1985) scheme of the development of the infant's self, the other three being the 'sense of an emergent self', 'sense of a core self', and 'sense of a subjective self', in that order (see separate entries). This fourth step is taken during the second year of life and coincides with the appearance of language. This gives the child a tool for further organizing his experience and to be with others in newer ways. However, as Stern notes, language is a double-edged sword. On the one hand, it facilitates communication with others and, by the act of verbally labelling and sorting out experiences, increases self-knowledge. On the other hand, the experiences in the domains of the three earlier modes of self and their relatedness often escape the grasp of spoken words. The linguistic self is thus both more related to, and more alienated from, others. Moreover, the advent of language enhances the capacity for symbolic thinking and imaginative constructions; these, in turn, can serve the purposes of wishful neurotic formations, or creativity, or both.

Separateness anxiety: see 'Separation anxiety'.

Separation anxiety: phenomenon described by Margaret Mahler (1965, 1968) and her colleagues (Mahler, Pine, & Bergman, 1975) in connection with the growing child's psychic differentiation from the mother. The loss of erstwhile symbiotic 'dual unity' (see separate entry) resulted in the threat of disorganization; this, in turn, mobilized the need to return to the mother for 'emotional refuelling' (see separate entry). Gradually, this anxiety diminished and the internalization of a more sustained image of mother became the source of psychic strength. The term 'separation anxiety', coined in this particular context, became a bit too 'popular'. Clinicians began using it for any sign of nervousness shown by an analysand who was facing a separation from his or her analyst. In sorting out this conundrum, Fred Pine (1979) emphasized that all anxiety at separation is not 'separation anxiety'. For instance, a patient who feels anxious upon learning of his analyst's vacation may be responding to a drive upsurge consequent upon the removal of an externalized superego, or he may be responding to an anticipated incoherence and disorganization of the self. The former anxiety is precipitated by separation but is not really 'separation anxiety'. Similarly, the anxiety stirred up at termination of analysis is not true 'separation anxiety', since such separation is from a well-differentiated object. 'Separation anxiety' involves a relationship with an undifferentiated other and is therefore 'separateness anxiety' or an 'anxiety over the sense of separateness' (p. 230).

Separation–individuation: term given by Margaret Mahler (Mahler, 1968, Mahler, Pine, & Bergman, 1975) to the four-step process (differen-

tiation, practising, rapprochement, on the road to object constancy) by which the infant emerges from existential symbiosis with the mother to develop his psychic separateness and individuality. The two tracks (*separation* and *individuation*) are overlapping, but distinct. The former refers to the autonomy of ego function, the latter to the distinct and unique direction and texture of psychic contents. In the West, the two tracks are intertwined while in the East, considerable individuation is possible without comparable separation (Bonovitz, 1998). Separation–individuation is preceded by the 'symbiotic phase' (see separate entry) and spans from about 4–5 months of age to the early third year of life. It has four subphases. First among these is the *differentiation subphase* (from about 4–5 to 8–9 months), in which the child starts to learn about his psychological separateness through rudimentary explorations of the self as well as the mother's environment. Next is the *practising subphase* (from 9 to 16–18 months), in which the toddler elatedly enjoys his newfound psychomotor autonomy and appears to be involved in the 'conquest of the world'. Then comes the rapprochement subphase (from about 16 to about 24 months), in which the child learns that his separateness, autonomy, and motor abilities have their limits. The realities of the external world appear harsh and the child regresses in the hope of re-establishing the lost symbiotic bliss with the mother. This return, however, is ambivalent, since the drive of individuation is at work with greater force. The resulting 'ambitendency' accounts for the alternating cycles of dependence and flight characteristic of a child in this phase. If overcome, the rapprochement phase is followed by a period designated *on the road to object constancy*, in which a deeper, somewhat ambivalent, but more sustained object representation is internalized, the libidinal attachment to which does not become seriously compromised by temporary frustrations. This is accompanied by a more realistic and less shifting view of the self. The attainment of 'object constancy' assures the mother's lasting presence in the child's mental structure. The attainment of self constancy establishes a coherent, single self-representation with minimal fluctuations under drive pressures.

Septet of baby fears: Edmund Bergler's (1961) delineation of seven fears that a human infant is subject to: (1) fear of starvation, (2) fear of being eaten, (3) fear of being poisoned, (4) fear of being choked, (5) fear of being chopped to pieces, (6) fear of being drained, and (7) fear of being castrated. According to Bergler, the infant responds to these fears by anger but, unwilling to attack his mother, discharges this anger upon himself. This forms the earliest basis of the masochistic propensity in human beings.

Sequence constancy: see 'Spatial representations'.

Severe personality disorders: this broad rubric includes narcissistic, borderline, schizoid, antisocial, paranoid, histrionic ('infantile'), and hypomanic characters. Individuals with this group of personality disorders show overt and covert symptoms in six areas of psychosocial functioning: self-concept; interpersonal relations; social adaptation; ethics, standards, and ideals; love and sexuality; and cognitive style. Overt and covert designations in this context do not imply conscious or unconscious existence, although such topographical distribution might exist. In general, these designations denote contradictory phenomenological aspects that are more or less discernible. This manner of organizing the symptomology emphasizes the centrality of splitting and identity diffusion (Akhtar, 1984, 1992b; Kernberg, 1975, 1984) in these conditions.

Sexual deviations: while Krafft-Ebing (1892) and Havelock Ellis (1894) had catalogued 'sexual deviations' or 'perversions' in great detail, Sigmund Freud (1905a) provided a comprehensive theoretical substrate to their development. He posited that adult sexuality emerges only gradually, and does so by the confluence of 'component instincts' under the dominance of 'genital primacy' (see separate entries). When this fails to occur and the aims of a partial instinct (e.g., biting, looking, smelling, inflicting pain) establish an erotic fiefdom of their own, the result is a perversion. The individual thus afflicted begins to draw major sexual gratification from the pre-genital aims, which constitute only a part of foreplay for his more fortunate counterparts. Even when such total replacement of genital sexual pleasure by pre-genital acts does not take place, the latter becomes a mandatory condition for arousal and orgasm in genital intimacy. Such 'sexual deviation' could result from fixation upon pre-genital aims (e.g., voyeurism, exhibitionism) or from the choice of inappropriate sexual objects (e.g., children, animals). Later, Freud (1927c) added the psychic inability (in fact, anxiety-based refusal) to accept anatomical difference between the sexes lay at the root of all sexual deviations; in this scheme, 'fetishism' (see separate entry) was accorded the status of perversion *par excellence*. With the assimilation of his idea that overcoming the Oedipus complex and establishing the incest barrier (Freud, 1924d, 1925j) was integral to 'mature love' (see separate entry) into the analytic perspective on 'sexual deviations', refinement of what actually constituted a 'perversion' occurred. The advent of the 'object relations theory' (see separate entry) also helped in this regard. The contemporary position on 'sexual deviations' is the composite result of these developments. In today's psychoanalytic understanding, a perversion displays an admixture of pre-genital drive fixation, defensive or counterphobic warding off of castration anxiety, disturbed intrapsychic generational boundaries, incapacity for genuine and deep relations with whole objects, and a dramatized reversal of real and imagined childhood trauma and over-stimulation with the help of disavowal of reality and splitting of aggression. Among the psychoanalysts who have made the most significant contributions to the understanding of 'sexual deviations' are William Gillespie (1952, 1956a,b), Robert Stoller (1975), Masud Khan (1979), Janine Chasseguet-Smirgel (1984), and Charles Socarides (1988). On a phenomenological level, it is now generally agreed upon that perverse fantasies are universal, perverse behaviour frequent, and that these occur along the spectrum of psychopathology, ranging from neurosis through character disorders to psychosis.

Sexual dysfunction: while greater attention was paid during the early days of psychoanalysis to specific symptoms involving sexual life (Abraham, 1917; Ferenczi, 1925b; Fenichel, 1945; Greenacre, 1950), the contemporary attitude is to view 'sexual dysfunction' like anything else, i.e., multiply-determined and existing in the larger biopsychosocial context of the individual. The explosion of knowledge regarding the scope and diversity of 'normal' sexual practices that resulted from the publication of the Kinsey report (1948, 1953) and the gradual shift of psychoanalysis from its psychosexual theory base to a more object relational perspective led to the diminution of interest in specific sexual symptoms. Three broad categories along a spectrum of increasing severity of psychopathology continue to be recognized: (1) *disorders of sexual satisfaction*, which involve the inability to achieve orgasm; these are often related to technical clumsiness (e.g., abbreviated foreplay), neurotic inhibitions (e.g., due to guilty equation of orgasm with oedipal triumph), and narcissistic resistances (e.g., refusal to give the partner the gratification of having brought one to climax); (2) *disorders of sexual performance*, which include psychogenic vaginismus in women, erectile dysfunction and premature ejaculation in men; these and other inhibitions and anxieties affecting lovemaking generally arise out of oedipal fixations, castration anxiety, and guilt, though sexual inexperience and cultural injunctions against sexual pleasure can also play a role in their genesis; (3) *disorders of sexual desire*, which range from total absence of erotic longing to ravaging hunger and 'sex addiction'. These conditions usually reflect deep disturbances in the early mother–child relationship. In assessing 'sexual dysfunction', the important things to keep in mind are the following: (1) biological factors, (2) cultural attitudes, (3) the extent of sexual experience, and (4) the 'fit' between partners in terms of their preferences and proficiencies. It should be remembered that an overwhelmed ego (e.g., during grief) and secretly brewing hostility within the dyad are frequent contributors to 'sexual dysfunction'. These ideas are derived from the work of many psychoanalysts, which include Burness Moore (1964), Gustav Bychowski (1963), Ralph Fishkin (cited in Ficher, Fishkin, & Jacobs, 1984), and Otto Kernberg (1995a).

Sexual instinct: in his first dual instinct theory, Sigmund Freud (1905a, 1915c) juxtaposed 'sexual instinct' with the self-preservatory 'ego instinct'. In his second dual instinct theory, he (1920g) placed these two instincts under 'life instinct' which, in turn, he paired with 'death instinct' (see 'instinct theory' for details). In either case, 'sexual instinct' remained a powerful explanatory force for a wide range of motivations, gratifications, fantasies, and behaviours. Among its most important characteristics are the following: (1) it is fuelled by an energy called 'libido'; (2) its source is constituted by various 'erogenous zones' which acquire psychic dominance according to a pre-programmed epigenetic schedule; (3) because of its varied somatic origins, the aims of this instinct are diverse; (4) it is constituted by 'component instincts', which only gradually come to lie under the dominance of 'genital primacy'; (5) the rudimentary and part-object relations associated with the early working of component sexual instincts slowly give way to deeper and whole object relationships and the capacity for 'mature love'; and (6) while sexual instinct does use 'aggression' for its purposes, an admixture of the two under the dominance of the latter gives rise to 'sadism' and 'masochism' (see separate entries on the terms in quotation marks).

Sexualization: while not listed in other psychoanalytic glossaries (Eidelberg, 1968; English & English, 1958; Laplanche & Pontalis, 1973; Moore & Fine, 1968, 1990), the term 'sexualization' is too frequently used by psychoanalysts to be ignored. Otto Fenichel (1945) employed it in connection with stuttering and intellectual inhibitions. He declared that 'the sexualization of the function of thinking always has special anal connotations' (p. 181). This type of use of the term implies that sexualization refers to finding sexual pleasure in non-sexual activities and then reacting to its presence by counter-cathexis. An additional sense in which Fenichel used the term pertains to the 'sexualization of fear' (p. 483). Here a displeasure turns into a source of erotic excitement. 'Sexualization' thus seems to have two meanings. One involves an inferred unconscious investment and the other a conscious sexual pleasure in non-sexual situations.

Shadowing and darting away: during the rapprochement subphase (from 14–15 months to about 24 months of age), at times the child follows his or her mother's every single move. In other words, he or she 'shadows' her and seems unable to let her out of sight and/or the immediate vicinity. At other times, however, the child displays the exactly opposite behaviour. He or she 'darts away' and waits for the mother to swoop him or her up in her arms. Both 'shadowing' and 'darting away' are intended to undo the feeling of separateness on the psychological level (Mahler, Pine, & Bergman, 1975).

Shame: refers to a painful experience which can be broken down into five components: (1) collapse of self-esteem, (2) feeling of humiliation, (3) rupture of self-continuity, whereby what one was, in one's mind, a moment ago is experientially lost, (4) sense of isolation and standing apart from the group, and (5) feeling of being watched by critical others. 'Shame' originates in shocked and disbelieving parental responses to ordinary psychomotor failures, social clumsiness, and loss of control during the early formative years. Too dramatic a response to a child's ego advancements can also increase self consciousness painfully and lay the groundwork for future vulnerability to 'shame'. In essence, the genesis of 'shame' boils down to how the discontinuities within the evolving self are handled by the child's parents. Sudden increase in the gap between actual and wishful self-representations can also fill one up with 'shame'. Unlike 'guilt' (see separate entry) which is predominately auditory, 'shame' is predominately visual. Guilt pushes for confession and shame pushes for hiding and concealment. Defences against shame involve narcissistic self-inflation and turning passive into active by shaming others, distortion of reality by lying and 'sliding of meanings' (Horowitz, 1975) of events and/or of one's statements, and withdrawal into a narcissistc cocoon. These important insights in the nature of 'shame' and their technical implications are to be found in the works of Roy Grinker, Sr (1955), Sidney Levin (1967, 1971), Moshe Halevi Spero (1984), Andrew Morrison (1989), Samuel Abrams (1990), Leon Wurmser (1994), and Benjamin Kilborne (2005).

Shared ethnic scotoma: Edith Shapiro and Henry Pinsker's (1973) phrase for blind spots in the therapeutic alliance and countertransference collusions with the patient when the therapist and the patient are the same ethnicity; under such circumstances, deeper understanding of the patient's psychopathology can suffer and aggression can be displaced on to ethniculturally different ones.

Shared implicit relationship: term used by Daniel Stern and colleagues (1998) for the existence of 'implicit relational knowing' (see separate entry) of each other on the part of both the analyst and the analysand. Such knowledge exists parallel to, but apart from, their respective technical 'roles' and their connection via the transference–countertransference axis. While one partner's implicit knowledge about the relationship might be different from that of the other, it is the area of their overlap that is of crucial significance. This is because it is only in the crucible of a 'shared implicit relationship' that the mutative 'moments of meeting' (see separate entry) arise.

Shared meanings : see ' We-ness'.

Shift in time perspective: Elliot Jaques' (1965) and Otto Kernberg's (1980) reminder that with the arrival of midlife, the individual becomes aware that more of life has gone and less is still to be lived. Increased understanding of one's now ageing parents and a renewed emotional contact with one's own childhood and youth strengthens the 'temporal continuity of the self' (Erik Erikson, 1950) and prepares one for having a vision for the future. Time enters life experience in a new, deep, and permanent way.

Shinkeishitsu personality: a syndrome of psychopathology first described by Shoma Morita (1960), the Japanese founder of 'Morita Therapy'. The 'Shinkeishitsu personality', is characterized by self-blame for symptoms of extreme perfectionism and hypersensitivity to oneself and others. An obsessional nucleus is covered over by a mildly masochistic persona. Anal fixation is prominent and the superego is harsh.

Shy narcissist: Salman Akhtar's (2000) designation for a less-recognized type of narcissistic character whose grandiose aspirations are largely covert. Like the ordinary narcissist, the shy narcissist is ambitious, involved with fantasies of glory and fame, and defective in his capacity for empathy with others. Unlike the usual narcissist, the shy narcissist appears modest and superficially uninterested in social success. He also possesses a stricter conscience. He feels gnawing remorse at his oedipal transgressions and at his incapacity to feel for others. Consequently, he is forever helpful to them. Unlike the ordinary narcissist, who discards others after having used them, the shy narcissist is capable of feeling grateful and offering reparations to them. The strict conscience responsible for this also pushes his grandiosity and ambitiousness into hiding. Unlike the usual narcissist, who feels humiliated upon the exposure of his blemishes, the shy narcissist experiences shame upon the unmasking of his secret grand plans. Indeed, he might live them out by playing 'second fiddle' to someone whose success he has himself silently engineered. Glen Gabbard's (1989) 'hypervigilant' type, James Masterson's (1993) 'closet' type, and Winslow Hunt's (1995) 'diffident' type of narcissistic personalities are subsumed under the broader rubric of the 'shy narcissist'. Akhtar (2000) underscores the possibility of constitutional shyness and cultural premium on modesty as possible vectors that shift the ordinary narcissistic phenomenology in the direction of reticence.

Sibling loss: the death of a sibling, both during childhood and adult life, can have a powerful impact upon the psyche. This impact is more marked when the siblings are twins (Engel, 1975), are close because they lack parents (Kramer & Akhtar, 1999), or one has had marked death wishes towards the other. Of historical as well as psychodynamic significance in this last mentioned context are Sigmund Freud's reactions to the death of his younger brother, Julius (Agger, 1988; Blum, 1999). In a fascinating paper, Peter Rudnytsky (1988) has compared and contrasted Freud's reactions with those of Harry Guntrip's, who had also lost a brother in childhood.

Sibling relationship: Sigmund Freud (1900a) noted that 'the elder child ill-treats the younger, maligns him and robs him of his toys; while the younger is consumed with impotent rage against the elder, envies him and fears him, or meets his oppressor with the first stirrings of a love of liberty and the sense of justice' (p. 202). Despite Freud's eloquence, 'sibling relationship' did not receive much attention from subsequent analysts. Feelings and fantasies involving siblings were regarded by then as mere displacements from the relationship with parents. Gradually, however, analysts began to realize that the 'sibling relationship' can have meanings and effects of its own (Colonna & Newman, 1983; Neubauer, 1983; Balsam, 1988, 1989; Parens, 1999; Provence & Solnit, 1983; Kernberg & Richards, 1988; Shapiro, 1999; Solnit, 1983; Volkan & Ast, 1997). While a panoply of emotional configurations, including 'twinning reactions', 'womb fantasies', and 'oedipal sibling triangles' (see separate entries for each) were described, the one that has received the most attention is 'sibling rivalry'. This consists of aggressive competition between siblings for the love of their parents. Selma Kramer and Salman Akhtar (1999) have delineated *eight factors* that determine the extent of sibling rivalry and, indeed, the overall flavour of relationship between siblings. These factors include (1) parental availability, (2) relationship between parents, (3) parental behaviour towards their children, (4) twinship, (5) sex of the siblings, (6) age difference or, more importantly, the 'developmental distance' (Solnit, 1983) between siblings, (7) their birth order, and (8) the existence of something 'special' (extraordinary talent or, conversely, an illness) in a sibling.

Sibling rivalry: see 'Sibling relationship'.

Sibling transferences: the early psychoanalytic inclination to regard all transferences of the analysand to be replications of real or imagined scenarios (or defences against them) involving parents has given way to the recognition that early relationships with siblings can play an independent role in generating transference phenomena. Such 'sibling transferences' might involve the narcissistic search for a twin (see 'Twinship transference') or, more often, the usual themes of envy, jealousy, and rivalry that prevail in relationships between brothers and sisters (Neubauer, 1983; Akhtar & Kramer, 1999). On the other hand, there might be an oedipal colouring to these transferences. In that case, the distinction between 'oedipal sibling triangles' (see separate entry) from the usual oedipal triangle involving parents becomes a matter of vital clinical importance.

Sibling triangle: see 'Oedipal sibling triangles'.

Signal affects: see 'Signal anxiety'.

Signal anxiety: Sigmund Freud's (1926d) term for the vague feeling of dread experienced in anticipation of an intrapsychic danger. 'Signal anxiety' is different from fear, which is a response to an

actual threat emanating from external reality. It is also different from 'automatic anxiety' (see separate entry), which results from overstimulation that overwhelms the immature ego and cannot be managed by it. 'Signal anxiety' is subclinical in threshold and serves as a trigger for mobilizing ego defences. While Freud had only referred to anxiety as serving this function, later analysts (Klein, 1935; Jacobson, 1994) pointed out that rage, shame, and depressive emotions can also function as 'signal affects'.

Signifier: Jacques Lacan's (1977) term for a linguistic element (e.g., a syllable, word, or phrase) that gives meaning to that which is signified by it. However, objects, relationships, and acts can also serve as 'signifiers'. 'The single condition which characterizes something as a signifier, for Lacan, is that it is inscribed in a system in which it takes on value purely by virtue of its difference from the other elements in the system' (Evans, 1996, p. 187). Since all psychic systems are context-bound, internally or externally, and therefore forever shifting, a 'signifier' can never have a single or fixed meaning.

Silence: in light of the fact that psychoanalytic treatment relies upon the patient's free associations and the analyst's spoken interventions, it is not surprising that silence during the sessions has mostly been considered a resistance to its progress. However, silence can also be a form of communication (Khan, 1963b). Like any other psychological phenomenon, silence is multiply determined. Silence can deplete the ego by banishing useful psychic content into the unconscious, or it can replenish the ego by permitting quiet, preconscious synthesis of subclinical conflicts (Shafii, 1973). It can serve primarily the function of defence or primarily the function of discharge (Zeligs, 1960). As a result, silence can represent (1) *unconscious resistance*, (2) *deliberate withholding*, (3) *a form of communication* (Leira, 1995), (4) *transference of defence*, (5) *enactment of fantasies* (e.g., those involving identification with a stubbornly silent parent, or playing possum to avoid an imagined murderous assault from the analyst), (6) *sadistic attack on the analyst or on the analytic process*, (7) *moment of hesitation* (Winnicott, 1960), (8) *contemplation*, and (9) *genuinely blank, contentless states of mind* (Khan, 1983b). Jacob Arlow (1961), in a seminal paper on this topic, concludes that there are no set rules of technique to deal with a patient's silence. 'Nothing can replace the sensitivity of the therapist nor his empathic response to the unfolding concatenation of influences at any moment in the transference' (p. 53).

Arlow goes on to say that there are silences that need (1) interpretation of the discharge tendencies contained in them, (2) interpretation of the defensive function of the ego, and (3) to be simply respected as such. Nina Coltart (2000) has also written meaningfully on dealing with the 'silent patient', and, more recently, Elsa Ronningstam (2006) has provided a thought-provoking update on the clinical and cultural aspect of silence.

Silence in the service of ego: see 'Silence'.

Silent patient: see 'Silence'.

Simple and complex selves: two dynamic levels of self-functioning described by Christopher Bollas (1992). 'The simple experiencing self and the complex reflecting self enable the person to process life according to different yet interdependent modes of engagement: one immersive, the other reflective' (p. 15). The aim of the 'simple self' is to experience, fully and deeply, what is offered from within or outside. The aim of the 'complex self' is to reflect on that experience and objectify it. In life, one moves back and forth between these two states. At times one is self-observant and, at another time, one yields to wordless experience. In some people, the observing tendency is more developed; in others, the experiencing tendency is. The former narrow their lives and avoid situational triggers to spontaneous unfolding of the intrapsychic. The latter actively 'seek objects with evocative integrity that challenge and stretch the self' (p. 31).

Simple self: see 'Simple amd complex selves'

Sinking feeling: in a contribution on the 'sinking feeling' or the 'hollow in the pit of the stomach', John Hitchcock (1984) suggests that it reflects the acceptance of a repudiated piece of reality and that 'this event, while manifested at any libidinal level of organization, has separation as a common denominator' (p. 328). Essentially, the 'sinking feeling' is a 'screen sensation' (see separate entry) and serves simultaneously as a somatic defence and a somatic recall of experiences of separation and loss.

Sita–Shakti: concept originated by Jaswant Guzder and Meenakshi Krishna (1991, 2005) to elucidate the duality inherent in mature female identity. Guzder and Krishna note that, in Hindu mythology, femininity is represented with two deities: Sita and Shakti. Sita, the heroine of the great epic Ramayana, is not only nurturant and generative but also—by following her husband,

Lord Rama—is a positive ego-ideal in the realm of gender identity. In contrast, Shakti, the consort of Lord Shiva, is transgressive , dangerous, phallic, and at times, even castrating. The figures of both Sita and Shakti, however, contain hidden qualities of the opposite nature. Sita can be quite wilful and Shakti profoundly protective. The two imagos are not split off from each other like the 'Madonna–whore' bifurcation of the West or like the 'good' and 'bad' breasts of the Kleinian pantheon. Indeed, it is the existence of duality that underscores the richness of female identity and provides a conduit for finer integration of self-representations during a girl's development.

Sitting in judgement: see 'Delusion of clarity of insight'.

Skin colour anxiety: phrase coined by Marjorie McDonald (1970) to denote that a dark-skinned child in a predominately white society might experience a sense of inordinate difference from others and thus feel distressed. While plausible, this explanation needs broadening along the following lines: (1) exposure to parents and other relatives of a particular skin colour during childhood lays down a dermatological 'waking screen' (see separate entry) against which other's complexion is assessed as familiar or different; this contributes to the early foundations of 'xenophobia' (see separate entry); (2) a child who feels unloved by his parents, especially the mother, might project that sense upon others and find his different skin colour as a rationalization for it ('They do not like me because I have a different skin colour') or, the child might turn the aggression upon his own self ('I am not good enough because I have this or that skin colour'). In the end, what seems to matter is the sense of safety and love provided by the child's family and the manner in which the society looks upon skin colour differences. Clearly, Sigmund Freud's celebrated statement that 'anatomy is destiny' (1924d, p. 178) only reflects one half of the truth; how 'anatomy' is handled by early caretakers and by the society at large constitutes the other half of the equation. The clinical significance of skin colour has recently been elucidated by Pratyusha Tummala-Narra (2007).

Slips of the tongue: see 'Parapraxis'.

Smell: that the function of smell is of considerable psychological significance is evident in *six different ways*: (1) smell plays an important role in infant–mother bonding; neonates smile when made to smell a vial containing milk squeezed from their

267

mother's breast while remaining indifferent to one containing another woman's milk, (2) the anal phase toddler's fascination with faeces extends to flatus and faecal smells; other bodily odours can later be enlisted for expressing anal phase conflicts and regressions, (3) urethral, vaginal, and phallic sensations and fantasies of childhood also contain a dimension of smell, (4) smell can also acquire intense romantic and sexual (especially during foreplay) connotations, (5) regression during paranoid schizophrenia is often associated with olfactory hallucinations, and (6) finally, smells associated with the environmental surroundings of one's childhood and youth often retain a powerful potential to trigger feelings of nostalgia among immigrants. In light of such multifaceted psychological importance of smell, it is suprising to note that psychoanalytic literature on the topic is meagre. Sigmund Freud noted that (1) smell and memory are often connected (1895d), (2) repressed 'coprophilic pleasure in smelling' (1905a, p. 151) contributes to the formation of fetish objects, and (3) civilization drives the pleasure in smelling faeces underground (1920g), leading to defensive disgust and/or overvaluation of 'good' smells. Among other psychoanalysts who have contributed to this topic are the Father of Indian psychoanalysis, Girindrashekhar Bose (1921), as well as Abraham Brill (1932), Paul Friedman (1959), and Jean Rosenbaum (1961); the last mentioned especially elucidated the role of olfactory sensations in clinical transferences.

Smiling response: term originated by René Spitz (1950) to denote the appearance of social smiling around the second or third month of life. Smiling in response to social interactions differs from endogenous smiling, which is present from birth. At first, the 'smiling response' can be elicited by presenting the infant with the gestalt of the human face in the form of a drawing. Soon, the mother becomes the most reliable elicitor of such smiling. Spitz regarded 'smiling response' to be a turning point in the infant's development and called it the 'first organizer of the psyche', as it implied a greater ego organization, beginning capacity for object relations, and the onset of some internal regulation of affects (see also the related entry on 'organizers of the psyche').

Social-fittedness: term coined by Robert Emde (1983, 1988) for the human neonate's pre-adapted stance for participating in human interactions. Among the capacities that are present at birth and facilitate such interactions are 'a propensity for participating in eye-to-eye contact; a state of responsivity for being activated and soothed by human holding, touching, and rocking; and a propensity for showing prolonged alert attentiveness to the stimulus features contained in the human voice and face' (p. 171). Such 'social fittedness' of the infant has a counterpart in the mother as well, who directs speech and gestures to her infant in a simple and repetitive pattern; this helps to establish a rudimentary sense of mutuality between them. Emde includes 'social fittedness' among the four 'basic motives of infancy'; the other three are 'activity', 'self regulation', and 'affective monitoring' (see separate entries on each).

Somatic compliance: term first used by Sigmund Freud in 1905 to underscore that hysterical conversion symptoms involve the participation of both the mind and body. The latter often shows a 'particular aptitude for signifying the repressed' (Laplanche & Pontalis, 1973, p. 423). Its actual vulnerabilities as well as its symbolic capacities can be enlisted by unconscious conflicts for their expression.

Somatization: term first used by Max Schur (1955) for the tendency to react to stressful stimuli by physical rather than psychological means. 'Somatization' encompasses both the highly symbolic pathways of conversion (see separate entry) and the more diffuse non-specific responses leading to psychosomatic disorders. Related concepts involve 'desomatization' (the growing child's replacing physical sensation by thought as a response to external stimuli) and 'resomatization' (movement in the opposite direction).

'Someday . . .' and 'If only . . .' fantasies: Salman Akhtar's (1996) designation for two fantasies that are ubiquitous in the human psyche but acquire tenacious and ego-depleting qualities in severe character pathology. The 'someday . . .' fantasy idealizes the future and propels either fierce ambition or a chronic attitude of waiting. The 'if only . . .' fantasy idealizes the past and lays the groundwork for nostalgia and regret. The two fantasies orginate in the narcissistic disequilibrium caused by early separation trauma, though the oedipal experience also contributes to them. Akhtar elucidated their metapsychology and phenomenology in detail, adding that six tasks are especially important in working with such material (1) providing a meaningful holding environment, (2) employing 'affirmative interventions' (see separate entry), (3) unmasking these fantasies and interpreting their defensive and instinctual aspects, (4) rupturing the patient's excessive hope and facilitating the mourning of this rupture, (5) reconstructing the origins of these fantasies, and (6) paying careful attention to the countertransference experience during this work. The work of Jacqueline Amati-Mehler and Simona Argentieri (1989) and Anna Potamianou (1992) on the defensive uses of hope is also pertinent in this context.

Soul murder: Leonard Shengold (1989) has traced the history of this term and made the most important contemporary contribution to the subject. According to him, 'soul murder' is a particular kind of traumatic experience resulting from repetitive and chronic overstimulation, alternating with emotional deprivation, that is deliberately brought about by another individual. Important components of such trauma are: (1) attack on the capacity for rational thought, (2) erasure of an individual's identity, and (3) brain-washing that leads to confusion in the victim's mind about what actually took place and that it was highly pathological. While 'soul murder' is frequent in the setting of torture and political imprisonment, the clinical situations associated with it arise from a child being cruelly treated by sadistic parents who often are paranoid, psychopathic, or psychotic themselves.

Source of the instinct: see 'Instinct'.

Spatial representations: in a paper outlining the close relationship between levels of psychological organization and the manner in which people perceive spatial relationships, David Roth and Sidney Blatt (1974) elucidated the concept of five 'spatial representations': (1) boundary constancy, (2) relation constancy, (3) sequence constancy, (4) object constancy, and (5) self constancy. The level to which these representations are developed gives valuable clues to the level of an individual's cognitive and psychostructural organization. A related contribution, not mentioned by the authors, is John Frosch's (1964) concept of 'reality constancy' (see separate entry). Also pertinent, are Oliver Flournoy's (1974) and Judit Szekacs (1985) views on spatial structures, and with a different slant, Thomas Wolman's (2007) essay on various human relationships with space.

Spatula game: a diagnostic technique evolved by Donald Winnicott (1941) while he was working as a paediatrican and had become qualified as a psychoanalyst. Essentially, the 'spatula game' consisted of putting a shiny spatula within easy reach of an infant and observing how he reacts to it. Under normal circumstances, the infant's response consisted of three steps: (1) noticing the the spatula, reaching for it, and then, in a 'moment of hesitation' gauging his mother's response, as if seeking her permission to proceed further; (2) picking the spatula up and mouthing it; and (3) dropping it, as if by mistake. If the spatula is offered again, the child is pleased and repeats the same sequence, though with greater intentionality. Absence or unevenness of this sequence suggests some disturbance within the infant or, more likely, within the infant–mother dyad.

Sphincter morality: term coined by Sandor Ferenczi (1925b) to denote a growing child's compliance with parental demands and expectations for proper control of excretory functions. Such compliance is largely in the service of gaining love and recognition from parents; it lacks a genuine anchor in one's own internal sense of reality and propriety in this regard. However, the achievement of 'sphincter morality' does indicate a certain degree of structure formation and can, therefore, be recognized as a early step in superego formation.

Spirituality, mysticism, and psychoanalysis: Sigmund Freud's (1930a) unease about the transcendent 'oceanic feeling' described to him by Romain Rolland, the French biographer of great Indian mystics Sri Ramakrishna Paramhansa and Swami Vivekauauda, led to a long chain of subservient psychoanalytic thinking which took Freud's atheism at face value and regarded psychoanalysis and religion (and mysticism and spirituality) as antagonistic. More recently, however, the trend has shifted. Doubts have been cast on Freud's avowed atheism (Nicholi, 2002; Akhtar, 2009b). Books, monographs, and papers have appeared on the concepts of 'God representation' (Rizzuto, 1979), 'faith' (Meissner, 1992a; Eigen, 1981), 'transference gods and gods of transference' (Rao, 2005), 'religious instinct' (Ostow, 1995, 2001), and mysticism (Meissner, 2005) and whether belief in God helps or not (Akhtar & Parens, 2001). While wide ranging, the discourse boils down to two important matters. The first pertains to the phenomenology of experiences variously labelled as 'religious', spiritual', 'divine', 'transcendent', or 'mystical'. The core of such descriptions involves selflessness, humility, and gratitude, as well as the feeling of being at one with the universe. On this first variable, there seems to be reasonable consensus. The second matter, namely, whether experiences of this sort are to be regarded as somehow different, or beyond psychoanalytic underrating, as it were, that is the source of contention. These experiences represent regressive reactivations of early states of mother–infant merger or defensive idealization against aggression. Or, are they genuinely transcendent and even suggestive of God's existence? A truly wise comment that can show one a path out of this conundrum, or at least help one bear the complexities involved more peacefully, has been made by highly respected New York based psychoanalyst, Sheldon Bach (1985). He says that 'whether such fantasies are viewed as defensive regressions or as creative expressions depends not only on whether one consults a psychiatrist or guru but also on the meaning of this experience in the context of the person's life, a complicated issue which forms part of a psychology as yet scarely begun of creative and mystical states. But perhaps we may assume that every narcissistic fantasy, omnipotent and transcendent as it may be, expresses in some distorted form an attainable human possibility as well as an unattainable divine one' (pp. 87–88).

Spirituality within sexuality: phrase originated by the Indian psychoanalyst, Sudhir Kakar, who has made wide-ranging contributions to the complex interface between psychoanalysis and cultural anthroplogy (1978, 1985, 1989a,b, 1995, 2001). Kakar's notion of 'spirituality within sexuality' emanates from the Hindu doctrine that, at its base, all desire and pleasure must be channelled towards achieving unity with the universe at large. According to Kakar (2001), this is 'a tradition which does not reduce sexual love to copulation but seeks to elevate it into a celebration, even a ritual that touches the partners with a sense of sacred, and where orgasm is experienced as a symbolic blessing of man by his ancestors and by the nature of things' (p. 250). Whether such an 'anagogic interpretation' (see separate entry) is a defensive idealization to ward off anxieties embedded in raw sexuality is certainly a fair question to ask. In her critical assessment of Kakar's corpus of work, Manasi Kumar (2005) links his 'spirituality within sexuality' notion with the more 'psychoanalytic' ideas of Ruth Stein (1988a,b) and André Green (2002).

Split treatment: 'Medication and psychoanalysis'.

Splitting: a term used by Sigmund Freud in many different ways. First, he spoke of 'splitting of consciousness' (1895d) to denote the alternating states of awareness in hysterical patients. Later, he described 'splitting of the ego' (1927c) in the fetishist who simultaneously acknowledged and disavowed the absence of the penis in women. Still later, Freud (1924f, 1940a [1938]) noted the existence of two contrary and independent attitudes in psychoses. One takes account of reality and the other, under the influence of the instincts, detaches the ego from reality. For an update on Freud's views on splitting, see Thierry Bokanowski and Sergio Lewkowicz (2009).

Splitting of self- and object-representations: in contrast to the above, the current use of the term 'splitting' is in connection with severe personality disorders. Some authors (e.g., Volkan, 1976) emphasize this distinction by labelling splitting, in this context, 'primitive splitting'. This view was developed by psychoanalysts who followed Freud: especially Melanie Klein (1935, 1940), Ronald Fairbairn (1952), Heinz Kohut (1971, 1977), Margaret Mahler (Mahler, Pine, & Bergman, 1975), and Otto Kernberg (1975, 1984). Mahler, for instance, observed that the collapse of the toddler's omnipotence during the rapprochement subphase, coupled with emotional unavailability of the mother, creates hostile dependency on the mother. The resulting intense ambivalence calls for keeping the 'good' and the 'bad' mother images apart, and is turning aggression against the self. This becomes the basis for habitually responding to stress with negative mood swings, as well as for the relentless pursuit of perfection in the self and/or others. According to Kernberg (1975), splitting begins as an inevitable means by which the infantile ego categorizes its pleasurable and unpleasurable experiences. Later, this same separation can come to serve a defensive purpose against intense ambivalence. 'This defensive division of the ego, in which what was at first a simple defect in integration is then used actively for other purposes, is in essence the mechanism of splitting' (p. 25). The use of splitting results in five clinical manifestations (Akhtar & Byrne, 1983): (1) inability to experience ambivalence, (2) marked and convincing oscillations of self esteem, (3) intensification of affects, (4) reckless decision making, and (5) ego-syntonic loss of impulse control (e.g., promiscuity, kleptomania) that produces little guilt. While better organized personalities might display occasional and focal splitting, its extensive use is a clinical marker of severe character pathology.

Squiggle game: a playful child therapy technique originated by Donald Winnicott in the 1960s, though the paper describing it was published posthumously in 1989. Essentially, the 'squiggle game' consisted of Winnicott drawing a wave-like line or figure on a paper and inviting the child patient to add to it or to draw something of his own, to which Winnicott could add. He and the child then took turns to 'complete' some sort of a picture from their random 'drawings'. The result of this game could be likened to dreams, since it was a representation of the unconscious. The game helped in diagnosing a child's problem but could also be therapeutic itself. Winnicott emphasized that, while the game is initiated by the therapist, the two partners must remain equally active in playing it. Spontaneity and surprise are necessary elements to such interaction.

State-of-affairs dreams: W. R. D. Fairbairn's (1952) designation of dreams which depict the current status of the inner psychic structure. For instance, a grieving individual might see an empty and dark house in his dream. Or, a pregnant woman might dream of a full refrigerator. Such dreams merely portray the current mental 'state-of-affairs'. This hypothesis of dream formation, replicated in Heinz Kohut's (1977) later description of 'self-state dreams' (see also Slap & Trunnell, 1987), is distinct from the wish-fulfilment dynamics of dreams proposed by Sigmund Freud (1900a).

Stimulus barrier: this term is derived from Sigmund Frued's (1920g, p. 27) notion of a 'protective shield' (see separate entry) against stimuli. It was first used by David Rapaport in 1951. Since then a number of investigators, especially René Spitz (1955), Margaret Mahler (1958), Helen Gediman (1971), Sidney Furst (1978), and Aaron Esman (1983), have elaborated and refined this concept. Some of them (e.g., Furst, 1978) use it in a structural sense while others (e.g., Gediman, 1971) refer to it as an ego function. Esman (1983) offers a revised formulation that supplants Freud's innate exclusionary barrier by a 'regulation of stimulus intake within the framework of object attachments and information processing, structure building concepts' (p. 205). He suggests that the metaphor of a 'stimulus screen' rather than of a 'stimulus barrier' is more appropriate for such a nuanced function.

Stimulus screen: see 'Stimulus barrier'.

Stockholm syndrome: see 'Identification with the aggressor'.

Stolen child: surveying the literature and mythology pertaining to the 'stolen child', Rita Frankiel (1985) proposed that the wish to steal a baby is a joint expression of two universal wishes: the wish for a baby and the wish to rescue (see 'Rescue fantasy'). 'Themes of rescue through replacing parents and especially the wish to kidnap a child in order to rescue him have a special relevance to the child treatment situation, sometimes stimulating guilty and wishful fantasies in the parents, the child, and/or the therapist' (p. 428).

Strachey–Loewald divergence: in an eloquent paper on psychoanalytic technique, Arnold Cooper (1988b) compared James Strachey's (1934) and Hans Loewald's (1960) seminal contributions, underscoring the profound difference between the two. Strachey's model is based on instinct theory and resistance analysis from a technically neutral position. The analyst's role is that of a 'benign interpreter of reality, internalized as a temporary new object, helping to make the unconscious conscious, and modifying the superego' (Cooper, 1988b, p. 19). In contrast, the model analyst for Loewald offers himself to the patient as a contemporary and emotionally related object. He is 'mindful of the patient's core of potential being, which he senses as a parent does, oriented towards the future, offering the patient opportunities to create new integrations on the armature of maturity that the analyst provides' (Cooper, 1988b, p. 26). Cooper concluded that the unification of these two models is a major task facing contemporary psychoanalysis.

Stage of concern: see 'Capacity for concern'.

Strain trauma: Ernst Kris' (1956) term for a gradually accumulating burden on the ego as a result of chronic frustrations. A series of events in childhood or, more likely, an ongoing set of parental attitudes that tax the child's capacity to metabolize painful affects collectively lead to such trauma. See also 'Cumulative trauma'.

Stranger anxiety: René Spitz's (1963) term for an infant beginning to show fear and distress around strangers; this happens at about eight months of age and, paradoxically, demonstrates that the child has developed a firm capacity to distinguish his primary love object (mother) from strangers. 'Stranger anxiety' is sometimes also called 'Eighth month anxiety' and constitutes what Spitz called the 'second organizer of the psyche' (see also the related entry on 'organizers of the psyche'.

Structure: while Sigmund Freud's (1900a) 'topographic theory' portrayed the mind as being composed of 'conscious', 'preconscious', and 'unconscious' (see separate entries), these were called 'systems' and not 'structures'. The term 'structure' arose in connection with his later (1923b) 'structural theory' which portrayed the mind as being composed of 'id', 'ego', and 'superego' (see separate entries). However, with the emergence of competing models of the mind, other entities began to lay claim to the designation of 'structure'. Melanie Klein's (1940) 'paranoid and depressive positions', Heinz Hartmann's (1952) 'object constancy' and Donald Winnicott's (1960) 'true and false selves' were among the concepts that could readily be added to the list of 'structures'. It was clear that a more explicit definition of the term was needed. This was provided by David Rapaport (1960), who reserved the term 'structure' for psychic phenomena whose 'rates of change are slow' (p. 28) and which are 'relatively abiding determiners of behavior and symptom' (p. 53). Robert Holt (1967) emphasized that the parts of a 'structure' are arranged in an organized pattern. Joseph Sandler and William Joffe (1969) carried these ideas further, dividing mental function into the experiential (e.g., wishes, memories, fantasies) and non-experiential (e.g., forces, energies, mechanisms) realms. According to them, 'the more stable components of the non-experiential realm can be considered to be "structures" in the sense in which they have been defined by Rapaport i.e. as organizations which are permanent or have a relatively slow rate of change' (p. 82). Two other points need to be mentioned here. First, there are important psychoanalytic contributors (e.g., Lichtenberg, 1989) who eschew the term 'structure' and prefer to view mental functioning in terms of 'motivational–functional systems' (p. 57). And second, besides the normative structures listed above, there are also pathological structures, including, for instance, the 'grandiose self' (see separate entry).

Structural change: setting aside the inevitable difficulty of defining 'structural change' if what is to be regarded as 'structure' (see separate entry) itself remains a bit unclear, one resorts to seeking a consensus view via a review of literature. Sigmund Freud's early declaration that the purpose of psychoanalysis is to make the unconscious conscious and to ascertain that 'where the id was there ego shall be' (1923b, p. 7) carry implicit definitions of 'structure change'. Edward Bibring (1937) elaborated in detail the kind of changes in id, ego, and superego result for a successful psychoanalysis. However, as Robert Wallerstein (1988) has noted, these are experience-distant, global abstractions; they are difficult to operationalize. Actually, the place of 'structural change' in psychoanalytic thought has become somewhat ambiguous. In the end, it has acquired the status of a 'highly prized goal but also kind of slogan' (Weinshel, 1984, p. 70). On the other hand, its definition is not agreed upon (see Wallerstein, 1988) and prominent analytic investigators favour using other terms, like 'psychoanalytic change' (Weinshel, 1988), 'characterologic change' (Modell, 1988), and 'change in psychological capacities' (Wallerstein, 1988) in its place. They suggest

'structural change' (or some equivalent of it) depends heavily upon the resolution of transference, improved reality testing, enhanced capacity to tolerate psychic pain and to resolve it through mourning, increased self-reflection, and sustained difference in the capacities for self esteem, zest for life, empathy, commitment, reciprocity, sexuality, effectance, self-assertion, and mastery. These later mentioned capacities , as will be noted, are anchored in deeper 'structures'. To come back full circle, one can say that a sustained alteration of content, firmness, and cohesion of id, ego, and superego, as well as of their mutual influences and relations, constitutes 'structural change'. However, such language limits 'structural change' to one conceptual model. Using a different model, for instance that of Margaret Mahler, Fred Pine, and Anni Bergman (1975), the achievement of 'object constancy' (see separate entry) by a borderline individual as a result of treatment can legitimately be called 'structural change'. It is to avoid such conceptual narrowness and experience-distant formulations that Robert Wallerstein (1988) emphatically endorsed a clinical, dynamic, and capacities-based assessment of 'structural change'.

Structural conflict: a state of tension between the three major psychic agencies, namely id, ego, and superego. In elaborating the nature of such 'intersystemic conflict' or 'structual conflict', Otto Fenichel (1945) delineated two constellations: (1) the ego and the superego joined together in opposition to the id, and (2) the ego standing in opposition to the id, which is supported by the superego. The former was typical of hysteria and the latter of compulsive neurosis. However, the concept of 'structual conflict' is crucial to understanding a wide spectrum of seemingly normal mental phenomena. Leo Rangell (1963a) emphasizes this point by stating that 'the ego–id opposition is the more usual and constant one, while the inter-systemic ego–superego tension is, comparatively speaking, more likely to be one of vigilant alertness rather than of constant interaction' (p. 110). The superego and the id generally initiate conflict, the ego largely suffers it. While Jacob Arlow and Charles Brenner (1964) have applied the model of 'structural conflict' to all types of psychopathology, and Sander Abend, Michael Porder, and Martin Willick (1983) have similarly sought to understand borderline conditions, this construct seems most suitable for explaining higher level, neurotic formations (e.g., obsession, phobia, hysteria) and the 'psychopathology of everyday life'.

Structural model of the mind: see 'Structural theory'.

Structural perspective: see 'Metapsychology'.

Structural theory: term applied to the theory of mental organization and functioning proposed by Sigmund Freud in 1923. Though the term 'ego' existed long before it (Freud, 1894a, 1896, 1900a, 1911b), the 'structural model of the mind' consisting of 'id', 'ego', and 'superego' was introduced later. It more or less replaced the earlier 'topographic theory', which had proposed that the mind is made up of three systems, namely 'conscious', 'preconscious', and 'unconscious'. The essence of 'structural theory' can be summarized along five dimensions: (1) *Function*: each 'structure' has its own function. The 'id' is the reservoir of instincts and constitutes the somatic engine of the mind. The 'superego' is the mind's moral compass. The 'ego' is the rational mediator and executive *par excellence*, attempting to create compromise formations and safe instinctual discharges. (2) *Methods*: the 'id' operates according to 'pleasure principle' and 'primary process'; it has little regard for reason. The 'ego' operates mostly through 'secondary process' and takes concerns of safety and reality into account. The 'superego' tends to be midway between the other two agencies; it can have rationality, but is largely made up of archaic patterns. (3) *Origin*: the 'id' is constitutional and somatic in its origin; the 'ego' arises from an undifferential id–ego matrix and contains both somatic underpinnings as well as precipitates of 'identification' with early caretakers. The 'superego' arises predominantly from the 'internalization' of the parental dictates during childhood but the forces of id colour the perception of parents and hence contributes to the 'instinctual' character of the 'superego'. (4) *Topography*: the 'id' is unconscious, while the 'ego' and 'superego' have both conscious and unconscious elements. (5) *Mutual relationship*: the three structures can be in complete harmony (e.g., in the wish to sleep after a hard day of work) or in conflict (e.g., the wish to steal a piece of art while visiting a museum and the inner moral outrage at it resulting in guilt and anxiety, leading to a hurried exit from the scene); most often, the 'ego' seeks to make compromises between the fun and frown of 'id' and 'superego' respectively. While first enunciated in *The Ego and The Id* (Freud, 1923b), the nuances of 'structural theory' took time to evolve. Freud's own subsequent writings (1924d, 1933a, 1940a [1938]) and those of others (A. Freud, 1936; Hartmann, 1939, 1952, 1956; Hartmann, Kris, & Loewenstein, 1946; Brenner, 1974, 1976, 1982) added detail and texture to the original description (see separate entries on all the terms in quotations marks here).

Structural violence: term coined by Bas Schreuder (1999) to denote the psychostructurally deleterious effect of political confinement and torture; such violence breaks through the boundaries of the self and the source of the destructive stimulus can then just as easily be ascribed to the self as to the external object causing it.

Struggle against the introjects: Gustav Bychowski (1958) described the complex relationship between the ego as an organized whole and the internal images, resulting from early introjections, contained within it. According to him, an ideal condition would be to have a complete and harmonious assimilation of all important introjects within the ego. However, because of ambivalence, this hardly ever takes place. Thus, the ego struggles against the introjects, attempting to do away with some and submit to others. Despite their externalization and attempted destruction, internal objects do not cease to exist; the ego is thus compelled to act out its destructive impulses over and over again. It is a testimony to Bychowski's broad-minded genius that he illustrated his ideas by sources as diverse as the life of Marcel Proust and the great Hindu religious tracts, the *Upanishads*.

Subjective disengagement: among the operations constituting the 'work of the negative' (see separate entry), André Green (1993) included this particular mechanism. A patient using it shows a peculiar detachment from the analytic process and his participation in it. He shows indifference to the analyst's intervention and to his response to them. He shows indifference even to the deleterious impact his indifference has upon his intrapsychic and external life.

Subjective object: Donald Winnicott's (1962) term for the infant's internal experience of the mother as against his objective perception of her. The mother who is in a state of 'primary maternal preoccupation' (see separate entry) facilitates the baby's illusion of omnipotence and thus becomes a 'subjective object'. As the baby grows and becomes capable of objective perception, the internalized illusion of the mother who made him feel omnipotent becomes a new 'subjective object' (Winnicott, 1971). The overlap between subjective object *vs.* the object that is objectively perceived and 'environment mother *vs.* object mother' (see separate entry) is also to be noted.

Sublimation: term introduced by Sigmund Freud (1908d) for the capacity of the sexual instinct to alter its original aim into a non-sexual aim that yields socially valued activities. Freud especially referred to intellectual and artisitic pursuits as products of 'sublimation'. His own additional insights (Freud, 1923b) as well as the contributions of subsequent psychoanalysts (Bernfeld, 1931; Fenichel, 1945; Hartmann, 1955; Kubie, 1962) led to the emergence of *six important features* of the concept: (1) activities resulting from sublimation are ego-syntonic; (2) like 'aim-inhibition' (see separate entry), sublimation involves a change in the instinctual aim. However, aim-inhibition results in partial and sublimation in full discharge of instinctual tension; (3) behaviours caused by sublimation lack the rigidity typical of those associated with 'reaction formation' (see separate entry); (4) sublimation contributes to, but is not exclusively responsible for, man's social and creative achievements; exercise of autonomous ego functions, inborn talents, and healthy identifications with creative family members and mentors also contribute to artisitic and literary achievements; (5) since social value lies at the centre of the definition of 'sublimation', the concept has some cultural specificity built into it; and (6) while the original definition referred to only the transformations of sexual instinct, sublimation can also result from alterations of aggressive aims (e.g., carpentry, surgery). Indeed, even in sublimations derived from sexual instinct, the energy of aggressive instinct might be co-mingled (e.g., sculpture).

Subsidiary egos: see 'Fairbairn's description of endopsychic structure'.

Substitute for objects: see 'Substitute objects'.

Substitute objects: by shortening Otto Fenichel's (1945) phrase 'substitute for objects' (p. 436), Vamik Volkan (1976) coined the term 'substitute objects'. Such objects need not be concrete; they might comprise religious or political ideologies, for instance. Their purpose is to help the patient, usually psychosis-prone, to maintain or regain a semblance of object contact. 'Substitute objects themselves may, however, like human objects, become sources of either fear or security, and maybe similarly clung to or avoided' (p. 207).

Success neurosis: see 'Those wrecked by success'.

Suggestibility: refers to the psychological capacity to be influenced by others, especially those in positions of authority and power over the subject. Under the sway of this tendency, the individual puts his own perception and judgement aside and begins to believe what he is told. As a conse-

quence, the trait of 'suggestibility' has a more problematic twin, namely 'corruptibility'. Ubiquitous to some extent, 'suggestibility' is more marked in certain personality disorders. In 'hysterical personality', it is pronounced, but confined to triangulated and sexualized situations with an oedipal tinge. In 'histrionic personality', it is more diffuse; the vulnerability to influence by others is less discriminating. It is, however, in 'as-if personality' (Deutsch, 1942) that the trait of 'suggestibility' reaches its zenith. Rapid identification with others leads to mimicking them. Also evident are profound inauthenticity and readiness to be used by others. Within the clinical situation, patient's 'suggestibility' and the analyst's penchant for using 'suggestion' (see separate entry) can collude and interfere with deeper interpretive work. The relevance of this for the hypnotic aspects of treatment, handling of delicate forensic situations, and reconstructions of childhood sexual abuse are obvious; an article by Michael Good (1996) is quite instructive in this regard. See the related entries on 'as-if personality' and 'hysterical and histrionic personalities'.

Suggestion: a concept that seems to occupy a curious place in the literature on psychoanalytic technique. On the one hand, it has been discussed from the earliest days of psychoanalytic enterprise and was accorded pride of place by Edward Bibring's (1954) including it among his fine therapeutic tools of psychoanalysis and psychodynamic psychotherapy (see 'Bibrings' five therapeutic principles'). On the one hand, most major psychoanalytic glossaries (Rycroft, 1968; Moore & Fine, 1968, 1990; Laplanche & Pontalis, 1973) do not contain an entry on it. Sigmund Freud used 'suggestion' freely during the era when he practised hypnosis and 'pressure technique' (see separate entry) but gave it up as he discovered that patients' 'free association (see separate entry) can provide access to unconscious mental contents. Or, to put it more accurately, he felt that a certain amount of 'suggestion'—which he defined as a conviction which is not based upon perception and reasoning, but upon an erotic tie (1921c)—was a necessary and unavoidable component of the analytic situation. It constituted an element of the 'unobjectionable positive transference' (see separate entry). However, Freud emphasized that such built-in 'suggestion' only led the patient to trust the analyst and any additional influence it had was dissolved by the interpretation of transference. Later analysts (Glover, 1931; Bibring, 1954; Greenson, 1967; Gill, 1994; Schlesinger, 2003) added further insights to this realm: (1) a judicious and occasional use of 'suggestion' for 'technical' and not 'therapeutic' purposes (i.e., for encouraging the patient to participate in the analytic work , not 'curing' his symptoms) might be an acceptable part of analytic technique; (2) two dangers in using 'suggestion' are its over-use and its unwitting use; (3) all interventions, even what are clearly intended to be interpretations, can be heard by the patient as 'suggestions'; this is especially true for patients with marked 'suggestibilty' (see separate entry); (4) recognizing the ubiquity of the potential for 'suggestion' helps one analyse the way in which one's interventions are being received by the analysand; and (5) patient's disagreements with the analyst's interventions might at times be a good sign in so far as these might reflect a healthy and 'unobjectionable negative transference' (see separate entry).

Suicide: the psychodynamics of suicidal threats and acts, like all other mental phenomena, is multiply determined. Issues of sadomasochism (an id variable), compromised reality testing and weakened impulse control (an ego variable), guilt-driven need for punishment (a superego variable), collapse of self-esteem under the burden of shame (an ego ideal variable), and hopelessness born out of social isolation and ecomonic hardship (a reality variable) often work synergistically and contribute to suicide. Sigmund Freud (1910g) wondered whether suicide 'can only come about with the help of a disappointed libido or whether the ego can renounce its self-preservation for its own egoistic motives' (p. 232). Later, he said that 'the ego can kill itself only, if owing to the return of object cathexis, it can treat itself as an object—if it is able to direct against itself the hostility which relates to an object and which represents the ego's original reaction to objects in the external world' (Freud, 1917e, p. 252). The view of suicide as a retroflexed murder thus became widely accepted. However, the emphasis upon the view that suicide was a murder *of* a bad internal object eclipsed the fact that suicide could also be a murder of the self *by* a bad object. Indeed, Freud had hinted at such surrender to an exalted bad object in his 1917 paper and laid the ground for his later (1920g, 1923b) view of suicide as the culmination of a guilty need for self punishment. Melanie Klein (1935) then proposed an additional possibility by stating that the suicidal individual 'hates not only his bad objects, but his id as well and that vehemently. In committing suicide, his purpose may be to make a clean breach in his relation to the outside world because his desire to rid some real object—or the good object that the whole world represents and which the ego is identified with—of himself, or of that part of his ego which is identified with his bad objects and his id' (p. 276). Such suicide was altruistic. A flip side was the suicide committed as a 'kindness' to oneself. This view is implicit in Donald Winnicott's (1960) statement that, under suffocating circumstances, suicide is 'the destruction of total self in avoidance of annihilation of the true self' (p. 143). All in all, the psychodynamics of suicide turns out to be a complex and multifactorial matter. Forces of sadism, masochism, altruism, narcissism, and, occasionally, rationality are all involved in the genesis of such behaviour. Karl Menninger's (1938) classification of the motives underlying suicide (namely, the wish to die, the wish to kill, and the wish to be killed) is also helpful in advancing clinical understanding. One will also benefit by looking up Otto Kernberg's (1984) essay on the management of chronically suicidal individuals, John Buckman's (1985) overview of self-destructive behaviours in general, Roger Lewin and Clarence Schulz's (1992) elucidation of the existentially useful functions of chronic suicidality, Donald Campbell's (1995) elucidation of the role of the father in a pre-suicide state, and the responses of thirteen eminent practitioners to clinical questions regarding suicide collected in a volume edited by Gerben Hellinga, Bert van Luyn, and Henk-Jan Dalewijk (2000).

Suitable reservoirs: writing about ethnic, religious or national large group identity, Vamik Volkan (1988, 1999a) introduced the term *suitable reservoirs*. Such reservoirs have two characteristics: (1) they are shared by all children in the large group and (2) they are constant. They intertwine children's core personal and large-group identities. Every ethnic, religious, national, or other large group shares a set of recognizable suitable reservoirs. For example, they include items such as kilts and bagpipes for Scottish children, the sauna for a Finnish child. A child uses many things when externalizing—both animate and inanimate objects are innocently used to promote and protect individual core identity. Some of these suitable reservoirs have a special historical significance to the child's large group; he or she receives conscious and unconscious guidance from parents and others in choosing them as depositories of 'good' self and object representations. This transgenerational guidance in object selection differentiates 'suitable reservoirs' from the ordinary transitional object. The latter is self-discovered and does not link the child to his or her ethnic group.

Sum of excitation: an early concept of Sigmund Freud (1894a) by which he tried to explain the: (1) derivation of psychic energy from internal stimuli that were more or less continuous and, being internal, could not be evaded by flight, and (2) energic imbalance that perpetually threatens the 'principle of constancy'. These two factors resulted in a 'sum of excitation' that had to be discharged, transformed into symptoms, channelled into productive actions, let loose to fuel wishful imagery in dreams and day-dreams, and so on. In essence, it was the substance which formed the central concern for the economic perspective of 'metapsychology' (see separate entry).

Sunday neurosis: term used by Sandor Ferenczi (1919b) for the exacerbation of neurotic and psychosomatic symptoms on Sundays. While physiological changes due to altered patterns of behaviour were contributory to it, 'Sunday neurosis' was mostly caused by the impact of 'inner liberation' (p. 176) associated with the day off from work. The holiday activated instinctual impulses, and self punishment fantasies followed. The result was an increase in neurotic symptoms. While Ferenczi's description was restricted to Sundays, similar dynamics often underlie the worsening of psychopathology during major holidays.

Superego: the psychic structure that comes into being with the resolution of the Oedipus complex (Freud 1923b, 1924d) and is the depository of parental injunctions and prohibitions, hence a source of inner guilt. That benevolent aspects of parental support also give structure to the superego and that its specific dictates should get more or less 'depersonified' (i.e., rendered abstract) during later periods of development, especially adolescence, was pointed out by Edith Jacobson (1964).

Superego analysis: term introduced by Otto Fenichel (1939b) to denote interpretative work directed at defensive attitudes undertaken at the instigation of the superego. According to him, 'superego analysis is partly an analysis of emotional relationships to persons in the environment who have been incorporated into the superego, and partly, an analysis of the early history of the instincts' (p. 180); this is especially true in the case of 'moral masochism' (see separate entry). Charles Brenner (1976) emphasized that when superego commands are allied with defences against instinct, there is little difference between 'superego analysis' and 'defence analysis' (see separate entry), but when the superego dictates are themselves defended against, the work becomes more complicated. Paul Gray (1994) extended these ideas and gave a more inclusive and nuanced definition of 'superego analysis'. He said that it

consists of 'systematically making available to consciousness those repetitions of defensive formations in the analytic situation—including pre- and post-internalizations—which were earlier mobilized, especially in connection with the oedipal situation, to the end that compromised ego function components can be progressively reclaimed, from the beginning of the analysis, by the relatively autonomous ego' (p. 120). For this to occur, superego activities, manifested as part of ego defences, have to be interpreted on an ongoing basis. Gray added that 'superego analysis is possible only to the extent that aggressive drive derivatives are truly returnable to the ego's voluntary executive powers' (p. 126). Lawrence Levenson (1998) has emphasized the importance of such 'superego defence analysis' during the termination phase of treatment.

Superego defence: refers to the superego's role in mobilizing ego defences against instinctual impulses. Transference of such superego activity on to the analyst endows him with authority. It also acts as a 'resistance' (see separate entry) against self-revelation, since any effort at opening up the inner world to scrutiny involves the emergence of instinctual derivatives in the associative material. As a result, a proper analysis of the 'superego defence' is essential. Such 'superego analysis' (see separate entry) or ' superego defence analysis' (Levenson, 1998) is what permits the patient's ego to gain conscious control of the hitherto repressed instinctual impulses.

Superego defence analysis: see 'Superego analysis'.

Superego dreams: see 'Punishment dreams'.

Superego forerunners: see 'Superego precursors'.

Superego lacunae: Adelaide Johnson and Martin Szurek's (1952) proposition that some forms of antisocial behaviour result not from generalized superego weakness, but from a lack of superego in certain circumscribed areas. To these, they applied the term 'superego lacunae'. One child in a family is subtly chosen as the scapegoat and unconsciously encouraged by the parents to act out their own forbidden impulses. The parents obtain vicarious gratification while maintaining an unconsciously permissive attitude toward the child. However, since such behaviour is contrary to their conscious self-image, it may also evoke severe punishments. The child is therefore trapped. Unconsciously, he is encouraged by the parents to act in certain ways (e.g., steal, be promiscuous, lie) and consciously discouraged to do the same. The paths open to such a child, and later adult, are a paralysis of intention or increasing cleverness in carrying out the delinquent acts. The former is one explanation of the antisocial individual's bouts of laziness. The latter contributes to the manipulative skills of the psychopath.

Superego precursors: while hints of this concept can be found scattered in earlier psychoanalytic writings (e.g., Ferenczi, 1925b; Freud, 1939a; Schafer, 1960; Jacobson, 1964) under the varying designations of 'superego forerunners' or 'superego precursors', its most lucid description is provided by Elsa Blum and Harold Blum (1990). According to them, 'superego precursors' make their appearance in the latter part of the first year and are related more to issues of safety and parental approval than to those of abstract morality. Parental control of the child's intentionality and mobility leads to the earliest internalizations of commands directed at the ego. Subsequently, 'rapprochement subphase' (see separate entry) struggles and the injunctions involved in toilet training are taken in and added to the emerging islets of inner control. However, such 'identification with the aggressor' (see separate entry) is not the only origin of the 'superego precursors'; positive identifications with the comforting and benevolent features of the parent's attitude toward the child also contribute to their genesis. At the same time, it should be underscored that 'superego precursors, because of the infant's drives, defences, and ego immaturity, may be far removed from the reality of the caregiver's attitudes and intent' (p. 594).

Superego resistance: see 'Resistance'.

Supervising analyst: an experienced psychoanalyst who is recognized by his local analytic society or institute as suitable to oversee the clinical work of those training to become psychoanalysts (see also 'Analytic supervision' and 'Training analyst').

Supervising and training analyst: see 'Training analyst' and 'Supervising analyst'.

Supervisory field: see 'Parallelism phenomena in psychoanalysis and supervision'.

Supportive psychotherapy: while some literature did exist on the role of persuasion, suggestion, environmental manipulation, and appealing to willpower (Schilder, 1938; Alexander & French, 1946), explicit descriptions of 'supportive psycho-

therapy' began only with the works of Merton Gill (1951, 1954), Edward Bibring (1954) and Sidney Tarachow (1963). Further light on the topic was shed by later contributors, especially John Gedo (1964), Paul Dewald (1971), and Otto Kernberg (1984). While the ideas proposed by these authors do not always correspond with each other, the picture of 'supportive psychotherapy' that emerges from pooling them is as follows: (1) 'supportive psychotherapy' usually involves one session per week. However, at times of crises and under constraints of the time period available to accomplish some therapeutic goals, the frequency can be greater; (2) sessions are conducted face to face and the couch is not used; (3) technical methods include suggestion, environmental intervention or 'manipulation', facilitation of 'abreaction', and some attempt at 'clarification' (see separate entries). Interpretation is not employed; (4) transference is handled in ways that are different from those of psychoanalytic psychotherapy or psychoanalysis. Positive transference, unless it is grotesque and primitive, is left unquestioned; it might even provide leverage for 'suggestion' (see separate entries) and encouragement of impulse control. Unconscious negative transference is silently noted and factored in to planning the patient's overall care and specific interventions. Conscious negative transference is minimized by clarifications and help with reality testing; (5) adjunct measures of both psychosocial (e.g., sex therapy, couples therapy) and biological (e.g., antidepressant medication) might be used; (6) there is less 'neutrality' (see separate entry) and the therapist is more active and 'real' in his interactions with the patient; and, finally (7) 'supportive psychotherapy' is useful for crisis situations, adjustment reactions, developmentally phase-specific but somewhat undue anxieties, circumscribed life problems, and patients who are either not sufficiently psychologically minded or too ill to participate in psychologically exploratory work. To be sure, different authors take exceptions to one or another aspect of this portrayal of 'supportive psychotherapy'. Herbert Schlesinger (1969), for instance, finds it preferable to think of supportive effects, purposes, and interventions which could be used even within psychoanalysis rather than to think of 'supportive psycotherapy' *per se*. Otto Kernberg (1984) believes that 'supportive psychotherapy' is a 'treatment of last resort' (p. 151), while also suggesting that it is easier to move from expressive to supportive treatment than vice versa. Significant contributions have also been made to the understanding of 'supportive psychotherapy' by David Stafford-Clark (1952) and David Werman (1988).

Suppression as a defence: the conscious attempt to put something out of one's mind, called 'suppression', has received relatively little attention in the psychoanalytic literature. An outstanding exception to this is the remarkable paper by David Werman (1983). Werman points out the interchangeable use of 'suppression' and 'repression' (see separate entry) in early psychoanalytic writings (e.g., Freud 1900a, p. 235, 1905c, p. 134) as well as in the English language. He cites Charles Brenner (1955), who suggests that the two concepts might lie on a continuum and that there might be intermediate stages between them, and George Vaillant (1977) who regards 'suppression' among the major mature defence mechanisms. All in all, he concludes that suppression involves the 'volitional elimination from consciousness, by any means, of undesirable thoughts, feelings, or bodily sensations . . . (this) may be the conscious equivalent of certain unconscious defence mechanisms such as isolation or reaction formation' (p. 413). As an ego mechanism, 'suppression' might be of help in affect regulation, conflict avoidance, and the unfolding of developmental and adaptive processes (Hsu, 1949).

Survival of the object: Donald Winnicott's (1962) concept for the mother's preserving her devotion and care while being the recipient of the 'ruthless love' (see separate entry) of the baby. It is her 'survival' in the face of such ruthlessness that makes it possible for the baby to advance from the 'pre-ruth' stage to a stage of having the 'capacity for concern' (see separate entry). This concept has great significance in the treatment of all psychiatric patients but especially those with marked aggression, since the therapist's 'surviving' their attacks over time makes them internalize a modified image of him. This, in turn, begins to alter their internal world and their capacity to contain ambivalence and relate well to others.

Survivor's guilt: While coined in the context of 'survivor syndrome' (see separate entry), this type of guilt is seen not only in those who have outlived comrades killed in combat and loved ones in an accident, but also in individuals whose parents died during their childhood and individuals raised with a grossly impaired sibling. The death of a child almost invariably leaves a residue of 'survivor's guilt' in his or her parents. One variable that might determine the intensity of guilt in such situations is whether the avoidance of ill-fortune is the result of an active decision made by the survivor or due to mere happenstance (Mark Moore, personal communication, 3 April 2008).

Survivor syndrome: term coined by William Niederland (1968) for a symptom cluster seen in individuals who have outlived someone close to them in the course of war, natural disaster, or an automobile accident or plane crash in which the bereaved could also have died. Prominent among the symptoms of 'survivor syndrome' are depression, anxiety, somatization, and chronic feelings of guilt. Preoccupation with the dreadful event, irritability, and 'flashbacks' typical of a 'post traumatic stress disorder' (see separate entry) can also be evident. Traumatic overwhelming of the ego and guilt at having outlived the deceased form the dynamic basis of this syndrome. Stephen Sonnenberg (1972) added the idea that the individual who died was in fact a recipient of guilt-expiating activity; there was much unconscious hostility towards him and the hope was to diminish this guilt by kindness and indulgence. The loss precluded this possibility and accentuated the pre-existing guilt.

Symbiotic need: term used by Robert Savitt (1969) to denote a life-long persistence of a desperate readiness to fuse with others through actual or symbolic pleas for love, the insatiable desire to suck and be sucked, to eat and to be eaten, and the sensation of merger and loss of ego boundaries during the slightest degree of intimate contact. Such object hunger resulted from an impoverished 'symbiotic phase' (see separate entry) during infancy and the lack of ameliorative experiences during the subsequent childhood. See also the related entries on 'mother–infant symbiosis' and 'merger fantasies'.

Symbiotic omnipotence: term used by Masud Khan (1969) for a particular sort of affectivity that manifests in the clinical hour as inertia, helpless dependence, and subtle coercion for the analyst to 'fit in' and provide the vitality missing from the patient's own experience. Khan traced the origin of such a state to an early and special bond between a highly intelligent mother and her gifted and sensitive child. This led to (1) imbalance in articulation of ego capacities with hyper-development of some functions and arrest of others, (2) a precocious awareness of mother's moods, (3) exaggerated self-awareness, owing to the hypercathexis of self by the mother, and (4) intensification of libidinal development and non-integration of aggression. This type of ego distortion can stay secret and unmodified by later developmental processes. Such children are usually hypersensitive and highly intelligent, and grow up into withdrawn and excessively self-absorbed adolescents. As adults, they are creative but inwardly passive and inert. They make constant efforts to actualize relationships where a focal specialness of two parties can be achieved; this 'reliving' of their early 'symbiotic omnipotence' both vitalizes them and leaves them unintegrated all over again.

Symbiotic orbit: for an infant and and a growing child, mother is the centre of the universe. Tied to her by an 'invisible bond' (Mahler, Pine, & Bergman, 1975, p. 25) or a 'psychic tether' (Akhtar, 1992a), he or she can only venture a certain distance away. The circumference of this imaginary circle of the child's sojourn constitutes the 'symbiotic orbit'. According to Margaret Mahler, Fred Pine, and Anni Bergman (1975), this orbit includes not only the mother but 'all parts and attributes of mother—her voice, her gestures, her clothes, and the space in which she comes and goes—which form the magic circle of the symbiotic mother–infant world' (p. 203).

Symbiotic phase: term coined by Margaret Mahler (1968) to denote the blissful, psychological merger between an infant and his or her mother that lasts from birth until about 4–5 months of age. The current view, however, is that rather than there being an autistic phase (an idea Mahler originally proposed but had begun to concede as untenable towards the end of her career) and a symbiotic phase, there are quasi-autistic and symbiotic moments sprinkled throughout early infancy, moments in which the infant is withdrawn and in which the infant is merged with the mother. Daniel Stern (1985) has, however, challenged even this view, suggesting that an emergent self is present from birth. He has questioned whether the infant's self arises out of a mother–child symbiotic matrix or whether the experience of (and even the capacity for) such merger is itself dependent upon having a separate self.

Symbolic: see 'Real, symbolic, and imaginary'.

Symbolic equation: while both Sandor Ferenczi (1912) and Ernest Jones (1916) had earlier mentioned that sometimes the distinction between a symbol and the thing it stands for vanishes, the term 'symbolic equation' owes its origins to Hanna Segal (1950). She provided lucid clinical illustrations of how an object and another object that is symbolically representing it become one and the same in mind. Such 'symbolic equation' is part of a disturbance in the ego's relationship to the object world. 'Parts of the ego and internal objects are projected into an object and identified with it. The differentiation between the self and

object is obscured' (Segal, 1957, p. 53). This is most clearly seen in psychotic patients.

Symbolism: within psychoanalysis, 'symbolism' stands for representing a body part (e.g., penis), activity (e.g., eating), feeling (e.g., hate) or idea (e.g., patriotism) by a concrete object. Thus the mind can come to be symbolized by a house, breast by a fruit, penis by a tower, and so on. The process of 'symbolism' displays the following characteristics: (1) the symbol is conscious, but that it stands for something else is often unconscious; (2) the symbol is concrete, but the symbolized may be concrete or abstract; (3) the formation of a symbol is dependent upon its partial equation with the symbolized, in accordance with primary process thinking (see 'primary and secondary processes'); (4) there exists a 'constant relation' between a symbol and its unconscious equivalent so that 'an individual may choose among the senses of a symbol but he can not create new ones' (Laplanche & Pontalis, 1973, p. 444) ; and (5) while dreams show the work of symbolism most clearly, neurotic symptoms and creativity also rely heavily upon this mechanism.

Symmetric logic: see 'Bi-logic'.

Symptom formation: careful reading of psychoanalytic literature (e.g., Freud, 1895a, 1900a, 1905a, 1915a, 1915c, 1926a; Fenichel, 1945; Arlow & Brenner, 1964; Pulver, 1995) makes the following seven points regarding 'symptom formation' clear: (1) a symptom is a distressing manifestation of psychopathology and is therefore, by definition, ego dystonic; (2) there might be 'negative' symptoms or 'inhibitions' where the performance of a healthy function is impeded and 'positive' symptoms where something new has cropped up in the field of mentation, affect, or behaviour; (3) symptoms reflect the end-product of a compromise between the repressed derivatives of instinctual desires and ego defencese directed against them; these defences are mobilized at the behest of the superego or due to concerns of external reality; (4) the threat of a 'return of the repressed' (see separate entry) plays a central role in the formation of neurotic symptoms in so far as it mobilizes secondary defences such as displacement, conversion, undoing, etc.; (5) compromises between drives and defences are psychically ubiquitous and ordinarily do not give rise to symptoms; this only happens when the instinctual drives are strengthened (e.g., during puberty) or the repressive forces weakened (e.g., during illness, grief, overwhelming work commitments); (6) despite an appearance to the contrary, symptoms do not cause anxiety; it is the other way around: anxiety causes symptoms and, if it cannot be 'bound' by symptoms, then the left over amount is consciously experienced as as a dysphoric affect; and (7) the dynamics of 'symptom formation' in neurotic and psychotic conditions is similar, although a less differentiated psychic structure and greater ferocity of aggression result in more severe disturbances of reality testing and gross behavioural manoeuvres to stabilize a crumbling self.

Symptom replacement: this concept is a natural corollary of viewing psychological symptoms as manifesting a compromise between conflicting unconscious forces. It implies that removal of symptoms by suggestion, hypnosis, or 'transference cure' does not alter the underlying dynamic, which sooner or later reasserts itself through a different symptomatic configuration.

Syndrome of narcissistic tranquillity: Mortimer Ostow's (1967) delineation of a clinical state characterized by (1) retreat from object relations, (2) narcissistic preoccupation, (3) weight gain, and (4) afternoon sleepiness. This syndrome comes about when object-relations are severely frustrating and represents 'an attempt to substitute a local, walled-off lesion for a general, arousing, psychic stress' (p. 582).

Synthetic function of the ego: refers to the ego's attempts to bring diverse forces (e.g., drive pressures, superego dictates, opposite constitutional tendencies) together in a harmonious gestalt. 'Synthetic function of the ego' is a manifestation of libido, or, more correctly, the 'life instinct' (see separate entry), which seeks to create unity, meaning, linkages, and higher forms of abstractions (Hartmann, 1958). When the compromise affected is relatively conflict-free, the behaviour is 'ego-syntonic'. At times, however, the synthesis achieved by the ego is clumsy and imbalanced; such is the case in parapraxes and neurotic symptoms. Greater problems arise when the strength of drives, especially destructive drives, makes the ego's task of synthesis difficult; the psychic structure then implodes into psychosis. On the other end of the spectrum lies artistic creativity, which is the amalgamated end-product of instinctual drives, unconscious fantasies, day-dreams, affects, pre-verbal residues in the deepest layers of the psyche, and the deft use of inherent talents. Here, the 'synthetic function of the ego' seems to have achieved its goal in a masterful way.

System unconscious: see 'Unconscious'.

Tact: while both Sigmund Freud (1926e) and Sandor Ferenczi (1928) regarded 'tact' to be integral to the correct timing of interpretation, it was Rudolph Loewenstein (1951) who clarified what it actually means. According to him, 'tact' is 'an intuitive evaluation of the patient's problems which leads the analyst to choose, among many possible interventions or interpretations, the one which is right at a given moment. Consequently, tact equally entails evaluation of the extent to which optimally a patient should be gratified or frustrated through an interpretation' (p. 8). In a more thorough study of the subject, Warren Poland (1975) noted that tact follows empathy. 'We learn with empathy and understanding and we interpret with tact' (p. 156). Poland traced tact's developmental origins to the loving presence of mother during the separation experiences of the child and also to the early handling of the child's exhibitionism by the parents. Tact is associated with emotional relatedness, but not the 'excessive warmth of denied hostility' (p. 157) which gives rise to 'pseudo-tact' or cowardly pussyfooting around conflictual matters.

Talking cure: aphoristic label assigned to psychoanalysis by Sigmund Freud's celebrated patient Anna O. (Breuer & Freud, 1895d). She was right in so far as psychoanalysis does place verbal exchange at the centre stage. However, besides 'talking', the treatment also relies upon 'listening'. In essence, psychoanalysis is a talking *and* 'listening cure' (see separate entry).

Teacher transference: Yasuhiko Taketomo's (1989) designation of the Japanese analysand's respectful desires to be mentored by his or her analyst; the basis of such feelings is in the important connection a Japanese child makes with the kindergarten teacher (often a male!) since he is the first major extra-familiar and truly paternal object in the child's experience. A subtle implication here is that Japanese fathers are often more maternal and, hence, the child's first 'father-like' experience occurs in the relationship with the kindergarten teacher.

Technical neutrality: see 'Neutrality'.

Telepathic dreams: Sigmund Freud (1922a) declared that he never had a 'telepathic dream' and that 'telepathy has no relation to the essential nature of dreams' (p. 219). This led to his followers losing interest in this topic. However, the matter resurfaced, some seven decades later, in an unpublished paper of Robert Stoller. The text of this paper has been posthumously incorporated in a comprehensive report by Elizabeth Lloyd Mayer (2001). Facing squarely the possibilities of defensive tricks of mind, conscious or unconscious self-deception, and utter serendipity, Stoller concluded that some dreams he himself had and some that his patients reported were 'telepathic' in so far as they depicted real life events that could not have been known to the dreamer. Almost all these dreams occurred during a separation, and the patients had few associations to the dream elements which reproduced the actual events in Stoller's life. Moreover, these details were different from any that had appeared in the patient's earlier dreams and they never recurred. Mayer (2001) added that such dreams are not as rare as Stoller felt, and that they are more commonly reported by patients with childhood experiences of traumatic separations and loss.

Telepathy and psychoanalysis: in a series of four papers, Sigmund Freud (1941d [1921]), 1922a, 1925b, 1933a) offered his thoughts about various telepathic phenomena including thought transference, extrasensory perception, prophetic dreams, and even character assessment via handwriting analysis. Fervently given to logic and rationality, Freud felt highly ambivalent about the veracity of telepathic occurrences; he traced the coincidences and mysteries involved in them to repressed associative links that had been overlooked. However, Freud's doubts about telepathy diminished over the course of his writing and his last paper on the subject, 'Dreams and occultism' (1933a, pp. 31–56) was quite sympathetic to the idea of thought-transference. Little follow-up of this was, however, evident in the subsequent psychoanalytic literature until Elizabeth Lloyd Mayer (2001) revived interest in the potential links between telepathy and psychoanalysis. The field of study is perhaps more ripe than ever before, especially in light of the contemporary emphasis upon 'two person' psychology, intersubjectivity, transgenerational transmission of trauma, and the co-created nature of psychological facts.

Telephone analysis: Sigmund Freud's bypass of face-to-face contact with his patients via the use of the couch has found a new counterpart in the contemporary patient's communicating via the telephone. Previously restricted to an occasional refuelling device, the use of the telephone has blossomed into a clinical diversity of astonishing range (Saul, 1954; Robertiello, 1972; Aronson, 2002). Most often, however, 'telephone analysis' is a therapeutic compromise and not a treatment of choice. It is resorted to because it is impractical for the patient to have sessions in person; the patient lives at a long distance, travels extensively, or has moved out of town during the course of treatment. John Lindon (1988) and Sharon Zaluksy (1998) have comprehensively discussed the pros and cons of such work.

Temperament: see 'Personality'.

Temperature eroticism: an essential component of all love relationships is to have skin-to-skin contact with one's partner and to feel the warmth of his or her body. However, in some individuals, the need for such 'warmth' becomes quite literal. Early deprivation of maternal care often lurks in their background. 'Intense pleasure in warmth, frequently manifested in neurotic bathing habits, is usually encountered in persons who simultaneously show other signs of a passive–receptive orientation, particularly in regard to the regulation of their self-esteem' (Fenichel, 1945, p. 70). Such individuals 'thaw' in a 'warm' atmosphere, take long hot showers, and can sit for hours in a warm bath. Such 'thermal sensitivity (is also) found in narcissistic patients for whom chill often represents the coldness of non-recognition and death, as opposed to the warmth of adequate reflection' (Bach, 1977, p. 20).

Temporal fracture of the self: an experiential discontinuity between the memories, feelings, and relationships from different eras of one's life. In younger patients, such rupture manifests as an inability to project themselves into the future, and in middle aged patients, it manifests as a peculiar disassociation from their own younger selves. In either case, all experience becomes uncannily contemporary. Time acquires a personalized yet fragmented quality and a longitudinal anamnesis reveals 'a life lived in pieces' (Pfeiffer, 1974).

Temporal order of life: beginning with the original oedipal experience which brought one into contact with the existence of generational boundaries (Chassaguet-Smirgel, 1984) and ending with the midlife sharpening of the time perspective in life, the individual gains knowledge that life is lived within the dimension of time and this has a profound impact on the instinctual, reality, and moral aspects of our existence.

Temporal regression: see 'Regression'.

Tenderness: Veikko Tahka (1993) described this affect as arising from 'empathic sharing of the object's pleasure and subsequent leaving of the pleasure for him. In a loving relationship, this letting the object keep the pleasure for himself is followed by a second repleasure in the subject for the loved person's feeling good and for the knowledge of having contributed to that oneself' (p. 244). Tenderness has a maternal quality and is integral to mature love between adults, parenthood, and also to the analyst's relationship with the analysand.

Tent of the large-group identity: because of their clinical interests, psychoanalysts have focused more on small groups and the psychodynamics involved when seven to fifteen individuals gather for a series of meetings. Wilfred Bion's (1961) work is among the best known of such studies. Also, in the psychoanalytic literature, the term 'large group' often refers to 30 to 150 members who meet in order to deal with a given issue. Vamik Volkan (1997, 2004, 2006) uses the term of large group to refer to tens, hundreds of thousands, or millions of individuals—most of whom will never meet during their lifetimes—who belong to a large group from childhood onwards. Thus, for Volkan, ethnic, national, religious, and some ideological groups are large groups. According to him, essential psychodynamics of such groups are *different* from the psychodynamics of 'small groups' and what have been conventionally called 'large groups' (composed of 30 or 150 individuals). He states that when we think of the classical Freudian theory of large groups, we can visualize people arranged around a gigantic maypole, which represents the group leader. Individuals in the large group dance around the pole/leader, identifying with each other and idealizing the leader. He has expanded this maypole metaphor by imagining a canvas extending from the pole out over the people, forming a huge tent. This canvas represents the large-group identity, a permanent sense of shared sameness. Thousands or millions of persons living under this huge tent may get together in subgroups: they may be poor or rich or women or men and they may belong to certain clans or professional organizations, but all of them exist under this huge 'tent'. Everyone under its canvas wears the garment of individual identity, but everyone under the tent shares the tent canvas as a second garment. However, in routine lives, most individuals are not keenly aware of this shared second garment. Under societal stress, they 'regress' and become more conscious of their common ethno-national identity signified by this 'tent'.

Termination: see 'Termination phase'.

Termination phase: the notion that bringing an analysis to its end requires a 'phase' of its own owes its origin to Edward Glover (1955). Before his proposal, the issue of 'termination' was elusive, due, at least in part, to the fact that Sigmund Freud did not develop a consistent technique to end an analysis. In a masterful essay on the topic, Martin Bergmann (2005) gives Harold Blum (1989) the credit for making this explicit. To be sure, Freud (1933a) had stated that the pupose of analysis was to make sure that 'where id was, there ego shall be' (p. 80), but it is also true that he grew increasingly pessimistic as to whether an analysis can truly be ended. In 'Analysis terminable and interminable', Freud (1937c) cited the tenacity of instincts and the capacity of life events to stir up new conflicts as the reasons for the 'interminability' of psychoanalysis. Among those who departed from Freud's notions were Sandor Ferenczi and Otto Rank (1924). They advocated a pre-set termination date (see the entry on 'active technique'). Otto Fenichel (posthumously published in 1974) also felt that it was possible for the ego to control undesirable impulses and an analysis to end on an optimistic note. Later literature began to list various criteria for 'termination' including (1) resolution of transference neurosis, (2) ascendancy of the ego, (3) enhanced capacity for impulse control and sublimation, (4) improved affect modulation, (5) alteration of defences from immature to mature ones, (6) cessation of repetitive dreams and diminished capacity of dreams to affect the next day's mind, (7) improved object relations, and (8) reconstruction of a plausible life narrative (Sharpe, 1930, 1931; Rangell, 1966; Shane & Shane, 1984; Ticho, 1972). At the same time, it was agreed upon that attempts to achieve perfect results and to do a truly complete analysis (on the part of the patient or the analyst or both) was undesirable. Some limitations have to be accepted. This is agreed upon by all. However, the precise technique of terminating is far from uniform. The analyst might begin to sense before the patient that termination is coming (Pulver, 1991) with diminished transference–countertransference pressure and with a shift of the patient's attention from past and present to future. At times, a dream might herald the patient's readiness for ending analysis (Cavenar & Nash, 1976).

Usually, however, the analyst waits for the patient to bring up the desire to finish and after exploring the defensive and discharge functions of the request itself, he might agree to end their work. A proper 'termination phase' is now set into motion with occasional resurgence of symptoms, 'review dreams' (see separate entry), and a mourning process which lasts until the very end. Most clinicians break up the termination process into two steps: agreeing to terminate and then, a few weeks later, setting a precise date for termination. The work, however, goes on until the last hour. Most analysts hold on to their interpretive stance until the very last minute (see Samuel Lipton's 1961 paper on the 'last hour'). Others (e.g., Bergman, 2005) suggest that 'it may well be indicated in certain cases to devote the last few hours to the evaluation of the analytic work. When this approach is followed, the patient should be asked to sit up and not necessarily free-associate but rather discuss his or her own understanding of the whole analytic procedure, what has been achieved, and what further work there still for him or her to do after the analysis is finished. The analyst should feel free to participate in the discussion. During this time, the two partners are speaking to each other more as equals than they did during the analysis itself' (p. 251). Still others (e.g., Schacter, 1992) make the discussion of potential 'post termination contacts' (see separate entry) also a part of the 'termination phase' work.

Termination phase dreams: see 'Termination related dreams'.

Termination related dreams: dreams associated with termination of analysis can be divided into two categories: (1) 'termination signal dreams' (Cavenar & Nash, 1976), which make their appearance before the possibility of termination has been overtly considered by the analyst or analysand. Such dreams usually depict finishing a task, clearing an attic or basement, and encountering the undisguised analyst in a matter of fact manner. 'Review dreams' (Glover, 1955, p. 157), whose manifest content can be readily interpreted as an assessment of the patient's progress in overcoming his or her difficulties also belong in this category. While Jesse Cavenar and James Nash (1976) regard all such dreams as indicators of the patient's unconscious readiness for termination, Jack Novick (1988) considers them to indicate an overdue or belated termination. (2) 'termination phase dreams', which appear *after* the decision to terminate has been undertaken. These usually depict the patient's primary symptoms, albeit in a markedly improved state, and the analyst in undisguised form being directly involved with those symptoms (Oremland, 1973). Dreams of rebirth and of coming out of a tunnel, as well as 'dreams of resolution' (Saul, 1953) that deal with solving the patient's main problem, also belong in this category.

Termination signal dreams: see 'Termination related dreams'.

Tertiary narcissism: term coined by Judith Kestenberg and Ira Brenner (1995) in the context of survival in the Nazi concentration camps. According to them, a certain redistribution of narcissistic libido is necessary in order to live through such a horrific experience. This might result in selective hypercathexis of certain ego functions, the memory of a specially good but lost object, or simply a strong sense of group affliation. This redistribution of narcissism constitutes an antithesis of fixation; 'primary narcissism coalesces with secondary narcissism . . . which is forged into tertiary narcissism. Tertiary narcissism then provides for additional resilience which, in the case of child survivors, enabled them to endure until liberation' (p. 43). Kestenberg and Brenner's definition of 'secondary narcissism' (see also the related entry on 'narcissism') includes not only the defensive withdrawal of cathexis from objects to ego, but also the increase in self-esteem that is a consequence of feeling loved by valued others. It is the latter tributary of 'secondary narcissism' that, in combination with 'primary narcissism', gives rise to 'tertiary narcissism'. The fate of this highly adaptive shift in narcissistic economy after liberation from the concentration camps remains a topic of continual investigation. See also Sverre Varvin's (2003a) paper on the strategies for mental survival in states of extreme traumatization.

Tertiary process: term originated by André Green (1972) to underscore the binding elements between the 'primary and secondary processes' (see separate entry). Green observed that, after a certain level of psychic complexity, duality as the foundation of conceptualization becomes insufficient. His concept of 'tertiary process' belongs to this realm. It links primary and secondary processes with each other. 'Without a structure making it possible to pass from one field to the other, one can see how neither of the two series (primary and secondary) can be linked up with the other; nor how analytic progress can be conceived of' (Green, 2005, p. 189).

Tether fantasy: first described by Salman Akhtar (1992a), the 'tether fantasy' refers to an unconscious belief that a rope or chain keeps one bound to a central reference point and thus assures one's staying within certain bounds. In dilute and largely subterranean forms, the tether fantasy might be ubiquitous. Its more explicit and intense versions are seen in individuals who are chronically concerned about their distance from an anchoring person or environment. They want to assert themselves and experiment with a wider segment of the world, but fear losing touch with the 'home base'. At the same time, they fear moving too close to the centre of their orbit since it stirs up merger anxieties. Their distancing attempts reassure them against such dread of fusion, while their imaginary psychic 'tethers' provide them 'distance contact' (Mahler, Pine, & Bergman, 1975, p. 67) with the anchoring person, who remains available despite their comings and goings.

Thanatos: a term coined by Wilhelm Stekel in 1908 and wholeheartedly advocated by Paul Federn (according to Ernest Jones, 1957, p. 295) to denote the death instinct. Intended to be analogous to 'Eros' (the life instinct), the term is not to be found in Sigmund Freud's written works though, according to Jones (*ibid.*), he sometimes used it in conversations. Subsequently, the term fell by the wayside. This was partly because of Freud's lukewarm response to it and partly because of the overall unpopularity of his death instinct concept. Even those theorists who upheld the death instinct did not use this term to any significant extent.

Theory of opposite wishes: forms the central thesis of the book titled *The Concept of Repression*, authored by the Calcutta based psychoanalyst, Girindrashekhar Bose in 1921. According to this theory, no wish exists in the psyche without its counterpart. A wish to love, for instance, is always accompanied by a wish to be loved. Similarly, a wish to hate is always accompanied by a wish to be hated. Unpleasure arises only from the conflict between such opposite wishes. The mind resolves such conflict by vacillation between the two wishes, by compromise formation, or, most often, by fulfilling one of the wishes and repressing the other. The latter, however, continues to seek expression. 'The latent wish, which in its manifest form, would exactly correspond to the situation of the object, finds satisfaction by the subject identifying himself with the object. Unless this identification takes place, the object is not apprehended by the psyche of the subject and remains a non-entity as far as the subject is concerned. This identity is the bond of relation between the object and the subject and on it depends the the true appreciation of the nature of the object' (p. 123). In a critical evaluation of Bose's contributions to psychoanalysis, including his decades-long correspondence with Sigmund Freud, Salman Akhtar and Pratyusha Tummala-Narra (2005) state that 'this remarkable passage contains the seeds of ideas regarding projective identification and intersubjectivity long before these concepts were explicitly developed in the West. Given the fact that in any interaction, each partner has a subjectivity and is treating the other as an object, Bose's statement that "the aim of all reactions is to bring about a state of identity between the subject and the object" (p. 126) seems to be the unknown precursor of the current relational and intersubjective emphasis in North American psychoanalysis' (p. 5).

Theory of thinking: phrase associated with Wilfred Bion's (1962b, 1967) explication of how thinking originates, how it functions, and what purposes it serves. Bion proposed that thinking originates in the conflict between the psyche's desire to rid itself of accumulating instinctual tensions on the one hand, and its encounter with reality on the other. Locating this in the course of development, Bion saw the earliest step in thinking being 'preconception'. This refers to a prior knowledge on the infant's part, which, by finding its counterpart in external reality called 'realization', is transformed into 'conception'. In constrast, when 'preconception' does not find 'realization', or, in Bion's words, finds 'negative realization', 'thinking' emerges. It is this moment of frustration that gives rise to psychic creativity in the form of imagination and thinking. The 'negative realization' becomes a 'thought' and provides a foundation for 'thinking'. Here Bion reversed the conventional wisdom, which holds that thinking produces thoughts; he assested that it is 'thought' that produces 'thinking'. All this is, however, contingent upon the psyche being able to bear the absence of 'realization'. If it cannot, it tries to evade such absence; what would have given rise to a 'thought' now becomes a 'bad object' itself and has to be voided. Thinking does not develop; instead, the tendency towards getting rid of parts of the psyche via 'projective identification' becomes intensified. If the mother can 'contain' and metabolize such projections and return them to the infant in a palatable form, 'thinking' can resume. If not, the infant is compelled to use projective mechanisms on a continuous basis, to the impoverishment of his personality.

Therapeutic alliance: term coined by Elizabeth Zetzel (1956) to denote the reality based, harmonious, and collaborative aspect of the analyst–analysand relationship which makes their ongoing clinical work possible. Ralph Greenson's (1965) 'working alliance' and Helmut Thoma and Horst Kachele's (1994) 'helping allliance' are roughly similar concepts. Essentially, the components of such an alliance are trust, mutuality of purpose, and ethics (Meissner, 1992c). While not explicitly mentioned by Sigmund Freud, the concept seems to have evolved from his idea that the analyst and the analysand 'form a pact with each other' (Freud, 1940a [1938], p. 173) to help the patient's ego from being burdened with inordinate instinctual demands and harsh superego reprisals. Freud's (1915a) notion of 'unobjectionable positive transference' and Richard Fox's (1998) 'unobjectionable positive countertransference' can be seen as the two halves of the concept of therapeutic alliance. But what gives rise to such a relationship? Is 'therapeutic alliance' a recapitulation of the non-conflictual and generative aspect of the early mother–child relationship (Zetzel, 1956), or does it evolve from mature ego functions which safeguard useful adult relationships (Curtis, 1979)? Or, do childish wishes to please or comply with a parent lurk behind the patient's collaborative attitude? This would blur the distinction between alliance and transference. Indeed, many analysts (Brenner, 1979; Curtis, 1979) find the concept of therapeutic alliance problematic. In Herbert Schlesinger's (2003) words, 'the closer one looks at the therapeutic relationship, with the hope of discriminating the real aspects from the transference aspects, the fuzzier the distinction becomes' (p. 256). Clearly, there are technical stakes to all this. If one views alliance as being a subtle form of transference, one might be inclined to explore its meanings and origins. If, on the other hand, one regards the patient's collaboration as realistic, then the analysis of its origins would appear inappropriate.

Therapeutic conscience: see 'Analyst's work ego'.

Therapeutic dissociation of the ego: concept first proposed by Richard Sterba (1934) to highlight that, during the course of his work, the analyst 'endeavours to oppose those elements in the ego which are focused on reality to those which have a cathexis of instinctual or defensive energy' (p. 118). Sterba declared that states where the ego is permanently fused with the id (e.g., severe narcissism, psychosis) are not amenable to psychoanalysis since the co-operation of ego is required to overcome its own neurotic entanglements. 'The therapeutic dissociation of the ego is a necessity if the analyst is to have the chance of winning over part of it to his side, conquering it, strengthening it by means of identification with himself, and opposing it in the transference to those parts which have a cathexis of instinctual and defensive energy' (p. 119). Sterba noted that calling on the analysand to co-operate with the analyst against something in himself sets the ground for such ego dissociation. The analyst's frequent use of the term 'we' for this collaborative compact buttresses the spirit. However, it is the act of interpretation, especially transference interpretation that most potently shifts the analysand's attention from his affective experience to a new point of intellectual contemplation about that experience.

Therapeutic misalliance: Robert Langs' (1982) term for a situation where both the analyst and analysand strive to treat the latter's symptoms by means other than interpretation, insight, and structural change. Deviations of setting and technique as well as a vague sense that things are actually not going well marks the situation. The cause of such 'therapeutic misalliance' (pp. 586–592) resides in the collusion of psychopathology of the two partners in the dyad. The patient, however, always remains unconsciously aware of the misalliance (even while not participating in it) and seeks to correct it. That these efforts might be feeble does not rule out their significance.

Therapeutic pseudo-alliance: term coined by Moises Rabih (1981) to denote a superficially compliant and co-operative attitude on the analysand's part underneath which lurk hatred and megalomania. These deeper currents attack and destroy analytic work. Rabih sees 'therapeutic pseudo-alliance' as a phenomenon derived from what Wilfred Bion (1957) called the 'psychotic part of the personality' (see the entry on 'psychotic and non-psychotic parts of personality).

Therapeutic regression: see 'Anaclitic regression'.

Therapeutic strategy and psychoanalytic technique: emphasizing that carefully thought out measures 'to foster the progress of an analysis rather than to themselves effect some lasting change in the patient' (p. 451) were his focus, Steven Levy (1987) elucidated the role of 'therapeutic strategy' in psychoanalytic technique. He noted that strategic elements, however nonspecific, were inherent in the use of the couch, and the stance of neutrality, abstinence, and anonymity. More palpable presence of 'therapeutic strategy' was to be found in the contemporary

approaches to the treatment of narcissistic and borderline patients (Kohut, 1971, 1977; Kernberg, 1975, 1984) and even in the relatively 'sober ego oriented defences analyses' (Gray, 1982; Weinshel, 1984). Levy emphasized that the prevalent anti-strategy bias has resulted in overlooking that clinical work involves an admixture of spontaneity and deliberateness; the analyst's interventions are derived as often from flashes of intuition as they are from methodical 'lines of exploration' (p. 459). He concluded that 'formal study of the tactical or strategic choices the analyst makes and how they interact with the analyst's more immediate, spontaneous responsiveness is needed if a truly encompassing theory of technique is to be evolved' (p. 459). See also the related entry on 'Heirarchy of interpretations'.

Thing presentation: see 'Thing presentation and word presentation'.

Thing presentation and word presentation: Sigmund Freud's (1891, 1895d, 1900a) notions regarding the two ways in which objects are mentally represented. 'Thing presentation' means that an object is represented concretely and visually, and 'word presentation' means that it is additionally represented lexically and aurally. The system Unconscious is replete with 'thing presentations', and the systems Preconscious and Conscious with 'word presentations'. In states of severe regression (e.g., schizophrenia), 'word representation' itself comes to be used as a thing, giving rise to the propensity for concretization of thought and formation of delusions.

Third individuation: extrapolating the ideas derived from the study of childhood 'separation–individuation' (Mahler, Pine, & Bergman, 1975) and adolescent 'second individuation' (Blos, 1967) has resulted in the expression 'third individuation'. Salman Akhtar (1995) gave this designation to the identity transformation consequent upon immigration. Unbeknown to him (see Akhtar, 1995, p. 1052), the San Diego based psychoanalyst, Calvin Colarusso (1990) had used the same label for the adult life working through of the 'separation–individuation' (see separate entry) conflicts reactivated at the time of becoming a parent. Regardless of the context, the 'third individuation' has only a phenomenological resemblance and not genetic equation with the infantile processes it is named after. Much psychic structuralization has ensued by the time the 'third individuation' takes place. Drives have attained fusion and genital primacy. The ego is better organized and a post-adolescent superego is in place.

The term 'third individuation', therefore, links an adult life reorganization of identity to a childhood phenomenon in a playful and metaphorical way. However, the potential of reworking earlier separation–individuation conflicts through this process cannot altogether be ruled out.

Third organizer of the psyche: see 'Organizers of the psyche'.

Those wrecked by success: a character type described by Sigmund Freud (1916d). These are individuals who fall apart when a 'long cherished wish has come to fulfilment' (p. 316). They are not able to tolerate the happiness that results from achievement and success. Indeed, they have a tendency to become morose and even self-destructive when their dreams come true. Freud elucidated the psychodynamics underlying this seemingly curious and paradoxical occurrence with the help of many clinical vignettes and literary examples. He concluded that it is the 'forces of conscience' (p. 318) that forbid the enjoyment of success, since success is unconsciously equated by the individual with the actualization of incestuous and murderous wishes typical of the oedipal phase. Notable in Freud's description is the fact that it was written seven years before the concept of the 'superego' (see separate entry) was to appear in the psychoanalytic lexicon. Moreover, the phenomenologic validity of his concept has stood the test of time, as all clinicians have time and again encountered such self-defeating characters. An additional twist to the dynamics of such 'success neurosis' has been recently offered by Dorothy Holmes (2002), who suggests that internalized communal dictates of ceilings upon what a particular race or socio-economic class is 'supposed' to or 'expected' to achieve, can also contribute to an individual from those groups fearing (and hence thwarting) accomplishment and success. Holmes' conceptualization equips the analyst dealing with minority patients with a technical stance that can be extremely useful for both empathic attunement and interpretive interventions.

Thought identity: see 'Perceptual identity and thought identity'.

Three box model of the mind: proposed by Joseph Sandler and Anne-Marie Sandler in 1983, this model proposes that the mind is divided into three 'boxes' or systems: (1) the *first box* is the 'past unconscious'. It consists of 'those infantile reactions, infantile wishes or wishful fantasies that developed early in life and are the outcome of all the transformations that defensive activities and modifying processes have brought about during that period' (p. 418). This box is not restricted to id impulses; it also contains ego's defensive and problem solving fantasies. Not directly accessible to consciousness, this system is, by and large, unchangeable; (2) the *second box* is the 'present unconscious'. It also contains unconscious fantasies but these are geared towards the present and future. Conflict-solving compromises are created in this box, and so are here-and-now adaptations to the tensions stirred up in the first box. Such fantasies are also more modifiable in light of current experience; (3) the *third box* is conscious, largely rational, and adapted to social realities. The first and second boxes are separated by the 'first censorship', which is erected to avoid shame and embarrassment; after all, the first box contains the child within the adult, with all its freedom from logic and morality. The second and third boxes are separated by the 'second censorship', which is akin to the classical repression barrier. As a result, the contents of the second box are more accessible to interpretation. Interventions that address the first box, without fleshing out its derivatives in the second box, are based upon a confusion of the 'past unconscious' with the 'present unconscious'. Interventions along these lines are less effective and their impact is soon eclipsed by newly cropped up resistances.

Three person psychology: see 'One, two, three, four, and multi-person psychologies'.

Time binding: Morton Beiser's (1997) term for the ego's attempt to maintain connectedness and links between the past, present, and future; this is disrupted in immigrants and refugees; time is often experienced by them as stagnating or fragmented.

Time collapse: Vamik Volkan's (1997) term for the rupture of boundaries between the past and present; the emotions and perceptions associated with the past begin to be experienced as if the trauma has just occurred, and they are even projected on to the future. What is remembered, felt, and expected come together. In the setting of large groups, time collapse might exaggerate the need and justification for taking revenge for old injuries to the group's collective narcissism.

Time dominance: Morton Beiser's (1997) term for the predominant valence of a particular era (past, present, or future) in an individual's psychic life; in immigrants and refuges, the past continues to dominate the present and there is little affective investment in the future.

287

Titrating the asymmetry gradient: see 'Titration'.

Titration: although the concept was employed earlier by Helmut Thoma and Horst Kachele (1994) in their thorough book on psychoanalytic technique under the rubric of 'titrating the asymmetry gradient', the term 'titration' itself owes its origin to Jerome Winer and Eric Ornstein (2001). The former set of authors use the idea in the context of regulating the degree of asymmetry in the clinical dyad in accordance with the patient's ego needs and always attempting to protect the patient from feeling inferior and alienated due to aspects of the therapeutic frame.The latter authors define 'titration' as 'a conscious decision by the analyst to increase or decrease assistance (or gratification) gradually, in order to facilitate the analytic process' (p. 891). There seems to be considerable overlap in these ideas emerging from clinical experience in Germany and the USA, respectively.

Too good mother: phrase coined by Robert Shields (1964) for the type of mother for whom 'primary maternal preoccupation' (see separate entry) is not temporary, but sustained over a period of years. The only satisfying role such a woman can play is that of fully devoted mother. 'The "too good" mother can not accept her child as a developing and differentiating organism. The nursing couple becomes a permanent state, subtly preserving an all-pervading mutual identification which actually amounts to infusion. The mother sees herself only as a supplier of infantile satisfactions and is herself unable to tolerate the notion that her child can bear dissatisfaction, frustration, or hate' (p. 85). As a consequence, the child does not achieve separateness and finds delineation of his personality as an overriding life-long task.

Topographic theory: though implicit in Sigmund Freud's (1895d) earliest works, the 'topographic theory' was made explicit in the celebrated chapter VII of his 1900a *Interpretation of Dreams*; it was further elaborated upon in later papers, especially those on the unconscious (1915e) and repression (1915d). Essentially, the 'topographic theory' proposes the existence of three psychic systems: 'conscious', 'preconscious', and 'unconscious' (see separate entries). The mental contents of the system 'conscious' are readily available to awareness while the mental contents of the system 'unconscious' are not; those belonging to 'system preconscious' are also out of awareness, but can be readily brought into it by effort. These systems are differentiated by: (1) *their location* in the psychic realm is along a vertical continuum from surface, then the 'preconscious', followed by the 'unconscious'; and (2) *their operational mode*, with the systems 'conscious' and 'preconscious' working along the 'primary process' and the system 'unconscious' working along the 'secondary process' (see 'primary and secondary processes'). The next consideration is that of 'censorship' (see separate entry), or the barriers that exist between these systems. Freud termed the barrier between 'conscious' and 'preconscious' as 'secondary censorship', and that between the 'preconscious' and 'unconscious' as 'censorship proper'; the former was more permeable than the latter. Freud (1920g, 1923b) later replaced the 'topographic theory' by his 'structural theory' (see separate entry) with id, ego, and superego as the main agencies of the mind. However, this 'replacement' was hardly complete, since the two models had some overlaps (e.g., ego having conscious, preconscious, and unconscious aspects). Besides, the concept of 'unconscious' remained irresistibly appealing and thus 'outlasted' Freud's theoretical shift. Cecilio Paniagua (1985) has commented upon the resulting technical 'lure' of the topographic model and the potential handicaps of such approach.

Topographical model of the mind: see 'Topographic theory'.

Topographic perspective: see 'Metapsychology'

Topographical regression: see 'Regression'.

Touch : see 'Physical contact between analyst and the patient'.

Traditional continuity: see 'Generational continuity'.

Tragic man: see 'Guilty Man *vs*. Tragic Man'.

Training analysis: the requirement that each aspiring analyst undergo a personal psychoanalysis was made 'official' at the 1922 IPA Congress in Berlin. It emanated from a sense that the experience of undergoing analysis oneself offers the best opportunity to witness the workings of the unconscious mind; it is, therefore, the best way to produce conviction in psychoanalytic theory and technique. Alongside didactic courses and supervised clinical work, 'training analysis' became the third pillar of the 'tripartite system' (see separate entry) of psychoanalytic training. While this is still the case, problems and difficulties with such analyses became evident as experience accrued over time. These include the inherent tensions between (1) *reporting and confidentiality*: analysis requires complete trust in the analyst and total self-revelation. However, in the early days of analysis (and, in some places, even today), the training analyst reported to the institute about the candidate's progress. This led to profound anxieties on everyone's part, especially the analysand; a tendency to be circumspect and to withhold information from one's analyst developed. The joke that one has to have two analyses, one for the institute and one for oneself, was the dark result of this tension; (2) *technical and collegial relationship*: the fact that the candidate in analysis is also a junior colleague and will one day be a fully participating member of one's analytic society also created difficulties and dilemmas in conducting such analyses; (3) *clinical and social information*: both the training analyst and the candidate know more about each other than a 'civilian' analytic dyad does. The principle of 'anonymity' (see separate entry) is compromised. Moreover, the candidate, who is attending classes taught by one's colleagues and is being supervised by one's peers, often talks about them during his analytic sessions. This secret window in the professional lives of one's colleagues can offer information to the training analyst that might be burdensome. A greater effort is necessary to not let such knowledge seep into social discourse and to keep one's mind attuned to the material's clinical significance; (4) *ordinary and extraordinary transferences and countertransferences*: in addition to the usual and inevitable transference and countertransference developments, the training analysis creates possibilities of professional idealization, supervision seeking, turning the analyst into a mentor, comparing and contrasting him or her with other senior analysts, on the part of the analysand. The training analyst, too, is vulnerable to viewing the analysand as a protégé to be 'groomed' to be a future successor; the fantasy of the candidate carrying on one's analysing style into the future generations can especially become a source of narcissistic impediment to technique; (5) *termination and transformation*: the fact that the training analyst's analysand becomes a colleague upon completion of analysis renders termination more complicated. Fortunately, the profession is aware of such difficulties arising from these five sources. As a result, much discussion is centring upon them (see the IPA Newsletter of June 2007, for instance, which contains six articles on the challenges of training analysis), including the proposal that training analysis be entirely delinked from the insititute functions of supervision and didactic teaching.

Training analyst: designation reserved for experienced psychoanalysts who have been appointed by their respective institutes to conduct 'training analysis' (see separate entry), i.e., the analytic treatment of psychoanalytic candidates. The term 'training analyst' made its first appearance in Edward Glover's (1927) article on technique, though the requirement that each aspiring analyst undergo a personal psychoanalysis had been agreed upon at the 1922 IPA Congress at Berlin. Currently, the training analyst function, especially in North America, is combined with supervisory function. As a result, the more frequently used designation is 'supervising and training analyst'. The position carries a certain prestige and important offices in a given institute are often held by training analysts. This has led to some discontent. A growing pressure to delink 'training analysis' and psychoanalytic education *per se*, or to eliminate the designation altogether is in evidence.

Transference: concept introduced by Sigmund Freud, who elaborated and deepened his understanding of the phenomenon in a series of papers. In *Studies on Hysteria* (1895a), he referred to the 'false connection' (p. 303) that a patient's wish establishes with the person of the treating physician. In the Dora case (1905e), he stated that transferences are 'new editions or facsimiles of the impulses and fantasies [which] replace some earlier person by the person of the physician' (p. 116). In the Ratman case (Freud, 1909d), he mentioned that both positive and negative feelings can be part of transference. However, it was his 1912b paper 'The dynamics of transference' that gave a composite and most clearly formulated account of 'transference'. In it, Freud made the following points: (1) transference emanates from the portion of libidinal impulses that has remained unexpressed and/or unconscious; (2) transference in the course of analysis is no more strong than outside of it; the difference is that it is made a subject of study; (3) transference poses a challenge to treatment; in fact, it is 'the strongest weapon of resistance' (p. 104); (4) transference can be positive or negative; (5) the former can be divided into an affectionate type, which is an 'unobjectionable' ally of the treatment, and an erotic type, which needs interpretive resolution; (6) successful treatment is unlikely if the predominant transference is negative; and (7) the patient's getting insight into how the transference based wishes fit into 'the nexus of treatment and of his life history' (p. 108) freeze him from the tendency to re-create such situations. This is necessary to dissolve early fixations since 'it is impossible to destroy anyone in absentia or in effigie' (p. 108). The move from transference as resistance to 'transference interpretation' (see separate entry) as a central element of technique is implicit here. It became explicit with the concept of 'transference neurosis', which appeared, in its technical sense, in Freud's (1914g) paper titled 'Remembering, repeating, and working through'. While literature on the topic of transference continued to grow after Freud, his central ideas have survived the test of time. The reader might benefit, though, by looking up the contributions of Leo Stone (1961), Merton Gill (1982), Heinz Kohut (1971, 1977), and Otto Kernberg (1975, 1984), to name a few. The contemporary view that, besides the re-creation of old object-relations, transference involves a search for developmentally new objects and that transference phenomena are co-created in the dialectics of analyst–analysand interaction (Mitchell, 1988; Stolorow, Brandschaft, and Atwood, 1987; Hoffman, 1983, 1994; Ogden, 1994) is also worthy of consideration.

Transference addiction: described by Horacio Etchegoyen (2005), this constellation develops during the psychoanalytic treatment of addicts. It comprises an affective bond in which 'the analyst is both drug and anti-drug; the addict can really relate to his analyst only when he transforms him into the drug (saving and destroying); and, at the same time, the bond of (healthy) analytical dependence is misunderstood (mainly through envy) as a threat of the worst addiction' (p. 199).

Transference depression: introduced by André Green (1982) and elaborated upon by Thierry Bokanowski (1996), this concept refers to the re-activation of a sense of abandonment, betrayal, and depression in response to feeling deprived by the analyst, a feeling that falls upon the fertile ground of an ontogenetically earlier experience-cum-fantasy of similar loss.

Transference focused psychotherapy: a special form of treatment for borderline patients derived from the work of Otto Kernberg (1967, 1975, 1984). The term 'transference focused psychotherapy' is new, though the interventions subsumed under it have been evident in the earlier descriptions of treating borderline patients by Kernberg and his colleagues (Kernberg, Selzer, Koenigsberg, Carr, & Applebaum, 1989; Yeomans, Selzer, & Clarkin, 1992). Essentially, the approach consists of (1) establishing a firm initial contract with the patient acting as a collaborator in the process, (2) exploring the split in the borderline psyche which divides the self and object world into 'all good' and 'all bad' categories; (3) conducting this work in the specific context of

moment-to-moment shifts in transference; (4) helping the patient understand the nature of anxiety which perpetuates the splitting of self and others, with the aim of achieving a psychological state; and (5) utilizing adjunct measures such as medications and hospitalization when and if necessary. For a through overview of 'transference focused psychotherapy', see the recent paper by Otto Kernberg, Frank Yeomans, John Clarkin, & Kenneth Levy (2008).

Transference hunger: expression first used by Peter Blos, Sr (1989) for the rapidity with which some analysands develop collaborative attachment to the analyst. In his own words, 'transference hunger or "transference compulsion" is a reflection, in and of itself, of a symptom in formation within the benign context of the analytic situation' (p. 126). While not mentioned by Blos, intensity of unresolved conflicts (especially those involving childhood deprivations), developmental pressures, and relative ego-weakness seem to be the factors that contribute to the readiness to develop transferences both within and outside of the clinical situation. Individuals with these tendencies have been called 'transference addicts' by Christopher Bollas (2000, p. 146).

Transference interpretation: term for the analyst's intervention directed at unmasking the 'transference' (see separate entry) basis of a particular attitude, feeling, fantasy, or behaviour of the analysand. The clinical significance of recognizing and resolving transference was noted by Sigmund Freud (1912b) and later by James Strachey (1934), who emphasized that truly mutative interpretations were the ones which had a sense of 'immediacy' (see separate entry) and credibility owing to their pointing out the transference experience. The concept of 'transference interpretation' was further elaborated later on. Prominent among the various contributions made then are: (1) Otto Fenichel's (1941) distinction between 'transference interpretation', which says, for instance, that 'the feeling you are having towards me is actually directed at your father' and 'reversed transference interpretation' which says that 'you are not feeling this about your father at this moment but about me'; (2) Merton Gill's (1979; Gill & Muslin, 1976: Gill & Hoffman, 1982) pointing out that the 'resistance to awareness of transference' needs interpretation before the transference itself; (3) Leo Stone's (1961, 1967, 1981) reminder that establishment of a genetic prototype is the ultimate aim of 'transference interpretation' and that there is a great variability of technique in this regard; (4) Ralph Greenson's

(1967) amendation to Freud's dictum of interpreting transference only when it becomes a resistance that one does so when a proper 'therapeutic alliance' (see separate entry) is in place. Greenson emphasized that one interprets transference to impart new insights to the patient and does so when there are strong affects, optimally intense resistance, contradictions in the material, symbolic communication, and repetition of key associations; (5) the emerging relational and intersubjective perspectives in psychoanalysis (Ehrenberg, 1974; Mitchell, 1993; Ogden, 1994; Benjamin, 1995, 2004, 2007; Bromberg, 1998) have led to a paradoxical dilution of transference as a re-creation idea and intensification of the focus upon the co-created here-and-now interactions. For further details on how the concept of 'transference interpretation' has evolved over the course of psychoanalytic history and where it stands now, see Arnold Cooper's sophisticated article in the 1987 *Journal of the American Psychoanalytic Association*. According to him, 'our once straight-forward historical understanding of transference interpretation has yielded to a more polymorphous and confusing, but more interesting modernist view' (p. 97).

Transference neurosis: term introduced into the psychoanalytic literature by Carl Jung (1907) during the early days of psychoanalysis when neuroses were divided into 'actual neuroses' (which resulted from contemporary sexual excess or deprivation) and 'psychoneuroses' (which were caused by childhood psychological trauma). The former included neuraesthenia and anxiety neurosis. The latter were subdivided into 'narcissistic neurosis' (where libido turned towards the ego and was not amenable for transference) and 'transference neurosis' (where libido was readily displaceable and the possibility of developing transference existed) and included anxiety hysteria, conversion hysteria, and obsessional neurosis. In contrast to this early nosological usage is the psychodynamic connotation of the term 'transference neurosis' which later emerged. This was enunciated by Sigmund Freud (1914g) in connection with the observation that the patient repeats his or her infantile conflicts within the transference. He stated that 'we succeed in giving all the symptoms of the illness a new transference meaning and in replacing (the patient's) ordinary neurosis by a "transference neurosis" of which he can be cured by the therapeutic work' (p. 154). *Five characteristics* of such 'transference neurosis' include (1) the development of relative calm in the patient's outside life, (2) the coalescence of the patient's conflicts around the person of the analyst, (3) the replacement of fleeting transference reactions by an intense and ongoing transference 'relationship', (4) the self-stabilitzing nature of this experience, which, like the original neurosis, resists change, and (5) its midway position between the manifest neurosis and infantile neurosis; in other words, manifest neurosis is replaced by transference neurosis, which leads to the unearthing of the infantile neurosis. The establishment of transference neurosis shows movement from the 'beginning phase' (see separate entry) to the 'middle phase' (see separate entry) of treatment. Clinical work of greatest importance involves the resolution of transference neurosis by means of interpretation and working through.

Transference perversion: term introduced thirty-one years ago by Ricardo Horacio Etchegoyen (1978) to bring together the diverse clinical phenomena encountered in the treatment of perverse individuals. Etchegoyen succinctly put the situation in the following words: 'In a quasi-satanic way, these patients try to pervert the analytical relationship and test our tolerance' (p. 47). Citing earlier authors, especially Betty Joseph (1971) and Donald Meltzer (1973), but also some from the French school, Etchegoyen underscored that work with such patients is characterized by erotization of transference, deployment of both words and silence to induce excitement in the analyst, and of passivity to provoke his intrusive interpretations. The patient also constructs an illusory but tenacious unity with the analyst. Ego splitting is pronounced and the tendency to transform impulse into ideology is great. Echoes of Etchegoyen's contribution can be heard in the later work by North American psychoanalysts, such as Owen Renik (1992), Lee Grossman (1992, 1993), and Gail Reed (1996). The last mentioned, especially, provides a detailed description of 'transference perversion' emphasizing the patient's tendency to turn analysis into a magical, circumscribed world with the accompanying loss of the as-if character of transference. She notes, however, that 'these are not psychotic phenomena. The sequestration of the illusory world, its maintenance as an island untouched by rational considerations at the same time that those considerations are left free to be applied in other areas of functioning differentiates this material from a psychotic transference' (p. 66). That such disavowal results from a major split in the ego that is both warding off and expressing sadism is agreed upon by all authors. To be sure, such a situation posed a great clinical challenge. 'Persistent confrontation, no matter how gentle, satisfies patient's masochistic wishes. Persistent patience in the face of the undermining of the analysis gratifies his or her sadistic wishes' (p. 70). After holding, containing, affirming, and interpreting approaches fail to reduce the result, the analyst might have to actively confront and rupture the patient's illusion, including by way of initiating termination. See also 'Analyst induced termination' and 'If only . . .' entries.

Transference psychosis: term originated by Margaret Little (1960) to denote the transference reaction of patients who (1) respond with derision or pseudo compliance to transference interpretation, (2) show concrete thinking and weak capacity to symbolize, (3) are not responsive to dream analysis, (4) act out violently or, inhibiting such inclination, become very passive, (5) view the relationship with the analyst as not one of give and take, but of dominance and submission; when they have to 'give', they feel enraged, and when they receive, they feel guilty, (6) develop an 'addiction to analysis' (see separate entry) and (7) treat their analyst as an actual re-creation or replacement of their parents. The background history of such patients reveals a mother who did not value the patient as a child, did not play with him or her, did not encourage thinking, and could not bear developmentally necessary fusion or separation with her child.

Transference resistance: see 'Resistance'.

Transferences of deception: in a paper with this very title, Lucy Lafarge (1995) described three transferences that are characteristic of patients in whom deception and inauthenticity are central organizing themes. These transferences include: (1) *imposturous transference*, in which the patient actively enjoys deceiving the analyst by his fabrications; (2) *psychopathic–paranoid transference*, in which the patient is intensely involved with the analyst, whom he feels is lying to him and will betray him; and (3) *psychopathic–unreal transference*, in which the patient feels disconnected with the analyst and automaton-like in his own experience. In a published discussion of Lafarge's contribution, Salman Akhtar (2007e) noted that the majority of literature on patients who lie to their analysts is contributed by women analysts: Helene Deutsch, Phyllis Greenacre, Christine Oldem, Janine Chasseguet-Smirgel, Edna O'Shaughnessy, and Helen Gediman, to name a few. To be sure, male analysts (e.g., Abraham, 1925b; Weinshel, 1979; Blum, 1983b; Kernberg, 1992) have also written on the topic, but the proportion of female analysts writing about male patients who tell them lies somehow seems greater. Perhaps impostrous men deliberately

seek a woman analyst to avoid passive homosexual urges and unconscious guilt *vis-à-vis* the father and to realize an oedipal victory that they experienced as children all over again.

Transferences of hatred: Otto Kernberg (1992) has delineated three transference constellations associated with hatred: (1) *Schizoid transference* is characterized by an attitude of tenacious withdrawal, which, in the setting of devoted attendance of sessions, can be quite striking. The patient develops intractable silences, leaving an empty shell of a person in his place. When he does talk, the material remains superficial, factual, and merely interpersonal. All this has a mind-numbing and maddening impact on the analyst, who feels placed in a technical straitjacket. Often, there is a non-humanness to the entire experience (Lafarge, 1995; Akhtar, 1995). (2) *Psychopathic transference* is characterized by patient's deliberate deceptiveness, which might include withholding information, lying, or, more frequently, telling half-truths. The projection of such dishonesty leads the patient to experience the analyst as dishonest as well. (3) *Paranoid transference* is characterized by the patient's conviction that the analyst dislikes or even hates him. The patient distorts reality to fit his mistrustful belief and his repeated attacks on the analyst's benevolence can, at times, produce the 'desired result', in so far as the analyst might develop countertransference hatred on his part. While these descriptions seem valid, it should be remembered that all feelings and fantasies are ultimately multifaceted. Salman Akhtar (1999c, p. 118) has noted that (1) *schizoid transference* reflects a hostile erasure of relatedness but also a loving protection of the analyst from one's 'bad' inner contents, (2) *psychopathic transference* reflects a destruction of intimacy but also a desperate search for smooth relatedness with the analyst, and (3) *paranoid transference* reflects a mistrustful attack upon the analyst as well as a fierce clinging to him for a reliable unreliability (see separate entry on 'Inconstant object', in this connection). The complex combination of emotions inherent in these transferences therefore warrants a multifaceted attention.

Transformational object: term coined by Christopher Bollas (1979) for the profoundly influential role of maternal object *vis-à-vis* the infant's life. Not only does the mother sustain and safeguard that life, she also imparts to it a particular 'aesthetic of being' (p. 97) via her way of caring, relating and being. The transformative potential of mother and of experiences with her is imbued with a reverential and near-sacred quality. And, one looks for such encounters later in life as well, especially if there were early breaches in infant–mother relationship.

Transitional objects: Donald Winnicott's (1953) term for a child of about 4–6 to 8–12 months old (p. 232) finding an object to carry, affectionately cuddle, excitedly mutilate, and to maintain unchangingly an attitude of personal ownership, even friendship, with it. The fate of such an object, usually a teddy bear or a blanket, 'is to be gradually allowed to be decathected so that in the course of years, it becomes not so much as forgotten as relegated to limbo' (p. 233); see also Winnicott (1959). The developmental, phenomenological, and sociocultural aspects of 'transitional objects' have been further elaborated after Winnicott (see especially the edited volume by Grolnick, Barkin, & Muensterberger, 1978). Their spontaneous emergence (re-emergence?) during therapeutic work with borderline patients have also been noted (Akhtar, 1992b, 2003).One especially moving paper in this realm is that by the analyst–photographer Barbara Young (2004), which describes how her photographs served as 'transitional objects' for a very ill patient in supplying, as it were, the 'transitional space' (see separate entry) for him to achieve emotional growth.

Transitional phenomena: Donald Winnicott's (1953) term for those affective and perceptual psychic experiences that are largely subjectively 'created', experienced, and enjoyed; they are neither questioned nor left unquestioned for their material verity. Poetry, games, fiction, movies, love, faith, and spiritual and religious experiences belong in the category of transitional phenomena.

Transitional space: extrapolating from the above, Donald Winnicott (1953) proposed the existence of an area of mind where reality and unreality co-exist, which is both simple and contradictory, which is to be observed but left unquestioned, and about which there develops a 'gentlemanly agreement' that permits its origins and nature to remain private. This 'intermediate area of experience' is where imagination is born and paradox reigns supreme. It contains the space for creativity and play, and, thus, forms the 'location of cultural experience' at large.

Transitory developmental neurotic conflicts: see 'Developmental conflict'.

Transcultural identity: see 'Biculutral identity'.

Transgenerational transmission of trauma: it is well known by now that a massive trauma to a group is not entirely 'mournable' by those directly affected by it and that its long-term effects are passed on for further psychosocial processing to the next generation. The Nazi Holocaust, which resulted in the genocidal destruction of nearly two-thirds of the European Jewish population, is by far the most studied trauma of this sort. This does not mean that other massive group traumas might not have similar long-term effects. Indeed, 'transgenerational transmission of trauma' is likely to be seen as a result of the centuries-long cold and ruthless tyranny of slavery in North America, the bloodshed that accompanied the Partition of India, the mass killings in the battle-fields of Vietnam, Cambodia, and Laos, the geno-cidal atrocities in Bosnia, Rwanda, and Darfur, and even the current American pillage of Iraq. However, the available psychoanalytic information is largely based upon the study of adult and child survivors of the Holocaust and their subsequent generations. Prominent analysts, such as Judith Kestenberg (1972, 1980, 1982; Kestenberg & Brenner, 1996), Henry Krystal (1968, 1981, 1988, 2007), Henri Parens (2004, 2007b), Anna Ornstein (1985), Dori Laub (1998), Ilse Grubrich-Simitis (1984), Ira Brenner (2002, 2004), amd Ilany Kogan (1995, 2002, 2007), among others, have studied the complex and varied phenomena in this realm. The parental inability to mourn, coupled with a desire to protect the offspring from the dark shadow of persecution, results in all sorts of subtle and gross avenues for a transgenerational transmission of trauma. Secrets, unexplained flare-ups of temper, constant 'transposition' (see separate entry) of the past on the present, survival anxiety, piling up of food supplies, avoidances of topics pertaining to the Second World War and/or to Germany, overprotectiveness towards children combined with covert (and, sometimes, overt) devaluation of their problems as trivial, and holding up an unrealistically high ideal (for children, that is) of stoicism and resilience, all contribute to how the parental Holocaust trauma can be transmitted to the second or even third generation of the survivors.

Transitive vitalization: Richard Atkins's (1984) term for the myriad ways in which mothers convey the father's image to their children. Allusions to him during his absence, display of affectionate respect, upholding his authority and even valorizing him are among the various maternal behaviours included here. These help the child develop respect for the father. In John Munder Ross's (1994) words, mother is a 'myth maker who conveys in word and deed distinct impressions of the who the father is' (p. 68). This facilitates what

Janine Chasseguet-Smirgel (1984) has called the child's 'forward projection of narcissism' (see separate entry). Such development is especially beneficial for the boy's sense of paternal affliation and later evolving masculine identity.

Transmuting internalization: Heinz Kohut's (1971) term for the process that involves decathexis of the 'idealized parent imago' (see separate entry) and its internalization in the form of a psychic structure based upon realistic and healthy narcissism. Three factors play an important role here: (1) the psychic apparatus must be maturationally ready for such internalization, (2) before the internalization takes place, the qualities of the object must be broken up as a result of optimal frustration with it; this 'fractionalized withdrawal of cathexis' (p. 50) facilitates internalization, and (3) the introjected aspect of the object's image must be depersonalized; functional principles rather than specific personality traits should be internalized. If the process goes well, the child renounces the idealized view of the parent and replaces it with a strong psychic structure which provides him with sustenance and direction. If, however, disappointments with parents are premature, excessive, and *en-bloc*, 'transmuting internalization' is prevented. Reliance upon highly idealized elders then persists into adulthood. Kohut also explicated the technical yield of these developmental notions, especially in the psychoanalytic treatment of individuals with narcissistic personality disorder.

Transparent screens: concept delineated by Richard Rosenthal (1988) to describe a defensive device used by borderline patients. Preoccupied with maintaining 'optimal distance' (see separate entry) from their objects, in order to minimize the anxiety of merger on the one hand and the dread of isolation on the other, these individuals interpose imaginary, 'transparent screens' between themselves and others. These screens also help to keep unacceptable parts of their own selves hidden. According to Rosenthal, the failure of such a screen can manifest in several ways: 'it may create too great a distance, isolating the individual and keeping him from life; it may become contaminated by projection and turn into a persecutor, or trap the individual in a state of intolerable claustrophobia; most dramatically, it may suddenly shatter. The latter is associated with psychosis and death, and its appearance may be a harbinger of suicide' (p. 295).

Transposition: term originated by Judith Kestenberg (1982) to describe the experience of living in two separate worlds on the part of the children of Holocaust survivors. While not directly affected by the Holocaust, and born in lands far away from the scene of this great tradegy, many such individuals feel as if they, too, are living a Holocaust reality. This is the consequence of the myriad forms of 'transgenerational transmission of trauma' (see separate entry). 'Transposition' of the past contributes to 'preoccupation with survival, loss, persecution, and Jewish identity. The resulting feeling of almost "being there" can have a surreal, uncanny, or dissociative quality' (Brenner, 2001, p. 94).

Transsexualism: a sexual perversion characterized by (1) a fervent desire to change one's sex; (2) absence of gross anatomical abnormalities of genitalia in almost all cases; (3) denial not of one's given anatomical sex, but of its significance and 'ownership'; (4) insistence upon receiving hormones and surgery in order to extirpate one's genitals and their associated secondary sexual characteristics; (5) similar pressure to hormonally and surgically construct the facsimiles of the genitalia and secondary sexual characteristics of the opposite sex, and (6) striking lack of ambivalence about one's thoughts, feelings, and behaviour. Based upon clinical interviews with 526 transsexual patients and a comprehensive review of literature, Jon Meyer (1982) noted that there are three aetiological hypotheses regarding 'transsexualism': (1) *biological imprint hypothesis* (Money & Gaskin, 1970), which views 'transsexualism' as the unfolding of a biological vulnerability; (2) *nonconflictual identity hypothesis* (Stoller, 1968, 1970, 1975, 1979), which suggests that 'transsexualism' grows out of prolonged blissful symbiosis between a depressed, bisexual mother and her physically and emotionally beautiful son; a strong and non-conflictual female identification in the boy results and there is no oedipal phase and/or castration anxiety; (3) *conflict hypothesis* (Socarides, 1970; Ovessey & Person, 1973; Person & Ovessey, 1974a,b; Volkan, 1976, 1979; Meyer, 1974, 1980a,b,c; Limentani, 1979; Kavanaugh & Volkan, 1980), which regards the wish for transsexual surgery to be a pathological compromise function. The desire is to merge with the split-off, idealized mother figure and to keep intense hostility towards her in abeyance; sex-reassignment surgery is thus actually an 'aggression-reassignment surgery' (see separate entry). The transsexual also seeks to repair the maternal body image and to demonstrate the interconvertibility of the sexes. 'When the transsexual says that he is a girl trapped in a man's body, he sincerely means what he says. As with other symptoms, it takes a long time before he begins to say what he means' (Meyer, 1982, p. 413).

Transvestism: a sexual deviation in which erotic gratification depends upon wearing the clothes of the opposite sex; reliance upon other accoutrements and enacting the opposite gender's role are also present. The condition is more frequent in men. Its overt symptomatology serves many deeper purposes. According to Otto Fenichel (1945), the male transvestite cohabits not with a woman, but with her clothes; there is, thus, an object–erotic dimension to his behaviour, though its narcissistic side is more marked. Robert Stoller (1975) discerned four dynamic features in male 'transvestism': (1) reversal of inferiority by exhibitionistic superiority; (2) revenge against women; (3) 'actualization' (see separate entry) of the subjective sense of being a woman anyway; and (4) identification 'not only with the humiliated male but with the masterful aggressor, the phallic woman' (p. 78). The childhood background of such an individual shows seduction and sexual overstimulation by the mother; this intensifies incestuous desire and the consequent castration anxiety. It also mobilizes hostility towards her. All three (longing, fear of castration, and hostility) are denied by a magical identification with her. The female transvestite struggles with intense 'penis envy' (see separate entry), which is displaced on to the masculine appearance in general. Cross-dressing offers a way to distinguish one's self from a devalued mother and to play at being a man.

Trauma: see 'Psychic trauma'.

Trauma of geographical dislocation: a significant environmental change involves loss of relatedness to human as well as non-human constituents of the surroundings. Meaningful psychological aspects of the latter include (1) separation from a familiar ecology, (2) loss of valued personal possessions, (3) alteration in man–animal relationship, and (4) encounter with new utensils of living. Working in unison, these factors mobilize anxiety of adjustment and ache of mourning. They also cause subtle disturbances in the perceptual functions of the ego. Individuals suffering from such 'trauma of geographical dislocation' (Akhtar, 2007f) experience a figure–ground disharmony, constriction of the transitional realm, pallor of metaphor, disjunction between actions and their context, undue awareness of one's whereabouts, and discordance with the prevalent attitudes towards time. To cope with all this, they mobilize defensive measures, including fantasies

and actions of repudiation, return, replication, reunion, and reparation. The analyst who is treating such individuals should keep in mind that they need (1) a greater amount of physical settling in the office, (2) validation of their feelings of dislocation, (3) combined affirmative and interpretive approach to their nostalgia, (4) 'developmental work' (see separate entry) in regard to their new physical realities, and (5) receptivity to their non-human transferences. Together, these guidelines help the analyst to sustain and deepen analytic work with dislocated individuals.

Traumatic dreams: according to Sigmund Freud (1920g), dreams that re-create a traumatic experience betray a 'fixation' (see separate entry) on trauma and arise 'in obedience to the compulsion to repeat' (p. 32). Such dreams are not based upon the hypothesis of wish fulfilment and are primarily an expression of 'repetition-compulsion' (see separate entry). Freud did wonder if an attempt to master the effects of a traumatic situation fuelled such dreams, but put this possilbility aside in favour of his compulsion to repeat hypothesis; the latter was, in the end, related to the 'daemonic force' (p. 35) of the 'death instinct' (see separate entry). Later authors, however, moved away from this idea. Some (Silverberg, 1948; Loewenstein, 1949; Stewart, 1967) emphasized the ego's attempt to master a traumatic event by repetition as the main dynamic of 'traumatic dreams'. Others (e.g., Garma, 1946) noted that even in such dreams, some wishful distortions of trauma are always present. Still others conceptualized traumatic dreams as satisfying the dreamer's need for punishment (Wisdom, 1949) or reflecting a combination of attempts at mastery and drawing unconscious pleasure from a disturbing experience (Adams-Silvan & Silvan, 1990). A fascinating distinction was made by Owen Renik (1981) between (1) 'post-traumatic dreams' in which the traumatic event has been reworked and wishfully distorted so as to contradict what was an unpleasant reality, and (2) 'traumatic dreams' in which 'a traumatic event is accurately repeated in faithful detail by the dream's manifest content' (p. 175). The former are intended for mastery as well as all varieties of wish-fulfilment, including the gratification of masochistic desires. The latter tend to occur in association with a traumatic event whose outcome in reality was not too bad; it was actually somewhat reassuring, since worse could have happened. Renik suggests that an indidivual wakes up with a feeling of relief after a 'traumatic dream', thinking that it was 'only a dream'. In this way, a 'traumatic dream' is akin to a typical 'examination dream' (see 'Universal dreams') from which one wakes up with the thought 'but I passed that test!'.

Traumatism, traumatic, and trauma: Thierry Bokanowski's (2005) distinctions between three concepts in the realm of 'psychic trauma' (see separate entry). 'Traumatism' refers to 'sudden and brutal encounter between an unconscious fantasy and external reality (the traumatic event) ... the disruptive action of the traumatism does not engage the primacy of the pleasure–unpleasure principle but the drive-related impulse—thereby curtailing the movement towards the preconscious and conscious systems' (p. 256). 'Traumatic' refers more specifically to economic aspects of the traumatic event and rests upon the variables of unpreparedness and the rupture of the 'protective shield' (see separate entry) against overstimulation. 'Trauma' refers to the negative impact of the traumatic event and the psychic disruption caused by it.

Traumatophilia: the tendency to actively repeat highly traumatic experiences in the hope of getting rid of them while also dreading their recurrence. What distinguishes this condition from 'counterphobia' (see separate entry) is its unconscious libidinization of the traumatic repetition; this also imparts a sadomasochistic quality to the object relations of these individuals. Having been subject to profound frustrations in their childhood, 'they feel themselves to be miserable creatures, helplessly exposed to a dreadful world which heaps traumatic experiences upon them' (Fenichel, 1945, p. 545). Their suffering resembles those with 'fate compulsion' (see separate entry) and 'addiction to near-death' (see separate entry).

Traumatic neuroses: while environmental events frequently act as triggers for activating a dormant neurotic tendency, the designation 'traumatic neurosis' is reserved for situations where trauma is the decisive, not the precipitating, factor in causing symptoms. The term itself predates psychoanalysis. However, the role of trauma, as both precipitating and causative factor, in the genesis of neurosis was clearly recognized by Sigmund Freud; his concept of 'complemental series' (see separate entry) underscores this point. More specifically, he (Freud, 1920g) referred to 'traumatic neurosis' as a condition arising out of an individual's being exposed to overwhelming psychosomatic stimulation that he is incapable of psychically or motorically discharging. 'War neuroses' (see separate entry) constituted an example *par excellence* of 'traumatic neuroses'. In current psychiatric nosology, the entity 'Post traumatic stress disorder' (see separate entry) encompasses the psychoanalytic 'traumatic neuroses'.

Treatment goals *vs.* life goals: a distinction highlighted by Ernst Ticho (1972) that is of great importance to the conduct of clinical work, especially in regard to terminating an analysis. *Treatment goals* involve the removal of obstacles to the patient's discovery of what his potentials are and what his life's course, if pursued with authenticity and newly formed compromises could be. *Life goals* are tasks and achievements in external reality if the patient could put his new found psychic freedom to use; the accomplishment of the latter might depend upon variables outside the patient's control (other people's will, employment opportunities, money, age, and so on). Decision to end an analysis should emanate from an assessment of whether the patient has achieved the 'treatment goals' (e.g., reduction of transference intensity, dissolution of major symptoms, renunciation of omnipotence and perfectionism, diminution of rigidity, tolerance of separation), and not whether he has realized his 'life goals'.

Tree Model: term referring to an applied psychoanalytic paradigm developed by Vamik Volkan (1999c) for bringing opposing ethnic groups together for peaceful coexistence. The roots of the conceptual 'tree' stand for a psychopolitical assessment of the conflict between the 'enemy' groups, the trunk represents a protracted psychopolitical dialogue between high-level representatives of the opposing groups, and the branches refer to taking what has been learnt from such a dialogue to both the grassroots and official levels in order to institutionalize peaceful coexistence.

Triad of cathexis: Stanley Cath's (1965) term for the elderly person's finding secure anchors in connectedness other than that with loved ones; these include cathexis of one's own body, cathexis of nostalgically constructed 'good old days', and cathexis of transitional objects such as things, pets, and plants, as well as cultural history and civic institutions.

Triad of silence: first described by Jerome Weinberger (1964), this triad consists of silence, masochism, and depression. The three tendencies are evident both within and outside the clinical situation. Together, they appear to express the loss of a very close and unique relationship with the mother; this loss usually happened between 18 months of age and the third year of life and was unmitigated by compensatory affection from others. A pattern was thus established of 'easily injured feelings expressed through silence, masochism as manifested in suffering and withdrawl from emotional contact with others, and depression'.

Triadic conflicts: see 'Dyadic *vs.* triadic conflicts'

Triadic intersubjectivity matrix: see 'Parallelism phenomena in psychoanalysis and supervision'.

Triadic match: term coined by Judy Kantrowitz (2002) for the interaction among analytic candidate, supervising analyst, and patient. 'Overlapping or diverging characteristics of candidate and supervisor may influence the candidate's learning for good or ill depending upon the way the patient's and candidate's character and conflicts interact' (p. 937).

Triadic reality: according to James Herzog (2005), an individual's 'self' (see separate entry) is constructed by three separate, though overlapping, sets of representations. These include 'self with mother', 'self with father', and 'self with mother and father together' representations. The last mentioned reflects the 'triadic reality' of the parental couple in interaction with the child as well as the psychosocial attributes of each parent as they interact with each other. This representation allows for the optimal development of the ego capacity to play, and thus equips the child to better manage both intrapsychically and interactively that with which he must contend. Herzog's 'triadic reality' is a benign, more differentiated, and psychologically useful counterpart of the aggressively charged and psychologically deleterious 'combined parent figure' described by Melanie Klein (1929).

Trial analysis: a vestige of the early clinical practice whereby the analyst could start an analysis on a 'trial' basis for a few weeks before committing to undertake the full treatment. This period was felt to assess the tenacity of a potential analysand's resistances and his ability to co-operate with the rigours of analytic treatment. Sigmund Freud (1913c) set this practice into motion by stating that 'I have formed the practice of first undertaking analysis only provisionally for one or two weeks . . . No other kind of preliminary examination is possible' (p. 124). A trial analysis was conducted according to customary rules, but the analyst's attention was directed towards judging whether psychoanalysis was actually indicated or feasible (Ekstein, 1950; Fenichel, 1945). With the gradual evolution of assessments of 'analysability' (see separate entry) and the dwindling list of

patients waiting to be analysed, the notion of 'trial analysis' fell into disfavour. At the same time, it remains true—though certainly on a different level of abstraction—that all analyses are, in essence, trial analyses, since the degree of analytic ability on the patient's part, the 'fit' between the analyses and the analyst's own capacity to handle this or that type of psychopathology becomes clear only as the analysis proceeds.

Trial identification: see 'Analyst's work ego'.

Trial interpretation: refers to a tentatively formulated comment offered to the patient, usually during the initial evaluative interviews, in order to assess his readiness to see symbolic meanings in his communication and enter into a metaphorical dialogue about it. A 'trial interpretation' must only invoke the consciously held material that the patient has produced and/or rather overt and noticeable parapraxes in the 'here and now' of the clinical situation. It should not refer to deep unconscious fantasies and genetic or transference material that can be inferred, but is far removed from the patient's conscious awareness. In essence, a 'trial interpretation' is more akin to 'clarification' (see separate entry) than to interpretation proper. Its value lies not in its therapeutic impact, but in its testing the patient's observing ego and its strengthening his or her psychological-mindedness.

Triangle of clinical judgment: Charles Spezzano (1998) coined this phrase to indicate that the analyst is never in a purely dyadic relationship with the analysand, since the relationship he has with his analytic community also impacts upon the clinical situation. Responding to the patient, the analyst does (or, at least, tries to do) what seems indicated and useful. Responding to the analytic community, the analyst tries to stay with practices that are consensually agreed upon. While the analyst's interventions may oscillate between these two poles, synthesize contradictions between them, or take sides, the tension between patient-stimulated practicality and community-dictated compliance never fully goes away.

Tripartite model: see 'Analytic training'.

Triple instinct theory: see 'Instinct theory.

Trisexual: see 'Trisexuality'.

Trisexuality: term coined by Christopher Bollas (1987) for 'a state of desire characterized by identification with and seduction of both sexes in order to appropriate genital sexuality by redirecting it into a threesome's love of one' (p. 82). The 'trisexual' individual acts seductively towards both men and women alike, trying to co-opt their desire for him as an erotic element of a family triangle. In Bollas's words, such a person 'appropriates his lovers to become that psychic income that generates his narcissitic wealth' (p. 84).

Trishanku complex: according to *Bhagwat Puran*, the Hindu Book of Gensis, Trishanku wanted to go to Heaven but did not want to die. He enlisted the help of many Gurus and one finally agreed to help. After twelve years of ritual and worship, however, this Guru could not send Trishanku alive to Heaven; the Gods simply would not accept this. The Guru then created a separate Heaven, but the Gods intervened and sent Trishanku back from there as well. A series of back-and-forth measures led Trishanku to be shunted repeatedly between Heaven and Earth. Finally, he became suspended midway forever. The Mumbai-based analyst, Shailesh Kapadia, uses the Trishanku myth as an explanatory metaphor for the borderline patient's dilemma. According to Kapadia (1998), the borderline does not swing from one pole to another; 'he is perched on the border because, like Trishanku, he is being pulled equally from both ends' (p. 513). Among the polarities between which the borderline is stuck are '(1) intervention–action; (2) cause–effect; (3) association–interpretation; (4) patient–analyst; (5) self–object; (6) mouth–nipple; (7) mother–father; (8) form–content; (9) paranoid–schizoid and depressive position; and (10) voyeurism–exhbitionism etc.' (p. 516). Kapadia then goes on to delineate technical guidelines for working with borderline patients.

True self: one of Donald Winnicott's (1960) twin concepts of 'True' and 'False' selves. True self, fascinatingly, was never defined by Winnicott. He simply states that true self, by which most likely he meant living authentically with a lambent corporeality and unimpeded psychic life (both operating silently and in peaceful unison) cannot be described. It is in the essence of living. Indeed, it is incognito.

Turning round upon the self: see 'Reversal into the opposite'.

Twinship transference: see 'Alter-ego transference'.

Twinning reaction: a number of psychoanalytic observers and clinicians (Joseph & Tabor, 1961; Shopper, 1974; Ainslie, 1997) have noted that children born as twins have a tendency to (1) polarize identity characteristics in order to buttress their own selves, and (2) blur the boundaries between them and feel incomplete upon being separated from each other. Such 'twinning reaction' is, however, not restricted to biological twins and can, at times, be seen in siblings born less than two years apart, or even in individuals who are not siblings but have otherwise remained close over long periods of time (e.g., marital partners). Phyllis Greenacre (1958) used the term 'pseudo-twining' and Ricardo Ainslie (1997), who has extensive experience in this realm, the term 'psychological twinning' for such a development. In the case of non-twin siblings, twinning reactions are facilitated by proximity in age and by the conscious and unconscious attitudes of parents towards the two children.

Two-ness: term coined by Wilfred Bion (1967) for the 'pre-conception' (see separate entry) finding a 'realization' (see separate entry) and, thus, getting paired. Bion drew the idea of such pairing from observing the natural occurance of pairs (e.g., two eyes, two hands, two ears).

Two person psychology: see 'One person *vs.* two person psychology'.

$$\boxed{U}$$

Uncanny: Sigmund Freud (1919h) included various forms of self–other and animate–inanimate blurrings of perception, including what Otto Rank (1914) had described as the *Doppelganger* ('the double') among 'uncanny' experiences. An encounter with a dead body, *déjà-vu*, or the unintended recurrence of the same situation also produced this sort of effect. Such experiences were accompanied by a sense that one is seeing or feeling something unfamiliar (*Unheimlich*) and yet vaguely known, even 'fateful and inescapable' (Freud, 1919h, p. 237). Freud concluded that such experiences grew out of the revival of the repressed, infantile complexes and/or the sudden and unexpected 'confirmation', through an experience in reality, of primitive beliefs (e.g., omnipotence of thoughts) that had been laid to rest. The theme of the 'uncanny' also drew the attention of René Spitz (1963) and Heinz Kohut (1972) who, respectively, underscored a transient loss of the capacity for animate–inanimate distinction, and a defensive assertion that the inanimate can also have vitality, as the basis of the 'uncanny'. Their views were based upon observations pertaining to feelings about puppets and wax figurines. Sheldon Bach (1975), in contrast, provided detailed clinical material relevant to this theme and concluded that the 'uncanny' resulted from 'discontinuities of the self-experience such that the self–object world and the self do not remain continuously alive for each other' (p. 180).

Uncommon mirror dreams: see 'Mirror dreams'.

Unconscious: Jean Laplanche and Jean-Bertrand Pontalis (1973) rightly declare that if Sigmund Freud's discoveries 'had to be summed up in a single word, that word without doubt would have to be "unconscious"' (p. 474). However, the term 'unconscious' is used in three different ways: (1) *descriptive unconscious*, which refers to the simple fact that a mental content is not accessible to reflective self-awareness; (2) *system unconscious*, which refers to an aspect of mind operating solely according to 'pleasure–unpleasure principle' and 'primary process' thinking (see entries on these concepts); (3) *dynamic unconscious*, which refers to the actively repressed material that exerts 'pressure in the direction of the conscious' (Freud, 1915d, p. 151) and includes the highly organized 'unconscious fantasy' (see separate entry). However, 'the repressed does not cover everything

that is unconscious' (Freud, 1915e, p. 166). This brings up the contents of the unconscious which can be divided into four categories: (1) instinctual representatives, (2) material accrued due to 'primal repression' (see separate entry), (3) contents pushed down by the forces of 'repression' (see separate entry), and (4) phylogenetic schemata that manifest through 'primal phantasies' (see separate entry). Finally, it should be noted that the term 'unconscious' is not synonymous with id, and aspects of ego and superego are also unconscious.

Unconscious affects : see 'Affect'

Unconscious fantasy: while the powerful role of 'unconscious fantasy' in the creation of daydreams, parapraxes, and neurotic symptoms is present throughout Sigmund Freud's work (e.g., 1901b, 1908c, 1915d, 1919h, 1927c) and in the contributions of almost all subsequent analysts, it is Jacob Arlow (1969) who is credited with elucidating and widely disseminating this concept. As a result, the following features of 'unconscious fantasy' came to the forefront: (1) although unconscious, it contains fixed verbal elements; (2) in contrast to the operating principles of the system unconscious, it is internally consistent and organized; (3) in tandem with fixed fantsies, there is an ongoing unconscious fantasy life; (4) external events can trigger 'unconscious fantasy' which, in turn, can colour the perception of external events; (5) 'unconscious fantasies' are grouped together around basic childhood wishes, though their different versions, evolved during different phases of life, can serve as defences against each other; (6) elements of both drive and defence are contained in an 'unconscious fantasy'; (7) encroachment of 'unconscious fantasy' upon the realistic ego may be complete or partial; and (8) while 'unconscious fantasy' is usually quite personal in nature, it is not uncommon to discern a certain 'communality of elements' (Arlow, 1969, p. 6) in members of the same cultural or social group. Arlow's ideas have recently been reviewed and reassessed by Theodore Shapiro (1990, 2008b), Frederic Levine (1993), and Donald Moss (2008). Levine elucidates the ways in which 'unconscious fantasy' intersects with various theories of psychoanalytic technique. Moss finds Arlow's proposals, and especially his way of discerning the encroachment of 'unconscious fantasy' upon conscious experience, as theoretically declarative, emotionally non-participatory, and epistemologically suspect and one-sided. Shapiro, in contrast, lauds Arlow's relentless emphasis upon 'discovering' unconscious elements and contrasts it with the current views that associations and fantasies emerging during the clinical hour are 'co-created'. He underscores that even an 'enactment' (see separate entry) is nothing but a 'fortuitious interplay of mutual or complementary unconscious fantasies' (2008b,p. 58). It is clear that Moss and Shapiro, respectively, are representing what is euphemistically called 'two person' and 'one person' psychologies, and, thus, see Arlow's contribution in differing terms.

Unconscious guilt: see 'Need for punishment'.

Unconscious hope: see 'Hope'.

Unconscious phantoms: term coined by Fritz Wittels (1939) for the figure that comes to exist within one's internal world as a result of 'identification' (see separate entry) with an external object. Such 'unconscious phantoms' can be integrated with other intrapsychic figures or remain discrete and sequestered. In either case, they contribute to the structure of one's personality. Wittels noted that 'there are phantoms that we have to live up to; there are others we fear, some we hate or secretly love. Some of them we consider to be our real selves. Some of them must be punished, others cajoled . . . Our conflicts are battles between two or more incompatible phantoms and can be appeased by throwing the searchlight of our minds upon them' (p. 142). Wittels' term did not gain much popularity. And, in today's terminology, his notion of 'unconscious phantoms' is subsumed under the rubrics of 'internal objects' and 'introjects' (see separate entries).

Unconscious recognition: see 'Recognition and misrecognition'.

Undifferentiated energy: see 'Psychic energy'.

Undoing: an unconsciously operative defence mechanism by which the ego wards off anxiety via committing an act opposite to that which is charged with powerful id impulses and, therefore, with superego prohibitions. The act almost always follows an internally or externally induced increase in the conflicted drive. For instance, someone arriving at a friend's door can find himself saying 'please do not ask me to stay long', or 'please do not offer me a drink', in a rather transparent effort to reverse the morally conflicted and

shy desire to stay long and ask for a drink. Undoing is typically seen in obsessive–compulsive symptoms, where a prohibited or unsavoury act is done in imagination only to be reversed, as it were, by a second act in reality. As ego defence, undoing and reaction formation (see separate entry) are related; undoing is to reaction formation what weather is to season. The former pertains to a single act, the latter to a changed characterlogical constellation.

Unforgettable and unrememberable: see 'Primal repression'.

Unmentalized xenophobia: see 'Xenophobia'.

Unitary theory: with the advancement of psychoanalysis from an 'id' or 'drive psychology' through 'ego psychology' to the later perspectives of 'object relations' and the 'self' (see 'four psychologies of psychoanalysis'), it was inevitable that the question would arise as to whether psychoanalysis was one theory or two or more theories that had some common elements. George Klein's (1973) separation of 'clinical' and 'abstract' theory and Robert Wallerstein's (1988) 'official' (he was, at that time, the President of the International Psychoanalytic Association) endorsement of theoretical plurality paved the way for further developments in this regard. A more or less comfortable consensus gradually emerged. Not much different from the 'gentleman's agreement' that ended the mid-twentieth century 'controversial discussions' (see separate entry) between the Kleinians and Freudians in the UK, this consensus allows different schools to exist in peace under the large umbrella of psychoanalysis. It holds that psychoanalysis has many theories whose overlap is greater in the clinical than in the metapsychological dimension. In sharp contrast to this position are the views of the renowned psychoanalyst Leo Rangell. Having contributed over 450 papers and seven books to the discipline's literature and having been twice the President of both the American and International Psychoanalytic Associations, Rangell has earned the right to speak with authority. In a series of publications (Rangell, 1988, 1996, 2004, 2007), he argues for 'total composite psychoanalytic theory, unifed and cumulative: total because it contains all non-expendable elements, composite because it is a blend of the old and all valid new concepts and discoveries, and psychoanalytic as fulfilling the criteria for what is psychoanalysis' (2007, p. 85). Rangell lists concepts that he regards as central to the 'unitary theory' (e.g., drives, objects, preoedipal and oedipal development, infantile and transference neurosis, interplay between constitution and environment, conflict and deficit, narcissism and psychic trauma) and what can be left out, either because it is already present in theory and does not need a new name (e.g., self object), or because it is too idiosyncratic (e.g., the infantile phantasies described by the Kleinians). While Rangell regards his proposal as theoretically economic and pragmatically sound, others consider his rejection of 'modern polytheoretical psychoanalysis' (Shapiro, 1990, p. 53) as essentially 'utopian' (Bergmann, 2004, p. 26) or as a stance that risks 'foreclosing consideration of potentially revolutionary departures that are fundamental aspects of the system or the system itself' (Richards, 1999, p. 18).

Universal dreams: while dream imagery is highly individualized and meanings of a dream can only be deciphered by knowing the dreamer as a person and listening to his own thoughts about the dream, there are some dreams that are seen by all human beings at one or the other point in their lives. Such 'universal dreams' (Freud, 1900a) include: (1) the dream of flying, (2) the dream of falling, (3) the dream of being naked or inadequately dressed in a public place, (4) the dream of being chased, (5) the dream of teeth falling out, (6) the examination dream, and (7) the dream of a loved one's death. The *dream of flying* gives expression to the ubiquitous childhood wish to be able to fly. A sense of 'familiarity' to the gratification of this wish is given by fathers and uncles (mothers and aunts generally do not do such things) throwing children in the air and then catching them or simply spinning them around. The *dream of falling*, in contrast, exposes childhood fears of high places. Equipped with our mammalian heritage with its 'hard-wired' alarm button vis-à-vis depth perception, human beings fear a sudden lowering of the ground under their feet. During childhood, this manifests as uneasiness with steps and looking down from balconies. Older children turn such fears upside down and start 'enjoying' the thrills of roller-coasters and other scary rides in amusement parks. The *dream of falling* actualizes infantile dreads (instead of our adulthood fears) in a form of moral plea-bargaining. The 'punishment' this dream metes out over real and imaginary adulthood transgressions is mild compared to that which one could receive from the real world at large. The *dream of being naked in a public place* has the interesting feature that those around the person react to this vestimentary inadequacy with indifference. This is a reversal of the childhood scenario, where two–three year olds sometimes take off their clothes

and gleefully run around naked as their parents look at them in exasperation, if not horror. The dream of being naked in public places is a disguised but essentially nostalgic longing for that early childhood play with parents. The same applies to the *dream of being chased*, which recapitulates the pleasure of being pursued by a parent who is pretending to look for the child in the wrong places and then catches him by delightful surprise. But, then, why the usual horror of such dreams? After all, the chase in the dream is often frightening and unpleasant. The reason for this is that, at times, the child was indeed 'chased' to be punished by parents. The *dream of teeth falling out* symbolizes a longing to be 'toothless' i.e., unable to bite; in other words, this dream imagery is in the direction of turning us into toothless babies, innocent, harmless, and ready to be nourished by the maternal breast. In men, this dream often symbolizes a fear of sexual inadequacy and in women it implies a wish to be pregnant. The *examination dream*, which invariably is about a test one has already passed in reality, makes us confront anxieties of performance but its true message is felt upon awakening: 'Ah, but I have already passed this examination in reality'. The dream thus tells one that the dread one felt was ill-founded. The task facing one in the day ahead will go well. Finally, there is the *dream of a loved one's death*. Despite the anxiety it causes, the hostile wish implicit in the dream is almost never about the person who 'dies' in the dream. It is not even a destructive wish from contemporary adult life. It is a residue of a childhood hostile wish directed toward someone whom the individual in the dream has come to symbolize. Putting the seven dreams together, one can see the common thread that runs through them. All of them, it turns out, hark back to our childhood feelings and our childhood modes of thinking. They portray the sharpness of perception, the intensity of emotion, the ruthlessness of desire, and the urgency of action that characterizes the experience of childhood. These seven dreams are nightly chariots which take one away from the arduous land of adulthood, with all its pretence and labour, to the magical kingdom of childhood.

Unobjectionable negative countertransference: used *en passant* by Merton Gill (1994, p. 37), this term lacks a proper definition. Coupled with 'unobjectionable positive countertransference', it seems to symbolize a protest against the analyst's so-called blank-screen stance. Together, the two concepts emphasize a more humane, helpful, and emotionally engaged stance on the analyst's part. This is the minimal implication of the term.

However, it is possible to view 'unobjectionable negative countertransference' as a benign form of what Donald Winnicott (1947) subsumed under his concept of 'countertransference hatred' (see separate entry).

Unobjectionable negative transference: term coined by Nella Guidi (1993) for the potential for the patient's healthy opposition to the analyst. The 'unobjectionable negative transference' is conscious, expresses self-respect, and protects self-realization. It creates the possibility of safeguarding the patient's goals (see entry on 'treatment goals *vs.* life goals') 'even in opposition to the analyst and the analyst's rules, idiosyncracies, possible errors, and inflexibility' (p. 108). Accepting the fact that the patient might rightly disagree with the analyst creates psychic space for the former's detaching from the analyst's authority and developing autonomous thinking. Paradoxically, this very recognition creates genuine mutuality and also sets up a background for discerning real negative transference; this is hostile, partly unconscious, and a resistance to recall and collaborative work. The issue boils down to distinguishing 'assertion' from 'aggression' (see separate entries). Also pertinent in this context is the concept of the adversarial 'selfobject' (see separate entry) experience deemed I for optimal personality growth.

Unobjectionable positive countertransference: while this term was mentioned earlier in passing by Merton Gill (1994, p. 37), it was Richard Fox (1998) who truly elucidated its connotation. According to Fox, it denotes the professionally appropriate and personally ego syntonic affectionate feelings of analysts towards their analysands. Extrapolating Sigmund Freud's (1912b, p. 105) phrase 'unobjectionable transference' to the realm of countertransference, Fox noted that 'unobjectionable positive countertransference plays a comparable role in the development and maintenance of the analytic bond. The analyst's loving feelings for the patient, as reflected in acceptance and caring, are a necessary precondition for the development of this analytic bond' (p. 1077). Fox declares that doing analysis is a form of sublimated love.

Unobjectionable positive transference: according to Sigmund Freud (1912b) positive transference has two components: 'transference of friendly or affectionate feelings which are admissible to consciousness and transference of prolongation of those feelings into the unconscious' (p. 105). While the latter component needs ana-

lytic unmasking and interpretation, the former, also called 'unpronounced positive transference' (1914g, p. 153), is largely outside the purview of such analysis. It is 'the vehicle of success in analysis' and, therefore, 'unobjectionable' (1912b, p. 105). Not that childhood experiences do not enter into the construction of this 'unobjectionable positive transference'; it is only that they do not distort the patient–analyst relationship. Analysts following Freud took this concept in two directions. Some (e.g., Zetzel, 1956; Greenson, 1965) subsumed it under their concepts of 'working' or 'therapeutic alliance' (see separate entry). Others (e.g., Stein, 1981; Gill, 1994) regarded the concept sceptically and noted that seemingly rational and friendly feelings towards the analyst can hide formidable resistance. This is more marked in the treatment of candidates for analytic training.

Unobtrusive analyst: Michael Balint's (1968) characterization of the correct technical attitude on the analyst's part when the patient is regressed and the area of 'basic fault' (see separate entry) is reached. The analyst, working under circumstances in which spoken words become unreliable, must bear the patient's regression for the time being, without attempting to organize or interpret the patient's material. He should 'sincerely give up, for the time being, any attempt to force the patient back to the verbal level' (p. 177). The analyst must, therefore, create a clinical climate in which regression can be tolerated and acting out accepted as a valid means of communication. There should be only minimal clash of interest between the patient and the analyst. Balint emphasized that the analyst need not provide extra love, attention, or gratification; he only needs to act as a 'provider of time and milieu' (p. 179) in which the patient can find himself, accept himself, and get on with himself, without external impingements.

Unpleasure: a concept belonging to the economic perspective of Freudian 'metapsychology' (see separate entry). The word itself is 'not a neologism since it was used by Coleridge in 1841' (Rycroft, 1968, p. 174). Used in place of the German *Unlust*, it denotes the uncomfortable build-up of instinctual (sexual or aggressive) tension in the psyche.

Unpleasure principle: see 'Pleasure–unpleasure principle'.

Unthinkable anxieties: Donald Winnicott's (1962) designation of the dreads experienced by the baby's immature psyche, especially when unsupported by the mother's care. Indeed, Winnicott suggested that the baby is all the time on the brink of 'unthinkable anxiety', though it is kept away by the vitally important function of the maternal care. There are four varieties of such anxiety: '(1) going to pieces, (2) falling forever, (3) having no relationship to the body, and (4) having no orientation' (p. 58). Winnicott regarded these to be the 'stuff of the psychotic anxieties' (p. 58); such fears are overt in schizophrenia but can also be found hidden in an otherwise non-psychotic personality. See also the related entries on 'annihilation anxiety' and 'psychotic anxiety'.

Unthought known: Christopher Bollas' (1987) term for the traces of very early object relations and their attendant 'memories of being and relating' (p. 3), all of which are known to the individual at a deep level, but have not yet been the subject of thought. Such 'inarticulate elements of psychic life' (p. 210) are largely discerned through countertransference experience. Sigmund Freud's (1895d) concept of 'primal repression' and its later elaboration by Alvin Frank (1969) under the title of the 'unrememberable and the unforgettable' are also pertinent in this context.

Urethral eroticism: while Sigmund Freud (1905a) had termed it 'urinary eroticism', Isidor Sadger's (1910) term 'urethral eroticism' gained wider acceptance. Perhaps this was because 'organ pleasure' (see separate entry) was more emphasized in those days than the enjoyment of an action. In any case, 'urethral eroticism' is a concept which relates to the pleasure derived from urination. Both excretory and retentive pleasures exist in relation to urination. Primarily autoerotic, 'urethral eroticism' soon shifts to involve objects and gets associated with fantasies about 'urinating at objects, being urinated on by objects, or with fantasies in which the connection with urination is more concealed' (Fenichel, 1945, p. 69). Urethral eroticism can have active and passive forms. The active form involves pleasures of forcefully urinating to damage something, to make it wet, to put a fire out, to compete with others about the strength and duration of urinary stream, and so on. The passive form involves the pleasures of gently letting go of urinary control and foregoing any sense of agency for the act. The active form of urethral eroticism, especially in boys, frequently becomes condensed with phallic penetrative fantasies, and the passive form with anal receptive aims or fantasies of being a woman. In girls, the idea of letting the urine flow passively is sometimes placed upwards and causes frequent teariness. In both sexes, loss of bladder control is closely linked with shame, which, in turn, is defended by ambition, though clearly ambition itself is derived from many childhood roots.

Urinary eroticism: see 'Urethral eroticism'.

Use of an object: Donald Winnictt's (1968a) notion which implies that it is only after the destruction of an object in phantasy and its subsequent survival, that a subject can actually 'use' it. Winnicott noted that such destruction 'places the object outside the area of the subject's omnipotent control . . . the object develops its own autonomy and life, and (if it survives) contributes in to the subject, according to its own properties' (p. 90). Winnicott emphasized that by 'use' he does not mean 'exploitation'. He felt that, while most patients come prepared to use the analyst, there are others 'who need us to able to give them a capacity to use us' (p. 94) by surviving their destructiveness. As a historical aside, Winnicott's presentation of these ideas at the New York Psychoanalytic Society in 1968 was met with a harsh discussion by Bernard Fine and an icy silence by the audience (Winnicott, Shepherd, and Davis, 1989; Kahr, 1996). This rejection caused him much pain and led him to write two more papers (Winnicott, 1968b, 1970) on 'use of an object' or 'object usage'.

$$\boxed{\textbf{V}}$$

Vagina dentata: a male fantasy that the vagina has teeth and can bite off the penis that is inserted into it. 'Vagina dentata' has two ontogenetic origins: (1) projection of oral–sadistic impulses upon women followed by their 'downwards' displacement to create the retaliatory fear of the vagina, and (2) the displacement of castration fear from father to mother. The fantasy is more common among men with pre-oedipal frustrations with the mother and the rage consequent upon them.

Vagina man: term coined by Adam Limentani (1989) for a particular kind of male sexual identity problem in which the individual harbours (1) a powerful wish to be a woman, (2) profound envy of everything female, and (3) a jealously guarded secret of possessing a fantasy vagina. For such a man, 'not only the anus and the mouth, but also the eye, the ear, and urethral orifice are endowed with receptive qualities similar to that of the vagina' (p. 192). The 'vagina man' is intelligent, charming, and friendly. He reads voraciously, looks at things intently, and insatiably seeks the company of others, especially women. He is feminine, but femininity is hidden behind attentiveness towards women. Owing to this attentiveness, his sexual performance is better than average. But his own pleasure is compromised 'by the envy of what the partner is experiencing, coupled with a desire to know exactly what that experience is' (p. 201). According to Limentani, such men have been raised by mothers who were somewhat masculine, while also treating their child as their phallus. The 'vagina man' constellation results from an identification with such a mother. It also serves as a defence against homosexuality. Moreover, the fantasy of belonging to the other sex helps avoid the fear of castration.

Vengeance: Charles Socarides (1966) has offered a sophisticated and detailed description of 'vengeance', or the desire to get even. The conscious aim of this desire is retribution, punishment, and a longed-for state of peace. Its unconscious aim is to undo a damage to the ego, originally experienced in childhood and revived by a traumatic event in current life. Its surface manifestations include grudge-holding, unforgiveness, inconsolability, and ruthlessness. With astounding 'narrow-mindedness' (see separate entry), the individual driven by vengeance shows little concern for the possible moral and social conse-

quences of his actions. Genetic exploration in such cases routinely reveals early oral deprivation. Given this, the patient's revenge-seeking appears to have defensive aims of concealing, if not magically undoing, the deepest traumata of his childhood. Four other aspects of vengeance need recognition: (1) while preoedipal injury to the self mostly underlies this affect, castration fantasies and the pain of oedipal exclusion also contribute to it; (2) 'vengeance masked by love' (Menninger, 1959) manifests in men as sexual promiscuity by which women are repeatedly seduced and abandoned; (3) a chronically humiliating and 'castrating' attitude towards men, especially one's husband, is a parallel manifestation of vengeance in women; and (4) groups and nations can also carry vengeance, often passing the hateful need to redress a group trauma from one generation to the other; victimized nations of yesterday can become harsh oppressors of today.

Vengeance masked by love: see 'Vengeance'.

Vertical split: see 'Horizontal and vertical splits'.

Villain hunger: Salman Akhtar's (2007c) term for the need to have someone (an individual or a group) to blame for one's problems. Such externalization of aggression blocks the awareness of one's own contributions to the hardship being faced; sadness and mourning are thus kept in abeyance. Anger makes one feel strong. Paranoia becomes a psychic vitamin for threatened identity and a powerful anodyne against the pain that results from genuine self-reflection. This is the essential dynamic of 'villain hunger'. And this hunger is readily activated when a large group's identity is threatened from external or internal sources. Most such threats are constituted by economic upheaval, but sometimes the sudden disappearance of a well-known enemy can also destabilize the group. The fall of the Soviet Union, for instance, created a vacuum in the American large group dynamics and, in part, led to it finding a new enemy in the form of Islamic fundamentalism (not that some Muslims did not invite such an occurrence themselves).

Visual images during psychoanalytic sessions: as Sigmund Freud advanced from his early 'pressure technique' (see separate entry) to unobtrusively utilizing patients' free associations in order to access his or her unconscious, the emphasis upon reporting visual images diminished in favour of verbal trains of thought. Mark Kanzer (1958) and Max Warren (1961) revived interest in the visual images that occur to a patient during the analytic hour. They noted that such images might be (1) reported spontaneously by the patient, (2) elicited by active inquiry during, and interruption in, the patient's flow of talk, and (3) at times, totally replace his or her verbalization. In general, there is less distortion in such images than in dreams; 'the interval between the image and the patient's talking about it minimizes the time available for secondary elaboration' (Warren, 1961, p. 517). Visual phenomena are less object-related than verbalization, though both can be used for narcissistic purposes. Three technical manoeuvres to utitlize them for analytic purposes are (1) encouraging the patient to put movement into static images, (2) linking the images to preceding verbal material, and (3) facilitating free associations to the image itself. See also Bennett Simon's (1981) interesting paper on the communicative function of confluence of visual images between the patient and analyst.

Von Domarus principle: according to Emile Von Domarus (1944), an individual with normal thinking accepts identity based upon identical subjects, but one given to paleological thought (e.g., a schizophrenic) accepts identity based upon identical predicates. Thus, a normal individual can conclude that Dr X is a psychoanalyst by putting the following two statements together: 'Those who are members of the International Psychoanalytic Association (IPA) are psychoanalysts' and 'Dr X is a member of the IPA'. A schizophrenic , however, may put two statements like 'Claudio Laks Eizirik, the President of the IPA, lives in Brazil' and 'Dr X lives in Brazil', and conclude that 'Dr X is the President of the IPA'. This conclusion appears 'crazy' to the normal person and is drawn by equating the identity of two predicates ('lives in Brazil') with the identity of subjects. Such thinking is a major contributor to the development of delusions in schizophrenia. Silvano Arieti (1974) has elucidated these ideas in great details with the help of vivid clinical illustrations.

Voyeurism: term employed in two, overlapping ways: (1) *defined narrowly*, 'voyeurism' stands for the predominant and mandatory mode of obtaining sexual gratification by watching nude women or two individuals engaged in sexual acts; the interest in watching genital activity can be displaced to foreplay and pregenital acts; (2) *defined broadly*, 'voyeurism' is but one of the pregenital erotic instincts (Freud, 1905a) which, along with its twin, 'exhibitionism' (see separate entry), succumbs to 'genital primacy' (see separate entry) over the course of development. Voyeurism as a sexual deviation is seen (pun unintended!) almost exclusively in men; unlike the notorious 'Peeping Tom', there is no 'Peeping Maria'. This is perhaps because the central dynamic in the perversion is a libidinized, counterphobic defence against castration anxiety. However, there is something 'organically' different between men and women in this regard as well. Women are far less dependent upon visual cues for romantic and sexual arousal. Besides these counterphobic and constitutional factors, early deprivation of libidinal ministrations by the mother can also intensify vision as a modality of contact (Spitz, 1965; Greenacre, 1953). This, in turn, can contribute to the later development of voyeurism. Finally, it should be noted that, while children 'spy' on parents and older relatives, the adult voyeur prefers looking at unsuspecting strangers and at pornographic material. Moreover, the epistemic vector in children's pursuit is missing from the adult's perversion; a modicum of superego defiance and sadism (Socarides, 1974) often accompanies the latter.

$$\boxed{\textbf{W}}$$

Waiting syndrome: Leon Altman's (1957) designation of a clinical constellation consisting of (1) prolonged suspension of effort and a tendency towards postponement of decisions, and (2) a reliance on time to come to one's aid and solve one's problems. Such a 'waiting syndrome' represents infantile ideas of omnipotence, pleasure in anal retention, denial of oedipal limits, and pregenital satisfaction in general. The syndrome seems to have overlaps with the 'Someday . . .' fantasy (see separate entry).

Waking screen: term originated by Joseph Kepecs (1952) for a sensation of being surrounded or enveloped by transparent substances which separate one from the outer world. The individual with a 'waking screen' might feel that objects do not appear vivid and clear; he might experience the analyst as also blurred. According to Kepecs, the 'waking screen', is regularly a manifestation of defence. Joseph Slap (1974) added that the appearance of a 'waking screen' is expressive of a wish to sleep, often accompanied by a fantasy of being in the womb. Accordingly, the substances constituting the screen are symbolic of the claustral wall. Six years later, Bernard Pacella (1980) used the same term in an entirely different context. In this usage, 'waking screen' denotes the background of perceptual experience derived from the earliest exposure to the external world (e.g., its smells, sounds, skin colour of significant others, types of trees and houses, etc.). The background of expectations plays 'an active role in scanning, integrating, rejecting, or modifying all the new percepts of object representations throughout life' (p. 130).

War neuroses: a traumatic neurosis precipitated by experiences during a war. The phenomenon had first been noted in connection with the First World War. Sigmund Freud (1918) regarded it to be the result of 'the conflict between two ego ideals: the customary one and the one war had compelled the person to build' (cited in Jones, 1955, p. 283). The former abhorred violence and the latter, under the mesmerizing influence of the military superiors, exalted it. More experience accrued with the Second World War and the symptomatology of the disorder was further elucidated by Abraham Kardiner (1941) and Roy Grinker Sr (1945) among others. Social withdrawal, irritability, flashbacks, and difficulties in interpersonal relationships constitute its main features. Clinical data from later wars, especially the Vietnam war (Schwartz, 1984), was then added to the mix. A finding that gradually emerged was that the veterans not only suffered from the direct effects of ego-overwhelming stress, but also from guilt at what they had done to others during the war. 'War neuroses' can be subsumed under the current psychiatric entity 'Post traumatic stress disorder' (see separate entry). However, the latter is a broad category that includes reactions to traumatic events of civilian life as well.

We-go: see 'We-ness'.

We-ness: in a posthumously published paper, George Klein (1967) proposed that psychoanalysis needs a therapy of 'we-go' as a counterpart of its theory of 'ego'. The internalized sense of 'we-ness' implied here has been elaborated upon by Anni Bergman (1980) and Robert Emde (1988). Bergman suggests that the feeling of 'we' is 'psychically experienced as the "we" of primary narcissism which still dominates the symbiosis. Only gradually does this archaic "we" experience develop to include differentiated "me" and "we" experiences' (p. 205). Robert Emde (1988) notes that, around three years of age, children demonstrate the capacity to follow internalized rules in the physical absence of parents. Such injunctions carry with them an autonomous sense of 'we-ness'. The concurrent consolidation of 'shared meanings' by matching gestures and actions with the caretaking other enhances such 'we-ness'. Emde adds, however, that it is unclear whether 'the three year old's "executive we" is more characteristic of optimal or of normative development' (p. 36). In a different context, Salman Akhtar (1999b) has elucidated the development of 'we-ness' in the immigrant as he or she moves thinking in 'mine' and 'yours' terms to that of 'ours'.

We-self: a term used by Alan Roland (1996) to denote the intrapsychic experience of Asian Indians who live in an ongoing state of partial merger with others, with an emotional flow back and forth. Some aspects of the self are clearly demarcated from others, while some other aspects are merged with them. Such an organization might be regarded as manifesting insufficient 'separation–individuation' (see separate entry). However, affixing labels of this sort betrays a theoretical colonialism which declares that what takes place in the West *vis-à-vis* separation–individuation is truly optimal and correct. Roland avoids this trap and offers his observations in an impartial manner.

Whole object: Melanie Klein's (1935) term for the perception of a person in his totality. This means that (1) the person is seen in his or her complete physical existence, (2) the 'good' and 'bad' aspects of the person are integrated, (3) the person is seen to have motivations, independent of oneself, and (4) the person is 'allowed' to have feelings of his own, including those of suffering. Such perception is characteristic of the 'depressive position' (see separate entry).

Widening scope of psychoanalysis: shortened version of 'The widening scope of indications for psychoanalysis', which was the title of the celebrated 1954 paper by Leo Stone which made the following points: (1) the scope of analytic treatment has gradually gone beyond neurotics who are capable of developing proper and analysable transference neurosis, (2) while difficulties in treatment increase as the nosological periphery is reached, psychoanalysis can be used for some very ill people who are inaccessible to other treatments and well-motivated to get better, and (3) 'both extranosological factors and therapist's personal tendencies may profoundly influence the indications and prognosis' (p. 593). While work with the 'widening scope patients' (as borderline, narcissistic, schizoid, and perverse individuals subsequently came to be known) have now become commonplace, in the setting of 1954 North America psychoanalysis, Stone's paper was indeed bold and dramatic. In fact, Anna Freud (1954), who wrote an accompanying discussion said 'I have nourished the secret ambition to write a really exhaustive, theoretically well-founded paper on the practical, technical aspects of psychoanalysis. Naturally, I feel envious that, in my place, Dr. Stone has made the attempt and has succeeded brilliantly in its execution' (p. 608).

Wild analysis: while Sigmund Freud has alluded to the notion earlier (1905a), he used the terms 'wild analysis' and 'wild psychoanalysis' *per se* for the first time in 1910. He emphasized that two conditions must be met before an analysand can become able to understand and accept his repressed, unconscious wishes. These conditions were (1) the patient should himself become able to approach 'the neighbourhood of what he has repressed' (1910k, p. 226), and (2) the relationship with the analyst should be reasonably well-established. In the absence of these conditions, attempts to rush the patient 'by brusquely telling him the secrets which have been discovered by the physician are technically objectionable' (p. 226). This was 'wild analysis'. Freud emphasized that the patient's resistances must be worked through before content based interpretations are made. 'If knowledge about the unconscious were as important for the patient as people inexperienced in psychoanalysis imagine, listening to lectures or reading books would be enough to cure them. Such measures, however, have as much influence on the symptoms of neurosis illness as a distribution of menu cards in a time of famine has upon hunger' (p. 225). Wild analysis is not only helpful, it can harm an individual by destabilizing their psychic equilibrium. None the less, there remain analysts who do not hesitate to make rapid and deep pronouncements on their patient's dynamics and, indeed, take pride in doing so. In Freud's own lifetime, Georg Groddeck is known to have boastfully declared: 'I am a wild psychoanalyst!' (Kiell, 1988).

Wild psychoanalysis: see 'Wild analysis'.

Wish: Sigmund Freud (1900a) formally explicated the concept of 'wish' (*Wunsch*), the cornerstone of the psychoanalytic motivational theory, in his book on dreams. He stated that, after an experience of satisfaction, the mnenic image of a perception remains with the memory trace of the excitation produced by that need. Freud went on to say that 'next time this need arises a psychical impulse will seek to re-cathect the mnemic image of the perception itself, that is to say to restablish the situation of the original satisfaction. An impulse of this kind is what we call a wish' (pp. 565–566). While at times using the two terms interchangeably, in principle, Freud distinguished a 'wish' from a 'need'. 'Need' is the psychical representative of a stimuli originating from within the organism, whereas 'wish' is inextricably bound with memory traces of previous gratification. 'Need' was basic and 'wish' a way of obtaining its satisfaction. Also, Freud implied that a 'need' could not be repressed while a 'wish' was subject to repression (Harold Blum, personal communication, December 1993). Salman Akhtar (1999a) has elucidated the complexities involved in the 'need–wish distinction' (see separate entry) in detail.

Wish fulfilment: a psychological formation which makes it appear that a wish has been realized. The notion was first mentioned by Sigmund Freud (1900a) in connection with dreams, which he regarded as fulfilment of repressed wishes. Later, he extended the idea to all neurotic symptoms. These, too, were forms of 'wish fulfilment', though often the wishes they gratify were contradictory or include aspects of defences erected against them. The relationship of 'wish fulfilment' to 'pleasure principle' (see 'pleasure–unpleasure principle') and 'primary process' (see 'primary and secondary processes') is also worthy of attention, since the urgency of discharge and collapse of reality characterize all three concepts. This does not mean 'wish fulfilment' cannot be brought about in actuality with the help of 'reality principle' (see separate entry) and 'secondary process' (see 'primary and secondary processes'), but that is not what 'wish fulfilment' as a psychoanalytic concept means; this concept refers to an intrapsychic and hallucinatory equation of wish and its gratification.

Withdrawal of cathexis: see 'Decathexis'.

Witnessing and the analytic process: Warren Poland's (2000) term for the analyst's recognizing and 'getting' 'what the patient is saying without doing anything more active about it' (p. 21). Such 'witnessing' has four other aspects: (1) it involves the active observing presence of the analyst, who is experienced by the patient as a distinctly separate person, (2) it evolves from 'holding' (see separate entry), but implies letting go and 'respecting the patient's essential aloneness' (p. 21), (3) it has a dialectical relationship with interpreting; interpreting enhances self-object differentiation and thus allows for more 'witnessing', which, in turn, yields material for interpretation, and (4) it actualizes the patient's growing autonomy and is therefore more evident as the analysis approaches termination. The issue of the *Journal of the American Psychoanalytic Association* that carried Poland's paper also contained commentaries on it by Jorge Ahumada, Emanuel Berman, Marcia Cavell, André Green, Edgar Levenson, and Alfred Margulies.

Without memory or desire: Wilfred Bion's (1967) celebrated phrase for the mental attitude he deemed ideal for an analyst during the analytic session. According to Bion, psychoanalytic observation is concerned 'neither with what has happened nor with what is going to happen but what is happening' (p, 271). An analyst must therefore cultivate a 'wilful avoidance of memory' (p. 273) and not have desires for results, causes, and even understanding. Sounding quite like J. Krishnamurti, the renowned Indian mystic and philosopher, Bion stated that a psychoanalyst 'should aim at achieving a state of mind so that at every session he feels he has not seen the patient before. If he feels he has, he is treating the wrong patient' (p. 280). Bion's conceptual overlap with Krishnamurti here is especially intriguing considering the fact that Bion was also born in India!

Without-ness: Wilfred Bion's (1962) expression for the decrease in knowledge (−K) and love (−L) that result from a container–contained relationship (see entry on 'Container') controlled by envy. Instead of removing fear and ignorance, the container (e.g., the breast, the analyst) is felt to enviously remove love and knowledge and thus create anxiety (see entry on the related concept of 'Nameless dread').

Womb fantasies: Bertram Lewin (1935), Jacob Arlow (1969), and Vamik Volkan (1997) have described unconscious fantasies in which one enters the mother's womb and encounters and destroys the father or sibling there. Often such a fantasy underlies claustrophobia in an adult patient. The patient displaces the mother's womb on to an enclosed place (e.g., a closet, aeroplane) and then avoids being there. The term 'womb fantasy' does not refer to imaginary scenarios about one's blissful existence in the mother's uterus; these Freud derided as 'retrospective fantasying' (1918b, p. 103).

Word presentation: see 'Thing presentation and word presentation'.

Work: in a much quoted statement, Sigmund Freud (1930a) declared that 'no other technique for the conduct of life attaches the individual so firmly to reality as laying emphasis on work; for his work at least gives him a secure place in a portion of reality, in the human community' (p. 80). Besides its central significance to a healthy existence, work has the following notable features: (1) it is not synonymous with holding a job or making money, though it may be involved in them; (2) it involves physical or mental activity aimed at producing a desired effect; (3) it may yield narcissistic, object related, sexualized, and aggressive pleasure but these are secondary, since work has its own rewards for the ego (see 'Work principle'); (4) it plays a role in regulating self esteem and maintaining identity; and (5) it follows a 'developmental line' (see separate entry) from infancy to old age with the phases of latency and young adulthood being most important to its consolidation. Charles Socarides and Selma Kramer's (1997) edited volume titled *Work and Its Inhibitions* deals with these matters (and their pathological variants) in a truly comprehensive manner.

Work compulsion: while Karen Horney (1937) had talked of 'the compulsive passion for work', it was Yale Kramer (1977) who wrote the first paper specifically focused upon 'work compulsion'. In his view, the driven and overwhelmingly preoccupying dedication to work was a multi-determined symptom. It served as a defence against (1) feelings of low self-esteem, (2) castration anxiety, and (3) anxieties consequent upon aggression and guilt. The last mentioned dynamic brings 'work compulsion' under the overall umbrella of 'manic defence' (see separate entry).

Work group: see 'Basic assumption group and work group'.

Work inhibition: Sigmund Freud's (1926d, p. 89) dictum that 'the ego function of an organ is impaired if its erogenicity—its sexual significance—is increased' applies as much to 'work inhibition' as it does to inhibitions in other areas of functioning. In Freud's view, this dynamic might acquire further strength from the fact that 'men are not spontaneously fond of work' (Freud, 1927c, p. 8). The topic of 'work inhibition' was taken up by many subsequent analysts. Melanie Klein (1928) emphatically stated that 'in both sexes, one of the principal rules of inhibitions is the anxiety and sense of guilt associated with the femininity phase' (p. 191). Otto Fenichel (1945) added that conflicts around autonomy, ambition, exhibitionism, and success frequently give rise to inhibitions of the capacity to work. More recently, Dorothy Holmes (2006a,b) traced problems of work-related success to parental psychic investment in work, social class, race, and gender and Selma Kramer (1997) traced the roots of learning difficulties to childhood sexual abuse. Charles Socarides and Selma Kramer's (1997) edited volume on the topic of work sheds further light on work inhibition as it crops up at different times in life and in different social and occupational realms.

Work of the negative: André Green's (1993) collective designation for mental functions that aim to reject objects, disinvest perception, and impoverish the ego. Green subsumes the Freudian idea that neurosis is the inverse of perversion and the concept of 'negative therapeutic reaction' (Freud, 1923b) as well as the mechanisms of 'repression', 'negation', 'splitting', and 'disavowal'. Under the broad rubric of the 'work of the negative', to this list he adds five additional notions of his own,

namely (1) 'negative hallucination', (2) 'negative hallucination of thought', (3) 'subjective disengagement by the ego', (4) 'negative narcissism', and (5) the ego's sense of self disappearance. Fuelled by destructive drives, these processes impel the individual towards a decision to accept or reject something: an object, a perception, a thought, or even one's own subjective existence (for more details, see separate entries on the various concepts mentioned here, including the four novel concepts of Green).

Work pleasure: see 'Work principle'.

Work principle: term coined by Ives Hendrick (1943a) for 'the principle that primary pleasure is sought by efficient use of the central nervous system for the performance of well-integrated ego functions which enabled the individual to control or alter his environment' (p. 311). This lays bare the fact that sexualized and narcissistic pleasures derived from work, regardless of their intensity, are actually by-products. Work has its own rewards in terms of ego gratification; this is 'work pleasure', pure and simple. This idea is replicated in George Klein's (1976) concept of 'pleasure in effectiveness' and Ernest Wolf's (1988) description of the self-enhancing role of 'efficacy experiences'.

Working alliance: see 'Therapeutic alliance'.

Working off: term introduced by Edward Bibring (1943) for the ego aspect of 'repetition compulsion' (see separate entry) that is predominantly aimed at diminishing the need for traumatic re-creations and does so by detaching libido from the pertinent memory traces over time and by establishing increasing familiarity with the anxiety-producing situation. This notion was further developed by Daniel Lagache (1957) who emphasized that, unlike ego defences, 'working off' mechanisms were not governed by 'primary process' (see 'primary and secondary processes') and were directed at resolving ego's own defensive operations.

Working out: borrowing from Jean-Martin Charcot (1889), who talked of 'working out' as the process between the end points of trauma and its appearance in symptoms, Sigmund Freud (1895d) proposed that it is the lack of associative binding and inadequate 'working our' of traumatic events that leads to hysterical conversion symptoms. A similar use of the concept is evident in his later descriptions of 'actual neurosis' (see separate entry).

Working through: term coined by Sigmund Freud (1914c) in connection with the piecemeal metabolism of newly gained insights during the psychoanalytic process. This means that resistances which have been overcome keep cropping up again and again and their interpretations have to be repeated afresh. There is an inherent 'laziness' involving change and a tenacity to 'id resistance' (see 'resistance'). Both the analyst and the analysand have to revisit material that has been analysed countless numbers of times and expand, fine-tune, and deepen the insights in this process. A quick agreement and rapid behavioural change following interpretation is suspect. It is the gradual and painstaking assimilation of insights gained as a result of repeated dissolution of resistances that ultimately matters. This is the essence of 'working through'. To this well-accepted meaning of the term, Charles Rycroft (1968) has added the slowly evolving psychic adjustment to any and all changed inner and/or outer realities. This extension seems to equate 'working through' with 'mourning' (see separate entry) and appears to unnecessarily dilute a useful technical concept.

World destruction fantasies: phrase originated by Paul Schilder (1925) for the feeling frequently associated with the onset of schizophrenia that everything has lost meaning and that the world is coming to an end. This results from (1) massive narcissistic withdrawal and decathexis of object representations, (2) domination of the subject's psyche with hostile and destructive drives, mentally represented as a destroyed world. William Spring (1939) pointed out that it is more pleasant to think of the end of the whole world than only of one's own. The idea that the world is coming to an end thus involves the simultaneous gratification of sadistic and masochistic impulses; that is the 'gratification of a destructive wish without distinction between the ego and external objects' (p. 56).

World reconstruction fantasies: originally described by Paul Schilder (1925), these imaginary scenarios of early schizophrenia consist of a sense that every little thing in the external reality is suffused with meaning. The world, which seemed to have lost all meaning (see 'world destruction fantasies') now comes alive. The patient might develop 'psychotic insight' (Arieti, 1955) and attribute this rejuvenation to mysterious, cosmic forces. Or, he might take it upon himself to reconstruct the world. Regardless of their specific content, 'world reconstruction fantasies' represent an effort at massive, if haphazard, re-cathexis of reality from which only a little while ago the patient had become so hatefully and regressively detached.

Wound of return: expression coined by the Spanish journalist Maruja Torres (cited in Leon Grinberg and Rebecca Grinberg, 1989) to denote the disappointments and difficulties faced by the immigrant who moves back to his original country; the person himself is changed and the country is no longer what he left behind, making the 'return' yet another immigration.

Writer's block: phrase introduced into psychoanalytic literature by the prolific psychoanalyst, Edmund Bergler in 1947. Coined to denote the drying up a writer's wellspring of creative imagination, the phrase gained wide currency owning to its brevity and self-evident nature. Bergler noted that writer's block may be total or partial, and its earliest manifestation may be feelings of insecurity regarding one's creativity, the development of a certain terseness of style, and looking to others for ideas for future projects. Bergler traced the origins of writer's block to oral masochism and superego driven need for punishment (see also the related entry on 'Publication anxiety').

X

Xenophobia: term applied to fear, mistrust and avoidance of those who are culturally, racially, or religion-wise different from one's self. The xenophobic individual lacks knowledge of others and makes no use of the opportunities that can provide such knowledge. The circle of socialization is restricted to those of his own group. An inevitable correlate of this is a smug self-acceptance. Such restriction of the ego's social surface buttresses repression of shameful and unwanted aspects of one's own ethnocultural self-representation. Often the avoidances caused by 'xenophobia' remain outside of the awareness of the individual. One simply does not think about discordant cultures and people, nor does one pay attention to the inner voices that do not fit with a highly sanitized view of oneself. This constitutes the syndrome of 'unmentalized xenophobia' (Akhtar, 2007c).

Y

Yearning: an emotion of helpless craving associated, on a crude and colloquial level, with addictions and infatuations and, on a psychoanalytically sophisticated level, with the sense of longing seen in relation to 'mental pain' (see separate entry).

Z

Zac's constants: according to Joel Zac (1971), there are three constants in the analytic treatment: (1) those emanating from the theory of psychoanalysis; (2) dependent on the analyst (e.g., his character, office, holiday schedule), and (3) those arising out of the specific nature of a particular analytic dyad. Each of these constants can be drawn into conflict, with the latter to being especially likely to contribute to transference-countertransference developments.

Zoerastia: see 'Bestiality'.

Zoerasty: see 'Bestiality'.

Zone of proximal development: concept introduced by the Russian psychologist Lev Vygotsky (1956, 1978) under the title of *zona blizaishego razvitia*. Translated into English as the 'zone of proximal development', the concept addressed the fact that two people, working in an atmosphere of mutuality, can create the possibility of psychological growth of the weaker member of the dyad. Arnold Wilson and Lisa Weinstein (1996) were the first to meaningfully extrapolate the Vygotskian concept to clinical psychoanalysis. They define the 'zone of proximal development' as the space which contains 'the processes that beget the differences between an analsand's ability to advantageously make use of the dyadic nature of the clinical situation as contrasted with solitary introspection or self-analysis, in order to acquire insight and capacities that promote self-knowledge and ultimately self-regulation' (p. 171). In the clinical setting, the 'zone of proximal development' and the patient's transferences create a partnership allowing for insight and mutative internalizations.

Zoophilia: see 'Bestiality'.

An Annotated List of Psychoanalytic Glossaries

The first psychoanalytic glossary

Handwörterbuch der Psychoanalyse, by Richard Sterba. Vienna: Internationaler Psychoanalytischer Verlag, 1932.

This German language book is the first surviving glossary of psychoanalysis. A glossary had been published some twelve years before it by the Hungarian Psychoanalytic Society, according to Sandor Lorand (personal communication, Eidelberg, 1968, p. 344) but all its copies were destroyed by the Nazis during their takeover. Sterba's book is therefore of great historical importance. Its story should be riveting for all those who live and breathe psychoanalysis. Sterba was encouraged to compile a collection of psychoanalytic terms, along with their definitions, by Adolf Strofer, who at that time was the Director of Internationale Psychoanalytischer Verlag, the publishing house set up at the behest of Sigmund Freud. However, by the time Sterba prepared the first instalment of the manuscript, Strofer had been replaced by Martin Freud as the person in charge of the press; the latter is thus the 'official' publisher of the book. The book itself appeared in five instalments of some twenty-five pages each. By the time the fifth instalment was published, Freud was turning eighty. It was therefore decided to put the five booklets together in the form of a solid and continuous volume. Freud was not only pleased by it, but also agreed to write a brief Foreword for it. With characteristically wry exhortation, Freud instructed Sterba to undertake this work not for any external rewards, but only as a submission to some 'internal obligation' (Freud, 1932, p. 253). Freud also suggested that each German language entry should be accompanied by its English and French translation. The English translations were done by Edith Jackson in consultation with the 'informal glossary committee' (Ornston, 1985, p. 391) headed by Ernest Jones. The French translations were done by La Commission linguistique pour l'unification du vocabulaire psychanalytique française, Paris, under the supervision of Eduard Pichon and Princess Marie Bonaparte. The book contains a total of 421 entries. Contrary to Ludwig Eidelberg's (1968, p. 344) declaration that the entries go up to the letter F, the book contains a full thirty-eight pages of terms beginning with letter G. Although Sterba's autobiography (1982), written several decades later, hints that he never gave up the desire to bring the dictionary to its 'completion' by writing entries from letters H to Z, this somehow never happened. To what extent the travails of his migration from Europe and resettlement in the USA were responsible for this lapse is unclear. Having received an endorsement from Freud for what he had already accomplished, and then Freud's passing away, could also have contributed to Sterba's diminished zeal towards this project. These are matters of speculation, however. What matters is that the book is truly a treasure trove of psychoanalytic ideas. One comes across the early formulations of terms that are now widely accepted and familiar. The greater pleasure comes from the encounter with notions that are unfamiliar. Two illustrations should suffice: *Auffrischung* ('revivification') denoting the re-cathexis of old memories and fantasies that had lost their emotional valence, and *Familienkomplex* ('family complex'), referring to the involvement of non-parental figures in oedipal fantasies when the child is growing in an extended family or has many older siblings. This quick tasting of the material contained in the book is simply to whet the reader's appetite. There is obviously much more of value, intrigue, and utility in the book. It is fortunate that the book survived the dark events in Europe around the time of its publication. It is rare, though. Only twelve copies of it exist; nine of these are in distinguished libraries in the USA and one each in the UK, Japan, and, to wit, Germany (Dwarkanath Rao, personal communication, 22 June 2008). Need a confession now be made that now a tenth, Xeroxed copy also exists in the USA and is a prized possession of the writer of the book that is in your hands?

Single authored glossaries

A Critical Dictionary of Psychoanalysis, by Charles Rycroft. London: Nelson, 1968 (revised edn. Penguin, 1972).

This is first single-authored psychoanalytic dictionary in English language. From its publication in 1968 until 2009, when the book in your hands appeared in print, it was the only book of its kind. Charles Rycroft, the analyst of R. D. Laing and a Consultant in Psychotherapy at the Tavistock Clinic in London, produced this 189-page readable collection of definitions of psychoanalytic terms largely for the educated laity. He included not only psychoanalytic concepts but also basic terms from psychiatry, Jungian psychology, existentialism, anthropology, biology, and medicine. Circumventing jargon, Rycroft wrote in a simple and straightforward manner. The entries are brief and only a few have references to pertinent literature. Their quality ranges from satisfactory to excellent. An occasional witticism (e.g., see the entry on 'analysand') makes the reading enjoyable. A superb introduction by the author elucidates the stumbling blocks to gaining entry into the psychoanalytic literature and boldly tackles the difficulty that English readers of psychoanalysis face in light of the fact that the original texts of the discipline are in German. Rycroft concludes that 'psychoanalytical theory will eventually have to be reformulated as a communication theory and that it will have to reflect conceptually the source of its own data' (p. xx). This sobering caution aside, Rycroft's clarity is no mean achievement and his book is a pleasure to browse through.

Kompendum Psychoanalytischer Grundbegeriffe, by Wolfgang Mertens. Munich: Quintessenz, 1992.

This single-authored book declares itself to be a 'supplement' to the widely respected *The Language of Psychoanalysis* by Jean Laplanche and Jean-Bertrand Pontalis (see below). It contains 109 alphabetically arranged entries on psychoanalytic terms. The selection is, however, idiosyncratic. Claudia Frank (1996), in her review of the book, states that she searched 'in vain for terms like psychoanalytic process, free association, dream (or dream thoughts), transference and countertransference, narcissism, psychic change, primal fantasies (innate knowledge, perception), and symbol formation' (p. 1291). Besides these omissions, there is little mention of how the same term has been used in different ways by various psychoanalytic schools. Frank concluded her review by saying that 'this is a compendium—a "supplement"—that requires further supplementing' (p. 1294).

Co-authored glossaries

Freud: Dictionary of Psychoanalysis, by Nandor Fodor and Frank Gaynor. New York: The Philosophical Library, 1950, pp. 208.

Equipped with a laudatory foreword by Theodore Reik, this early dictionary is largely a collection of terms associated with Sigmund Freud. A vast ground is covered and the length of entries ranges from one sentence to four pages, with most of

them being rather brief. The readability of these definitions is quite good, especially for the beginner. At the same time, the material reflects a particular era of psychoanalysis and is not really up to date. One puzzling thing is that Fodor and Gaynor call themselves 'editors' of the book, but there is no list of contributors anywhere and the book seems to have been written by these two individuals.

A Comprehensive Dictionary of Psychological and Psychoanalytical Terms, by Horace B. English and Ava Champney English. New York: Longmans, Green, and Company, 1958.

While it often gets mentioned alongside the major psychoanalytic dictionaries, owing perhaps to the inclusion of the phrase 'psychoanalytical terms' in its title, this book is a general psychological dictionary with a sprinkling of a few psychoanalytic terms. It has little to offer to a psychoanalytic readership.

The Language of Psychoanalysis, by Jean Laplanche and Jean-Bertrand Pontalis (translated by Donald Nicholson-Smith). London: Hogarth Press, 1973.

Amply deserving of all the respect and accolades it has received, this remarkable book offers a highly sophisticated and deep elucidation of concepts originated by Sigmund Freud. The level of scholarship is superb and each entry is historically layered and conceptually fleshed out. Although an occasional Kleinian, Winnicottian, and Lacanian concept is thrown in, it is not a glossary of psychoanalytic terms at large. The authors' attention is exclusively upon the ideas of the Master. These are described in 327 alphabetically arranged entries. Each entry is divided into two parts: a succinct definition (laid out in bold type face) and an essay. Painstakingly, these essays trace the origins of each important idea of Freud and demonstrate how it evolved over the course of his professional life and how the indication of what was to come had been implicit in earlier writings. There are, however, a few puzzling omissions with the 'need–wish distinction', 'homosexuality' (or, 'inversion', to use Freud's preferred term) and 'insight' being the most prominent among them. The book has a foreword by Masud Khan.

Edited glossaries

Encyclopedia of Psychoanalysis, edited by Ludwig Eidelberg. New York: Free Press, 1968.

The dust cover of this book says it all: 'This unique one volume work contains the terms, concepts, and biographical data relevant to the understanding of Freudian psychoanalysis. Included are 643 clinically defined and illustrated entries, detailed examinations of history, opinions, and evaluations that clarify current psychoanalytic theory, complete bibliography and list of related concepts with each entry, 1500 title bibliography, and 6000 item inde;. Yes, it is all on the front cover. The back cover lists the 17 individuals who, along with the Editor-in-Chief, Ludwig Eidelberg, wrote the entries; this translates into approximately 36 entries per person. Published in 1968, the book can hardly avoid appearing a bit dated at this point in our field's evolution. The contributing editors are all from New York. This now appears an illustration of sad but naïve provincialism. It should not detract one from noticing the impressive amount of amount of ground covered by these authors. The quality of entries is, by and large, good, though, as happens in edited volumes of this sort, a little uneven in depth of coverage. The inclusion of clinical vignettes from time to time distinguishes the glossary from all others in this genre.

A Glossary of Psychoanalytic Terms and Concepts, edited by Burness E. Moore and Bernard D. Fine. New York: American Psychoanalytic Association, 1968.

Published by the American Psychoanalytic Association, 'this small book represents an attempt by organized psychoanalysis to clarify for the public in simple, understandable language what is meant by its terms and concepts' (p. 7). Seventy-four contributors have authored the definitions, the total number of which stands at 164. While some entries (e.g., 'character disorders', 'ego development', 'instinctual drives', and 'Oedipus complex') are more than a page long, most others are limited to four or five sentences. Terms and concepts selected to be defined are exclusively from 'classical' psychoanalysis and ego psychology; the contributions of Melanie Klein, Ronald Fairbairn, Donald Winnicott, and Michael Balint are not included. The quality of what does exist is quite good, though little pretence is made of being scholarly. The entire text occupies 79 pages and the bibliography is restricted to 16 references. 'The usual format has been employed. Words printed in italics are defined elsewhere in the glossary. Words in the text in boldface are terms subsumed under the heading of the major concept being defined' (p. 8).

Psychoanalytic Terms and Concepts, edited by Burness E. Moore and Bernard D. Fine. New Haven, CT: Yale University Press, 1990.

Published by the American Psychoanalytic Association in conjunction with the Yale University Press, this 1990 compendium is the second incarnation of the earlier slim volume edited by the team of Burness Moore and Bernard Fine. Its 210 pages contain 490 entries written by 296 contributors. The definitions are solid and informative. The tone is sombre, the approach straightforward, and the conceptualizations steeped in ego psychology and mindful of the principle of multiple function. There is a tendency towards 'ghettoization' of concepts associated with British analysis, with entries like ' Bionian theory', 'Kleinian theory', and 'Winnicott's theory'. Latin American and French contributions are not included and there is little of 'applied' psychoanalysis here. Cross-referencing between various entries is inoptimal. The placement of references following each entry has the advantage of providing easy access to further sources of information but the repeated rupture of text is not easy on the eye.

International Dictionary of Psychoanalysis, edited by Alain de Mijolla. Detroit, Thomas Gale, 2005.

This magisterial work consists of three beautifully printed volumes with 1,569 entries written by 463 contributors. Now available in a somewhat enlarged version in English, the book was originally published in French in 2002. Indeed, two-thirds of the entries are by French authors and the French edition indicates that 96 entries have been written by Sophie D. Mijolla-Mellor, 83 by Roger Perron, and 40 by Bernard Golse; the book does not tell how many entries are authored by Alain de Mijolla himself. Peter Rudnytsky (2007) called the dictionary 'a heroic achievement, one that should be celebrated by everyone who lives and breathes psychoanalysis' (p. 371). His comprehensive review identifies the 'gems' in the prodigious number of entries. Included are Jean-Bertrand Pontalis's essay on the capacity to be alone, Malcolm Pines' on Trigant Burrow, Jacques Sedat's on Lacan, John Simmons's on the Washington Psychoanalytic Society, and Jean-Louis Brenot's on the Laplanche and Pontalis book (see above), which contains an engaging narrative personal relationship between the two authors. Rudnytsky also notes the dictionary's shortcomings. Among these are the omission of an index of entries by each author, 'an alarming number of typographical errors' (p. 73), some historical mistakes of major and minor proportions. Most importantly, Rudnytsky faults the book for its insistant tendency towards idealization, the result of which is that unpleasant and inconvenient truths, to use a phrase popularized by Al Gore, are glossed over.

On a more plebian note, another reviewer (Chessick, 2006) noted that the books are very heavy and hard to read on one's lap.

Glossaries pertaining to specific areas in psychoanalysis

The Encyclopedia of Evolving Techniques in Dynamic Psychotherapy by Irving Solomon. Northvale, NJ: Jason Aronson, 1992.

As a mirror image of the English book (mentioned above), which has psychoanalysis in its title but hardly any of it in its content, Solomon's book has a lot of psychoanalysis in its content but not in its title. The book has 235 entries, which is not an insignificant number for a single authored book. The emphasis is unabashedly clinical and pragmatic, though theoretical matters are not altogether dropped. The quality of discourse is good and the provision of clinical vignettes improves the explanatory power of the entries. Two problems, however, exist. One pertains to the fact that the literature coverage is not comprehensive and deeply anchored in the discipline's history. The second involves the titles of entries themselves, with many of them (e.g., 'best attitude towards psychoanalytic theory and technique', 'family background of patient', and 'free association's complexities') having a somewhat cooked up and *ad hoc* flavour. The fact that the titles of each entry are placed in boxes also takes something away from the seriousness of the endeavour.

Feminism and Psychoanalysis: A Critical Dictionary edited by Elizabeth Wright. Oxford: Blackwell, 1992.

Bringing together a diverse body of feminist literature posing a radical challenge to the phallocentrism of classical psychoanalysis, this book is quite readable, though theoretically it leaves something to be desired. Most of the contributors are academics and scholars of humanities. This makes the book weak on the clinical front. In her review of it, Susan Lipshitz-Phillips (1995) concluded that 'the book seems more successful in its rethinking of the image of women and the female body in art, cinema, literary criticism, and history, where the data are publicly accessible, than in its discussion, for example, of the intricacies of sadomasochism evident in the individual psychic life and its enactment in relationships' (p. 868).

One Hundred and One Defenses: How the Mind Shields Itself by Jerome S. Blackman. New York: Brunner-Routledge, 2004.

Replete with clinical vignettes and examples from day-to-day life, Blackman's book should have enormous appeal for beginners. This is especially true for psychiatric residents, whose training these days suffers from didactic anaemia when it comes to psychoanalysis. The insufficient distinction between intrapsychic defences (e.g., repression, undoing) and defensive manoeuvres (e.g., garrulousness, fatigue) might not rankle the novice but remains noticeable to the experienced eye. Such conflation is, in part, the reason for the overgrown list of defences. Wanting to be ever helpful, the book includes chapter length sections on interpretive and supportive techniques in psychotherapy.

Glossaries pertaing to the work of specific authors

The Work of W. R. Bion, by R. E. Lopez-Corvo. London: Karnac, 2005.

This book is far from a mere compilation of psychoanalytic concepts associated with the work of Wilfred Bion. It is a scholarly treatise where Bion's ideas are finely elucidated and linked with each other. They are also located within the context of psychoanalytic literature at large, especially in regard to the corresponding ideas of Sigmund Freud, Otto Rank, Melanie Klein, Ronald Fairbairn, Max Gitelson, and Henrich Racker. Lopez-Corvo has done a lot of original research for this book. This appears in the form of novel explanations as well as previously unreported anecdotes; the one about Bion's reaction to hearing *Mahabharata*, the great Hindu epic, being recited is especially heartwarming in the light of Bion's traumatic departure at the age of eight from India. A biographical sketch at the outset of the book sets the ground for empathy in this regard.

The Language of Winnicott: A Dictionary of Winnicott's Use of Words, by Jan Abram. London: Karnac, 2007.

Far from being a simple listing of the meaning of the terms used by Donald Winnicott, Jan Abram's book is a rich and multilayered discourse on his ideas. In the author's own words, 'each entry is a journey through the writings spanning almost forty years . . . to guide impartially so that the reader may make a personal discovery of the evolution of Winnicott's thought' (p. xxiii). Thomas Ogden confirms this in his Foreword. He states that 'the reader comes away from a history of usage of language not with a definition or even a set of definitions, but with a sense of language as a very living thing. I believe that such an approach to language is the only approach that could possibly be adequate to a study of Winnicott's thinking and writing. This is so in large part because of the paradoxical structure of Winnicott's most important ideas' (pp. xxv–xxvi). The book is divided into 23 sections, including aggression, antisocial tendencies, creativity, dependence, holding, playing, and so on. Each section has 3–12 entries. The book also contains a chronological list of every known published work by Winnicott; this has been prepared by Knud Hjumland, a clinical psychologist from Denmark. The main text of the book contains ample passages in Winnicott's own language, which brings the ideas under consideration truly alive. This is a superb book indeed.

An Introductory Dictionary of Lacanian Psychoanalysis by Dylan Evans. New York: Routledge, 1996.

Making the work of Jacques Lacan understandable to Anglophone readers is no simple task, and yet Dylan Evans has admirably accomplished it. The dictionary he has authored provides a chronological listing of major events in Lacan's life alongside more than 200 entries explaining Lacan's own terminology (e.g. 'factor c', 'mirror stage', 'object petit a', and 'name-of-the-father') and his use of common French words as well as the handed-down psychoanalytic expressions (e.g., 'ego' and 'Oedipus complex'). Evans distils comprehensibility from Lacan's dense and idiosyncratic writing style and places his concepts in their historical context, especially in their relation to the work of Sigmund Freud.

A Dictionary of Kleinian Thought by Robert Hinshelwood. Northvale, NJ: Jason Aronson, 1991.

This book constitutes an outstanding contribution to psychoanalytic literature. It has all the advantages of a single-authored book over an edited volume, including consistency of tone, ample cross-referencing, and avoidance of repetition. Its level of scholarship is impressive and the resulting discourse truly sophisticated. Of the 163 entries, 13 are designated 'main entries' and the remaining 150 'general entries'. This categorization is puzzling. What, for instance, dictates placing 'femininity phase' in the ' main entries' section and 'depressive anxiety' in 'general entries'? Why is 'envy' deserving and ' reparation' not deserving of being included among the 'main entries'? In a book devoted to Mrs Klein's contributions, it might be acceptable to find Wilfred

Bion, Susan Isaacs, and Hanna Segal as 'general entries', but to have 'Melanie Klein' in the same category appears disconcerting. Does not the old lady deserve to be in the 'main entries' section? Minus such quibbles and minus the publisher's penchant for font variation, there is little that is negative or weak about this book. The 22-page section on Kleinian technique would especially prove to be an exemplary aid in teaching courses on Mrs Klein 's work

General glossaries as appendices to psychoanalytic books

Glossary. In: *The American Psychiatric Publishing Textbook of Psychoanalysis*, edited by Ethel Person, Arnold Cooper, and Glen Gabbard, pp. 547–562. Washington, DC: American Psychiatric Press.

Four editors and 37 contributors are responsible for this 296-item glossary, which appears as an appendix to this recent American textbook of psychoanalysis. The entries are brief but do accomplish their goal in a workmanlike fashion. There are no references, since the terms and concepts defined in the glossary find greater explication, with proper bibliographic citations, in the main text of the book. The only concepts whose originators are named are those of Margaret Mahler, Otto Kernberg, Heinz Kohut, and Melanie Klein; the concepts of all other analysts remain unattributed. The reason for this is unclear.

Topical glossaries as appendices to psychoanalytic books

Glossary. In: *The Psychological Birth of the Human Infant* by Margaret Mahler, Fred Pine, and Anni Bergman, pp. 289–293. New York: Basic Books, 1975.

This 28-item glossary provides succinct definitions of the various concepts involving the symbiosis and separation–individuation process described by the authors. While scattered papers on the topic by the senior author existed, this book brought together her and her colleagues' observations in composite form. Some 35 years later, when these concepts have become part and parcel of psychoanalytic lexicon, it is hard to imagine the need for such a glossary. At the time of its publication however, the provision of clearly spelled out definitions of concepts (e.g., 'emotional refuelling', 'optimal distance') that were still unfamiliar to a large number of psychoanalysts was indeed a great service. In fact, the potential use of this glossary for teaching purposes, especially for beginners in the study of psychoanalysis and child development, has survived the test of time.

Glossary. In: *Psychotherapy: A Basic Text* by Robert Langs, pp. 720–751. New York: Jason Aronson.

This thirty-page appendix to the over 700-page book on psychodynamic psychotherapy contains brief definitions of psychoanalytic terms that are well-established (e.g., introject, neurosis, transference) as well as terms coined by the book's author himself (e.g., alliance sector, bastion, misalliance). The entries are brief, mostly unreferenced, and, from time to time, simplistic and idiosyncratic. 'Emotional disturbance', for instance, is defined as 'synonymous with neurosis when it is used in its broadest sense to include all forms of psychologically and emotionally founded disorders' (p. 726), and 'Identification' as 'an intrapsychcic process through which the self-representations and other aspects of the subjective internal world and defences are unconsciously modified in keeping with a model derived from an external object' (pp. 728–729). The exuberance of the writitng is hard to ignore. For readers who like the Langs malt, this is vintage stuff indeed!

Glossary. In: *In Search of Self in India and Japan: Toward a Cross-Cultural Psychology* by Alan Roland, pp. 335–347. Princeton, NJ: Princeton University Press, 1988.

Appearing as an appendix to a wonderful book on cross-cultural psychoanalysis, this twelve page glossary has 152 entries; this should give some idea about the length of each entry. Psychoanalytic concepts are intermingled with notions, phrases, and facts regarding Indian and Japanese culture and history. Some entries have bibliographic citations, but overall the bent is towards simplicity and minimalism.

Glossary. In: *Immigration and Identity: Turmoil, Treatment, and Transformation* by Salman Akhtar, pp. 167–181. Northvale, NJ: Jason Aronson, 1999.

This is a collection of terms specifically pertaining to the psychosocial experience of immigration and exile. General psychoanalytic terms (e.g., repression, Oedipus complex) are not included. By focusing upon terms such as 'accidental immigrants', 'bicultural self', 'disorienting anxieties', 'fake refugees', and 'negative acculturation', an attempt is made to collate and underscore a context-specific vocabulary of migration.

Other books in this genre

A Guide to the Language of Psychoanalysis: An Empirical Study of the Relationships Among Psychoanalytic Terms and Concepts, by George Klumpner. Madison, CT: International Universities Press, 1992.

This is a fascinating index to psychoanalytic terminology organized along the principles of a thesaurus. The author had a data base of 64,000 terms (in 32,000 pairs) that had been placed in relation to each other by some earlier indexer or compiler of a lexicon. Avoiding duplication by selecting one 'preferred term' for all its synonyms (e.g., 'instinct aim' for 'aim of the instinct') and linking that term with 'associated terms' (words that had appeared in relation to the former on at least two occasions), the list was reduced to 16,000 pairs of terms. The primary purpose of this Guide, in its author's words, is 'to present, and to support with empirical evidence, the thesis that psychoanalysis in its broadest sense consist of a set of central interrelated concepts. These central concepts can be said to define psychoanalysis and distinguish it from other disciplines' (p. 1).

Glossary: Vocabulary of Psychoanalysis, by Jean Laplanche and Jean Bertrand Pontalis, revised and updated by Gabriele Junkers, on behalf of The Committee on Languages, European Psychoanalytic Federation (Chair: Jacqueline Amati-Mehler). London: Karnac, 1997.

Formed in 1997 under the able Chairmanship of Jacqueline Amati-Mehler (Italy), the European Psychoanalytic Federation's Committee on Languages produced this volume. Working with her colleagues on the Committee—Betty Denzler (Switzerland), Duveken Engels (Holland), Avigail Golomb (Israel), Gabriele Junkers (Germany), Luisa Munoz (Spain), Eva Pragai (Hungary), and Sverre Varvin (Sweden)—Amati-Mehler sought to address the communication problems caused by the multilingualism of European psychoanalysts. In the words of the Committee itself, 'there is no doubt that in a discipline such as ours, in which the shades and nuances as well as hidden allusions of language have great significance, the difficulty of understanding colleagues with different mother tongues assumes particular significance' (p. 52). Adapting a laudably pluralistic approach, the Committee decided to try to match psychoanalytic terms in six different languages: English, German, French, Spanish, Italian, and Portuguese. A total of 324 terms were arranged in seven parallel and corresponding columns. Six of these were filled with

Glossaries

matching terms in the languages above, while the seventh, in a gesture of openness and large-heartedness, was left blank. Indeed, the beautifully printed (on white art paper and red, blue, and green divider pages) *Glossary* says that 'tomorrow or the day after tomorrow we may need to have Japanese, Chinese, Indian, Russian, Polish, Rumanian, etc., translations in our meetings' (p. 52). This well-intentioned remark is turning out to be impressively prescient as well. But *Indian*?

The Freud Encyclopedia: Theory, Therapy, and Culture, edited by Edward Erwin. New York: Routledge, 2002.

A colllection of 296 brief essays on diverse topics in psychoanalysis, this book has a misleading title. It is not restricted to Sigmund Freud's work and extends far beyond it to include topics that range from 'feminism and psychoanalysis' to 'symbiosis', from 'clinical ethics' to 'Marxism' and 'Freudianism', and from 'delusions' to 'psychoanalytically oriented psychotherapy'. Entries also exist on the important figures that had formative influence on Freud (e.g., Jean-Martin Charcot, Gustav Fechner, Wilhelm Fleiss) and his early pupils (e.g., Karl Abraham, Sandor Ferenczi). Significant figures from later analysis (e.g., Melanie Klein, Karen Horney, Harry Stack Sullivan) also have essays devoted to them. The spread of psychoanalysis to different regions of the world is well-covered, with entries such as 'Africa and psychoanalysis', 'Korea and psychoanalysis', and 'Philippines and psychoanalysis', 'Sweden and psychoanalysis', and the like being especially informative. A striking feature of the book is that, of its 193 contributors, 57 are from countries other than the USA, including Australia, Belguim, Denmark, France, Holland, South Africa, and the UK, among others. While cross-referencing between the articles is inoptimal, their overall quality is quite good. The book is handsomely produced with a striking picture of young Freud on its cover.

And, finally . . .

A New German–English Psycho-Analytical Vocabulary. by Alix Strachey. *International Journal of Psychoanalysis* Research Supplement No.1, pp. 1–84 .London: Bailliere, Tindall,and Cox, 1943.

Laboriously prepared by Alix Strachey, this compendium contains the original German psychoanalytical terms and their English counterparts as agreed upon by the 'Informal Glossary Committee' comprising Ernest Jones, Joan Riviere, James Strachey ,and Alix Strachey. The slim volume was published as a supplement to the *International Journal of Pyschoanalysis* in 1943 and is mentioned in the *Standard Edition* (Volume 1, p. XIX) as the source of all the English terms. While the collection contains over 1800 words, there is little attempt made to define the concepts involved. All that is provided is an 'agreed upon' English equivalent of the German word used by Sigmund Freud. While lacking explication, the book is of fundamental importance for those interested in reading Freud across languages and those involved in translating Freud from his original German.

The Concordance to the Standard Edition of the Complete Psychological Works of Sigmund Freud, Volumes I–VI, Samuel Guttman, Randall Jones, and Stephen Parrish (Eds.). Boston, MA: GK Hall, 1980.

A work of magesterial proportions, this is a 4,725-page, six-volume, oversized (12" × 9") compendium meticulously documenting the Master's usage of nearly two million words. The entries, which are simply too numerous to count, are alphabetically arranged. The number of times Freud used a particular word, regardless of it being technical or colloquial, is noted alongside the title of the entry. For instance, 'abandon' 107 times, 'advice' 66 times, 'back' 1394 times, and so on. Each word is accompanied by a few preceding and a few following words. Each such entry is then followed by the volume number of the *Standard Edition* in which it appears, the pertinent page number, an abbreviated title of the paper or the book, and the date of its publication. A further adjunct provided is the key to move directly from the quoted line in the *Standard Edition* to the corresponding passage in *GesammelteWerke*. The authors state that 'moving to the German text from the English helps open access to one of the richest sources of insight into Freud's mind, that is, his use of metaphors, particularly those in which his theoretical concepts are presented' (p. xii). For anyone interested in locating Freud quotations, discerning patterns of thought through the veil of linguistic choices (e.g., Freud's use of 'punishment'—253 times, and 'forgiveness'— 5 times), and conducting research on conceptual precedence as well as the accuracy of James Strachey's translation of Freud's writings, this *Concordance* is indispensable. To realize that the work was done with the aid of relatively primitive computers during the 1970s makes one's amazement at what has been accomplished even greater. At the risk of using a hackneyed phrase, if there was anything like a 'labour of love', by God, this is it!

REFERENCES

ALEXANDER AARONS

(1975). The analyst's relocation: its effect on the transference—parameter or catalyst. *International Journal of Psychoanalysis, 56*: 303–319.

ERNEST ABELIN

(1971). The role of father in the separation–individuation process. In: J. B. McDevitt & C. F. Settlage (Eds.), *Separation–Individuation* (pp. 229–252). New York: International Universities Press.
(1975). Some further observations and comments on the earliest role of the father. *International Journal of Psychoanalysis, 56*: 293–302.

SANDER ABEND

(1967). An analogue of negation. *Psychoanalytic Quarterly, 44*: 631–637.
(1982). Serious illness in the analyst: countertransference considerations. *Journal of the American Psychoanalytic Association, 30*: 365–379.

SANDER ABEND, MICHAEL PORDER, & MARTIN WILLICK

(1983). *Borderline Patients: Psychoanalytic Perspectives*. New York: International Universities Press.

KARL ABRAHAM

(1907a). On the significance of sexual trauma in childhood for the symptomatology of dementia praecox. In: *Clinical Papers and Essays on Psychoanalysis* (pp. 13–20). New York: Brunner/Mazel, 1955.
(1907b). The experiencing of sexual traumas as a form of sexual activity. In: *Selected Papers on Psychoanalysis* (pp. 47–63). New York, Brunner/Mazel, 1955.
(1908). The psychological relations between sexuality and alcoholism. In: *Selected Papers on Psychoanalysis* (pp. 80–89). New York: Brunner/Mazel Publishing.
(1911). Notes on the psychoanalytic investigation and treatment of manic–depressive insanity and allied conditions. In: *Selected Papers on Psychoanalysis* (pp. 137–156). London: Hogarth Press, 1927.
(1913a). Some remarks on the role of grandparents in the psychology of neuroses. In: *Clinical Papers and Essays on Psychoanalysis* (pp. 44–47). New York: Brunner/Mazel, 1955.
(1913b). A constitutional basis of locomotor anxiety. In: *Selected Papers on Psychoanalysis* (pp. 235–249). New York: Brunner/Mazel.
(1913c). On neurotic exogamy: a contribution to the similarities in the psychic of neurotics and of primitive man. In: *Clinical Papers and Essays on Psycho-Analysis* (pp. 48-50). London: Hogarth, 1955.
(1917). Ejaculatio praecox. In: *Selected Papers of Karl Abraham, M.D.* (pp. 280–298). London: Hogarth, 1927.
(1919). The applicability of psychoanalytic treatment to patients at an advanced age. In: *Selected Papers on Psychoanalysis* (pp. 312–317). New York: Brunner/Mazel.
(1921). Contributions to the theory of the anal character. In: *Selected Papers on Psychoanalysis* (pp. 370–392). New York: Brunner/Mazel.
(1924a). A short study of the development of the libido viewed in light of mental disorders. In: *Selected Papers of Karl Abraham, M.D.* (pp. 407–417). London: Hogarth, 1927.
(1924b). The influence of oral erotism on character formation. In: *Selected Papers of Karl Abraham, M.D.* (pp. 393–406). New York: Brunner/Mazel.
(1925a). Character formation on the genital level of libido. In: *Selected Papers on Psychoanalysis* (pp. 407–417). New York: Brunner/Mazel.
(1925b). The history of an impostor in the light of psychoanalytical knowledge. In: *Clinical Papers and Essays on Psychoanalysis* (pp. 291–305). New York: Brunner/Mazel, 1955.

JAN ABRAM

(2007). *The Language of Winnicott: A Dictionary of Winnicott's Use of Words* (2nd edn). London: Karnac.

SAMUEL ABRAMS

(1978). The teaching and learning of psychoanalytic developmental psychology. *Journal of the American Psychoanalytic Association, 26*: 387–406.
(1983). Development. *Psychoanalytic Study of the Child, 38*: 113–139.
(1986). Disposition and the environment. *Psychoanalytic Study of the Child, 41*: 41–60.
(1990). Psychoanalytic process: the developmental and the integrative. *Psychoanalytic Quarterly, 59*: 650–677.

DAVID WILFRED ABSE

(1974). Hysterical conversion and dissociative syndromes and the hysterical character. In: S. Arieti & E. B. Brodie (Eds.), *The American Handbook of Psychiatry, Volume 3* (pp. 155–194). New York: Basic Books.

References

(1977). The dream screen: phenomenon and noumenon. *Psychoanalytic Quarterly, 46*: 256–286.

(1983). Multiple personality. In: S. Akhtar (Ed.), *New Psychiatric Syndromes: DSM-III and Beyond* (pp. 339–361). New York: Jason Aronson.

(1987). *Hysteria and Related Mental Disorders* (2nd edn). Bristol: Wright.

WILFRED ABSE

(1966). *Hysteria and Related Mental Disorders: An Approach to Psychological Medicine*. Baltimore, MD: Williams & Wilkins.

LAWRENCE ABT & STUART WEISSMAN

(1965). (Eds.) *Acting Out: Theoretical and Clinical Aspects*. New York: Grune and Stratton.

ABBY ADAMS-SILVAN & MARK SILVAN

(1990). 'A dream is the fulfillment of a wish': traumatic dream, repetition compulsion, and the pleasure principle. *International Journal of Psychoanalysis, 71*: 513–529.

GERALD ADLER

(1985). *Borderline Psychopathology and its Treatment*. Northvale, NJ: Jason Aronson.

ELOISE AGGER

(1988). Psychoanalytic perspectives on sibling relationships. *Psychoanalytic Inquiry, 8*: 3–30.

THOMAS AGOSTON

(1946). The fear of post-orgastic emptiness. *Psychoanalytic Review, 33*: 197–214.

KARIN AHBEL-RAPPE

(2006). 'I no longer believe': did Freud abandon the seduction theory? *Journal of the American Psychoanalytic Association, 54*: 171–199.

AUGUST AICHHORN

(1925). *Wayward Youth*. New York: Viking.

RICARDO AINSLIE

(1997). *The Psychology of Twinship*. Northvale, NJ: Jason Aronson.

MARY AINSWORTH, MARY BLEHAR, EVERETT WATERS, & SALLY WALL

(1978). *Patterns of Attachment : A Psychological Study of the Strange Situation*. Hillsdale, NJ: Lawrence Erlbaum.

SALMAN AKHTAR

(1984). The syndrome of identity diffusion. *American Journal of Psychiatry, 141*: 1381–1385.

(1985). The other woman: phenomenological, psychodynamic, and therapeutic considerations. In: D. Goldberg (Ed.), *Contemporary Marriage* (pp. 215–240). Homeswood, IL: Dow Jones-Irwin.

(1987). Schizoid personality disorder: a synthesis of developmental, dynamic, and descriptive features. *American Journal of Psychotherapy, 41*: 499–518.

(1990). Paranoid personality disorder: a synthesis of developmental, dynamic, and descriptive features. *American Journal of Psychotherapy, 44*: 5–25.

(1991a). Panel report: sadomasochism in the perversions. *Journal of the American Psychoanalytic Association, 39*(3): 741–755.

(1991b). Three fantasies related to unresolved separation–individuation: a less recognized aspect of severe character pathology. In: S. Akhtar & H. Parens (Eds.), *Beyond the Symbiotic Orbit: Advances in Separation–Individuation Theory* (pp. 261–284). Northvale, NJ: Jason Aronson.

(1992a). Tethers, orbits, and invisible fences: clinical, developmental, sociocultural, and technical aspects of optimal distance. In: S. Kramer & S. Akhtar (Eds.), *When the Body Speaks: Psychological Meanings in Kinetic Clues* (pp. 21–57). Northvale, NJ: Jason Aronson.

(1992b). *Broken Structures: Severe Personality Disorders and Their Treatment*. Northvale, NJ: Jason Aronson.

(1994). Object constancy and adult psychopathology. *International Journal of Psychoanalysis, 75*: 441–455.

(1995). Some reflections on the nature of hatred and its emergence in the treatment process. In: S. Akhtar, S. Kramer & H. Parens (Eds.), *The Birth of Hatred: Developmental, Clinical, and Technical Aspects of Intense Aggression* (pp. 83–102). Northvale, NJ: Jason Aronson.

(1996). 'Someday . . ,' and 'If only . . .' fantasies: pathological optimism and inordinate nostalgia as related forms of idealization. *Journal of the American Psychoanalytic Association, 44*: 723–753.

(1997). The psychodynamic dimension of terrorism. *Psychiatric Annals, 29*: 350–355.

(1998). From simplicity through contradiction to paradox: the evolving psychic reality of the borderline patient in treatment. *International Journal of Psychoanalysis, 79*: 241–252.

(1999a). The distinction between needs and wishes: implications for psychoanalytic theory and technique. *Journal of the American Psychoanalytic Association, 47*: 113–151.

(1999b). *Immigration and Identity: Turmoil, Treatment, and Transformation.* Northvale, NJ: Jason Aronson.

(1999c). *Inner Torment: Living Between Conflict and Fragmentation.* Northvale, NJ: Jason Aronson.

(2000). Mental pain and the cultural ointment of poetry. *International Journal of Psychoanalysis, 81*: 229–243.

(2001). From mental pain through manic defense to mourning. In: S. Akhtar (Ed.), *Three Faces of Mourning: Melancholia, Manic Defense, and Moving On* (pp. 95–113). Northvale, NJ: Jason Aronson.

(2002). Forgiveness: origins, dynamics, psychopathology, and technical relevance. *Psychoanalytic Quarterly, 71*: 175–212.

(2003a). Things: developmental, psychopathological, and technical aspects of inanimate objects. *Canadian Journal of Psychoanalysis, 11*: 1–44.

(2003b). Mentor: a developmental object of young adulthood. In: R. S. Murthy (Ed.), *Mental Health in India 1950–2000: Essays in Honor of Professor N. N. Wig* (pp. 2–8). Bangalore, India, 2001: PAHN

(2005). *Objects of Our Desire.* New York: Harmony Press.

(2006). Experiencing oneness: pathological pursuit or normal necessity? In: S. Akhtar (Ed.), *Interpersonal Boundaries: Variations and Violations* (pp. 87–97). Lanham, MD: Jason Aronson.

(2007a). Four roadblocks in approaching Masud Khan. *Psychoanalytic Quarterly, 76*: 991–995.

(2007b). Disruptions in the course of psychotherapy and psychoanalysis. In: B. van Luyw, S. Akhtar & W. J. Livesley (Eds.), *Severe Personality Disorders* (pp. 93–108). Cambridge: Cambridge University Press.

(2007c). From unmentalized xenophobia to messianic sadism: some reflections on the phenomenology of prejudice. In: H. Parens, A. Mahfouz, S. W. Twemlow & D. E. Scharff (Eds.), *The Future of Prejudice: Psychoanalysis and the Prevention of Prejudice* (pp. 7–19). Lanham, MD: Jason Aronson.

(2007d). (Ed.) *Listening to Others: Developmental and Clinical Aspects of Empathy and Attunement.* Lanham, MD: Jason Aronson.

(2007e). Discussion of Lucy Lafarge's paper 'Transferences of deception'. In: *Regarding Others: Reviews, Responses, and Reflections* (pp. 80-84). Charlottesville, VA: Pitchstone.

(2007f). The trauma of geographical dislocation: leaving, arriving, mourning, and becoming. In: M. T. Hooke & S. Akhtar (Eds.), *The Geography of Meanings: Psychoanalytic Perspectives on Place, Space, Land, and Dislocation* (pp. 165–190). London: International Psychoanalytic Association.

(2008). (Ed.) *The Crescent and the Couch: Crosscurrents Between Islam and Psychoanalysis.* Lanham, MD: Jason Aronson.

(2009a). Love, sex, and marriage in the setting of pathological narcissism. *Psychiatric Annals, 39*: 185–191.

(2009b). (Ed.) *Good Feelings: Psychoanalytic Reflections on Positive Attitudes and Emotions.* London: Karnac.

SALMAN AKHTAR & ANDREW SMOLAR

(1998). Visiting the father's grave. *Psychoanalytic Quarterly, 67*: 474–483.

SALMAN AKHTAR & GLENDA WRENN

(2008). The biopsychosocial miracle of human resilience: an overview. In: H. Parens, H. Blum & S. Akhtar (Eds.), *The Unbroken Soul: Tragedy, Trauma, and Resilience* (pp. 1–20). Lanham, MD: Jason Aronson.

SALMAN AKHTAR & HENRI PARENS

(2001). (Eds.) *Does God Help?* Northvale, NJ: Jason Aronson.

SALMAN AKHTAR & JAMES ANDERSON THOMSON, JR

(1982). Overview: narcissistic personality disorder. *American Journal of Psychiatry, 139*: 12–20.

SALMAN AKHTAR & JESSICA PRICE BYRNE

(1983). The concept of splitting and its clinical relevance. *American Journal of Psychiatry, 140*: 1016–1018.

SALMAN AKHTAR & JODIE BROWN

(2005). Animals in psychiatric symptomatology. In: S. Akhtar & V. Volkan (Eds.), *The Mental Zoo* (pp. 3–38). Madison, CT: International Universities Press.

SALMAN AKHTAR & LOIS CHOI

(2004). When evening falls: the immigrant's encounter with middle and old age. *American Journal of Psychoanalysis, 64*: 183–191.

SALMAN AKHTAR & PRATYUSHA TUMMALA-NARRA

(2005). Psychoanalysis in India. In: S. Akhtar (Ed.), *Freud Along the Ganges: Psychoanalytic Reflections on the People and Culture of India* (pp. 3-25). New York: Other Press.

References

SALMAN AKHTAR & SELMA KRAMER

(1999). Beyond the parental orbit: brothers, sisters, and others. In: S. Akhtar & S. Kramer (Eds.), *Brothers and Sisters: Developmental, Dynamic, and Technical Aspects of the Sibling Relationship* (pp. 1–24). Lanham, MD: Jason Aronson.
(2000). *Thicker than Blood: Bonds of Fantasy and Reality in Adoption*. Northvale, NJ: Jason Aronson.

SALMAN AKHTAR & STEVEN SAMUEL

(1996). The concept of identity: developmental origins, phenomenology, clinical relevance, and measurement. *Harvard Review of Psychiatry, 3*: 254–267.

SALMAN AKHTAR, SELMA KRAMER, & HENRI PARENS

(1995). (Eds.) *The Birth of Hatred: Developmental, Clinical, and Technical Aspects of Intense Aggression*. Northvale, NJ: Jason Aronson.

FRANZ ALEXANDER

(1925). Dreams in pairs and series. *International Journal of Psychoanalysis, 6*: 446–451.
(1933). The relation of the structural and instinctual conflicts. *Psychoanalytic Quarterly, 2*: 181–194.
(1948). *Fundamentals of Psychoanalysis*. New York: W. W. Norton.

FRANZ ALEXANDER & THOMAS FRENCH

(1946). *Psychoanalytic Therapy*. New York: Ronald Press.

FRANZ ALEXANDER, THOMAS FRENCH, & GEORGE POLLOCK

(1968). *Psychosomatic Specificity*. Chicago, IL: University of Chicago Press.

*JON ALLEN

(2006). Mentalization in practice. In: J. G. Allen & P. Fonagy (Eds.), *Handbook of Mentalization-Based Treatment* (pp. 3–30). Chichester: John Wiley.

JON ALLEN & PETER FONAGY

(2006). (Eds.) *Handbook of Mentalization-Based Treatment*. Chichester: John Wiley.

RENATO ALMANSI

(1960). The face–breast equation. *Journal of the American Psychoanalytic Association, 8*: 43–70.

LEON ALTMAN

(1957). The waiting syndrome. *Psychoanalytic Quarterly, 36*: 508–518.
(1980). *The Dream in Psychoanalysis*. New York: International Universities Press.

NEIL ALTMAN

(2004). *The Analyst in the Inner City: Race, Class, and Culture through a Psychoanalytic Lens*. New York: The Analytic Press.

JACQUELINE AMATI-MEHLER & SIMONA ARGENTIERI

(1989). Hope and hopelessness: a technical problem? *International Journal of Psychoanalysis, 70*: 295–304.

JACQUELINE AMATI-MEHLER, SIMONA ARGENTIERI, & JORGE CANESTRI

(1993). *The Babel of the Unconscious: Mother Tongue and Foreign Languages in the Psychoanalytic Dimension*. New York: International Universities Press.

AMERICAN PSYCHIATRIC ASSOCIATION

(1980). *Diagnostic and Statistical Manual of Mental Disorders* (3rd edn) (*DSM-III*). Arlington, VA: American Psychiatric Association.
(2005). *Diagnostic and Statistical Manual of Mental Disorders* (4th edn, Text Revised) (*DSM-IV-TR*). Arlington, VA: American Psychiatric Association.

AMY ANGEL

(1934). Einige bemerkungen uber den optimismus. *International Journal of Psychoanalysis, 20*: 191–199.

KLAUS ANGEL

(1967). On symbiosis and pseudo-symbiosis. *Journal of the American Psychoanalytic Association, 15*: 294–316.

JAMES ANTHONY

(1961). A study of screen sensations. *Psychoanalytic Study of the Child, 16*: 211–245.

DIDIER ANZIEU

(1986). *Freud's Self Analysis*. Madison, CT: International Universities Press.
(1992). A sound image of the self. *International Review of Psychoanalysis, 6*: 23–32.

STEPHEN APPELBAUM

(1966). Speaking with the second voice: evocativeness. *Journal of the American Psychoanalytic Association, 14*: 462–477.
(1973). Psychological-mindedness: word, concept, and essence. *International Journal of Psychoanalysis, 54*: 35–46.
(2000). *Evocativeness: Moving and Persuasive Interventions in Psychotherapy*. Northvale, NJ: Jason Aronson.

ADRIENNE APPLEGARTH

(1997). Aggression, envy, and ambition: circulating tensions in women's psychic life. *Gender and Psychoanalysis, 2*: 291–325.

JEFFREY APPLEGATE & JENNIFER BONOWITZ

(1995). *The Facilitating Partnership: A Winnicottian Approach for Social Workers and Other Helping Professionals*. Northvale, NJ: Jason Aronson.

MAURICE APPREY

(1988). Concluding remarks: from an inchoate sense of entitlement to a mature attitude of entitlement. In: V. D. Volkan & T. C. Rodgers (Eds.), *Attitudes of Entitlement* (pp. 93–98). Charlottesville, VA: University Press of Virginia.

SILVANO ARIETI

(1955). *Interpretation of Schizophrenia*. New York: Brunner.
(1974). *Interpretation of Schizophrenia* (2nd edn). New York: Basic Books.

JACOB ARLOW

(1953). Masturbation and symptom formation. *Journal of the American Psychoanalytic Association, 1*: 45–58.
(1961). Silence and the theory of technique. *Journal of the American Psychoanalytic Association, 9*: 44–55.
(1963). The supervisory situation. *Journal of the American Psychoanalytic Association, 11*: 576–593.
(1966). Depersonalization and derealization. In: R. M. Loewenstein, L. M. Newman, M. Schur & A. J. Solnit (Eds.), *Psychoanalysis—A General Psychology: Essays in Honor of Heinz Hartmann* (pp. 456–478). New York: International Universities Press.
(1969). Fantasy, memory, and reality testing. *Psychoanalytic Quarterly, 38*: 28–51.
(1969). Unconscious fantasy and disturbances of mental experience. *Psychoanalytic Quarterly, 38*: 1–27.
(1971). Character perversion. In: I. W. Marcus (Ed.), *Currents in Psychoanalysis* (pp. 317–336). New York: International Universities Press.
(1986). The poet as a prophet: a psychoanalytic perspective. *Psychoanalytic Quarterly, 64*: 215–233.
(1995). Stilted listening: psychoanalysis as discourse. *Psychoanalytic Quarterly, 64*: 215–233.

JACOB ARLOW & CHARLES BRENNER

(1964). *Psychoanalytic Concepts and the Structural Theory*. New York: International Universities Press.

LEWIS ARON & ADRIENNE HARRIS

(1993). Sandor Ferenczi: discovery and rediscovery. In: L. Aron & A. Harris (Eds.), *The Legacy of Sandor Ferenczi* (pp. 1–35). Hillsdale, NJ: Analytic Press.

LEWIS ARON & ANNABELLA BUSHRA

(1998). Mutual regression: altered states in the psychoanalytic situation. *Journal of the American Psychoanalytic Association, 46*: 389–412.

JOYCE ARONSON

(2002). (Ed.) *Use of the Telephone in Psychotherapy*. Northvale, NJ: Jason Aronson.

STUART ASCH

(1976). Varieties of negative therapeutic reactions and problems of technique. *Journal of the American Psychoanalytic Association, 24*: 383–407.
(1988). The analytic concepts of masochism: a re-evaluation. In: R. A. Glick & D. I. Meyers (Eds.), *Masochism: Current Psychoanalytic Perspectives* (pp. 93–116). Hillsdale, NJ: Analytic Press.

RICHARD ATKINS

(1984). Transitive vitalization and its impact on father representation. *Contemporary Psychoanalysis, 20*: 663–675.

References

NANETTE AUERHAHN & DORI LAUB

(1987). Play and playfulness in Holocaust survivors. *The Psychoanalytic Study of the Child*, 42: 45–58.

SONIA AUSTRIAN & TONI MANDELBAUM

(2008). Attachment theory. In: S. G. Austrian (Ed.), *Developmental Theories Through the Life Cycle* (2nd edn) (pp. 365–414). New York: Columbia University Press.

GEORGE AWAD

(2001). Effects of medication on the psychoanalytic process. *Psychoanalytic Study of the Child*, 56: 263–285.
(2007). Prejudice between Palestinians and Israelis. In: H. Parens, A. Mahfouz, S. W. Twemlow, & D. E. Scharff (Eds.), *The Future of Prejudice: Psychoanalysis and the Prevention of Prejudice* (pp. 181–200). Lanham, MD: Jason Aronson.

HOWARD BACAL

(1985). Optimal responsiveness and the therapeutic process. In: A. Goldberg (Ed.), *Progress in Self Psychology* (pp. 202–226). Hillsdale, NJ: Analytic Press.
(1987). British object relations theorists and self psychology: some critical reflections. *International Journal of Psychoanalysis*, 68: 81–98.

SHELDON BACH

(1975). Narcissism, continuity, and the uncanny. *International Journal of Psychoanalysis*, 56: 77–86.
(1977). On narcissistic state of consciousness. *International Journal of Psychoanalysis*, 58: 209–233.
(1985). *Narcissistic States and the Therapeutic Process*. New York: Jason Aronson.

HENRY BACHRACH & LOUIS LEAFF

(1978). Analyzability: a systematic review of the clinical and quantitative literature. *Journal of the American Psychoanalytic Association*, 26: 881–920.

KATHLEEN BACON & JOHN GEDO

(1993). Ferenczi's contributions to psychoanalysis: essays in dialogue. In: L. Aron & A. Harris (Eds.), *The Legacy of Sandor Ferenczi* (pp. 121–139). Hillsdale, NJ: Analytic Press.

MICHAEL BAILY & DEANNA BENISHAY

(1993). Familial aggregation of female sexual orientation. *American Journal of Psychiatry*, 150: 272–277.

ROBERT BAK

(1968). The phallic woman, the ubiquitous fantasy in perversions. *Psychoanalytic Study of the Child*, 23: 15–36.

RONALD BAKER

(1993). The patient's discovery of the psychoanalyst as a new object. *International Journal of Psychoanalysis*, 74: 1223–1233.

MICHAEL BALINT

(1932). Character analysis and new beginnings. In: *Primary Love and Psychoanalytic Technique* (pp. 33–55). London: Tavistock.
(1937). Early developmental states of the ego: primary object-love. In: *Primary Love and Psycho-Analytic Technique* (pp. 74–90). London: Hogarth Press, 1955.
(1948). On genital love. *International Journal of Psychoanalysis*, 29: 34–40.
(1959). *Thrills and Regressions*. London: Hogarth.
(1968). *The Basic Fault*. London: Tavistock.

ROSEMARY BALSAM

(1984). A special transference: the perfect patient. *Psychoanalytic Study of the Child*, 39: 285–299.
(1988). On being good: the internalized sibling with examples from late adolescent analyses. *Psychoanalytic Inquiry*, 8: 66–87.
(1989). Styles of connection in analysis—clinical instances. *Psychoanalytic Study of the Child*, 44: 191–198.
(1996). The pregnant mother and the body image of the daughter. *Journal of the American Psychoanalytic Association*, 44: 401–427.
(1999). Sisters and their disappointing brothers. In: S. Akhtar & S. Kramer (Eds.), *Brothers and Sisters: Developmental, Dynamic, and Technical Aspects of the Sibling Relationship* (pp. 69–100). Northvale, NJ: Jason Aronson.
(2000). The mother within the mother. *Psychoanalytic Quarterly*, 69: 465–492.
(2003). The vanished pregnant body in psychoanalytic female developmental theory. *Journal of the American Psychoanalytic Association*, 51: 1153–1171.

LEON BALTER

(2005). Nested ideation and the problem of reality: dreams and works of art in dreams. *Psychoanalytic Quarterly, 74*: 661–701.
(2006). Nested ideation and the problem of reality: dreams and works of art in works of art. *Psychoanalytic Quarterly, 75*: 405–445.

LEON BALTER, ZVI LOTHANE, & JAMES SPENCER

(1980). On the analyzing instrument. *Psychoanalytic Quarterly, 49*: 474–504.

MADELINE BARANGER & WILLY BARANGER

(1966). Insight and the analytic situation. In: R. Litman (Ed.), *Psychoanalysis in the Americas* (pp. 56–72). New York: International Universities Press.

SIMON BARON-COHEN

(1995). *Mindblindness: An Essay on Autism and Theory of Mind*. Cambridge, MA: MIT Press.

BARNABY BARRATT

(1978). Critical notes on Schafer's 'action language'. *The Annual of Psychoanalysis, 6*: 287–303.

RUSSELL BARTON & JOHN WHITEHEAD

(1969). The gaslight phenomenon. *Lancet, 1*: 1258–1260.

ANTHONY BATEMAN & PETER FONAGY

(2006). *Mentalization-Based Treatment for Borderline Personality Disorder: A Practical Guide*. London: Oxford University Press.

GREGORY BATESON

(1972). *Steps to an Ecology of Mind*. New York: Chandler.

GREGORY BATESON, DONALD JACKSON, JAY HALEY, & JOHN WEAKLAND

(1956). Toward a theory of schizophrenia. *Behavioral Science, 1*: 251–264.

FRANCIS BAUDRY

(1989). Character, character type, and character organization. *Journal of the American Psychoanalytic Association, 37*: 655–686.
(1995). Character. In: B. E. Moore & B. D. Fine (Eds.), *Psychoanalysis: The Major Concepts* (pp. 196–208). New Haven, CT: Yale University Press.

RONALD BAYER

(1981). *Homosexuality and American Psychiatry: The Politics of Diagnosis*. New York: Basic Books.

HILARY BEATTIE

(2005). Panel report: revenge. *Journal of the American Psychoanalytic Association, 53*: 513–524.

BEATRICE BEEBE & DANIEL STERN

(1977). Engagement-disengagement and early object experiences. In: M. Freedman & S. Grand (Eds.), *Communicative Structures and Psychic Structures* (pp.38–77). New York: Plenum Press.

REBECCA BEHRENDS & SIDNEY BLATT

(1985). Internalization and psychological development throughout the life cycle. *Psychoanalytic Study of the Child, 40*: 11–39.

MORTON BEISER

(1997). Coping with past and future: a study of adaptation to social change in West Africa. *Journal of Operational Psychiatry, 11*: 140–154.

ANITA BELL

(1961). Some observations on the role of the scrotal sac and testicles. *Journal of the American Psychoanalytic Association, 9*: 261–286.

SANDRA BEMESDERFER

(1996). A revised psychoanalytic view of menopause. *Journal of the American Psychoanalytic Association, 44*: 351–369.

References

THERESE BENEDEK

(1938). Adaptation to reality in early infancy. *Psychoanalytic Quarterly, 7*: 200–214.

JESSICA BENJAMIN

(1988). *The Bonds of Love*. New York: Pantheon Books.
(1995). Recognition and destruction: an outline of intersubjectivity. In: *Like Subjects, Love Objects*. New Haven, CT: Yale University Press.
(2004). Beyond doer and done-to: an intersubjective view of thirdness. *Psychoanalytic Quarterly, 73*: 5–46.
(2007). Listening together: intersubjective aspects of the analytic process of losing and restoring recognition. In: S. Akhtar (Ed.), *Listening to Others: Developmental and Clinical Aspects of Empathy and Attunement* (pp. 53–76). Lanham, MD: Jason Aronson.

STAVROULA BERATIS

(1988). The personal myth as a defense against internal primitive aggression. *International Journal of Psychoanalysis, 69*: 475–482.

MORTON BERG

(1977). The externalizing transference. *International Journal of Psychoanalysis, 58*: 235–244.

EDMUND BERGLER

(1944). Eight pre-requisites for psychoanalytic treatment of homosexuality. *Psychoanalytic Review, 31*: 253–286.
(1947). The psychopathology of bargain hunters. *Journal of Clinical Psychology, 8*: 623–627.
(1956). *Homosexuality: Disease or Way of Life*. New York: Hill & Wang.
(1959). *1000 Homosexuals: Conspiracy of Silence on Curing and Deglamorizing Homo-sexuality*. Patterson, NJ: Pageant.
(1961). *Curable and Incurable Neurosis: Problems of Neurotic Versus Malignant Masochism*. New York: Liveright.

ANNI BERGMAN

(1980). Ours, yours, mine. In: R. F. Lax, S. Bach & J. A. Berlin (Eds.), *Rapprochement: The Critical Subphase of Separation–Individuation* (pp. 199–216). New York: Jason Aronson.

ANNI BERGMAN, MICHAEL SCHWARTZMAN, PHYLLIS SLOATE, & ARNOLD WILSON

(1983). Oral deadlock: treatment of a psychotic child. *Journal of the American Psychoanalytic Association, 31*: 443–465.

MARTIN BERGMANN

(1982). Thoughts on superego pathology of survivors and their children. In: M. S. Bergmann & M. E. Jucovy (Eds.), *Generations of the Holocaust* (pp. 287–311). New York: Basic Books.
(2004). Rethinking dissidence and change in the history of psychoanalysis. In: M. Bergmann (Ed.), *Understanding Dissidence and Controversy in the History of Psychoanalysis* (pp. 1–110. New York: Other Press.
(2005). Termination and reanalysis. In: E. Person, A. Cooper & G. Gabbard (Eds.), *The American Psychiatric Publishing Textbook of Psychoanalysis* (pp. 241–253). Washington, DC: American Psychiatric Press.

OWEN BERKELY-HILL

(1921). The anal erotic factor in the religion, philosophy, and character of the Hindus. *International Journal of Psychoanalysis, 2*: 306–338.

BERNHARD BERLINER

(1947). On some psychodynamics of masochism. *Psychoanalytic Quarterly, 16*: 459–471.
(1958). The role of object relations in moral masochism. *Psychoanalytic Quarterly, 27*: 38–56.
(1966). Psychodynamics of the depressive character. *Psychoanalytic Forum, 1*: 244–251.

SIEGFRIED BERNFELD

(1928). Uber faszination. *Imago, 14*: 31–40.
(1931). Zur sublimierungstheorie. *Imago, 17*: 1–22.

DORIS BERNSTEIN

(1983). The female superego: a different perspective. *International Journal of Psychoanalysis, 64*: 187–201.
(1990). Female genital anxieties, conflicts, and typical mastery modes. *International Journal of Psychoanalysis, 71*: 151–165.

ISODORE BERNSTEIN & JOHN GLENN

(1978). The child analyst's emotional reactions to his patients. In: J. Glenn (Ed.), *Child Analysis and Therapy* (pp. 375–392). New York: Jason Aronson.

STEPHEN BERNSTEIN

(1983). Treatment preparatory to psychoanalysis. *Journal of the American Psychoanalytic Association*, 31: 363–390.

SUSAN BERS

(2006). Learning about psychoanalysis combined with medication: a non-physician's perspective. *Journal of the American Psychoanalytic Association*, 54: 805–831.

MANFRED BEUTEL, EMILY STERN, & DAVID SILBERSWEIG

(2003). The emerging dialogue between psychoanalysis and neuroscience: neuroimaging perspectives. *Journal of the American Psychoanalytic Association*, 51: 773–801.

EDWARD BIBRING

(1937). On the theory of the therapeutical results of psychoanalysis. *International Journal of Psychoanalysis*, 18: 170–189.
(1943). The concept of the repetition compulsion. *Psychoanalytic Quarterly*, 12: 486–519.
(1953). The mechanism of depression. In: P. Greenacre (Ed.), *Affective Disorders* (pp. 13–48). New York: International Universities Press.
(1954). Psychoanalysis and the dynamic psychotherapies. *Journal of the American Psychoanalytic Association*, 2: 745–770.

GRETA BIBRING

(1940). On an oral component in masculine inversion. *Internationale Zeitschrift fur Psychoanalyse*, 25: 124–130.

GRETA BIBRING, THOMAS DWYER, DOROTHY HUNTINGTON, & ARTHUR VALENSTEIN

(1961). A study of the psychological processes in pregnancy and of the earliest mother–child relationship—1. Some propositions and comments. *Psychoanalytic Study of the Child*, 16, 9–72.

ESTHER BICK

(1964). Notes on infant observation in psychoanalytic training. *International Journal of Psychoanalysis*, 45: 558–566.
(1968). The experience of the skin in early object relations. *International Journal of Psychoanalysis*, 49: 484–486.

WILFRED BION

(1950). The imaginary twin. In: *Second Thoughts* (pp.). London: Karnac, 1993.
(1957). Differentiation of the psychotic from the non-psychotic personalities. *International Journal of Psychoanalysis*, 38: 266–275.
(1958). On arrogance. *International Journal of Psychoanalysis*, 39: 144–146.
(1961). *Experiences in Groups and Other Papers*. New York: Basic Books.
(1962a). *Learning from Experience*. London: Karnac, 1984.
(1962b). A theory of thinking. *International Journal of Psychoanalysis*, 43: 306–310.
(1963). *Elements of Psychoanalysis*. London: Karnac, 1984.
(1965). *Transformations*. London: Karnac, 1984.
(1967). Notes on memory and desire. In: *Cogitations*. London: Karnac, 1992.
(1970). *Attention and Interpretation*. London: Karnac, 1984.
(1974). *Brazilian Lectures: Rio/Sao Paulo Number 2*. Rio De Janeiro: Imago Editora.
(1977). *Seven Servants*. New York: Jason Aronson.

DANA BIRKSTED-BREEN

(1996a). Unconscious representation of femininity. *Journal of the American Psychoanalytic Association*, 44: 119–132.
(1996b). Phallus, penis, and mental space. *International Journal of Psychoanalysis*, 77: 649–657.
(2009). 'Reverberation time', dreaming and the capacity to dream. *International Journal of Psychoanalysis* 90: 35-51.

KAY BLACKER

(1981). Panel report: insight: clinical considerations. *Journal of the American Psychoanalytic Association*, 29: 659–671.

JEROME BLACKMAN

(2004). *101 Defenses: How the Mind Shields Itself*. New York: Brunner-Routledge.

GERTRUDE BLANCK & RUBIN BLANCK

(1974). *Ego Psychology: Theory and Practice*. New York: Columbia University Press.

RACHEL BLASS & ZVI CARMELLI

(2007). The case against neuropsychoanalysis. *International Journal of Psychoanalysis*, 88: 19–40.

References

GERARD BLEANDONU

(1994). *Wilfred Bion: His Life and Works 1897–1979*. New York: Guilford Press.

EUGEN BLEULER

(1911). *Dementia Praecox, or the Group of Schizophrenias*. J. Zinkin (Trans.). New York: International Universities Press.

MANFRED BLEULER

(1968). A twenty-three year longitudinal study of 208 schizophrenics and impressions in regard to the nature of schizophrenia. In: D. Rosenthal & S. Katy (Eds.), *The Transmission of Schizophrenia* (pp. 3–12). London: Pergamon Press.

MARCIANNE BLEVIS

(2008). *Jealousy: Love's Favorite Decoy*. New York: Other Press.

MARCIANNE BLEVIS & JUDITH FEHER-GUREWICH

(2003). The jouissance of the other and the prohibition of incest: a Lacanian perspective. *Psychoanalytic Quarterly*, 72: 241–261.

PETER BLOS, SR

(1958). Preadolescent drive organization. *Journal of the American Psychoanalytic Association*, 6: 47–56.
(1967). The second individuation process of adolescence. *Psychoanalytic Study of the Child*, 22: 162–186.
(1968). Character formation in adolescence. *Psychoanalytic Study of the Child*, 23: 245–263.
(1984). Son and father. *Journal of the American Psychoanalytic Association*, 32: 301–324.
(1985). *Son and Father*. New York: Free Press.
(1989). The place of the adolescent process in the analysis of the adult. *Psychoanalytic Study of the Child*, 44: 3–18.

ELSA BLUM & HAROLD BLUM

(1990). The development of autonomy and superego precursors. *International Journal of Psychoanalysis*, 71: 585–595.

HAROLD BLUM

(1964). Color in dreams. *International Journal of Psychoanalysis*, 45: 519–529.
(1971). On the conception and development of the transference neurosis. *Journal of the American Psychoanalytic Association*, 19: 41–53.
(1973). The concept of erotized transference. *Journal of the American Psychoanalytic Association*, 21: 61–84.
(1979). The curative and creative aspects of insight. *Journal of the American Psychoanalytic Association*, 27(Suppl.): 41–69.
(1980a). The value of reconstruction in adult psychoanalysis. *International Journal of Psychoanalysis*, 61: 39–52.
(1980b). Paranoia and beating fantasy: psychoanalytic theory of paranoia. *Journal of the American Psychoanalytic Association*, 28: 331–361.
(1981a). Object inconstancy and paranoid conspiracy. *Journal of the American Psychoanalytic Association*, 29: 789–813.
(1981b). Some current and recurrent problems of psychoanalytic technique. *Journal of the American Psychoanalytic Association*, 29: 47–68.
(1983a). The position and value of extra transference interpretation. *Journal of the American Psychoanalytic Association*, 31: 587–617.
(1983b). The psychoanalytic process and analytic inference: a clinical study of a lie and loss. *International Journal of Psychoanalysis*, 64: 17–33.
(1987a). Countertransference: concepts and controversies. In: E. Slakter (Ed.), *Countertransference* (pp. 87–104). Northvale, NJ: Jason Aronson.
(1987b). The role of identification in the resolution of trauma: The Anna Freud Lecture. *Psychoanalytic Quarterly*, 56: 609–627.
(1989). The concept of termination and the evolution of psychoanalytic thought. *Journal of the American Psychoanalytic Association*, 37: 275–295.
(1995). Sanctified aggression, hate, and alteration of standards and values. In: S. Akhtar, S. Kramer & H. Parens (Eds.), *The Birth of Hatred: Developmental, Clinical, and Technical Aspects of Intense Aggression* (pp. 15–38). Northvale, NJ: Jason Aronson.
(1996). Female psychology in progress. *Journal of the American Psychoanalytic Association*, 44: 3–9.
(1999). The legacy of the defective and dead sibling. In: S. Akhtar & S. Kramer (Eds.), *Brothers and Sisters: Developmental, Dynamic, and Technical Aspects of the Sibling Relationship* (pp. 101–112). Lanham, MD: Jason Aronson.

LAWRENCE BLUM

(1996). Egocentricity and infidelity. In: S. Akhtar & S. Kramer (Eds.), *Intimacy and Infidelity: Separation-Individuation Perspectives* (pp. 133–144). Northvale, NJ: Jason Aronson.

References

FELIX BOEHM

(1930). The femininity-complex in men. *International Journal of Psychoanalysis*, 11: 444–469.

DALE BOESKY

(1973). Déjà raconte as a screen defense. *Psychoanalytic Quarterly*, 42: 491–524.
(1989). The questions and curiosity of the psychoanalyst. *Journal of the American Psychoanalytic Association*, 37: 579–603.

THIERRY BOKANOWSKI

(1995). The concept of psychic homosexuality. *International Journal of Psychoanalysis*, 76: 793–804.
(1996). Freud and Ferenczi: trauma and transference depression. *International Journal of Psychoanalysis*, 71: 519–536.
(2005). Variations on the concept of traumatism: traumatism, traumatic, and trauma. *International Journal of Psychoanalysis*, 86: 251–266.

THIERRY BOKANOWSKI & SERGIO LEWKOWICZ

(2009). (Eds.) *On Freud's Splitting of the Ego in the Process of Defence*. London: Karnac.

CHRISTOPHER BOLLAS

(1979). The transformational object. *International Journal of Psychoanalysis*, 60: 97–107.
(1987). *The Shadow of the Object*. London: Free Association.
(1989). *Forces of Destiny*. London: Free Association.
(1992). *Being a Character: Psychoanalysis and Self Experience*. New York: Hill and Wang.
(1996). Figures and their functions: on the oedipal structure of a psychoanalysis. *Psychoanalytic Quarterly*, 65: 1–20.
(1999). *The Mystery of Things*. London: Routledge.
(2000). *Hysteria*. London: Routledge.
(2009). *The Evocative Object World*. London: Routledge.

STEFANO BOLOGNINI

(1994). Transference: erotized, erotic, loving, affectionate. *International Journal of Psychoanalysis*, 75: 73–86.

JENNIFER BONOVITZ

(1998). Reflections of the self in the cultural looking glass. In: S. Akhtar & S. Kramer (Eds.), *The Colors of Childhood: Separation–Individuation across Cultural, Racial, and Ethnic Differences* (pp. 169–198). Northvale, NJ: Jason Aronson.

BERTA BORNSTEIN

(1951). On latency. *Psychoanalytic Study of the Child*, 6: 279–285.
(1953). Masturbation in latency period. *Psychoanalytic Study of the Child*, 8: 65–78.

MELVIN BORNSTEIN

(1983). Values and neutrality in psychoanalysis. *Psychoanalytic Inquiry*, 3: 547–550.

GIRINDRASHEKHAR BOSE

(1921). *The Concept of Repression*. Calcutta: Sri Gouranga Press.

MAURICE BOUVET

(1958). Technical variation and the concept of distance. *International Journal of Psychoanalysis*, 39: 211–221.

JOHN BOWLBY

(1940). The influence of early environment in the development of neurosis and neurotic character. *International Journal of Psychoanalysis*, 21: 154–178.
(1944). Forty-four juvenile thieves: their characters and home life. *International Journal of Psychoanalysis*, 25: 19–53.
(1958). The nature of the child's tie to his mother. *International Journal of Psychoanalysis*, 39: 350–373.
(1960). Separation anxiety. *International Journal of Psychoanalysis*, 41: 89–113.
(1961). Process of mourning. *International Journal of Psychoanalysis*, 42: 317–340.
(1963). Pathological mourning and childhood mourning. *Journal of the American Psychoanalytic Association*, 11: 500–541.
(1980). *Attachment and Loss I: Attachment*. New York: Basic Books.

BRYCE BOYER

(1955). Christmas neurosis. *Journal of the American Psychoanalytic Association*, 3: 467–488.
(1961). Provisional evaluation of psychoanalysis with few parameters employed in the treatment of schizophrenia. *International Journal of Psychoanalysis*, 42: 389–403.

References

(1971). Psychoanalytic technique in the treatment of certain characterlogical and schizophrenia disorders. *International Journal of Psychoanalysis, 52*: 67–85.

PAUL BRADLOW

(1973). Depersonalization, ego splitting, non human fantasy, and shame. *International Journal of Psychoanalysis, 54*: 487–492.

PAUL BRADLOW & STANLEY COEN

(1975). The analyst's undisguised appearance in the initial dream in psychoanalysis. *International Journal of Psychoanalysis, 56*: 415–425.

LINDA BRAKEL

(1990). A misperceived misperception: towards a technical recommendation in self-analysis. *International Journal of Psychoanalysis, 71*: 611–613.
(1993). Shall drawing become part of free association? Proposal for a modification in psychoanalytic technique. *Journal of the American Psychoanalytic Association, 41*: 359–394.

BERRY BRAZELTON

(1980). New knowledge about the infant from current research: implications for psychoanalysis. Paper presented at the American Psychoanalytic Association Meeting, San Francisco, CA.

KATI BRECKENRIDGE

(2000). Physical touch in psychoanalysis. *Psychoanalytic Inquiry, 20*: 2–20.

ERIC BRENMAN

(1985). Cruelty and narrowmindedness. *International Journal of Psychoanalysis, 66*: 273–281.

BROOKS BRENNEIS

(1975). Theoretical notes on manifest dream. *International Journal of Psychoanalysis, 56*: 197–206.

CHARLES BRENNER

(1955). *Elementary Textbook of Psychoanalysis*. New York: International Universities Press.
(1959). The masochistic character: genesis and treatment. *Journal of the American Psychoanalytic Association, 7*: 197–226.
(1974). *An Elementary Textbook of Psychoanalysis*. New York: International Universities Press.
(1975). Affects and psychic conflicts. *Psychoanalytic Quarterly, 44*: 5–28.
(1979). Working alliance, therapeutic alliance, and transference. *Journal of the American Psychoanalytic Association, 27*: 137–157.
(1982). *The Mind in Conflict*. New York: International Universities Press.
(1996). The nature of knowledge and the limits of authority in psychoanalysis. *Psychoanalytic Quarterly, 65*: 21–31.
(2000). Brief communication: evenly hovering attention. *Psychoanalytic Quarterly, 69*: 545–549.

IRA BRENNER

(1988). Multisensory bridges in response to object loss during the Holocaust. *Psychoanalytic Review, 75*: 573–587.
(1994). The dissociative character: a reconsideration of 'multiple personality'. *Journal of the American Psychoanalytic Association, 42*: 819–846.
(1996). On trauma, perversion, and 'multiple personality'. *Journal of the American Psychoanalytic Association, 44*: 785–814.
(2001). *Dissociation of Trauma: Theory, Phenomenology, and Technique*. Madison, CT: International Universities Press.
(2002). Foreword. In: V. D. Volkan, G. Ast, & W. Greer, Jr (Eds.), *The Third Reich in the Unconscious: Transgenerational Transmission and Its Consequences* (pp.xi–xvii). New York: Brunner/Routledge.
(2004). *Psychic Trauma: Dynamics, Symptoms, and Treatment*. Northvale, NJ: Jason Aronson.
(2009a). A new view from Acropolis: dissociative identity disorder. *Psychoanalytic Quarterly, 78*: 57–105.
(2009b). Geopolitical identity disorder. *American Journal of Psychoanalysis, 69*: 62–71.

INGE BRETHERTON

(1987). New perspectives on attachment relationships: security, communication, and internal working models. In: J. Osofsky (Ed.), *Handbook of Infant Development* (pp. 1061–1101). New York: John Wiley and Sons.

MARTIN BREZIN

(1967). Panel report: the theory of genital primacy in the light of ego psychology. *Journal of the American Psychoanalytic Association, 17*: 968–987.

ABRAHAM A. BRILL

(1932). The sense of smell in the neuroses and psychoses. *Psychoanalytic Quarterly, 1*: 7–42.
(1941). Necrophilia. *Journal of Criminal Psychopathology, 3*: 51–73.

RONALD BRITTON

(1994). Publication anxiety: conflict between communication and affiliation. *International Journal of Psychoanalysis, 75*: 1213–1224.

RONALD BRITTON & JOHN STEINER

(1994). Interpretation: selected fact or overvalued idea? *International Journal of Psychoanalysis, 75*: 1069–1078.
(1998). Naming and containing. In: *Belief and Imagination: Explorations in Psychoanalysis* (pp. 19–28). London: Routledge.

MORRIS BRODY

(1959). *Observations on 'Direct Analysis', The Therapeutic Technique of Dr. John N. Rosen*. New York: Vantage Press.

PHILLIP BROMBERG

(1980). Sullivan's concept of consensual validation and the therapeutic action of psychoanalysis. *Contemporary Psychoanalysis, 16*: 237–238.
(1988). Interpersonal psychoanalysis and self psychology: a clinical comparison. In: D. W. Detrich & S. P. Detrich (Eds.), *Self Psychology: Comparisons and Contrasts* (pp. 275–291). Hillsdale, NJ: Analytic Press.
(1998). Staying the same while changing: reflections on clinical judgment. *Psychoanalytic Dialogues, 8*: 225–236.

WALTER BROMBERG & PAUL SCHILDER

(1933). Death and dying. *Psychoanalytic Review, 20*: 133–185.
(1936). The attitude of psychoneurotics towards death. *Psychoanalytic Review, 23*: 1–25.

LAWRENCE BROWN & MARTIN MILLER

(2002). The triadic intersubjective matrix in supervision. *International Journal of Psychoanalysis, 83*: 811–823.

HILDE BRUCH

(1978). *The Golden Cage The Enigma of Anorexia Nervosa*. Cambridge, MA: Harvard University Press.

RUTH MACK BRUNSWICK

(1928). A supplement to Freud's 'History of an infantile neurosis'. *International Journal of Psychoanalysis, 9*: 437–476.

JOHN BUCKMAN

(1985). Self-destructive behaviors. In: V. D. Volkan (Ed.), *Depressive States and Their Treatment* (pp. 221–234). Northvale, NJ: Jason Aronson.

DAN BUIE

(1981). Empathy: its nature and limitations. *Journal of the American Psychoanalytic Association, 29*: 281–307.

ALEXIS BURLAND

(1986). The vicissitudes of maternal deprivation. In: R. Lax, S. Bach, & J. A. Burland (Eds.), *Self and Object Constancy* (pp. 324–348). New York: Guilford Press.

DOROTHY BURLINGHAM

(1973). The preoedipal infant–father relationship. *Psychoanalytic Study of the Child, 28*: 23–47.

DONALD BURNHAM, ARTHUR GLADSTONE, & ROBERT GIBSON

(1969). *Schizophrenia and the Need–Fear Dilemma*. New York: International Universities Press.

BEN BURSTEN

(1973). Some narcissistic personality types. *International Journal of Psychoanalysis, 54*: 287–300.

FRED BUSCH

(1997). Understanding the patient's use of the method of free association: an ego psychological approach. *Journal of the American Psychoanalytic Association, 45*: 407–423.
(1998). Self-disclosure ain't what it's cracked up to be, at least not yet. *Psychoanalytic Inquiry, 18*: 518–529.
(2000). What is a deep interpretation? *Journal of the American Psychoanalytic Association, 48*: 237–254.
(2004). *Ego at the Center of Technique*. Northvale, NJ: Jason Aronson.

References

(2007). 'I noticed': the emergence of self-observation in relationship to pathological attractor sites. *International Journal of Psychoanalysis, 88*: 423–442.

BUTLER, J.

(1998). Moral sadism and doubting one's own love. In: L. Stonebridge & J. Phillips (Eds.), *Kleinian Reflections on Melancholia* (pp. 179–189). London: Routledge.

GUSTAV BYCHOWSKI

(1953). The problem of latent psychosis. *Journal of the American Psychoanalytic Association, 1*: 484–503.
(1954). On the handling of some schizophrenic defense mechanisms and reaction patterns. *International Journal of Psychoanalysis, 35*: 147–153.
(1958). Struggle against the introjects. *International Journal of Psychoanalysis, 39*: 182–187.
(1962). Escapes: a form of discussion. *Psychoanalytic Quarterly, 31*: 155–174.
(1963). Frigidity and object relationship. *International Journal of Psychoanalysis, 44*: 57–62.

ALBERT CAIN & BARBARA CAIN

(1964). On replacing a child. *Journal of the American Academy of Child Psychiatry, 3*: 443–456.

VICTOR CALEF

(1982). An introspective on training and non-training analysis. *Annual of Psychoanalysis, 10*: 93–114.

VICTOR CALEF & EDWARD WEINSHEL

(1980). The analyst as the conscience of analysis. *International Review of Psychoanalysis, 7*: 279–280.
(1981). Some clinical consequences of introjection: gaslighting. *Psychoanalytic Quarterly, 50*: 44–66.

LUZ CALVO

(2008). Racial fantasies and the primal scene of miscegenation. *International Journal of Psychoanalysis, 89*: 55–70.

DONALD CAMPBELL

(1995). The role of the father in a pre-suicide state. *International Journal of Psychoanalysis, 76*: 315–323.

DONALD CAMPBELL, & HENRIK ENCKELL

(2005). Metaphor and the violent act. *International Journal of Psychoanalysis, 86*: 801–823.

KAY CAMPBELL, DONALD SILVER, KERRY KELLY NOVICK, JACK NOVICK, MARY MITTLESTAEDT, & ANNE WALTON

(1995). The application of Lichtenberg's five motivational systems to the analysis of mother-infant interaction. *Psychoanalytic Inquiry, 15*: 481–492.

JORGE CANESTRI

(1994). Transformations. *International Journal of Psychoanalysis, 75*: 1079–1092.
(2005). Some reflections on the use and meaning of conflict in contemporary psychoanalysis. *International Journal of Psychoanalysis, 74*: 295–326.

DAVID CARLSON

(2002). Free-swinging attention. *Psychoanalytic Quarterly, 71*: 725–750.

PATRICK CASEMENT

(1982). Some pressures on the analyst for physical contact during the re-living of an early trauma. *International Review of Psychoanalysis, 9*: 279–286.
(1991). *Learning from the Patient*. New York: Guilford.

DIANNE CASONI

(2002). 'Never twice without thrice': an outline for the understanding of traumatic neurosis. *International Journal of Psychoanalysis, 83*: 137–159.

STANLEY CATH

(1965). Some dynamics of middle and later years: a study of depletion and restitution. In: M. Berezin & S. H. Cath (Eds.), *Geriatric Psychiatry: Grief, Loss, and Emotional Disorders in Aging Process* (pp. 21–72). New York: International Universities Press.
(1966). Beyond depression, the depleted state: a study in ego psychology in the aged. *Canadian Psychiatric Association Journal, 2*(Suppl.): 329–339.

(1990). The awareness of the nearness of death, depletion, and the senescent cell antigen: a reconsideration of Freud's death instinct on the new frontier between psychodynamic theory and biology. In: R. A. Nemiroff & C. A. Colarusso (Eds.), *New Dimensions in Adult Development* (pp. 420–442). New York: Basic Books.

(1997). Loss and restitution in late life. In: S. Akhtar & S. Kramer (Eds.), *The Seasons of Life: Separation–Individuations Perspectives* (pp. 125–156). Northvale, NJ: Jason Aronson.

JESSE CAVENAR & JAMES NASH

(1976). The dream as a signal of termination. *Journal of the American Psychoanalytic Association*, 24: 425–436.

ANDREA CELENZA

(2005). Vis-à-vis the couch: where is psychoanalysis? *International Journal of Psychoanalysis, 86*: 1645–1660.

(2007). *Sexual Boundary Violations: Therapeutic, Supervisory, and Academic Contacts*. Lanham, MD: Jason Aronson.

ALFRED CHAPMAN

(1959). The concept of nemesis in psychoneurosis. *Journal of Nervous and Mental Disease, 129*: 29–34.

JEAN-MARTIN CHARCOT

(1889). *Clinical Lectures on Diseases of the Nervous System Delivered at the Infirmary of La Salpetriere, Vols. I-III.* Paris: New Syndenham Society.

JANINE CHASSEGUET-SMIRGEL

(1984). *Creativity and Perversion.* New York: W. W. Norton.

(1988). The triumph of humor. In: H. P. Blum, Y. Kramer, A. K. Richards & A. D. Richards (Eds.), *Fantasy, Myth, and Reality: Essays in Honor of Jacob Arlow, M.D.* (pp. 197–213). Madison, CT: International Universities Press.

JOSEPH CHASSELL

(1955). Panel report: psychoanalysis and psychotherapy. *Journal of the American Psychoanalytic Association, 3*: 528–533.

CHARLES CHEDIAK

(1979). Counter-reactions and countertransference. *International Journal of Psychoanalysis, 60*: 117–129.

RICHARD CHESSICK

(2006). Review of *International Dictionary of Psychoanalysis*, Alain de Mijolla (Ed.). *Journal of the American Academy of Psychoanalysis and Dynamic Psychiatry, 34*: 570–574.

NANCY CHODOROW

(1989). *Feminism and Psychoanalytic Theory.* New Haven, CT: Yale University Press.

(1992). Heterosexuality as a compromise formation: reflections on the psychoanalytic theory of sexual development. *Psychoanalysis and Contemporary Thought, 15*: 267–304.

GEORGE CHRISTIE

(1994). Some psychoanalytic aspects of humor. *International Journal of Psychoanalysis, 75*: 479–489.

JUDITH CHUSED

(1982). The role of analytic neutrality in the use of the child analyst as a new object. *Journal of the American Psychoanalytic Association, 30*: 3–28.

GIUSEPPE CIVITARESE

(2006). Dreams that mirror the session. *International Journal of Psychoanalysis, 87*: 703–723.

VIRGINIA CLOWER

(1976). Theoretical implications of the current views of masturbation in latency age girls. *Journal of the American Psychoanalytic Association, 24*(Suppl.): 109–125.

STANLEY COEN

(1988). Superego aspects of entitlement (in rigid characters). *Journal of the American Psychoanalytic Association, 36*: 409–427.

(1994). Barriers to love between patient and analyst. *Journal of the American Psychoanalytic Association, 42*: 1107–1135.

(1995). Narcissistic temptations to cross boundaries and how to manage them. *Journal of the American Psychoanalytic Association, 55*: 1169–1190.

(1996). The passions and perils of interpretation (of dreams and texts): an appreciation of Erik Erikson's dream specimen paper. *International Journal of Psychoanalysis, 77*: 537–548.

References

(1997). Negative acting-in: how to help patients (and analysts) bear the unbearable. *Journal of the American Psychoanalytic Association*, 45: 1183–1207.

(1998). Perverse defenses in neurotic patients. *Journal of the American Psychoanalytic Association*, 46: 1169–1194.

(2000). The wish to regress in patient and analyst. *Journal of the American Psychoanalytic Association*, 48: 785–810.

(2002). *Affect Intolerance in the Patient and the Analyst*. Northvale, NJ: Jason Aronson.

STANLEY COEN & PAUL BRADLOW

(1985). The common mirror dream, dreamer, and the dream mirror. *Journal of the American Psychoanalytic Association*, 33: 797–820.

MABEL COHEN, GRACE BAKER, ROBERT COHEN, FRIEDA FROMM-REICHMANN, & EDITH WEIGERT

(1954). An intensive study of twelve cases of manic–depressive psychosis. *Psychiatry*, 17: 103–138.

BERTRAM COHLER & ROBERT GALATZER-LEVY

(2000). *The Course of Gay and Lesbian Lives*. Chicago, IL: University of Chicago Press.

CALVIN COLARUSSO

(1990). The third individuation: the effect of biological parenthood on separation–individuation processes in adulthood. *Psychoanalytic Study of the Child*, 45: 170–194.

(1997). Separation–individuation processes in middle adulthood: the fourth individuation. In: S. Akhtar & S. Kramer (Eds.), *The Seasons of Life: Separation–Individuation Perspectives* (pp. 73–93). Northvale, NJ: Jason Aronson.

(2005). The evolution of paternal identity in late adulthood. *Journal of the American Psychoanalytic Association*, 53: 51–81.

CALVIN COLARUSSO & ROBERT NEMIROFF

(1979). Some observations and hypotheses about the psychoanalytic theory of adult development. *International Journal of Psychoanalysis*, 60: 59–71.

(1981). *Adult Development: A New Dimension in Psychodynamic and Practice*. New York: Plenum.

ALICE COLONNA & LOTTIE NEWMAN

(1983). The psychoanalytic literature on siblings. *Psychoanalytic Study of the Child*, 38: 285–309.

NINA COLTART

(1988). The assessment of psychological mindedness in the diagnostic interview. *British Journal of Psychiatry*, 153: 819–820.

(2000). *Slouching Towards Bethlehem*. New York: Other Press.

MICHAEL CONRAN

(1976). Incestuous failure. *International Journal of Psychoanalysis*, 57: 477–481.

ARNOLD COOPER

(1983). The place of self-psychology in the history of depth psychology. In: A. Goldberg (Ed.), *The Future of Psychoanalysis* (pp. 3–17). New York: International Universities Press.

(1987). Changes in psychoanalytic ideas: transference interpretation. *Journal of the American Psychoanalytic Association*, 35: 77–98.

(1988a). The narcissistic–masochistic character. In: R. A. Glick & D. I. Meyers (Eds.), *Masochism: Current Psychoanalytic Perspectives* (pp. 117–138). Hillsdale, NJ: The Analytic Press.

(1988b). Our changing views of the therapeutic action of psychoanalysis: comparing Strachey and Loewald. *Psychoanalytic Quarterly*, 57: 15–27.

STEVEN COOPER

(1998). Analyst's subjectivity, analyst's disclosure, and the aims of psychoanalysis. *Psychoanalytic Quarterly*, 67: 379–406.

(2000). *The Objects of Hope*. Hillsdale, NJ: Analytic Press.

RICHARD CORNFIELD

(1999). Panel on applied psychoanalysis: psychoanalytic concepts in communication with other fields. *Journal of Applied Psychoanalytic Studies*, 1: 367–371.

JEAN COURNUT

(1991). *L'Ordinaire de la passion*. Paris: Presses Universitaires de France.

PAUL COURTRIGHT

(1985). *Ganesha: Lord of Obstacles, Lord of Beginnings.* New York: Oxford University Press.

HOMER CURTIS

(1979). The concept of therapeutic alliance: implications for the 'widening scope'. *Journal of the American Psychoanalytic Association, 27*(Suppl): 159–192.

HEATHER CRAIGE

(2002). Mourning analysis: the post-termination phase. *Journal of the American Psychoanalytic Association, 50*: 507–550.

JOACHIM DANCKWARDT & PETER WEGNER

(2007). Performance as annihilation or integration? *International Journal of Psychoanalysis, 88*: 1117–1133.

CLAUDE DANGAR-DALY

(1930). The psychology of revolutionary tendencies. *International Journal of Psychoanalysis, 11*: 193–210.

CHARLES DARWIN

(1859). *On the Origin of Species by Means of Natural Selection.* London: John Murray.

WALTER DAVISON, MONROE PRAY, & CURTIS BRISTOL

(1990). Mutative interpretation and close process monitoring in a study of psychoanalytic process. *Psychoanalytic Quarterly, 59*: 599–628.

ANTHONY DECASPER & MELANIE SPENCE.

(1986). Pre-natal speech influences newborn's perception of speech sounds. *Infant Behavior and Development, 9*: 133–150.

JULIA GRINBERG DE EKBOIR & ANA LICHTMANN

(1982). Genuine self analysis is impossible. *International Review of Psychoanalysis, 9*: 75–83.

EDDY DE KLERK

(2003). Het trauma van Freud besnijdenis. *Tijdschrift voor Psychoanalyse, 9*: 136–152.
(2004). Kastrationsangst und beschneidung. *Psyche, 58*: 464–470.

BEATRIZ DE LEON DE BERNARDI

(2000). The countertransference: a Latin American view. *International Journal of Psychoanalysis, 81*: 331–351.

JACQUES DERRIDA

(1998). 'Geopsychoanalysis' . . . and the rest of the world. In: C. Lane (Ed.), *The Psychoanalysis of Race* (pp. 65–90). New York: Columbia University Press.

FELIX DEUTSCH

(1952). Analytic posturology. *Psychoanalytic Quarterly, 21*: 196–214.

HELENE DEUTSCH

(1925). The psychology of women in relation to the functions of reproduction. *International Journal of Psychoanalysis, 6*: 405–418.
(1929). The genesis of agoraphobia. *International Journal of Psychoanalysis, 10*: 51–69.
(1933). The psychology of manic–depressive states with particular reference to chronic hypermania. In: *Neuroses and Character Types* (pp. 203–217). New York: International Universities Press, 1965.
(1942). Some forms of emotional disturbance and their relationship to schizophrenia. *Psychoanalytic Quarterly, 11*: 301–321.
(1966). *A Developmental Approach to Problems of Acting Out.* Washington, DC: American Academy of Child Psychiatry.

GEORGE DEVEREUX

(1951). Some criteria for the timing of confrontation and interpretation. *International Journal of PsychoAnalysis, 32*: 19–24.

PAUL DEWALD

(1966). Forced termination of psychoanalysis: transference, countertransference, and reality responses in five patients. *Bulletin of the Menninger Clinic, 30*: 98–110.

References

(1971). *Psychotherapy: A Dynamic Approach*. New York: Basic Books.

(1982a). Serious illness in the analyst: transference, countertransference, and reality aspects. *Journal of the American Psychoanalytic Association*, 30: 347–363.

(1982b). Psychoanalytic perspectives on resistance. In: P. Wachtel (Ed.), *Resistance: Psychodynamics, and Behavioral Approaches* (pp. 25–68). New York: Plenum Press.

MICHAEL DIAMOND

(2006). Masculinity unraveled: the roots of male gender identity and the splitting of male ego ideals throughout life. *Journal of the American Psychoanalytic Association*, 54: 1099–1130.

ROBERT DICKES

(1965). The defensive function of an altered state of consciousness. *Journal of the American Psychoanalytic Association*, 13: 356–403.

M. DOEHRMAN

(1976). Parallel processes in supervision and psychotherapy. *Bulletin of the Menninger Clinic*, 60: 3–10.

TAKEO DOI

(1962). Amae: a key concept for understanding Japanese personality structure. In: R. J. Smith & R. K. Beardsley (Eds.), *Japanese Culture: Its Development and Characteristics*. Chicago, IL: Aidine.

(1989). The concept of amae and its psychoanalytic implications. *International Review of Psychoanalysis*, 16: 349–354.

NORMAN DOIDGE

(2001). Diagnosing 'The English Patient': schizoid fantasies of being skinless and being buried alive. *Journal of the American Psychoanalytic Association*, 49: 279–309.

WENDY DONIGER

(1976). *Origins of Evil in Hindu Mythology*. Los Angeles, CA: University of California Press.

(1981). *Siva: The Erotic Ascetic*. New York: Oxford University Press.

S. DONOVAN & STEVEN ROOSE

(1995). Medication use during psychoanalysis: a survey. *Journal of Clinical Psychiatry*, 56: 177–179.

ROBERT DORN

(1967). Crying at weddings and 'when I grow up . . .'. *International Journal of Psychoanalysis*, 48: 298–307.

THEODORE DORPAT

(1976). Structural conflict and object relations conflict. *Journal of the American Psychoanalytic Association*, 24: 855–874.

(1978). Psychological aspects of accidents. *The Annual of Psychoanalysis*, 6: 273–283.

(1984). The technique of questioning. In: J. S. Raney (Ed.), *Listening and Interpreting* (pp. 55–74). New York: Jason Aronson.

DENISE DORSEY

(1996). Castration anxiety or feminine genital anxiety? *Journal of the American Psychoanalytic Association*, 44(suppl): 283–302.

JENNIFER DOWNEY & RICHARD FRIEDMAN

(1998). Female homosexuality: classical psychoanalytic theory reconsidered. *Journal of the American Psychoanalytic Association*, 46: 471–505.

FLANDERS DUNBAR

(1954). *Emotions and Bodily Changes*. New York: Columbia University Press.

JONATHAN DUNN

(1995). Intersubjectivity in psychoanalysis: a critical review. *International Journal of Psychoanalysis*, 76: 723–738.

MARCO ANTONIO DUPONT

(1984). On primary communication. *International Review of Psychoanalysis*, 11: 303–311.

BARBARA RUTH EASSER & STANLEY LESSER

(1965). Hysterical personality: a reevaluation. *Psychoanalytic Quarterly*, 34: 390–405.

HENRY EDELHEIT

(1974). Crucifixion fantasies and their relation to the primal scene. *International Journal of Psychoanalysis, 55*: 193–199.

ROSE EDGCUMBE

(1981). Toward a developmental line for the acquisition of language. *Psychoanalytic Study of the Child, 36*: 71–103.

JOYCE EDWARDS, N. RUSKIN, & PATSY TURINI

(1981). *Separation–Individuation Theory and Application.* New York: Gardener.

DARLENE EHRENBERG

(1974). The intimate edge in therapeutic relatedness. *Contemporary Psychoanalysis, 10*: 423–437.
(1992). *The Intimate Edge.* New York: W. W. Norton.
(1995). Self-disclosure: therapeutic tool or indulgence? *Contemporary Psychoanalysis, 31*: 213–228.

FRIEDRICH WILHELM EICKHOFF

(1989). On the 'borrowed unconscious sense of guilt' and the palimpsestic structure of a symptom. *International Review of Psychoanalysis, 16*: 323–329.

LUDWIG EIDELBERG

(1945). A contribution to the study of the masturbation fantasy. *International Journal of Psychoanalysis, 26*: 127–137.
(1948). *Studies in Psychoanalysis.* New York: International Universities Press.
(1954). *An Outline of the Comparative Theory of the Neuroses.* New York: International Universities Press.
(1957). An introduction to the study of the narcissistic mortification. *Psychoanalytic Quarterly, 31*: 657–668.
(1959). Humiliation in masochism. *Journal of the American Psychoanalytic Association, 7*: 274–283.
(1968). (Ed.). *Encyclopedia of Psychoanalysis.* New York: The Free Press.

MICHAEL EIGEN

(1981). The area of faith in Winnicott, Lacan, and Bion. *International Journal of Psychoanalysis, 62*: 413–433.

ALAN EISNITZ

(1961). Mirror dreams. *Journal of the American Psychoanalytic Association, 9*: 461–479.
(1980). The organization of the self-representation and its influence on pathology. *Psychoanalytic Quarterly, 49*: 361–392.

KURT EISSLER

(1949). Some problems of delinquency. In: K. R. Eissler (Ed.), *Searchlights on Delinquency* (pp. 3–25). New York: International Universities Press.
(1950). Ego psychological implications of the psychoanalytic treatment of delinquents. *Psychoanalytic Study of the Child, 5*: 97–121.
(1953). The effect of the structure of the ego on psychoanalytic technique. *Journal of the American Psychoanalytic Association, 1*: 104–143.
(1959). On isolation. *Psychoanalytic Study of the Child, 14*: 29–60.
(1960). The efficient soldier. In: W. Muensterburger & S. Axelrod (Eds.), *The Psychoanalytic Study of Society.* New York: International Universities Press.
(1971). Death drive, ambivalence, and narcissism. *Psychoanalytic Study of the Child, 26*: 25–78.

MAX EITINGON

(1925). Announcement by the general executive. *Bulletin of the International Psychoanalytical Association, 6*: 235–237.

CLAUDIO LAKS EIZIRIK

(1996). Panel report: psychic reality and clinical technique. *International Journal of Psychoanalysis, 77*: 37–41.
(1997). Psychoanalysis and culture: some contemporary challenges. *International Journal of Psychoanalysis, 78*: 789–800.

RUDOLPH EKSTEIN

(1950). Trial analysis in the therapeutic process. *Psychoanalytic Quarterly, 19*: 52–63.

RUDOLPH EKSTEIN & ROBERT WALLERSTEIN

(1958). *The Teaching and Learning of Psychotherapy.* New York: Basic Books.

HAVELOCK ELLIS

(1894). *Man and Woman: A Study of Human Secondary Sexual Characteristics.* Kila, MT: Kessinger, 1964.

References

(1903). *Analysis of Sexual Impulse, Love and Pain: The Sexual Impulse in Women*. Philadelphia, PA: F. A. Davis Co.

(1905). *Studies in the Psychology of Sex: Sexual Selection in Man*. Honolulu, HI: University Press of the Pacific, 2001.

PAUL ELOVITZ & CHARLOTTE KAHN

(1997). *Immigrant Experiences: Personal Narrative and Psychological Analysis*. Cranbury, NJ: Associated University Presses.

ROBERT EMDE

(1980). The developmental orientation in psychoanalysis. *Psychoanalysis and Contemporary Thought, 3*: 123–131.

(1981). Changing models of infancy and the nature of early development: remodeling the foundation. *Journal of the American Psychoanalytic Association, 29*: 179–219.

(1983). The pre-representational self and its affective core. *Psychoanalytic Study of the Child, 38*: 165–192.

(1988). Development terminable and interminable: innate, motivational factors. *International Journal of Psychoanalysis, 69*: 23–42.

(1990). Mobilizing fundamental modes of development: empathic availability and therapeutic action. *Journal of the American Psychoanalytic Association, 38*: 881–913.

(1999). Moving ahead: integrating influences of affective processes for development and for psychoanalysis. *International Journal of Psychoanalysis, 80*: 317–339.

GEORGE ENGEL

(1971). Attachment behaviour, object relations and the dynamic-economic points of view: critical review of Bowlby's 'Attachment and Loss'. *International Journal of Psychoanalysis, 52*: 183–196.

(1975). The death of a twin: mourning and anniversary reactions—fragments of ten years of self analysis. *International Journal of Psychoanalysis, 56*: 23–40.

HORACE ENGLISH & AVA ENGLISH

(1976). *A Comprehensive Dictionary of Psychological and Psychoanalytical Terms*. New York: Longman, Green.

SPURGEON ENGLISH, WILLIAM HAMPE, CATHERINE BACON, & CALVIN SETTLAGE

(1961). *Direct Analysis and Schizophrenia*. New York: Grune and Stratton.

LAWRENCE EPSTEIN

(1979). Countertransference with borderline patients. In: L. Epstein & A. H. Feiner (Eds.), *Countertransference* (pp. 375–406). New York: Jason Aronson.

LAWRENCE EPSTEIN & ARTHUR FEINER

(1979). *Countertransference*. New York: Jason Aronson.

ERIK ERIKSON

(1950). *Childhood and Society*. New York: Norton, 1963.

(1954). The dream specimen of psychoanalysis. *Journal of the American Psychoanalytic Association, 2*: 5–56

(1956). The problem of ego identity. In: *Identity and the Life Cycle* (pp. 104–164). New York: International Universities Press, 1959.

(1958). *Young Man Luther: A Study in Psychoanalysis and History*. New York: W. W. Norton.

(1959). *Identity and the Life Cycle: Psychological Issues Monograph: I*. New York: International Universities Press.

(1969). *Gandhi's Truth: On the Origins of Militant Nonviolence*. New York: W. W. Norton.

(1975). *Life History and the Historical Moment*. New York: W. W. Norton.

(1980). Elements of a psychoanalytic theory of psychosocial development. In: S. I. Greenspan & G. H. Pollock (Eds.), *The Course of Life: Psychoanalytic Contributions Toward Understanding Personality Development, Volume I: Infancy and Early Childhood* (pp. 11–61). Adelphi, MD: National Institute of Mental Health.

(1982). *The Life Cycle Completed: A Review*. New York: W. W. Norton.

JOAN ERLE

(1979). An approach to the study of analyzability and analyses: the course of forty consecutive cases selected for supervised analysis. *Psychoanalytic Quarterly, 48*: 198–228.

JOAN ERLE & DANIEL GOLDBERG

(1984). Observations on assessment of analyzability by experienced analysts. *Journal of the American Psychoanalytic Association, 32*: 715–737.

EDWARD ERWIN

(2002). *The Freud Encyclopedia: Theory, Therapy, and Culture*. New York: Routledge.

PHILIP ESCOLL

(1992). Vicissitudes of optimal distance through the life cycle. In: S. Kramer & S. Akhtar (Eds.), *When the Body Speaks: Psychological Meanings in Kinetic Clues* (pp. 59–87). Northvale, NJ: Jason Aronson.
(2001). A to Z: awe, cabalism, and zohar. In: S. Akhtar & H. Parens (Eds.), *Does God Help?: Developmental and Clinical Aspects of Religious Belief* (pp. 235–252). Northvale, NJ: Jason Aronson.

OFRA ESHEL

(1998). 'Black holes', deadness and existing analytically. *International Journal of Psychoanalysis*, 79: 1115–1130.

AARON ESMAN

(1983). Stimulus barrier: a review and reconsideration. *Psychoanalytic Study of the Child*, 38: 193–207.
(1987) Rescue fantasies. *Psychoanalytic Quarterly*, 56: 263–270.

ALICIA ETCHEGOYEN

(1993). The analyst's pregnancy and its consequences on her work. *International Journal of Psychoanalysis*, 74: 141–149.

HORACIO ETCHEGOYEN

(1978). Some thoughts on transference perversion. *International Journal of Psychoanalysis*, 59: 45–53.
(2005). *The Fundamentals of Psychoanalytic Technique*. London: Karnac.

HORACIO ETCHEGOYEN & JORGE AHUMADA

(1990). Bateson and Matte-Blanco: bio-logic and bi-logic. *International Review of Psychoanalysis*, 17: 493–502.

HOSSEIN ETEZADY

(1995). Narcissism: primary–secondary, fundamental, or obsolete? In: T. B. Cohen, M. H. Etezady & B. L. Pacella (Eds.), *The Vulnerable Child, Volume 2* (pp. 3–9). Madison, CT: International Universities Press.

DYLAN EVANS

(1996). *An Introductory Dictionary of Lacanian Psychoanalysis*. New York: Routledge.

RONALD FAIRBAIRN

(1931). Features in the analysis of a patient with a genital abnormality. In: *Psychoanalytic Studies of the Personality* (pp. 197–222). London: Routledge & Kegan Paul, 1952.
(1940). Schizoid factors in the personality. In: *An Object Relations Theory of Personality* (pp. 3–27). New York: Basic Books, 1952.
(1943). The repression and the return of bad objects. In: *Psychoanalytic Studies of the Personality* (pp. 59–81). London: Routledge & Kegan Paul, 1952.
(1944). Endopsychic structure considered in terms of object relationships. In: *Psychoanalytic Studies of the Personality* (pp. 82–137). London: Routledge & Kegan Paul, 1952.
(1952). *Psychoanalytic Studies of the Personality*. London: Routledge & Kegan Paul, 1952.

SUSAN FAIRFIELD

(1994). The kore complex: the myths and some unconscious fantasies. *International Journal of Psychoanalysis*, 75: 243–264.

AVNER FALK

(1974). Border symbolism. *Psychoanalytic Quarterly*, 43: 650–660.

FRANTZ FANON

(1952). *Black Skin, White Masks*, R. Philcox (Trans.). New York: Grove Press, 2008.
(1959). *A Dying Colonialism*, H. Chevalier (Trans.). New York: Grove Press, 1994.

DENNIS FARRELL & MICHAEL HOYT

(1982). On speaking of one's self by name. *International Journal of Psychoanalytic Psychotherapy*, 9: 601–619.

IRENE FAST

(1974). Multiple identities in borderline personality organization. *British Journal of Medical Psychology*, 47: 291–300.

GUSTAV FECHNER

(1873). *Einige Ideen zur Schopfungs - und Entwicklungsgeshichte der Organismen*. Leipzig: Bretikopf und Hartel.

References

LOUIS FEDER

(1974). Adoption trauma: oedipal myth/clinical reality. *International Journal of Psychoanalysis, 55*: 491–493.

PAUL FEDERN

(1928). Narcissism in the structure of the ego. *International Journal of Psychoanalysis, 9*: 401–419.
(1932). The ego feeling in dreams. *Psychoanalytic Quarterly, 1*: 511–542.
(1934). The analysis of psychotics. *International Journal of Psychoanalysis, 15*: 209–214.
(1952) *Ego Psychology and the Psychoses*. New York: Basic Books.

MICHAEL FELDMAN

(1993). The dynamics of reassurance. *International Journal of Psychoanalysis, 74*: 275–285.

SANDOR FELDMAN

(1958). Blanket interpretations. *Psychoanalytic Quarterly, 37*: 205–216.

OTTO FENICHEL

(1927). Economic functions of screen memories. In: *The Collected Papers of Otto Fenichel—Volume I* (pp. 113–116). New York: W. W. Norton, 1953.
(1928). The dread of being eaten. In: *The Collected Papers of Otto Fenichel—Volume 1* (pp. 158–159). New York: W. W. Norton, 1953.
(1931). Specific types of Oedipus complex. *International Journal of Psychoanalysis, 12*: 412–430.
(1934). Defense against anxiety, particularly by libidinization. In: H. Fenichel & D. Rapaport (Eds.), *The Collected Papers of Otto Fenichel, First Series* (pp. 303–317). New York: W. W. Norton, 1953.
(1938). The drive to amass wealth. *Psychoanalytic Quarterly, 7*: 69–95.
(1939a). The economics of pseudologia phantastica. In: *The Collected Papers of Otto Fenichel—Volume II* (pp. 129–140). New York: W. W. Norton, 1954.
(1939b). Problems of psychoanalytic technique: IV. *Psychoanalytic Quarterly, 8*: 164–185.
(1941). *Problems of Psychoanalytic Technique*. Albany, NY: Psychoanalytic Quarterly Press.
(1945). *The Psychoanalytic Theory of Neurosis*. New York: W. W. Norton [reprinted 1972].
(1974). A review of Freud's 'Analysis terminable and interminable'. *International Review of Psychoanalysis, 1*: 109–116.

SHERI FENSTER, SUZANNE PHILLIPS, & ESTELLE RAPOPORT

(1986). *The Therapist's Pregnancy: Intrusion in Analytic Space*. Hillsdale, NJ: Analytic Press.

SANDOR FERENCZI

(1909). Introjection and transference. In: *First Contributions to Psychoanalysis*, E. Mosbacher (Trans.) (pp. 35–93). London: Karnac, 1980.
(1911). On obscene words. In: *Final Contributions to the Problems and Methods of Psychoanalysis*, E. Mosbacher (Trans.). London: Karnac, 1980.
(1912). Transitory symptom-constructions during the analysis. In: *First Contributions to Psychoanalysis*, E. Mosbacher (Trans.) (pp. 193–212). London: Karnac, 1980.
(1913). The grandfather complex. In: *Further Contributions to the Theory and Technique of Psycho-Analysis* (pp. 323–324). New York: Boni and Liveright, 1926.
(1914). The origin of the interest in money. In: *First Contributions to the Problems and Methods of Psychoanalysis*, E. Mosbacher (Trans.). London: Karnac, 1980.
(1915). Polycratism. In: *Further Contributions to the Theory and Technique of Psycho-Analysis* (p. 423). New York: Boni and Liveright, 1926.
(1919a). On the technique of psychoanalysis. In: *Further Contributions to the Theory and Technique of Psychoanalysis*, J. Suttie (Trans.) (pp. 177–189). London: Karnac, 1980.
(1919b). Sunday neuroses. In: *Further Contributions to the Theory and Technique of Psycho-Analysis* (pp. 174–177). New York: Boni and Liveright, 1926.
(1921). The further development of the active therapy in psychoanalysis. In: *Further Contributions to the Theory and Technique of Psychoanalysis* (pp. 198–217). London: Hogarth Press, 1955.
(1923). The dream of the 'clever baby'. In: *Further Contributions to the Theory and Technique of Psychoanalysis*, J. Suttie (Trans.) (pp. 349–350). London: Karnac, 1980.
(1925a). Contraindications to the active psychoanalytical technique. In: *Further Contributions to the Theory and Technique of Psychoanalysis*, J. Suttie (Trans.) (pp. 217–230). London: Karnac, 1980.
(1925b). Psychoanalysis of sexual habits. In: *Further Contributions to the Theory and Technique of Psychoanalysis*, J. Suttie (Trans.) (pp. 259–297). London: Karnac, 1980.
(1928). The elasticity of psychoanalytic technique. In: *Final Contributions to the Problems and Methods of Psychoanalysis*, E. Mosbacher (Trans.) (pp. 87–101). London: Karnac, 1980.

(1929). The principle of relaxation and neocatharsis. In: *Final Contributions to the Problems and Methods of Psychoanalysis*, E. Mosbacher (Trans.) (pp. 108–125). London: Karnac, 1980.

(1932). *The Clinical Diary of Sandor Ferenczi*, M. Balint & N. Jackson (Trans.). Cambridge, MA: Harvard University Press, 1988.

(1933). On the confusion of tongues between adults and the child. In: *Final Contributions to the Problems and Methods of Psychoanalysis* (pp. 155–167). New York: Basic Books, 1955.

SANDOR FERENCZI & OTTO RANK

(1924). *The Development of Psychoanalysis*. New York: Nervous and Mental Disease Publishing.

JOSEPH FERNANDO

(2000). The borrowed sense of guilt. *International Journal of Psychoanalysis*, 81: 499–512.

MIGUEL FICHER, RALPH FISHKIN, & JOSEPH JACOBS

(1984). *Sexual Arousal: New Concepts in Basic Sciences, Diagnosis, and Treatment*. Chicago, IL: Charles Thomas.

GERMANO FILHO, ANTONIO PIRES, GERSON BERLIM, RAUL HARTKE, & SERGIO LEWKOWICZ

(2007). The supervisory field and projective identification. *International Journal of Psychoanalysis*, 88: 681–689.

HERBERT FINGARETTE

(1960). Stages in screen sensations. In: M. R. Stein, A. J. Vidich, & D. M. White (Eds.), *Identity and Anxiety* (p. 234). Glencoe, IL: Free Press.

PAUL FINK

(1970). Correlations between 'actual' neurosis and the work of Masters and Johnson. *Psychoanalytic Quarterly*, 39: 38–51.

STEPHEN FIRESTEIN

(1978). *Termination in Psychoanalysis*. New York: International Universities Press.

(1990). Death of the analyst: termination, interruption, what? In: A. J. Schwartz & A. S. Silver (Eds.), *Illness and the Analyst: Implications for the Treatment Relationship* (pp. 333–340). Washington, DC: American Psychiatric Press.

NEWELL FISCHER

(1971). An interracial analysis; transference and countertransference significance. *Journal of the American Psychoanalytic Association*, 19: 736–745.

(1989). Anorexia nervosa and unresolved rapprochement conflicts: a case study. *International Journal of Psychoanalysis*, 70: 41–54.

NEWELL FISCHER & RUTH FISCHER

(1991). Adolescence, sex, and neurosogenesis: a clinical perspective. In: S. Akhtar & H. Parens (Eds.), *Beyond the Symbiotic Orbit: Advances in Separation Individuation Theory* (pp. 209–226). Hillsdale, NJ: Analytic Press.

RUTH FISCHER

(1991). The unresolved rapprochement crisis: an important constituent of the incest experience. In: S. Kramer & S. Akhtar (Eds.), *Trauma of Transgression: Psychotherapy of Incest Victims* (pp. 39–55). Northvale, NJ: Jason Aronson.

(2002). Lesbianism: some developmental and psychodynamic considerations. *Psychoanalytic Inquiry*, 22: 278–295

B. FISH & R. HAGIN

(1972). Visual–motor disorders in infants at risk for schizophrenia. *Archives of General Psychiatry*, 27: 594–600.

CHARLES FISHER

(1987). Panel report: conversion of psychotherapy to psychoanalysis. *Journal of the American Psychoanalytic Association*, 35: 713–726.

MARGARET ANN FITZPATRICK-HANLY

(1986). Keats' oral imagination: ''tis not through envy'. *Psychoanalytic Quarterly*, 55: 618–639.

(1993). Sadomasochism in Charlotte Bronte's *Jane Eyre*: a ridge of lighted heath. *International Journal of Psychoanalysis*, 74: 1049–1061.

(2003). Creativity and oedipal fantasy in Austen's *Emma*: an ingenious and animating suspension. *International Journal of Psychoanalysis*, 84: 969–984.

(2005). Submission, inhibition, and sexuality: masochistic and psychic change in Austen's *Mansfield Park*. *International Journal of Psychoanalysis*, 86: 483–501.

References

ROBERT FLIESS

(1935). The hypnotic evasion. *Psychoanalytic Quarterly, 22:* 497–511.
(1942). The metapsychology of the analyst. *Psychoanalytic Quarterly, 11:* 211–227.

OLIVER FLOURNOY

(1974). A discussion of David Roth's and Sidney Blatt's paper 'Spatial representations of transparency and the suicide potential'. *International Journal of Psychoanalysis, 55:* 295–296.

PETER FONAGY

(1998). Moments of change in psychoanalytic theory: discussion of a new theory of psychic change. *Infant Mental Health Journal, 19:* 163–171.
(1999). Memory and therapeutic action. *International Journal of Psychoanalysis, 80:* 215–223.
(2001). *Attachment Theory and Psychoanalysis.* New York: Other Press.

PETER FONAGY & ARNOLD COOPER

(1999). Joseph Sandler's intellectual contributions to theoretical and clinical psychoanalysis. In: P. Fonagy, A. Cooper, & R. Wallenstein (Eds.), *Psychoanalysis on the Move: The Work of Joseph Sandler* (pp. 1–27). London: Routledge.

PETER FONAGY & MARY TARGET

(1996). Playing with reality: I. theory of mind and the normal development of psychic reality. *International Journal of Psychoanalysis, 77:* 217–233.
(1997). Attachment and reflective function: their role in self-organization. *Development and Psychopathology, 9:* 679–700.

PETER FONAGY, GYÖRGY GERGELY, ELLIOT JURIST, & MARY TARGET

(2002). *Affect Regulation, Mentalization and the Development of the Self.* New York: Other Press.
(2005). *Mentalization, and the Development of Self.* New York: Other Press.

DAVID FORREST

(1973). On one's own onymy. *Psychiatry, 36:* 266–290.

JAMES FOSSHAGE

(2000). The meanings of touch in psychoanalysis. *Psychoanalytic Inquiry, 20:* 21–43.

RICHARD FOX

(1998). The 'unobjectionable' countertransference. *Journal of the American Psychoanalytic Association, 46:* 1067–1087.

SELMA FRAIBERG

(1959). *The Magic Years: Understanding and Handling the Problems of Early Childhood.* New York: Charles Scribner's Sons.

ALVIN FRANK

(1969). Unrememberable and unforgettable: passive primal repression. *Psychoanalytic Study of the Child, 24:* 48.

ALVIN FRANK & HYMAN MUSLIN

(1967). The development of Freud's concept of primal repression. *Psychoanalytic Study of the Child, 22:* 55.

CLAUDIA FRANK

(1996). Review of 'Kompendium Psychoanalytischer Grundbegeriffe' by Wolfgang Martens. *Journal of the American Psychoanalytic Association, 44:* 1291–1295.

JUSTIN FRANK

(2004). *Bush on the Couch: Inside the Mind of the President.* New York: Regan Books.

RITA FRANKIEL

(1985). The stolen child: a fantasy, a wish, a source of countertransference. *International Review of Psychoanalysis, 12:* 417–430.

LISELOTTE FRANKL

(1963). Self-preservation and the development of accident proneness in children and adolescents. *Psychoanalytic Study of the Child, 18:* 464–483.

References

ABRAHAM FREEDMAN

(1990). Death of the psychoanalyst as a form of termination of psychoanalysis. In: H. J. Schwartz & A. S. Silver (Eds.), *Illness in the Analyst: Implications for the Treatment Relationship* (pp. 299–332). Washington, DC: American Psychiatric Press.

DANIEL FREEMAN

(1998). Emotional refueling in development, mythology, and cosmology: the Japanese separation–individuation experience. In: S. Akhtar & S. Kramer (Eds.), *The Colors of Childhood: Separation Individuation across Cultural, Racial, and Ethnic Differences* (pp. 17–60). Northvale, NJ: Jason Aronson.

THOMAS FREEMAN

(1962). The etiology of schizophrenia. *International Journal of Psychoanalysis, 43*: 182–184.
(1963). The concept of narcissism in schizophrenic states. *International Journal of Psychoanalysis, 44*: 293–303.
(1977). On Freud's theory of schizophrenia. *International Journal of Psychoanalysis, 58*: 383–388.
(1981). The psychoanalytic examination of a psychotic state. *International Review of Psychoanalysis, 8*: 315–324.
(1982). Schizophrenic delusions and their prepsychotic antecedents. *International Journal of Psychoanalysis, 63*: 445–448.
(1985). Nosography and the theory of schizophrenias. *International Journal of Psychoanalysis, 66*: 237–243.

THOMAS FRENCH

(1945). The integration of social behavior. *Psychoanalytic Quarterly, 14*: 149–161.

ANNA FREUD

(1927). Four lectures on child analysis. In: *The Writings of Anna Freud, Vol. I* (pp. 3–69). New York: International Universities Press, 1974.
(1936). *The Ego and the Mechanisms of Defense.* New York: International Universities Press, 1966.
(1946). The psychoanalytic study of infantile feeding disturbances. *Psychoanalytic Study of the Child, 2*: 119–132.
(1951). Homosexuality. *Bulletin of the American Psychoanalytic Association, 7*: 117–118.
(1954). Psychoanalysis and education. *Psychoanalytic Study of the Child, 9*: 9–15.
(1960). Discussion of Dr John Bowlby's paper (Grief and mourning in infancy). *Psychoanalytic Study of the Child, 15*: 53–62.
(1962). Assessment of childhood disturbances. *Psychoanalytic Study of the Child, 17*: 149–158.
(1963). The concept of developmental lines. *Psychoanalytic Study of the Child, 18*: 245–265.
(1965). *Normality and Pathology in Childhood.* New York: International Universities Press.
(1981a). The concept of developmental lines: their diagnostic significance. *Psychoanalytic Study of the Child, 36*: 129–136
(1981b). Insight: its presence and absence as a factor in normal development. *Psychoanalytic Study of the Child, 36*: 241–250.
(1984). About losing and being lost. *Psychoanalytic Study of the Child, 39*: 9–19.

SIGMUND FREUD

(1891). *Hypnosis. S.E., 1*: 103–115. London: Hogarth
(1892–1899). Extracts from the Fliess papers. *S.E., 1*: 173–280. London: Hogarth.
(1893a). On the psychical mechanism of hysterical phenomena: a lecture. *S.E., 3*: 25–41. London: Hogarth.
(1894a). The neuro-psychoses of defence. *S.E., 3*: 45–61. London: Hogarth.
(1895 [1950]). *Project for a Scientific Psychology. S. E., 1*: 295–343.
(1895d). *Studies on Hysteria* (with Joseph Breuer). *S.E., 2*: 1–323. London: Hogarth.
(1896). The 'specific' aetiology of hysteria. *S.E., 3*: 163–168. London: Hogarth.
(1897). *The Complete Letters of Sigmund Freud to Wilhelm Fliess, 1887–1904*, J. M. Masson (Ed. & Trans.). Cambridge, MA: Harvard University Press, 1985.
(1897). Letter 75 to Wilhelm Fliess. *S.E., 1*: 268–271.
(1898a). Sexuality in the aetiology of the neuroses. *S.E., 3*: 263–285. London: Hogarth.
(1899a). Screen memories. *S.E., 3*: 301–323. London: Hogarth.
(1900a). *The Interpretation of Dreams. S.E., 4–5*: 1–626. London: Hogarth.
(1901b). *The Psychopathology of Everyday Life. S.E., 6*: 1–310. London: Hogarth.
(1903). Letter to the Editor. *Die Zeit* (Vienna). 27 October.
(1905a). *Three Essays on the Theory of Sexuality. S.E., 7*: 135–243. London: Hogarth.
(1905c). *Jokes and their Relation to the Unconscious. S.E., 8*: 9–236. London: Hogarth.
(1905e). *Fragment of an Analysis of a Case of Hysteria. S.E., 7*: 1–122. London: Hogarth.
(1906a). My views on the part played by sexuality in the aetiology of the neuroses. *S.E., 7*: 271–282. London: Hogarth.
(1907a). Delusions and dreams in Jensen's 'Gradiva.' *S.E.., 9*: 1–96. London: Hogarth.

References

(1908b). Character and anal erotism. *S.E., 9*: 167–176. London: Hogarth.

(1908c). On the sexual theories of children. *S.E., 9*: 209–226. London: Hogarth.

(1908d). Civilized sexual morality and modern nervous illness. *S.E., 9*: 177–204. London: Hogarth.

(1908e). Creative writers and daydreaming. *S.E., 9*: 141–154. London: Hogarth.

(1909a). Some general remarks on hysterical attacks. *S.E., 9*: 231–232. London: Hogarth.

(1909b). *Analysis of a Phobia in a Five-year-old Boy. S.E., 10*: 5–149. London: Hogarth.

(1909c). Family romances. *S.E., 9*: 237–241. London: Hogarth.

(1909d). Notes upon a case of obsessional neurosis. *S.E., 10*: 155–318. London: Hogarth.

(1910d). The future prospects of psychoanalytic therapy. *S.E., 11*: 139–152. London: Hogarth.

(1910g). Contributions to a discussion on suicide. *S.E., 11*: 231–232. London: Hogarth.

(1910h). A special type of object choice made by men. *S.E., 11*: 163–165. London: Hogarth.

(1910i). The psycho-analytic view of psychogenic disturbances of vision. *S.E., 11*: 214–218. London: Hogarth.

(1910k). 'Wild' psycho-analysis. *S.E., 11*: 219–228. London: Hogarth.

(1911b). Formulations on the two principles of mental functioning. *S.E., 12*: 213–226. London: Hogarth.

(1911c). Psycho-analytic notes on an autobiographical account of a case of paranoia. *S.E., 12*: 9–88. London: Hogarth.

(1911e). The handling of dream-interpretation in psycho-analysis. *S.E., 12*: 89–96.

(1912–1913). *Totem and Taboo. S.E., 13*: 1–161. London: Hogarth.

1912a). On the universal tendency to debasement in the sphere of love. *S.E., 11*: 178–190. London: Hogarth.

(1912b). The dynamics of transference. *S.E., 12*: 97–108. London: Hogarth.

(1912e). Recommendations to physicians practising psycho-analysis. *S.E., 12*: 109–120. London: Hogarth.

(1913c). On beginning the treatment. *S.E., 12*: 123–144. London: Hogarth.

(1913i). The disposition to obsessional neurosis. *S.E., 12*: 317–326. London: Hogarth.

(1914b). *The Moses of Michelangelo. S.E.., 13*: 209-236. London: Hogarth.

(1914c). On narcissism. *S.E., 14*: 67–103. London: Hogarth.

(1914d). On the history of the psycho-analytic movement. *S.E., 14*: 7–66.

(1914g). Remembering, repeating, and working through. *S.E., 12*: 145–156. London: Hogarth.

(1915a). Observations on transference love. *S.E., 12*: 157–171. London: Hogarth.

(1915c). Instincts and their vicissitudes. *S.E., 14*: 117–140. London: Hogarth.

(1915d). Repression. *S.E., 14*: 141–158. London: Hogarth.

(1915e). The unconscious. *S.E., 14*: 159–216. London: Hogarth.

(1915–1916). *Introductory Lectures on Psychoanalysis (Parts I & II). S.E., 15*. London: Hogarth.

(1916d). Some character types met with in psychoanalytic work. *S.E., 14*: 310–333. London: Hogarth.

(1916–1917). *Introductory Lectures on Psychoanalysis. S.E., 16*. London: Hogarth.

(1917b). A childhood recollection from Dichtung und Wahrheit. *S.E., 17*: 145–157. London: Hogarth.

(1917d). A metapsychological supplement to the theory of dreams. *S.E., 14*: 222–235. London: Hogarth.

(1917e). Mourning and melancholia. *S.E., 14*: 237–260. London: Hogarth.

(1915f). A case of paranoia running counter to the psycho-analytic theory of the disease. *S.E., 14*: 261–272.

(1918a). The taboo of virginity. *S.E., 11*: 193–208. London: Hogarth.

(1918b). *From the History of an Infantile Neurosis. S.E., 17*: 1–122. London: Hogarth.

(1919a). Lines of advance in psychoanalytic therapy. *S.E., 17*: 157–168. London: Hogarth.

(1919d). Introduction to 'Psycho-Analysis and the War Neuroses'. *S.E., 17*: 205–217. London: Hogarth.

(1919e). 'A child is being beaten': a contribution to the study of the origin of sexual perversions. *S.E., 17*: 179–204.

(1919h). The 'uncanny'. *S.E., 17*: 217–252. London: Hogarth.

(1920a). The psychogenesis of a case of homosexuality in a woman. *S.E., 28*: 145–174. London: Hogarth.

(1920g). *Beyond the Pleasure Principle. S.E., 18*: 7–64. London: Hogarth.

(1921c). *Group Psychology and the Analysis of the Ego. S.E., 18*: 65–143. London: Hogarth.

(1922a). Dreams and telepathy. *S.E., 18*: 195–220. London: Hogarth.

(1922b). Some neurotic mechanisms in jealousy, paranoia, and homosexuality. *S.E., 18*: 221–233. London: Hogarth.

(1923a). Two encyclopaedia articles. *S.E., 18*: 235–259. London: Hogarth.

(1923b). *The Ego and the Id. S.E., 17*: 3–68. London: Hogarth.

(1923e). The infantile genital organization. *S.E., 19*: 139–145. London: Hogarth.

(1924c). The economic problem of masochism. *S.E., 19*: 157–170. London: Hogarth.

(1924d). The dissolution of the Oedipus complex. *S.E., 19*: 171–188. London: Hogarth.

(1924e). Neurosis and psychosis. *S.E., 19*: 149–153. London: Hogarth.

(1924f). A short account of psycho-analysis. *S.E., 19*: 189–209. London: Hogarth.

(1925a). A note upon the 'mystic writing-pad'. *S.E., 19*: 227–232. London: Hogarth.

(1925d). An autobiographical study. *S.E., 20*: 7–74. London: Hogarth.

(1925h). Negation. *S.E., 19*: 235–239. London: Hogarth.

(1925j). Some psychical consequences of the anatomic distinction between the sexes. *S.E., 19*: 241–258. London: Hogarth.

(1926d). *Inhibitions, Symptoms, and Anxiety. S.E., 20*: 77–174. London: Hogarth.

(1926e). The question of lay analysis. *S.E., 20*: 179–250. London: Hogarth.

(1927c). *The Future of an Illusion*. S.E., 21: 3–56. London: Hogarth.
(1930a). *Civilization and Its Discontents*. S.E., 21: 59–145. London: Hogarth.
(1931a). Libidinal types. S.E., 21: 215–220. London: Hogarth.
(1931b). Female sexuality. S.E., 21: 223–243. London: Hogarth.
(1932). Preface to Richard Sterba's *Dictionary of Psycho-Analysis*. S.E., 22: 253. London: Hogarth.
(1933a). *New Introductory Lectures on Psycho-Analysis* [On femininity (pp. 112–134)]. S.E., 22: 3–182. London: Hogarth.
(1935). Letter to the Editor. *American Journal of Psychiatry*, 107: 786.
(1937c). Analysis terminable and interminable. S.E., 23: 211–253. London: Hogarth.
(1937d). Constructions in analysis. S.E., 23: 255–269. London: Hogarth.
(1939a). *Moses and Monotheism*. S.E., 23: 7–137. London: Hogarth.
(1940a [1938]). *An Outline of Psychoanalysis*. S.E., 23: 139–207. London: Hogarth.
(1941d). Psycho-analysis and telepathy. S.E., 18: 177–193. London: Hogarth.

BETTY FRIEDAN

(1963). *The Feminine Mystique*. New York: Dell.

LAWRENCE FRIEDMAN

(1996). Overview: knowledge and authority in the psychoanalytic relationship. *Psychoanalytic Quarterly*, 65: 254–265.
(2005). Is there a special form of psychoanalytic love? *Journal of the American Psychoanalytic Association*, 53: 349–375.

PAUL FRIEDMAN

(1959). Some observations on the sense of smell. *Psychoanalytic Quarterly*, 28: 307–329.

RICHARD FRIEDMAN & JENNIFER DOWNEY

(1993). Psychoanalysis, psychobiology, and homosexuality. *Journal of the American Psychoanalytic Association*, 41: 1159–1198.
(1998). Psychoanalysis and the model of homosexuality as psychopathology: a historical overview. *American Journal of Psychoanalysis*, 58: 249–270.

MARTIN FROMMER

(2000). Offending gender: being and wanting in male same-sex desire. *Studies in Gender and Sexuality*, 1: 191–206.

FRIEDA FROMM-REICHMAN

(1950). *Principles of Intensive Psychotherapy*. Chicago, IL: University of Chicago Press.

JOHN FROSCH

(1960). Psychotic character. *Journal of the American Psychoanalytic Association*, 8: 544–551.
(1964). The psychotic character. *Psychiatric Quarterly*, 38: 81–96.
(1970). Psychoanalytic considerations of the psychotic character. *Journal of the American Psychoanalytic Association*, 18: 24–50.
(1977). The morning ruminative state—the flash phenomenon. *International Journal of Psychoanalysis*, 58: 301–309.

ERNA FURMAN

(1980). Early latency: normal and pathological aspects. In: S. I. Greenspan & G. H. Pollack (Eds.), *The Course of Life, Volume II: Latency, Adolescence, and Youth* (pp. 1–32). Adelphi, MD: National Institute of Mental Health.
(1996). On motherhood. *Journal of the American Psychoanalytic Association*, 44(suppl): 429–447.

ROBERT FURMAN

(1980). Some vicissitudes of the transition into latency. In: S. I. Greenspan & G. H. Pollack (Eds.), *The Course of Life, Volume II: Latency, Adolescence, and Youth* (pp. 33–43). Adelphi, MD: National Institute of Mental Health.

ROBERT FURMAN & ERNA FURMAN

(1984). Intermittent decathexis: a type of parental dysfunction. *International Journal of Psychoanalysis*, 65: 423–433.

SIDNEY FURST

(1967). *Psychic Trauma*. New York: Basic Books.
(1978). The stimulus barrier and the pathogenicity of trauma. *International Journal of Psychoanalysis*, 59: 345–352.
(1995). Trauma. In: B. Moore & B. Fine (Eds.), *Psychoanalysis: The Major Concepts* (pp. 306–316). New Haven, CT: Yale University Press.

References

GLEN GABBARD

(1982). The exit line: heightened transference–countertransference manifestations at the end of the hour. *Journal of the American Psychoanalytic Association*, 30: 579–598.
(1989). Images in our souls, Cavell, psychoanalysis and cinema: psychiatry and humanities. *Psychoanalytic Quarterly*, 58: 496–501.
(1997). Challenges in the analysis of adult patients with histories of childhood sexual abuse. *Canadian Journal of Psychoanalysis*, 5: 1–25.
(1999). Boundary violations and the psychoanalytic training system. *Journal of Applied Psychoanalytic Studies*, 1: 207–221.

GLEN GABBARD & KRIN GABBARD

(1999). *Psychiatry and Cinema* (2nd edn). Washington, DC: American Psychiatric Press.

GLEN GABBARD & EVA LESTER

(1995). *Boundaries and Boundary Violations in Psychoanalysis*. Washington, DC: American Psychiatric Press.

GLEN GABBARD & STUART TWEMLOW

(1994). The role of mother-son incest in the pathogenesis of narcissistic personality disorder. *Journal of the American Psychoanalytic Association*, 42: 171–189.

RICHARD GALDSTON

(1987). The longest pleasure: a psychoanalytic study of hatred. *International Journal of Psychoanalysis*, 68: 371–378.

ELEANOR GALENSON

(1980). Characteristics of psychological development during the second and third years of life. In: S. I. Greenspan & G. H. Pollock (Eds.), *The Course of Life: Psychoanalytic Contributions Toward Understanding Personality Development, Volume I: Infancy and Early Childhood* (pp. 443–458). Adelphi, MD: National Institute of Mental Health.
(1988). The precursors of masochism: protomasochism. In: R. Glick & D. Meyers (Eds.), *Masochism: Current Psychoanalytic Perspective* (pp. 189–204). Hillsdale, NJ: The Analytic Press.

ELEANOR GALENSON & HERMAN ROIPHE

(1976). Preodipal development of the boy. *Journal of the American Psychoanalytic Association*, 28: 805–827.

YOLANDA GAMPEL

(1999). Between the background of safety and the background of the uncanny in the context of social violence. In: P. Fonagy, A. Cooper, & R. Wallenstein (Eds.), *The Work of Joseph Sandler* (pp. 54–67). London: Routledge.

MOHANDAS KARAMCHAND GANDHI

(1940). *An Autobiography: The Story of My Experiments with Truth*. M. Desai (Trans.). Boston, MA: Beacon Press, 1957.

MURIEL GARDINER

(1964). The Wolfman grows older. *Journal of the American Psychoanalytic Association*, 12: 80–92.
(1983). Wolfman's last years. *Journal of the American Psychoanalytic Association*, 31: 867–897.

RUTH GARFIELD

(2004). Making a case for father hunger in girls. In: S. Akhtar & H. Parens (Eds.), *Real and Imaginary Fathers: Development, Transference, and Healing* (pp. 31–44). Lanham, MD: Jason Aronson.

PAUL GARFINKEL

(1995). Eating disorders. In: H. I. Kaplan & B. J. Sadock (Eds.), *Comprehensive Textbook of Psychiatry, Volume 2* (6th edn) (pp. 1361–1371). Baltimore, MD: William and Wilkins.

ANGEL GARMA

(1946). The traumatic situation in the genesis of dreams. *International Journal of Psychoanalysis*, 27: 134–139.
(1950). On the pathogenesis of peptic ulcer. *International Journal of Psychoanalysis*, 31: 53–72.
(1966). *The Psychoanalysis of Dreams*. New York: Jason Aronson [reprinted, 1974].
(1968). The deceiving superego and the masochistic ego in mania. *Psychoanalytic Quarterly*, 37: 63–79.

NORMAN GARMENZY

(1985). Stress-resistant children: the search for protective factors. In: J. E. Sevens (Ed.), *Recent Research in Developmental Psychopathology* (pp. 213–233). Oxford: Pergamon Press.

CESAR GARZA-GUERRERO

(1974). Culture shock: its mourning and the vicissitudes of identity. *Journal of the American Psychoanalytic Association*, 22: 408–429.

PETER GAY

(1988). *Freud: A Life for Our Time*. New York: W. W. Norton.

DANIEL GEAHCHAN

(1968). Deuil et nostalgie. *Revue Française de Psychanalyse*, 32: 39–65.

HELEN GEDIMAN

(1971). The concept of stimulus barrier: its review and reformulation as an adaptive ego function. *International Journal of Psychoanalysis*, 52: 243–257.
(1985). Impostor, inauthenticity, and feeling fraudulent. *Journal of the American Psychoanalytic Association*, 33: 911–936.

HELEN GEDIMAN & FRED WOLKENFELD

(1980). Parallelism phenomena in psychoanalysis and supervision: its reconsideration as a triadic system. *Psychoanalytic Quarterly*, 49: 234–255.

JOHN GEDO

(1964). Concepts for a clarification of the psychotherapies. *International Journal of Psychoanalysis*, 45: 530–539.
(1975). Review of *The History of the Concept of Association of Ideas* by David Rapaport. *Journal of the American Psychoanalytic Association*, 23: 667–668.
(1997). *Spleen and Nostalgia: A Life and Work in Psychoanalysis*. Northvale, NJ: Jason Aronson.

JOHN GEDO & ARNOLD GOLDBERG

(1973). *Models of the Mind*. Chicago: University of Chicago Press.

MARY GEDO

(1983). Archaeology of painting: city of dead beneath Picasso's 'La Vie'. *Psychoanalytic Inquiry*, 3: 371–394.

MARK GEHRIE

(1993). Psychoanalytic technique and the development of the capacity to reflect. *Journal of the American Psychoanalytic Association*, 41: 1083–1111.

J. GERRARD

(2007). Enactments in the countertransference. *British Journal of Psychotherapy*, 23: 217–230.

AMAR GHORPADE

(2009). State-dependent self-representations: a culture-bound aspect of identity. *American Journal of Psychoanalysis*, 69: 72–79.

HARWANT SINGH GILL

(1987). Effects of oedipal triumph: collapse or death of the rival parent. *International Journal of Psychoanalysis*, 68: 251–260.

MERTON GILL

(1951). Ego psychology and psychotherapy. *Psychoanalytic Quarterly*, 20: 62–71.
(1954). Psychoanalysis and exploratory psychotherapy. *Journal of the American Psychoanalytic Association*, 2: 771–797.
(1979). The analysis of the transference. *Journal of the American Psychoanalytic Association*, 27(Suppl.): 263–288.
(1982). *Analysis of Transference, Volume I: Theory and Technique*. New York: International Universities Press.
(1994). *Psychoanalysis in Transition: A Personal View*. Hillsdale, NJ: Analytic Press.

MERTON GILL & HYMAN MUSLIN

(1976). Early interpretation of transference. *Journal of the American Psychoanalytic Association*, 24: 779–794.

MERTON GILL & IRWIN HOFFMAN

(1982). A method for studying the analysis of aspects of the patient's experience of the relationship in psychoanalysis and psychotherapy. *Journal of the American Psychoanalytic Association*, 30: 137–168.

WILLIAM GILLESPIE

(1940). A contribution to the study of fetishism. *International Journal of Psychoanalysis*, 21: 401–415.

References

(1952). Notes on the analysis of sexual perversions. *International Journal of Psychoanalysis, 33*: 397–402.

(1956a). The general theory of sexual perversion. *International Journal of Psychoanalysis, 37*: 396–403.

(1956b). The structure and aetiology of sexual perversion. In: S. Lorand & M. Balint (Eds.), *Perversions: Psychodynamics and Therapy* (pp. 33–51). New York: Random House.

CAROL GILLIGAN

(1982). *In a Different Voice: Psychological Theory and Women's Development*. Cambridge, MA: Harvard University Press.

KAREN GILMORE

(1998). Cloacal anxiety in female development. *Journal of the American Psychoanalytic Association, 46*: 443–470.

PETER GIOVACCHINI

(1967). The frozen interject. *International Journal of Psychoanalysis, 48*: 61–67.

(1972). The symbiotic phase. In: *Tactics and Techniques in Psychoanalytic Therapy* (pp. 137–169). New York: Science House.

(1997). *Schizophrenia and Primitive Mental States*. Northvale, NJ: Jason Aronson.

MAX GITTLESON

(1954). The analysis of the 'normal' candidate. *International Journal of Psychoanalysis, 35*: 174–183.

PETER GLAUBER

(1955). On the meaning of agoraphilia. *Journal of the American Psychoanalytic Association, 3*: 701–709.

(1968). Dysautomatization: a disorder of preconscious ego functioning. *International Journal of Psychoanalysis, 49*: 89–99.

JULES GLENN

(1991). Transformation in normal and pathological latency. In: S. Akhtar & H. Parens (Eds.), *Beyond the Symbiotic Orbit: Advances in Separation–Individuation Therapy* (pp. 171-187). Hillsdale, NJ: Analytic Press.

ROBERT GLICK

(1987). Forced termination. *Journal of the Academy of Psychoanalysis and Dynamic Psychiatry, 15*: 449–463.

ROBERT GLICK & DONALD MEYERS

(1988). Introduction. In: R. Glick & D. Meyers (Eds.), *Masochism: Current Psychoanalytic Perspectives* (pp. 1–26). Hillsdale, NJ: The Analytic Press.

ROBERT GLICK & STEVEN ROOSE

(2006). Talking about medication. *Journal of the American Psychoanalytic Association, 54*: 745–762.

LETICIA GLOCER FIORINI

(2007). *Deconstructing the Feminine: Psychoanalysis, Gender and Theories of Complexity*. London: Karnac.

EDWARD GLOVER

(1925). Notes on oral character formations. *International Journal of Psychoanalysis, 6*: 131–153.

(1927). Further contributions to the theory and technique of psychoanalysis. *International Journal of Psychoanalysis, 8*: 417–421.

(1929). The screening function of traumatic memories. *International Journal of Psychoanalysis, 10*: 90–93.

(1931). The therapeutic effect of inexact interpretation. *International Journal of Psychoanalysis, 12*: 397–418.

(1939). Psychoanalysis of affects: *International Journal of Psychoanalysis, 20*: 297–307.

(1954). Therapeutic criteria of psychoanalysis. *International Journal of Psychoanalysis, 35*: 91–101.

(1955). *The Technique of Psychoanalysis*. New York: International Universities Press.

(1956a). Grades of ego differentiation. In: *On the Early Development of Mind: Collected Papers of Edward Glover* (pp. 112–122). New York: International Universities Press.

(1956b). Medico-psychological aspects of normality. In: *On the Early Development of Mind: Collected Papers of Edward Glover* (pp. 129–137). New York: International Universities Press.

ARNOLD GOLDBERG

(1983). On the nature of the 'misfit'. In: A. Goldberg (Ed.), *The Future of Psychoanalysis* (pp. 293–308). New York: International Universities Press.

(1999). Between empathy and judgment. *Journal of the American Psychoanalytic Association, 47*: 351–365.

(2002). Enactment as understanding and as misunderstanding. *Journal of the American Psychoanalytic Association, 50*: 869–883.

EUGENE GOLDBERG , WAYNE MYERS AND ISRAEL ZEIFMAN

(1974). Some observations on three inter-racial analyses. *International Journal of Psychoanalysis*, *55*: 495–500.

MARIANNE GOLDBERGER & DOROTHY EVANS

(1985). On transference manifestations in male patients with female analysts. *International Journal of Psychoanalysis*, *66*: 295–310.

FRIEDA GOLDMAN-EISLER

(1953). Breast feeding and character formation. In: C. Kluckhohn & H. A. Murray (Eds.), *Personality in Nature, Society, and Culture* (pp. 31–56). New York: Alfred Knopf.

SCOTT GOLDSMITH

(1995). Oedipus or Orestes? Aspects of gender identity development in homosexual men. *Psychoanalytic Inquiry*, *15*: 112–124.
(2001). Oedipus or Orestes? Homosexual men, their mothers, and other women revisited. *Journal of the American Psychoanalytic Association*, *49*: 1269–1287.

MICHAEL GOOD

(1995). Karl Abraham, Sigmund Freud, and the fate of the seduction theory. *Journal of the American Psychoanalytic Association*, *43*: 1137–1167.
(1996). Suggestion and veridicality in the reconstruction of sexual trauma ,or can a bait of suggestion catch a carp of falsehood? *Journal of the American Psychoanalytic Association*, *44*: 1189–1224.
(1998). Screen reconstructions: traumatic memory, conviction, and the problem of verification. *Journal of the American Psychoanalytic Association*, *46*: 149–183.

GREGG GORTON & SALMAN AKHTAR

(1990). The literature on personality disorders—1985–88: trends, issues, and controversies. *Hospital and Community Psychiatry*, *41*: 39–51.

RICHARD GOTTLIEB

(2006). Mind, madness, and medications: situating psychoanalysis. *Journal of the American Psychoanalytic Association*, *54*: 739–744.

SUE GRAND

(2002). *The Reproduction of Evil: A Clinical and Cultural Perspective*. Mahwah, NJ: Analytic Press.

PAUL GRAY

(1973). Psychoanalytic technique and the ego's capacity for viewing intrapsychic conflict. *Journal of the American Psychoanalytic Association*, *21*: 474–494.
(1982). Developmental lag in the evolution of technique for psychoanalysis of neurotic conflict. *Journal of American Psychoanalytic Association*, *30*: 621–655.
(1986). On helping analysands observe intrapsychic activity. In: A. Richards & M. Willick (Eds.), *Psychoanalysis: The Science of Mental Conflicts* (pp. 245–262). Hillsdale, NJ: Analytic Press.
(1994). *The Ego and the Analysis of Defense*. Northvale, NJ: Jason Aronson.

ANDRÉ GREEN

(1972). Note sur les processus tertiaires. In: *Propedeutique, La metapsychologie revisitée* (Annexe D). Paris: Champ Vallon [reprint, 1995].
(1980). The dead mother. In: *Life Narcissism, Death Narcissism*, A. Weller (Trans.). London: Free Association.
(1982). La mère morte. In: *Narcissisme de Vie, Narcissisme de Mort* (pp. 222–253). Paris: Editions de Minuit.
(1983). *Narcissisme de vie, Narcissisme de mort*. Paris: Minuit.
(1986). Réponses à des questions inconcevables. *Topique*, *37*: 11–30.
(1993). *The Work of the Negative*. London: Free Association.
(1999). The death drive, negative narcissism and the disobjectalising function. In: *The Work of the Negative*, A. Weller (Trans.). London: Free Association.
(2000).The central phobic position: a new formulation of the free association method. *International Journal of Psychoanalysis*, *81*: 429–451.
(2001). *Life Narcissism, Death Narcissism*, A. Weller (Trans.). London: Free Association.
(2002). A dual conception of narcissism: positive and negative organizations. *Psychoanalytic Quarterly*, *71*: 631–649.
(2005). *Key Ideas for a Contemporary Psychoanalysis: Misrecognition and Recognition of the Unconscious*. London: Routledge.

References

RICHARD GREEN

(1974). *Sexual Identity Conflict in Children and Adults*. New York: Basic Books.
(1975). Sexual identity research strategies. *Archives of Sexual Behavior*, 4: 337–352.

PHYLLIS GREENACRE

(1945). Pathological weeping. *Psychoanalytic Quarterly*, 16: 62–75.
(1949). A contribution to the study of screen memories. *Psychoanalytic Study of the Child*, 3: 73–84.
(1950). Special problems of early female sexual development. *Psychoanalytic Study of the Child*, 5: 122–138.
(1953). Certain relationships between fetishes and the faulty development of the body image. *Psychoanalytic Study of the Child*, 8: 79–97.
(1956). Experience of awe in childhood. *Psychoanalytic Study of the Child*, 11: 9–30.
(1958). Early physical determinants in the development of the sense of identity. *Journal of the American Psychoanalytic Association*, 6: 612–627.
(1959). On focal symbiosis. In: *Emotional Growth, Volume I* (pp. 145–161). New York: International Universities Press, 1971.

RALPH GREENSON

(1953). On boredom. *Journal of the American Psychoanalytic Association*, 1: 7–21.
(1958a). Variations in classical psychoanalytic technique. *International Journal of Psychoanalysis*, 39: 200–201.
(1958b). On screen defenses, screen hunger and screen identity. *Journal of the American Psychoanalytic Association*, 6: 242–262.
(1965). The working alliance and the transference neurosis. *Psychoanalytic Quarterly*, 34: 155–181.
(1967). *The Technique and Practice of Psychoanalysis*. New York: International Universities Press.
(1968). Dis-identifying from mother: its special importance for the boy. *International Journal of Psychoanalysis*, 49: 370–374.
(1974). Loving, hating, and indifference towards the patient. *International Review of Psychoanalysis*, 1: 259–266.

STANLEY GREENSPAN

(1977). The oedipal–preoedipal dilemma: a reformulation in the light of object relations theory. *International Review of Psychoanalysis*, 6: 612–627.
(1980). *Intelligence and Adaptation: An Integration of Psychoanalytic and Piagetian Developmental Psychology*. New York: International Universities Press.

STANLEY GREENSPAN & SERENA WIEDER

(2005). *Infant and Early Childhood Mental Health: A Comprehensive Developmental Approach to Assessment and Intervention*. Washington, DC: American Psychiatric Press.

STANLEY GREENSPAN & STUART SHANKER

(2005). Developmental research. In: E. S. Person, A. M. Cooper, & G. O. Gabbard (Eds.), *Textbook of Psychoanalysis* (pp. 335–360). Washington, DC: American Psychiatric Publishing.

JOANNE MARIE GREER

(1994). 'Return of the repressed' in the analysis of an adult incest survivor. *Psychoanalytic Psychology*, 11: 545–561.

LEON GRINBERG

(1962). On a specific aspect of countertransference due to the patient's projective identification. *International Journal of Psychoanalysis*, 43: 436–440.

LEON GRINBERG, & ELIZABETH DE BIANCHEDI

(1977). *New Introduction to the Work of Bion*. E. De Bianchedi (Ed.). New York: Jason Aronson.

LEON GRINBERG & REBECCA GRINBERG

(1989). *Psychoanalytic Perspectives on Migration and Exile*, N. Festinger (Trans.). New Haven, CT: Yale University Press.

LEON GRINBERG, DARIO SOR, & ELIZABETH DE BIANCHEDI

(1972). (Eds.) *Introduccion a las ideas de Bion*. Buenos Aires, Argentina: Nueva Vision.

ROY GRINKER

(1945). Psychiatric disorders in combat crews overseas and in returnees. *Medical Clinics of North America*, 29: 729–739.

(1955). Growth inertia and shame: their therapeutic implications and dangers. *International Journal of Psychoanalysis, 36*: 242–253.

ROY GRINKER, BEATRICE WERBLE, & ROBERT DRYE

(1968). *The Borderline Syndrome: A Behavioral Study of Ego Functions.* New York: Basic Books.

ALEXANDER GRINSTEIN

(1956). *Index of Psychoanalytic Writings, Volumes I–IX.* New York: International Universities Press.

GEORG GRODDECK

(1923). *The Book of the It.* London: Vision, 1949.

SIMON GROLNICK, LEONARD BARKIN, & WERNER MUENSTERBERGER

(1978). (Eds.) *Between Reality and Fantasy: Transitional Objects and Phenomena.* New York: Jason Aronson.

ALBERT GROSS

(1951). The secret. *Bulletin of the Menninger Clinic, 15*: 37–44.

LEE GROSSMAN

(1992). An example of character perversion in a woman. *Psychoanalytic Quarterly, 61*: 581–589.
(1993). The perverse attitude towards reality. *Psychoanalytic Quarterly, 62*: 422–436.
(1996). Psychic reality and reality testing in the analysis of perverse defense. *International Journal of Psychoanalysis, 77*: 509–518.

JAMES GROTSTEIN

(1977a). The psychoanalytic concept of schizophrenia: I the dilemma. *International Journal of Psychoanalysis, 58*: 403–425.
(1977b). The psychoanalytic concept of schizophrenia: II reconciliation. *International Journal of Psychoanalysis, 58*: 427–452.
(1986). The psychology of powerlessness: disorders of self-regulation and interactional regulation as a newer paradigm for psychopathology. *Psychoanalytic Inquiry, 6*: 93–118.
(1987). Schizophrenia as a disorder of self-regulation and interactional regulation. Presented at The Regressed Patient Conference at the Boyer House Foundation, San Francisco, March 21, 1987, cited in T. Ogden, 1987.
(1989). A revised psychoanalytic conception of schizophrenia: an interdisciplinary update. *Psychoanalytic Psychology, 6*: 253–275.
(1990). Nothingness, meaninglessness, and the black hole. *Contemporary Psychoanalysis, 26*: 257–290.
(1997). Integrating one-person and two-person psychologies: autochthony and alterity in counterpoint. *Psychoanalytic Quarterly, 66*: 403–430.
(2005). 'Projective *transidentification*': an extension of the concept of projective identification. *International Journal of Psychoanalysis, 86*: 1051–1069.

ILSE GRUBRICH-SIMITIS

(1984). From concretism to metaphor: thoughts on some theoretical and technical aspects of the psychoanalytic work with child of Holocaust survivors. *Psychoanalytic Study of the Child, 39*: 301–319.

URSULA GRUENERT

(1979). The negative therapeutic reaction as a reactivation of a disturbed process of separation in the transference. *Bulletin of the European Psychoanalytical Foundation, 16*: 5–9.

BELA GRUNBERGER

(1989). *New Essays on Narcissism,* D. Macey (Trans.). London: Free Association.

MING DONG GU

(2006). The filial piety complex: variations on the oedipus theme in Chinese literature and culture. *Psychoanalytic Quarterly, 75*: 163–196.

JOHN GUNDERSON & MARGARET SINGER

(1975). Defining borderline patients: an overview. *American Journal of Psychiatry, 133*: 1–10.

NELLA GUIDI

(1993). Unobjectionable negative transference. *Annual of Psychoanalysis, 21*: 107–124.

References

HARRY GUNTRIP

(1969). *Schizoid Phenomena, Object Relations, and the Self*. New York: International Universities Press.

DAVID GUTTMAN

(1980). Psychoanalysis and aging: a developmental view. In: S. I. Greenspan & G. H. Pollack (Eds.), *Adulthood amd Aging Process* (pp. 489–517). Washington, DC: NIMH Publications.

JASWANT GUZDER & MEENAKSHI KRISHNA

(1991). Sita-shakti: cultural paradigms for Indian women. *Transcultured Psychiatric Research Review, 28*: 257–301.
(2005). Sita-shakti @ cultural collision: issues in the psychotherapy of diaspora Indian women. In: S. Akhtar (Ed.), *Freud Along the Ganges: Psychoanalytic Reflections on the People and Culture of India* (pp. 205–233). New York: Other Press.

FREDERICK HACKER

(1962). The discriminating function of the ego. *International Journal of Psychoanalysis, 43*: 395–405.

LUDWIG HAESLER

(1993). Adequate distance in the relationship between supervisor and supervisee—the position of the supervisor between 'teacher' and 'analyst'. *International Journal of Psychoanalysis, 74*: 547–555.

FORREST HAMER

(2006). Racism as a transference state: episodes of racial hostility in the psychoanalytic context. *Psychoanalytic Quarterly, 75*: 197–214.
(2007). Anti-Black racism and the conception of Whiteness. In: H. Parens, A. Mahfouz, S. W. Twemlow, & D. E. Scharff (Eds.), *The Future of Prejudice: Psychoanalysis and the Prevention of Prejudice* (pp. 131–140). Lanham, MD: Jason Aronson.

GREGORY HAMILTON

(1986). Positive projective identification. *International Journal of Psychoanalysis, 67*: 489–496.

JAMES HAMILTON

(1969). Object loss, dreaming, and creativity: the poetry of John Keats. *Psychoanalytic Study of the Child, 24*: 488–531.
(1976). Early trauma, dreaming, and creativity: works of Eugene O'Neill. *International Review of Psychoanalysis, 3*: 341–364.
(1979). Transitional phenomena and the early writings of Eugene O'Neill. *International Review of Psychoanalysis, 6*: 49–60.

STEVEN HAMMERMAN

(1961). Masturbation and character. *Journal of the American Psychoanalytic Association, 9*: 287–311.

CHARLES HANLY

(1978). A critical consideration of Bowlby's ethological theory of anxiety. *Psychoanalytic Quarterly, 67*: 364–380.
(1982). Narcissism, defense, and the positive transference. *International Journal of Psychoanalysis, 63*: 427–444.
(1990). The concept of truth in psychoanalysis. *International Journal of Psychoanalysis, 71*: 375–384.
(1992). *The Problem of Truth in Applied Psychoanalysis*. New York: Guilford Press.
(1996). Reflections on feminine and masculine authority: a developmental perspective. *Psychoanalytic Quarterly, 65*: 84–101.
(1998). Reflections on the analyst's self-disclosure. *Psychoanalytic Inquiry, 18*: 550–565.

MARJORIE HARLEY & ANNMARIE WEIL

(1979). Introduction. In: *The Selected Papers of Margaret S. Mahler, Volume I: Infantile Psychosis and Early Contributions* (pp. ix–xx). New York: Jason Aronson.

HELENA HARRIS

(1990). A critical view of three psychoanalytic positions on menopause. In: R. Formanek (Ed.), *The Meanings of Menopause* (pp. 65–77). Hillsdale, NJ: Analytic Press.

IRVING HARRISON

(1975). On the maternal origins of awe. *Psychoanalytic Study of the Child, 30*: 181–195.

HEINZ HARTMANN

(1939). *Ego Psychology and the Problem of Adaptation*, D. Rapaport (Trans.). New York: International Universities Press, 1958.

(1948). Comments on the psychoanalytic theory of instinctual drives. In: *Essays on Ego Psychology* (pp. 69–89.) New York: International Universities Press, 1964.

(1950). Comments on the psychoanalytic theory of the ego. In: *Essays on Ego Psychology* (pp. 113–141). New York: International Universities Press, 1964.

(1952). The mutual influences in the development of ego and id. *Psychoanalytic Study of the Child*, 7: 9–30.

(1955). Notes on the theory of sublimation. *Psychoanalytic Study of the Child*, 10: 9–29.

(1956). Notes on the reality principle. *Psychoanalytic Study of the Child*, 11: 31–53.

(1958). Comments on the scientific aspects of psychoanalysis. *Psychoanalytic Study of the Child*, 13: 127–146.

(1964). *Essays on Ego Psychology*. New York: International Universities Press.

HEINZ HARTMANN, ERNST KRIS, & RUDOLPH LOEWENSTEIN

(1946). Comments on the formation of psychic structure. *Psychoanalytic Study of the Child*, 2: 11–38.

ANNE HAYMAN

(1989). What do we mean by 'phantasy'? *International Journal of Psychoanalysis*, 70: 105–114.

ANDRE HAYNAL

(1988). *The Technique at Issue: Controversies in Psychoanalysis from Freud and Ferenczi to Michael Balint*, E. Holder (Trans.). London: Karnac.

(2005). In the shadow of a controversy: Freud and Ferenczi 1925–33. *International Journal of Psychoanalysis*, 86: 457–466.

SUSANN HEENEN-WOLFF

(2005). The countertransference dream. *International Journal of Psychoanalysis*, 86: 1543–1558.

GERT HEILBRUNN

(1955). The basic fear. *Journal of the American Psychoanalytic Association*, 3: 447–466

PAULA HEIMANN

(1950). On countertransference. *International Journal of Psychoanalysis*, 31: 81–84.

(1952). Preliminary notes on some defense mechanisms in paranoid states. *International Journal of Psychoanalysis*, 33: 206–213.

GERBEN HELLINGA, BERT VAN LUYN & HENK-JAN DALEWIJK

(2000). *Personalities: Master Clinicians Confront the Treatment of Borderline Personality Disorder*. Amsterdam: Boom.

JANET HELMS

(1990). *Black and White Racial Identity Development: Theory, Research, and Practice*. Westport, CT: Greenwood Press.

JANET HELMS & DONELDA COOK

(1999). *Using Race and Culture in Counseling and Psychotherapy: Theory and Process*. Boston: Allyn and Bacon.

IVES HENDRICK

(1943a) Work and the pleasure principle. *Psychoanalytic Quarterly*, 12: 311–329.

(1943b). The discussion of the 'instinct to master'. *Psychoanalytic Quarterly*, 12: 561–565.

JOHN SHANNON HENDRIX

(2006). *Architecture and Psychoanalysis: Peter Eisenman and Jacques Lacan*. New York: Peter Lang.

JAMES HERZOG

(1980). Sleep disorder and father hunger: the Erlkönig syndrome. *Psychoanalytic Study of the Child*, 35: 219–235.

(1984). Fathers and young children: fathering daughters and fathering sons. In: J. D. Call, E. Galenson, & R. Tyson (Eds.), *Foundations of Infant Psychiatry, Volume 2* (pp. 335-343). New York: Basic Books.

(2001). *Father Hunger: Clinical and Developmental Explorations*. Hillsdale, NJ: The Analytic Press.

(2004). Father hunger and narcissistic deformation. *Psychoanalytic Quarterly*, 73: 893–914.

(2005). Triadic reality and the capacity to love. *Psychoanalytic Quarterly*, 74: 1029–1052.

JOSEPHINE HILGARD

(1953). Anniversary reactions in parents precipitated by children. *Psychiatry*, 16: 73–80.

JOSEPHINE HILGARD & MARTHA NEWMAN

(1959). Anniversaries in mental illness. *Psychiatry*, 22: 113–121.

References

ROBERT HINSHELWOOD

(1989). *A Dictionary of Kleinian Thought*. Northvale, NJ: Jason Aronson.

IRWIN HIRSCH

(1998). The concept of enactment and theoretical convergence. *Psychoanalytic Quarterly, 67*: 78–100.

JOHN HITCHCOCK

(1984). The sinking feeling. *Psychoanalytic Study of the Child, 39*: 321–329.

AXEL HOFFER

(1985). Toward a definition of psychoanalytic neutrality. *Journal of the American Psychoanalytic Association, 33*: 771–795.
(1991). The Freud–Ferenczi controversy: a living legacy. *International Review of Psychoanalysis, 18*: 465–472.
(2006). What does the analyst want?: free association in relation to the analyst's activity, ambition, and technical innovation. *American Journal of Psychoanalysis, 66*: 1–23.

AXEL HOFFER & PETER HOFFER

(1999). Ferenczi's fatal illness in historical context. *Journal of the American Psychoanalytic Association, 47*: 1257–1268.

PETER HOFFER

(2003). The wise baby meets the enfant terrible: the evolution of Ferenczi's views on development. *Psychoanalytic Psychology, 20*: 18–29.
(2005). Reflections on cathexis. *Psychoanalytic Quarterly, 74*: 101–109.
(2008). Ferenczi's collaboration with Rank: on paradigm shift and the origins of complementarity in psychoanalysis. *American Journal of Psychoanalysis, 68*: 128–138.

WILLIE HOFFER

(1949). Mouth, hand, and ego integration. *Psychoanalytic Study of the Child, 3*: 49–58.
(1950). Development of body ego. *Psychoanalytic Study of the Child, 5*: 18–23.

IRWIN Z. HOFFMAN

(1983). The patient as interpreter of the analyst's experience. *Contemporary Psychoanalysis, 19*: 389–422.
(1994). Dialectical thinking and therapeutic action in the psychoanalytic process. *Psychoanalytic Quarterly, 63*: 187–215.
(2006). The myths of free association and the potentials of the analytic relationship. *International Journal of Psychoanalysis, 87*: 43–61.

MOHAMMEDREZA HOJAT

(2007). *Empathy in Patient Care: Antecedents, Development, Measurement, and Outcomes*. New York: Springer.

ALEX HOLDER

(2000). To touch or not to touch. *Psychoanalytic Inquiry, 20*: 44–64.

DOROTHY HOLMES

(1992). Race and transference in psychoanalysis and psychotherapy. *International Journal of Psychoanalysis, 73*: 1–11.
(2006a). The wrecking effects of race and social class on self and success. *Psychoanalytic Quarterly, 75*: 215–235.
(2006b). Success neurosis: what race and social class have to do with it? In: R. Moodley (Ed.), *Race, Culture, and Psychotherapy* (pp. 189–199). London: Routledge.

JEREMY HOLMES

(1993). Attachment theory: a biological basis for psychotherapy? *British Journal of Psychiatry, 163*: 430–438.
(2006). Mentalizing from psychoanalytic perspective: what is new? In: J. G. Allen & P. Fonagy (Eds.), *Handbook Mentalization-Based Treatment* (pp. 31–50). Chichester, UK: John Wiley and Sons.

ROBERT HOLT

(1967). *The Development of the Primary Process*. Psychological Issues Monograph 18/19. New York: International Universities Press.

DEANNA HOLTZMAN & NANCY KULISH

(1996). Nevermore: the hymen and the loss of virginity. *Journal of the American Psychoanalytic Association, 44*: 303–332.
(2000). The feminization of the female oedipal complex, part I: a reconsideration of the significance of separation issues. *Journal of the American Psychoanalytic Association, 48*: 1413–1437.

MARIA TERESA HOOKE & SALMAN AKHTAR (Eds.)

(2007). *The Geography of Meanings: Psychoanalytic Perspectives on Place, Space, Land, and Dislocation*. London: International Psychoanalytic Association.

LINDA HOPKINS

(2000). Masud Khan's application of Winnicott's 'play' technique to analytic consultation and treatment of adults. *Contemporary Psychoanalysis, 36*: 639–663.

KAREN HORNEY

(1926). The flight of womanhood. *International Journal of Psychoanalysis, 7*: 324–329.
(1932). The dread of woman. *International Journal of Psychoanalysis, 13*: 348–366.
(1933). The denial of the vagina—a contribution to the problem of the genital anxieties specific to women. *International Journal of Psychoanalysis, 14*: 57–70.
(1937). *The Neurotic Personality of Our Times*. New York: W. W. Norton.

MARDI HOROWITZ

(1975). Sliding meanings: a defense against threat in narcissistic personalities. *International Journal of Psychoanalytic Psychotherapy, 4*: 167–180.
(1982). Self-naming. *International Journal of Psychoanalytic Psychotherapy, 9*: 621–624.
(2002). Defining character integrity. *Journal of the American Psychoanalytic Association, 50*: 551–573.

LEONARD HORWITZ

(1990). Psychotherapy as a trial for psychoanalysis. *Psychoanalytic Inquiry, 10*: 43–56.
(2005). The capacity to forgive: intrapsychic and developmental perspectives. *Journal of the American Psychoanalytic Association, 53*: 485–511.

FRED HSU

(1949). Suppression versus repression. *Psychiatry, 12*: 223–242.

WINSLOW HUNT

(1995). The diffident narcissist: a character-type illustrated in *The Beast in The Jungle* by Henry James. *International Journal of Psychoanalytic, 76*: 1252–1267.

MARVIN HURVICH

(1989). Traumatic moment, basic dangers and annihilation anxiety. *Psychoanalytic Psychology, 6*: 309–323.
(2003). The place of annihilation anxieties in psychoanalytic theory. *Journal of the American Psychoanalytic Association, 51*: 579–616.

PEGGY HUTSON

(2002). From ego psychology to psychoanalysis in the year 2000: one analyst's journey. *Psychoanalytic Inquiry, 22*: 106–123.

BURTON HUTTO

(1998). A self-report contrasting concentrated and standard psychoanalysis [Letter to Editor]. *International Journal of Psychoanalysis, 79*: 171–173.

JULIAN HUXLEY

(1966). *From An Antique Land: Ancient and Modern in the Middle East*. New York: Harper and Row.

LAWRENCE INDERBITZIN & STEVEN LEVY

(1994). On grist for the mill: external reality as defense. *Journal of the American Psychoanalytic Association, 42*: 763–788.

SUSAN ISAACS

(1948). The nature and function of phantasy. *International Journal of Psychoanalysis, 29*: 73–97.

AMNON ISSACHAROFF

(1979). Barriers to knowing. In: L. Epstein & A. H. Feiner (Eds.), *Countertransference* (pp. 27–44). New York: Jason Aronson.

OTTO ISAKOWER

(1938). A contribution to the patho-psychology of phenomena associated with falling asleep. *International Journal of Psychoanalysis, 19*: 331–345.

References

(1963). Minutes of the Faculty Meeting, New York Psychoanalytic Institute, 14 October [unpublished, cited in T. Jacobs (2007)].

RICHARD ISAY

(1985). On the analytic therapy of homosexual men. *Psychoanalytic Study of the Child*, 40: 235–254.
(1987). Fathers and their homosexually inclined sons in childhood. *Psychoanalytic Study of the Child*, 42: 275–290.
(1989). *Being Homosexual: Gay Men and Their Development*. New York: Farrar, Straus, and Giroux.
(1991). The homosexual analyst: clinical considerations. *Psychoanalytic Study of the Child*, 46: 199–216.

GAVIN IVEY

(2008). Enactment controversies: a critical review of current debates. *International Journal of Psychoanalysis*, 88: 19–38.

DANIEL JACOBS

(1986). On negotiating fees with psychotherapy and psychoanalytic patients. In: D. W. Krueger (Ed.), *The Last Taboo: Money as Symbol and Reality in Psychotherapy and Psychoanalysis* (pp. 121–131). New York: Brunner/Mazel.

THEODORE JACOBS

(1983). The analyst and the patient's object world: notes on an aspect of countertransference. *Journal of the American Psychoanalytic Association*, 31: 619–642.
(1986a). Transference relationships, the relationships between transferences and reconstruction. In: A. Richards & M. Willick (Eds.), *Psychoanalysis: The Signs of Mental Conflict* (pp. 301–320). Hillsdale, NJ: The Analytic Press.
(1986b). On countertransference enactments. *Journal of the American Psychoanalytic Association*, 34: 289–307.
(1990). The corrective emotional experience—its place in current technique. *Psychoanalytic Inquiry*, 10: 433–454.
(1994). Nonverbal communications: some reflections on their role in the psychoanalytic process and psychoanalytic education. *Journal of the American Psychoanalytic Association*, 42: 741–762.
(1999). On the question of self-disclosure by the analyst: error or advance in technique? *Psychoanalytic Quarterly*, 68: 159–183.
(2007). Listening, dreaming, sharing: on the uses of the analyst's inner experiences. In: S. Akhtar (Ed.), *Listening to Others: Developmental and Clinical Aspects of Empathy and Attunement* (pp. 93–112). Lanham, MD: Jason Aronson.

EDITH JACOBSON

(1946). The effect of disappointment on ego and superego formation in normal and depressive development. *Psychoanalytic Review*, 33: 129–147.
(1950). Development of the wish for a child in boys. *Psychoanalytic Study of the Child*, 5: 139–152.
(1953). Contribution to the metapsychologically of cyclothymic depression. In: P. Greenacre (Ed.), *Affective Disorders*. New York: International Universities Press.
(1954). The self and the object world: vicissitudes of their infantile cathexes and their influence on ideation and affective development. *Psychoanalytic Study of the Child*, 9: 75–127.
(1959). The 'exceptions': an elaboration of Freud's character study. *Psychoanalytic Study of the Child*, 14: 135–154.
(1964). *The Self and The Object World*. New York: International Universities Press.
(1971). *Depression*. New York: International Universities Press.

JOHN JACOBSON

(1994). Signal affects and our psychoanalytic confusion of tongues. *Journal of the American Psychoanalytic Association*, 42: 43–64.

DAN JAFFE

(1983). Some relations between the negative oedipus complex and aggression in the male. *Journal of the American Psychoanalytic Association*, 31: 957–984.

PIERRE JANET

(1889). *Psychological Healing: A Historical and Clinical Study, Vols. I–II*. New York: Arno Press, 1976.

ELLIOTT JAQUES

(1965). Death and the mid-life crisis. *International Journal of Psychoanalysis*, 46: 502–514.

WILLIAM JOFFEE & JOSEPH SANDLER

(1965). Pain, depression, and individuation. In: J. Sandler (Ed.), *From Safety to Superego* (pp. 154–179). New York: Guilford Press.

ADELAIDE JOHNSON & MARTIN SZUREK

(1952). The genesis of antisocial acting out in children and adults. *Psychoanalytic Quarterly*, 21: 323–343.

ADELAIDE JOHNSON & SPURGEON ENGLISH

(1953). Panel report: the essentials of psychotherapy as viewed by the psychoanalyst. *Journal of the American Psychoanalytic Association*, 1: 550–561.

ERNEST JONES

(1908). Rationalisation in everyday life. *Journal of Abnormal Psychology*, 3: 161–169.
(1913a). The God complex. In: *Essays in Applied Psychoanalysis, Volume II* (pp. 244–265). New York: International Universities Press, 1973.
(1913b). The significance of the grandfather for the fate of the individual. In: *Papers on Psychoanalysis* (pp. 519–524). Baltimore, MD: Williams and Wilkins.
(1916). The theory of symbolism. *British Journal of Psychology*, 9: 181–229.
(1918). Anal erotic character traits. In: *Papers on Psychoanalysis* (pp. 413–437). Baltimore, MD: Williams and Wilkins, 1950.
(1927). The early development of female sexuality. *International Journal of Psychoanalysis*, 8: 459–472.
(1929). Fear, guilt, and hate. *International Journal of Psychoanalysis*, 10: 383–397.
(1931). The concept of a normal mind. In: E. Jones (Ed.), *Papers on Psychoanalysis* (pp. 201–216). Baltimore, MD: Williams and Wilkins, 1950.
(1933). The phallic phase. *International Journal of Psychoanalysis*, 14: 1–33.
(1935). Early female sexuality. *International Journal of Psychoanalysis*, 16: 263–273.
(1955). *The Life and Work of Sigmund Freud, Volume II*. New York: Basic Books.
(1957). *The Life and Work of Sigmund Freud, Volume III*. New York: Basic Books.

BETTY JOSEPH

(1971). A clinical contribution to the analysis of a perversion. In: E. Spillius & M. Feldman (Eds.), *Psychic Equilibrium and Psychic Change: Selected Papers of Betty Joseph* (pp. 51–67). London: Tavistock/Routledge, 1989.
(1981). Towards the experiencing of psychic pain. In: M. Feldman & E. B. Spillius (Eds.), *Psychic Equilibrium and Psychic Change: Selected Papers of Betty Joseph* (pp. 88–97). London: Routledge, 1989.
(1982). Addiction to near-death. *International Journal of Psychoanalysis*, 63: 449–456.
(1987). Projective identification: some clinical aspects. In: E. B. Spillius (Ed.), *Melanie Klein Today Volume I: Mainly Theory* (pp. 138–150). London: Routledge, 1988.

EDWARD JOSEPH & JACK TABOR

(1961). The simultaneous analysis of a pair of identical twins and the twinning reaction. *Psychoanalytic Study of the Child*, 16: 275–299.

LAWRENCE JOSEPHS

(2001). The seductive superego: the trauma of self-betrayal. *International Journal of Psychoanalysis*, 82: 701–712.

MILTON JUCOVY

(1976). Initiation fantasies and transvestitism. *Journal of the American Psychoanalytic Association*, 24: 525–546.

CARL JUNG

(1907). *Uber die Psychologie der Dementia Praecox*. Zurich: Halle.
(1915). *The Theory of Psychoanalysis*. New York: Nervous & Mental Disease Publishing.
(1916). The structure of the unconscious. In: H. Read, M. Fordham & G. Adler (Eds.), *The Collected Works of Carl Jung, Volume VII*. Princeton, NJ: Princeton University Press, 1967.

ELLIOT JURIST

(2005). Mentalized affectivity. *Psychoanalytic Psychology*, 22: 426–444.

JOHN KAFKA

(1989). *Multiple Realities in Clinical Practice*. New Haven, CT: Yale University Press.

BRETT KAHR

(1996). *D. W. Winnicott: A Biographical Portrait*. London: Karnac.

SUDHIR KAKAR

(1978). *The Inner World: A Psychoanalytic Study of Childhood and Society*. Delhi: Oxford University Press.
(1985). Psychoanalysis and non-Western cultures. *International Review of Psychoanalysis*, 12: 441–448.
(1989a). *Intimate Relations: Exploring Indian Sexuality*. Chicago, IL: University of Chicago Press.
(1989b). The maternal–feminine in Indian psychoanalysis. *International Review of Psychoanalysis*, 16: 355–362.

References

(1991). *Shamans, Mystics and Doctors: A Psychological Inquiry into India and its Healing Traditions*. Chicago, IL: University of Chicago Press.
(1995). The clinical work and cultural imagination. *Psychoanalytic Quarterly, 64*: 265–281.
(2001). *The Essential Writings of Sudhir Kakar*. New York: Oxford University Press.

LILA KALINICH & STUART TAYLOR

(2008). *The Dead Father: A Psychoanalytic Inquiry*. London: Routledge.

JUDY KANTROWITZ

(1993). Impasses in psychoanalysis: overcoming resistances in situations of stalemate. *Journal of the American Psychoanalytic Association, 41*: 1021–1050.
(2002). The triadic match: the interactive effect of supervisor, candidate, and patient. *Journal of the American Psychoanalytic Association, 50*: 939–968.

MARK KANZER

(1955). The communicative function of the dream. *International Journal of Psychoanalysis, 36*: 260–266.
(1958). Image formation during free association. *Psychoanalytic Quarterly, 27*: 465–481.

SHAILESH KAPADIA

(1998). On borderline phenomena. *International Journal of Psychoanalysis, 79*: 513–528.

LOUISE KAPLAN

(1978). *Oneness and Separateness: From Infancy to Individual*. New York: Simon and Shuster.

ABRAHAM KARDINER

(1941). *The Traumatic Neuroses of War*. New York: Hoebar.

JON KARLSSON

(1966). *The Biologic Basis of Schizophrenia*. Springfield, IL: Charles Thomas.

LAILA KARME

(1979). The analysis of a male patient by a female analyst: the problem of the negative oedipal transference. *International Journal of Psychoanalysis, 60*: 253–262.

ANNIE KATAN

(1961). Some thoughts about the role of verbalization in early childhood. *Psychoanalytic Study of the Child, 16*: 184–188.

JAMES KAVANAUGH & VAMIK VOLKAN

(1980). Transsexualism and a new type of surgery: thoughts on MacVicar's paper. *International Journal of Psychoanalytic Psychotherapy, 7*: 366–372.

SYLVAN KEISER

(1969). Superior intelligence: its contribution to neurosogenesis. *Journal of the American Psychoanalytic Association, 17*: 452–473.

HARVEY KELMAN

(1975). The 'day precipitate' of dreams: the Morris hypothesis. *International Journal of Psychoanalysis, 56*: 209–218.

JOSEPH KEPECS

(1952). A waking screen analogous to the dream screen. *Psychoanalytic Quarterly, 21*: 167–171.
(1957). The oral triad applied to psychosomatic disorders. *Psychoanalytic Quarterly, 26*: 461–475.

HANSI KENNEDY

(1950). Cover memories in formation. *Psychoanalytic Study of the Child, 5*: 275–284.

OTTO KERNBERG

(1967). Borderline personality organization. *Journal of the American Psychoanalytic Association, 14*: 641–685.
(1970). A psychoanalytic classification of character pathology. *Journal of the American Psychoanalytic Association, 18*: 800–822.
(1974a). Barriers to falling and remaining in love. In: *Object Relations Theory and Clinical Psychoanalysis* (pp. 185–213). New York: Jason Aronson, 1976.

References

(1974b). Mature love: prerequisites and characteristics. In: *Object Relations Theory and Clinical Psychoanalysis* (pp. 215–239). New York: Jason Aronson.
New York: Jason Aronson,1976.
(1975). *Borderline Conditions and Pathological Narcissism*. New York: Jason Aronson.
(1976a). *Object Relations Theory and Clinical Psychoanalysis*. New York: Jason Aronson.
(1976b). Technical considerations in the treatment of borderline personality organization. *Journal of the American Psychoanalytic Association, 30*: 795–829.
(1978). The diagnosis of borderline conditions in adolescence. *Adolescent Psychiatry, 6*: 298–319.
(1980). *Internal World and External Reality*. New York: Jason Aronson.
(1982). Self, ego, affects, and drives. *Journal of the American Psychoanalytic Association, 30*: 893–918.
(1984). *Severe Personality Disorders: Psychotherapeutic Strategies*. New Haven, CT: Yale University Press.
(1989). The narcissistic personality disorder and the differential diagnosis of antisocial behavior. *Psychiatric Clinics of North America, 12*: 533–570.
(1991). Sadomasochism, sexual excitement, and perversion. *Journal of the American Psychoanalytic Association, 39*: 333–362.
(1992). *Aggression in Personality Disorders and Perversions*. New Haven, CT: Yale University Press.
(1994). Love in the analytic setting. *Journal of the American Psychoanalytic Association, 42*: 1137–1157.
(1995a). Hatred as a core affect of aggression. In: S. Akhtar, S. Kramer & and H. Parens (Eds.), *The Birth of Hatred: Clinical, Developmental, Clinical, and Technical Aspects of Intense Aggression* (pp. 53–82). Northvale, NJ: Jason Aronson.
(1995b). *Love Relations: Normality and Pathology*. New Haven, CT: Yale University Press.
(1996). The analyst's authority in the psychoanalytic situation. *Psychoanalytic Quarterly, 65*: 137–157.
(2000). Concerned critique of psychoanalytic education. *International Journal of Psychoanalysis, 81*: 97–120.
(2006). The coming changes in psychoanalytic education: part I. *International Journal of Psychoanalysis, 87*: 1649–1673.
(2007). The coming changes in psychoanalytic education: part II. *International Journal of Psychoanalysis, 88*: 183–202.
(2008). The destruction of time in pathological narcissism. *International Journal of Psychoanalysis, 89*: 299–312.

OTTO KERNBERG, FRANK YEOMANS, JOHN CLARKIN, & KENNETH LEVY

(2008). Transference focused psychotherapy: overview and update. *International Journal of Psychoanalysis, 89*: 601–620.

OTTO KERNBERG, MICHAEL SELZER, HAROLD KOENIGSBERG, ARTHUR CARR, & ANN APPLEBAUM

(1989). *Psychodynamic Psychotherapy of Borderline Patients*. New York: Basic Books.

PAULINA KERNBERG & ARNOLD RICHARDS

(1988). Siblings of preadolescents: their role in development. *Psychoanalytic Inquiry, 8*: 51–65.

JUDITH KESTENBERG

(1972). Psychoanalytic contributions to the problems of children of survivors from Nazi persecution. *Israel Annals of Psychiatry and Related Disciplines, 10*: 311–325.
(1980). Psychoanalyses of children of Holocaust survivors. *Journal of the American Psychoanalytic Association, 28*: 775–804.
(1982). A metapsychological assessment based on an analysis of a survivor's child. In: M. Bergmann & M. Jucovy (Eds.), *Generations of the Holocaust* (pp. 137–158). New York: Basic Books.

JUDITH KESTENBERG & IRA BRENNER

(1995). Narcissism in the service of survival. In: T. Cohen, M. H. Etezady & B. L. Pacella (Eds.), *The Vulnerable Child, Volume 2* (pp. 35–50). Madison, CT: International Universities Press.
(1996). *The Last Witness: The Child Survivor of the Holocaust*. Washington, DC: American Psychiatric Press.

JUDITH KESTENBERG & YOLANDA GAMPEL

(1983). Growing up in the Holocaust culture. *Israel Journal of Psychiatry, 29*: 129–146.

MASUD KHAN

(1960). Regression and integration in the analytic setting. In: *The Privacy of the Self* (pp. 136–167). London: Hogarth, 1974.
(1962). Dream psychology and the evolution of the psychoanalytic situation. In: *The Privacy of the Self* (pp. 27–41). London: Hogarth, 1974.
(1963a). The concept of cumulative trauma. *Psychoanalytic Study of the Child, 18*: 286–306.
(1963b). Silence as communication. In: *The Privacy of the Self* (pp. 168–180). New York: International Universities Press, 1974.
(1969). On symbiotic omnipotence. In: *The Privacy of the Self* (pp. 82–92). New York: International Universities Press, 1974.

References

(1971). Infantile neurosis as a false self organization. *Psychoanalytic Quarterly, 40*: 245–263.

(1979). *Alienation in Perversions*. New York: International Universities Press.

(1983a). Infancy, aloneness, and madness. In: *Hidden Selves* (pp. 181–182). New York: International Universities Press.

(1983b). Lying fallow. In: *Hidden Selves* (pp. 183–188). New York: International Universities Press.

RANJANA KHANNA

(2004). *Dark Continents: Psychoanalysis and Colonialism*. Chapel Hill, NC: Duke University Press.

CHRISTINE KIEFFER

(2004). Selfobjects, oedipal objects, and mutual recognition: a self-psychological reappraisal of the female 'oedipal victor'. *Annual of Psychoanalysis, 32*: 69–80.

(2008). From selfobjects to mutual recognition: towards optimal responsiveness in father–daughter relationships. *Psychoanalytic Inquiry, 28*: 76–91.

NORMAN KIELL

(1988). *Freud Without Hindsight: Reviews of His Work (1893–1939)*. Madison, CT: International Universities Press.

BENJAMIN KILBORNE

(2005). Shame conflicts and tragedy in *The Scarlet Letter*. *Journal of the American Psychoanalytic Association, 53*: 465–483.

BJORN KILLINGMO

(1989). Conflict and deficit: implications for technique. *International Journal of Psychoanalysis, 70*: 65–79.

PEARL KING

(1978). Affective response of the analysis to the patient's communications. *International Journal of Psychoanalysis, 59*: 329–334.

PEARL KING & RICCARDO STEINER

(1991). *The Freud–Klein Controversies: 1941–45*. London: Routledge.

ALFRED KINSEY, WARDELL POMEROY, & CLYDE MARTIN

(1948). *Sexual Behavior in the Human Male*. New York: W. B. Saunders.

(1953). *Sexual Behavior in the Human Female*. New York: W. B. Saunders.

WARREN KINSTON & JONATHAN COHEN

(1986). Primal repression: clinical and theoretical aspects. *International Journal of Psychoanalysis, 67*: 337–353.

JAMES KLEEMAN

(1967). The peek-a-boo game. *Psychoanalytic Study of the Child, 22*: 239–273.

GEORGE KLEIN

(1958). Cognitive control and motivation. In: G. Lindzey (Ed.), *Assessment of Human Motives* (pp. 87–118). New York: Reinhardt.

(1967). Preemptory ideation: structure and force in motivated ideas. *Psychological Issues, 5*(2–3): 18–19.

(1973). Is psychoanalysis relevant? *Psychoanalytic Contemporary Science, 2*: 3–21.

(1976). *Psychoanalytic Theory*. New York: International Universities Press.

MELANIE KLEIN

(1921). The development of a child. *International Journal of Psychoanalysis, 1*: 200–203.

(1923). Zur frühanalyse. *Imago, 9*: 222–259.

(1924). The role of the school in libidinal development of the child. *International Journal of Psychoanalysis, 9*: 323–344.

(1926). The psychological principles of early analysis. *International Journal of Psychoanalysis, 8*: 25–37.

(1927). Criminal tendencies in normal children. *British Journal of Medical Psychology, 7*: 177–192.

(1928). Early stages of the oedipus conflict. In: *Love, Guilt and Reparation and Other Works—1921–1945*. New York: The Free Press, 1975.

(1929). Personification in the play of children. *International Journal of Psychoanalysis, 19*: 193–214.

(1930). The psychotherapy of the psychoses. *British Journal of Medical Psychology, 10*: 242–244.

(1931). A contribution to the theory of intellectual inhibition. In: *Love, Guilt and Reparation and Other Works—1921–1945* (pp. 236–247). New York: Free Press, 1975.

(1932). *The Psychoanalysis of Children*. New York: The Free Press, 1975.

(1933). The early development of conscience in the child. In: *Love, Guilt and Reparation and Other Works—1921–1945* (pp. 248–257). New York: Free Press, 1975.

(1934). A contribution to the psychogenesis of manic-depressive states. In: *Love, Guilt, and Reparation and Other Works—1921–1945* (pp. 262–289). New York: The Free Press, 1984.

(1935). A contribution to the psychogenesis of manic depressive states. In: *Love, Guilt and Reparation and Other Works—1921–1945* (pp. 262–289). New York: Free Press, 1975.

(1937). Love, guilt, and reparation. In: *Love, Guilt and reparation and Other Works—1921–1945* (pp. 306–343). New York: Free Press, 1975.

(1940). Mourning and its relation to manic depressive states. In: *Love, Guilt and Reparation and Other Works - 1921–1945* (pp. 344–369). New York: Free Press, 1975.

(1946). Notes on some schizoid mechanisms. In: *Envy and Gratitude and Other Works—1946–1963* (pp. 1–24). New York: Free Press, 1975.

(1948a). A contribution to the theory of anxiety and guilt. *International Journal of Psychoanalysis*, 29: 114–123.

(1948b). *Contributions to Psychoanalysis (1921–1945)*. London: Hogarth.

(1952). The mutual influences in the development of ego and the id. In: *Envy and Gratitude and Other Works—1946–1963* (pp.57–60). New York: Free Press, 1975.

(1957). Envy and gratitude. In: *Envy and Gratitude and Other Works—1946–1963* (pp. 176–235). New York: Free Press, 1975.

(1960). On mental health. *British Journal of Medical Psychology*, 33: 237–241.

MILTON KLEIN & DAVID TRIBICH

(1981). Kernberg's object-relations theory: a critical evaluation. *International Journal of Psychoanalysis*, 62: 27–43.

JACK KLEINER

(1970). On nostalgia. *Bulletin of the Philadelphia Association for Psychoanalysis*, 20: 11–30.

RICHARD KLUFT

(1984). Treatment of multiple personality: a study of 33 cases. *Psychiatric Clinics of North America*, 7: 9–29.

(1985). Childhood multiple personality disorder: predictors, clinical findings, and treatment results. In: R. P. Kluft (Ed.), *Childhood Antecedents of Multiple Personality* (pp. 167–196). Washington, DC: American Psychiatric Press.

(1986). Personality unification in multiple personality disorder: a follow-up study. In: B. G. Braun (Ed.), *Treatment of Multiple Personality Disorder* (pp. 29–60). Washington, DC: American Psychiatric Press.

(1993). Clinical approaches to the integration of personalities. In: R. P. Kluft & C. G. Fine (Eds.), *Clinical Perspectives on Multiple Personality Disorder* (pp. 101–134). Washington, DC: American Psychiatric Press.

GEORGE KLUMPNER

(1992). *A Guide to The Language of Psychoanalysis: An Empirical Study of the Relationships Among Psychoanalytic Terms and Concepts*. Madison, CT: International Universities Press.

DANIELLE KNAFO & KENNETH FEINER

(1996). Primal scene. *Journal of the American Psychoanalytic Association*, 44: 549–569.

ROBERT KNIGHT

(1940). Introjection, projection, and identification. *Psychoanalytic Quarterly*, 9: 334–341.

ILANY KOGAN

(1990). A journey to pain. *International Journal of Psychoanalysis*, 71: 629–640.

(1995). *The Cry of Mute Children: A Psychoanalytic Perspective of the Second Generation of the Holocaust*. London: Free Association.

(2002). Enactment in the lives and treatment of Holocaust survivors' offspring. *Psychoanalytic Quarterly*, 71: 251–273.

(2006). Breaking of boundaries and craving for oneness. In: S. Akhtar (Ed.), *Interpersonal Boundaries: Variations and Violations* (pp. 61–86). Lanham, MD: Jason Aronson.

(2007). *The Struggle Against Mourning*. Lanham, MD: Jason Aronson.

HEINZ KOHUT

(1971). *Analysis of the Self*. New York: International Universities Press.

(1972). Thoughts on narcissism and narcissistic rage. *Psychoanalytic Study of the Child*, 27: 360–400.

(1977). *Restoration of the Self*. New York: International Universities Press.

(1980). Summarizing reflections. In: A. Goldberg (Ed.), *Advances in Self Psychology* (473–554). New York: International Universities Press.

(1982). Introspection, empathy, and the semi-circle of mental health. *International Journal of Psychoanalysis*, 63: 395–407.

References

HEINZ KOHUT & ERNEST WOLF

(1978). The disorders of the self and their treatment: an outline. *International Journal of Psychoanalysis, 59*: 413–425.

HAROLD KOLANSKY

(1960). Treatment of a three year old girl's severe infantile neurosis. *Psychoanalytic Study of the Child, 15*: 261–285.

HAROLD KOLANSKY & HENRY EISNER

(1974). The psychoanalytic concept of preoedipal developmental arrest. Paper presented at the Fall Meetings of the American Psychoanalytic Association. Cited in: S. Akhtar (Ed.), *Inner Torment: Living Between Conflict and Fragmentation* (p. 231). Northvale, NJ: Jason Aronson, 1999.

HEISAKU KOSAWA

(1931). Two kinds of guilt feelings: the Ajase complex. *Gonryo: Newsletter of the Alumni Association of Tohoku Teikoku University*, 15 June issue: 2–5).

EMIL KRAEPELIN

(1921). *Manic Depressive Insanity and Paranoia*. Edinburgh: Livingston Press.

RICHARD VON KRAFFT-EBING

(1892). *Psychopathia Sexualis with Special Reference to Contrary Sexual Instinct: A Medico–Legal Study*. Philadelphia, PA: Davis.

PAUL KRAMER

(1955). On discovering one's identity: a case report. *Psychoanalytic Study of the Child, 10*: 47–74.

SELMA KRAMER

(1983). Object coercive doubting: a pathological defensive response to maternal incest. *Journal of the Psychoanalytic Association, 31*(Suppl.): 325–351.
(1987). A contribution to the concept 'the exception' as a developmental phenomenon. *Child Abuse and Neglect, 11*: 367–370.
(1991). Psychopathological effects of incest. In: S. Kramer & S. Akhtar (Eds.), *The Trauma of Transgression: Psychotherapy of Incest Victims* (pp. 1–10). Northvale, NJ: Jason Aronson.
(1997). Work and its inhibitions as seen in children and adolescents. In: C. Socarides & S. Kramer (Eds.), *Work and Its Inhibitions: Psychoanalytic Essays* (pp. 159–179). Madison, CT: International Universities Press.

SELMA KRAMER & JOSEPH RUDOLPH

(1980). The latency stage. In: S. I. Greenspan & G. H. Pollack (Eds.), *The Course of Life, Volume II,: Latency, Adolescence, and Youth* (pp. 109–119). Adelphi, MD: National Institute of Mental Health.

SELMA KRAMER & SALMAN AKHTAR

(1991). *The Trauma of Transgression: Psychotherapy of Incest Victims*. Northvale, NJ: Jason Aronson.

YALE KRAMER

(1977). Work compulsion: a psychoanalytic study. *Psychoanalytic Quarterly, 46*: 361–385.

MERTON KRAUSE

(1961). Defensive and non-defensive resistance. *Psychoanalytic Quarterly, 30*: 221–231.

RAINER KRAUSE & JORG MERTEN

(1999). Affects, regulation of relationship, transference and countertransference. *International Forum of Psychoanalysis, 8*: 103–114.

LEON KREISLER

(1984). Fundamentals for a psychosomatic pathology of infants. In: J. D. Call, E. Galenson, & R. L. Tyson (Eds.), *Frontiers of Infant Psychiatry*, Volume II (pp. 447–454). New York: Basic Books.

EMILE KRETSCHMER

(1925). *Physique and Character*, W. J. H. Sprott (Trans.). New York: Harcourt-Brace.

ANTON KRIS

(1977). Either-or dilemmas. *Psychoanalytic Study of the Child, 32*: 91–117.
(1981). On giving advice to parents in analysis. *Psychoanalytic Study of the Child, 36*: 151–162.

(1982). *Free Association*. New Haven, CT: Yale University Press.
(1984). The conflicts of ambivalence. *Psychoanalytic Study of the Child, 39*: 213–234.
(1985). Resistance in convergent and in divergent conflicts. *Psychoanalytic Quarterly, 54*: 537–568.
(1988). Some clinical applications of the distinction between divergent and convergent conflicts. *International Journal of Psychoanalysis, 69*: 431–441.
(1992). Interpretation and the method of free association. *Psychoanalytic Inquiry, 12*: 208–224.

ERNST KRIS

(1947). The structure of psychoanalytic propositions and their validation. In: *Selected Papers of Ernst Kris*. New Haven, CT: Yale University Press, 1975.
(1951). Ego psychology and interpretation in psychoanalytic therapy. *Psychoanalytic Quarterly, 20*: 15–30.
(1952). *Psychoanalytic Explorations in Art*. New York: International Universities Press.
(1956). The recovery of childhood memories in psychoanalysis. *Psychoanalytic Study of the Child, 11*: 54–88.

JULIA KRISTEVA

(1982). *Powers of Horror: An Essay in Abjection*, L. S. Roudiz (Trans.). New York: Columbia University Press.
(1987). *In the Beginning Was Love: Psychoanalysis and Faith*, A. Goldhammer (Trans.). New York: Columbia University Press.

DAVID KRUEGER

(1986). (Ed.)*The Last Taboo: Money as Symbol and Reality in Psychotherapy and Psychoanalysis*. New York: Brunner/Mazel.

HENRY KRYSTAL

(1968). *Massive Psychic Trauma*. New York: International Universities Press.
(1981). The aging survivor of the Holocaust. *Journal of Geriatric Psychiatry, 14*: 165–189.
(1985). Trauma and the stimulus barrier. *Psychoanalytic Inquiry, 5*: 131–161.
(1988). *Integration and Self-Healing*. Hillsdale, NJ: Analytic Press.
(2007). Resilience: accommodation and recovery. In: H. Parens, H. P. Blum, & S. Akhtar (Eds.), *The Unbroken Soul: Tragedy, Trauma, and Resilience* (pp. 47–64). Lanham, MD: Jason Aronson.

HENRY KRYSTAL & HERBERT RASKIN

(1970). *Drug Dependence: Aspects of Ego Function*. Detroit, MI: Wayne State University Press.

LAWRENCE KUBIE

(1954). The fundamental distinction between normality and neurosis. *Psychoanalytic Quarterly, 23*: 167–204.
(1962). The fallacious misuse of the concept of sublimation. *Psychoanalytic Quarterly, 31*: 73–79.
(1968). Unresolved problems in the resolution of transference. *Psychoanalytic Quarterly, 37*: 331–352.

ELISABETH KUBLER-ROSS

(1969). *On Death and Dying*. London: Macmillan.

NANCY KULISH

(2000). Primary femininity: clinical advances and theoretical ambiguities. *Journal of the American Psychoanalytic Association, 48*: 1355–1379.

NANCY KULISH & DEANNA HOLTZMAN

(1998). Persephone, the loss of virginity, and the female oedipal complex. *International Journal of Psychoanalysis, 79*: 57–71.

MANASI KUMAR

(2005). In a bid to restate the culture–psyche problematic: revisiting the essential writings of Sudhir Kakar. *Psychoanalytic Quarterly, 74*: 561–587.

LARRY KUNSTADT

(2001). Neuropsychoanalytic research. *Psychoanalytic Association of New York Bulletin, 9*: 10–12.

STEPHEN KURTZ

(1989). *The Art of Unknowing*. New York: Jason Aronson.

JACQUES LACAN

(1938). Les complexes familiaux dans la formation de l'individu. In: *Essai d'Analyse d'une Function en Psychologie* (pp. 3–37). Paris: Navarin, 1984.

References

(1949). The mirror stage as formative of the function of the 'I'. In: J. Lacan (Ed.), A. Sheridan (Trans.), *Ecrits: A Selection* (pp. 1–7). London: Tavistock, 1977.

(1950). Introduction theorique aux fonctions de la psychanalyse en criminologie. In: *Ecrits* (pp. 125–149). Paris: Seuil, 1966.

(1951). Some reflections on the ego. *International Journal of Psychoanalysis, 34*: 11–17.

(1955). *The Seminar Book-II: The Ego in Freud's Theory and in the Technique of Psychoanalysis, 1954–55* (p. 321), S. Tomaselli (Trans.). Cambridge: Cambridge University Press, 1988.

(1956). *The Seminar Book-III: The Psychoses*, R. Grigg (Trans.). London: Routledge, 1993.

(1957). *Le Seminaire-Livre IV: La relation d' object* (pp. 374–408), J.-A. Miller (Trans.). Paris: Seuil, 1994.

(1958). Le Seminaire-Livre V: Les formations de l'inconsistant. Unpublished and summarized by J.-B. Pontalis in *Bulletin de Psychologie, 12*: 182–192.

(1959). *The Seminar-Book VII: The Ethics of Psychoanalysis* (pp. 139, 165, 171), D. Porter (Trans.). London: Routledge, 1992.

(1960). *The Seminar-Book VII: The Ethics of Psychoanalysis* (p. 184), D. Porter (Trans.). London: Routledge, 1992.

(1964). *The Seminar Book-XI: The Four Fundamental Concepts of Psychoanalysis* (pp. 21–22), A. Sheridan (Trans.). London: Hogarth Press and the Institute of Psychoanalysis, 1977.

(1974). *Le Seminaire. Livre XXII*, J.-A. Miller (Ed.). Paris: Seuil.

(1977). *Ecrits: A Selection*, A. Sheridan (Trans.). London: Tavistock.

PIERRE LACOMBE

(1958). A special meaning of pathological weeping. *Psychoanalytic Quarterly, 27*: 246–251.

LUCY LAFARGE

(1995). Transferences of deception. *Journal of the American Psychoanalytic Association, 43*: 765–792.

(2004). The imaginer and the imagined. *Psychoanalytic Quarterly, 73*: 591–625.

(2006). The wish for revenge. *Psychoanalytic Quarterly, 75*: 447–475.

(2009). Authentication, lying and malicious deception. In: S. Akhtar & H. Parens (Eds.), *Lying, Cheating, and Carrying On: Developmental, Clinical, and Sociocultural Aspects of Dishonesty and Deceit* (pp. 43–57). Lanham, MD: Jason Aronson.

DANIEL LAGACHE

(1957). La psychanalyse et la structure de la personnalité. *La Psychanalyse, 3*: 33–46.

(1968). Acting out et action: difficultés terminologiques. *Revue française de Psychanalyse, 32*: 1055–1066.

RONALD LAING

(1964). *The Divided Self*. London: Tavistock.

(1971). *Politics of Family and Other Essays*. London: Tavistock.

JEANNE LAMPL-DE-GROOT

(1949). Neurotics, delinquents and ideal formation. In: K. R. Eissler (Ed.), *Searchlights on Delinquency* (pp. 225–245). New York: International Universities Press.

JANET LANDMAN

(1993). *Regret: The Persistance of the Possible*. New York: Oxford University Press.

CHRISTOPHER LANE

(1998). The psychoanalysis of race: an introduction. In: C. Lane (Ed.), *The Psychoanalysis of Race* (pp. 1–37). New York: Columbia University Press.

ROBERT LANGS

(1971). Day residues, recall residues, and dreams: reality and the psyche. *Journal of the American Psychoanalytic Association, 19*: 499–523.

(1976). *The Bipersonal Field*. New York: Jason Aronson.

(1979). The interactional dimension of countertransference. In: L. Epstein & A. H. Feiner (Eds.), *Countertransference* (pp. 71–103). New York: Jason Aronson.

(1981). *Technique of Psychoanalytic Psychotherapy: Initial Contact: Theoretical Framework: Understanding the Patients Communications: Therapist's Intervention*. New York: Jason Aronson.

(1982). *Psychotherapy: A Basic Text*. New York: Jason Aronson.

MELVIN LANSKY

(2001). Hidden shame: working through and the problem of forgiveness in 'The Tempest'. *Journal of the American Psychoanalytic Association, 49*: 1004–1033.

(2005). The impossibility of forgiveness: shame fantasies as instigators of vengefulness in Euripides' 'Medea'. *Journal of the American Psychoanalytic Association, 53*: 437–464.

JEAN LAPLANCHE & JEAN-BERNARD PONTALIS

(1973). *The Language of Psychoanalysis*. D. Nicholson-Smith (Trans.). New York: W. W. Norton.

RICHARD LASKY

(1984). Dynamics and problems in the treatment of the 'oedipal winner'. *Psychoanalytic Review*, 71: 351–374.

DORI LAUB

(1998). The empty circle: children of survivors and the limits of reconstruction. *Journal of the American Psychoanalytic Association*, 46: 507–529.

MOSES LAUFER

(1968). The body image, the function of masturbation and adolescence: problem of the ownership of the body. *Psychoanalytic Study of the Child*, 23: 114–137.

RUTH LAX

(1980). The rotten core: a defect in the formation of the self during the rapprochement subphase. In: R. F. Lax, S. Bach, & J. A. Burland (Eds.), *Rapprochement: The Critical Phase of Separation–Individuation* (pp. 439–456). New York: Jason Aronson.
(1982). The expectable depressive climacteric reaction. *Bulletin of the Menninger Clinic*, 46: 151–167.
(1994). Aspects of primary and secondary genital feelings and anxieties in girls during the preoedipal and early oedipal phases. *Psychoanalytic Quarterly*, 63: 271–296.
(2007). Psychoanalysis and psychotherapy with the aging and the aged. *Issues in Psychoanalytic Psychology*, 29: 79–86.

RALPH LAYLAND

(1981). In search of a loving father. *International Journal of Psychoanalysis*, 62: 215–223.

AARON LAZARE.

(1971). The hysterical character in psychoanalytic theory. *Archives of General Psychiatry*, 25: 131–137.

LOUIS LEAFF

(1991). Separation individuation and adolescence with special reference to character formation. In: S. Akhtar & H. Parens (Eds.), *Beyond the Symbiotic Orbit: Advances in Separation–Individuation Theory* (pp. 189–208). Hillsdale, NJ: Analytic Press.

JONATHAN LEAR

(2007). Working through the end of civilization. *International Journal of Psychoanalysis*, 88: 291–308.

KIMBERLY LEARY

(1995). Interpreting in the dark: race and ethnicity in psychoanalytic psychotherapy. *Psychoanalytic Psychology*, 12: 127–140.
(1997). Race, self-disclosure, and 'forbidden talk': race, ethnicity in contemporary practice. *Psychoanalytic Quarterly*, 66: 163–189.
(2006). In the eye of the storm. *Psychoanalytic Quarterly*, 75: 345–363.

JOHANNES LEHTONEN

(1997). On the origins of the body ego and its implications for psychotic vulnerability. In: V. D. Volkan & S. Akhtar (Eds.), *The Seed of Madness: Constitution, Environment, and Fantasy in the Organization of the Psychotic Core* (pp. 19–57). Madison, CT: International Universities Press.

TORHILD LEIRA

(1995). Silence and communication: nonverbal dialogue and therapeutic action. *Scandinavian Psychoanalytic Review*, 18: 41–65.

ALESSANDRA LEMMA

(2000). *Humour on the Couch: Exploring Humour in Psychotherapy and Everyday Life*. London: Whurr.
(2005). The many faces of lying. *International Journal of Psychoanalysis*, 86: 737–753.

EVA LESTER & BRIAN ROBERTSON

(1995). Multiple interactive processes in psychoanalytic supervision. *Psychoanalytic Inquiry*, 15: 211–223.

EVA LESTER, ROSE-MARIE JODOIN, & BRIAN ROBERTSON

(1989). Countertransference dreams reconsidered: a survey. *International Review of Psychoanalysis*, 16: 305–314.

References

LAWRENCE LEVENSON

(1998). Superego defense analysis in the termination phase. *Journal of the American Psychoanalytic Association, 46*: 847–866.

ALAN LEVETON

(1961). The night residue. *International Journal of Psychoanalysis, 17*: 506–516.

FRED LEVIN

(1995). Psychoanalysis and the brain. In: B. Moore & B. Fine (Eds.), *Psychoanalysis: The Major Concepts* (pp. 537–552). New Haven, CT: Yale University Press.

JEROME LEVIN

(1987). *Treatment of Alcoholism and Other Addictions: A Self-Psychology Approach.* Northvale, NJ: Jason Aronson.

SIDNEY LEVIN

(1967). Some metapsychological considerations on the differentiation between shame and guilt. *International Journal of Psychoanalysis, 48*: 267–276.
(1970). On the psychoanalysis of attitudes of entitlement. *Bulletin of the Philadelphia Association for Psychoanalysis, 20*: 1–10.
(1971). The psychoanalysis of shame. *International Journal of Psychoanalysis, 52*: 355–362.

FREDERIC LEVINE

(1993). Unconscious fantasy and theories of technique. *Psychoanalytic Inquiry, 13*: 326–342.
(2003). The forbidden quest and the slippery slope of authoritarianism in psychoanalysis. *Journal of the American Psychoanalytic Association, 51*(Suppl.): 203–245.

HOWARD LEVINE

(1985). Psychotherapy as the initial phase of psychoanalysis. *International Review of Psychoanalysis, 12*: 285–297.
(2005). The sins of fathers: narcissistic boundaries and the power politics of psychoanalysis. Paper presented at the Fall Meetings of the American Psychoanalytic Associations, January 19, 2005.

HOWARD LEVINE & RAYMOND FRIEDMAN

(2000). Intersubjectivity and interaction in the analytic relationship. *Psychoanalytic Quarterly, 69*: 63–92.

STEVEN LEVINE

(1995). *Monet, Narcissus, and Self-Reflection: The Modernist Myth of the Self.* Chicago, IL: University of Chicago Press.

SUSAN LEVINE

(2001). On the mirror stage with Henry and Eliza or playing with Pygmalion in five acts. *Journal of Applied Psychoanalytic Studies, 3*: 103–125.
(2004). To have and to hold: the experience of having an other. *Psychoanalytic Quarterly, 73*: 939–969.
(2007). Nothing but the truth: self-disclosure, self-revelation, and the persona of the analyst. *Journal of the American Psychoanalytic Association, 55*: 81–104.

DANIEL LEVINSON, CHARLOTTE DARROW, EDWARD KLEIN, MARIA LEVINSON, & BRAXTON MCKEE

(1978). *The Seasons of a Man's Life.* New York: Alfred Knopf.

NADINE LEVINSON

(2003). Panel on 'acting out and/or enactment'. *International Journal of Psychoanalysis, 84*: 151–155.

KATA LEVY

(1949). The eternal dilettante. In: K. R. Eissler (Ed.), *Searchlights on Delinquency* (pp. 65–76). New York: International Universities Press.

STEVEN LEVY

(1984). Psychoanalytic perspectives on emptiness. *Journal of the American Psychoanalytic Association, 32*: 387–404.
(1987). Therapeutic strategy and psychoanalytic technique. *Journal of the American Psychoanalytic Association, 35*: 447–466.

STEVEN LEVY & LAWRENCE INDERBITZIN

(1990). The analytic surface and the theory of technique. *Journal of the American Psychoanalytic Association, 38*: 371–391.
(1992). Neutrality, interpretation, and therapeutic intent. *Journal of the American Psychoanalytic Association, 40*: 989–1011.

BERTRAM LEWIN

(1935). Claustrophobia. *Psychoanalytic Quarterly, 4*: 227–233.
(1946). Sleep, the mouth, and the dream screen. *Psychoanalytic Quarterly, 15*: 419–434.
(1950). *The Psychoanalysis of Elation*. New York: W. W. Norton.
(1968). *The Image and the Past*. New York: International Universities Press.

ROGER LEWIN & CLARENCE SCHULZ

(1992). *Losing and Fusing: Borderline Transitional Object and Self Relations*. Northvale, NJ: Jason Aronson.

AUBREY LEWIS

(1936). Problems of obsessional illness. *Proceedings of the Royal Society of Medicine, 29*: 325–328.

JOSEPH LICHTENBERG

(1982). Reflections on the first year of life. *Psychoanalytic Inquiry, 1*: 695–730.
(1989). *Psychoanalysis and Motivation*. Hillsdale, NJ: Analytic Press.
(1992). Interpretive sequence. *Psychoanalytic Inquiry, 12*: 248–274.
(1996). Caregiver–infant, analyst–analysand exchanges: models of interaction. *Psychoanalytic Inquiry, 16*: 54–66.
(2005). Sanderian activation waves: a hypothesis of a nonsymbolic influence on moods. *Psychoanalytic Quarterly, 74*: 485–505.

JOSEPH LICHTENBERG & DAVID LEVI

(1990). Psychotherapy to psychoanalysis: a method of study. *Psychoanalytic Inquiry, 10*: 7–20.

JOSEPH LICHTENBERG & FLOYD GALLER

(1987). The fundamental rule: a study of current usage. *Journal of the American Psychoanalytic Association, 35*: 47–76.

JOSEPH LICHTENBERG, FRANK LACHMAN, & JAMES FOSSHAGE

(1996). *The Clinical Exchange*. Hillsdale, NJ: The Analytic Press.

HEINZ LICHTENSTEIN

(1963). The dilemma of human identity: notes on self-transformation, self-objectivation, and metamorphosis. *Journal of the American Psychoanalytic Association, 11*: 173–223.

THEODORE LIDZ

(1968). *The Person: His and Her Development Throughout the Life Cycle*. New York: Basic Books (revised edn), 1983.
(1973). *The Origin and Treatment of Schizophrenic Disorders*. New York: International Universities Press, 1990.

JANICE LIEBERMAN

(2000). *Body Talk: Looking and Being Looked at in Psychotherapy*. Northvale, NJ: Jason Aronson.

LAWRENCE LIFSON & RICHARD GEIST

(1999). *The Psychology of Investing*. London: John Wiley.

LAWRENCE LIFSON & ROBERT SIMON

(1998). *The Mental Health Practitioner and the Law*. Cambridge, MA: Harvard University Press.

ADAM LIMENTANI

(1979). The significance of transsexualism in relation to some basic psychoanalytic concepts. *International Review of Psychoanalysis, 6*: 139–153.
(1989). *Between Freud and Klein: The Psychoanalytic Quest for Knowledge and Truth*. London: Free Association.

JOHN LINDON

(1958). Castrophilia as a character neurosis. *International Journal of Psychoanalysis, 39*: 525–534.
(1988). Psychoanalysis by telephone. *Bulletin of the Menninger Clinic, 52*: 521–528.

SUSAN LIPSHITZ-PHILLIPS

(1992). Review of *Feminism and Psychoanalysis: A Critical Dictionary*, Elizabeth Wright (Ed.), *International Journal of Psychoanalysis, 76*: 867–868.

SAMUEL LIPTON

(1961). The last hour. *Journal of the American Psychoanalytic Association, 9*: 325–341.

References

BONNIE LITOWITZ

(1998). An expanded developmental line for negation: rejection, refusal, denial. *Journal of the American Psychoanalytic Association, 46*: 121–148

MARGARET LITTLE

(1951). Countertransference and the patient's response to it. *International Journal of Psychoanalysis, 32*: 32–40.
(1960). On basic unity. *International Journal of Psychoanalysis, 41*: 377–384; 637.
(1990). *Psychotic Anxieties and Containment: A Personal Record of an Analysis with Winnicott*. Northvale, NJ: Jason Aronson.

HANS LOEWALD

(1960). On the therapeutic action of psychoanalysis. *Journal of the American Psychoanalytic Association, 41*: 16–33.
(1970). Psychoanalytic theory and psychoanalytic process. *Psychoanalytic Study of the Child, 25*: 45–68.
(1971). Some considerations on repetition and repetition compulsion. *International Journal of Psychoanalysis, 52*: 59–66.
(1974). Discussion: current status of the concept of infantile neurosis. *Psychoanalytic Study of the Child, 29*: 183–188.

PETER LOEWENBERG

(1995). *Fantasy and Reality in History*. London: Oxford University Press.

RUDOLPH LOEWENSTEIN

(1949). A post-traumatic dream. *Psychoanalytic Quarterly, 18*: 449–454.
(1951). The problem of interpretation. *Psychoanalytic Quarterly, 20*: 1–23.
(1957). A contribution to the psychoanalytic theory of masochism. *Journal of the American Psychoanalytic Association, 5*: 197–234.

RAFAEL LOPEZ-CORVO

(2003). *The Work of W. R. Bion*. London: Karnac.

LESTER LUBORSKY

(1976). Helping alliances in psychotherapy: the groundwork for a study of their relationship to its outcome. In: J. L. Claghorn (Ed.), *Successful Psychotherapy* (pp. 92–116). New York: Brunner/Mazel.
(1977). Measuring a perverse psychic structure in psychotherapy: the core-conflictual relationship theme. In: N. Freedman & S. Grand (Eds.), *Communicative Structures and Psychic Structures* (pp. 367–395). New York: Plenum.
(1988). *Who Will Benefit from Psychotherapy?: Predicting Therapeutic Outcomes*. New York: Basic Books.

LESTER LUBORSKY & PAUL CRITS-CHRISTOPHER

(1989). A relationship pattern measure: the core conflictual relationship theme. *Psychiatry, 52*: 250–259.
(1990). *Understanding Transference: The CCRT Method*. New York: Basic Books.

LESTER LUBORSKY & ELLEN LUBORSKY

(1993). The era of measures of transference: the CCRT and other measures. *Journal of the American Psychoanalytic Association, 41*(Suppl.): 329–351.

RICHARD LUCAS

(2003a). Psychoanalytic controversies: the relationship between psychoanalysis and schizophrenia. *International Journal of Psychoanalysis, 84*: 3–15.
(2003b). The relationship between psychoanalysis and schizophrenia: a response to the commentary by Robert Michels. *International Journal of Psychoanalysis, 84*: 12–15.

IDA MACALPINE

(1950). The development of the transference. *Psychoanalytic Quarterly, 19*: 501–539.

HOUSTON MACINTOSH

(1994). Attitudes and experiences of psychoanalysts in analyzing homosexual patients. *Journal of the American Psychoanalytic Association, 42*: 1183–1205.

JOHN MACK

(1976). *A Prince of Our Disorder: The Life of T. E. Lawrence*. Cambridge, MA: Harvard University Press.
(1981). Alcoholism: A. A., and the governance of the self. In: M. H. Bean & N. E. Zinberg (Eds.), *Dynamic Approaches to the Understanding and Treatment of Alcoholism* (pp. 128–162). New York: Free Press.

ROGER MACKINNON & ROBERT MICHELS

(1971). *The Psychiatric Interview in Clinical Practice*. Philadelphia, PA: Saunders.

LEO MADOW

(1997). On the way to a second symbiosis. In: S. Akhtar & S. Kramer (Eds.), *The Seasons of Life: Separation–Individuation Perspectives* (pp. 157–170). Northvale NJ: Jason Aronson.

MARGARET MAHLER

(1942). Pseudo-imbecility: a magic cap of invisibility. *Psychoanalytic Quarterly, 11*: 149–164.
(1952). On child psychosis and schizophrenia: autistic and symbiotic infantile psychoses. *Psychoanalytic Study of the Child, 7*: 286–305.
(1955). Discussion of papers by Kanner and Isenberg, Despert, and Lourie. In: P. H. Hoch & J. Zubin (Eds.), *Psychopathology of Childhood* (pp. 285–289). New York: Grune & Stratton.
(1958). On two crucial phases of integration of the sense of identity: separation–individuation and bisexual identity. *Journal of the American Psychoanalytic Association, 6*: 136–139.
(1963). Thoughts about development and individuation. In: *The Selected Papers of Margaret S Mahler, Vol. II* (pp. 3–19. New York: Jason Aronson.
(1965). On the significance of the normal separation–individuation phase with reference to research in symbiotic child psychosis. In: M. Schur (Ed.), *Drives, Affects, Behavior—Volume II* (pp. 161–169). New York: International Universities Press.
(1966). Notes on the development of basic moods: the depressive affect. In: R. M. Loewenstein, L. M. Newman, M. Schur & A. J. Solnit (Eds.), *Psychoanalysis: A General Psychology* (pp. 152–168). New York: International Universities Press.
(1968). *On Human Symbiosis and The Vicissitudes of Individuation—Volume I: Infantile Psychosis*. New York: International Universities Press.
(1971). A study of the separation–individuation process and its possible application to borderline phenomena in the psychoanalytic situation. In: *The Selected Papers of Margaret S. Mahler, Volume Two, Separation–Individuation* (pp. 169–187). New York: Jason Aronson.
(1972). On the first three subphases of the separation–individuation process. *International Journal of Psychoanalysis, 53*: 333–338.
(1974). Symbiosis and individuation: the psychological birth of the human infant. In: *The Selected Papers of Margaret S. Mahler, Volume 2* (pp. 149–165). New York: Jason Aronson, 1979.

MARGARET MAHLER & BERTRAM GOSLINER

(1955). On symbiotic child psychoanalysis: genetic, dynamic and restitutive aspects. *Psychoanalytic Study of the Child, 10*: 195–212.

MARGARET MAHLER, FRED PINE, & ANNI BERGMAN

(1975). *The Psychological Birth of the Human Infant*. New York: Basic Books.

PATRICK MAHONY

(1979). The boundaries of free association. *Psychoanalysis and Contemporary Thought, 2*: 151–198.

MARY MAIN, NANCY KAPLAN, & JUDE CASSIDY

(1985). Security of attachment in infancy, childhood, and adulthood. In: I. Bretherton & E. Waters (Eds.), *Growing Points of Attachment Theory and Research*. SRCD Monograph, Vol. 9, No. 6, serial number 209.

NEIL MAIZELS

(1985). Self envy, the womb and the nature of goodness. *International Journal of Psychoanalysis, 66*: 185–192.

GEORGE MAKARI & THEODORE SHAPIRO

(1993). On psychoanalytic listening: language and unconscious communication. *Journal of the American Psychoanalytic Association, 41*: 991–1020.

FRANK MALESON

(1984). Multiple meanings of masochism in psychoanalytic discourse. *Journal of the American Psychoanalytic Association, 32*: 325–356.

HENRY MALLARD

(1987). Ambiguities of self analysis. *Psychoanalytic Quarterly, 56*: 523–527.

JOHN MALTSBERGER & DAN BUIE

(1974). Countertransference hate in the treatment of suicidal patients. *Archives of General Psychiatry, 30*: 625–633.

References

ELI MARCOVITZ

(1966). Discussion of psychodynamics of the depressive character. *Psychoanalytic Forum*, 1: 251–254.

GERALD MARGOLIS

(1966). Secrecy and identity. *International Journal of Psychoanalysis*, 47: 517–522.
(1974). The psychology of keeping secrets. *International Review of Psychoanalysis*, 1: 291–296.

MARVIN MARGOLIS

(1977). A preliminary report of a case of consummated mother–son incest. *Annual of Psychoanalysis*, 5: 267–293.
(1984). A case of mother–adolescent son incest: a follow-up study. *Psychoanalytic Quarterly*, 53: 355–385.
(1991). Parent–child incest: analytic treatment experiences with follow-up data. In: S. Kramer & S. Akhtar (Eds.), *The Trauma of Transgression* (pp. 55–91). Northvale, NJ: Jason Aronson.

PAOLOA MARIOTTI

(1993). The analysts' pregnancy: the patient, the analyst, and the space of the unknown. *International Journal of Psychoanalysis*, 74: 151–164.

JUDD MARMOR

(1953). Orality in the hysterical personality. *Journal of the American Psychoanalysis Association*, 1: 656–671.

KAREN MARODA

(1991). *The Power of Countertransference*. New York: John Wiley.

PETER MARTIN

(1960). On scierneuropsia: a previously unnamed psychogenic visual disturbance. *Journal of the American Psychoanalytic Association*, 8: 71–81.

DIANE MARTINEZ

(1989). Pains and gains: a study of forced terminations. *Journal of the American Psychoanalytic Association*, 37: 89–115.

PIERRE MARTY

(1958). The allergic object relationship. *International Journal of Psychoanalysis*, 39: 98–103.

JEFFEREY MOUSSAIEFF MASSON

(1984). *The Assault on Truth: Freud's Suppression of the Seduction Theory*. New York: Farrar, Straus, and Giroux.

JEFFEREY MOUSSAIEFF MASSON

(1985). (Ed.) *The Complete Letters of Sigmund Freud to Wilhelm Fliess*. Cambridge, MA: Harvard University Press.

JAMES MASTERSON

(1967). *The Psychiatric Dilemma of Adolescence*. Boston, MA: Little, Brown.
(1993). *The Emerging Self: A Developmental, Self, and Object Relations Approach to the Treatment of the Closet Narcissistic Disorder of the Self*. New York: Brunner/Mazel.

DONNA MATHIAS

(2008). The analyst's fears: open scientific meeting, 15 November, 2008. *Newsletter of the Psychoanalytic Society of New England East*, 20: 9–12.

IGNACIO MATTE-BLANCO

(1975). *The Unconscious as Infinite Sets*. London: Duckworth.

JUNQUIERA MATTOS

(1996). Concentrated analysis: a three decades experience. In: *Psychoanalysis and Process: Method, Theory, Applications. Festschrift in Homage to R. Horacio Etchegoyen*. New York: Jason Aronson.

ELIZABETH LLOYD MAYER

(1985). 'Everybody must be just like me': observations on female castration anxiety. *International Journal of Psychoanalysis*, 66: 331–347
(2001). On 'telepathic dreams'?: an unpublished paper by Robert J. Stoller. *Journal of the American Psychoanalytic Association*, 49: 630–657.

References

LINDA MAYES & DONALD COHEN

(1995). Constitution. In: B. Moore & B. Fine (Eds.), *Psychoanalysis The Major Concepts* (pp. 271–292). New Haven, CT: Yale University Press.

ALAN MAYLON

(1982). Psychotherapeutic implications of internalized homophobia in gay men. *Journal of Homosexuality*, 7: 59–70.

VIRGINIA MCDERMOTT

(2003). Panel report: is free association still fundamental? *Journal of the American Psychoanalytic Association*, 51: 1349–1356.

JOHN MCDEVITT

(1983). The emergence of hostile aggression and its defensive and adaptive modification during the separation-individuation process. *Journal of the American Psychoanalytic Association*, 31(Suppl.): 273–300.

MARJORIE MCDONALD

(1970). *Not By the Color of Their Skin*. New York: International Universities Press.

JOYCE MCDOUGALL

(1974). The psychosoma and the psychoanalytic process. *International Review of Psychoanalysis*, 1: 437–459.
(1982). Alexithymia: a psychoanalytic viewpoint. *Psychotherapy and Psychosomatics*, 38: 81–90.
(1989a). *Theaters of the Body: Illusion and Truth on the Psychoanalytic Stage*. New York: W. W. Norton.
(1989b). The dead father. *International Journal of Psychoanalysis*, 70: 205–221.

FRANCIS MCLAUGHLIN

(1959). Problems of reanalysis. *Journal of the American Psychoanalytic Association*, 7: 537–547.

JAMES MCLAUGHLIN

(1975). The sleepy analyst: some observations on states of consciousness in the analyst at work. *Journal of the American Psychoanalytic Association*, 23: 363–382.
(1987). The play of transference: some reflections on enactment in the psychoanalytic situation. *Journal of the American Psychoanalytic Association*, 35: 557–582.
(1992). Non-verbal behaviors in the analytic situation: the search for meaning in non-verbal cues. In: S. Kramer & S. Akhtar (Eds.), *When the Body Speaks: Psychological Meanings in Kinetic Clues* (pp. 131–161). Northvale, NJ: Jason Aronson.

JAMES MCLAUGHLIN & MORTON JOHAN

(1985). Reanalysis. *Journal of the American Psychoanalytic Association*, 33: 187–200.

NABUKO MEADERS.

(1997). The transcultural self. In: P. H. Elovitz & C. Kahn (Eds.), *Immigrant Experiences* (pp. 47–59). Cranbury, NJ: Associated University Presses.

MURRAY MEISELS & ESTHER SHAPIRO

(1990). *Tradition and Innovation in Psychoanalytic Training for Psychologists*. Hillsdale, NJ: Erlbaum.

WILLIAM MEISSNER

(1978). *The Paranoid Process*. New York: Jason Aronson.
(1979). Internalization and object relations. *Journal of the American Psychoanalytic Association*, 27: 345–360.
(1985). Phallic narcissistic personality. *Journal of the American Psychoanalytic Association*, 33: 437–469.
(1992a). Religious thinking as transitional conceptualization. *Psychoanalytic Review*, 79: 175–196.
(1992b). The pathology of belief systems. *Psychoanalysis and Contemporary Thought*, 15: 99–128.
(1992c). The concept of the therapeutic alliance. *Journal of the American Psychoanalytic Association*, 40: 1059–1087.
(2002). The problem of self-disclosure in psychoanalysis. *Journal of the American Psychoanalytic Association*, 50: 827–867.
(2005). On putting a cloud in a bottle: psychoanalytic perspectives on mysticism. *Psychoanalytic Quarterly*, 74: 507–559.

DONALD MELTZER

(1967). *The Psychoanalytical Process*. London: Tavistock.
(1973). *Sexual States of the Mind*. Strath Tay, Perthshire: Clunie Press.
(1975). Adhesive identification. *Contemporary Psychoanalysis*, 11: 289–310.

References

(1976). The delusion of clarity of insight. *International Journal of Psychoanalysis*, 57: 141–146.
(1979). Routine and inspired interpretations. In: L. Epstein & A. H. Feiner (Eds.), *Countertransference* (pp. 129–145). New York: Jason Aronson.

HERMAN MELVILLE.

(1851). *Moby Dick; Or, the Whale*. Berkeley, CA: University of California Press, 1979.

MYER MENDELSON

(1974). *Psychoanalytic Concepts of Depression* (2nd edn). New York: Spectrum Publications.

KARL MENNINGER

(1938). *Man Against Himself*. New York: Harcourt and Brace.
(1941). Some observations on the psychological factors in urination and genito-urinary afflictions. *Psychoanalytic Review*, 28: 91–110.
(1945). *The Human Mind* (3rd edn). New York: Alfred Knopf.
(1959). *A Psychoanalyst's World*. New York: Viking.

KARL MENNINGER & PHILIP HOLZMAN

(1973). *Theory of Psychoanalytic Technique*. New York: Basic Books.

BERNARD MEYER

(1970). *Joseph Conrad: A Psychoanalytic Biography*. Princeton, NJ: Princeton University Press.
(1976). *Houdini: A Mind In Chains: A Psychoanalytic Portrait*. New York: Dutton.

JON MEYER

(1974). Clinical variants among applicants for sex reassignment. *Archives of Sexual Behavior*, 3: 527–558.
(1980a). Psychotherapy in sexual dysfunctions. In: T. Karasu & L. Bellak (Eds.), *Specialized Techniques in Individual Psychotherapy* (pp. 199–219). New York: Brunner/Mazel.
(1980b). Body image, selfness, and gender sense. *Psychiatric Clinics of North America*, 3: 21–36.
(1980c). Paraphilia. In: H. Kaplan, A. Freedman, & B. Sadock (Eds.), *Comprehensive Textbook of Psychiatry* (pp. 1770–1782). Baltimore, MD: Williams and Wilkins Company.
(1982). The theory of gender identity disorders. *Journal of the American Psychoanalytic Association*, 30: 381–418.

HELEN MEYERS

(1988). A consideration of treatment techniques in relation to the functions of masochism. In: R. Glick & D. Meyers (Eds.), *Masochism: Current Psychoanalytic Perspectives* (pp. 175–188). Hillsdale, NJ: The Analytic Press.

PAUL MEYERSON

(1965). Modes of insight. *Journal of the American Psychoanalytic Association*, 13: 771–792.

ROBERT MICHELS

(1995). Medication use during psychoanalysis: a survey. *Journal of Clinical Psychiatry*, 56: 179.
(2003). 'The relationship between psychoanalysis and schizophrenia' by Richard Lucas: a commentary. *International Journal of Psychoanalysis*, 84: 9–12.

IVAN MILAKOVIC

(1967). The hypothesis of a deglutitive (prenatal) stage in libidinal development. *International Journal of Psychoanalysis*, 48: 76–82.

IRA MILLER

(1963). Confrontation, conflict, and the body image. *Journal of the American Psychoanalytic Association*, 11: 66–83.

MILTON MILLER

(1948). Ego functioning in two types of dreams. *Psychoanalytic Quarterly*, 17: 346–355.

STUART MILLER

(1964). The manifest dream and the appearance of color in dreams. *International Journal of Psychoanalysis*, 45: 512–518.

BARBARA MILROD, FRED BUSCH, ARNOLD COOPER, & THEODORE SHAPIRO

(1997). *Manual of Panic-Focused Psychodynamic Psychotherapy*. Washington DC: American Psychiatric Press.

ELIZABETH MINTZ

(1969). Touch and the psychoanalytic tradition. *Psychoanalytic Review*, 56: 365–376.

References

STEPHEN MITCHELL

(1988). *Relational Concepts in Psychoanalysis: An Integration.* Cambridge, MA: Harvard University Press.
(1993). *Hope and Dread in Psychoanalysis.* New York: Basic Books.

STEPHEN MITCHELL & LEWIS ARON

(1999). *Relational Psychoanalysis: The Emergence of a Tradition.* Hillsdale, NJ: Analytic Press.

JUDITH MITRANI

(1994). On adhesive pseudo-object relations. *Contemporary Psychoanalysis, 30*: 348–366.
(2001). *Ordinary People and Extraordinary Protections.* London: Brunner-Routledge.

ARNOLD MODELL

(1963). Primitive object relationships and the predisposition to schizophrenia. *International Journal of Psychoanalysis, 44*: 282–292.
(1965). On aspects of the superego's development. *International Journal of Psychoanalysis, 46*: 323–331.
(1975a). A narcissistic defense against affects and the illusion of self-sufficiency. *International Journal of Psychoanalysis, 56*: 275–282.
(1975b). The ego and the id. *International Journal of Psychoanalysis, 56*: 57–68.
(1976). The holding environment and the therapeutic action of psychoanalysis. *Journal of the American Psychoanalytic Association, 24*: 285–307.
(1981). Does metapsychology still exist? *International Journal of Psychoanalysis, 62*: 391–402.
(1988). Changing psychic structure through treatment: preconditions for the resolution of the transference. *Journal of the American Psychoanalytic Association, 36S*: 225–239.

KATHLEEN MOGUL

(1982). Overview: the sex of the therapist. *American Journal of Psychiatry, 139*: 1–11.

JOHN MONEY & R. GASKIN

(1970). Sex reassignment. *International Journal of Psychiatry, 9*: 249–269.

BURNESS MOORE

(1964). Fridigity: a review of psychoanalytic literature. *Psychoanalytic Quarterly, 33*: 323–371.

BURNESS MOORE & BERNARD FINE

(1968). (Eds.) *A Glossary of Psychoanalytic Terms and Concepts.* New York: American Psychoanalytic Association.
(1990). *Psychoanalytic Terms and Concepts.* New Haven, CT: Yale University Press.
(1995). *Psychoanalysis: The Major Concepts.* New Haven, CT: Yale University Press.

SHOMA MORITA

(1960). *Morita Therapy and the True Nature of Anxiety-Based Disorders (Shinkeishitsu),* A. Kondo (Trans.). Buffalo, NY: State University of New York Press, 1998.

ANDREW MORRISON

(1989). *Shame: The Underside of Narcissism.* Hillsdale, NJ: The Analytic Press.

RENA MOSES-HRUSHOVSKI

(1994). *Deployment: Hiding Behind Power Struggles As a Character Defense.* Northvale, NJ: Jason Aronson.

PAUL MOSHER

(1990). *Title Key Word and Author Index to Psychoanalytic Journals (1920–1990).* New York: The American Psychoanalytic Association.

DONALD MOSS

(1997). On situating homophobia. *Journal of the American Psychoanalytic Association, 45*: 201–215.
(2008). Two readings of Arlow's 'Unconscious fantasy and disturbances of conscious experience': one old and one 'green'. *Psychoanalytic Quarterly, 77*: 61–75.

JOHN MURRAY

(1964). Narcissism and the ego ideal. *Journal of the American Psychoanalytic Association, 12*: 477–511.

WAYNE MYERS

(1977). The significance of the colors black and white in the dreams of black and white patients. *Journal of the American Psychoanalytic Association, 25*: 163–181.

References

PATRICIA NACHMAN

(1991). Contemporary infant research and the separation-individuation theory of Margaret S. Mahler. In: S. Akhtar & H. Parens (Eds.), *Beyond the Symbiotic Orbit: Advances in Separation–Individuation Theory* (pp. 121–149). Hillsdale, NJ: The Analytic Press.

JULIE JAFFE NAGEL

(2008). Psychoanalytic perspectives on music: an intersection on the oral and aural roads. *Psychoanalytic Quarterly*, 77: 507–530.

JULIE JAFFE NAGEL & LOUIS NAGEL

(2005). Animals, music, and psychoanalysis. In: S. Akhtar & V. D. Volkan (Eds.), *Cultural Zoo: Animals in the Human Mind and Its Sublimations* (pp. 145–176). Madison, CT: International Universities Press.

HUMBERTO NAGERA

(1963). The developmental profile: notes on some practical considerations regarding its use. *Psychoanalytic Study of the Child*, 18: 511–540.
(1964). On arrest in development, fixation, and regression. *Psychoanalytic Study of the Child*, 19: 222–239.
(1966). *Early Childhood Disturbances, The Infantile Neurosis, and The Adulthood Disturbances*. New York: International Universities Press.
(1967). *Vincent van Gogh: A Psychological Study*. London: George Allen and Unwin.

ASHOK NAGPAL

(2000). Cultural continuity and change in Kakar's works: some reflections. *International Journal of Group Tensions*, 29: 285–321.

ASHIS NANDY

(2007). *An Ambiguous Journey to the City*. New Delhi: Oxford University Press.

MONISHA NAYAR

(2008). Technical considerations in the psychotherapy of traumatized individuals: a psychoanalytic perspective. *American Journal of Psychoanalysis*, 68: 50–65.

ENRIQUE NEBLETT, JR, NICOLE SHELTON, & ROBERT SELLERS

(2004). The role of racial identity in managing daily racial hassles. In: G. Philogene (Ed.), *Racial Identity in Context: The Legacy of Kenneth B. Clark*. Washington, DC: American Psychological Association.

WILLIAM NEEDLES

(1966). The defilement complex: a contribution to psychic consequences of the anatomical distinction between the sexes. *Journal of the American Psychoanalytic Association*, 14: 700–710.

JOHN NEMIAH & PETER SIFNEOS

(1970). *Modern Trends in Psychosomatic Medicine, Volume 2*. London: Butterworth.

EDWARD NERSESSIAN & RICHARD KOPFF

(1996). *Textbook of Psychoanalysis*. Washington, DC: The American Psychiatric Press.

PETER NEUBAUER

(1983). The importance of the sibling experience. *Psychoanalytic Study of the Child*, 38: 325–336.

M. NG

(1985). Psychoanalysis for the Chinese: applicable or not applicable? *International Review of Psychoanalysis*, 12: 449–460.

ARMAND NICHOLI, JR

(2002). *The Question of God: C. S. Lewis and Sigmund Freud Debate God, Love, Sex, and the Meaning of Life*. New York: The Free Press.

DAVID NICHOL

(2006). Buddhism and psychoanalysis: a personal reflection. *American Journal of Psychoanalysis*, 66: 157–172.

WILLIAM NIEDERLAND

(1965). Narcissistic ego impairment in patients with early physical malformations. *Psychoanalytic Study of the Child*, 20: 518–534.
(1968). Clinical observations on the 'survivor syndrome'. *International Journal of Psychoanalysis*, 49: 313–315.

MALKAH NOTMAN

(1984). Psychiatric disorders of menopause. *Psychiatric Annals, 14*: 448–453.

JACK NOVICK

(1980). Negative therapeutic motivation and negative therapeutic alliance. *Psychoanalytic Study of the Child, 35*: 299–320.
(1988). The timing of termination. *International Review of Psychoanalysis, 15*: 307–318.

JACK NOVICK & KERRY KELLY NOVICK

(1970). Projection and externalization. *Psychoanalytic Study of the Child, 25*: 69–75.
(1994). Postoedipal transformations: latency, adolescence, and pathogenesis. *Journal of the American Psychoanalytic Association, 42*: 143–169.
(2000). Love in the therapeutic alliance. *Journal of the American Psychoanalytic Association, 48*: 189–218.
(2006). *Good Goodbyes: Knowing How to End in Psychotherapy and Psychoanalysis.* Lanham, MD: Jason Aronson.

ERIC NUETZEL

(2003). Idiodynamics and psychoanalysis. *Journal of Applied Psychoanalytic Studies, 5*: 395–404.

HERMAN NUNBERG

(1926). The will to recovery. *International Journal of Psychoanalysis, 7*: 64–78.
(1931). The synthetic function of the ego. *International Journal of Psychoanalysis, 12*: 123–140.

CLARENCE OBERNDORF

(1941). Co-conscious mentation. *Psychoanalytic Quarterly, 10*: 44–65.

HONEY OBEROI

(2009). *Lives in Exile: Exploring the World of Tibetan Refugees.* New Delhi: Routledge.

DANIEL OFFER

(1969). *The Psychological World of the Teenager.* New York: Basic Books.
(1971). Rebellion and antisocial behaviour. *American Journal of Psychoanalysis, 31*: 13–19.

DANIEL OFFER & MELVIN SABSHIN

(1974). *Normality: Theoretical and Clinical Concepts of Mental Health.* New York: Basic Books.

THOMAS OGDEN

(1986). *The Matrix of the Mind: Object Relations and the Psychoanalytic Dialogue.* Northvale, NJ: Jason Aronson.
(1989). On the concept of an autistic–contiguous position. *International Journal of Psychoanalysis, 70*: 127–140.
(1994). *Subjects of Analysis.* Northvale, NJ: Jason Aronson.
(1996). Reconsidering three aspects of psychoanalytic technique. *International Journal of Psychoanalysis, 77*: 883–899.

CHRISTINE OLDEN

(1943). The psychology of obstinacy. *Psychoanalytic Quarterly, 12*: 240–255.
(1946). Headline intelligence. *Psychoanalytic Study of the Child, 2*: 263–269.

WENDY OLESKER

(2006). Thoughts on medication and psychoanalysis: a lay analyst's view. *Journal of the American Psychoanalytic Association, 54*: 763–779.

STANLEY OLINICK

(1954). Some considerations of the use of questioning as a psychoanalytic technique. *Journal of the American Psychoanalytic Association, 2*: 57–66.
(1969). On empathy and regression in the service of the other. *British Journal of Medical Psychology, 42*: 41–49.
(1976). Parallel analyzing functions in work ego and observing ego. *Journal of the Philadelphia Association for Psychoanalysis, 3*: 3–21.

STANLEY OLINICK, WARREN POLAND, KENNETH GRIGG, & WILLIAM GRANATIR

(1973). The psychoanalytic work ego: process and interpretation. *International Journal of Psychoanalysis, 54*: 143–151.

PETER OLSSON

(2007). *The Cult of Osama: Psychoanalyzing Bin Laden and His Magnetism for Muslim Youth.* New York: Praeger.

References

MARY KAY O'NEIL & SALMAN AKHTAR

(2008). (Eds.) *On Freud's* The Future of an Illusion. London: Karnac.

BARRY OPATOW

(1997). The real unconscious: psychoanalysis as a theory of consciousness. *Journal of the American Psychoanalytic Association*, 45: 865–890.

JEROME OREMLAND

(1973). Specific dreams during the termination phase. *Journal of the American Psychoanalytic Association*, 21: 285–311.

SHELLY ORGEL

(1974). Fusion with the victim and suicide. *International Journal of Psychoanalysis*, 55: 531–541.

ANNA ORNSTEIN

(1974). The dread to repeat and the new beginning: a contribution to the psychoanalysis of the narcissistic personality disorders. *The Annual of Psychoanalysis*, 2: 231–248.
(1985). Survival and recovery. *Psychoanalytic Inquiry*, 5: 99–130.

PAUL ORNSTEIN & ANNA ORNSTEIN

(1980). Formulating interpretations in clinical psychoanalysis. *Journal of the International Psychoanalytic Association*, 61: 203–211.

DARIUS ORNSTON

(1985). The invention of 'cathexis' and Strachey's strategy. *International Review of Psychoanalysis*, 12: 401–410.

DOUGLAS ORR

(1942). Is there a homeostatic instinct? *Psychoanalytic Quarterly*, 11: 322–335.

EDNA O'SHAUGHNESSY

(1990). Can a liar be psychoanalyzed? *International Journal of Psychoanalysis*, 71: 187–196.

MORTIMER OSTOW

(1962). *Drugs in Psychoanalysis and Psychotherapy*. New York: Basic Books.
(1967). The syndrome of narcissistic tranquility. *International Journal of Psychoanalysis*, 48: 573–583.
(1995). *Ultimate Intimacy, The Psychodynamics of Jewish Mysticism*. Madison, CT: International Universities Press.
(2001). Three archaic contributions to the religious instinct: awe, mysticism, and apocalypse. In: S. Akhtar & H. Parens (Eds.), *Does God Help? Developmental and Clinical Aspects of Religious Belief* (pp. 197–233). Northvale, NJ: Jason Aronson.

LIONEL OVESSEY

(1969). *Homosexuality and Pseudohomosexuality*. New York: Science House.

LIONEL OVESSEY & ETHEL PERSON

(1973). Gender identity and sexual psychopathology in men: a psychodynamic analysis of homosexuality, transsexualism, and transvestism. *Journal of the American Academy of Psychoanalysis*, 1: 53–72.

BERNARD PACELLA

(1980). The primal matrix configuration. In: R. Lax, S. Bach, & J. A. Burland (Eds.), *Rapprochement: The Critical Subphase of Separation–Individuation* (pp. 117-131). New York: Jason Aronson.

REGINA PALLY

(2000). Introduction. In: *Mind–Brain Relationship* (pp. v–vi). London: Karnac.

STANLEY PALOMBO

(1984). Deconstructing the manifest dream. *Journal of the American Psychoanalytic Association*, 32: 405–420.

CECILIO PANIAGUA

(1985). A methodological approach to surface material. *International Review of Psychoanalysis*, 12: 311–325.
(1997). Negative acting in. *Journal of the American Psychoanalytic Association*, 45: 1209–1223.
(1998). Acting-in revisited. *International Journal of Psychoanalysis*, 79: 499–512.

PING-NE PAO

(1965). The role of hatred in the ego. *Psychoanalytic Quarterly*, 434: 257–264.

(1977). On the formation of schizophrenic symptoms. *International Journal of Psychoanalysis, 58*: 389–401.

(1979). *Schizophrenic Disorders: Theory and Treatment from a Psychodynamic Point of View.* New York: International Universities Press.

HENRI PARENS

(1970). Inner sustainment: metapsychological considerations. *Psychoanalytic Quarterly, 39*: 223–239.

(1979). Developmental considerations of ambivalence—part 2 of an exploration of the relations of instinctual drives and the symbiosis-separation-individuation process. *Psychoanalytic Study of the Child, 34*: 385–420.

(1989). Toward an epigenesis of aggression in early childhood. In: S. I. Greenspan & G. H. Pollock (Eds.), *The Course of Life: Volume 2 Early Childhood* (pp. 689–721). New York: International Universities Press.

(1998). The impact of cultural holding environment on psychic development. In: S. Akhtar & S. Kramer (Eds.), *The Colors of Childhood: Separation–Individuation Across Cultural, Racial, and Ethnic Differences* (pp. 199–230). Northvale, NJ: Jason Aronson.

(2004). *Renewal of Life: Healing from the Holocaust.* Rockwell, MD: Schreiber.

(2007a). Toward understanding prejudice: benign and malignant. In: H. Parens, A. Mahfouz, S. W. Twemlow, & D. E. Scharff (Eds.), *The Future of Prejudice: Psychoanalysis and the Prevention of Prejudice* (pp. 21–36). Lanham, MD: Jason Aronson.

(2007b). An autobiographical study of resilience: healing from the Holocaust. In: H. Parens, H. P. Blum, & S. Akhtar (Eds.), *The Unbroken Soul: Tragedy, Trauma, and Resilience* (pp. 85–116). Lanham, MD: Jason Aronson.

HENRI PARENS & LEON SAUL

(1971). *Dependence in Man: A Psychoanalytic Study.* New York: International Universities Press.

HENRI PARENS, AFAF MAHFOUZ, STUART TWEMLOW, & DAVID SCHARFF

(2007). *The Future of Prejudice: Psychoanalysis and the Prevention of Prejudice.* Lanham, MD: Jason Aronson.

HENRI PARENS, ELIZABETH SCATTERGOOD, WILLIAM SINGLETARY, & ANDRINA DUFF

(1987). *Aggression in Our Children: Coping With It Constructively.* Northvale, NJ: Jason Aronson.

HENRI PARENS, HAROLD BLUM, & SALMAN AKHTAR

(2008). *The Unbroken Soul: Tragedy, Trauma, and Resilience.* Lanham, MD: Jason Aronson.

HENRI PARENS, LEAFY POLLOCK, JOAN STERN, & SELMA KRAMER

(1976). On girls' entry into oedipus complex. *Journal of the American Psychoanalytic Association, 24*(Suppl): 79–107.

COLIN PARKES

(1972). *Bereavement: Studies of Grief in Adult Life.* New York: International Universities Press.

MICHAEL PARSONS

(2000). *The Dove that Returns, The Dove that Vanishes: Paradox and Creativity in Psychoanalysis.* London: Routledge.

GERALD PEARSON

(1966). The importance of peer relationships in the latency period. *Bulletin of the Philadelphia Association for Psychoanalysis, 16*: 109–121.

MARY JO PEEBLES-KLEIGER, LEONARD HORWITZ, JAMES KLEIGER, & RICHARD WAUGAMAN

(2006). Psychological testing and analyzability: bringing new life to an old issue. *Psychoanalytic Psychology, 23*: 504–526.

LILLI PELLER

(1958). Reading and daydreams in latency: boy–girl differences. *Journal of the American Psychoanalytic Association, 6*: 57–70.

LINDA PENN

(1986). The pregnant therapist: transference and countertransference issues. In: J. Alpert (Ed.), *Psychoanalysis and Women* (pp. 287–315). Hillsdale, NJ: Analytic Press.

ROSEMARIE PEREZ-FOSTER, MICHAEL MOSKOWITZ, & RAFAEL JAVIER

(1996). *Reaching Across Boundaries of Culture and Class.* Northvale, NJ: Jason Aronson.

FREDERICO PERIERA & DAVID SCHARFF

(2002). *Fairbairn and Relational Theory.* London: Karnac.

References

ETHEL PERSON

(1976). Initiation fantasies and transvestitism: discussion. *Journal of the American Psychoanalytic Association, 24*: 547–551.

(2001). Knowledge and authority: the Godfather fantasy. *Journal of the American Psychoanalytic Association, 49*: 1133–1155.

ETHEL PERSON & LIONEL OVESSEY

(1974a). The transsexual syndrome in males I: primary transsexualism. *American Journal of Psychotherapy, 28*: 4–20.

(1974b). The transsexual syndrome in males II: secondary transsexualism. *American Journal of Psychotherapy, 28*: 174–193.

ETHEL PERSON, ARNOLD COOPER, & GLEN GABBARD

(2005). (Eds.) *American Psychiatric Publishing Textbook of Psychoanalysis*. Washington, DC: American Psychiatric Press.

BRADLEY PETERSON

(2002). Indeterminacy and compromise formation. *International Journal of Psychoanalysis, 83*: 1017–1035.

ERIC PFEIFFER

(1974). Borderline states. *Diseases of the Nervous System, 35*: 212–219.

RICHARD PHILLIPS

(1960). The nature and function of children's formal games. *Psychoanalytic Quarterly, 29*: 200–209.

SIDNEY PHILLIPS

(2001). The overstimulation of everyday life: I. new aspects of male homosexuality. *Journal of the American Psychoanalytic Association, 49*: 1195–1219.

JEAN PIAGET

(1937). *The Construction of Reality in the Child*. New York: Basic Books.

FRED PINE

(1979). The separation–individuation process. *International Journal of Psychoanalysis, 60*: 225–242.

(1987). *Developmental Theory and Clinical Process*. New Haven, CT: Yale University Press.

(1988). The four psychologies of psychoanalysis and their place in clinical work. *Journal of the American Psychoanalytic Association, 36*: 671–596.

(1995). On the origin and evolution of a species of hate: a clinical–literary excursion. In: S. Akhtar, S. Kramer & H. Parens (Eds.), *The Birth of Hatred: Developmental, Clinical, and Technical Aspects of Intense Aggression* (pp. 103–132). Northvale, NJ: Jason Aronson.

(1997). *Diversity and Direction in Psychoanalytic Technique*. New Haven, CT: Yale University Press.

(2005). Motivational theories in psychoanalysis. In: E. Person, A. Cooper & G. Gabbard (Eds.), *American Psychiatric Publishing Textbook of Psychoanalysis* (pp.3–20). Washington, DC: American Psychiatric Press.

MALCOLM PINES

(1984). Reflections on mirroring. *International Review of Psychoanalysis, 11*: 27–42.

HAROLD PINTER

(1975). *No Man's Land*. New York: Grove Press.

ALESSANDRA PIONTELLI

(1987). Infant observation from before birth. *International Journal of Psychoanalysis, 68*: 453–463.

(1988). Prenatal life reflected in the analysis of a psychotic girl at age two. *International Review of Psychoanalysis, 15*: 73–81.

(1992). *From Fetus to Child: An Observational and Psychoanalytic Study*. London: Routledge.

FRIEDA PLOTKIN

(2000). Treatment of the older adult. *Journal of the American Psychoanalytic Association, 48*: 1591–1616.

WARREN POLAND

(1975). Tact as a psychoanalytic function. *International Journal of Psychoanalysis, 56*: 155–161.

(1977). Pilgrimage, action, and tradition in self-analysis. *Journal of the American Psychoanalytic Association, 25*: 399–416.

(1988). Insight and the analytic dyad. *Psychoanalytic Quarterly, 57*: 341–369.

(1990). The gift of laughter: on the development of a sense of humor in clinical analysis. *Psychoanalytic Quarterly,* *59*: 197–225.

(2000). The analyst's witnessing and otherness. *Journal of the American Psychoanalytic Association, 48*: 17–34.

(2002a). On immediacy: 'vivid contrast between past and present'. *Psychoanalytic Quarterly, 71*: 113–115.

(2002b). The interpretive attitude. *Journal of the American Psychoanalytic Association, 50*: 807–826.

GEORGE POLLOCK

(1961). Mourning and adaptation. *International Journal of Psychoanalysis, 42*: 341–361.

(1970). Anniversary reactions, trauma, and mourning. *Psychoanalytic Quarterly, 39*: 347–371.

(1971). Temporal anniversary manifestations: hour, day, holiday. *Psychoanalytic Quarterly, 40*: 123–131.

(1980). Dying: a psychoanalytic study with special reference to individual creativity and defensive organization. *Psychoanalytic Quarterly, 49*: 704–706.

(1989). On migration: voluntary and coerced. *Annual of Psychoanalysis, 17*: 145–158.

ANNA POTAMIANOU

(1992). *Un bouclier dans l'economie des etats l'espoir.* Paris: Presses Universitaires de France.

E. POZNANSKI

(1972). The 'replacement child': a saga of unresolved parental grief. *Behavioral Pediatrics, 81*: 1190–1193.

SUDHA PRATHIKANTI

(1997). East Indian American families. In: E. Lee (Ed.), *Working with Asian Americans: A Guide to Clinicians* (pp. 79–100). New York: Guilford Press.

KARL PRIBRAM & MERTON GILL

(1976). *Freud's 'Project' Reassessed.* New York: Basic Books.

MORTON PRINCE

(1929). *The Unconscious.* New York: Macmillan.

WARREN PROCCI

(1987). Mockery through caricature: a variant of introjection utilized by a masochistic woman. *Journal of American Academy of Psychoanalysis, 15*: 51–66.

(2000). Panel report: clinical and theoretical uses of bi-logic. *International Journal of Psychoanalysis, 81*: 571–574.

SALLY PROVENCE & ALBERT SOLNIT

(1983). Development-promoting aspects of the sibling experience: vicarious mastery. *Psychoanalytic Study of the Child, 38*: 337–351.

KYLE PRUETT

(1988) *The Nurturing Father.* New York: Grand Central.

(2000). *Father Need: Why Father Care Is As Essential as Mother Care for Your Child.* New York: Free Press.

SYDNEY PULVER

(1970). Narcissism: the term and the concept. *Journal of the American Psychoanalytic Association, 52*: 347–354.

(1971). Can affects be unconscious? *International Journal of Psychoanalysis, 52*: 347–354.

(1974). Unconscious versus potential affects. *Psychoanalytic Quarterly, 43*: 77–84.

(1987). The manifest dream in psychoanalysis: a clarification. *Journal of the American Psychoanalytic Association, 35*: 99–116.

(1991). Termination and separation–individuation. In: S. Akhtar & H. Parens (Eds.), *Beyond the Symbiotic Orbit: Advances in Separation–Individuation Therapy* (pp. 389–404). Hillsdale, NJ: Analytic Press.

(1995). Symptomatology. In: B. E. Moore & B. D. Fine (Eds.), *Psychoanalysis: The Major Concepts* (pp. 186–195). New Haven, CT: Yale University Press.

(2003). On the astonishing clinical irrelevance of neuroscience. *Journal of the American Psychoanalytic Association, 51*: 755–772.

MARIO PUZO

(1969). *The Godfather.* New York: G. P. Putnam's Sons.

JEAN-MICHEL QUINODOZ

(1989). Female homosexual patients in psychoanalysis. *International Journal of Psychoanalysis, 70*: 55–63.

MOISES RABIH

(1981). La seudoalianza terapeutica. *Psicoanalisis, 3*: 169–191.

References

ARNOLD RACHMAN

(1993). Ferenczi and sexuality. In: L. Aron & A. Harris (Eds.), *The Legacy of Sandor Ferenczi* (pp. 81–100. Hillsdale, NJ: Analytic Press.

HENRICH RACKER

(1953). A contribution to the problem of countertransference. *International Journal of Psychoanalysis, 34*: 313–324.
(1957). The meanings and uses of countertransference. *Psychoanalytic Quarterly, 26*: 303–357.
(1958). Psychoanalytic technique and the analyst's unconscious masochism. *Psychoanalytic Quarterly, 37*: 555–562.
(1968). *Transference and counter-transference*. New York: International Universities Press.

SANDOR RADO

(1925). The economic principle in psycho-analytic technique. *International Journal of Psychoanalysis, 6*: 35–44.
(1926). The psychic effects of intoxicants: an attempt to evolve a psychoanalytical theory of morbid cravings. *International Journal of Psychoanalysis, 7*: 396–413.
(1928). The problem of melancholia. *International Journal of Psychoanalysis, 9*: 420–438.
(1933). The psychoanalysis of pharmacothymia (drug addiction). *Psychoanalytic Quarterly, 2*: 1–23.
(1942). Pathodynamics and treatment of traumatic war neuroses (traumatophobia). *Psychosomatic Medicine, 4*: 11–20.

ISHAK RAMZY

(1963). The role of plurality in psychoanalysis. *International Journal of Psychoanalysis, 44*: 444–453.

ISHAK RAMZY & HOWARD SHEVRIN

(1976). The nature of the inference process in psychoanalytic interpretation: a critical review of the literature. *International Journal of Psychoanalysis, 57*: 151–159.

LEO RANGELL

(1954). Similarities and differences between psychoanalysis and dynamic psychotherapy. *Journal of the American Psychoanalytic Association, 2*: 734–744.
(1959). The nature of conversion. *Journal of the American Psychoanalytic Association, 7*: 632–662.
(1963a). The scope of intrapsychic conflict: microscopic and macroscopic considerations. *Psychoanalytic Study of the Child, 18*: 75–102.
(1963b). On friendship. *Journal of the American Psychoanalytic Association, 11*: 3–54.
(1966). An overview of the ending of an analysis. In: R. Litman (Ed.), *Psychoanalysis in the Americas* (pp. 7–33). New York: International Universities Press.
(1969). Choice conflict and the decision-making function of the ego. *International Journal of Psychoanalysis, 50*: 599–602.
(1974). A psychoanalytic perspective leading currently to the syndrome of the compromise of integrity. *International Journal of Psychoanalysis, 55*: 3–12.
(1978). On understanding and treating anxiety and its derivatives. *International Journal of Psychoanalysis, 59*: 229–236.
(1981). Psychoanalysis and dynamic psychotherapy: similarities and differences twenty-five years later. *Psychoanalytic Quarterly, 50*: 665–693.
(1983). Defense and resistance in psychoanalysis and life. *Journal of the American Psychoanalytic Association, 31*(Suppl.): 147–174.
(1987). A core process in psychoanalytic treatment. *Psychoanalytic Quarterly, 56*: 222–249.
(1988). The future of psychoanalysis: the scientific crossroads. *Psychoanalytic Quarterly, 57*: 313–340.
(1995). Psychoanalytic realities and analytic goal. *International Journal of Psychoanalysis, 76*: 15–18.
(1996). The 'analytic' in psychoanalytic treatment: how analysis works. *Psychoanalytic Inquiry, 16*: 140–166.
(2004). *My Life in Theory*. New York: Other Press.
(2007). *The Road to Unity in Psychoanalytic Theory*. Northvale, NJ: Jason Aronson.

OTTO RANK

(1914). *The Double: A Psychoanalytic Study*. Chapel Hill, NC: University of North Carolina Press, 1971.
(1924). *The Trauma of Birth*. New York: Robert Brunner, 1952.

DWARKANATH RAO

(2005). Manifestations of God in India: a transference patheon. In: S. Akhtar (Ed.), *Freud Along the Ganges: Psychoanalytic Reflections on the People and Culture of India* (pp. 271–308). New York: Other Press.

DAVID RAPHLING

(1989). Fetishism in a woman. *Journal of the American Psychoanalytic Association, 37*: 465–491.

DAVID RAPHLING & JUDITH CHUSED

(1988). Transference across gender lines. *Journal of the American Psychoanalytic Association*, 36: 77–104.

DAVID RAPAPORT

(1951). Paul Schilder's contribution to the theory of thought processes. *International Journal of Psychoanalysis*, 32: 291–301.
(1953a). On the psychoanalytic theory of affects. *International Journal of Psychoanalysis*, 34: 177–198.
(1953b). The psychology of thinking. *Psychoanalytic Quarterly*, 22: 291–295.
(1960). The structure of psychoanalytic theory. *Psychological Issues*, 6: 39–72.
(1974). *The History of the Concept of the Association of Ideas*. New York: International Universities Press.

DAVID RAPAPORT & MERTON GILL

(1959). The points of view and assumptions of metapsychology. *International Journal of Psychoanalysis*, 40: 153–162.

JOAN RAPHAEL-LEFF

(1996). Pregnancy–procreative process, 'the placental paradigm' and perinatal therapy. *Journal of the American Psychoanalytic Association*, 44: 373–399.

ERNEST RAPPAPORT

(1958). The grandparent syndrome. *Psychoanalytic Quarterly*, 37: 518–539.

ERIC RAYNER & GERALD WOOSTER

(1990). Bi-logic in psychoanalysis and other disciplines: an introduction. *International Review of Psychoanalysis*, 17: 425–431.

SATISH REDDY

(2005). Psychoanalytic process in a sacred Hindu text: the *Bhagavad Gita*. In: S. Akhtar (Ed.), *Freud Along the Ganges: Psychoanalytic Reflections on the People and Culture of India* (pp. 309–333). New York: Other Press.

GAIL REED

(1994). *Transference Neurosis and Psychoanalytic Experience*. New Haven, CT: Yale University Press.
(1996). *Clinical Understanding*. Northvale, NJ: Jason Aronson.

ANNIE REICH

(1951). The discussion of 1912 on masturbation and our present day views. *Psychoanalytic Study of the Child*, 6: 80–94.

WILHELM REICH

(1927). Zur technik der deutung und der widerstandsanalyse. *Internationale Zeitschrift fuer Psychoanalyse*, 13: 141–159.
(1933). *Character Analysis*, V. R. Carfagno (Trans.). New York: Farrar, Strauss, and Giroux, 1972.

NORMAN REIDER

(1953). Reconstruction and screen function. *Journal of the American Psychoanalytic Association*, 1: 389–405.

MORTON REISER

(1971). Psychological issues in training for research in psychiatry. *Journal of Psychiatric Review*, 8: 531–537.
(1997). The art and science of dream interpretation. *Journal of the American Psychoanalytic Association*, 45: 891–905.

OWEN RENIK

(1981). Typical examination dreams, superego dreams, and traumatic dreams. *Psychoanalytic Quarterly*, 50: 159–189.
(1984). The clinical use of manifest dream. *Journal of the American Psychoanalytic Association*, 32: 157–162.
(1992). The use of the analyst as a fetish. *Psychoanalytic Quarterly*, 71: 197–204.
(1993). Analytic interaction: conceptualizing technique in light of the analyst's irreducible subjectivity. *Psychoanalytic Quarterly*, 62: 553–571.
(1995). The ideal of the anonymous analyst and the problem of self-disclosure. *Psychoanalytic Quarterly*, 64: 466–495.
(1996). Perils of neutrality. *Psychoanalytic Quarterly*, 65: 495–517.
(1998). Getting real in psychoanalysis. *Psychoanalytic Quarterly*, 67: 566–593.
(1999). Playing with one's cards face up in analysis. *Psychoanalytic Quarterly*, 68: 521–539.
(2006). *Practical Psychoanalysis for Therapists and Patients*. New York: Other Press.

HARVEY RICH

(1985). Psychoanalysis of a depressed woman. In: V. D. Volkan (Ed.), *Depressive States and Their Treatment* (pp. 237–254). Northvale, NJ: Jason Aronson.

References

ARLENE KRAMER RICHARDS

(1981). Self theory, conflict theory, and the problem of hypochrondriasis. *Psychoanalytic Study of the Child, 36*: 319–337.
(1996). Primary femininity and female genital anxiety. *Journal of the American Psychoanalytic Association, 44*(Suppl.): 261–281.

ARNOLD RICHARDS

(1985). Isakower-like experience on the couch: a contribution to the psychoanalytic understanding of regressive ego phenomena. *Psychoanalytic Quarterly, 54*: 415–434.
(1999). A. A. Brill and the politics of exclusion. *Journal of the American Psychoanalytical Association, 47*: 9–28.

JOHN RICKMAN

(1951). Number and the human sciences. *Psychoanalysis and Culture, 4*: 150–155.

SAMUEL RITVO

(1974). Current status of infantile neurosis: implications for diagnosis and technique. *Psychoanalytic Study of the Child, 29*: 159–180.

SAMUEL RITVO & ARTHUR ROSENBAUM

(1983). Reanalysis of child analytic patients. *Journal of the American Psychoanalytic Association, 31*: 677–688.

ANNA MARIE RIZZUTO

(1979). *The Birth of the Living God.* Chicago, IL: University of Chicago Press.
(1996). Psychoanalytic treatment and the religious person. In: E. Sahfranske (Ed.), *Religion and Clinical Practice of Psychology* (pp. 409–432). Washington, DC: American Psychological Association Books.
(2001). Does God help? Would God? Helping whom: the convolutions of divine help. In: S. Akhtar & H. Parens (Eds.), *Does God Help? Developmental and Clinical Aspects of Religious Belief* (pp. 19–51). Northvale, NJ: Jason Aronson.

BERNARD ROBBINS

(1937). Escape into reality: a clinical note on spontaneous social recovery. *Psychoanalytic Quarterly, 6*: 352–364.

MICHAEL ROBBINS

(1993). *The Experience of Schizophrenia: An Integration of the Personal, Scientific, and Therapeutic.* New York: Guildford Press.
(2002a). Psychoanalysis and schizophrenia. *Journal of the American Psychoanalytic Association, 50*: 310–314.
(2002b). The language of schizophrenia and the world of delusion. *International Journal of Psychoanalysis, 83*: 383–405.

RICHARD ROBERTIELLO

(1972). Telephone sessions. *Psychoanalytic Review, 59*: 633–634.

BRIAN ROBERTSON & MARY-ELEANOR YACK

(1993). A candidate dreams of her patient: a report and some observations on the supervisory process. *International Journal of Psychoanalysis, 74*: 993–1003.

GREGORY ROCHLIN

(1959). The loss complex. *Journal of the American Psychoanalytic Association, 7*: 299–316.

CARL ROGERS

(1942). *Counseling and Psychotherapy.* Boston, MA: Houghton Mifflin.

HERMAN ROIPHE

(1976). Book review: *Attachment and Loss, Vol. II: Separation,* by John Bowlby. *Psychoanalytic Quarterly, 45*: 307–309.

ALAN ROLAND

(1988). Indians in America: adaptation and the bicultural self. In: P. H. Elovitz & C. Kahn (Eds.), *Immigrant Experiences: Personal Narrative and Psychological Analysis* (pp. 148–157). Cranbury, NJ: Associated University Presses.
(1996). *Cultural Pluralism and Psychoanalysis: The Asian and North American Experience.* New York: Routledge.

ELSA RONNINGSTAM

(2006). Silence: cultural function and psychological transformation in psychoanalysis and psychoanalytic psychotherapy. *International Journal of Psychoanalysis, 87*: 1277–1296.

STEVEN ROOSE & ROBIN STERN

(1995). Medication use in training cases: a survey. *Journal of the American Psychoanalytic Association*, 43: 163–170.

GILBERT ROSE

(1969). Transference birth fantasies and narcissism. *Journal of the American Psychoanalytic Association*, 17: 1015–1029.
(1996). *Necessary Illusion: Art as Witness*. Madison, CT: International Universities Press.

HELEN ROSEN & ELAINE ZICKLER

(1996). Feminist psychoanalytic theory: American and French reactions to Freud. *Journal of the American Psychoanalytic Association*, 44(suppl): 71–92.

IRWIN ROSEN

(2007). Revenge—the hate that dare not speak its name: a psychoanalytic perspective. *Journal of the American Psychoanalytic Association*, 55: 595–619.
(2009). Relational masochism: the search for a 'bad-enough' object. *Psychoanalytic Inquiry*, 29: (in press).

JOHN ROSEN

(1947). The treatment of schizophrenia by direct analytic therapy. *Psychiatric Quarterly*, 2: 3–13.
(1953). *Direct Analysis*. New York: Grune and Stratton.

JEAN ROSENBAUM

(1961). The significance of the sense of smell in the transference. *Journal of the American Psychoanalytic Association*, 9: 312–324.

DAVID ROSENFELD

(1984). Hypochondriasis, somatic delusion, and body scheme in psychoanalytic practice. *International Journal of Psychoanalysis*, 65: 377–387.

HERBERT ROSENFELD

(1965). *Psychotic States: A Psychoanalytic Approach*. London: Hogarth.
(1971). Theory of life and death instincts: aggressive aspects of narcissism. *International Journal of Psychoanalysis*, 45: 332–337.
(1988). On masochism: a theoretical and clinical approach. In: R. Glick & D. Meyers (Eds.), *Masochism: Current Psychoanalytic Perspectives* (pp. 151–174). Hillsdale, NJ: The Analytic Press.

RICHARD ROSENTHAL

(1988). Transparent screens. *Journal of the American Psychoanalytic Association*, 36: 295–317.

JOHN MUNDER ROSS

(1975). The development of paternal identity: a critical review of the literature on nurturance and generativity in boys and men. *Journal of the American Psychoanalytic Association*, 23: 783–817.
(1979). Fathering: a review of some psychoanalytic contributions on paternity. *International Journal of Psychoanalysis*, 60: 317–327.
(1992). *The Male Paradox*. New York: Simon and Schuster.
(1994). *What Men Want: Mothers, Fathers, and Manhood*. Cambridge, MA: Harvard University Press.
(1996). Male infidelity in long marriages: second adolescences and fourth individuation. In: S. Akhtar & S. Kramer (Eds.), *Intimacy and Infidelity: Separation–Individuation Perspectives* (pp. 107–130). Northvale, NJ: Jason Aronson.
(1999). Psychoanalysis, the anxiety of influence, and the sadomasochism of everyday life. *Journal of Applied Psychoanalytic Studies*, 1: 57–78.
(2003). Preconscious defense analysis, memory, and structural change. *International Journal of Psychoanalysis*, 84: 59–76.

NATHANIEL ROSS

(1959). The face–genital equation. *Psychoanalytic Quarterly*, 28: 493–500.

DAVID ROTH & SIDNEY BLATT

(1974). Spatial representations and psychopathology. *Journal of the American Psychoanalytic Association*, 22: 854–872.

PRISCILLA ROTH

(1994). Being true to a false object: a view of identification. *Psychoanalytic Inquiry*, 14: 393–405.

PRISCILLA ROTH & ALESSANDRA LEMMA

(2008). (Eds.) *Envy and Gratitude Revisited*. London: International Psychoanalytic Association.

References

ARNOLD ROTHSTEIN

(1977). The ego attitude of entitlement. *International Review of Psychoanalysis, 4*: 409–417.
(1980). Toward a critique of the psychology of the self. *Psychoanalytic Quarterly, 49*: 423–455.
(1982). The implications of early psychopathology in the analyzability of narcissistic personality disorders. *International Journal of Psychoanalysis, 63*: 177–188.
(1984). Fear of humiliation. *Journal of the American Psychoanalytic Association, 32*: 99–116.
(1987). *The Interpretation of Dreams in Clinical Work*. New York: International Universities Press.

RALPH ROUGHTON

(2002). Rethinking homosexuality: what it teaches us about psychoanalysis. *Journal of the American Psychoanalytic Association, 50*: 733–763.

JEFFREY RUBIN

(1996). The analyst's authority. *Journal of the American Academy of Psychoanalysis, 24*: 257–283.

PETER RUDNYTSKY

(1988). Redefining the revenant: guilt and sibling loss in Guntrip and Freud. *Psychoanalytic Study of the Child, 43*: 423–432.
(2007). Review of *International Dictionary of Psychoanalysis*, edited by Alain de Mijolla. *Journal of the American Psychoanalytic Association, 55*: 371–379.

HOWARD RUDOMINER

(2002). Consummated mother–son incest in latency: a case report of an adult analysis. *Journal of the American Psychoanalytic Association, 50*: 909–935.

SALMAN RUSHDIE

(1989). *The Satanic Verses*. New York: Viking.

CHARLES RYCROFT

(1951). A contribution to the study of the dream screen. *International Journal of Psychoanalysis, 32*: 178–184.
(1968). *A Critical Dictionary of Psychoanalysis*. London: Penguin Books, 1972.

ANDREA SABBADINI

(2007). *Couch and the Silver Screen*. Philadelphia, PA: Taylor & Francis.

F. SACCO & STUART TWEMLOW

(1997). School violence reduction: a model Jamaican secondary school program. *Community Mental Health Journal, 33*(3): 229–234.

DAVID SACHS

(1977). Panel report: current concepts of normality. *Journal of the American Psychoanalytic Association, 25*: 679–692.

DAVID SACHS & STANLEY SHAPIRO

(1976). On parallel processes in therapy and teaching. *Psychoanalytic Quarterly, 45*: 394–415.

HANS SACHS

(1923). On genesis of sexual perversions. *Internationale Zeitschrift für Psychoanalyse, 9*: 172–182.

LISBETH SACHS

(1973). On crying, weeping, and laughing as defenses against sexual drives, with special consideration of adolescent giggling. *International Journal of Psychoanalysis, 54*: 477–484.

OSCAR SACHS

(1967). Fantasy and reality elements in memory and reconstructions. *International Journal of Psychoanalysis, 48*: 416–426.

J. SADGER

(1910). Ueber urethralerotik. *Jahrbuch fuer Psychoanalytische Forschungen, 2*: 5–15.

DESY SAFRAN-GERARD

(1998). Bearable and unbearable guilt: a Kleinian perspective. *Psychoanalytic Quarterly, 67*: 351–378.

EDWARD SAID

(1978). *Orientalism*. New York: Pantheon.

LOUIS SANDER

(1980). New knowledge about the patient from current research: implications for psychoanalysis. *Journal of the American Psychoanalytic Association*, 28: 181–198.

(1983). Polarity, paradox, and the organizing process of development. In: J. D. Call, E. Galenson, & R. L. Tyson (Eds.), *Frontiers of Infant Psychiatry* (pp. 333–345). New York: Basic Books.

(1988). The event–structure of regulation in the neonate–caregiver system as a biological background for early organization of psychic structure. *Progress in Self Psychology*, 3: 64–77.

JOSEPH SANDLER

(1960). The background of safety. *International Journal of Psychoanalysis*, 41: 352–365.

(1976). Countertransference and role-responsiveness. *International Review of Psychoanalysis*, 3: 43–47.

(1987). Internalization and externalization. In: J. Sandler (Ed.), *Projection, Identification, and Projective Identification* (pp. 101–122). Madison, CT: International Universities Press.

JOSEPH SANDLER & ANNA FREUD

(1983). Discussions in the Hampstead Index of 'The Ego and the Mechanisms of Defense'. *Journal of the Psychoanalytic Association*, 31(Suppl.): 19–146.

JOSEPH SANDLER & ANNE-MARIE SANDLER

(1983). The 'second censorship', the 'three box model' and some technical implications. *International Journal of Psychoanalysis*, 64: 413–425.

(1998). *Internal Objects Re-Visited*. London: Karnac.

JOSEPH SANDLER & BERNARD ROSENBLATT

(1962). Representational world. *Psychoanalytic Study of the Child*, 17: 128–145.

JOSEPH SANDLER & HUMBERTO NAGERA

(1963). Aspects of the metapsychology of fantasy. *Psychoanalytic Study of the Child*, 18: 159–194.

JOSEPH SANDLER & WILLIAM JOFFE

(1969). Towards a basic psychoanalytic model. *International Journal of Psychoanalysis*, 50: 79–90.

JOSEPH SANDLER, ALEX HOLDER, & DALE MEERS

(1963). The ego ideal and the ideal self. *Psychoanalytic Study of the Child*, 18: 139–158.

JOSEPH SANDLER, CHRISTOPHER DARE, & ALEX HOLDER

(1973). *The Patient and the Analyst*. New York: International Universities Press.

CHARLES SARNOFF

(1976). *Latency*. New York: Jason Aronson.

(1987). *Psychotherapeutic Strategies in Latency Years*. New York: Jason Aronson.

LOUIS SASS & ROBERT WOOLFOLK

(1988). Psychoanalysis and the hermeneutic turn: a critique of 'Narrative Truth and Historical Truth'. *Journal of the American Psychoanalytic Association*, 36: 429–454.

LEON SAUL

(1953). The ego in a dream. *Psychoanalytic Quarterly*, 22: 257–258.

(1954). A note on the telephone as a technical aid. *Psychoanalytic Quarterly* 20: 287–290.

(1970). Inner sustainment: the concept. *Psychoanalytic Quarterly*, 39: 215–222.

ROBERT SAVITT

(1969). Transference, somatization, and symbiotic need. *Journal of the American Psychoanalytic Association*, 17: 1030–1053.

JOSEPH SCHACHTER

(1990). Post-termination patient–analyst contact: I. analyst attitudes and experience. *International Journal of Psychoanalysis*, 71: 475–486.

(1992). Concepts of termination and post-termination contact. *International Journal of Psychoanalysis*, 73: 137–154.

References

JOSEPH SCHACHTER & HUGH BUTTS

(1968). Transference and countertransference in interracial analyses. *Journal of the American Psychoanalytic Association*, 16: 792–808.

ROY SCHAFER

(1959). Generative empathy in the treatment situation. *Psychoanalytic Quarterly*, 28: 342–373.
(1960). The loving and beloved superego in Freud's structural theory. *Psychoanalytic Study of the Child*, 15: 163–188.
(1970). The psychoanalytic vision of reality. *International Journal of Psychoanalysis*, 51: 279–297.
(1973a). Concepts of self and identity in relation to separation–individuation. *Psychoanalytic Quarterly*, 42: 42–59.
(1973b). Action: its place in psychoanalytic interpretation and theory. *The Annual of Psychoanalysis*, 1: 159–196.
(1976). *A New Language for Psychoanalysis*. New Haven, CT: Yale University Press.
(1983). *The Analytic Attitude*. London: Karnac.
(2002). Defenses against goodness. *Psychoanalytic Quarterly*, 71: 5–19.
(2005). Cordelia, Lear, and forgiveness. *Journal of the American Psychoanalytic Association*, 53: 389–410.

JILL SCHARFF & DAVID SCHARFF

(2005). *The Primer of Object Relations* (2nd edn). Lanham, MD: Jason Aronson.

PAUL SCHILDER

(1925). *Introduction to Psychoanalytic Psychiatry*. New York: International Universities Press, 1951.
(1938). Personality in formation and action. *International Journal of Psychoanalysis*, 19: 510–511.

HERBERT SCHLESINGER

(1969). Diagnosis and prescription for psychotherapy. *Bulletin of the Menninger Clinic*, 33: 269–278.
(2003). *The Texture of Treatment: On the Matter of Psychoanalytic Technique*. Hillsdale, NJ: Analytic Press.

NATHAN SCHLESSINGER

(1990). A developmental view of converting psychotherapy to psychoanalysis. *Psychoanalytic Inquiry*, 10: 67–87.

NATHAN SCHLESSINGER & FRED ROBBINS

(1974). Assessment and follow-up in psychoanalysis. *Journal of the American Psychoanalytic Association*, 22: 542–567.

CORDELIA SCHMIDT-HELLERAU

(2006a). Surviving in absence: on the preservative and death drives and their clinical utility. *Psychoanalytic Quarterly*, 75: 1057–1095.
(2006b). The role of consciousness in working with trauma: necessary condition or irrelevant distraction. *International Journal of Psychoanalysis*, 87: 559–561.
(2009). 'You've hurt me!': clinical reflections on moral sadism. *Psychoanalytic Quarterly* 78: 233–241.

ANITA SCHMUKLER & EMANUEL GARCIA

(1990). Special symbols in early female development: fantasies of folds and spaces, protuberances, and concavities. *International Journal of Psychoanalysis*, 71: 297–300.

ALLAN SCHORE

(1997). A century after Freud's project: is a rapprochement between psychoanalysis and neurobiology at hand? *Journal of the American Psychoanalytic Association*, 45: 807–840.

JANOS SCHOSSBERGER

(1963). Deanimation: a study of the communication of meaning by transient expressive configuration. *Psychoanalytic Quarterly*, 32: 479–532.

BAS SCHREUDER

(1999). The transitional space between inner and outer world in migration and psychodrama. Paper presented at the Symposium 'Migrants and Refugees: About Mourning, Coping, and Identity', co-sponsored by the Dutch Psychoanalytic Society and PHAROS (The Dutch Mental Health Organization for Migrants and Refugees, Amsterdam, March 23, 1999).

RITA SCHULMAN

(2009). Commentary [on Leo Rangell's paper on 'Friendship']. In: S. Akhtar (Ed.), *Good Feelings: Psychoanalytic Reflections on Positive Attitudes and Emotions* (pp. 267–274). London: Karnac.

MAX SCHUR

(1955). Comments on the metapsychology of somatization. *Psychoanalytic Study of the Child, 10*: 119–164.
(1966). *The Id and the Regulatory Principles of Mental Functioning.* New York: International Universities Press.

EVELYNE SCHWABER

(1983). Psychoanalytic listening and psychic reality. *International Review of Psychoanalysis, 10*: 379–392.
(1986). Reconstruction and perceptual experience: further thoughts on psychoanalytic listening. *Journal of the American Psychoanalytic Association, 34*: 911–932.
(1992). Countertransference: the analyst's retreat from the patient's vantage point. *International Journal of Psychoanalysis, 73*: 349–361.
(1995). A particular perspective on impasses in the clinical situation: further reflections on analytic listening. *International Journal of Psychoanalysis, 76*: 711–722.
(1996). Toward a definition of the term and concept of interaction: its reflection in analytic listening. *Psychoanalytic Inquiry, 16*: 5–24.
(1998). From whose point of view? A neglected question in analytic listening. *Psychoanalytic Quarterly, 67*: 645–661.
(2005). Pleasures of mind. *Journal of the American Psychoanalytic Association, 53*: 427–435.
(2007). The unending struggle to listen: locating one's self within the other. In: S. Akhtar (Ed.), *Listening to Others: Developmental and Clinical Aspects of Empathy and Attunement* (pp. 17–40). Lanham, MD: Jason Aronson.

HARVEY SCHWARTZ

(1984). (Ed.) *Psychotherapy of the Combat Veteran.* New York: Springer.
(1986). Bulimia: psychoanalytic perspectives. *Journal of the American Psychoanalytic Association, 34*: 439–462.
(1987). Illness in the doctor: implications for the psychoanalytic process. *Journal of the American Psychoanalytic Association, 35*: 657–692.

HARVEY SCHWARTZ & ANN-LOUISE SILVER (Eds.)

(1990). *Illness in the Analyst: Implications for the Treatment Relationship.* New York: International Universities Press.

GENE SCHWARZ

(1980). Forced termination of analysis revisited. *International Review of Psychoanalysis, 1*: 282–290.

HAROLD SEARLES

(1955). The informational value of the supervisor's emotional experiences. *Psychoanalytic Quarterly, 65*: 394–415.
(1960). *The Non-Human Environment in Normal Development and Schizophrenia.* New York: International Universities Press.
(1962). The differentiation between concrete and metaphorical thinking in the recovering schizophrenic patient. *Journal of the American Psychoanalytic Association, 10*: 22–49.
(1965). *Collected Papers on Schizophrenia and Related Subjects.* New York: International Universities Press.
(1977). The development of mature hope in the patient-therapist relationship. In: *Countertransference and Related Subjects: Selected Papers* (pp. 479–502). New York: International Universities Press, 1979.
(1979). The analyst's experience with jealousy. In: L. Epstein & A. H. Feiner (Eds.), *Countertransference* (pp. 305–327). New York: Jason Aronson.
(1986). *My Work with Borderline Patients.* Northvale, NJ: Jason Aronson.

BETH SEELIG

(1993). Panel report: the analytic surface. *Journal of the American Psychoanalytic Association, 41*: 179–190.

BETH SEELIG & LISA ROSOF

(2001). Normal and pathological altruism. *Journal of the American Psychoanalytic Association, 49*: 933–959.

HANNA SEGAL

(1950). Some aspects of the analysis of a schizophrenic. *International Journal of Psychoanalysis, 31*: 268–278.
(1956). Depression in the schizophrenic. *International Journal of Psychoanalysis, 28*: 139–145.
(1957). Notes on symbol formation. *International Journal of Psychoanalysis, 39*: 391–397.
(1974). *Introduction to the Work of Melanie Klein.* New York: Basic Books.
(1981). Manic reparation. In: *The Work of Hanna Segal* (pp. 147–158). New York: Jason Aronson.

NATHAN SEGAL

(1969). Repetition, acting out, and identification with the doer. *Journal of the American Psychoanalytic Association, 17*: 474–488.

References

CALVIN SETTLAGE

(1989). The interplay of therapeutic and developmental process in the treatment of children: an application of con-temporary object relations theory. *Psychoanalytic Inquiry*, 9: 375–396.
(1993). Therapeutic process and developmental process in the restructuring of object and self constancy. *Journal of the American Psychoanalytic Association*, 41: 473–492.
(1996). Transcending old age: creativity, development, and psychoanalysis in the life of a centenarian. *International Journal of Psychoanalysis*, 77: 549–564.
(2001). Defenses evoked by early childhood loss: their impact on life-span development. In: S. Akhtar (Ed.), *Three Faces of Mourning: Melancholia, Manic Defense, and Moving On* (pp. 47–93). Northvale, NJ: Jason Aronson.

MOHAMMAD SHAFII

(1973). Silence in the service of ego: psychoanalytic study of meditation. *International Journal of Psychoanalysis*, 54: 431–443.

MORTON SHANE & ESTELLE SHANE

(1984). The end phase of analysis. *Journal of the American Psychoanalytic Association*, 32: 739–772.

BARBARA SHAPIRO

(1999). Sibling rivalry: a phenomenon of construction and deconstruction. In: S. Akhtar & S. Kramer (Eds.), *Brothers and Sisters: Developmental, Dynamic, and Technical Aspects of the Sibling Relationship* (pp. 135–158). Lanham, MD: Jason Aronson.
(2003). Building bridges between body and mind: the analysis of an adolescent with paralyzing chronic pain. *International Journal of Psychoanalysis*, 84: 547–561.

DAVID SHAPIRO

(1965). *Neurotic Styles*. New York: Basic Books.

EDITH SHAPIRO & HENRY PINSKER

(1973). Shared ethnic scotoma. *American Journal of Psychiatry*, 130: 1338–1341.

THEODORE SHAPIRO

(1970). Interpretation and naming. *Journal of the American Psychoanalytic Association*, 18: 399–421.
(1979). *Clinical Psycholinguistics*. New York: Plenum Press.
(1984). On neutrality. *Journal of the American Psychoanalytic Association*, 32: 269–282.
(1990). Unconscious fantasy: introduction. *Journal of the American Psychoanalytic Association*, 37: 38–46.
(2008). Masturbation, sexuality, and adaptation: normalization in adolescence. *Journal of the American Psychoanalytic Association*, 56: 123–146.

ISAIAH SHARE, SHIRLEY RASHKIS, & BERTRAM RUTTENBERG

(1995). A developmental approach to narcissism. In: T. B. Cohen, M. H. Etezady, & B. L. Pacella (Eds.), *The Vulnerable Child, Volume 2* (pp. 11–23). Madison, CT: International Universities Press.

ELLA FREEMAN SHARPE

(1930). The technique of psycho-analysis: survey of defence mechanisms in general character traits and in conduct. *International Journal of Psychoanalysis*, 11: 361–386.
(1931). The technique of psycho-analysis: anxiety-outbreak and resolution. International *Journal of Psychoanalysis*, 12: 24-60.
(1949). *Dream Analysis*. London: Hogarth.

SHEILA SHARPE & ALLAN ROSENBLATT

(1994). Oedipal sibling triangles. *Journal of the American Psychoanalytic Association*, 42: 491–523.

LEONARD SHENGOLD

(1975). Soul murder. *International Journal of Psychoanalytic Psychotherapy*, 3: 366–373.
(1989). *Soul Murder: The Affects of Childhood Abuse and Deprivation*. New Haven, CT: Yale University Press.
(1980). Some reflections on a case of mother–adolescent son incest. *International Journal of Psychoanalysis*, 61: 461–476.
(1985). Defensive anality and anal narcissism. *International Journal of Psychoanalysis*, 66: 47–75.
(1988). *Halo in the Sky*. New York: Guilford Press.
(1991). A variety of narcissistic pathology stemming from parental weakness. *Psychoanalytic Quarterly*, 60: 86–92.

ROBERT SHIELDS

(1964). The 'too good' mother. *International Journal of Psychoanalysis*, 45: 85–88.

MERTON SHILL

(2004). Analytic neutrality, anonymity, abstinence, and elective self-disclosure. *Journal of the American Psychoanalytic Association*, 52: 151–187.

MOISY SHOPPER

(1974). Twinning reaction in non-twin siblings. *Journal of the American Academy of Child and Adolescent Psychiatry*, 13: 300–318.

SHAHRZAD SIASSI

(2000). Male patient–female analyst: elucidation of a controversy. *Journal of Clinical Psychoanalysis*, 9(1): 93–112.
(2004). Transcending bitterness and early paternal loss through mourning and forgiveness. *Psychoanalytic Quarterly*, 73: 915–937.
(2007). Forgiveness, acceptance, and a matter of expectation . *International Journal of Psychoanalysis*, 88: 1423–1240.

ALFRED SIEGMAN

(1954). Emotionality: a hysterical character defense. *Psychoanalytic Quarterly*, 23: 339–354.

PETER SIFNEOS

(1975). Problems of psychotherapy of patients with alexithymic characteristics and physical disease. *Psychotherapy and Psychosomatics*, 26: 65–70.

AUSTIN SILBER

(1970). Functional phenomenon: historical concept, contemporary defense. *Journal of the American Psychoanalytic Association*, 18: 519–538.
(1973). Secondary revision, secondary elaboration, and ego synthesis. *International Journal of Psychoanalysis*, 54: 161–168.
(1979). Childhood seduction, parental pathology, and hysterical symptomatology. *International Journal of Psychoanalysis*, 60: 109–116.
(1983). A significant 'dream within a dream'. *Journal of the American Psychological Association*, 31: 899–915.

HERBERT SILBERER

(1909a). Report on method of eliciting and observing certain symbolic hallucination-phenomena. In: D. Rapaport (Ed.), *Organization and Pathology of Thought* (pp. 208–233). New York: Columbia University Press, 1951.
(1909b). Zur Symboldindung. *Jahrbuch der Psychoanalyse*, 4: 610–615.
(1914). *Problem der Mystik und ihrer Symbolik*. Leipzig: Hugo Heller.

ISIDOR SILBERMANN

(1961). Synthesis and fragmentation. *Psychoanalytic Study of the Child*, 16: 90–117.

JOAN SILK

(1998). Making amends: adaptive perspectives on conflict remediation in monkeys, apes, and humans. *Human Nature*, 9: 341–368.

WILLIAM SILVERBERG

(1948). The concept of transference. *Psychoanalytic Quarterly*, 17: 304–321.

MARTIN SILVERMAN

(1985). Countertransference and the myth of the perfectly analyzed analyst. *Psychoanalytic Quarterly*, 54: 175–199.

ERNEST SIMMEL

(1925). A screen memory in statu nascendi. *International Journal of Psychoanalysis*, 6: 454–457.
(1948). Alcoholism and addiction. *Psychoanalytic Quarterly*, 17: 6–31.

JOSEPH SIMO

(1983). On Christianity and the oedipal winner. *Psychoanalytic Review*, 70: 321–329.

BENNETT SIMON

(1981). Confluence of visual image between patient and analyst: communication of failed communication. *Psychoanalytic Inquiry*, 1: 471–488.

MELVIN SINGER

(1977a). The experience of emptiness in narcissistic and borderline states: deficiency and ego defect versus dynamic–defensive models. *International Review of Psychoanalysis*, 4: 459–470.

References

(1977b). The experience of emptiness in narcissistic and borderline states: the struggle for a sense of self and the potential for suicide. *International Review of Psychoanalysis*, 4: 471–479.

(1988). Fantasy or structural defect? The borderline dilemma as viewed from analysis of an experience of nonhumanness. *Journal of the American Psychoanalytic Association*, 36: 31–59.

DIANA SISKIND

(1997). *Working with Parents: Establishing the Essential Alliance in Child Psychotherapy and Consultation*. Northvale, NJ: Jason Aronson.

EDMUND SLAKTER

(1987). *Countertransference*. Northvale, NJ: Jason Aronson.

JOSEPH SLAP

(1974). On waking screens. *Journal of the American Psychoanalytic Association*, 22: 844–853.

(1976). A note on the drawing of dream details. *Psychoanalytic Quarterly*, 45: 455–456.

(1987). Freud's assumptions about perception and the structural model. *Journal of the American Psychoanalytic Association*, 35: 629–641.

JOSEPH SLAP & ANDREW SAYKIN

(1983). Schema: basic concept in a non-metapsychological model of mind. *Psychoanalysis and Contemporary Thought*, 6: 305–321.

(1984). On the nature and organization of the repressed. *Psychoanalytic Inquiry*, 4: 107–124.

JOSEPH SLAP & LAURA SLAP-SHELTON

(1991). *The Schema in Clinical Psychoanalysis*. New York: Analytic Press.

JOSEPH SLAP & EUGENE TRUNNELL

(1987). Reflections on the self state dream. *Psychoanalytic Quarterly*, 56: 251–261.

JOYCE SLOCHOWER

(1996). Holding and the evolving maternal function. *Psychoanalytic Review*, 83: 195–218.

VICTOR SMIRNOFF

(1969). The masochistic contract. *International Journal of Psychoanalysis*, 50: 665–671.

HENRY SMITH

(2000). Countertransference, conflictual listening, and the analytic object relationship. *Journal of the American Psychoanalytic Association*, 48: 95–128.

(2002a). On psychic bisexuality. *Psychoanalytic Quarterly*, 71: 549–558.

(2002b). A footnote on forgiveness. *Psychoanalytic Quarterly*, 71: 327–329.

KENNETH SMITH

(1971). Homophobia: a tentative personality profile. *Psychological Report*, 29: 1–17.

SYDNEY SMITH

(1977). The golden fantasy: a regressive reaction to separation anxiety. *International Journal of Psychoanalysis*, 58: 311–324.

ANDREW SMOLAR

(1999). Bridging the gap: technical aspects of the analysis of an Asian immigrant. *Journal of Clinical Psychoanalysis*, 8: 567–594.

(2002). Reflections on gifts in the therapeutic setting: the gift from patient to therapist. *American Journal of Psychotherapy*, 56: 27–45.

(2003). When we give more: reflections on 'gifts' from therapist to patient. *American Journal of Psychotherapy*, 57: 300–323.

ANN SMOLEN

(2006). An analysis with a latency age girl with post-traumatic stress disorder resulting in a secondary narcissistic personality disorder. *Journal of Infant, Child, and Adult Psychotherapy*, 5: 175–195.

CHARLES SOCARIDES

(1960). The development of a fetishistic perversion: the contribution of preoedipal phase conflict. *Journal of the American Psychoanalytic Association*, 8: 281–311.

(1962). Panel report: theoretical and clinical aspects of female homosexuality. *Journal of the American Psychoanalytic Association*, *10*: 579–592.

(1966). On vengeance: the desire to get even. *Journal of the American Psychoanalytic Association*, *14*: 356–375.

(1970). A psychoanalytic study of the desire for sexual transformation (transsexualism): the plaster of paris man. *International Journal of Psychoanalysis*, *51*: 341–349.

(1974). The demonified mother: a study of voyeurism and sexual sadism. *International Review of Psychoanalysis*, *1*: 187–201.

(1978). *Homosexuality*. New York: Jason Aronson.

(1988). *The Preoedipal Origin and Psychoanalytic Therapy of Sexual Perversions*. Madison, CT: International Universities Press.

(1992). Sexual politics and scientific logic. *Journal of Psychohistory*, *19*: 307–329.

(1995). *Homosexuality: A Freedom Too Far*. Phoenix, AZ: Margrave Books.

CHARLES SOCARIDES & SELMA KRAMER

(1997). Eds. *Work and Its Inhibitions: Psychoanalytic Essays*. Madison, CT: International Universities Press.

LESLIE SOHN

(1983). Nostalgia. *International Journal of Psychoanalysis*, *64*: 203–210.

(1985). Narcissistic organization, projective identification, and the formation of the identificate. In: E. B. Spillius (Ed.), *Melanie Klein Today, Volume I: Mainly Theory* (pp. 271–292). London: Routledge.

MARK SOLMS

(1997). What is consciousness? *Journal of the American Psychoanalytic Association*, *45*: 681–703.

ALBERT SOLNIT

(1970). A study of object loss in infancy. *Psychoanalytic Study of the Child*, *25*: 257–272.

(1982). Developmental perspectives on self and object constancy. *Psychoanalytic Study of the Child*, *37*: 201–208.

(1983). The sibling experience. *Psychoanalytic Study of the Child*, *38*: 281–284.

IRVING SOLOMON

(1992). *The Encyclopedia of Evolving Techniques in Dynamic Psychotherapy: The Movement to Multiple Models*. Northvale, NJ: Jason Aronson.

STEPHEN SONNENBERG

(1972). A special form of survivor syndrome. *Psychoanalytic Quarterly*, *41*: 58–62.

STEPHEN SONNENBERG & WILLIAM MYERSON

(2007). The educational boundary. *International Journal of Psychoanalysis*, *88*: 203–217.

DONALD SPENCE

(1982). *Narrative Truth and Historical Truth: Meaning and Interpretation in Psychoanalysis*. New York: W. W. Norton.

DONALD SPENCE, LINDA MAYES, & HARTVIG DAHL

(1994). Monitoring the analytic surface. *Journal of the American Psychoanalytic Association*, *42*: 43–64.

JAMES SPENCER & LEON BALTER

(1990). Psychoanalytic observation. *Journal of the American Psychoanalytic Association*, *38*: 393–421.

MELITTA SPERLING

(1955). Psychosis and psychosomatic illness. *International Journal of Psychoanalysis*, *36*: 320–327.

OTTO SPERLING

(1963). Exaggeration as a defense. *Psychoanalytic Quarterly*, *32*: 533–548.

MOSHE HALEVI SPERO

(1984). Shame—an object-relational formation. *Psychoanalytic Study of the Child*, *39*: 259–282.

(1993). Phallic-patheticness. *International Journal of Psychoanalysis*, *74*: 519–534.

CHARLES SPEZZANO

(1998). The triangle of clinical judgement. *Journal of the American Psychoanalytic Association*, *46*: 365–368.

JOHN SPIEGEL

(1976). Cultural aspects of transference and countertransference revisited. *Journal of American Academy of Psychoanalysis*, *4*: 447–467.

References

LEO SPIEGEL

(1959). The self, the sense of the self, and perception. *Psychoanalytic Study of the Child*, 14: 81–112.

ELIZABETH BOTT SPILLIUS

(1988a). (Ed.) *Melanie Klein Today, Volume I: Mainly Theory*. London: Routledge.
(1988b). (Ed.) *Melanie Klein Today, Volume II: Mainly Practice*. London: Routledge.
(1993). Varieties of envious experience. *International Journal of Psychoanalysis*, 74: 1199–1212.
(2001). Freud and Klein on the concept of phantasy. *International Journal of Psychoanalysis*, 82: 361–373.

ELLEN HANDLER SPITZ

(1985). *Art and Psyche: A Study in Psychoanalysis and Aesthetics*. New Haven, CT: Yale University Press.

RENÉ SPITZ

(1946). Anaclitic depression: an inquiry into the genesis of psychiatric conditions in early childhood. *Psychoanalytic Study of the Child*, 2: 313–342.
(1950). Anxiety in infancy: a study of its manifestations in the first year of life. *International Journal of Psychoanalysis*, 31: 138–143.
(1955). The primal cavity: a contribution to the genesis of perception and its role for psychoanalytic theory. *Psychoanalytic Study of the Child*, 10: 215–240.
(1957). *No and Yes*. New York: International Universities Press.
(1959). *A Genetic Field Theory of Ego Formation*. New York: International Universities Press.
(1960). Discussion of Dr John Bowlby's paper (Grief and mourning in infancy). *Psychoanalytic Study of the Child*, 15: 85-94.
(1963). The evolution of the dialogue. In: M. Schur (Ed.), *Drives, Affects, Behavior*. New York: International Universities Press.
(1965). *The First Year of Life*. New York: International Universities Press.

MARIANNE SPITZFORM

(2000). The ecological self: metaphor and developmental experience. *Journal of Applied Psychoanalytic Studies*, 2: 265–286.

HYMAN SPOTNITZ

(1979). Narcissistic countertransference. In: L. Epstein & A. Feiner (Eds.), *Countertransference* (pp.329–343). New York: Jason Aronson.

MADELON SPRENGNETHER

(2005). Musing on forgiveness: a response to Roy Schafer. *Journal of the American Psychoanalytic Association*, 53: 411–424.

WILLIAM SPRING

(1939). Observations on world destruction fantasies. *Psychoanalytic Quarterly*, 8: 48–56.

LAURENCE SPURLING

(2008). Is there still a place for the concept of 'therapeutic regression' in psychoanalysis? *International Journal of Psychoanalysis*, 89: 523–540.

BHASKAR SRIPADA

(1999). A comparison of failed supervision and a successful supervision of the same psychoanalytic case. *Annual of Psychoanalysis*, 26: 219–241.
(2005). Psychic bisexuality, male homosexuality, plural oedipus complex, and Hinduism. In: S. Akhtar (Ed.), *Freud Along the Ganges: Psychoanalytic Reflections on the People and Culture of India* (pp. 235–268). New York: Other Press.

DAVID STAFFORD-CLARK

(1952). *Psychiatry for Students*. London: Penguin.

MARTHA STARK

(1994). *A Primer on Working with Resistance*. Northvale, NJ: Jason Aronson.

GERALD STECHLER

(1987). Clinical applications of a psychoanalytic systems model of assertion and aggression. *Psychoanalytic Inquiry*, 1: 348–363.

References

BRANDT STEELE

(1991). The psychopathology of incest participants. In: S. Kramer & S. Akhtar (Eds.), *The Trauma of Transgression* (pp. 13–37). Northvale, NJ: Jason Aronson.

DAVID STEERE

(1982). *Bodily Expressions in Psychotherapy*. New York: Brunner/Mazel.

MARTIN STEIN

(1958). The cliché: a phenomenon of resistance. *Journal of the American Psychoanalytic Association*, 6: 263–277.
(1981). The unobjectionable part of the transference. *Journal of the American Psychoanalytic Association*, 29: 869–892.
(1985). Irony in psychoanalysis. *Journal of the American Psychoanalytic Association*, 33: 35–58.

RUTH STEIN

(1998a). The poignant, the excessive, and the enigmatic in sexuality. *International Journal of Psychoanalysis*, 79: 253–268.
(1998b). The enigmatic dimension of sexual experience. *Psychoanalytic Quarterly*, 67: 594–625.
(2006). Father regression: clinical narratives and theoretical reflections. *International Journal of Psychoanalysis*, 87: 1005–1027.

BLEMA STEINBERG

(1993). The need to know and the inability to tolerate not knowing. *Canadian Journal of Psychoanalysis*, 1: 85–103.

JOHN STEINER

(1993). *Psychic Retreats: Pathological Organizations in Psychotic, Neurotic and Borderline Patients*. London: Routledge.
(1996). Revenge and resentment in the oedipus situation. *International Journal of Psychoanalysis*, 77: 434–444.
(2006). Interpretive enactments and the analytic setting. *International Journal of Psychoanalysis*, 87: 315–320.

RICCARDO STEINER

(1985). Some thoughts about tradition and change arising from an examination of the British Psychoanalytical Society's Controversial Discussions (1943–1944). *International Review of Psychoanalysis*, 12: 27–71.

IRVING STEINGART

(1995). *A Thing Apart: Love and Reality in the Therapeutic Relationship*. Northvale, NJ: Jason Aronson.

WILHELM STEKEL

(1908). *Neurotic Anxiety-States and Their Treatment*. New York: Liveright, 1950.

PAUL STEPANSKY

(1988). (Ed.) *The Memoirs of Margaret S. Mahler*. New York: Free Press.

KARIN STEPHEN

(1941). Aggression in early childhood. *British Journal of Medical Psychology*, 18: 178–190.

EDITH STERBA

(1940). Homesickness and the mother's breast. *Psychiatric Quarterly*, 14: 701–707.

RICHARD STERBA

(1934). The fate of the ego in analytic therapy. *International Journal of Psychoanalysis*, 15: 117–126.
(1940). Aggression in the rescue fantasy. *Psychoanalytic Quarterly*, 9: 505–508.
(1946). Dreams and acting out. *Psychoanalytic Quarterly*, 15: 175–179.
(1982). *Reminiscences of a Viennese Psychoanalyst*. Detroit, MI.: Wayne State University Press.

ADOLPH STERN

(1938). Psychoanalytic investigation and therapy in borderline group of neuroses. *Psychoanalytic Quarterly*, 7: 467–489.

DANIEL STERN

(1977). *The First Relationship: Infant and Mother*. Cambridge, MA: Harvard University Press.
(1985). *The Interpersonal World of the Infant*. New York: Basic Books.
(1995). *The Motherhood Constellation*. New York: Basic Books.

References

DANIEL STERN, LOUIS SANDLER, JEREMY NAHUM, ALEXANDRA HARRISON, KARLEN LYONS-RUTH, ALEC MORGAN, NADIA BRUSCHWELER-STERN, & EDWARD TRONICK

(1998). Non-interpretive mechanisms in psychoanalytic therapy: the 'something more' than interpretation. *International Journal of Psychoanalysis, 79*: 903–922.

HAROLD STERN

(1978). *The Couch: Its Use and Meaning in Psychotherapy.* New York: Human Sciences Press.

HAROLD STEWART

(1993). Clinical aspect of malignant regression. In: L. Aron & A. Harris (Eds.), *The Legacy of Sandor Ferenczi* (pp. 249–264). Hillsdale, NJ: The Analytic Press.

WALTER STEWART

(1967). Comments on the manifest content of certain types of unusual dreams. *Psychoanalytic Quarterly, 36*: 329–341.

ROBERT STOLLER

(1964). A contribution to the study of gender identity. *International Journal of Psychoanalysis, 45*: 220–226.
(1968). *Sex and Gender, Volume I.* New York: Science House.
(1970). The transsexual boy: mother's feminized phallus. *British Journal of Medical Psychology, 43*: 117–128.
(1973). *Perversion: The Erotic Form of Hatred.* New York: Pantheon Books.
(1975). *Sex and Gender, Volume II.* New York: Jason Aronson.
(1976). Primary femininity. *Journal of the American Psychoanalytic Association, 24*(Suppl): 59–79.
(1979). Fathers of transsexual children. *Journal of the American Psychoanalytic Association, 27*: 837–866.

ROBERT STOLOROW

(1973). Perspectives on death anxiety: a review. *Psychiatric Quarterly, 47*: 473–486.
(1977). Notes on the signal function of hypochondriacal anxiety. *International Journal of Psychoanalysis, 58*: 245–246.
(1979). Defensive and arrested developmental aspects of death anxiety, hypochondriasis and depersonalization. *International Journal of Psychoanalysis, 60*: 201–213.

ROBERT STOLOROW & GEORGE ATWOOD

(1978). *Faces in a Cloud: Subjectivity in Personality Theory.* New York: Jason Aronson.

ROBERT STOLOROW, BERNARD BRANDSCHAFT, & GEORGE ATWOOD

(1987). *Psychoanalytic Treatment: An Intersubjective Approach.* Hillsdale, NJ: The Analytic Press.

LEO STONE

(1954). The widening scope of indications for psychoanalysis. *Journal of the American Psychoanalytic Association, 2*: 567–594.
(1961). *The Psychoanalytic Situation.* New York: International Universities Press.
(1967). The psychoanalytic situation and transference: postscript to an earlier communication. *Journal of the American Psychoanalytic Association, 15*: 3–58.
(1971). Reflections on the psychoanalytic concept of aggression. *Psychoanalytic Quarterly, 40*: 195–244.
(1973). On resistance to the psychoanalytic process. In: B. B. Rubenstein (Ed.), *Psychoanalysis and Contemporary Science, Volume 2* (pp. 42–73). New York: Macmillan.
(1981). Notes on the noninterpretive elements in the psychoanalytic situation and process. *Journal of the American Psychoanalytic Association, 29*: 89–118.
(1984). *Transference and Its Context.* New York: Jason Aronson.

JAMES STRACHEY

(1934). The nature of therapeutic action of psychoanalysis. *International Journal of Psychoanalysis, 15*: 127–159.

ALLAN STRAUSS

(1955). Unconscious mental processes and the psychosomatic concept. *International Journal of Psychoanalysis, 36*: 307–318.

HERBERT STREAN

(1981). Extra-analytic contacts: theoretical and clinical considerations. *Psychoanalytic Quarterly, 50*: 238–259.

CARLO STRENGER

(1989). The classic and romantic visions in psychoanalysis. *International Journal of Psychoanalysis, 70*: 595–610.

(1998). *Individuality, The Impossible Project: Psychoanalysis and Self-Creation.* Madison, CT: International Universities Press.
(2004). *The Designed Self: Psychoanalysis and Contemporary Identities.* Northvale, NJ: Jason Aronson.

HARRY STACK SULLIVAN

(1947). *Conceptions of Modern Psychiatry.* Washington, DC: William Alanson White Foundation.
(1953). *The Interpersonal Theory of Psychiatry.* New York: W. W. Norton.

CARL SULZBERGER

(1953). Why it is hard to keep secrets. *Psychoanalysis, 2*: 37–43.

NEVILLE SYMINGTON

(2008). How belief in God affects my clinical work. In: M. K. O'Neil & S. Akhtar (Eds.), *On Freud's 'The Future of an Illusion'* (pp. 237–252). London: Karnac.

JUDIT SZEKACS

(1985). Impaired spatial structures. *International Journal of Psychoanalysis, 66*: 193–199.

LAJOS SZEKELY

(1967). The creative pause. *International Journal of Psychoanalysis, 48*: 353–367.

VEIKO TAHKA

(1993). *Mind and Its Treatment: A Psychoanalytic Approach.* Madison, CT: International Universities Press.

YASUHIKO TAKETOMO

(1989). An American–Japanese transcultural psychoanalysis and the issue of teacher transference. *Journal of the American Academy of Psychoanalysis, 17*: 427–450.

NADINE TANG & JACQUELIN GARDNER

(1999). Race, culture, and psychotherapy: transference to minority therapists. *Psychoanalytic Quarterly, 68*: 1–20.

SIDNEY TARACHOW

(1960). Judas, the beloved executioner. *Psychoanalytic Quarterly, 29*: 528–554.
(1963). *An Introduction to Psychotherapy.* New York: International Universities Press.
(1966). Coprohagia and allied phenomena. *Journal of the American Psychoanalytic Association, 14*: 685–699.

MARY TARGET & PETER FONAGY

(1996). Playing with reality: II. the development of psychic reality from a theoretical perspective. *International Journal of Psychoanalysis, 77*: 459–479.

ALEX TARNOPOLSKY

(1995). Teaching countertransference. *Canadian Journal of Psychoanalysis, 3*: 293–313.
(2000). Normal and pathological mourning: a Kleinian interpretation of Verdi and *Rigoletto. Canadian Journal of Psychoanalysis, 8*: 19–40.

WILLIAM TARNOWER

(1966). Extra-analytic contacts between the psychoanalyst and the patient. *Psychoanalytic Quarterly, 35*: 399–413.

HELEN TARTAKOFF

(1966). The normal personality in our culture and the Nobel Prize complex. In: R. M. Loewenstein, L. M. Newman, M. Schur, & A. J. Solnit (Eds.), *Psychoanalysis: A General Psychology* (pp. 222–252). New York: International Universities Press.

ALLAN TASMAN, MICHELLE RIBA, & KENNETH SILK

(2000). *The Doctor–Patient Relationship in Pharmacotherapy: Improving Treatment Effectiveness.* New York: Guilford Press.

VICTOR TAUSK

(1912). On masturbation. *Psychoanalytic Study of the Child, 6*: 61–79.
(1919). Uber die entsehung des beeinflussungsapparates in der schizphrenie. *International Journal of Psychoanalysis, 5*: 1–33.

References

JAGDISH TEJA & SALMAN AKHTAR

(1981). The psychosocial problems of FMGs with special reference to those in psychiatry. In: R. S. Chen (Ed.), *Foreign Medical Graduates in Psychiatry: Issues and Problems* (pp. 321–328). New York: Human Sciences Press.

LAURA TESSMAN

(1982). A note on the father's contribution to the daughter's way of loving and working. In: S. Cath, A. Gurwitt, & J. M. Ross (Eds.), *Father and Child*. Boston: Little Brown.

HELMUT THOMA & HORST KACHELE

(1994). *Psychoanalytic Practice, Volume 2: Clinical Studies*. Northvale, NJ: Jason Aronson.

TROY THOMPSON II

(1991). Psychosomatic phenomena. In: S. Akhtar & H. Parens (Eds.), *Beyond the Symbiotic Orbit: Advances in Separation-Individuation Theory* (pp. 243–261). Hillsdale, NJ: The Analytic Press.

JAMES ANDERSON THOMSON JR, MAX HARRIS, & VAMIK VOLKAN

(1993). *The Psychology of Western European Neo-Racism*. Charlottesville, VA: Center for the Study of Mind and Human Interaction.

HENRY DAVID THOREAU

(1854). *Walden; or Life in the Woods*. Boston, MA: Ticknor and Fields.

ERNEST TICHO

(1972). Termination of psychoanalysis: treatment goals, life goals. *Psychoanalytic Quarterly*, 41: 315–333.

GERTRUDE TICHO

(1967). On self analysis. *International Journal of Psychoanalysis*, 48: 308–323.

MARION TOLPIN

(1970). The Infantile Neurosis—a metapsychological concept and a paradigmatic case history. *Psychoanalytic Study of the Child*, 25: 273–305.
(1974). The Daedalus experience: a developmental vicissitude of the archaic grandiose fantasy. *Annual of Psychoanalysis*, 2: 213–228.
(1986). The self and its selfobjects: a different baby. In: A. Goldberg (Ed.), *Progress in Self Psychology, Volume 2* (pp. 115–128). New York: Guildford Press.

TOVE TRAESDAL

(2005). When the analyst dies: dealing with the aftermath. *Journal of the American Psychoanalytic Association*, 53: 1235–1255.

GEORGE TRAIN

(1953). Flight into health. *American Journal of Psychotherapy*, 7: 463–483.

DANIEL TRAUB-WARNER

(1986). The place and value of bestophilia in perversions. *Journal of the American Psychoanalytic Association*, 34: 975–992.

EDWARD TRONICK

(1989). Emotions and emotional communications in infants. *American Psychologist*, 44: 112–119.
(2002). A model of infant mood states and Sanderian activation waves. *Psychoanalytic Dialogues*, 12: 73–99.

LANDRUM TUCKER

(2006). Grandparent syndrome: a clinical study. *Psychoanalytic Study of the Child*, 61: 82–99.

DAVID TUCKETT

(2005). Does anything go? Towards a framework for the more transparent assessment. *International Journal of Psychoanalysis*, 86: 31–49.

DAVID TUCKETT & RICHARD TAFFLER

(2008). Phantastic objects and the financial market's sense of reality: a psychoanalytic contribution to the understanding of stock market instability. *International Journal of Psychoanalysis*, 89: 389–412.

PRATYUSHA TUMMALA-NARRA

(2004). Dynamics of race and culture in the supervisory encounter. *Psychoanalytic Psychology*, 21: 300–311.
(2007). Skin color and therapeutic relationship. *Psychoanalytic Psychology*, 24: 255–270.
(2009). Contemporary impingements on mothering. *American Journal of Psychoanalysis*, 69: 4–21.

FRANCES TUSTIN

(1980). Autistic objects. *International Review of Psychoanalysis*, 7: 27–39.
(1988). The 'black hole': a significant element in autism. *Free Associations*, 11: 35–50.
(1993). On psychogenic autism. *Psychoanalytic Inquiry*, 13: 34–41.

ADELE TUTTER

(2006). Medication as object. *Journal of the American Psychoanalytic Association*, 54: 781–804.

STUART TWEMLOW

(2000). The roots of violence: converging psychoanalytic explanatory models for power struggles and violence in schools. *Psychoanalytic Quarterly*, 69: 741–785.

ISAAC TYLIM

(2005). The power of apologies in transforming resentment into forgiveness. *International Journal of Applied Psychoanalytic Studies*, 2: 260–270.

PHYLLIS TYSON

(1980). The gender of the analyst: in relation to transference and countertransference manifestations in pre-latency children. *Psychoanalytic Study of the Child*, 35: 321–338.

PHYLLIS TYSON & ROBERT TYSON

(1984). Narcissism and superego development. *Journal of the American Psychoanalytic Association*, 32: 75–98.
(1990). *Psychoanalytic Theories of Development*. New Haven, CT: Yale University Press.
(1995). Development. In: B. Moore & B. Fine (Eds.), *Psychoanalysis The Major Concepts* (pp. 395–420). New Haven, CT: Yale University Press.

ROBERT URSANO, STEPHEN SONNENBERG, & SUSAN LAZAR

(1998). *Concise Guide to Psychodynamic Psychotherapy*. Washington, DC: American Psychiatric Press.

GEORGE VAILLANT

(1977). *Adaptation to Life*. Boston, MA: Little, Brown.
(1992). *Ego Mechanisms of Defense: A Guide for Clinicians and Researchers*. Washington, DC: American Psychiatric Press, Inc.

ARTHUR VALENSTEIN

(1962). The psychoanalytic situation: affects, emotional re-living, and insight in the psychoanalytic process. *International Journal of Psychoanalysis*, 43: 315–324.
(2000). The older patient in psychoanalysis. *Journal of the American Psychoanalytic Association*, 48: 1563–1589.

MADHUSUDANA RAO VALLABHANENI

(2005). Advaita Vedanta, psychoanalysis and the self. In: S. Akhtar (Ed.), *Freud Along the Ganges: Psychoanalytic Reflections on the People and Culture of India* (pp. 359–393). New York: Other Press.

CAREL VAN DER HEIDE

(1941). A case of pollakiuria nervosa. *Psychoanalytic Quarterly*, 10: 267–283.

BESSEL VAN DER KOLK

(1987). (Ed.) *Psychological Trauma*. Washington, DC: American Psychiatric Press.

ADELINE VAN WANING

(1991). 'To be the best or not to be, that is the question . . .' on enactment, play, and acting out. *International Journal of Psychoanalysis*, 72: 539–550.

SVERRE VARVIN

(2003a). Extreme traumatisation: strategies for mental survival. *International Forum of Psychoanalysis*, 12: 5–16.
(2003b). Which patients should avoid psychoanalysis, and which professional should avoid psychoanalytic training? *Scandinavian Psychoanalytic Review*, 26: 109–122.

References

SVERRE VARVIN & VAMIK VOLKAN (Eds.)

(2005). *Violence or Dialogue? Psychoanalytic Insights on Terror and Terrorism*. London: International Psychoanalytic Association.

SUSAN VAUGHAN

(1999). The hiding and revelation of sexual desire in lesbians. *Journal of Gay and Lesbian Psychotherapy*, 3: 81–90.

LILLA VESZY-WAGNER

(1961). The analytic screen: an instrument or an impediment in the psycho-analytic technique. *International Journal of Psychoanalysis*, 17: 32–42.

VAMIK VOLKAN

(1976). *Primitive Internalized Object Relations: A Clinical Study of Schizophrenic, Borderline, and Narcissistic Patients*. New York: International Universities Press.
(1979). *Cyprus: War and Adaptation*. Charlottesville, VA: University Press of Virginia.
(1981). *Linking Objects and Linking Phenomena: A Study of the Forms, Symptoms, Metapsychology, and Therapy of Complicated Mourning*. New York: International Universities Press.
(1982). Narcissistic personality disorder. In: J. O. Cavener & H. K. Brodie (Eds.), *Critical Problems in Psychiatry* (pp. 332–350). Philadelphia, PA: Lippincott.
(1985). (Ed.) *Depressive States and Their Treatment*. Northvale, NJ: Jason Aronson.
(1987). Psychological concepts useful in the building of political foundations between nations (Track II diplomacy). *Journal of the American Psychoanalytic Association*, 35: 903–935.
(1988). *The Need to Have Enemies and Allies: From Clinical Practice to International Relationships*. Northvale, NJ: Jason Aronson.
(1995). *The Infantile Psychotic Self and Its Fates*. Northvale, NJ: Jason Aronson.
(1997). *Bloodlines: From Ethnic Pride to Ethnic Terrorism*. New York: Farrar, Straus and Giroux.
(1999a). *Das Versagen der Diplomatie: Zur Psychoanalyse nationaler, ethnischer und religiöser Konflikte (The Failure of Diplomacy: The Psychoanalysis of National, Ethnic and Religious Conflicts)*. Gießen: Psychosozial-Verlag.
(1999b). Psychoanalysis and diplomacy, Part I: Individual and large-group identity. *Journal of Applied Psychoanalytic Studies*, 1: 29–55.
(1999c). The tree model: a comprehensive psychopolitical approach to unofficial diplomacy and the reduction of ethnic tension. *Mind & Human Interaction*, 10: 142–210.
(1999d). Nostalgia as a linking phenomenon. *Journal of Applied Psychoanalytic Studies*, 1: 169–179.
(2004). *Blind Trust: Large Groups and Their Leaders in Times of Crises and Terror*. Charlottesville, VA: Pitchstone.
(2006). *Killing in the Name of Identity: Terror, Trauma, Mourning, and Reconciliation*. Charlottesville, VA: Pitchstone.

VAMIK VOLKAN & GABRIELLE AST

(1997). *Siblings in the Unconscious and Psychopathology*. Madison, CT: International Universities Press.

VAMIK VOLKAN & NORMAN ITZKOWITZ

(1984). *The Immortal Atatürk*. Chicago, IL: University of Chicago Press.

VAMIK VOLKAN & ROBERT CORNEY

(1968). Some considerations of satellite states and satellite dreams. *British Journal of Medical Psychology*, 41: 283–290.

VAMIK VOLKAN & ROBERT SHOWALTER

(1968). Known object loss, disturbance in reality testing, and 're-grief work' as a method of brief psychotherapy. *Psychiatric Quarterly*, 42: 358–374.

VAMIK VOLKAN & TERRY RODGERS

(1988). *Attitudes of Entitlement*. Charlottesville, VA: University Press of Virginia.

VAMIK VOLKAN, NORMAN ITZKOWITZ, & ANDREW DODD

(2001). *Richard Nixon: A Psychobiography*. New York: Columbia University Press.

VAMIK VOLKAN, SALMAN AKHTAR, ROBERT DORN, JOHN KAFKA, OTTO KERNBERG, PETER OLSSON, RITA ROGERS, & STEPHEN SHANFIELD

(1998). Leaders and decision-making. *Mind and Human Interaction*, 9: 130–181.

EILHARD VON DOMARUS

(1944). Specific laws of logic in schizophrenia. In: J. S. Kassanin (Ed.), *Language and Thought in Schizophrenia* (pp. 104-114). Berkeley, CA: University of California Press.

LEV VYGOTSKY

(1956). *Selected Psychological Investigations*. Moscow: Izdatel'stvo Akademii Pedagogiceskikh Nauk.
(1978). *Mind in Society: The Development of Higher Psychological Processes*. Cambridge, MA: Harvard University Press.

CONRAD WADDINGTON

(1947). *Organizers and Genes*. Cambridge: Cambridge University Press.

ROBERT WAELDER

(1925). The psychoses, their mechanisms, and accessibility to influence. *International Journal of Psychoanalysis*, 6: 259–281.
(1933). The psychoanalytic theory of play. *Psychoanalytic Quarterly*, 2: 208–225.
(1936). The principle of multiple function; observations on multiple determination. *Psychoanalytic Quarterly*, 5: 45–62.

ROBERT WALLERSTEIN

(1969). Introduction to panel: psychoanalysis and psychotherapy. *International Journal of Psychoanalysis*, 50: 117–126.
(1983). Self psychology and 'classical' psychoanalytic psychology: the nature of their relationship. In: A. Goldberg (Ed.), *The Future of Psychoanalysis* (pp. 19–63). New York: International Universities Press.
(1986). *Forty-two Lives in Treatment: A Study of Psychotherapy and Psychoanalysis*. New York: Guilford Press.
(1988). Assessment of structural change in psychoanalytic therapy and research. *Journal of the American Psychoanalytic Association*, 36(Suppl.): 241–261.
(1992). Follow-up in psychoanalysis: what happens to treatment gain? *Journal of the American Psychoanalytic Association*, 40: 665–690.
(1993). Between chaos and petrification: a summary of the Fifth IPA Conference of Training Analysts. *International Journal of Psychoanalysis*, 74: 165–178.
(1999). *Lay Analysis: Life Inside the Controversy*. Hillsdale, NJ: Analytic Press.

ROBERT WALLERSTEIN & LEWIS ROBBINS

(1956). The psychotherapy research project of the Menninger Foundation. *Bulletin of the Menninger Clinic*, 20: 239–262.

MARTIN WANGH

(1962). The 'evocation of a proxy': a psychological maneuver, its use as a defense, its purposes and genesis. *Psychoanalytic Study of the Child*, 17: 451–469.

MAX WARREN

(1961). The significance of visual images during the analytic session. *Journal of the American Psychoanalytic Association*, 9: 504–518.

ROBERT WASKA

(2006). Addictions and the quest to control the object. *American Journal of Psychoanalysis*, 66: 43–62.

HELEN WATKINS & JOHN WATKINS

(1997). *Ego States: Theory and Therapy*. New York: W.W. Norton

EDITH WEIGERT

(1967). Narcissism: benign and malignant terms. In: R. W. Gibson (Ed.), *Crosscurrents in Psychiatry and Psychoanalysis* (pp. 222–238). Philadelphia: J. B. Lippincott.

ANNEMARIE WEIL

(1970). The basic core. *Psychoanalytic Study of the Child*, 25: 442–460.

JEROME WEINBERGER

(1964). A triad of silence: silence, masochism, and depression. *International Journal of Psychoanalysis*, 45: 304–309.

EDWARD WEINSHEL

(1979). Some observations on not telling the truth. *Journal of the American Psychoanalytic Association*, 27: 503–531.
(1984). Some observations on the psychoanalytic process. *Psychoanalytic Quarterly*, 53: 63–92.
(1988). Structural change in psychoanalysis. *Journal of the American Psychoanalytic Association*, 36(Suppl.): 263–280.

EDUARDO WEISS

(1947). Projection, extrajection, and objectivation. *Psychoanalytic Quarterly*, 16: 357–377.
(1957). The phenomenon of 'ego passage'. *Journal of the American Psychoanalytic Association*, 5: 267–281.

References

JOSEPH WEISS

(1988). Testing hypotheses about unconscious mental functioning. *International Journal of Psychoanalysis, 69*: 87–95.

STANLEY WEISS

(1972). Some thoughts and clinical vignettes on translocation of an analytic practice. *International Journal of Psychoanalysis, 53*: 505–513.

DAVID WERMAN

(1977). Normal and pathological nostalgia. *Journal of the American Psychoanalytic Association, 25*: 387–398.
(1979). Chance, ambiguity, and psychological mindedness. *Psychoanalytic Quarterly, 48*: 107–115.
(1983). Suppression as a defense. *Journal of the American Psychoanalytic Association, 31*(Suppl.): 405–415.
(1988). *The Practice of Supportive Psychotherapy*. New York: Routledge.

ALLEN WHEELIS

(1949). Flight from insight. *American Journal of Psychiatry, 105*: 915–919.
(1966). *The Illusionless Man*. New York: Harper Colophon.

ROY WHITMAN, MILTON KRAMER, & BILL BALDRIDGE

(1969). Dreams about the patient: an approach to the problem of countertransference. *Journal of the American Psychoanalytic Association, 17*: 707–727.

NARENDRA NATH WIG (2004). Hanuman complex and its resolution: an illustration of psychotherapy from Indian mythology. *Indian Journal of Psychiatry 46*: 25–29.

SALLYE WILKINSON

(1993). The female genital dress-rehearsal: a prospective process at the oedipal threshold. *International Journal of Psychoanalysis, 74*: 313–330.

GIANNA WILLIAMS

(1997). Reflections on some dynamics of eating disorders: 'no entry' defences and foreign bodies. *International Journal of Psychoanalysis, 78*: 927–941.

MIRIAM WILLIAMS

(1972). Problems of technique during latency. *Psychoanalytic Study of the Child, 27*: 598–617.

MARTIN WILLICK

(1983). On the concept of primitive defenses. *Journal of the American Psychoanalytic Association, 31S*: 175–200.

ARNOLD WILSON & LISA WEINSTEIN

(1996). The transference and the zone of proximal development. *Journal of the American Psychoanalytic Association, 44*: 167–200.

GEORGE WILSON

(1948). Further contribution to the study of olfactory repression with particular reference to transvestitism. *Psychoanalytic Quarterly, 17*: 322–339.

JEROME WINER

(1994). Panel report: hate in the analytic setting. *Journal of the American Psychoanalytic Association, 42*: 219–241.
(2005). Frank Lloyd Wright: power, powerlessness, and charisma. *Annual of Psychoanalysis, 33*: 179–190.

JEROME WINER & ERIC ORNSTEIN

(2001). Titration in the treatment of the more troubled patient. *Journal of the American Psychoanalytic Association, 49*: 891–908.

JEROME WINER, JAMES ANDERSON, & ELIZABETH DANZE (Eds.)

(2005). *Psychoanalysis and Architecture*. Catskill, NY: Mental Health Resources.

CLARE WINNICOTT, RAY SHEPHERD, & MADELINE DAVIS

(1989). *Psychoanalytic Explorations: D. W. Winnicott*. Cambridge, MA: Harvard University Press.

DONALD WINNICOTT

(1935). The manic defense. In: *Collected Papers: Through Paediatrics to Psychoanalysis* (pp. 129–144). New York: Basic Books, 1958.

(1941). The observation of infants in a set situation. *International Journal of Psychoanalysis*, 22: 229–249.

(1942). Why children play. In: The Child and the Outside World: Studies in Developing Relationships (pp. 149-152). London: Tavistock, 1957.

(1945). Primitive emotional development. *International Journal of Psychoanalysis*, 26: 137–143.

(1946). What do we mean by a normal child? In: The Child and the Family: First Relationships (pp. 100-106). London: Tavistock, 1957.

(1947). Hate in the countertransference. In: *Collected Papers: Through Paediatrics to Psychoanalysis* (pp. 306–316). New York: Basic Books, 1958.

(1953). Transitional objects and transitional phenomena. *International Journal of Psycho-Analysis*, 34: 89–97.

(1954). The depressive position in normal emotional development. In: *Collected Papers: Through Paediatrics to Psychoanalysis* (pp. 262–277). London: Tavistock.

(1956a). Antisocial tendency. In: *Collected Papers: Through Paediatrics to Psychoanalysis* (pp. 306–316). New York: Basic Books, 1958.

(1956b). Primary maternal preoccupation. In: *Collected Papers: Through Paediatrics to Psychoanalysis* (pp. 300–305). New York: Basic Books, 1958.

(1958). The capacity to be alone. *International Journal of Psychoanalysis*, 39: 416–420.

(1959). The fate of the transitional object. In: C. Winnicott, R. Shepherd, & M. Davis (Eds.), *Psychoanalytic Explorations* (pp. 53–58). Cambridge, MA: Harvard University Press.

(1960). Ego distortion in terms of true and false self. In: *Maturational Processes and Facilitating Environment* (pp. 140–152). New York: International Universities Press, 1965.

(1962). Ego integration in child development. In: *The Maturational Processes and the Facilitating Environment* (pp. 56–63). New York: International Universities Press.

(1963). Dependence in infant care, child care, and in the psychoanalytic setting. *International Journal of Psychoanalysis*, 44: 339–344.

(1965). *The Maturational Process and the Facilitating Environment*. New York: International Universities Press.

(1966). Ordinary devoted mother. In: C. Winnicott, R. Shepherd, & M. Davis (Eds.), *Babies and their Mothers* (pp. 3–4). Reading, MA: Addison-Wiley, 1987.

(1967). Playing: a theoretical statement. In: *Playing and Reality*, pp. 32–41. London: Tavistock, 1971.

(1968a). Breastfeeding as a communication. In: C. Winnicott, R. Shepherd & M. Davis (Eds.), *Babies and Their Mothers*. Reading, MA: Addison-Wiley, 1987.

(1968b). Play in the analytic situation. In: C. Winnicott, R. Shepherd & M. Davis (Eds.), *Psychoanalytic Explorations* (pp.28–29). Cambridge, MA: Harvard University Press.

(1969). The use of an object. *International Journal of Psychoanalysis*, 50: 711–716.

(1970). The place of the monarchy. In: *Home Is Where We Start From*. New York: W. W. Norton, 1990.

(1971). *Playing and Reality*. London: Penguin Books.

(1974). Fear of breakdown. *International Review of Psychoanalysis*, 1: 103–107.

(1989). Notes on play. In: C. Winnicott, R. Shepherd & M. Davis (Eds.), *Psychoanalytic Explorations* (pp. 59–63). Cambridge, MA: Harvard University Press.

DONALD WINNICOTT & MASUD KHAN

(1953). Review of *Psychoanalytic Study of the Personality* by W. R. D. Fairbairn. *International Journal of Psychoanalysis*, 34: 329–333.

JOHN WISDOM

(1949). A hypothesis to explain trauma re-enactment dreams. *International Journal of Psychoanalysis*, 30: 13–20.

FRANZ WITTELS

(1939). Unconscious phantoms in neurotics. *Psychoanalytic Quarterly*, 8: 141–163.

ERNEST WOLF

(1979). Countertransference in disorders of the self. In: L. Epstein & A. H. Feiner (Eds.), *Countertransference: The Therapist's Contribution to the Therapeutic Situation* (pp. 445–464). New York: Jason Aronson.

(1988). *Treating the Self: Elements of Clinical Self Psychology*. New York: Guilford Press.

(1994). Selfobject experiences: development, psychopathology, treatment. In: S. Kramer & S. Akhtar (Eds.), *Mahler and Kohut: Perspectives on Development, Psychopathology, and Technique* (pp. 65–96). Northvale, NJ: Jason Aronson.

THOMAS WOLMAN

(1990). The death of the analyst in the post-termination phase of analysis: impact and resolution. In: H. J. Schwartz & A. S. Silver (Eds.), *Illness in the Analyst: Implications for the Treatment Relationship* (pp. 253–266). Washington, DC: American Psychiatric Press.

References

(2007). Human space, psychic space, analytic space, geopolitical space. In: M. T. S. Hooke & S. Akhtar (Eds.), *The Geography of Meanings: Psychoanalytic Perspectives on Place, Space, Land, and Dislocation* (pp. 23–45). London: International Psychoanalytic Association.

ELIZABETH WRIGHT

(1992). *Feminism and Psychoanalysis: A Critical Dictionary.* Oxford: Blackwell.

JOSEPHINE WRIGHT

(2006). Psychoanalysis in conjunction with medication: a clinical research opportunity. *Journal of the American Psychoanalytic Association, 54*: 833–855.

KENNETH WRIGHT

(1991). *Vision and Separation.* Northvale, NJ: Jason Aronson.

LEON WURMSER

(1994). *The Mask of Shame.* Northvale, NJ: Jason Aronson.

HAROLD WYLIE JR & MAVIS WYLIE

(1987). The older analysand: countertransference issues in psychoanalysis. *International Journal of Psychoanalysis, 68*: 343–352.

SUZANNE YANG, EVE CALIGOR, DEBORAH CABANISS, BRUCE LUBER, JUSTINE DONOVAN, PAUL ROSEN, NICHOLAS FORAND, & STEVEN ROOSE

(2004). Poster abstract: post-termination contact: a survey of prevalence, characteristics, and analyst's attitudes. *Journal of the American Psychoanalytic Association, 52*: 455–457.

RICHARD YAZMAJIAN

(1966). Pathological urination and weeping. *Psychoanalytic Quarterly, 35*: 40–47.
(1983). The use of color for the secondary elaboration of the dream. *Psychoanalytic Quarterly, 52*: 225–236.

FRANK YEOMANS, MICHAEL SELZER, & JOHN CLARKIN

(1992). *Treating the Borderline Patient: A Contract-Based Approach.* New York: Basic Books.

BARBARA YOUNG.

(2004). Rebirth at 40: photographs as transitional objects. *International Journal of Applied Psychoanalytic Studies, 1*: 158–181.

VIRGINIA YOUNGREN

(2004). Panel report: is free association still at the core of psychoanalysis? *International Journal of Psychoanalysis, 85*: 1489–1492.

JOEL ZAC

(1971). Un enfoque metodologico del establecimiento del encuadre. *Revista de Psicoanalisis, 5*: 593–610.

SHARON ZALUSKY

(1998). Telephone analysis: out of sight but not out of mind. *Journal of the American Psychoanalytic Association, 46*: 1221–1242.

GEORGE ZAVITZIANOS

(1972). Homovestism: perverse form of behavior involving wearing clothes of the same sex. *International Journal of Psychoanalysis, 53*: 471–477.

MEYER ZELIGS

(1957). Acting in: a contribution to the meaning of some postural attitudes observed during analysis. *Journal of the American Psychoanalytic Association, 5*: 685–706.
(1960). The role of silence in transference, countertransference, and the psychoanalytic process. *International Journal of Psychoanalysis, 41*: 407–412.

SIEGFRIED ZEPF

(2006). Attachment theory and psychoanalysis: some remarks from an epistemological and from a Freudian viewpoint. *International Journal of Psychoanalysis, 87*: 1529–1548.

KATHARINE ZERBE

(1992). The phoenix rises from Eros, not ashes: creative collaboration in the lives of five Impressionist and Postimpressionist women artists. *Journal of the American Academy of Psychoanalysis, 20:* 295–315.

(2005). *Body Betrayed: A Deeper Understanding of Women, Eating Disorders, and Treatment.* New York: W. W. Norton.

(2008). *Integrated Treatment of Eating Disorders: Beyond Body Betrayed.* New York: W. W. Norton.

ELIZABETH ZETZEL

(1956). Current concepts of transference. *International Journal of Psychoanalysis, 37:* 369–375.

(1968). The so-called god hysteric. *International Journal of Psychoanalysis, 49:* 265–260.

GREGORY ZILBOORG.

(1952). The emotional problem and the therapeutic role of insight. *Psychoanalytic Quarterly, 21:* 1–24.

RICHARD ZIMMER, PETER BOOKSTEIN, EDWARD KENNY, & ANDREAS KRAEBER

(2005). Glossary. In: E. Person, A. Cooper, & G. Gabbard (Eds.), *The American Psychiatric Publishing Textbook of Psychoanalysis* (pp. 347–362). Washington, DC: American Psychiatric Press.

DAVID ZIMMERMAN

(1982). Analysability in relation to early psychopathology. *International Journal of Psychoanalysis, 63:* 189–200.

NORMAN ZINBERG

(1975). Addiction and ego function. *Psychoanalytic Study of the Child, 30:* 567–588.

JANET ZUCKERMAN & LISA HORLICK

(2006). The affective experience of the analyst in the extra-analytic moment. *American Journal of Psychoanalysis, 66:* 351–371.

RALPH ZWEIBEL

(1985). The dynamics of the countertransference dream. *International Review of Psychoanalysis, 12:* 87–99.